New Perspectives on

Adobe® Flash® CS3 Professional

Comprehensive

Luis A. Lopez

COURSE TECHNOLOGY
CENGAGE Learning™

Australia • Brazil • Japan • Korea • Mexico • Singapore • Spain • United Kingdom • United States

COURSE TECHNOLOGY
CENGAGE Learning™

New Perspectives on Adobe Flash CS3 Professional—Comprehensive
Luis A. Lopez

Executive Editor: Marie L. Lee
Senior Product Manager: Kathy Finnegan
Product Manager: Erik Herman
Associate Acquisitions Editor: Brandi Henson
Associate Product Manager: Leigh Robbins
Editorial Assistant: Patrick Frank
Director of Marketing: Cheryl Costantini
Marketing Manager: Ryan DeGrote
Marketing Specialist: Jennifer Hankin
Developmental Editor: Robin M. Romer
Content Project Manager: Heather Furrow
Composition: GEX Publishing Services
Text Designer: Steve Deschene
Art Director: Marissa Falco
Cover Designer: Elizabeth Paquin
Cover Art: Bill Brown
Copyeditor: Andrew Therriault
Proofreader: Brandy Lilly
Indexer: Alexandra Nicholson

For product information and technology assistance, contact us at
Cengage Learning Customer & Sales Support, 1-800-354-9706

For permission to use material from this text or product, submit all requests online at **cengage.com/permissions**
Further permissions questions can be emailed to
permissionrequest@cengage.com

ISBN-13: 978-1-4239-2539-2

ISBN-10: 1-4239-2539-4

Course Technology
25 Thomson Place
Boston, Massachusetts 02210
USA

Cengage Learning is a leading provider of customized learning solutions with office locations around the globe, including Singapore, the United Kingdom, Australia, Mexico, Brazil, and Japan. Locate your local office at: **international.cengage.com/region**

Cengage Learning products are represented in Canada by Nelson Education, Ltd.

For your lifelong learning solutions, visit **course.cengage.com**

Purchase any of our products at your local college store or at our preferred online store **www.ichapters.com**

Printed in Canada
2 3 4 5 6 7 8 9 12 11 10 09

Preface

The New Perspectives Series' critical-thinking, problem-solving approach is the ideal way to prepare students to transcend point-and-click skills and take advantage of all that Adobe Flash CS3 Professional has to offer.

Our goal in developing the New Perspectives Series was to create books that give students the software concepts and practical skills they need to succeed beyond the classroom. With this new edition, we've updated our proven case-based pedagogy with more practical content to make learning skills more meaningful to students.

With the New Perspectives Series, students understand *why* they are learning *what* they are learning, and are fully prepared to apply their skills to real-life situations.

"This text is filled with excellent explanations and activities. My students vary in their abilities, and this text covers exactly what they need in a logical, incremental fashion. It's a great reference book that students will find useful for years."

—Kenneth Wade
Champlain College

About This Book

This book offers a case-based, problem-solving approach to learning Adobe Flash CS3 Professional. Using Flash, students will learn how to create rich interactive experiences for the Web, ranging from banners and interactive menus to a complete Web site.

- Covers new features of Flash CS3, including the improved user interface consistent with other Adobe CS3 software, and the new Primitive Rectangle and Oval drawing tools.
- Follows the New Perspectives Series case-based, problem-solving approach to help students understand the how and the why behind software skills.
- Includes coverage of both ActionScript 2.0 and ActionScript 3.0 programming. The new ActionScript 3.0 programming language is covered in two tutorials.
- Students create a Flash Web site incorporating the use of ActionScript, components, and video.
- New case scenario used throughout six tutorials, as well as a new case scenario with new data files for one of the running Case Problems in the end-of-tutorial reinforcement material.
- Includes a new Appendix with an overview of the Adobe Certified Associate credential for Flash CS3. The appendix covers the objectives assessed with the Rich Media Communication Using Adobe Flash CS3 Exam. The Appendix is available in the Student Downloads and Instructor Downloads sections of www.course.com.
- *Guide to Using Adobe Flash CS3 on the Macintosh* is available in the Student Downloads and Instructor Downloads sections of www.course.com.

System Requirements

This book assumes that students have a default installation of Adobe Flash CS3 Professional, Adobe Flash Player 9, and a current Web browser.

The screenshots in this book were produced on a computer running Windows Vista Ultimate with Aero turned off and, for a browser, Internet Explorer 7. If students use a different operating system or browser, their screens might differ from those in the book.

"The New Perspectives Series approach, which combines definition and real-world application of content, makes it an easy choice for me when selecting textbooks. I am able to teach concepts that students can immediately apply."
—Brian Morgan
Marshall University

The New Perspectives Approach

Context
Each tutorial begins with a problem presented in a "real-world" case that is meaningful to students. The case sets the scene to help students understand what they will do in the tutorial.

Hands-on Approach
Each tutorial is divided into manageable sessions that combine reading and hands-on, step-by-step work. Screenshots help guide students through the steps. **Trouble?** tips anticipate common mistakes or problems to help students stay on track and continue with the tutorial.

InSight

InSight Boxes
New for this edition! InSight boxes offer expert advice and best practices to help students better understand how to work with Adobe Flash CS3 Professional and create interactive graphics, animations, and Web sites. With the information provided in the InSight boxes, students achieve a deeper understanding of the concepts behind the features and skills presented.

Tip

Margin Tips
New for this edition! Margin Tips provide helpful hints and shortcuts for more efficient use of Adobe Flash CS3 Professional. The Tips appear in the margin at key points throughout each tutorial, giving students extra information when and where they need it.

Reality Check

Reality Checks
New for this edition! Comprehensive, open-ended Reality Check exercises give students the opportunity to practice skills by completing practical, real-world tasks involved in planning and creating a personal Flash Web site.

Review

In New Perspectives, retention is a key component to learning. At the end of each session, a series of Quick Check questions helps students test their understanding of the concepts before moving on. Each tutorial also contains an end-of-tutorial summary and a list of key terms for further reinforcement.

Apply

Assessment
Engaging and challenging Review Assignments and Case Problems have always been a hallmark feature of the New Perspectives Series. Icons and brief descriptions accompany the exercises, making it easy to understand, at a glance, both the goal and level of challenge a particular assignment holds.

Reference Window

Task Reference

Reference
While contextual learning is excellent for retention, there are times when students will want a high-level understanding of how to accomplish a task. Within each tutorial, Reference Windows appear before a set of steps to provide a succinct summary and preview of how to perform a task. In addition, a complete Task Reference at the back of the book provides quick access to information on how to carry out common tasks. Finally, each book includes a combination Glossary/Index to promote easy reference of material.

Our Complete System of Instruction

Brief
Introductory
Comprehensive

Coverage To Meet Your Needs

Whether you're looking for just a small amount of coverage or enough to fill a semester-long class, we can provide you with a textbook that meets your needs.

- Brief books typically cover the essential skills in just 2 to 4 tutorials.
- Introductory books build and expand on those skills and contain an average of 5 to 8 tutorials.
- Comprehensive books are great for a full-semester class, and contain 9 to 12+ tutorials.

So if the book you're holding does not provide the right amount of coverage for you, there's probably another offering available. Visit our Web site or contact your Course Technology sales representative to find out what else we offer.

COURSECASTS

CourseCasts – Learning on the Go. Always available...always relevant.

Want to keep up with the latest technology trends relevant to you? Visit our site to find a library of podcasts, CourseCasts, featuring a "CourseCast of the Week," and download them to your mp3 player at http://coursecasts.course.com.

Ken Baldauf, host of CourseCasts, is a faculty member of the Florida State University Computer Science Department where he is responsible for teaching technology classes to thousands of FSU students each year. Ken is an expert in the latest technology trends; he gathers and sorts through the most pertinent news and information for CourseCasts so your students can spend their time enjoying technology, rather than trying to figure it out. Open or close your lecture with a discussion based on the latest CourseCast.

Visit us at http://coursecasts.course.com to learn on the go!

Instructor Resources

We offer more than just a book. We have all the tools you need to enhance your lectures, check students' work, and generate exams in a new, easier-to-use and completely revised package. This book's Instructor's Manual, ExamView testbank, PowerPoint presentations, data files, solution files, figure files, and a sample syllabus are all available on a single CD-ROM or for downloading at www.course.com.

Blackboard

Online Content

Blackboard is the leading distance learning solution provider and class-management platform today. Course Technology has partnered with Blackboard to bring you premium online content. Content for use with *New Perspectives on Adobe Flash CS3 Professional, Comprehensive* is available in a Blackboard Course Cartridge and may include topic reviews, case projects, review questions, test banks, practice tests, custom syllabi, and more. Course Technology also has solutions for several other learning management systems. Please visit http://www.course.com today to see what's available for this title.

Acknowledgments

I want to extend my gratitude to all of the members of the New Perspectives Team who made this book possible, especially Erik Herman, Product Manager, for his patience and guidance of this project. Thanks also to Heather Furrow, Content Project Manager, and Christian Kunciw and the Manuscript Quality Assurance Team, including John Freitas, Danielle Shaw, and Susan Whalen.

Special thanks to Robin M. Romer, Developmental Editor, for her hard work and dedication to this project. Her editorial and organizational skills, attention to detail, and great insight have made this project a success.

And, finally, without the love and support of my family this book would have been impossible to complete. I dedicate this book to my beautiful wife, Gloria, and to our wonderful daughter, Alyssandra.

- Luis A. Lopez

Brief Contents

Adobe Flash

Adobe Flash CS3 Professional

Table of Contents

Tutorial 9 Using Flash Components and Video, and Printing Flash Content

Tutorial 1

Objectives

Session 1.1
- Discover the types of Web media created in Flash
- Compare vector graphics and bitmap graphics
- Learn how Flash graphics are displayed in a Web page
- Start Flash and explore its main workspace components

Session 1.2
- Display grid lines, guides, and rulers
- Set a document's properties

Session 1.3
- Learn about strokes, fills, and colors
- Select and modify objects
- Use Flash Help

Introducing Adobe Flash CS3 Professional

Exploring the Basic Features of Flash

Case | Admiral Web Design

Admiral Web Design, founded in 2001, is a fast-growing Web site design and development company that specializes in building Web sites for small- to medium-sized businesses and organizations. This innovative Web design company has a growing list of clients from various industries, including a national sports equipment company and a local seafood restaurant. The company's rapid growth and success has largely been due to its energetic and creative staff.

Admiral Web Design is owned by Gloria Adamson and Jim Torres, both graduates of a Web design and multimedia program at a local college. The other full-time employees are Aly Garcia, Chris Johnson, and Raj Sharma. Gloria handles the bulk of the business decisions and oversees the Web site design and development projects. Jim is responsible for marketing and manages the company's finances. Aly is the graphic designer, and Chris and Raj are the site designers responsible for developing the content for the clients' Web sites.

Aly uses **Adobe Flash CS3 Professional (Flash)** to create visually exciting and interactive components, such as animated logos and online interactive advertising, to enhance the clients' Web sites. Flash was originally designed to create small, fast-loading animations that could be used in Web pages. Over the years, Flash has evolved into an advanced authoring tool for creating interactive Web media that range from animated logos to Web site navigational controls and interactive Web sites. Flash can also be used to develop engaging content for mobile devices. You will help Aly develop Flash graphics and animations.

Starting Data Files

Tutorial.01 →

Tutorial	Review	Case1	Case2	Case3	Case4
AC_RunActiveContent.js awdbanner.jpg awdflash.htm flashad1.swf flashad2.swf flashad3.swf flashad4.swf MyKite.fla Sample.fla	Sample.fla	Shapes.fla	Objects.fla	(none)	(none)

Session 1.1

Reviewing Types of Web Media

Web pages are made up text, graphics, animations, sounds, and videos. These elements are referred to as **Web media**. The different types of Web media are created by a variety of programs, and then pulled together to work as a cohesive whole on a Web page through XHTML, the underlying code used in creating Web pages. The most common types of Web media besides text are graphics and animations, which can be created in Flash.

Bitmap and Vector Graphics

Graphics fall into essentially two types: bitmap and vector. Each has advantages, disadvantages, and appropriate uses in Web page design.

> **Tip**
>
> Bitmap graphic files in the JPEG format have the file extension .jpg. Bitmap graphic files in the GIF format have the file extension .gif.

A **bitmap graphic** is a row-by-row list of every pixel in the graphic, along with each pixel's color. A **pixel** is the smallest picture element on the monitor screen that can be controlled by the computer. A 100×100-pixel bitmap graphic is simply a grid containing 10,000 colored pixels. As a result, resizing a bitmap graphic creates unattractive side effects. If you enlarge a bitmap graphic, for example, the edges become ragged as the pixels are redistributed to fit the larger grid. You cannot easily take a bitmap graphic apart to modify only one portion of the image. Bitmap graphics, however, provide blending and subtle variations in colors and textures. A common bitmap graphic is a digital photograph. You can also create bitmap graphics using imaging software such as Adobe Fireworks or Adobe Photoshop. The two most common file formats for bitmap graphics used in Web pages are JPEG (Joint Photographic Experts Group) and GIF (Graphic Interchange Format).

A **vector graphic** is a set of mathematical instructions that describe the color, outline, and position of all the shapes of the image. Each shape is defined by numbers that represent the shape's position in the window in which it is being displayed. Other numbers represent the points that establish the shape's outline. As a result, vector graphics scale well, which means you can resize a vector image proportionally and the quality remains the same. Vector graphics also appear uniform regardless of the size or resolution of the monitor on which they are displayed. Individual shapes within a vector graphic can be modified independently of the rest. Vector graphics excel at sharp lines, smooth colors, and precise detail. Vector graphic files are generally smaller than bitmap graphic files and take less time to download. Common examples of vector graphics are images created in drawing programs such as Adobe Illustrator as well as images created in Flash.

InSight | Combining Bitmap and Vector Graphics

Designers often import bitmap graphics into Flash and combine them with vector graphics. For example, bitmap images such as photographs often appear as the background to Flash vector graphics and animations. They tend to soften the overall effect, and add a little realism to Flash graphics. Using a bitmap graphic in a Flash document is best when you are developing an advertisement or banner for a Web site for a business or professional organization. You should also edit the bitmap graphic in an image-editing program such as Adobe Photoshop to reduce its size to match the size of the Flash document. Using large bitmap graphics will cause the resulting Flash graphic to download very slowly.

Figure 1-1 shows an image of a basketball as a bitmap graphic (left) and as a vector graphic (right). The bitmap graphic becomes distorted when enlarged whereas the vector graphic retains its quality.

Figure 1-1 Bitmap graphic compared to vector graphic

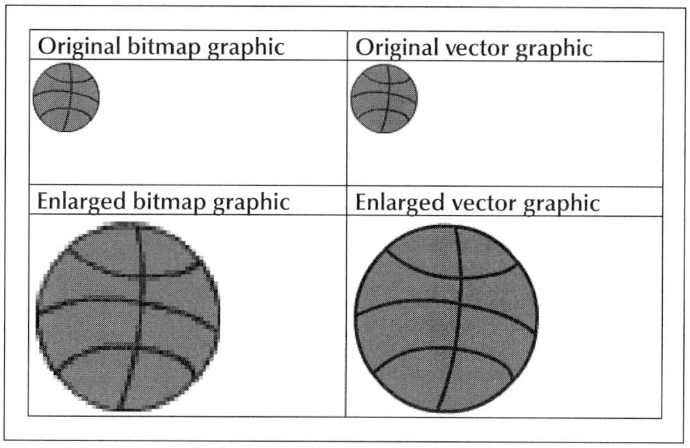

Bitmap and Vector Animation

Animation is a series of still images displayed in sequence to give the illusion of motion. Animation can be accomplished with both bitmap and vector images.

Bitmap animation is created by putting a sequence of bitmap images into one file and playing back the sequence. The playback of the bitmap images produces a perception of motion. Each change the viewer sees requires changing the colors of pixels in the frame. A lot of information is required to keep track of all of the pixel changes even for small images of short duration. The amount of information that must be stored increases dramatically for larger display sizes, longer sequences, or smoother motion. Because of the importance of rapid transmission over the Internet, bitmap motion graphics are usually limited to small display sizes and short sequences.

Vector animation lists shapes and their transformations that are played back in sequence to provide the perception of motion. The information required to describe the modification of shapes in a vector animation is usually less than the information required to describe the pixel changes in a bitmap animation. Also, because vector graphics are resolution independent, which means that they always appear with the optimum onscreen quality regardless of image size or the screen resolution, increasing the display size of the shapes in a vector animation has no effect on the file size.

Web Media in Flash

Flash allows developers to create media-rich elements that integrate with Web pages and that download quickly. Flash graphics also have streaming capability, which allows animations to start playing even before they download completely. Web media created in Flash are called **documents** and can include text, static images, sound and video as well as animations. Flash animations are created from a series of graphic objects such as lines, shapes, and text that are then sequenced. The graphics created in Flash are primarily vector graphics but can include bitmap graphics. Flash also supports many import formats so that developers can include media from a broad range of sources including Photoshop and Illustrator files.

InSight | Using Media in Flash Documents

A completed Flash document can include anything from silent, still imagery to motion graphics with sound and interactivity, as well as elements that incorporate video. Flash enables you to add sound—as sound effects, voiceovers, or music—to any element within a document. You can choose to have sound play all the time, be activated by a mouse click, be turned on and off by the user, or be synchronized with events in your document. You can also incorporate video into a Web page as part of a graphic or animation and add controls to the video elements to enable the viewer to manage the video playback.

Like other media files, a Flash file must be referenced in an XHTML file to be viewed in a Web page. You can publish the XHTML files and references automatically from within the Flash program. If you are experienced with XHTML, you can insert the reference manually or create your own XHTML file to reference and control the Flash file.

While developing content using Flash, you work with a Flash authoring document, referred to as an **FLA file**, which has the .fla file extension. When you're ready to deliver that content for viewing by end users, you publish the Flash document as an **SWF file**, which has the .swf file extension and can be displayed in a Web page. For example, if the Flash document in which you create and develop an animation for the Admiral Web Design Web site is named AWDanim.fla, the published file with the finished animation would be named AWDanim.swf.

> **Tip**
>
> The free Flash Player plug-in is available at *www.adobe.com/downloads.*

The SWF file plays in an XHTML file in a Web browser using the **Flash Player plug-in**. All current versions of the major Web browsers come with the Flash Player plug-in installed. Besides allowing Flash documents to be viewed in your browser, the Flash Player plug-in provides controls for zooming in and out of the document, changing the document's quality, printing the document, and other functions. The controls are accessed by right-clicking the animation to open the context menu shown in Figure 1-2.

Figure 1-2 Flash Player plug-in context menu

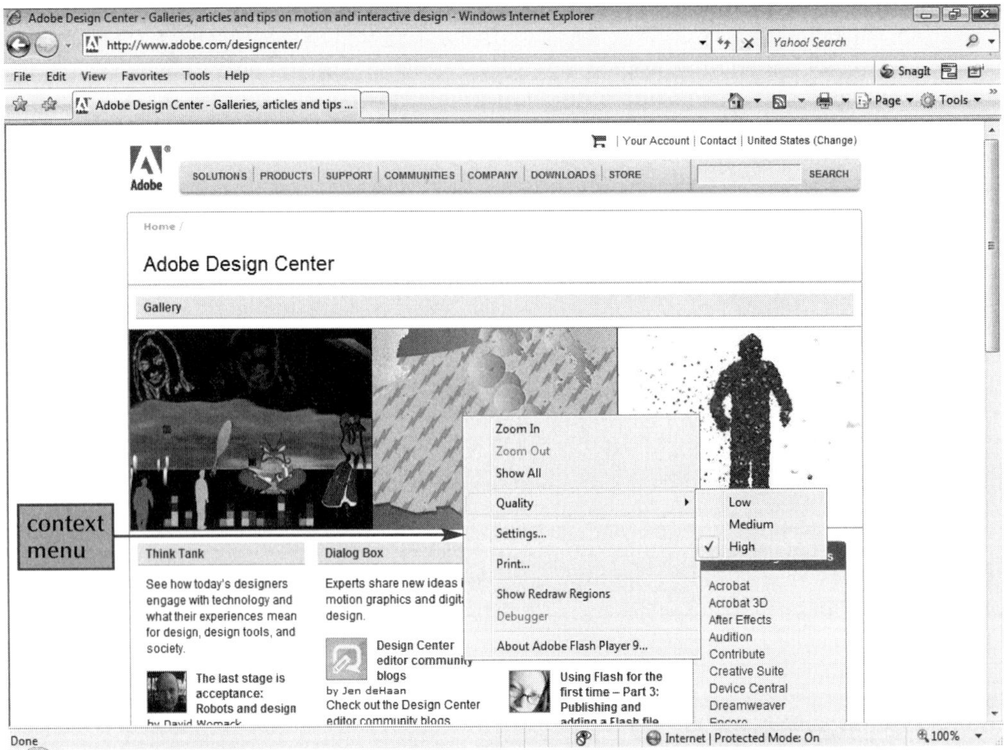

Another element of Flash is ActionScript, a scripting programming language that enables you to add interactivity to buttons and other Web media that users can click or select to control the Flash graphics or animation they are viewing. You will learn more about ActionScript in later tutorials.

Viewing Flash SWF Files

Aly wants you to look at several examples of Flash SWF files she has created and placed on the Admiral Web Design Web site. You open a Flash Web page in a Web browser the same way as you open any other page. If the Flash Player plug-in is installed, the streaming capability of a Flash file allows the player to begin playing the animation as soon as enough of the file has been downloaded. If the Flash Player plug-in is not installed, you can easily install it by downloading the plug-in from the Adobe download Web site.

To view examples of Flash SWF files in your browser:

1. Click the **Start** button on the taskbar, and then click **Internet Explorer**. The Web browser opens, displaying the default home page.

   Trouble? If you don't see Internet Explorer on the Start menu, click All Programs, and then click Internet Explorer. If you still don't see Internet Explorer, press the Esc key until the Start menu closes, and then click the Launch Internet Explorer Browser button on the Quick Launch toolbar or double-click the Internet Explorer icon on your desktop.

   Trouble? If you are using Mozilla Firefox or a different Web browser, use the Start menu or desktop icon to open that browser, and then modify any Web browser steps in these tutorials as needed.

2. If the Internet Explorer menu bar is not displayed, click the **Tools** button, and then click **Menu Bar**.

3. Click **File** on the menu bar, and then click **Open**. The Open dialog box opens.

4. Click the **Browse** button, navigate to the **Tutorial.01\Tutorial** folder included with your Data Files, click **awdflash.htm**, and then click the **OK** button. The Admiral Web Design sample page appears in the browser window. This page contains several examples of Flash SWF files that are available for Admiral's clients to review.

   Trouble? If you don't have the starting Data Files, you need to get them before you can proceed. Your instructor will either give you the Data Files or ask you to obtain them from a specified location (such as a network drive). In either case, make a backup copy of the Data Files before you start so that you will have the original files available in case you need to start over. If you have any questions about the Data Files, see your instructor or technical support person for assistance.

   Trouble? If a dialog box opens stating that Internet Explorer needs to open a new window to display the Web page, click the OK button.

   Trouble? If the Information Bar indicates that your Internet Security settings block the active content in the Admiral Web Design sample page, you need to allow blocked content here and whenever you open an XHTML page in these tutorials. Click the Information Bar, click Allow blocked content, and then click the Yes button in the security dialog box.

5. Right-click one of the animations on the page. The context menu with the controls for the Flash file opens. See Figure 1-3.

Figure 1-3 Sample Flash SWF files

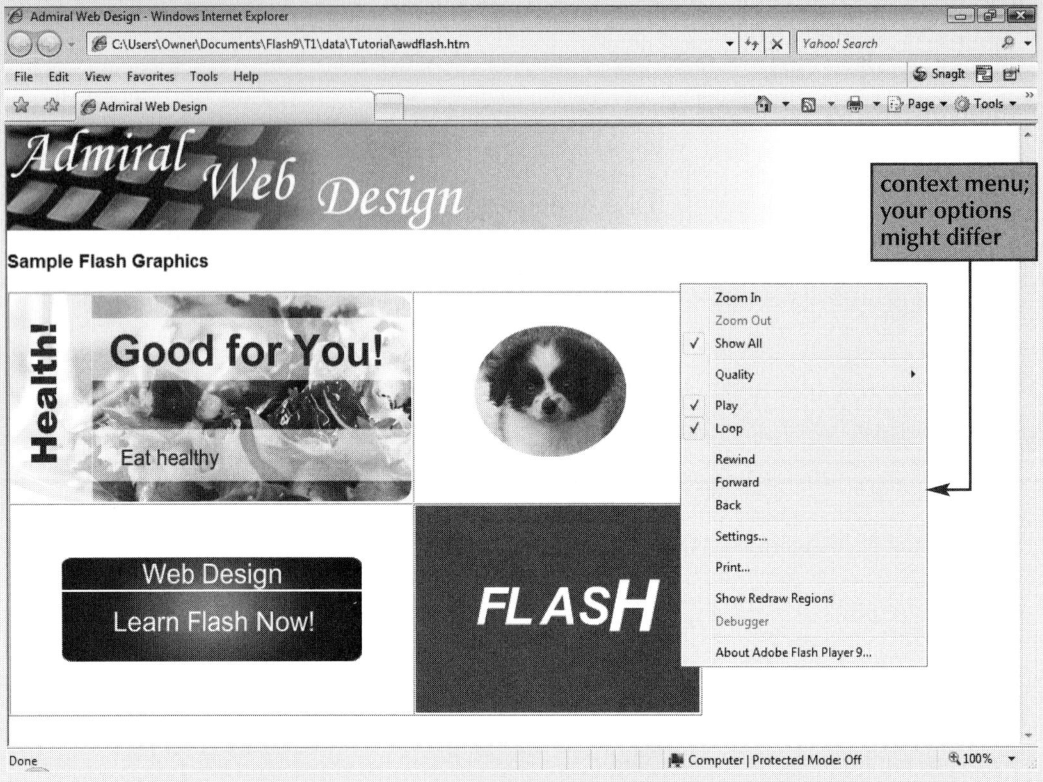

6. Click **Play** on the context menu to remove the check mark. The command is deselected, and the animation stops.
7. Right-click an animation, and then click **Zoom In** on the context menu. The graphic's magnification level increases.
8. Use the context menu controls to rewind, zoom out, and step forward and back through the animation.
9. Click the **Close** button on the browser's title bar. The browser window closes.

   Trouble? If a dialog box opens, prompting you to close all of the tabs, click the Close Tabs button.

Tip

When an SWF graphic is magnified, the pointer changes to a hand and you can drag the graphic to see different areas.

Starting Flash

When you first start Flash, or when the program is running but no documents are opened, the Start page appears. The Start page provides access to the most commonly used actions such as opening a recently used file, creating a new Flash document, or creating a document using a template. After you open a document or create a new one, the Flash program window, called the workspace appears. The workspace contains components, such as toolbars and panels, that you can organize to suit your work style and needs.

Aly wants you to set the workspace to its default layout.

To start Flash and set the workspace to its default layout:

1. Click the **Start** button on the taskbar, click **All Programs**, and then click **Adobe Flash CS3 Professional**. The Flash program window opens and displays the Start page.

   Trouble? If you do not see Adobe Flash CS3 Professional on the All Programs menu, look for and click an Adobe folder, and then click Adobe Flash CS3 Professional. If you can't find Adobe Flash CS3 Professional in an Adobe folder, press the Esc key twice to close the Start menu, and then double-click the Adobe Flash CS3 Professional program icon on your desktop. If you still can't find Adobe Flash CS3 Professional, ask your instructor or technical support person for help.

   Trouble? If the Adobe Product Activation dialog box opens, this is probably the first time Flash was started on this computer. Click the appropriate option button, click the Continue button, enter the information requested, and then click the Register button. If you do not know your serial number or need further assistance, ask your instructor or technical support person.

2. If necessary, click the **Maximize** button on the title bar to maximize the Flash program window.
3. In the Create New section of the Start page, click **Flash File (ActionScript 3.0)**. An untitled Flash file window opens.

   Trouble? If the Start page is hidden, click File on the menu bar, click New to open the New Document dialog box, and then click Flash File (ActionScript 3.0) in the Type box on the General tab of the New Document dialog box.

4. Click the **Maximize** button on the document's title bar to maximize the document window, if necessary.

   The Flash workspace is customizable, which means you can easily change the way different components are arranged. The figures in these tutorials show the Flash workspace in its default layout. You'll change the workspace to its default layout.

5. Click **Window** on the menu bar, point to **Workspace**, and then click **Default**. The panels in the Flash workspace reset to their default layout.
6. Click **Window** on the menu bar, point to **Toolbars**, and then make sure that **Main** and **Controller** do not have check marks next to them and that **Edit Bar** has a check mark next to it. If necessary, click a command to add or remove the check mark. See Figure 1-4.

Figure 1-4 Flash default workspace layout

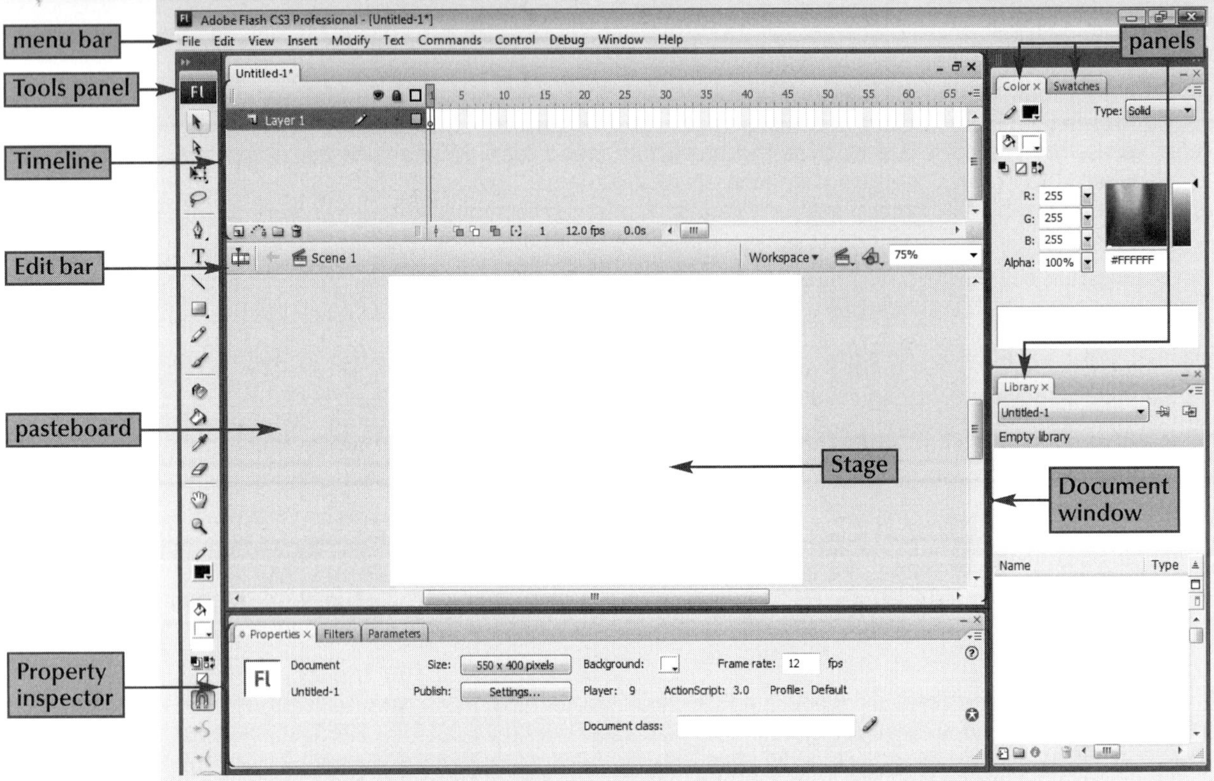

Figure 1-5 briefly describes each of the main components of the Flash workspace.

Figure 1-5 Main components of the Flash workspace

COMPONENT	DESCRIPTION
Menu bar	Lists the menu categories such as File, Edit, View, Insert, and Help, which include commands to access most of the Flash program features
Edit bar	Displays the Hide/Show Timeline button, current scene number, the Select Workspace Layout button, the Edit Scene button, the Edit Symbols button, and the Zoom control
Tools panel	Contains the Flash tools, such as the tools for drawing and painting lines and shapes, selecting objects, changing the view of the Stage, and choosing colors
Stage	Located in the Document window; the rectangular area where you assemble and position all of the viewable objects that are part of a Flash document
Pasteboard	Located in the Document window; used to place objects that are not part of the viewable Stage and to position objects that move onto or off the Stage as part of an animation
Timeline	Located in the Document window; displays and controls the layers and frames that make up an animation and organizes the objects that are part of the document
Panels	Contain controls for viewing and changing the properties of objects
Property inspector	Provides easy access to the most common attributes of the currently selected tool or object

The five most commonly used components of the Flash workspace are the Stage, pasteboard, Timeline, Tools panel, and panels. You'll learn more about these components in the next session.

Previewing Documents

As you develop a Flash document, you often need to preview it to check the results of your changes. You can preview your work in Flash in several ways. You can preview or play the document's animation within the Flash workspace, publish the file to play in a separate Flash Player window, or publish it to play in a Web page in your default Web browser. Previewing the document in the Flash workspace is the quickest method, although some animation effects and interactive functions only work in the published format.

You will view Aly's document from the Flash workspace. The MyKite.fla file is a Flash document consisting of a simple animation.

To preview the MyKite.fla document in the Flash workspace:

1. Click **File** on the menu bar, and then click **Close**. If a dialog box prompts you to save changes, click the **No** button. The document closes and the Start page appears.
2. Click **File** on the menu bar, and then click **Open**. The Open dialog box opens.
3. Navigate to the location where you store your Data Files, open the **Tutorial.01\Tutorial** folder, click **MyKite.fla** in the file list, and then click the **Open** button. The MyKite document opens on the Stage.

   Trouble? The MyKite file may include the FLA extension in its filename, depending on whether your computer's operating system is configured to display file extensions. If this is the case, just click MyKite in the file list.
4. Click **View** on the menu bar, point to **Magnification**, and then click **Show All**. The workspace changes to show the entire document. See Figure 1-6.

Figure 1-6 MyKite document

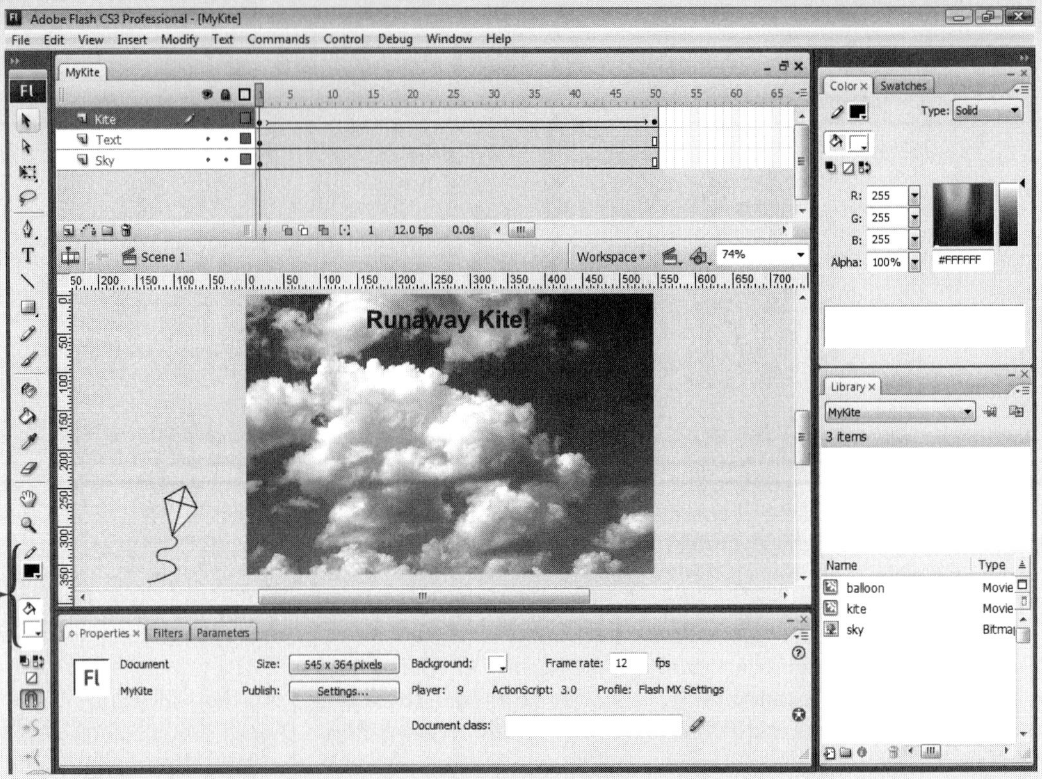

5. Click **Control** on the menu bar, and then click **Play**. As the animation plays, notice that the Timeline tracks the animation's progress. You will learn more about the elements in the Timeline later in the next session.

You can also preview the published file in a separate Flash Player window or in a browser window.

To preview the published file in a separate Flash Player window and then in a browser:

1. Click **Control** on the menu bar, and then click **Test Movie**. Flash creates a file in the SWF format, opens it in a separate window, and then plays it with the Flash Player. See Figure 1-7.

Tip

You can also test the movie by pressing the Ctrl+Enter keys.

Figure 1-7 MyKite document playing in Flash Player window

2. Click the **Close** button on the Flash Player window title bar to close the Flash Player and to return to the Flash document.

   Trouble? If Flash closes, you probably clicked the Close button on the Flash program window title bar. Restart Flash, and then open the MyKite document again.

   Next, you will preview the Flash file in a Web page.

3. Click **File** on the menu bar, point to **Publish Preview**, and then click **HTML**. The default browser on your computer opens and the SWF file plays in the browser window. See Figure 1-8.

Figure 1-8 MyKite.swf file playing in a Web browser

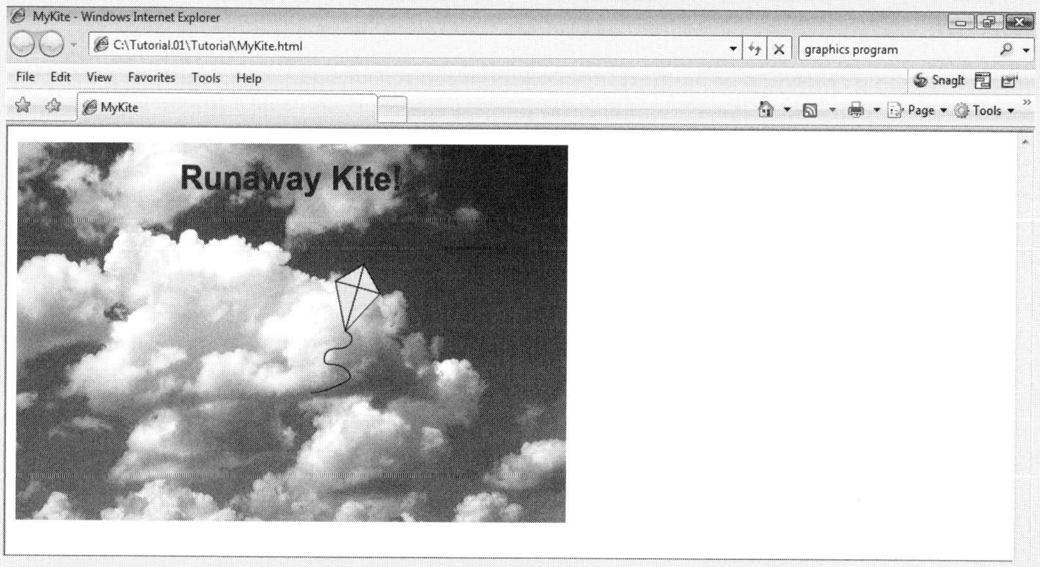

Trouble? If a dialog box opens, prompting you to overwrite the AC_RunActiveContent.js file, click the No button. Flash creates this file automatically, and the file is included with your Data Files.

Trouble? If your Web browser window does not appear, it might be minimized. Click the taskbar button for the Web browser.

Trouble? If the animation does not play in your browser window, start your Web browser and open the MyKite.html file located in the Tutorial.01\Tutorial folder included with your Data Files.

4. Close the browser window to return to Flash.

So far, you have learned about Web media and viewed sample Flash documents. In the next session, you will learn about the main components of the Flash workspace and how to change a document's settings.

Review | Session 1.1 Quick Check

1. Flash creates ______________ -based graphics.
2. What file extension does a Flash document have after it has been published for Web delivery?
3. List three things you might find in a Flash document.
4. True or False? Flash allows you to synchronize sound with events in your document.
5. Bitmap graphics store information as a grid of ______________ .
6. How does a vector graphic store image data?
7. Does the term *resolution-independent* apply to bitmap graphics, vector graphics, or both?
8. What are two common results of enlarging a bitmap image?

Session 1.2

Flash Workspace Components

The main components of the Flash workspace are the Stage, pasteboard, Timeline, Tools panel, and panels. The Stage, the pasteboard, and the Timeline make up the Document window.

Stage

The **Stage** is where you create, import, and assemble all of the graphic objects for a document. The Stage is the central area of the Document window. Any graphic object must be on the Stage to appear in the final document, whether that object is static or animated. The Stage shows only the objects that are visible at a particular point in an animation. In fact, the Stage in Flash is just like the stage in a dramatic production. As the production progresses, actors appear and disappear, and move around from place to place on the Stage.

Because Flash is used to create animations, you expect different objects to be visible at different times during playback. While you are working on a project, the Stage displays only those objects that are associated with the currently selected frame. Flash documents are divided into frames, which represent units of time, and each frame might contain different images or different states of the same image. If you select another frame, objects might appear or disappear, change position or change appearance.

Pasteboard

Surrounding the Stage is a gray area called the **pasteboard**. When you complete a Flash document and publish it to view it on a Web page, only the objects and portions of objects on the Stage appear. Objects and portions of objects in the pasteboard are not shown. You can also place a graphic in the pasteboard and then animate it to move onto the Stage.

Using the Pasteboard | InSight

Designers often place instructions or comments in the pasteboard for reference as they work with a Flash document. These instructions or comments are not visible when the document is published, but are only visible to the designer and help guide the designer in the development of the Flash document. The pasteboard is also a convenient place to store graphic objects until you are ready to add them to the Stage. So, you can use the pasteboard as a notes or storage area as you develop Flash documents.

Timeline

The **Timeline**, shown in Figure 1-9, controls and coordinates the layers and frames that make up a Flash document. Layers are used to organize the images, animations, and other objects that are part of a document. As mentioned above, a frame represents a unit of time. Another key element of the Timeline is the **playhead**, a marker that indicates which frame is currently selected in the Timeline.

Flash Timeline | Figure 1-9

Flash documents are divided into frames similar to a motion picture film. The Timeline is used to coordinate and control the timing of the animation by determining how and when these frames are displayed. Each frame can contain different images or different states of the same image. As the document's animation is played over time, the playhead moves from frame to frame and the contents of each frame appear in succession, achieving the perception of motion. You can play an animation using the commands on the

Control menu. You can also play the animation manually by **scrubbing**, or dragging the playhead back and forth through the frames. Scrubbing is useful when testing an animation during development. A new document in Flash contains one frame. You add more frames as you build an animation.

The Timeline also controls layers. The layers are listed in a column on the left side of the Timeline. Each row represents one layer. The frames for that layer are shown to the right of the layer name. A new Flash document starts with one layer. For each layer you add, another row is inserted into the Timeline. You can place different objects on the different layers. When you draw or change something on a layer, only the contents of the active layer are changed. The objects on the other layers are not affected.

Tip

To resize the layer name column of the Timeline, drag the right edge of the column left or right.

To explore the frames, layers, and playhead in the Timeline:

1. If you took a break after the previous session, make sure the MyKite document located in the Tutorial.01\Tutorial folder included with your Data Files is open, the Stage magnification is set to Show All, and the workspace layout is set to Default.
2. Scrub the playhead by dragging it back and forth along the Timeline header. The animation on the Stage changes based on the contents of the different frames as you scrub the playhead.
3. In the Timeline header, click **Frame 25**. Frame 25 is the current frame, and its contents appear on the Stage. See Figure 1-10.

Figure 1-10 Frame selected in the Timeline header

4. In the Kite layer under the Show/Hide All Layers column, click the dot. The dot changes to a Hidden Layer icon and the contents of the Kite layer are hidden.
5. In the Kite layer, click the **Hidden Layer** icon. The contents of the Kite layer are shown.

Tools Panel

The **Tools panel**, located on the left side of the Flash workspace, contains the tools that you use to draw, paint, select, and modify Flash graphics. The Tools panel also contains tools to change the magnification level of the Stage and to select colors.

You select a tool in the Tools panel by clicking the tool's button or pressing the tool's keyboard shortcut. A small arrow in the lower-right corner of a tool's button indicates that other tools are hidden behind the button. To access the hidden tools, click and hold the tool button to open a pop-up menu, and then click a tool on the pop-up menu to select it. The function of each tool and its corresponding button and shortcut are described in Figure 1-11.

Tools panel tools and their functions — **Figure 1-11**

TOOL NAME	BUTTON	SHORTCUT KEY	FUNCTION
Selection		V	Selects objects in the Document window; you must select an object to modify it
Subselection		A	Modifies specific anchor points in a line or curve
Free Transform		Q	Moves, scales, rotates, skews, or distorts objects
Lasso		L	Selects objects or a group of objects
Pen		P	Draws lines or curves by creating anchor points that connect them; clicking draws points for straight lines; clicking and dragging draws points for smooth, curved lines
Text		T	Creates and edits text
Line		N	Draws straight lines (strokes) of varying lengths, widths, and colors
Rectangle		R	Draws rectangles of different sizes and colors
Pencil		Y	Draws lines and shapes in a free-form mode
Brush		B	Paints fills with brush strokes
Ink Bottle		S	Applies color, thickness, and styles to lines
Paint Bucket		K	Fills enclosed areas of a drawing with color
Eyedropper		I	Picks up styles of existing lines, fills, and text and applies them to other objects
Eraser		E	Erases lines and fills
Hand		H	Moves the view of the Stage and pasteboard
Zoom		M, Z	Increases or reduces the view of the Stage and pasteboard
Stroke color control			Sets the stroke color; click control to display color palette
Fill color control			Sets the fill color; click control to display color palette
Black and white button			Sets the stroke color to black and the fill color to white
Swap colors button			Swaps the current stroke and fill colors
No color button			Specifies that no color be used; can be set for either the stroke or fill color

The first area of the Tools panel contains tools to select and modify graphic images in a Flash document. The Selection tool, Subselection tool, and Lasso tool are used to select one or more objects or to select part of an object by dragging a marquee around them. A **marquee** is an outline that encloses an area to be selected. The Selection and Subselection tools create rectangular marquees. The Lasso tool creates a free-form marquee. The Free Transform tool is used to rotate, skew, scale, or distort selected objects.

Tip

To arrange the tools in two columns, click the double-arrow icon at the top of the Tools panel.

The second area of the Tools panel contains tools that are used to create and modify the lines, shapes, and text that make up the graphic images of a Flash document. For example, you can draw ovals and rectangles, you can draw lines and curves, and you can create and edit text.

The third area of the Tools panel contains tools used to fill in shapes with color, copy color from one object to another, and to erase parts of an object.

Below this area are the Hand tool and the Zoom tool. The Hand tool converts the pointer to a hand that can then be dragged to move the view of the Stage. This is especially useful when you want to see a different area of a document that has been magnified. The Zoom tool changes the view of the Stage by reducing or enlarging it. Neither of these tools affects the way the Flash graphic is displayed to the end user.

Some tools have modifiers that change the way a specific tool functions. The modifiers appear at the bottom of the Tools panel when the tool is selected. For example, when you select the Zoom tool, the Enlarge and Reduce modifier buttons appear so you can choose whether the Zoom tool magnifies or shrinks the view of the Stage.

InSight | Using the Tools Panel Effectively

As you create documents in Flash, you most often will use the tools in the Tools panel. Always look carefully at which tool is selected before you click an object on the Stage. The pointer changes to reflect the function of the tool that is currently selected. For example, when the Zoom tool is selected, the pointer appears as a magnifying glass. Double-check which tool is selected to ensure you make the changes you intended.

Aly wants you to try using some of the tools in the Tools panel to modify the MyKite document.

To use tools in the Tools panel to modify the MyKite document:

1. Click **Control** on the menu bar, and then click **Rewind**. Frame 1 of the document becomes the current frame.
2. In the Tools panel, click the **Selection** tool, if necessary. The pointer changes to .
3. In the pasteboard to the left of the Stage, click the **kite**. A light blue box surrounds the kite to indicate that it is selected. See Figure 1-12.

Figure 1-12 Kite selected in the pasteboard

Trouble? If the rest of the document fades, you probably double-clicked the kite and entered a different editing mode. Click the Scene 1 link on the Edit bar.

4. Drag the kite up toward the top of the pasteboard just to the left of the Stage. This becomes the new starting point for the kite animation.

   You'll preview the animation to see how moving the kite changed its path.

5. Click **Control** on the menu bar, and then click **Play**. The animation changed based on the different starting point of the kite.

Panels

Flash puts most of the controls you need into panels that you can keep handy as you work. A **panel** contains controls for viewing and changing the properties of objects such as vector and bitmap graphics. Flash includes panels for aligning objects, transforming objects, and mixing and selecting colors. The Window menu lists all of the available panels. Panels with a check mark next to them appear in the Flash workspace. Each displayed panel has a tab with the name of the panel. Panels also have an options menu accessible from the options menu control located in the upper-right side of the panel. Two or more panels displayed together form a **panel group**. A **dock** is a collection of panels or panel groups. Figure 1-13 shows the panels in their default layout.

Figure 1-13 Panels in their default layout

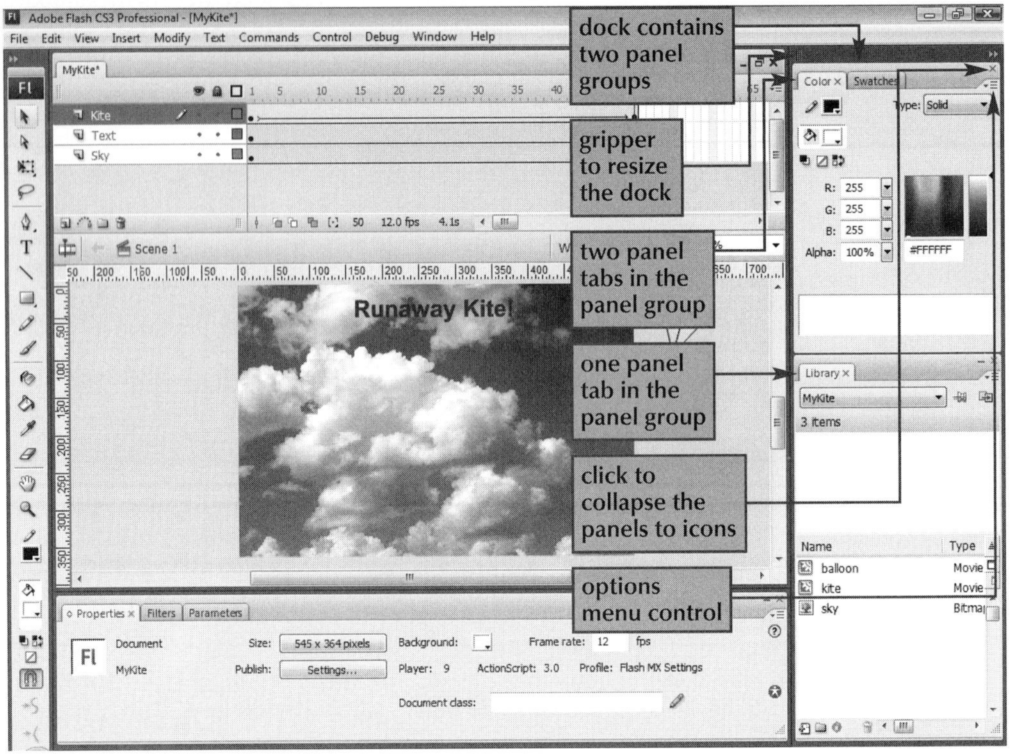

You can organize panels according to your preference. You can close a panel you don't use often, reposition panels to better fit how you work, and collapse panels to icons to minimize the space they occupy in the workspace. You can also move a panel into another dock or panel group or create a free-floating panel by moving it onto the workspace.

You can work with panel groups in much the same way. You can close, collapse, or expand a panel group. A collapsed panel group has only its title bar and panel tabs visible. You can move a panel group to a new location in a dock or create a free-floating panel group. You can also stack free-floating panels as one unit.

Finally, you can collapse a dock to reduce the amount of space it occupies. Each panel appears as a button in the dock, as shown in Figure 1-14. You click a panel's button to expand or collapse that panel. Also, you can drag the gripper to change the width of all the panels in a dock.

Figure 1-14 Panels collapsed to icons

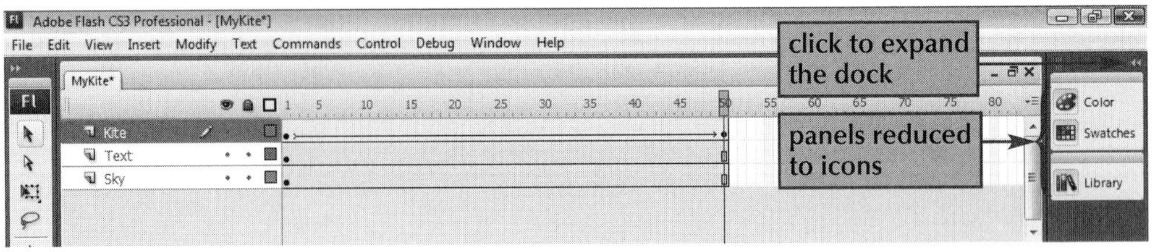

Organizing Panels and Panel Groups

| Reference Window

- To display or hide a panel, click Window on the menu bar, and then click the panel name.
- To move a panel, drag and drop its tab into another dock or panel group or the workspace.
- To collapse or expand a panel group, click its title bar (or click the Minimize or Maximize button on the panel title bar).
- To move a panel group, drag its title bar to another location in a dock or in the workspace.
- To minimize or maximize a dock, click the Collapse to Icons button or Expand Dock button in the upper-right corner of the dock.
- To resize a dock's width, drag the gripper in the upper-left corner of the dock.

After you customize the panels' arrangement, you can save the layout. The next time you start Flash, you can select the saved panel layout to quickly rearrange the panels to that layout.

To collapse, expand, and reposition panels:

1. Click **Window** on the menu bar, point to **Workspace**, and then click **Default**. The Color and Swatches panels appear at the top of the dock in the upper-right corner of the workspace and the Library panel appears in the lower-right corner.
2. Click the **Swatches** tab. The Swatches panel moves to the front of the panel group. See Figure 1-15.

Swatches panel **Figure 1-15**

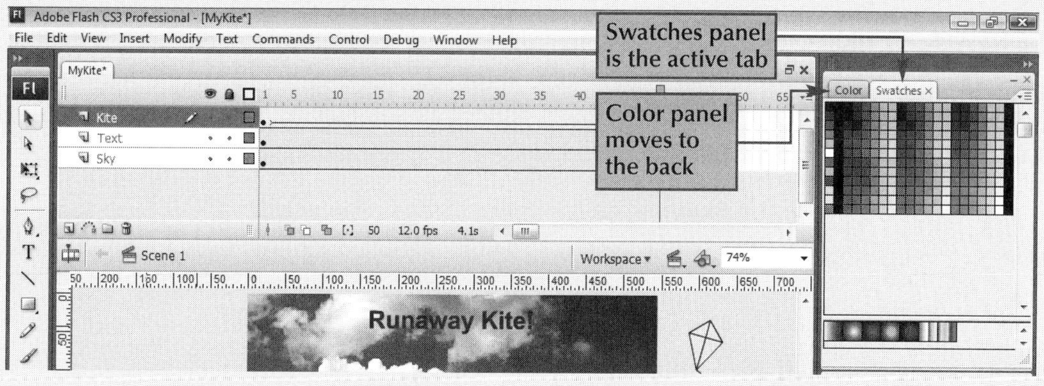

3. Click **Window** on the menu bar, and then click **Movie Explorer**. The Movie Explorer panel opens as a free-floating panel.

   You can combine two or more panels together as a free-floating panel group.

4. Drag the **Color panel** tab to the Movie Explorer panel title bar and drop the panel when the blue highlighted line appears around the Movie Explorer panel. The Movie Explorer panel and the Color panel are grouped as a free-floating panel group. See Figure 1-16.

Figure 1-16 Free-floating panel group

Panels collapsed to icons minimize the amount of space they occupy.

5. In the upper-right corner of the dock above the Swatches panel, click the **Collapse to Icons** button. The panels collapse to icons.
6. In the dock, click the **Swatches** button. The Swatches panel expands. See Figure 1-17.

Figure 1-17 Swatches panel expanded

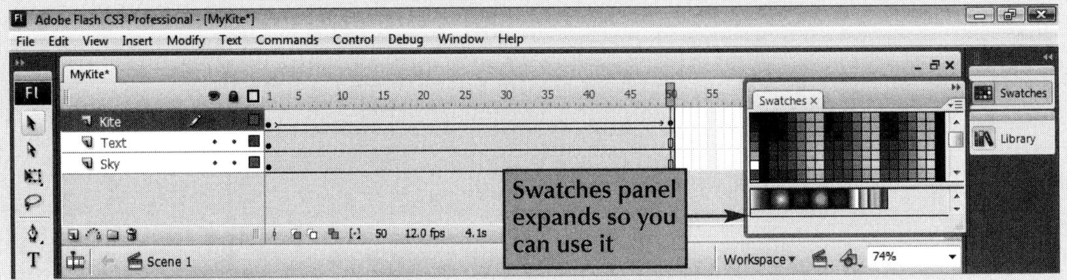

7. In the dock, click the **Swatches** button again. The panel collapses to an icon.

   The Workspace menu on the Edit bar contains options for quickly changing the layout of the panels.

8. On the Edit bar, click the **Workspace** button, and then click **Icons Only Default**. The panels are arranged as icons along the right side of the workspace and the Movie Explorer panel group moves to the dock.
9. On the Edit bar, click **Workspace**, and then click **Default**. The panels return to their default layout. The Color panel is again in the right dock.

The Property Inspector

Many of the most frequently used options are located in the Property inspector, which is located at the bottom of the Flash workspace. The **Property inspector** is a special panel that provides easy access to the most common attributes of the currently selected tool or object. The contents of the Property inspector change to reflect the selected tool. For example, if you click the Selection tool in the Tools panel, the Property inspector displays information about the document such as the background color or the frame rate. If you select an object on the Stage, such as the kite, the contents of the Property inspector display properties specific to the object, such as the name of the object, its X and Y coordinates (location on the Stage), and its width and height.

You'll use the Property inspector to change the kite's properties.

To use the Property inspector to change the kite's location and dimensions:

1. Click **Control** on the menu bar, and then click **Rewind**. Frame 1 is the current frame.
2. In the Tools panel, click the **Selection** tool, if necessary. The Property inspector displays information about the MyKite document. See Figure 1-18.

Property Inspector for the Selection tool **Figure 1-18**

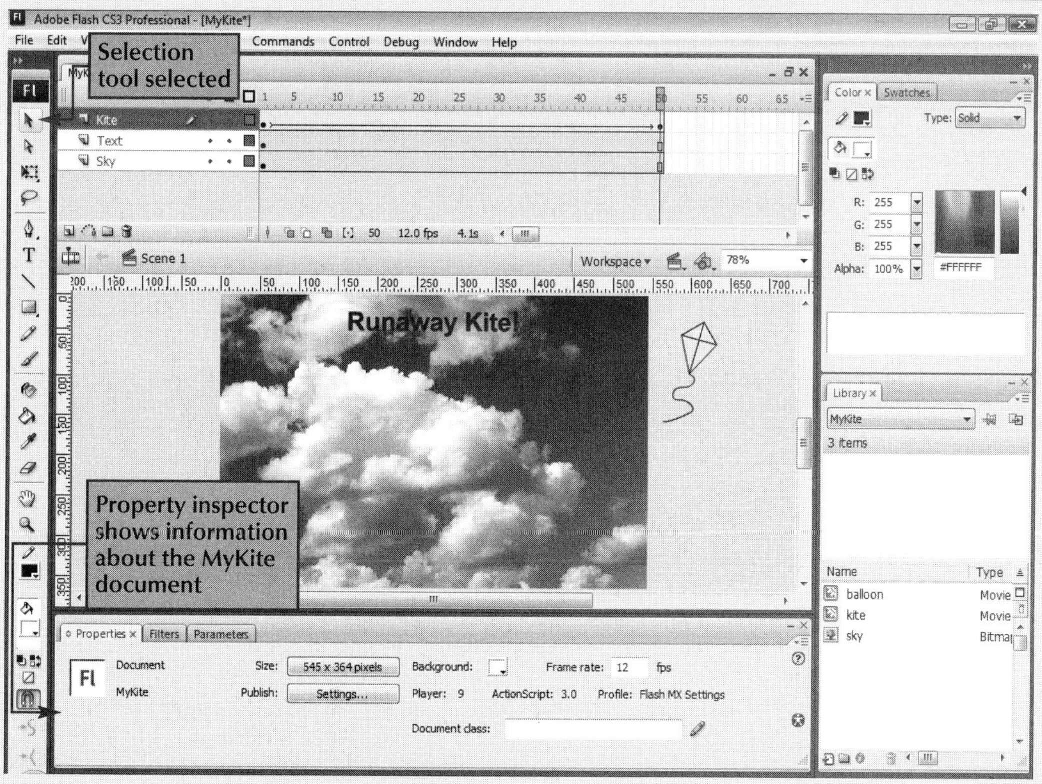

3. In the pasteboard, click the **kite**. The kite is selected, and information about the kite appears in the Property inspector.

   To reposition the kite, you will change its X and Y coordinates. These values represent the horizontal (X) and vertical (Y) position of the kite relative to the upper-left corner of the Stage.

4. In the Property inspector, double-click the value in the **X** box, type **50**, and then press the **Enter** key. The kite moves horizontally.
5. In the Property inspector, double-click the value in the **Y** box, type **200**, and then press the **Enter** key. The kite moves vertically. See Figure 1-19.

Figure 1-19 Kite repositioned in the pasteboard

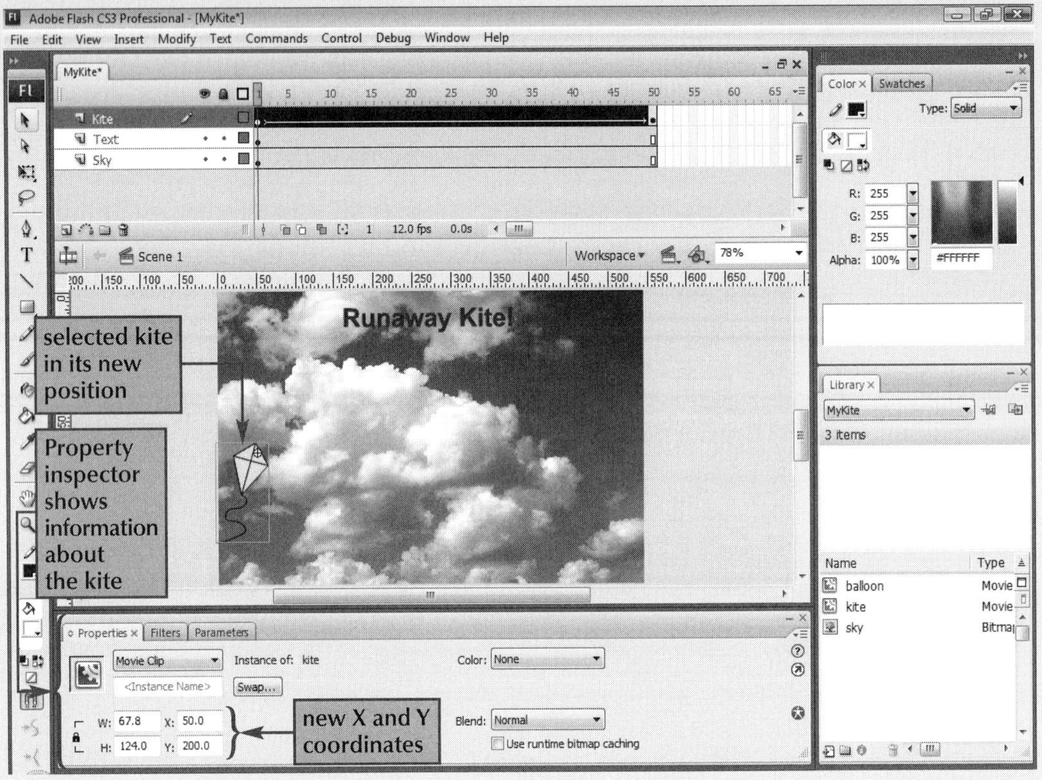

You can change the kite's dimensions by entering new values for the width (W) and the height (H).

6. In the Property inspector, click the **unlock** icon to lock it, if necessary.
7. In the Property inspector, double-click the value in the **W** box, type **25**, and then press the **Enter** key. The height (H) value adjusts proportionally to the new width value and the kite gets smaller.

   You will play the animation to see the effect of the changes you made to the kite's properties.

8. Click **Control** on the menu bar, and then click **Play**. The kite starts in its new position and moves to its end position as before. The kite gradually changes back to its original dimensions. Because you changed the dimensions of the kite only in Frame 1, Flash adjusted the rest of the frames to change the kite to its original dimensions in the last frame.

   You no longer need the MyKite file. You'll close it without saving any changes you made.

9. Click **File** on the menu bar, and then click **Close**. A dialog box prompts you to save the changes you made to the MyKite document.
10. Click the **No** button. The MyKite file closes and the Start page appears.

Changing the View of the Stage

As you develop graphics on the Stage, you will need to change the view of the Stage. You can adjust the magnification level and move different parts of the Stage into view. You can also display the grid, rulers, and guides to assist you as you draw or align graphics. And you can change a document's properties.

Magnifying and Moving the Stage

You can change the view of the Stage by using the Zoom tool in the Tools panel to adjust the magnification level. The Zoom tool includes the Enlarge and Reduce modifiers at the bottom of the Tools panel. The Enlarge modifier, selected by default, sets the Zoom tool to increase the magnification level. To reduce the magnification level of the Stage, you click the Reduce modifier. Then, you click the Zoom tool on the part of the Stage you want to enlarge or reduce. You can also select an area to enlarge by dragging the pointer over an area of the Stage to draw a marquee around it.

Another way to adjust the magnification level is with the View menu. The Zoom In and Zoom Out commands enlarge and reduce the view of the Stage, respectively. The Magnification command has a submenu of percentage levels that you can apply to the view of the Stage. The submenu also includes the Fit in Window, Show Frame, and Show All commands. The Fit in Window command adjusts the Stage to fit completely within the Document window. The Show All command changes the view of the Stage to display all the contents of the current frame, including objects in the pasteboard. The Show Frame command changes the magnification level to make the entire Stage is visible. A quick way to access the Magnification submenu commands is by clicking the Zoom control on the Edit bar.

Changing the View of the Stage | Reference Window

- In the Tools panel, click the Zoom tool.
- In the Tools panel, click the Enlarge or Reduce modifier.
- Click a part of the Stage (or drag the pointer to draw a marquee around the part of the Stage to enlarge or reduce).

or

- Click View on the menu bar (or click the Zoom control on the Edit bar).
- Click the appropriate command.

You'll try various ways to change the view of the Stage. You will use a document that contains objects Aly has drawn in Flash.

To open the Sample document and change the view of the Stage:

1. Click **File** on the menu bar, click **Open** to open the Open dialog box, navigate to the **Tutorial.01\Tutorial** folder included with your Data Files, click **Sample.fla** in the file list, and then click the **Open** button. The Sample document opens in the workspace.
2. Click **File** on the menu bar, and then click **Save As**. The Save As dialog box opens.
3. Navigate to the **Tutorial.01\Tutorial** folder included with your Data Files, type **MySample** in the File name box, and then click the **Save** button. The document is saved with the new name. You do not need to type the .fla extension when saving a document; Flash will enter the file extension for you.

Tip

You can also click the Open button on the Start page to open the Open dialog box.

You'll hide the Timeline because you will not use it in this tutorial. Hiding the Timeline provides more room for the Stage and pasteboard.

4. On the Edit bar, click the **Hide Timeline** button. The Timeline closes and the pasteboard expands to fill the space.
5. On the Edit bar, click the **Zoom control arrow**, and then click **50%**. The view of the Stage changes.

   Next, you'll use the Zoom tool to magnify the fish graphic.
6. In the Tools panel, click the **Zoom** tool, and then, if necessary, click the **Enlarge** modifier button. The pointer changes to .
7. On the Stage, click the middle of the **fish** object twice. The magnification level increases each time you click. The fish is centered in the Document window each time you click it. See Figure 1-20.

Figure 1-20 Magnified fish shape

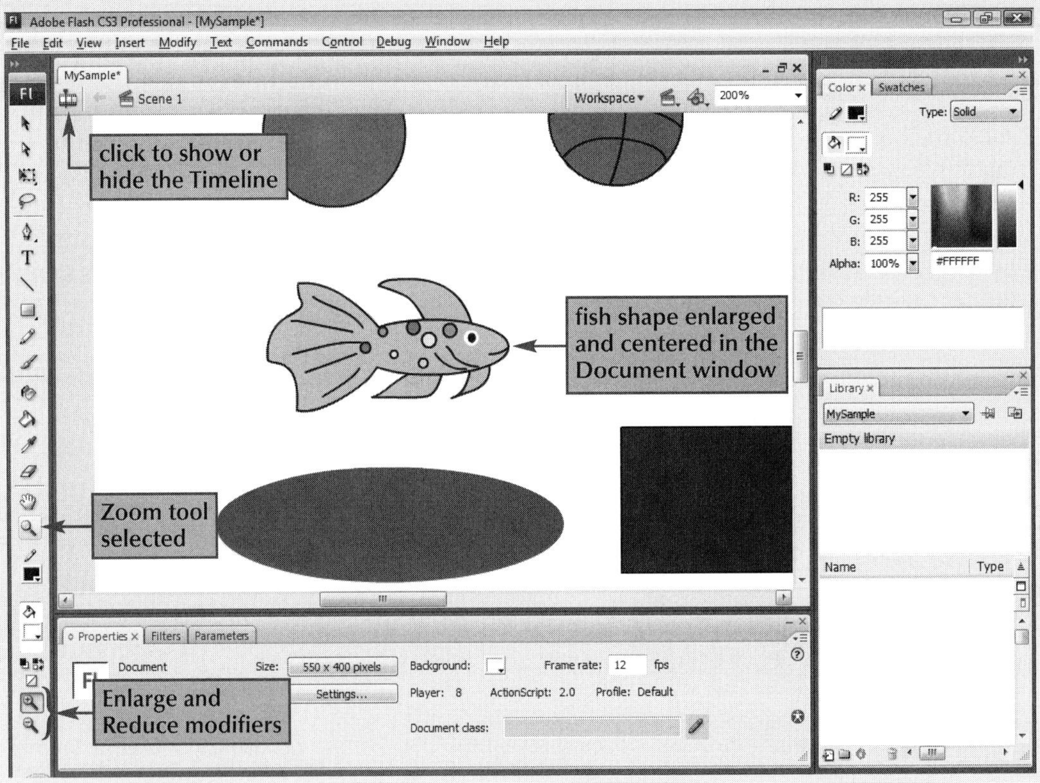

After you magnify the view of the Stage, some graphic objects shift out of sight. You can move the Stage without changing the magnification level by using the Hand tool to drag the part of the Stage you want to see into view. You'll shift the baseball graphic into view.

To use the Hand tool to view the baseball graphic on the Stage:

1. In the Tools panel, click the **Hand** tool. The pointer changes to as you move it over the Stage.
2. Drag the Stage to the left until you see the baseball in the middle of the Document window. See Figure 1-21.

Stage view shifted **Figure 1-21**

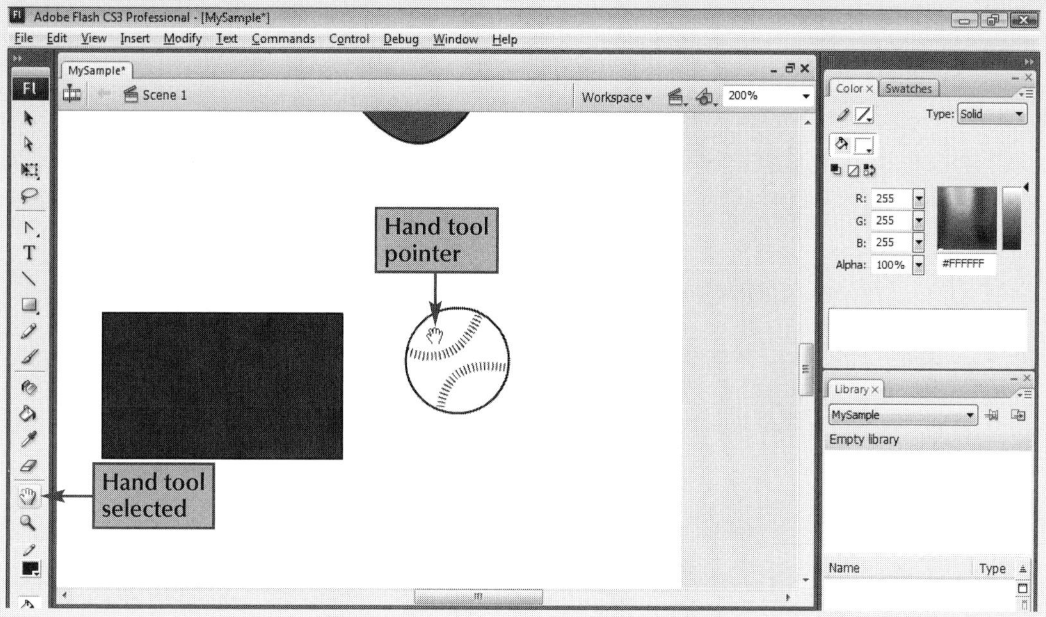

Next, you'll reduce the magnification of the Stage.

3. In the Tools panel, click the **Zoom** tool, and then click the **Reduce** modifier button. The pointer changes to .
4. Click the center of the **baseball**, and then click the center of the **basketball**. The magnification level of the Stage reduces each time you click.
5. In the Tools panel, double-click the **Hand** tool. The magnification level of the Stage is enlarged to show all of its contents centered in the Document window.

Displaying the Grid, Rulers, and Guides

The Stage includes grids, rulers, and guides, which are designed to help you create documents. You can lay out objects on the Stage more precisely if you display the grid. The **grid** appears as a set of lines on the Stage behind all of the objects you place or draw on the Stage. The grid lines are not part of the document. They are only visible as you develop the document. The Grid submenu, located on the View menu, offers commands for controlling the grid. The Show Grid command displays the grid on the Stage. The Edit Grid command opens the Grid dialog box so you can customize the grid. For example, you can select a color for the grid lines that is different from the document's background color to make the grid lines easier to see, and you can change the spacing between the lines. You can also select the Snap to Grid option to make objects attach to the grid lines as you move or draw them on the Stage. Snapping enables you to more accurately align objects vertically or horizontally. Changes you make to the grid are saved with the currently active document.

You will first display the grid in the MySample document.

To display and edit the grid for the MySample document:

1. Click **View** on the menu bar, point to **Grid**, and then click **Show Grid**. A check mark appears next to the command and the grid lines are displayed on the Stage. See Figure 1-22.

Figure 1-22 Grid shown on the Stage

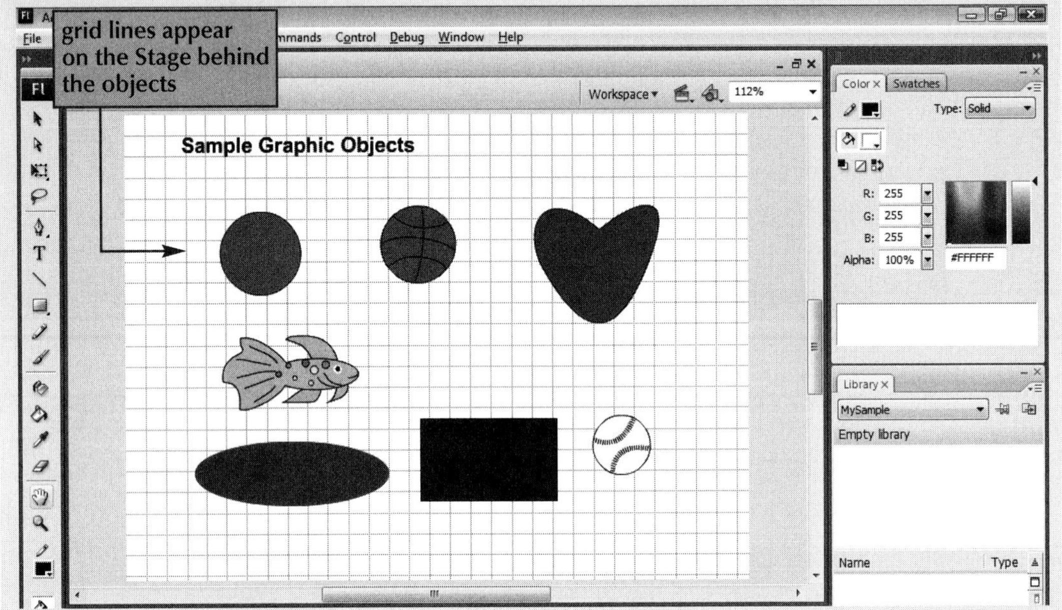

You'll use the Grid dialog box to modify how the grid appears on the Stage. You'll change the grid line color and turn on the Snap to grid option.

2. Click **View** on the menu bar, point to **Grid**, and then click **Edit Grid**. The Grid dialog box opens. See Figure 1-23.

Figure 1-23 Grid dialog box

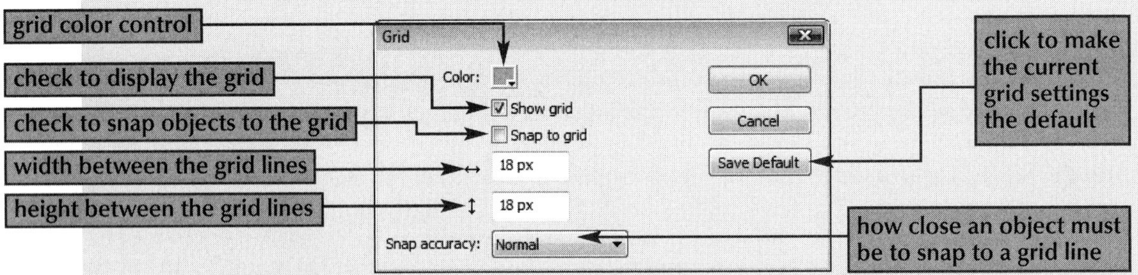

3. Click the **Color** control. The color palette opens and the pointer changes to [pointer icon].
4. Click the **blue** color swatch in the first column, ninth row of the color palette. The grid lines change to blue.

5. Click the **Snap to grid** check box to insert a check mark. With this option selected, objects will snap to, or align with, the nearest grid line when you move or draw them.
6. Click the **OK** button. The Grid dialog box closes, and the grid lines reflect the settings you selected.

Measuring in Pixels | InSight

You can use various units of measurement in Flash including inches, points, and centimeters. Because most elements in Web pages are measured in pixels, you should also use pixels to express the width and height values of Web graphics. A pixel, short for picture element, is the Flash default unit of measurement. Pixels represent the smallest picture element on the monitor that can be controlled by the computer. Each pixel is composed of three colors, red, green, and blue.

As you develop graphics, you might want to display the rulers. The **rulers** display the selected unit of measurement on the left and top edges of the Stage window. The rulers show the unit of measurement, such as pixels, that is specified in the Document Properties dialog box. The rulers are very helpful in placing objects on the Stage according to specific coordinates.

When the rulers are displayed, you can create vertical or horizontal guides. A **guide** is a line used to align objects that you move to a specific part of the Stage using the rulers for reference. To create a guide, click a ruler and drag a line onto the Stage. If you drag from the top ruler, a horizontal guide is created. If you drag from the left ruler, a vertical guide is created. You can edit the guides to change their color to make them easier to see against the background, snap objects to them, and lock them into place. Guides, like grid lines, do not become part of a document. They are visible only while you are working with the document. Guides can be created whether or not the grid is displayed.

Aly wants you to create guides in the MySample document. You'll need to display the rulers first.

To display the rulers and create guides in the MySample document:

1. Click **View** on the menu bar, and then click **Rulers**. The rulers appear along the left and top sides of the pasteboard.
2. In the Tools panel, click the **Selection** tool.
3. Click the **horizontal ruler** at the top of the pasteboard. The pointer changes to .
4. Click and drag the pointer down from the horizontal ruler to approximately **105** pixels on the vertical ruler. The horizontal guide you created snaps to the closest grid line. See Figure 1-24.

Figure 1-24 Horizontal guide

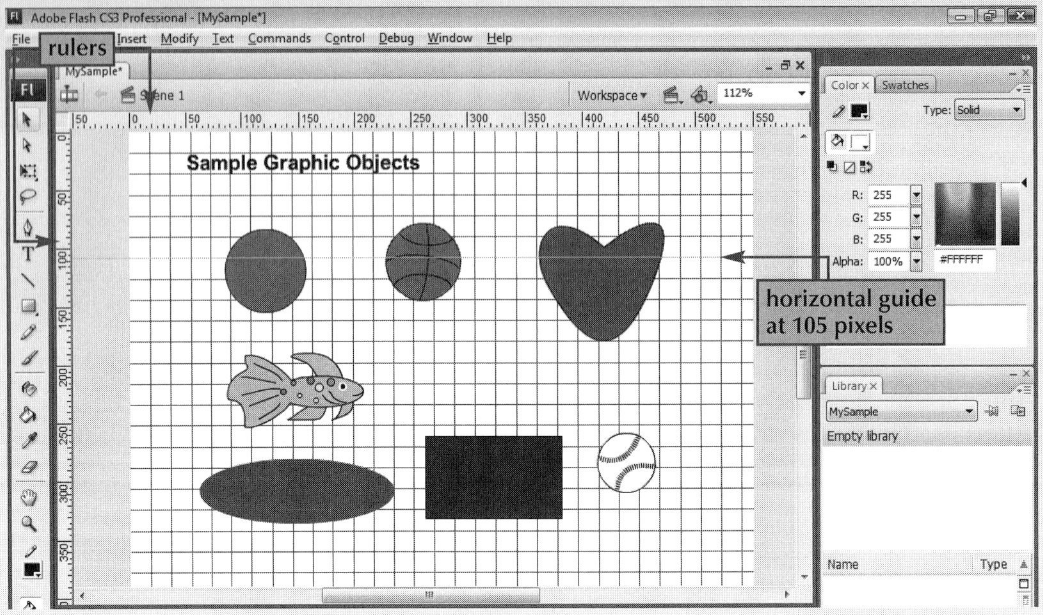

Next, you will create a vertical guide.

5. Click the **vertical ruler** and drag the pointer to the right to approximately **105** pixels on the horizontal ruler. The vertical guide you created snaps to the closest grid line.
6. Click **View** on the menu bar, point to **Guides**, and then click **Edit Guides**. The Guides dialog box opens. See Figure 1-25.

Figure 1-25 Guides dialog box

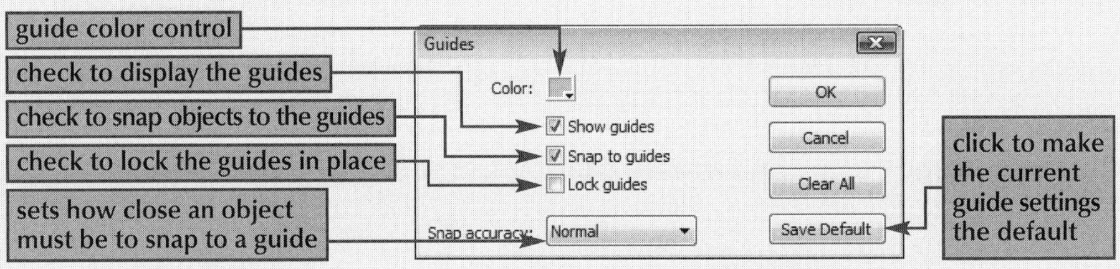

You'll change the color of the guides.

7. Click the **Color** control. The color palette opens and the pointer changes to (eyedropper icon).
8. Click the **red** color swatch located in the first column, seventh row of the color palette. The guides change to red.
9. Click the **OK** button. The Guides dialog box closes.

Changing the Document Properties

Every document in Flash has certain properties such as Title, Description, Stage size, background color, frame rate, and ruler unit. Title and Description are embedded within the SWF file and can be used by search engines to categorize Flash content on the Web.

The other document properties are set at default values when you open a new document. For example, the default Stage size is 550 pixels wide by 400 pixels high. In addition, the Stage background color is set to white, the frame rate is set to 12 frames per second, and the ruler units are set to pixels. (The frame rate specifies how many frames in an animation are displayed in one second.) You change a document's default properties in the Document Properties dialog box. Changes you make in the dialog box are reflected on the Stage.

Aly suggests you modify the MySample document's properties by changing its background color.

To change the MySample document's background color:

1. Click **Modify** on the menu bar, and then click **Document**. The Document Properties dialog box opens. See Figure 1-26.

Figure 1-26 Document Properties dialog box

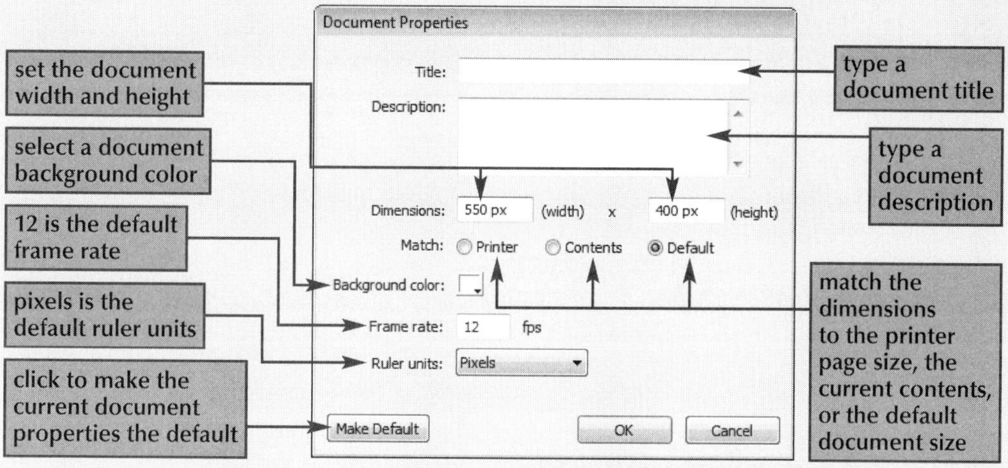

Tip

You can also open the Document Properties dialog box by clicking the Size button in the Property inspector.

You can use the options in this dialog box to change the background color of the document. The dimensions, frame rate, and ruler units are fine with the defaults.

2. Click the **Background color** control. The color palette opens and the pointer changes to .
3. Click the **gray** color swatch located in the first column, third row of the color palette.
4. Click the **OK** button. The dialog box closes, and the Stage has a gray background color.

   You can also change the document's background color in the Property inspector.

5. Click the pasteboard. The document properties appear in the Property inspector.
6. In the Property inspector, click the **Background** box, and then click the **white** color swatch located in the first column, sixth row of the color palette. The Stage returns to a white background.
7. Click **File** on the menu bar, then click **Save**. The changes you made to the document are saved.

You no longer need the rulers, grid, or guides. You'll hide them for now.

To hide the rulers, grid, and guides:

1. Click **View** on the menu bar, and then click **Rulers** to turn off the rulers.
2. Click **View** on the menu bar, point to **Grid**, and then click **Show Grid** to turn off the grid.
3. Click **View** on the menu bar, point to **Guides**, and then click **Show Guides** to turn off the guides.

In this session, you learned about the basic components of the Flash workspace. You learned how to open and reposition the panels, how to change the display of the Stage, how to modify the document settings, and how to use the tools in the Tools panel. In the next session, you will learn how graphic objects drawn in Flash interact with each other and how to select and group objects.

Review | Session 1.2 Quick Check

1. In what area do you position the objects that will appear in the document?
2. What area displays the document's frame and layer information?
3. What is the Hand tool used for?
4. ________________ is when you drag the playhead back and forth in the Timeline to test a document.
5. Which panel changes to display different options depending on the tool or object selected?
6. Describe two ways to change the magnification levels of the Stage.
7. True or False? The grid lines on the Stage become part of the document.
8. How do you create a horizontal guide?

Session 1.3

Working with Objects in Flash

The drawing and painting tools available in the Tools panel include the Line, Pen, Pencil, Oval, Rectangle, and Brush. These tools allow you to create the lines and shapes that make up the images in a Flash document. Before using these tools, it's important to understand how the objects you draw behave and how you can change their basic characteristics, such as their color. In particular, you need to be aware of how shapes or lines you draw interact with existing shapes or lines.

Creating Strokes and Fills

When drawing objects in Flash, you create strokes and fills. **Strokes** are the lines that make up a Flash graphic. These lines can be straight or curved and can be individual line segments or connected together to form shapes. The Flash drawing tools give you a great deal of flexibility and allow you to draw almost any type of line you need. **Fills** are the areas in a Flash graphic that you paint with color. These areas can be enclosed by strokes.

Before you draw a shape, such as an oval or a rectangle, you can specify whether you want the shape to have a stroke, a fill, or both. For example, you can draw a circle that has both a fill and a stroke. You can draw one that has a fill but has no stroke. Or, you can draw the circle with a stroke but no fill. See the examples in Figure 1-27. You can also add a stroke or fill after you draw an object, and you can always modify its stroke or fill properties.

Figure 1-27 Sample shapes with fills and strokes

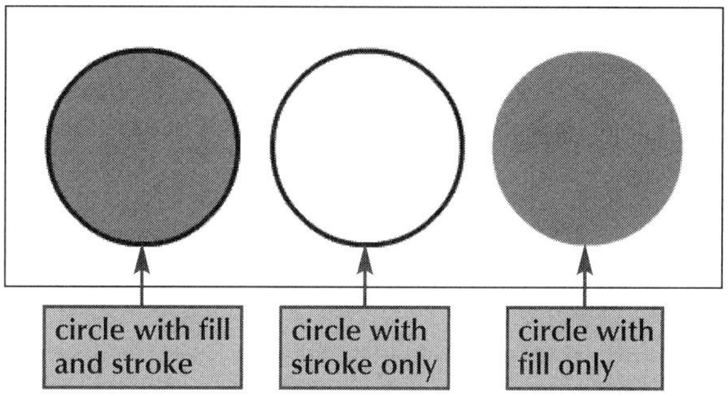

Drawing and Grouping Objects

Flash provides two models for how objects created with the drawing tools such as the Pencil, Line, Oval, and Rectangle tools interact: the Merge Drawing model and the Object Drawing model. By default, Flash uses the Merge Drawing model. The drawing model you use depends on how you want the objects to interact.

With the **Merge Drawing model**, objects drawn or moved on top of other objects merge with or segment the existing objects. (Objects on the same layer are not considered to be on top of or below one another.) For example, when you draw a line through an existing shape such as a circle, the line is split into line segments at the points where it intersects the circle. The circle is also split into separate shapes. These line segments and split shapes can be moved individually. If you draw or move a fill on top of another fill of the same color, the two fills merge and become one shape. If you draw a fill of one color on top of another fill of a different color, the new fill cuts away the existing fill.

With the **Object Drawing model**, the drawn shapes are treated as separate objects and do not merge with or alter other objects on the same layer. When you draw an object using the Object Drawing model, a blue outline appears around the object on the Stage. Figure 1-28 shows how drawn objects interact in each model.

Figure 1-28 Comparison of the drawing models

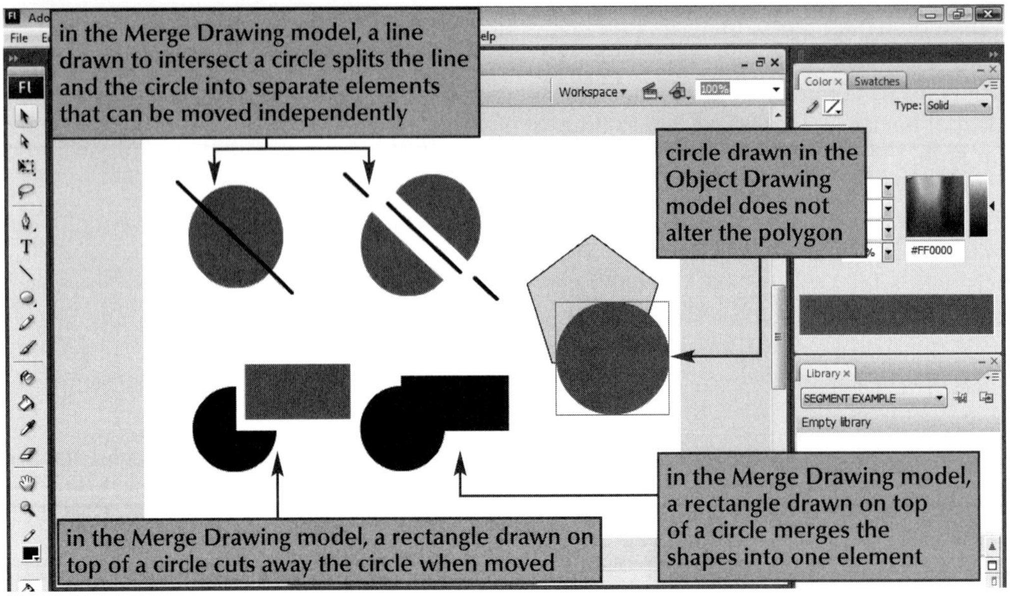

To prevent objects from impacting each other, you can **group** them, which treats two or more objects such as a stroke and a fill as one entity. A thin blue rectangle outlines the grouped object when it is selected. Grouped objects are on top of nongrouped objects so they do not alter or merge with other objects. To modify a grouped object, you must enter group-editing mode. You can then edit the individual objects within the group. When editing the objects within a group, the rest of the objects on the Stage are dimmed, indicating they are not accessible, as shown in Figure 1-29. After you finish modifying the individual objects, you exit group-editing mode.

Figure 1-29 Grouped object in group-editing mode

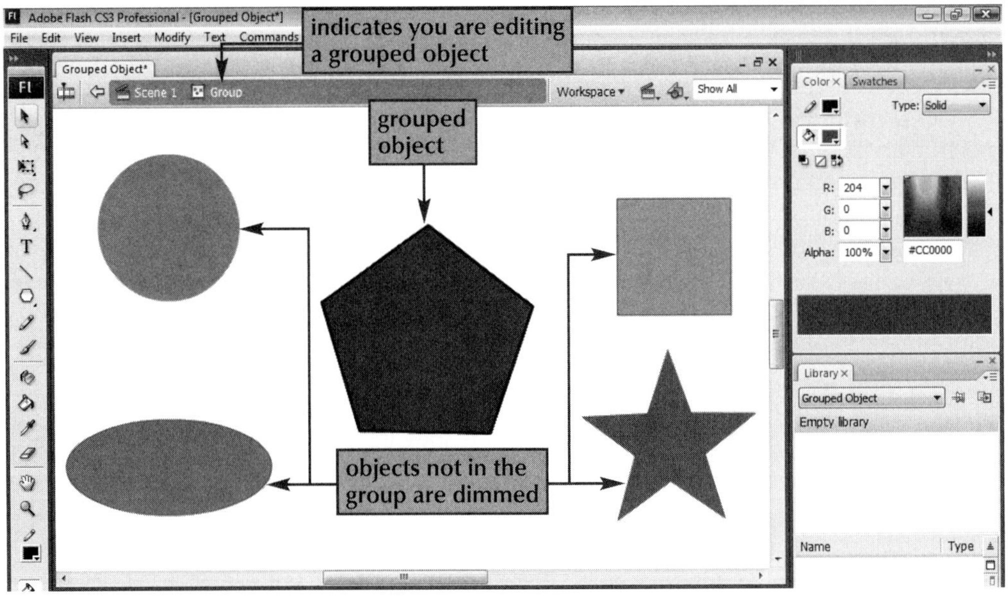

Grouping Fills and Strokes | InSight

When you create a complex object made up of multiple strokes and fills, group the strokes and fills together. This will prevent you from accidently changing one part of the object. It will also make it easier to resize or move the complex object at one time without having to modify the strokes and fills within the object individually.

You'll group the objects that make up the fish in the MySample document.

To group the fish in the MySample document:

1. If you took a break after the previous session, make sure the MySample document located in the Tutorial.01\Tutorial folder included with your Data Files is open, the workspace layout is set to Default, the Timeline is hidden, and the Stage magnification is set to Show All.
2. In the Tools panel, click the **Selection** tool, if necessary.
3. Draw a marquee around the fish graphic. The graphic is selected and a dotted pattern appears on the fish.

   You will group the selected fills and strokes next.
4. Click **Modify** on the menu bar, and then click **Group**. A blue rectangular outline appears around the fish, indicating it is a grouped object. See Figure 1-30.

Figure 1-30 Strokes and fills of fish graphic are grouped

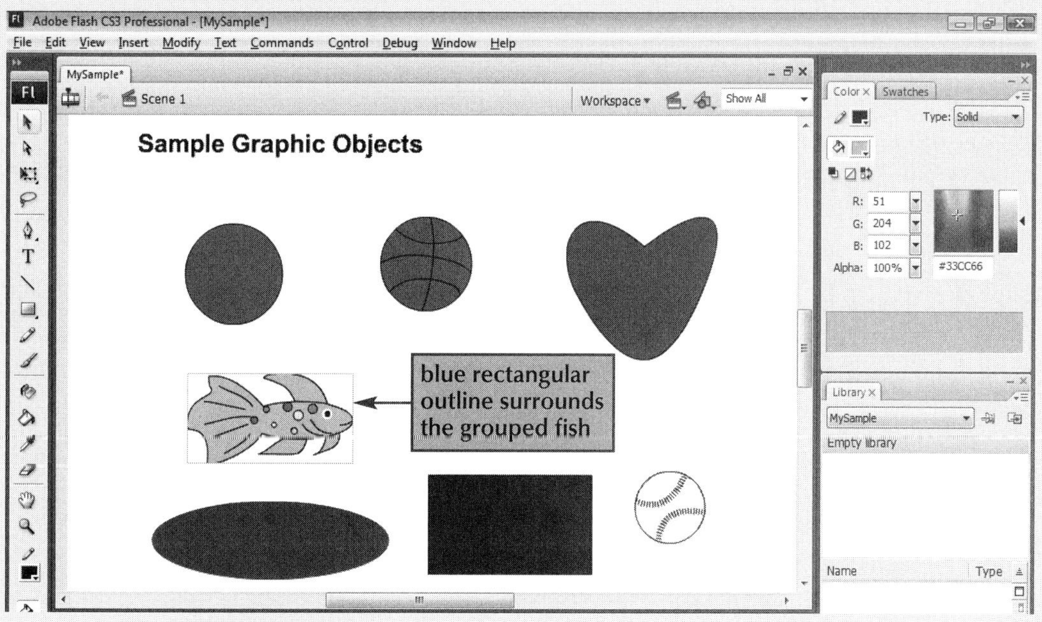

Using the Color Controls and the Color Panel

All strokes and fills can be drawn with different colors. You can specify the colors before you draw strokes and fills or you can change the colors of existing strokes and fills. The simplest way to change the color of a stroke or fill is by using the Stroke color control in the Tool panel to specify the color for strokes and the Fill color control in the Tools panel to specify the color for fills. Each of these controls opens a color palette from which you can select a particular color. Figure 1-31 shows the color palette for the Fill color control.

Figure 1-31 **Color palette for the Fill color control**

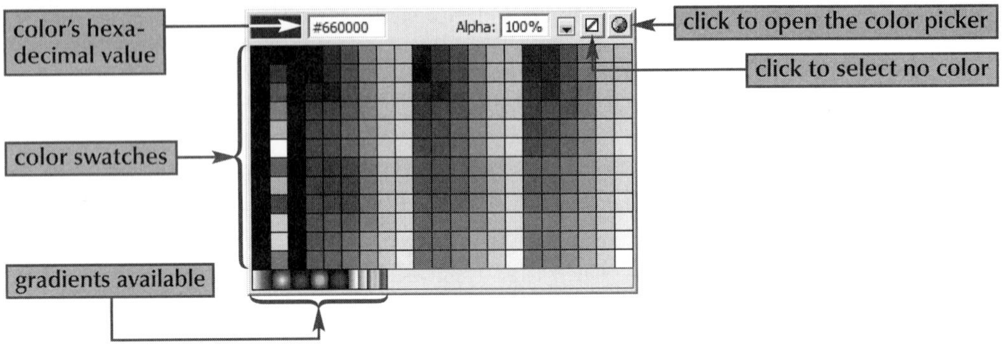

A color square in the palette is referred to as a **swatch**. By default, the color swatches in the color palette are the 216 **Web safe colors**. These colors were developed to display the same on both Internet Explorer and Netscape Navigator browsers, as well as on both Windows and Macintosh operating systems. Most graphic programs still use the Web safe colors but aren't limited to only those 216 colors.The Fill color palette also includes a set of preset gradients. A gradient is a blend of two or more colors. A linear gradient blends the colors from one point to another in a straight line. A radial gradient blends the colors in a circular pattern. Also, you can click the Color Picker button to open the Color dialog box, and create custom colors.

InSight | **Using Hexadecimal Codes**

All colors can be represented using hexadecimal codes. A color's hexadecimal value (such as #00FF00 for green) is based on the three basic colors used on computer monitors: red, green, and blue, referred to as RGB. The first two hexadecimal digits represent the amount of red, the next two digits represent the amount of green, and the last two digits represent the amount of blue. Values for each two-digit pair range from 00 to FF, which are numbers based on the hexadecimal numbering system. These three color values combine to form the desired color. You can enter a color's hexadecimal value into the box above the color swatches in the color palette. Today's computer monitors can display many more than the 216 Web safe colors, so you are not limited to using the Web safe colors.

You can also select colors using the Property inspector. When a strokes or fill tool is selected in the Tools panel or an existing stroke of fill is selected on the Stage, its color controls appear in the Property inspector. These controls work the same way as the Stroke color and Fill color controls in the Tools panel.

Finally, you can select colors using the Color panel shown in Figure 1-32. Using this panel, you can select colors in one of several ways. You can use the panel's color controls to open the color palette, you can enter a color's hexadecimal value, or you can create custom colors.

Figure 1-32 Color panel

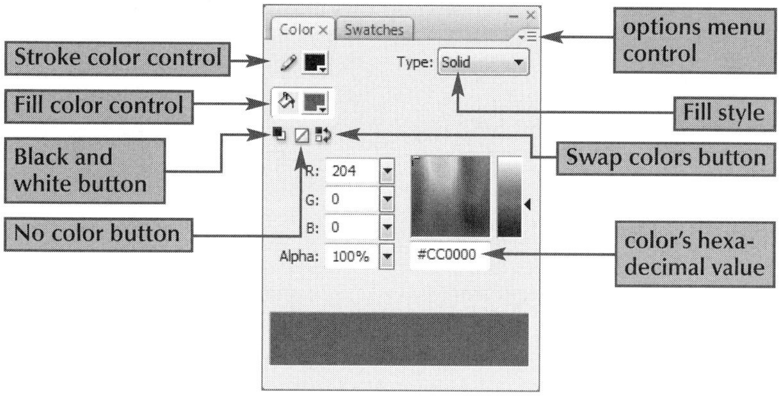

You'll change the color of the strokes in the fish.

To change the stroke color for the grouped fish object:

1. Double-click the **fish** graphic. The contents on the Stage are dimmed except for the fish, indicating you are in group-editing mode.
2. Draw a marquee around the fish graphic to select it, if necessary. The strokes and fills of the fish are selected.
3. On the Property inspector, click the **Stroke color** control to open the color palette, and then click the **red** swatch located in the seventh row, first column of the color palette. The strokes on the fish are red. See Figure 1-33.

Tip

To edit a grouped object, you can also select it and click Edit Selected on the Edit menu. To exit group-editing mode, you can also double-click a blank area of the Stage or click Edit All on the Edit menu.

Figure 1-33 Fish stroke color changed

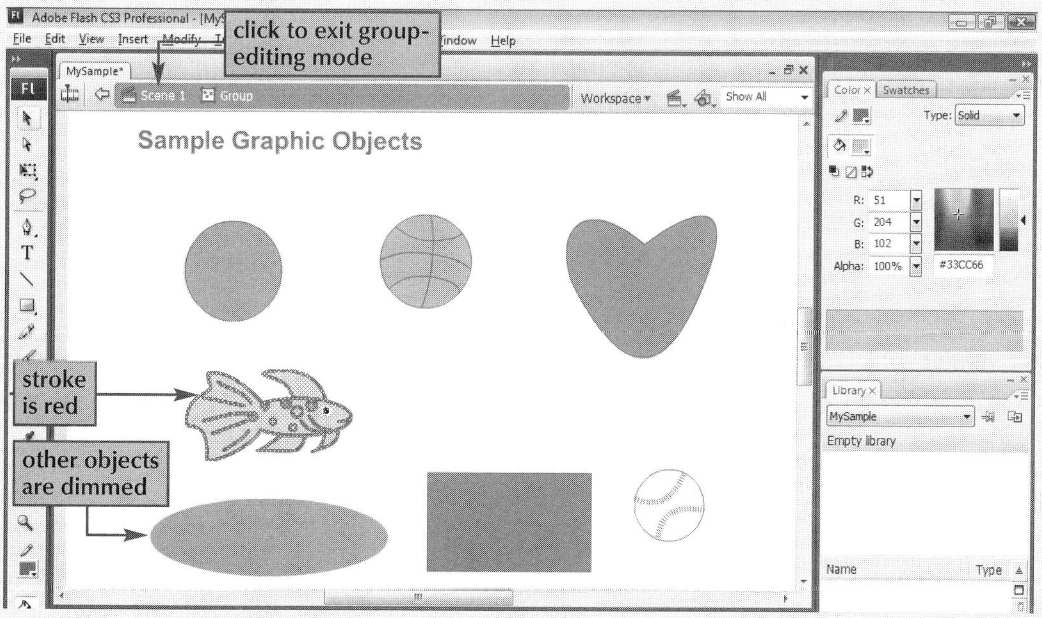

You'll exit group-editing mode.

4. On the Edit bar, click the **Scene 1** link. The contents on the Stage are no longer dimmed.

Selecting Objects

Before you can change the characteristics of a graphic object on the Stage, you must select the object. You can use the Selection, Subselection, and Lasso tools in the Tools panel to select part of an object, the entire object, or several objects at one time. You'll use these tools, especially the Selection tool, frequently as you create graphics.

Selection Tool

The **Selection tool** is used to select strokes or fills as well as a group of objects. You can also use the Selection tool to move selected objects on the Stage or in the pasteboard and to modify objects. You select objects by clicking them or by dragging the pointer to draw a marquee around the object, which is useful for selecting more than one object at a time. When you select a graphic object, a dot pattern covers it to indicate the object is selected. Some selected objects, such as text blocks, have a rectangular outline instead of a dot pattern. You can move a selected object to a new position by dragging it with the Selection tool. To change an object's shape with the Selection tool, deselect the object, move the pointer to one of the object's edges or corners, and then drag to change the object's shape. The pointer changes based on the object you are modifying. If you move the pointer to a corner of a star shape, for example, the pointer changes to , as shown in Figure 1-34.

Figure 1-34 Selection tool modifying an object

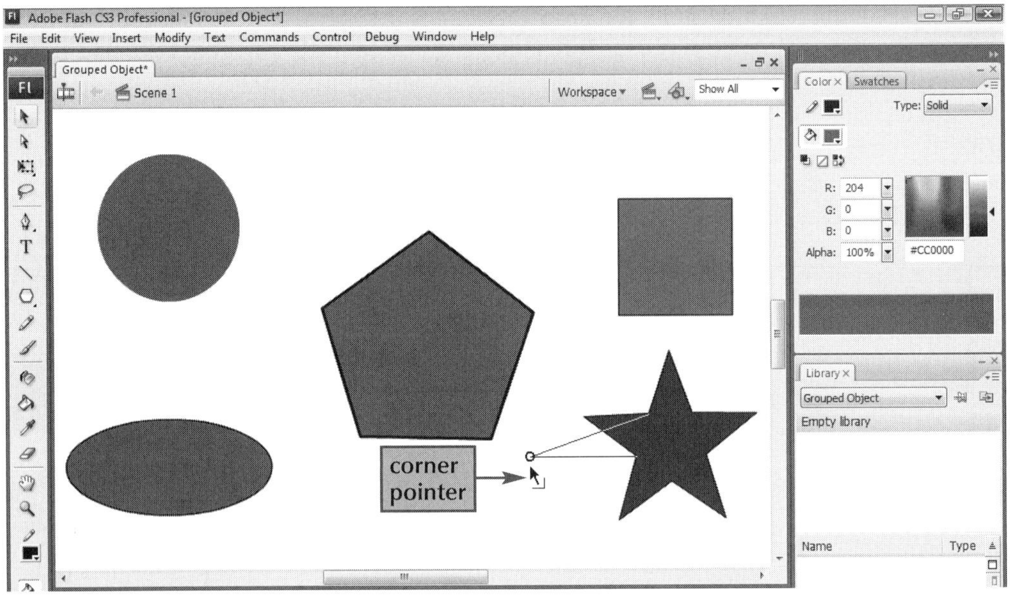

The Selection tool, like many of the tools in the Tools panel, has modifiers that change the way it works. The Selection tool includes the Snap to Objects, Smooth, and Straighten modifiers, which are shown in Figure 1-35.

Figure 1-35 Selection tool modifiers

MODIFIER ICON	MODIFIER	DESCRIPTION
	Snap to Objects	Snaps selected objects to other objects when they are moved close together
	Smooth	Smoothes the selected line or shape outline
	Straighten	Straightens the selected line or shape outline

Aly wants you to use the Selection tool to select and modify the graphics in her sample document.

To select and modify objects with the Selection tool:

1. In the Tools panel, click the **Zoom** tool, and then click the **Enlarge** modifier button.
2. Click the red circle to enlarge and center it in the Stage window.
3. In the Tools panel, click the **Selection** tool. The pointer changes to.
4. Click the center of the red circle and drag it to the right just before the basketball. The circle's fill is separated from its stroke and has a dot pattern to indicate it is selected. See Figure 1-36.

Figure 1-36 Circle's fill and stroke separated

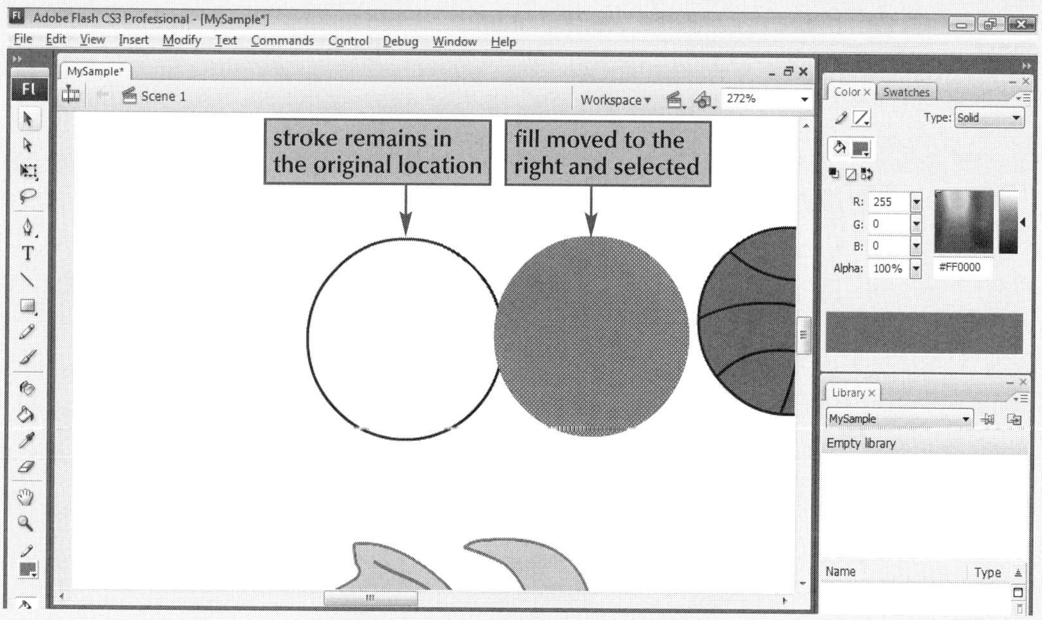

You'll undo this change.

5. Click **Edit** on the menu bar, click **Undo Move** to move the circle's fill back to its original location, and then click a blank area of the Stage to deselect the circle's fill.

You can use the Selection tool to select both the fill and the stroke of the circle simultaneously.

Tip

You can also undo a change by pressing Ctrl+Z keys.

6. Double-click the red circle to select its fill and its stroke, and then drag the selected circle to the right. The stroke and the fill move together.
7. Click a blank area of the Stage to deselect the circle.

   Next, you'll use the Selection tool to change the shape of the circle.
8. Move the pointer over the stroke of the circle until the pointer changes to ↖, and then drag the stroke of the circle away from the center of the circle to change its shape (but do not release the mouse button). See Figure 1-37.

Figure 1-37 Circle's shape being changed

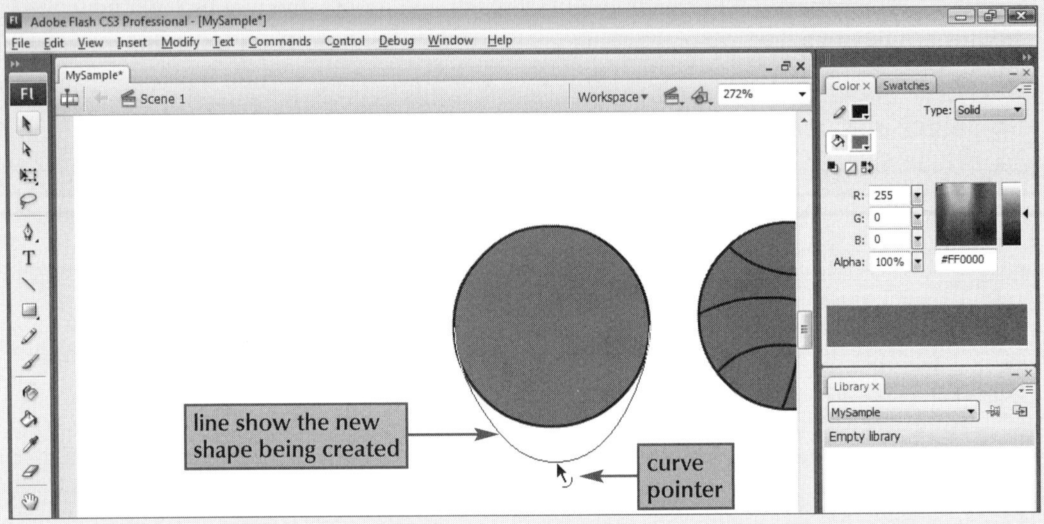

9. Release the mouse button. The fill expands to the new shape.

Subselection Tool

The **Subselection tool** is used to display and modify points, referred to as **anchor points**, on strokes and on the outlines of fills that have no stroke. The strokes and fills can then be modified by adjusting these points. If you click and drag an anchor point on a straight line segment, you can change the angle or the length of the line. If you click an anchor point on a curved line, **tangent handles** appear next to the selected point, as shown in Figure 1-38. You can change the curve by dragging the tangent handles.

Figure 1-38 Curve's anchor points and tangent handles

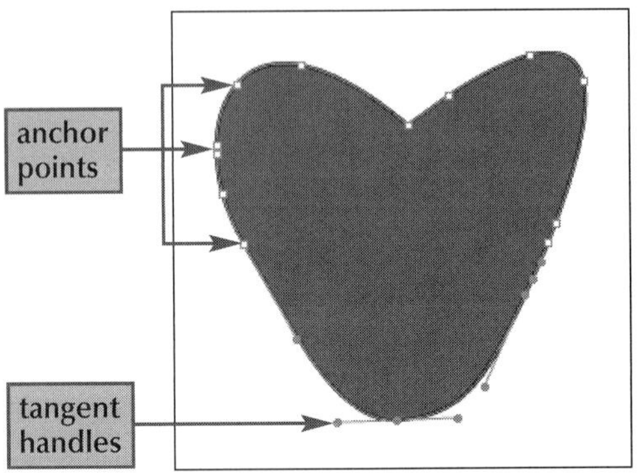

Using the Subselection Tool

| Reference Window

- In the Tools panel, click the Subselection tool.
- Click an object's stroke or its fill outline to display its anchor points.
- Drag the anchor points or tangent handles to modify the stroke or fill outline.

You'll use the Subselection tool to select and modify objects in the MySample document.

To use the Subselection tool to modify the brown rectangle and green oval:

1. In the Tools panel, click the **Hand** tool to change the pointer to , and then drag the view of the Stage until the brown rectangle is in the middle of the Document window.
2. In the Tools panel, click the**Subselection** tool . The pointer changes to .

   You'll use this tool to display the rectangle's stroke anchor points.
3. Click the stroke of the brown rectangle. A thin blue outline surrounds the rectangle, and square anchor points appear on the rectangle's corners.

   You'll drag an anchor point to modify the rectangle's stroke.
4. Drag the anchor point in the upper-right corner away from the center of the rectangle (but do not release the mouse button). See Figure 1-39.

Rectangle's shape being changed **Figure 1-39**

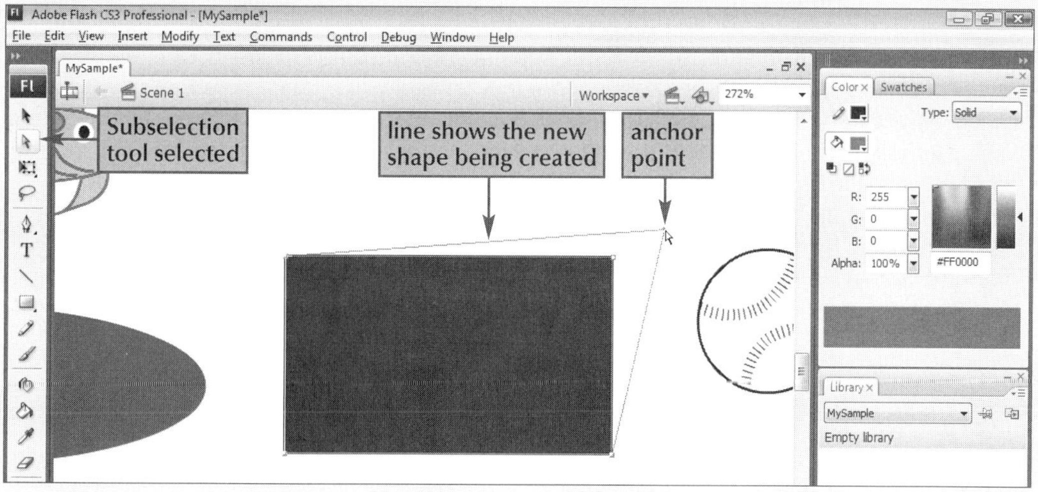

5. Release the mouse button. The rectangle's fill expands to fill the new shape.

   Next, you will use the Subselection tool to modify the blue oval.
6. In the Tools panel, click the **Hand** tool to change the pointer to , and then drag the view of the Stage until the blue oval is in the center of the Stage window.
7. In the Tools panel, click the **Subselection** tool , and then click the blue oval's outline. Anchor points appear along the oval's outline.
8. Click the anchor point at the bottom of the oval's outline. Because this is a curved outline, tangent handles appear. You use a tangent handle to modify the oval.

9. Drag the left tangent handle of the bottom anchor point down to change the oval's shape. The fill expands to fit the new shape. See Figure 1-40.

Figure 1-40 **Modified oval with tangent handles**

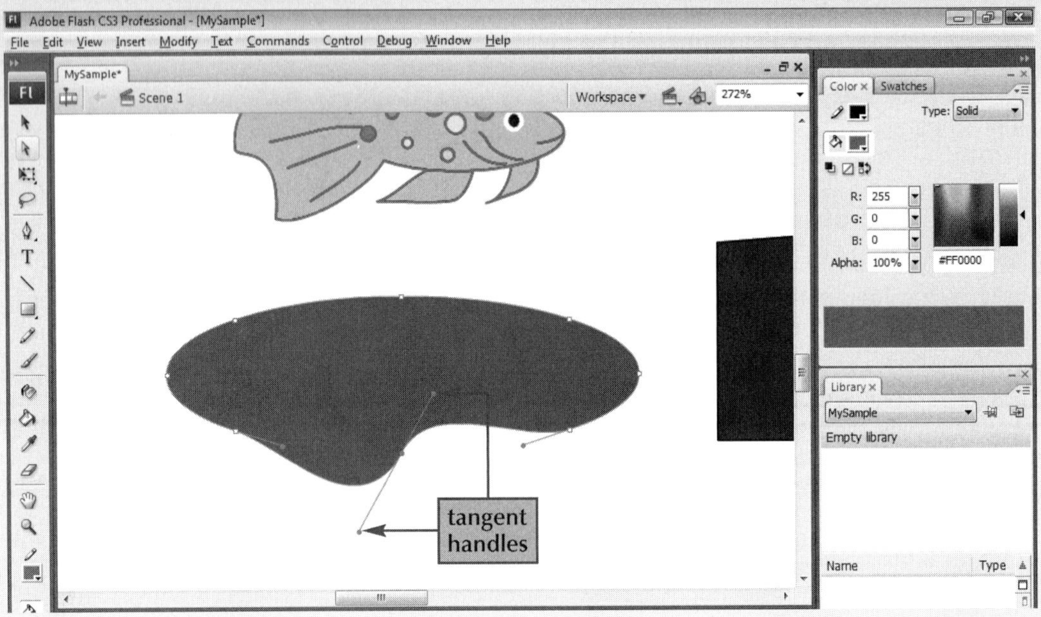

Lasso Tool

If you need to select part of a fill or a stroke, which you cannot do with the Selection or Subselection tools, you can use the Lasso tool. The **Lasso tool** is used to select an object, to select several objects at one time, or to select an irregularly shaped area of an object by drawing a free-form marquee. You can move the selection or apply other effects to it such as changing the color of all the selected fills at one time.

Aly wants you to use the Lasso tool with the objects in the MySample document.

To select objects in the MySample document with the Lasso tool:

1. In the Tools panel, double-click the **Hand** tool. The entire Stage becomes visible.
2. In the Tools panel, click the **Lasso** tool. The pointer changes to when moved over the Stage. You use this tool to select multiple objects at once.
3. Drag the pointer to create a free-form marquee that includes part of the modified brown rectangle, part of the baseball, part of the red heart, and part of the basketball (but do not release the mouse button). See Figure 1-41.

Figure 1-41 Free-form marquee

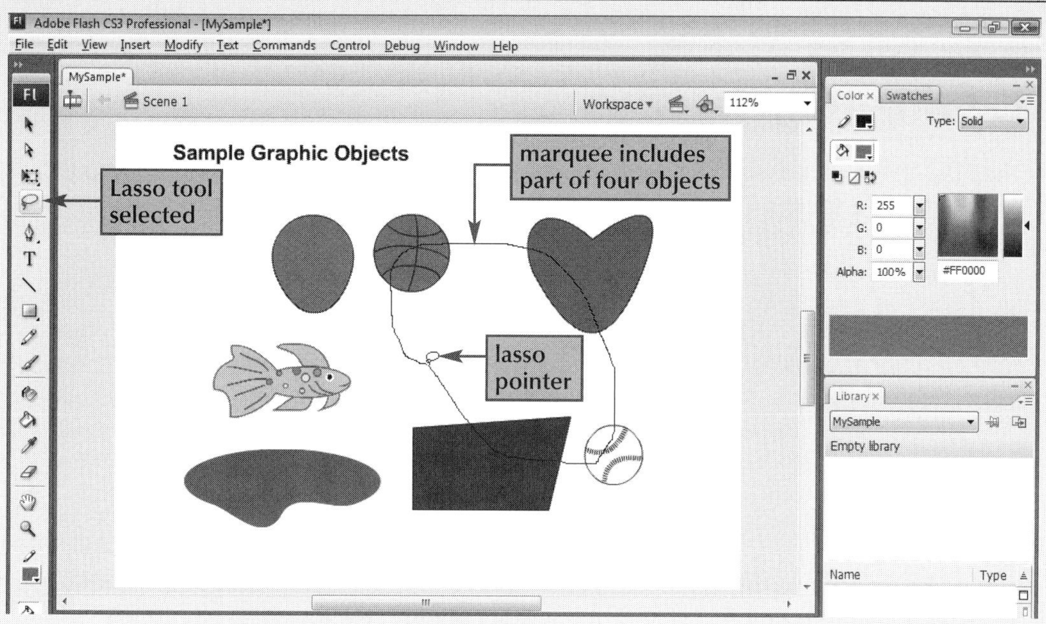

Trouble? If you cannot create a free-form marquee, the Polygon Mode modifieris probably selected in the Tools panel. Click the Polygon Mode modifier button in the Tools panel to deselect it, and then repeat Step 3.

4. Release the mouse button. All of the selected areas appear with a dot pattern.

   You will change the fill color for the selected area.

5. In the Tools panel, click the **Fill color** control to open the color palette, and then click the **yellow** color swatch located in the first column, tenth row of the color palette. The fill color of the selected areas in the rectangle, baseball, heart, and basketball change to yellow. The strokes are not affected because they are not fills. See Figure 1-42.

Figure 1-42 New fill color for the selected areas

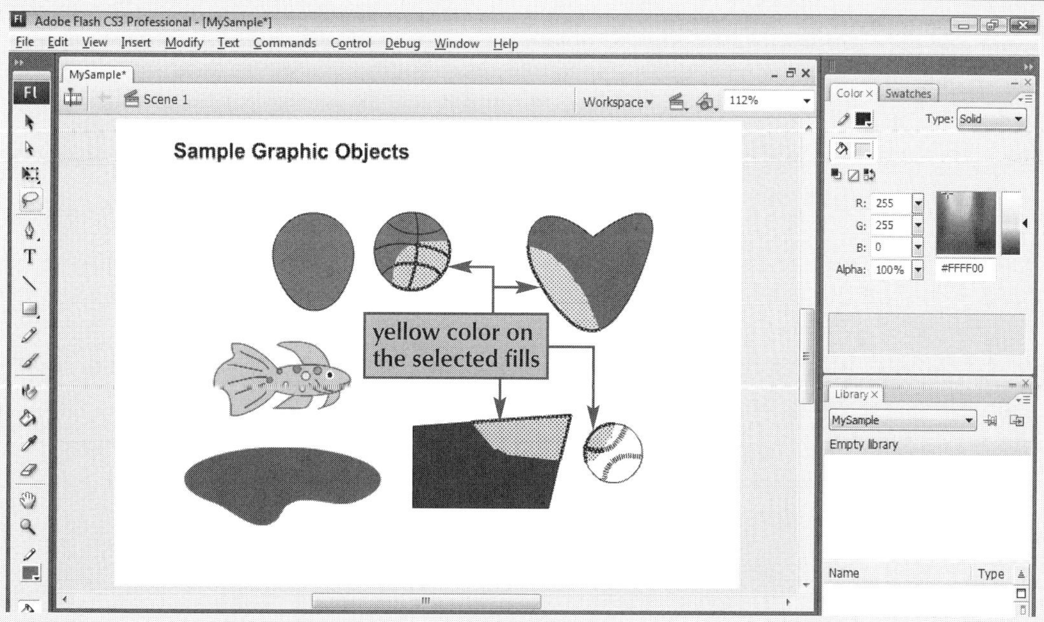

6. Click **File** on the menu bar, then click **Save**. The MySample document is saved with all of your changes.

Getting Help in Flash

The Flash Help system is useful for finding information about features in Flash as you work with a document. The Help system appears in the Help panel, which is organized topically.

The left pane of the Help panel shows a list of books that fall into the selected category. For example, when all books are displayed, the first available book is the Using Flash book, which provides information about the basics of Flash. Clicking a book displays additional books or help topics. When you click a help topic in the left pane, the associated help information appears in the right pane. The help information in the right pane also contains links to related topics. A history tracks the topics you have viewed; you can use the History Back button and the History Forward button to navigate between previously viewed topics.

You can also use the Search feature to find a list of books and topics that contain the keyword. You click a topic in the left pane of the Help panel to display its help information in the right pane. The keywords used in the search are highlighted in the text of the help information. To find topics containing exact phrases, enclose the keywords in quotes, such as "object drawing model". The search returns only topics containing the exact phrase. Without quotes, the search will return all topics that contain any of the words in the phrase.

Tip

To learn more about the Help system, click the Using Flash book, click the Getting started book, click the Using Help book, and then click the appropriate topics.

Reference Window | Using the Flash Help System

- Click Help on the menu bar, and then click Flash Help (or click a panel's options menu control icon, and then click Help).
- Click the book category button, and then click the book category you want to search.
- In the left pane, click books until you see the topic you want, and then click the topic.
- In the right pane, read the information and click links to additional information.
- Click the Close button in the Help panel tab.

You'll use the Flash Help system to obtain more information about the Property inspector.

To use the Flash Help system to get more information about the Property inspector:

1. Click **Help** on the menu bar, and then click **Flash Help**. The Help panel opens.
2. If necessary, click the **Table of Contents** button to clear the Search box and display the table of contents.
3. If necessary, click the **book category** button located below the Search button, and then click **Features**.
4. In the left pane, click the **Using Flash** book, if necessary, to display a list of books, click the **Workspace** book to display another list of books, and then click the **Using Flash authoring panels** book. Topics related to the panels appear.
5. Click the **About the Property inspector** topic. The help information for this topic appears in the right pane. See Figure 1-43.

Figure 1-43

About the Property inspector Help topic

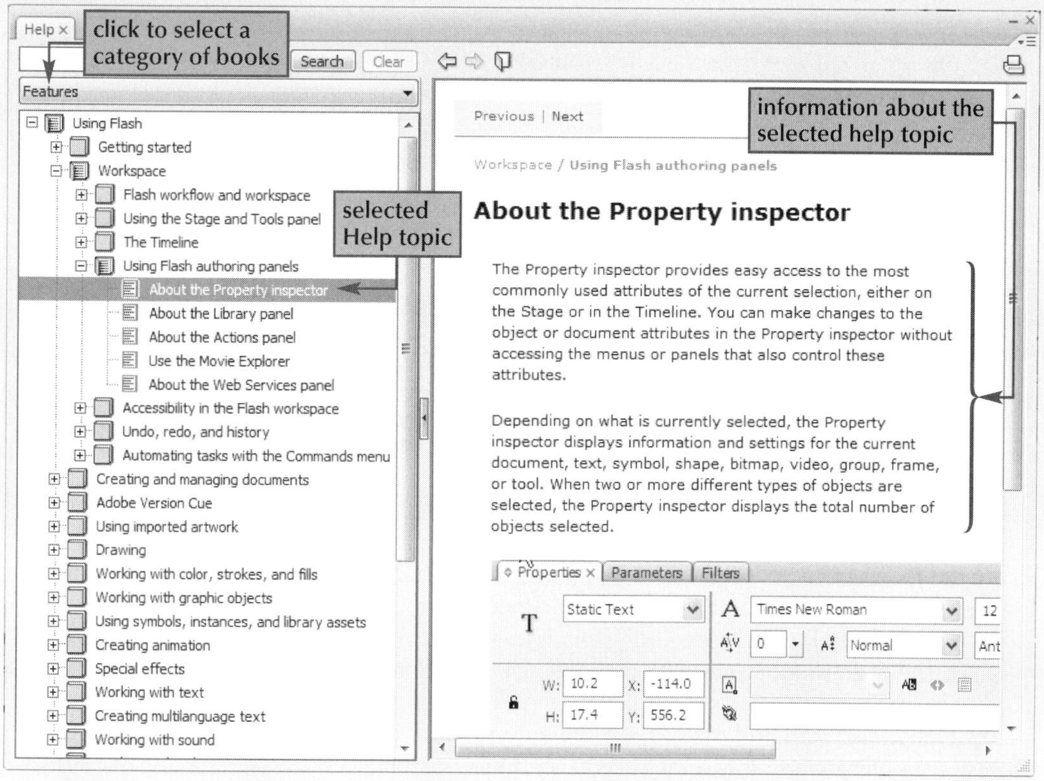

Tip

To display information associated with a specific panel, clicj the options menu control icon, and then click Help.

6. Read the help information, and then click the **Close** button on the Help panel's tab. The Help panel closes.

Closing a Document and Exiting Flash

After you finish working with a document in Flash, you should close it. If you haven't already saved the document before you try to close it, Flash prompts you to save the file.

To close the MySample document and exit Flash:

1. Click **File** on the menu bar, and then click **Close**. The MySample document closes and the Start page appears.

   Trouble? If you are prompted to save the file, you might have inadvertently made changes since the last time you saved. Click the No button.

2. Click **File** on the menu bar, and then click **Exit**. The Flash program exits.

In this session, you learned how objects interact when they are drawn or moved over each other on the Stage. You learned how to select and group objects, and you learned about an object's stroke, fill, and colors. You also learned how to use the Help system.

Review | Session 1.3 Quick Check

1. What is the difference between strokes and fills?
2. True or False? If you draw a blue oval on top of an ungrouped red rectangle drawn in Merge Drawing model, the rectangle will not be modified.
3. True or False? Grouped objects cannot be edited.
4. By default, how many colors are shown on the color palette?
5. What are the three basic colors used on computer monitors?
6. What two ways can the stroke and the fill of an oval be selected at the same time?
7. How can you select several objects at the same time using the Lasso tool?
8. When searching for information in the Help system, how can you find topics containing an exact phrase?

Review | Tutorial Summary

In this tutorial, you reviewed the Flash program and the types of Web media you can create using Flash. You previewed a document with a simple animation and you learned about the differences between bitmap and vector graphics. You became familiar with the Flash workspace components including the Stage, the tools in the Tools panel, and the panels. You selected tools in the Tools panel, customized the arrangement of the panels, changed the Stage settings and changed the document properties. You also learned how objects interact with each other on the Stage and how Flash treats objects drawn using the Merge Drawing model and the Object Drawing model. You selected objects and worked with strokes, fills, and colors. Finally, you used the Flash Help system.

Key Terms

Adobe Flash CS3 Professional (Flash)
anchor point
animation
bitmap animation
bitmap graphic
dock
document
fill
FLA file
Flash Player plug-in
grid
group
guide
Lasso tool
marquee
Merge Drawing model
Object Drawing model
panel
panel group
pasteboard
pixel
playhead
Property inspector
rulers
scrubbing
Selection tool
Stage
stroke
Subselection tool
swatch
SWF file
tangent handle
Timeline
Tools panel
vector animation
vector graphic
Web media
Web safe colors

Practice | Review Assignments

Practice the skills you learned in the tutorial.

Data File needed for the Review Assignments: Sample.fla

Aly wants you to work with some of the tools in Flash and to change the document settings by modifying the Sample document. You will use these skills to develop graphics for Admiral Web Design's clients.

1. Open the **Sample.fla** file located in the Tutorial.01\Review folder included with your Data Files. Set the workspace layout to Icons and Text Default. Hide the Timeline and change the magnification level to Show Frame.
2. Display the rulers and the grid.
3. Click the Selection tool in the Tools panel, and then double-click the red circle to select both its fill and stroke. Move the red circle to the upper-right corner of the Stage.
4. With the Selection tool, draw a marquee around the baseball to select it. Group the baseball's strokes and fills.
5. Move the baseball to the upper-left corner of the Stage so that it is approximately 50 pixels from the left of the Stage and 100 pixels from the top of the Stage.
6. Move the pointer to the top stroke of the brown rectangle. Use the curve pointer to drag the stroke slightly down toward the center of the rectangle to create a curved edge. Repeat to curve each of the other three sides of the rectangle toward its center.
7. Click the Lasso tool in the Tools panel. Drag around the fish and the basketball to select both shapes. Click the Fill color control on the Property inspector, and then click a light blue color in the color palette. The fills in the fish and the basketball change to light blue.
8. Click the Subselection tool in the Tools panel, and then click any stroke on the basketball to display its anchor points. Drag any anchor points to reshape the basketball. Click an empty area of the Stage to deselect the modified basketball.
9. Click the Background color control in the Property inspector, and then click a light yellow color in the color palette to change the background color of the Stage.
10. Save the revised document as **SampleRevised** in the Tutorial.01\Review folder included with your Data Files. Submit the finished document to your instructor, either in printed or electronic form, as requested.

Apply | Case Problem 1

Use the skills you learned to modify a Flash document for a scrapbook store.

Data File needed for this Case Problem: Shapes.fla

Sandy's Scrapbook Store Sandy Rodriguez is the owner of Sandy's Scrapbook Store, which specializes in supplies and products for every type of scrapbook project. The store sells scrapbook supplies such as albums, books, card stock, ribbons, and stickers. It sells card making kits, paper shapers, and cutters. It also hosts scrapbook classes to teach customers new techniques. To help promote the store, Sandy hired John Rossini to develop a Web site. The site will include graphics and animation in addition to textual information. John wants to use Flash to develop the elements for the site. John asks you to explore a sample Flash document to become more familiar with the program.

1. Open the **Shapes.fla** file located in the Tutorial.01\Case1 folder included with your Data Files. Arrange the workspace to its default layout and set the magnification level to 100%.

2. Display the rulers and the grid. Make sure that Snap to Grid is turned off and that Snap to Guides is turned on. Drag a horizontal guide line from the top ruler to the grid line about 100 pixels from the top of the Stage.
3. Use the Selection tool to move the triangle to the left side of the Stage. The bottom side of the triangle should rest on the guide line. Make sure to move both the triangle's fill and stroke together.
4. Select all of the baseball and move it to the right of the triangle. The baseball's top edge should rest below the guide.
5. Move the cube to the right of the baseball and place it so that its center is on the guide.
6. Select all of the basketball and move it to the right of the cube. The basketball's top edge should rest below the guide.
7. Select the red pentagon shape and move it to the right of the basketball and place it so that its bottom side rests on the guide. Make sure to move both the pentagon's fill and stroke together.
8. With the pentagon still selected, use the Stroke color control in the Property inspector to change the pentagon's stroke color to green.
9. Change the triangle's fill color to brown and its stroke color to red. Change the baseball's fill color to yellow and its stroke color to gray.
10. Save the document as **ShapesRevised** in the Tutorial.01\Case1 folder included with your Data Files, and then close it. Submit the finished document to your instructor, either in printed or electronic form, as requested.

Apply | Case Problem 2

Use the skills you learned to modify a Flash document for a local zoo.

Data File needed for this Case Problem: Objects.fla

Alamo City Zoo The Alamo City Zoo, established in 1965, provides animal exhibits for San Antonio and the surrounding area. The zoo is opened year-round and has special exhibits throughout the year. Alamo City Zoo staff also work with local schools to arrange field trips and guided tours for students. Janet Meyers, zoo director, commissioned Alex Smith to develop Flash graphics for the Alamo City Zoo Web site. Alex asks you to explore how objects interact with each other in Flash.

1. Open the **Objects.fla** file located in the Tutorial.01\Case2 folder included with your Data Files. Arrange the workspace to its default layout and set the magnification level to Show All.
2. Drag the red circle on the lower-left side of the Stage to overlay the left side of the blue circle. Click a blank area of the Stage to deselect the circle. Select the red circle again, and then move the circle back to the lower-left side of the Stage. Notice that part of the blue circle has been cut away.
3. Drag the red circle on the upper-left side of the Stage and place it on the green circle. Click a blank area of the Stage to deselect the circle. The red circle is behind the green circle. Move the red circle back to the upper-left side, and then deselect it. The green circle does not change.
4. Using the Selection tool, point to the bottom of the red circle on the upper-left side of the Stage, and then use the curve pointer to drag the line up slightly to curve it. Repeat this step to modify the bottom of the green circle. Notice that both objects are modified in the same manner with the Selection tool.

5. Using the Selection tool, point to the left point of the star in the upper-right side of the Stage, and then use the corner pointer to drag the star's point to the left slightly. Repeat this step to move the left point of the lower star. Notice that both objects are modified in the same manner with the Selection tool.
6. Record what you think are the differences and similarities between the two star objects. Also record why you think the circle shapes interact differently with each other.
7. Save the document as **ObjectsRevised** in the Tutorial.01\Case2 folder included with your Data Files, and then close it.
8. Submit your answers from Step 6 and the finished document to your instructor, either in printed or electronic form, as requested.

Challenge | Case Problem 3

Customize the Flash workspace for a gardening store.

There are no Data Files needed for this Case Problem.

Westcreek Nursery Alice Washington is the owner of Westcreek Nursery, a specialty store providing a variety of trees, plants, flowers, and gardening accessories. Alice has been in business for 10 years and has gradually expanded her store and services. Alice attributes her success to her focus on customer service. Customers are able to look through the nursery's inventory in a relaxing and inviting environment. A friendly and knowledgeable staff provides expert advice and answers to customers' gardening questions.

Alice contracted Amanda Lester to update the store's Web site. As other local nurseries have developed Web sites, Alice wants to make sure her store's Web site stays current and remains an effective marketing tool. You'll help Amanda develop Flash graphics for the Web site. She wants you to customize the Flash workspace and arrange the panels you will use regularly. She also instructs you to look for information in the Flash Help system.

1. Create a new Flash document, and then set the panels to their default layout.
2. Click Window on the menu bar, and then click Behaviors to open the Behaviors panel as a free-floating window. Move this window slightly to the left by dragging the panel's tab or title bar. Open the Movie Explorer panel and the Align panel. Note that the Align panel is docked on the right side of the workspace.
3. EXPLORE — Group the Movie Explorer and Behaviors panels into one window. First, drag the Movie Explorer panel from its window and into the Behaviors panel's window. The two panels are grouped into one window.
4. Drag the Align panel into the window with the Behaviors and Movie Explorer panels. All three panels are grouped.
5. EXPLORE — Click the Collapse to Icons button above the Color and Swatches panels. Drag the gripper above the Color panel to the right to reduce the width of the dock and display the panels as icons only.
6. EXPLORE — Click Workspace on the Edit bar, and then click Save Current. Type **My Layout** in the Name box, and then click the OK button.
7. Return the panels to their default layout.
8. Click Workspace on the Edit bar and then click My Layout, which now appears on the list of panel layouts. The panel arrangement reflects the changes you made.
9. Close the free-floating panel group with the three panels.

10. Delete the saved layout. Click Workspace on the Edit bar, and then click Manage. In the Manage Workspace Layouts dialog box, click My Layout and then click the Delete button. Click the Yes button to confirm you want to delete the workspace layout, and then click the OK button.

EXPLORE 11. Find out more about the Align panel. Open the Help panel, and then, if necessary, change the book category to Features. Type **Align panel** in the Search box, and then click the Search button. In the search results in the left pane, click the Align objects topic under the Using Flash book. In the right pane, read the information for aligning objects.

EXPLORE 12. Click the Print button in the Help panel to print the Align Objects topic. Close the Help panel.

13. Submit the finished document to your instructor, either in printed or electronic form, as requested.

Research | Case Problem 4

Explore drawing in Flash and Web Media for a nonprofit organization.

There are no Data Files needed for this Case Problem.

Regional Dietetic Association Richard Perez is the current president of the Regional Dietetic Association, a nonprofit organization of dietetic professionals in the San Antonio and south Texas area. The association is an advocate for the dietetics profession that serves the public through the promotion of optimal nutrition, health, and well-being. The association provides a forum for its members to meet and exchange ideas and to promote their profession.

Richard hired Katie Ellison to improve and maintain the association's Web site. He wants to add new graphics and animation to the site to improve its appeal to the association members. Katie plans to use Flash to develop the new elements for the site. She wants you to review information about drawing shapes and some of the tools used to draw graphics and then view examples of Web media.

1. Open the Help panel, and then clear the Search box and display the table of contents.
2. If necessary, click the Using Flash book in the table of contents to expand it. Click the Drawing book to display its contents. Read the information about drawing on the right pane of the Help panel.
3. If necessary, click the Drawing Basics book to expand it and then click the About vector and bitmap graphics topic in the table of contents. Read the information displayed in the right pane.
4. When you are done reading, click Next in the upper-left corner of the pane to display the About the Flash drawing models topic. Read the information displayed about the Merge Drawing model and the Object Drawing model. Record the definitions found in the Help topics for vector graphics and for bitmap graphics.
5. Click Next to display the About overlapping shapes topic. Read the information in the right pane.
6. Click the Using Flash drawing and painting tools book in the table of contents to expand it. Click the Draw with the Pencil tool topic and read the information displayed in the right pane.

7. Click the Reshaping lines and shape outlines book in the table of contents. Click the Reshape using the Selection tool topic. Read the information displayed in the right pane. Note the difference between reshaping an end point and a corner. Close the Help panel.

EXPLORE

8. Click Help on the menu bar, and then click Flash Developer Center. Your default browser opens and displays the Flash Developer Center Web site. Click the Samples tab (or the Samples link on the right side of the page). To view a sample, click its link. Read the information provided with the sample and then experiment with the interactive components, if available. To return to the list of sample files, use the browser's Back button. As you navigate to some of the samples, study and compare the animation effects you see. Listen for sound effects, music, and voiceovers. See if you can distinguish between bitmap and vector graphics.
9. In your browser, open the home page for the FlashKit site at *www.flashkit.com*. Review the various examples of Flash graphics and animations displayed on the home page. Look for a list of hyperlinks, usually located at the top of page. In this list of hyperlinks, explore several of the categories such as Movies, Tutorials, and Gallery. Note how the various examples make use of animation, colors, sound, and pictures.
10. Close any open files without saving. Submit the finished document to your instructor, either in printed or electronic form, as requested.

Review | Quick Check Answers

Session 1.1

1. vector
2. .swf
3. any three of the following: still imagery, sound, animation, hyperlinks, buttons, text, and scripted programming
4. True.
5. pixels
6. as a set of mathematical instructions that describe the color, outline, and position of all the shapes of the image
7. vector graphics
8. The enlarged bitmap looks jagged or blurred.

Session 1.2

1. the Stage
2. the Timeline
3. moving the view of the Stage and pasteboard
4. Scrubbing
5. the Property inspector
6. (1) click View on the menu bar, point to Magnification, and click a magnification level, or (2) click the Zoom control arrow on the Edit bar, and then click a magnification level.
7. False. The grid lines do not become part of the document.
8. Drag your pointer from the top ruler down to the Stage window.

Session 1.3

1. Strokes are lines and outlines; fills are the areas enclosed by lines and outlines.
2. False. The blue oval cuts away at the ungrouped red rectangle.
3. False. Grouped objects can be edited in group-editing mode.
4. the 216 Web safe colors
5. red, green, and blue
6. (1) double-click either the stroke or fill, or (2) draw a marquee around the oval with the Selection tool.
7. Draw a marquee around the objects to select.
8. Type the phrase enclosed in quotes in the Search box, and then click the Search button.

Ending Data Files

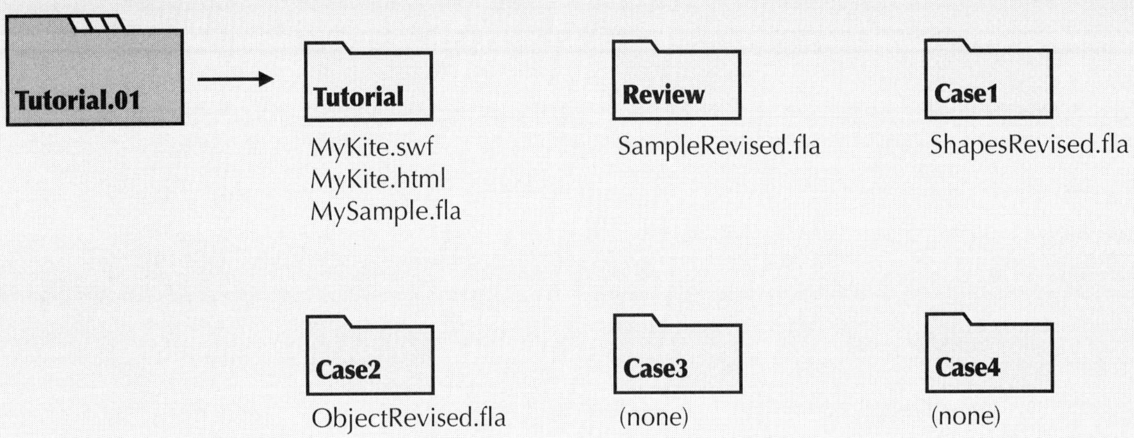

Objectives

Session 2.1
- Draw lines, curves, ovals, and rectangles
- Apply stroke and fill colors

Session 2.2
- Modify strokes and fills
- Transform graphic objects using the Free Transform tool
- Create text blocks

Session 2.3
- Export a graphic for use in a Web site
- Learn how to use the History panel
- Create symbols and instances of symbols
- Organize symbols in the Library panel

Drawing Shapes, Adding Text, and Creating Symbols

Creating and Exporting a Banner

Case | Admiral Web Design

Admiral Web Design focuses on designing easy-to-use, informative, and effective Web sites that meet the specific needs of each client. Several clients have requested enhancements to their Web sites. Jenny's Oyster Hut, a seafood restaurant that has been in operation for 10 years, has won numerous local and national awards for its special dishes, customer satisfaction, and contributions to the community. The restaurant's owner, Jenny Emerson, asks Admiral Web Design to develop a new banner for her Web site for a special promotion celebrating the restaurant's tenth anniversary. You will work on this project with Aly and Chris.

During the planning meeting, Jenny said that she wants a colorful banner with graphic images depicting a scene related to the sea. Aly suggests the banner include graphics of a beach scene with sand, the ocean, some fish, and several lines of text. Chris thinks this banner will blend well with the current design of the restaurant's home page. Jenny likes the idea, and approves Aly's final sketch of the new banner. You will use Flash to create the banner according to Aly's sketch.

As you create the banner for Jenny's Oyster Hut in Flash, you will use the drawing tools, text tools, and tools for modifying graphic objects. You will select and apply colors. You will modify existing graphics, create new graphics, and then export the banner for use on the restaurant's Web site.

Starting Data Files

Tutorial.02 →

Tutorial	Review	Case1	Case2	Case3	Case4
Jennys.htm sports.fla	Jennys Banner.fla	(none)	(none)	(none)	(none)

Session 2.1

Drawing Lines and Shapes

When working with Flash, you will often create graphic images from scratch. You draw lines and curves with the Line, Pen, and Pencil tools. If you create an enclosed shape, the enclosed area is filled with the fill color selected in the Fill color control in the Tools panel. You draw shapes with the Oval, Rectangle, PolyStar, Brush, Rectangle Primitive, and Oval Primitive tools. These tools allow you to create shapes of various sizes and colors. Ovals, rectangles, and polygons can include strokes as well as fills, or only a stroke or only a fill. The primitive tools create rectangles with modifiable corners and ovals that can be changed into pie shapes or half circles.

Figure 2-1 shows Aly's sketch of the banner you will create for Jenny's Oyster Hut. You will use the Oval, Pencil, Paint Bucket, and Eyedropper tools to create the fish and background graphics. You will use the Rectangle tool to create a frame around the banner, the Primitive Oval tool to create the umbrella, and the Selection tool to modify the shapes. You will display the guides, which will be useful as you draw and align objects on the Stage.

Figure 2-1 **Sketch of the Web site banner for Jenny's Oyster Hut**

You are ready to begin creating the banner for Jenny's Oyster Hut. You will first set the document properties and display the rulers. You will then save the banner file.

To set the document properties, show the rulers, and save the document:

1. Click **File** on the menu bar, and then click **New**. The New Document dialog box opens with the General tab active.
2. Click **Flash File (ActionScript 3.0)**, if necessary, and then click the **OK** button. The new document opens.

3. On the Edit bar, click the **Workspace** button, and then click **Default**. The panels return to their default layout.
4. On the Edit bar, click the **Hide Timeline** button . The Timeline disappears from view.

   Next, you will set the document title and dimensions according to the banner sketch.
5. Click **Modify** on the menu bar, and then click **Document**. The Document Properties dialog box opens.
6. Type **Jenny's Oyster Hut Banner** in the Title box, press the **Tab** key twice to select the value in the width box, type **400**, press the **Tab** key to select the value in the height box, and then type **300**.

   You will set the background color to light blue as shown in the sketch.
7. Click the **Background color** control to open the color palette, and then click the **light blue** color swatch (#66CCFF) in the second column from the right, sixth row of the color palette.

   You'll leave the frame rate at 12 frames per second and the ruler units at pixels.
8. Click the **OK** button. The dialog box closes and the document changes to match your document settings.
9. Click **View** on the menu bar, point to **Magnification**, and then click **Fit in Window**. The document enlarges to fill the pasteboard.
10. Click **View** on the menu bar, and then click **Rulers**. The rulers appear along the top and left of the pasteboard. See Figure 2-2.

Figure 2-2 Document window showing rulers and new document properties

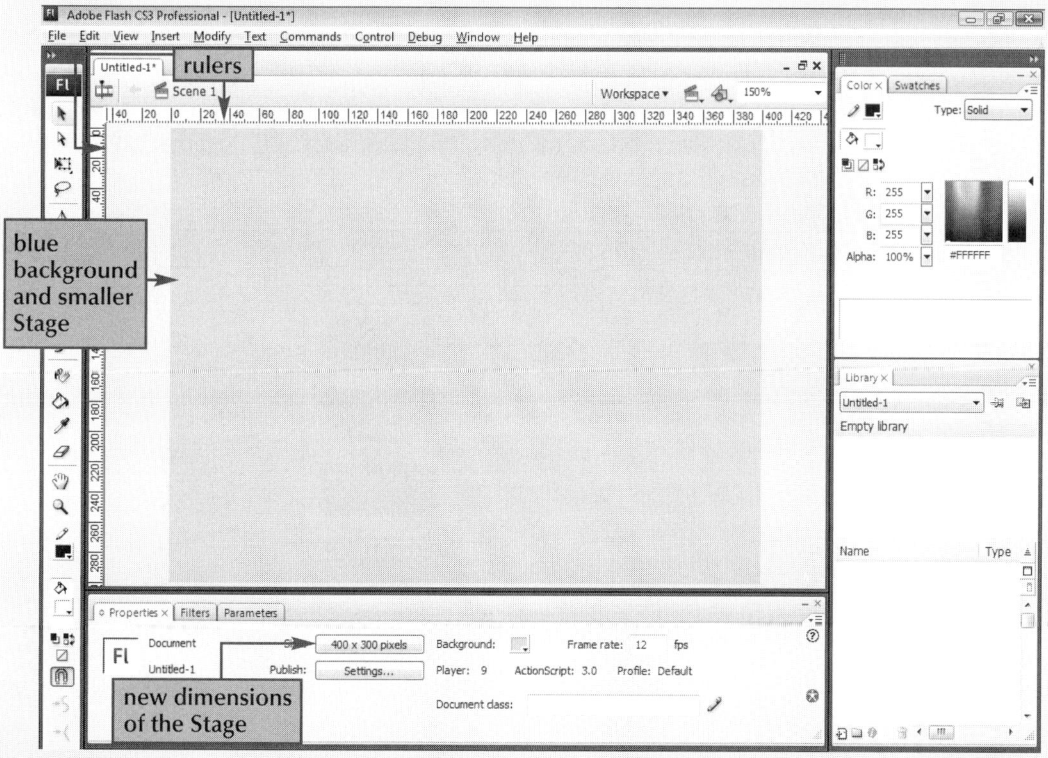

11. Save the document as **Banner** in the **Tutorial.02\Tutorial** folder included with your Data Files.

Using the Oval, Rectangle, and PolyStar Tools

Drawing simple shapes is easy with the Oval, Rectangle, and PolyStar tools. These tools all work in a similar manner. As you drag the pointer for the selected tool on the Stage, the size of the drawn shape changes until you release the mouse button. When you use the PolyStar tool, you choose whether to draw a polygon or a star shape. You can also indicate the number of sides the shape will have, which can range from 3 to 32. For star shapes, you can also specify the value of the star point size, which can range from 0 to 1. A number closer to 0 results in narrower star points, and a number closer to 1 results in wider star points, as shown in Figure 2-3.

Figure 2-3 **Star shapes with different point sizes**

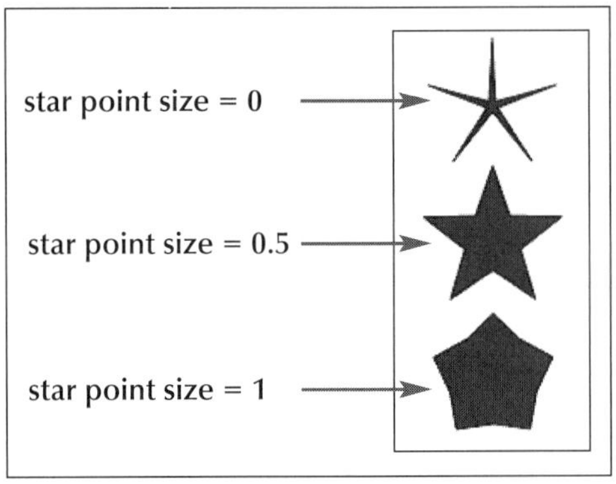

Tip

To create a rectangle with specific dimensions and a specific corner radius, select the Rectangle tool, press the Alt key as you click the Stage, enter values in the Rectangle Settings dialog box, and then click the OK button.

You can use the Oval and Rectangle tools to draw a perfect circle or a perfect square. You first select the Snap to Objects modifier. As you draw with the Oval or Rectangle tool, a small solid ring appears next to the pointer to let you know when you have drawn a perfect circle or a perfect square.

When you select the Rectangle tool, the Rectangle corner radius option appears in the Property inspector. The value you enter in the Rectangle corner radius box represents the number of pixels by which to round the corners of the rectangle shape. A 0 value results in square corners, higher values produce more rounded corners, and negative values create inward corners, as shown in Figure 2-4.

Figure 2-4 **Rectangles with different corner radii**

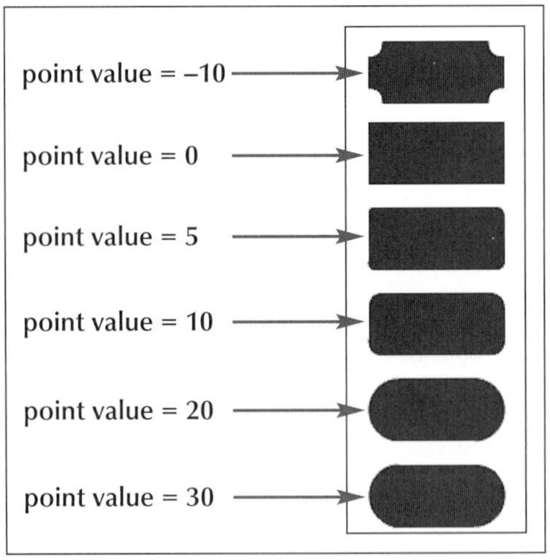

Using the Drawing Models to Create Graphics | InSight

Before you start creating graphics in Flash, carefully plan how you want the graphic objects to interact with each other. If you want to create graphic shapes that combine to form one shape, draw them using the Merge Drawing model. If you want to keep the shapes you draw separate from each other, use the Object Drawing model. You can also switch between drawing models as you draw the graphics for your document.

You will draw rectangle shapes for the beach and ocean graphics for the banner's background. You will draw another rectangle around the banner to provide a frame around all of the graphic elements. As indicated in Aly's sketch, the rectangle for the frame will have a stroke, no fill, and rounded corners. You will draw the background graphics using the Object Drawing model so that they won't merge with the fish you will create.

To draw the ocean rectangle using the Rectangle tool and guides:

1. Drag a horizontal guide from the horizontal ruler to approximately 150 pixels from the top of the Stage, and then drag another horizontal guide from the horizontal ruler to approximately 200 pixels from the top of the Stage.
2. In the Tools panel, click the **Rectangle** tool, and then click the **Object Drawing** button, if necessary. The rectangles you draw will not merge with other shapes.
3. In the Property inspector, select the **Rectangle corner radius** value, type **0**, and then press the **Enter** key. The rectangle you draw will have square corners.
4. In the Color panel, click the **Fill color** control to open the color palette, and then click the **blue** color swatch (#0000FF) in the first column, ninth row. The rectangle you draw will be blue.

   Trouble? If the first column of the color palette displays all black swatches, use the second column.
5. In the Color panel, double-click the **Alpha** value to select it, type **50**, and then press the **Enter** key. The reduced Alpha value of the fill color will make the rectangle partially transparent.
6. In the Color panel, click the **Stroke color** control to open the color palette, and then click the **No Color** button. The rectangles you draw will not have an outline.

   You are ready to draw the rectangle for the ocean.
7. Draw a rectangle from the left side of the Stage at the top guide to the lower-right corner of the Stage. See Figure 2-5.

Figure 2-5 **Rectangle for the ocean**

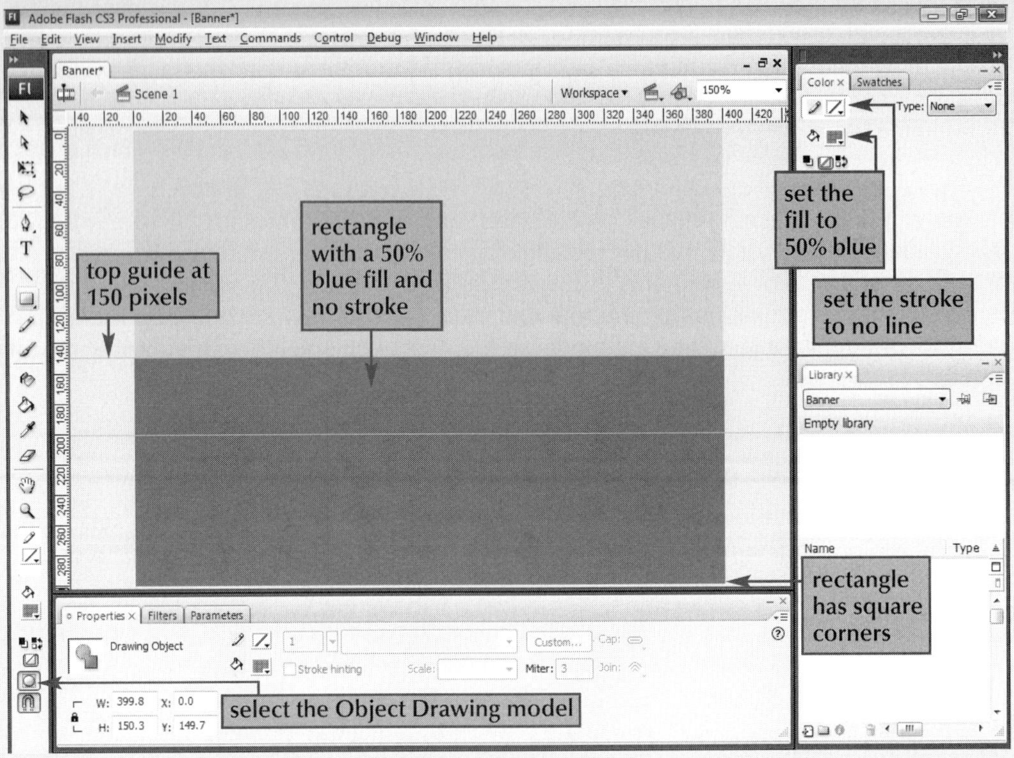

The second rectangle you draw will represent the beach. You need to deselect the ocean rectangle, and then change the fill color in the Color panel.

To draw the beach rectangle using the Rectangle tool and guides:

1. In the Tools panel, click the **Selection** tool, and then click in another area of the Stage to deselect the blue rectangle.
2. In the Color panel, click the **Fill color** control to open the color palette, and then click the **light yellow** color swatch (#FFFFCC) in the last column, second row from the bottom of the color palette. The yellow fill is for the sand.
3. In the Color panel, verify that the Alpha value is set to **100%** and the Stroke color is set to **No Color**.
4. In the Tools panel, click the **Rectangle** tool, and then draw a rectangle from the left side of the Stage at the lower guide to the lower-right corner of the Stage. See Figure 2-6.

Figure 2-6 Rectangle for the beach

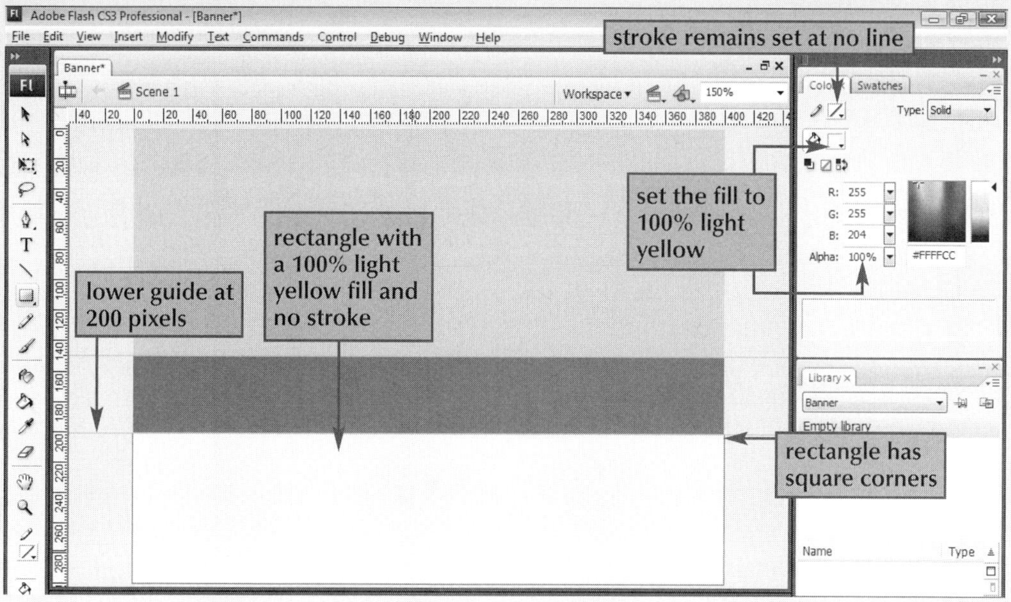

You will draw another rectangle to frame the banner. This rectangle will have a black stroke color and no fill color. It will also have rounded corners and a stroke height of 2.

To draw the frame rectangle using the Rectangle tool and guides:

1. In the Tools panel, click the **Selection** tool, and then click another area of the Stage to deselect the beach rectangle.
2. In the Color panel, click the **Stroke color** control to open the color palette, and then click the **black** color swatch (#000000) in the first column, first row of the color palette.
3. In the Color panel, click the **Fill color** control to open the color palette, and then click the **No Color** button.
4. In the Tools panel, click the **Rectangle** tool, and then, in the Property inspector, double-click the **stroke height** value, type **2**, and then press the **Enter** key. The stroke height is set to 2.
5. In the Property inspector, if necessary, click the **unlock** icon for the Rectangle corner radius to change it to a lock icon.
6. In the Property inspector, double-click the **Rectangle corner radius** value to select it, type **10**, and then press the **Enter** key. The value for each corner is set to 10.
7. In the Tools panel, click the **Snap to Objects** modifier button to deselect it, if necessary, so the rectangle won't snap to the edges of the Stage.
8. Draw a rectangle from just inside the upper-left corner of the Stage to just inside the lower-right corner of the Stage. See Figure 2-7.

Figure 2-7 **Rectangle for the frame**

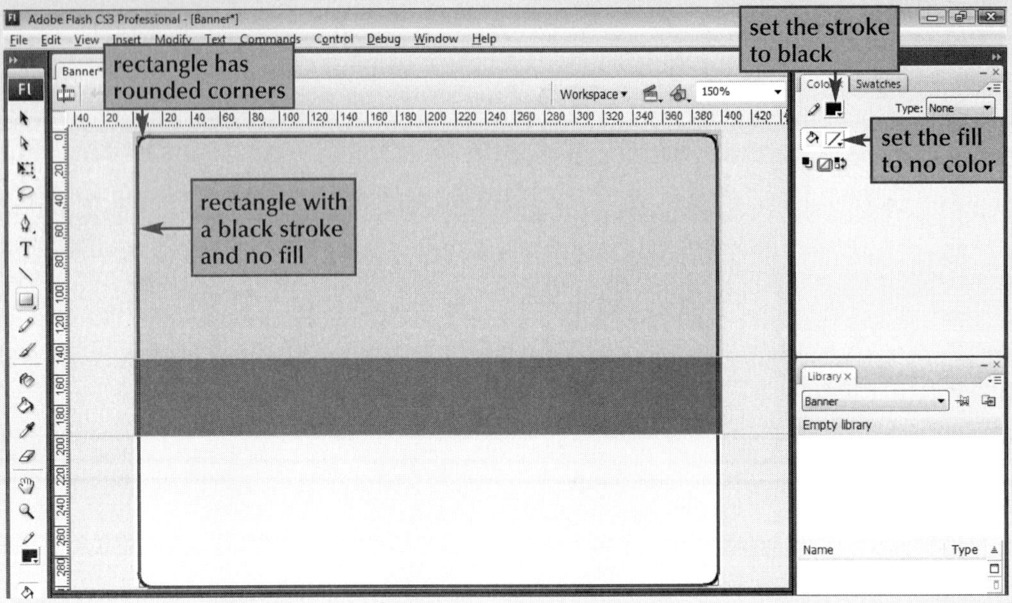

You will modify the yellow rectangle to more closely resemble the beach graphic that Aly sketched. You will do this by curving the top side of the rectangle using the Selection tool. You will hide the guides because you will not be using them.

To hide the guides and modify the yellow rectangle shape using the Selection tool:

1. Click **View** on the menu bar, point to **Guides**, and then click **Show Guides**. The guides are no longer visible.

   You will modify the bottom rectangle using the Selection tool.

2. In the Tools panel, click the **Selection** tool, and then click another area on the Stage to deselect the frame rectangle.
3. Move the pointer to the upper-middle side of the light yellow rectangle until the pointer changes to, and then drag the top of the rectangle down about 45 pixels to curve it. See Figure 2-8.

Curved rectangle created using the Selection tool

Figure 2-8

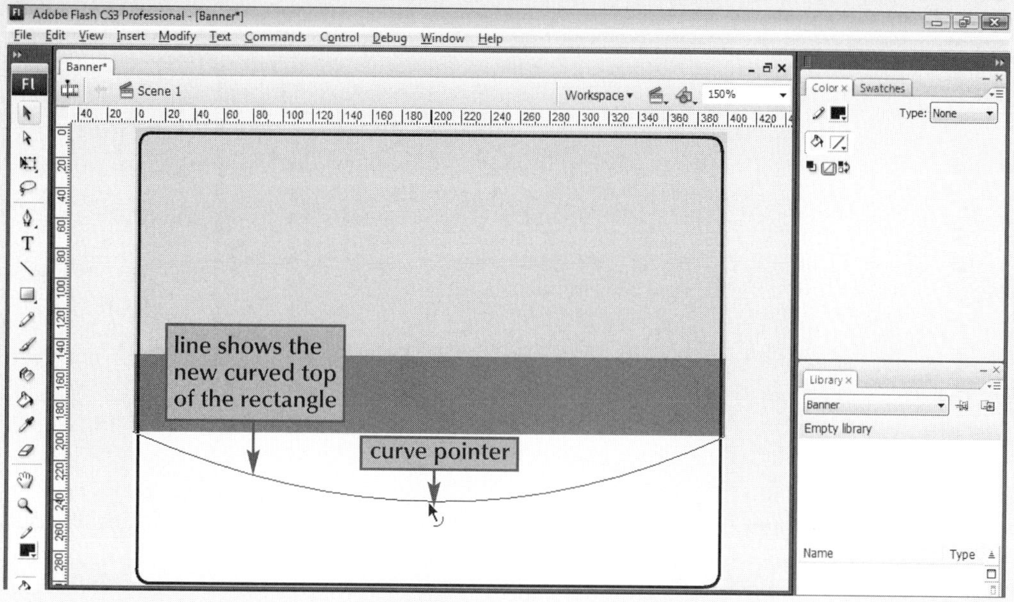

4. Release the mouse button.

Next, you will create the fish in the center of the banner that Aly sketched. You'll draw a large oval for the body of the fish and a rectangle that you will modify to become the fish's tail. You will use the Merge Drawing model so that the two shapes combine into one. Guides will help you draw these shapes.

To draw the fish using the Oval and Rectangle tools and guides:

1. Click **View** on the menu bar, point to **Guides**, and then click **Show Guides**. The guides are displayed.
2. Drag the top guide up to approximately 50 pixels from the top of the Stage, and then drag the bottom guide up to approximately 90 pixels from the top of the Stage.

   You'll create vertical guides.
3. Drag a vertical guide from the vertical ruler to approximately 150 pixels from the left of the Stage, and then drag another vertical guide from the vertical ruler to approximately 250 pixels from the left of the Stage. See Figure 2-9.

Figure 2-9 Guides for creating the fish

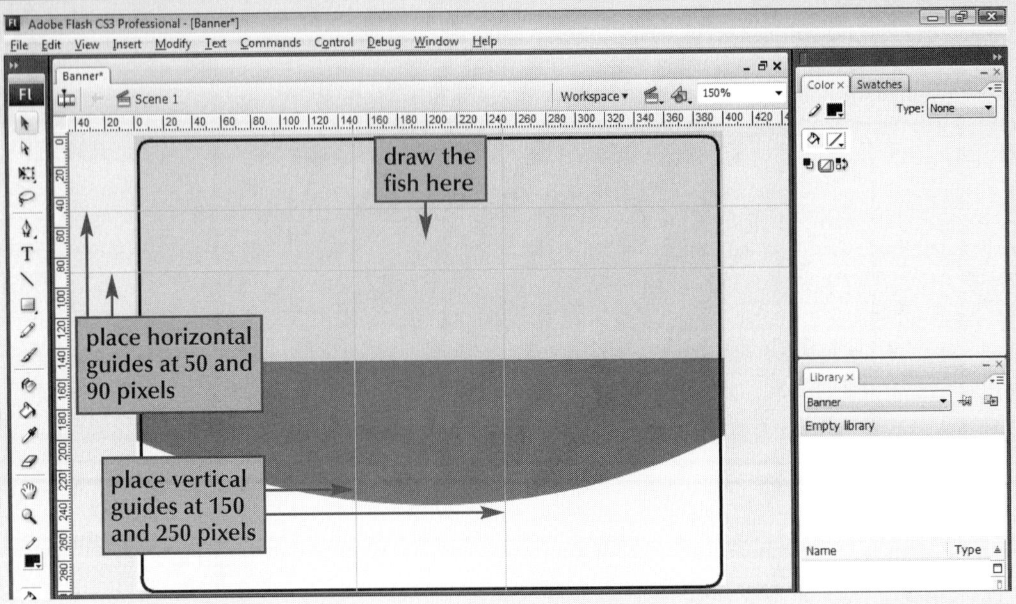

Using the guides to help you draw, you will create the fish body with the Oval tool and the Merge Drawing model.

4. In the Tools panel, click and hold the **Rectangle** tool to open the pop-up menu, and then click the **Oval** tool. The pointer changes to +.
5. In the Tools panel, click the **Object Drawing** button to deselect it. The Merge Drawing model is now in effect.
6. In the Property inspector, if necessary, click the **Stroke color** control to open the color palette, and then click the **black** color swatch (#000000) in the first column, first row of the color palette.
7. In the Property inspector, enter **1** in the Stroke height box, and then make sure the Stroke style is set to **Solid**.
8. In the Property inspector, click the **Fill color** control to open the color palette, and then click the **orange** color swatch (#FF9900) in the seventh row, third column from the right.

   You will draw the fish body.

9. Draw an oval from the upper-left corner of the rectangular area formed by the guides to the lower-right corner of the rectangular area formed by the guides. See Figure 2-10.

Figure 2-10 Oval for the fish body

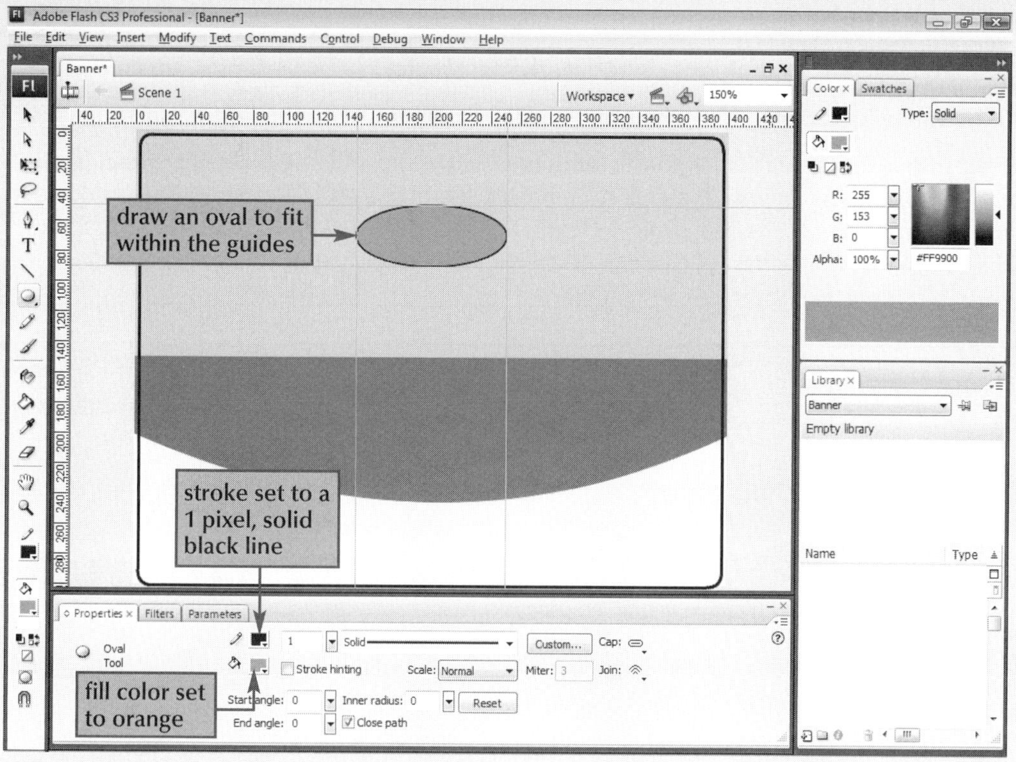

10. In the Tools panel, click and hold the **Oval** tool to open the pop-up menu, and then click the **Rectangle** tool.
11. In the Property inspector, set the value in the Rectangle corner radius box to **0**.
12. Draw a rectangle starting at approximately **40** pixels from the top of the Stage and **100** pixels from the left of the Stage and ending at approximately **100** pixels from the top of the Stage and **170** pixels from the left of the Stage. See Figure 2-11.

Figure 2-11 Overlapping oval and rectangle shapes

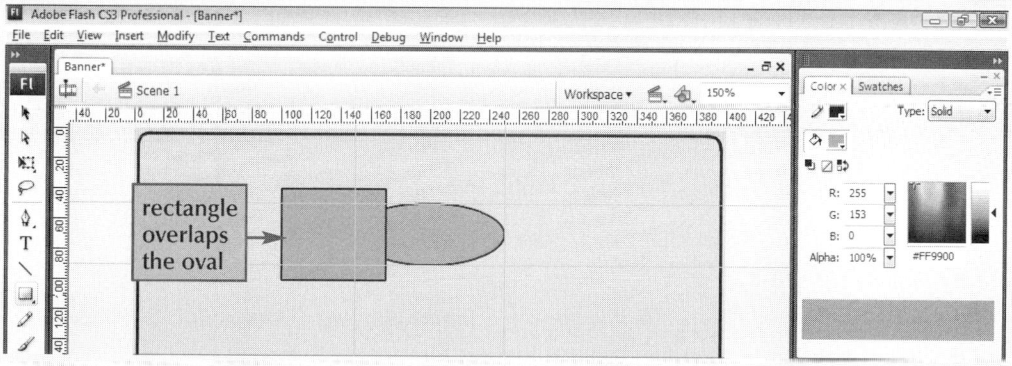

You will use the Selection tool to modify the two shapes so that they more closely resemble the fish Aly sketched. The right corners of the rectangle will be modified to connect to the oval and the sides of the rectangle will be curved. You will clear the guides because you don't need them anymore.

To modify the oval and rectangle shapes using the Selection tool:

1. Click **View** on the menu bar, point to **Guides**, and then click **Clear Guides**. The guides disappear.

   You will modify the right corners of the rectangle.

2. In the Tools panel, click the **Snap to Objects** modifier button to select it.
3. In the Tools panel, click the **Selection** tool, drag the upper-right corner of the rectangle down until it snaps to the top edge of the oval, and then drag the lower-right corner of the rectangle up until it snaps to the lower edge of the oval. See Figure 2-12.

Figure 2-12 Modified rectangle

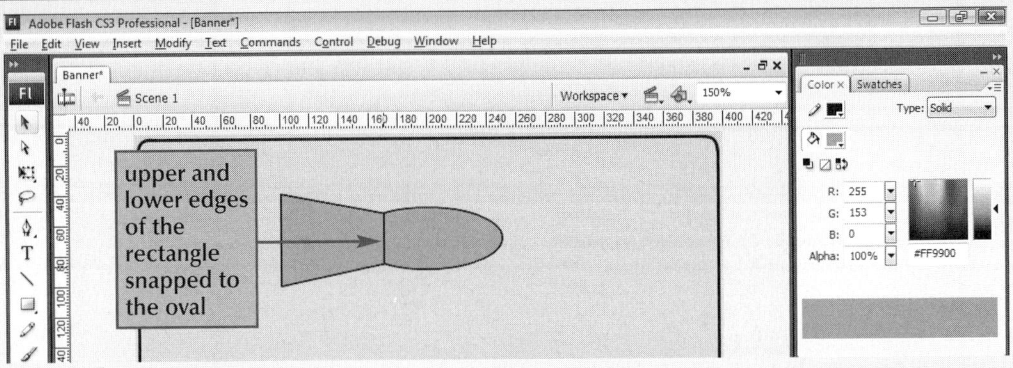

4. Move the pointer to the stroke on the left side of the modified rectangle shape until the pointer changes to , and then drag the line to the right to about the center point of the shape.
5. Drag the top line up slightly to curve it, drag the bottom line down slightly to curve it, and then drag the right side slightly to the left. See Figure 2-13.

Figure 2-13 Sides of the rectangle modified

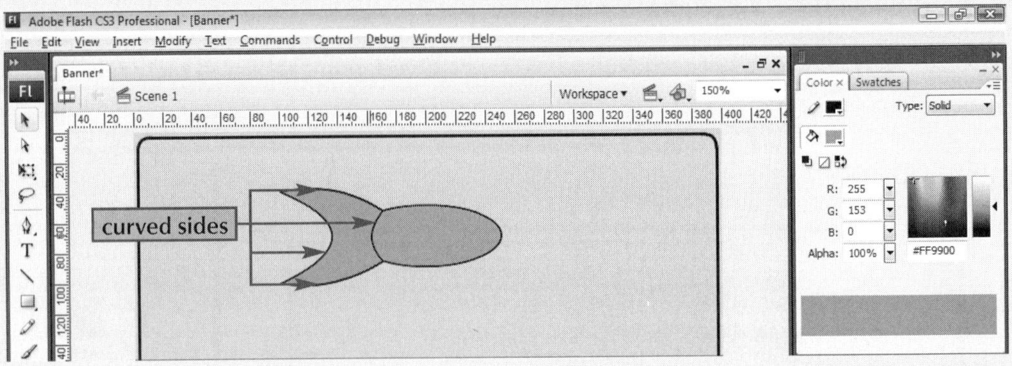

The modified rectangle and oval resemble a fish shape. You are ready to draw the eye for the fish. You can use the Oval tool for this. You'll turn on the Snap to Objects modifier so you can draw a perfect circle for the eye.

To use the Oval tool to draw the eye for the fish:

1. In the Tools panel, click the **Zoom** tool, make sure the **Enlarge** modifier button is selected, and then click the right side of the fish shape once to zoom in.

2. In the Tools panel, click and hold the **Rectangle** tool [icon] to open the pop-up menu, and then click the **Oval** tool [icon]. The pointer changes to [icon].
3. In the Property inspector, click the **Stroke color** control to open the color palette, click the **No Color** button [icon], click the **Fill color** control to open the color palette, and then click the **white** color swatch (#FFFFFF) in the first column, sixth row of the color palette.

   Trouble? If the first column of the color palette displays all black swatches, use the second column.

   You'll draw a perfect circle for the eye.
4. In the Tools panel, click the **Snap to Objects** modifier button [icon] to select it, if necessary.
5. Draw a small circle on the upper-right end of the fish shape. See Figure 2-14.

Figure 2-14 Fish eye drawn

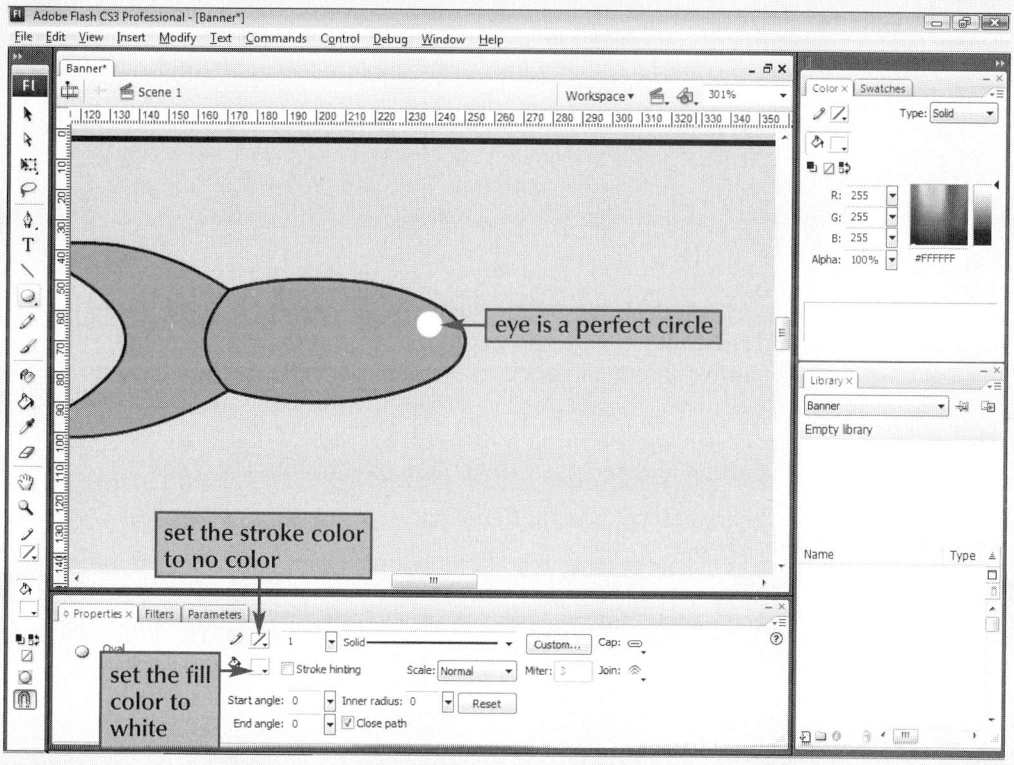

6. In the Tools panel, click the **Snap to Objects** modifier button [icon] to deselect it. Having the modifier off will make it easier to draw a small oval for the pupil.
7. In the Tools panel, click the **Fill color** control to open the color palette, and then click the **black** color swatch (#000000) in the first column, first row of the color palette.
8. Draw a smaller oval inside the eye to represent the eye's pupil. See Figure 2-15.

Figure 2-15 Pupil for fish eye

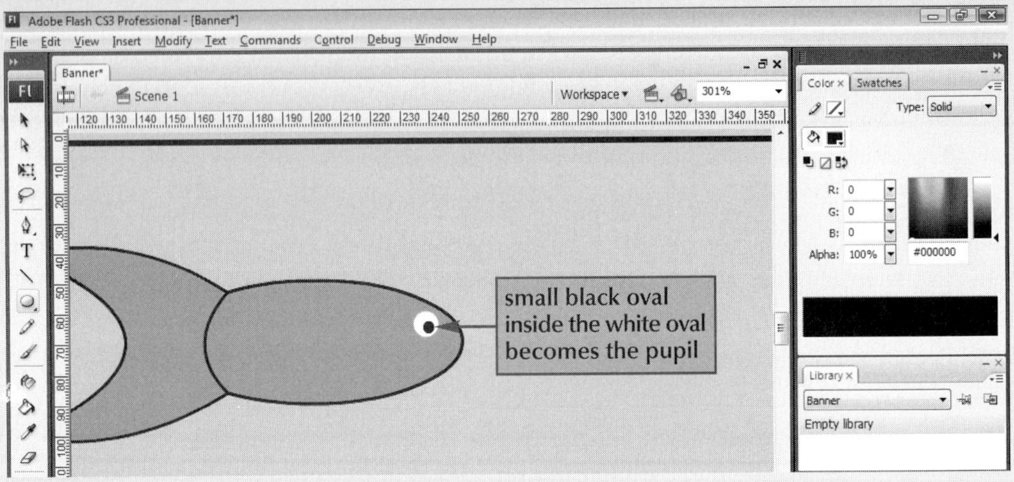

Trouble? If you make a mistake and draw over the orange fill of the fish, click Edit on the menu bar, click Undo Oval, and then repeat Step 8 to draw the oval for the pupil of the fish eye again.

Using the Pencil Tool

The Pencil tool works in a similar way to the Line tool, but it does not limit you to drawing straight lines. The **Pencil tool** allows you to draw lines and shapes in a free-form manner as if you were using an actual pencil to draw on paper. As is the case with the Line tool, you can select a color, height, and style for the lines drawn with the Pencil tool. The Pencil Mode modifier in the Tools panel lets you control the way lines appear as you draw them. Figure 2-16 summarizes the options for this modifier.

Figure 2-16 Pencil Mode modifier options

Modifier Button	Option	Description
	Straighten	The option helps straighten the lines you draw
	Smooth	The option smoothes out the lines and curves you draw
	Ink	The option provides minimal assistance as you draw

You'll use the Pencil tool to add a mouth and fins to the fish.

To add the fins, the mouth, and lines to the fish using the Pencil tool:

1. In the Tools panel, click the **Pencil** tool to select it. You want the Smooth option for the Pencil Mode modifier so that the lines you draw will be smooth.
2. In the Tools panel, click the **Pencil Mode** modifier button to open the menu of options, and then click **Smooth**.

   You'll use the Property inspector to set the stroke color, height, and style before drawing lines for the fins, mouth, and curves.
3. In the Property inspector, make sure the stroke color is **black** (#000000), the stroke height is **1**, and the stroke style is **Solid**.

4. Draw a fin on the top side of the fish and two fins on the bottom side, as shown in Figure 2-17. Be sure the strokes for the fins connect to the strokes for the fish.

Figure 2-17 **Fins on the fish**

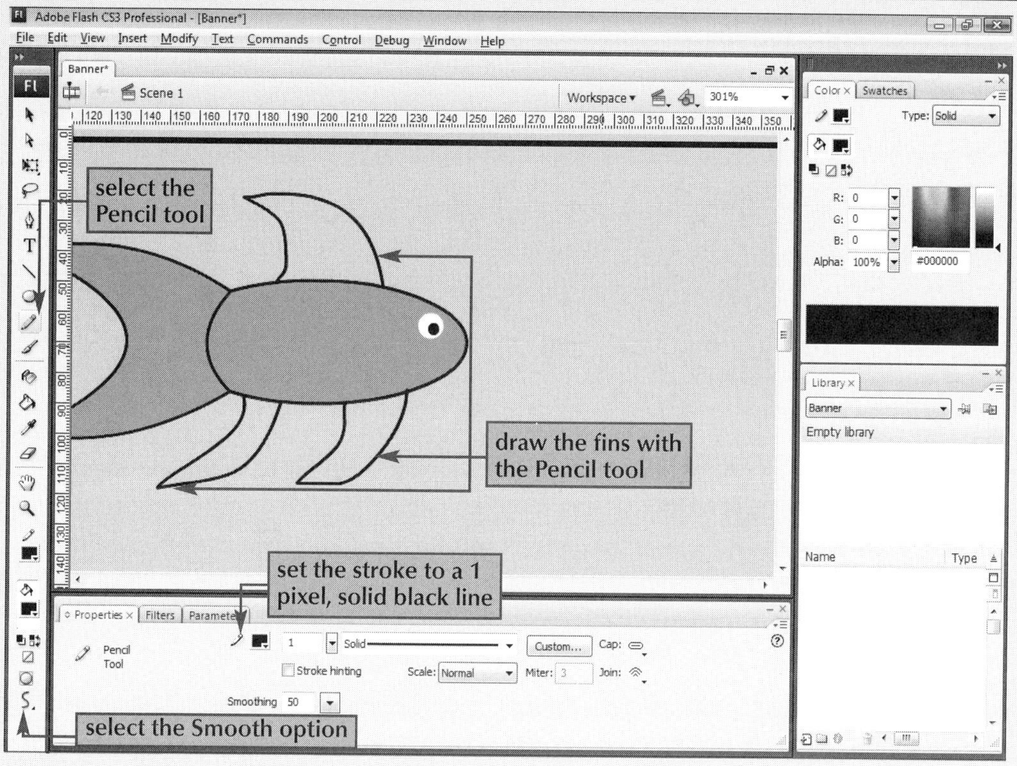

5. Draw a small curved line for the fish's mouth from right below the eye to the stroke in the lower-right side of the fish.

6. Draw a curved line segment in the top part of the fish, and then draw a curved line segment in the bottom part of the fish, as shown in Figure 2-18. Be sure the strokes for the curved line segments connect to the strokes for the fish.

Figure 2-18 **Fish with fins, mouth, and curved lines**

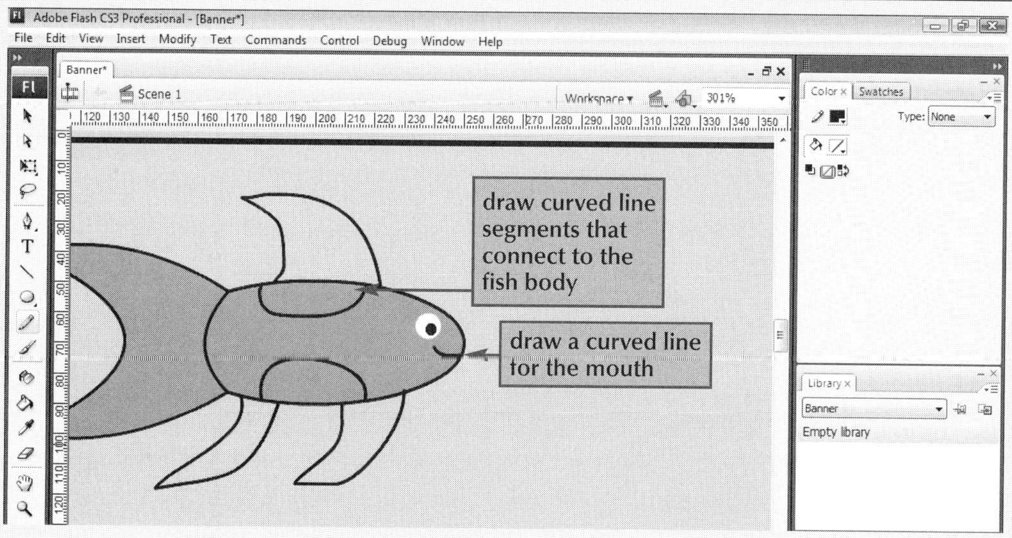

Changing Strokes and Fills

After you draw an object, you can still change its stroke and fill. You can change the stroke's color, height, or style, and you can change a fill's color. You can even add a fill or a stroke to an object that does not have one or the other. The Paint Bucket tool modifies an existing fill's color or applies a fill to an enclosed area that does not have a fill. The Ink Bottle tool changes the attributes or properties of a stroke, or it applies a stroke to an object that has no stroke. The Eyedropper tool copies the attributes of a stroke from one object to the stroke of another object. It also copies a fill's color from one object to another. You'll use the Paint Bucket and Eyedropper tools to complete the banner for Jenny's Oyster Hut. Based on the sketch of the banner, the curved lines on the fish should be areas of color. The fins and tail also need color added to them.

To keep the various parts of the fish together, you will group them. Recall that grouping combines the individual elements of an object so that they're treated as one object. After you group the elements that comprise the fish graphic, you can easily modify the fish graphic as a whole or create copies of the fish graphic. You can still modify individual elements of a grouped object in group editing mode.

To group the fish graphic:

1. Click **View** on the menu bar, point to **Magnification**, and then click **Show Frame** to view all of the contents of the Stage.
2. In the Tools panel, click the **Selection** tool, and then draw a marquee around the entire fish to select all of its parts.
3. Click **Modify** on the menu bar, and then click **Group**. The graphic elements are grouped. A thin rectangular line surrounds the grouped object to show it is selected. See Figure 2-19.

Tip

You can also press the Ctrl+G keys to group selected elements.

Figure 2-19 Grouped fish graphic

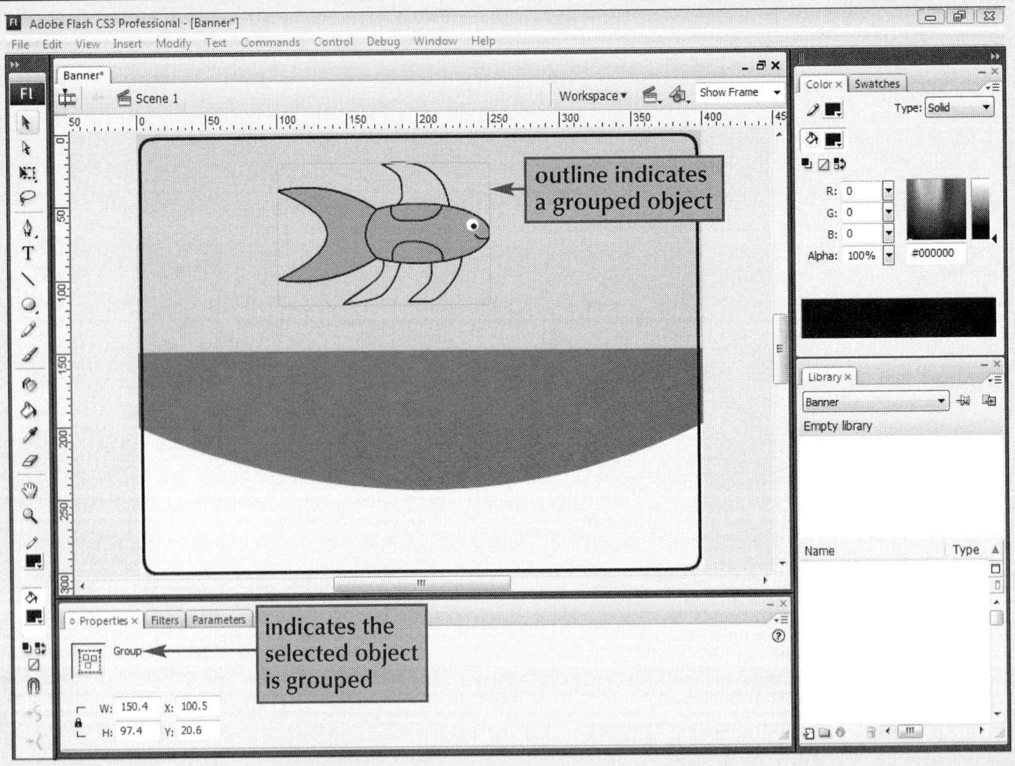

Using the Paint Bucket Tool

The **Paint Bucket tool** changes the color of an existing fill or adds a fill to an enclosed area. The fill color is selected with the Fill color control in the Tools panel, the Property inspector, or the Color panel. The Paint Bucket tool also has a Gap Size modifier and a Lock Fill modifier. The Gap Size modifiers—Don't Close Gaps, Close Small Gaps, Close Medium Gaps, and Close Large Gaps—determine how the tool will paint areas that are not completely enclosed. The Lock Fill modifier extends gradient and bitmap fills across multiple objects.

You will use the Paint Bucket tool to fill the bands on the fish with bright colors.

To apply fills to the fish with the Paint Bucket tool:

1. Double-click the grouped fish graphic to enter group-editing mode, and then click another area of the Stage to deselect the fish. In group-editing mode, you can modify each part of the fish independently.
2. In the Tools panel, click the **Paint Bucket** tool. The pointer changes to.
3. In the Tools panel, click the **Fill color** control to open the color palette, and then click the **light green** color swatch (#66FF00) in the last column, first row of the color palette.
4. Click inside the tail area of the fish to apply the fill color. The fish has a light green tail. See Figure 2-20.

Figure 2-20 Fill color applied with the Paint Bucket tool

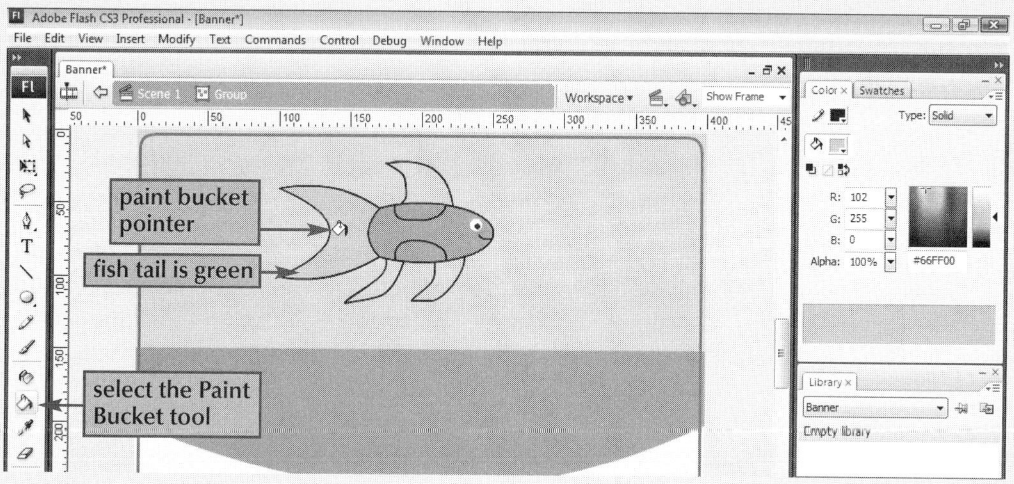

Trouble? If a padlock icon appears next to the paint bucket pointer, the Lock Fill modifier is selected. This does not affect the way the Paint Bucket tool works. Continue with Step 5.

5. In the Tools panel, click the **Fill color** control to open the color palette, click the **red** color swatch (#FF0000) in the first column, seventh row of the color palette, and then click the area enclosed by the curved line on the top part of the fish body to make a red spot.

Trouble? If the first column of the color palette displays all black swatches, use the second column.

Trouble? If the red color fills other areas of the fish, the endpoints of the strokes for the curved line segment are probably not connected to the strokes of the fish. Click Edit on the menu bar, and then click Undo Fill Color. In the Tools panel, click the Selection tool, select the line segment, and then press the Delete key. In the Tools panel, click the Pencil tool, click the Smooth modifier button, and then redraw the curved line segment so that its endpoints connect to the strokes of the fish. In the Tools panel, click the Paint Bucket tool, and then click the area enclosed by the curved line.

6. Repeat Step 5 to apply the **yellow** color (#FFFF00) in the first column, tenth row of the Fill color palette to the area enclosed by the curved line on the bottom part of the fish body to make a yellow spot. See Figure 2-21.

Figure 2-21 Fish with colored spots

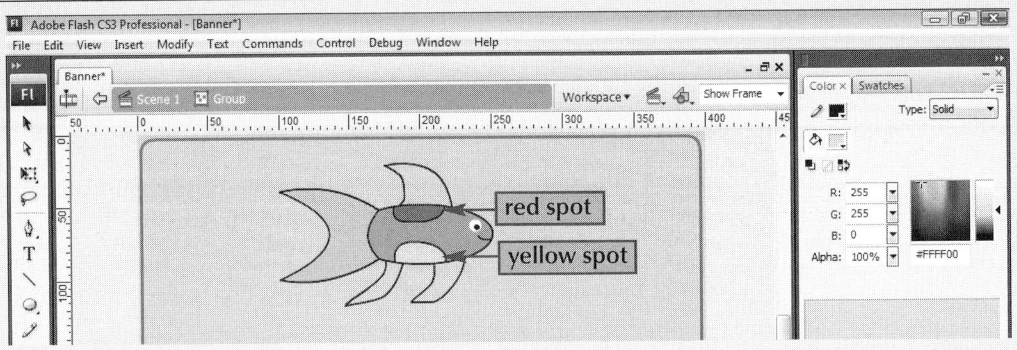

Using the Eyedropper Tool

The **Eyedropper tool** copies the fill or stroke properties of one object and applies them to another object. You can also use the Eyedropper tool to copy the properties of a text block and apply them to another text block. When you select the Eyedropper tool, the pointer changes to . If you move the eyedropper over a stroke, the pointer changes to to indicate that you are about to copy the stroke's attributes. After you click the stroke, the pointer changes to , which indicates that you can apply the copied stroke attributes to another object. If you move the eyedropper over a fill, the pointer changes to to indicate that you are about to copy the fill's attributes. After you click the fill, the pointer changes to and you can click another object to apply the copied fill attributes. The pointer includes a padlock when the Lock Fill modifier is selected.

Reference Window | Using the Eyedropper Tool

- In the Tools panel, click the Eyedropper tool.
- Click the stroke or fill whose attributes you want to copy.
- Click the stroke or fill to which you want to apply the copied attributes.

Based on to Aly's sketch, the fins of the fish need to be the same color as the fish's tail. You can use the Eyedropper tool to copy the fill color of the tail to the fins.

To copy the color from the fish's tail to the fins using the Eyedropper tool and exit group editing mode:

1. In the Tools panel, click the **Eyedropper** tool. The pointer changes to.
2. Click the green fill color in the tail of the fish. The pointer changes to or (depending on whether the Lock Fill modifier is selected) to indicate that you can apply the green color to another part of the fish.
3. Click the blank area enclosed by the top fin. The top fin now has the same color as the tail of the fish. See Figure 2-22.

Figure 2-22 **Fill color copied from the tail to the fin**

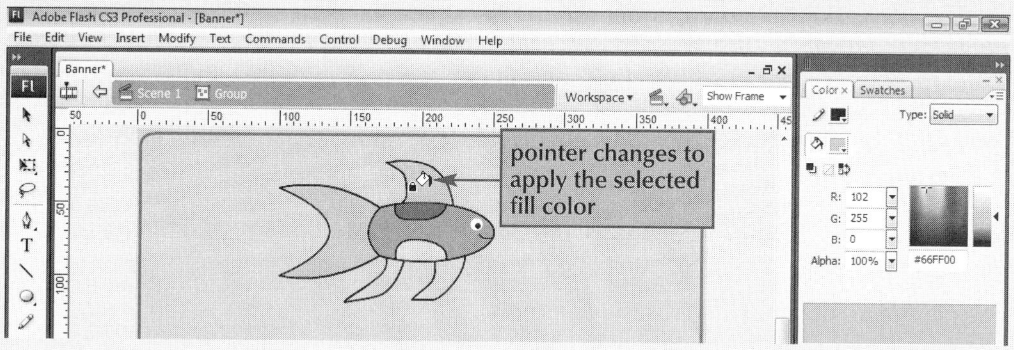

Trouble? If the green color does not fill the area enclosed by the fin, the endpoints of the strokes of the fin are probably not connected to the strokes of the fish. In the Tools panel, click the Selection tool, select the stroke of the fin, and press the Delete key. In the Tools panel, click the Pencil tool, click the Snap to Objects modifier button, and then redraw the fin so that its endpoints connect to the strokes of the fish. Repeat Steps 1, 2, and 3.

4. Click the bottom fins. The green fill color is applied to them.
5. On the Edit bar, click the **Scene 1** link to exit group-editing mode.

Using Primitive Tools

The **Rectangle Primitive** and **Oval Primitive tools** create rectangles and ovals that are treated as separate objects whose characteristics you can modify using the Property inspector without having to redraw the shapes from scratch. For example, after you draw a rectangle with the Rectangle tool, you cannot change the roundness of the rectangle's corners. However, if you create a rectangle with the Rectangle Primitive tool, you can easily modify the rectangle's corners by changing the values in the Rectangle corner radius boxes in the Property inspector. Similarly, after you draw an oval with the Oval Primitive tool, the Property inspector provides several controls for modifying the oval, as shown in Figure 2-23.

Figure 2-23 Oval Primitive controls in the Property inspector

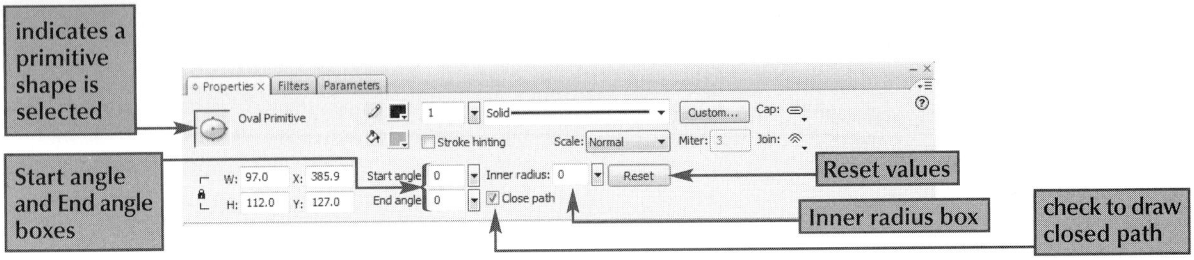

The Start angle and End angle values specify the angles of the starting and ending points of the oval. This can be used to create a pie or half circle shape. The Inner radius value specifies the percentage of the oval's fill that is removed. For example, you can change the Inner radius value to create a doughnut shape. The Close path option determines whether the path of the oval is closed or open. An open path results in an oval shape with no fill when the start angle and end angle are not set to zero. Reset returns the oval shape on the Stage to its original size and shape. Figure 2-24 shows shapes drawn with the Rectangle Primitive and Oval Primitive tools.

Figure 2-24 Sample shapes drawn with the primitive tools

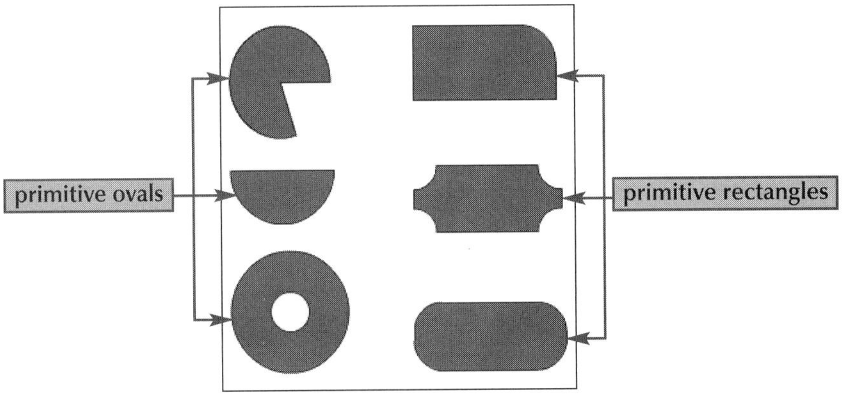

After you create a shape with the primitive tools, you can convert it to a drawing object to further modify the shape just as if you had drawn the shape using the Object Drawing model. If you convert a primitive shape into a drawing object, the object will no longer be a primitive shape and the primitive tool controls will not be available in the Property inspector.

According to Aly's sketch, the umbrella is still needed for the banner. You'll use the Oval Primitive tool to draw the umbrella so you can modify the oval's start and end angles to create the half circle that will form the umbrella. You'll draw the umbrella's pole using the Line tool.

Tip

Double-click a primitive object to convert it to a drawing object, modify the object, and then click the Scene 1 link on the Edit bar to exit Drawing Object mode.

To draw an oval for the umbrella with the Oval Primitive tool:

1. In the Tools panel, click the **Selection** tool, show the guides, and then drag a horizontal guide to about 150 pixels from the top of the Stage, and then drag another horizontal guide to about 250 pixels from the top of the Stage.
2. Drag a vertical guide to about 50 pixels from the left of the Stage, and then drag another vertical guide to about 150 pixels from the left of the Stage. You'll use the guides as you create the umbrella.

3. In the Tools panel, click and hold the **Oval** tool to open the pop-up menu, and then click the **Oval Primitive** tool. The Oval Primitive tool is selected.

   Before drawing an oval, you'll set the stroke and fill colors.

4. In the Tools panel, set the stroke color to **black** (#000000) and set the fill color to **red** (#FF0000).

5. In the Property inspector, if necessary, set the stroke height to **1**, set the stroke style to **Solid**, and then click the **Reset** button to reset the primitive oval controls.

   You are ready to draw an oval inside the square formed by the guides.

6. Drag + inside the square formed by the guides to create an oval. See Figure 2-25.

Figure 2-25 Primitive oval shape

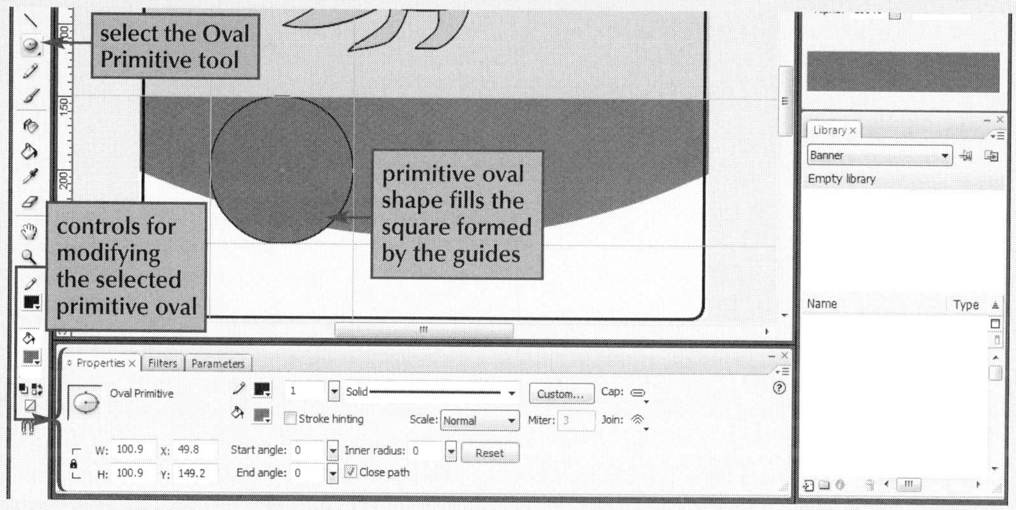

7. In the Property inspector, double-click the value in the Start angle box, type **180**, and then press the **Enter** key. The oval changes to a half circle based on the new value. See Figure 2-26.

Figure 2-26 Primitive oval changed to a half circle shape

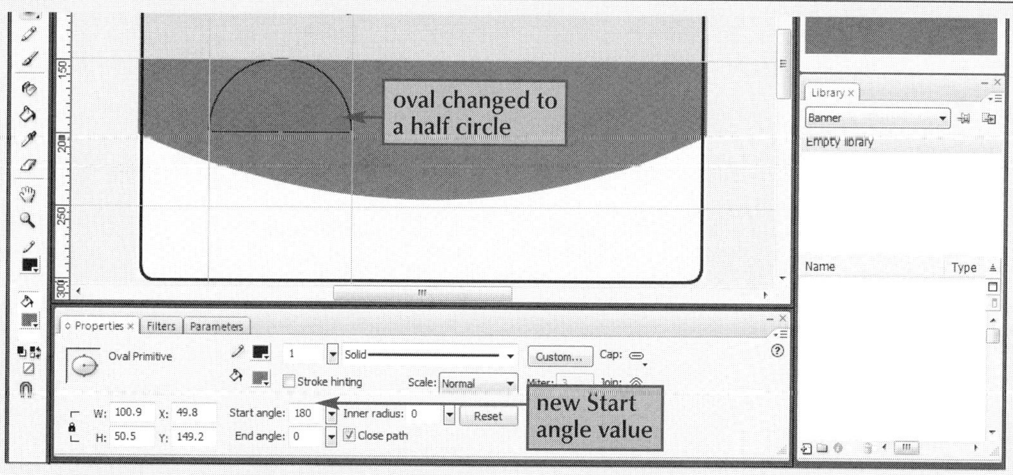

Tip

You can click the Start angle or End angle arrow in the Property inspector, drag the handle in the control to change the angle value, and see its effect on the shape on the Stage.

Next, you will convert the half circle shape to a drawing object and add lines to it so it resembles an umbrella.

8. In the Tools panel, click the **Selection** tool, double-click the half circle shape, and then, click the **OK** button in the dialog box that opens to inform you that the shape must be converted to a drawing object. The program switches to Drawing Object mode.

   Trouble? If a dialog box doesn't open, the warning was disabled for your installation. Continue with Step 9.

   You will add lines to the shape using the Line tool.

9. In the Tools panel, click the **Line** tool, and then, if necessary, set the stroke color to **black** (#000000), the stroke height to **1**, and the stroke style to **Solid**.
10. In the Tools panel, click the **Snap to Objects** button to select it, if necessary.
11. Draw three lines on the half circle, as shown in Figure 2-27.

Figure 2-27 Lines added to the half circle shape

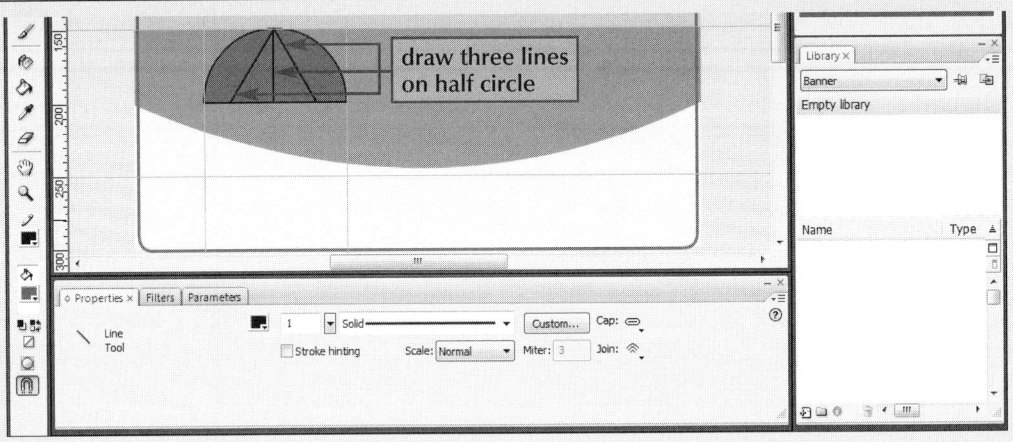

12. In the Property inspector, set the stroke height to **3**, and then draw a vertical line from the midpoint at the bottom edge of the half circle to the guide. See Figure 2-28.

Figure 2-28 Line added for the umbrella's pole

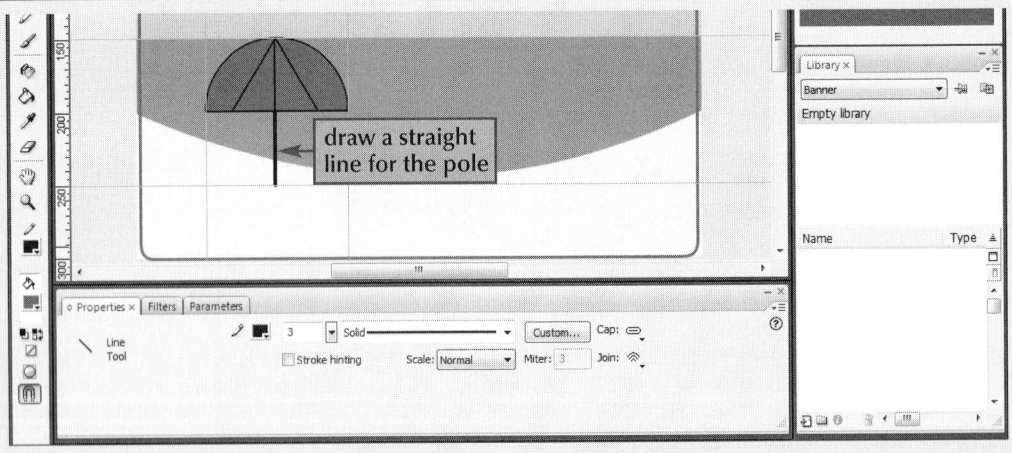

Based on Aly's sketch of the banner, two of the lines you drew on the umbrella should be curved lines. You'll use the Selection tool to modify the lines on the half circle.

To modify the lines on the umbrella using the Selection tool:

1. In the Tools panel, click the **Selection** tool, and then point to the straight line on the left side of the umbrella. The pointer changes to .
2. Drag the left line slightly to the left to curve it, and then drag the straight line on the right side of the umbrella slightly to the right to curve it. See Figure 2-29.

Figure 2-29 Lines modified with the Selection tool

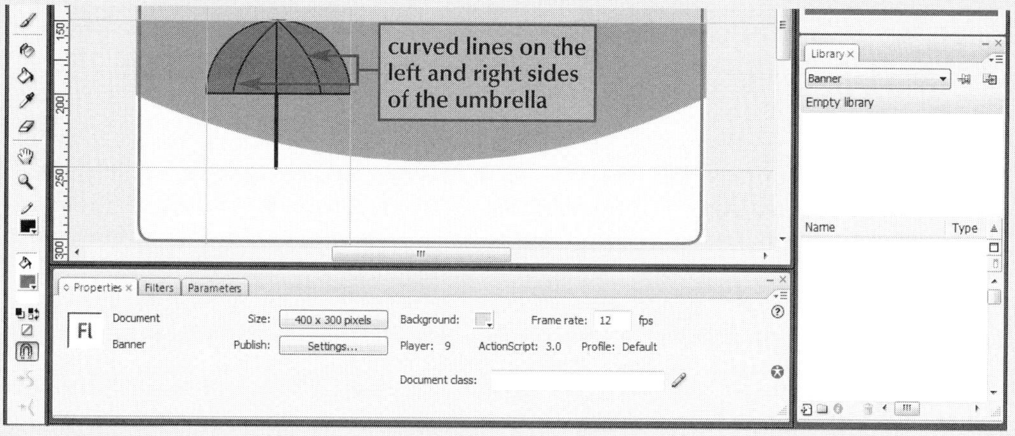

Next, you will modify the line segments on the bottom edge of the umbrella. You'll increase the magnification level of the umbrella first.

3. In the Tools panel, click the **Zoom** tool, and then, if necessary, click the **Enlarge** modifier button.
4. Click the umbrella once to zoom in and center the umbrella on the Stage.
5. In the Tools panel, click the **Selection** tool, point to the first line segment on the left side of the bottom edge of the umbrella to change the pointer to , and then drag the line slightly up to curve it.
6. Repeat Step 5 to drag each of the other three line segments at the bottom edge of the umbrella to curve them. See Figure 2-30.

Figure 2-30 Modified line segments

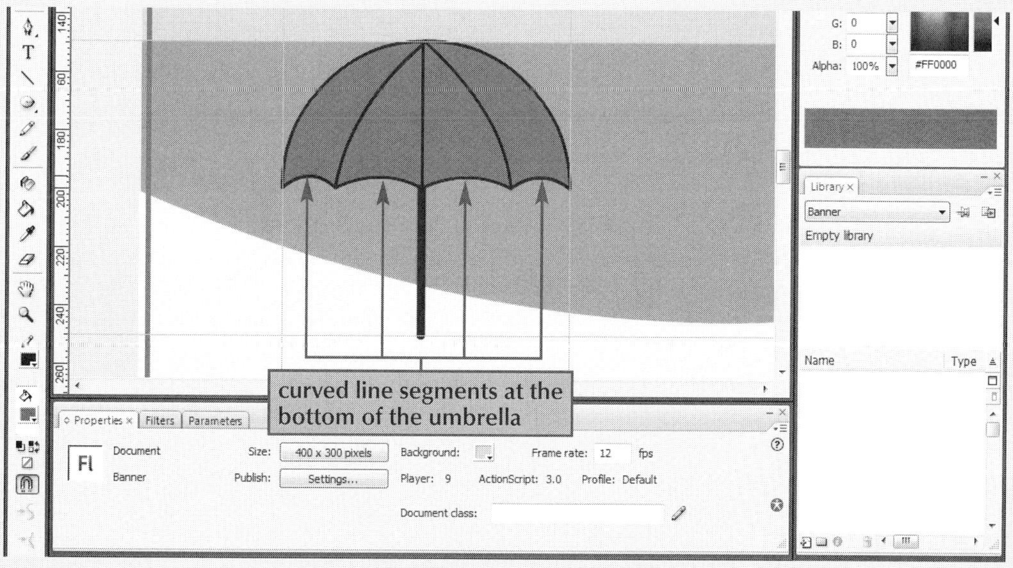

Next, you will clear the guides and exit Object Drawing mode.

7. Click **View** on the menu bar, point to **Guides** and click **Clear Guides**. The guides are removed from the Stage.
8. On the Edit bar, click the **Scene 1** link to exit Object Drawing mode.
9. On the Edit bar, click the **Zoom control arrow**, and then click **Show Frame** to set the magnification level so you can see all of the Stage.

Using the Free Transform Tool

You can modify the strokes and fills of objects you draw in ways other than just changing their colors. The **Free Transform tool** allows you to move, rotate, scale, skew, and even distort objects. You can transform a particular stroke or fill of an object, or you can transform the entire object at once. When you select an object with the Free Transform tool, a bounding box with transformation handles surrounds the object. These handles are different from the anchor points you used with the Subselection tool. The anchor points modify curves, lines, or specific shapes. The transformation handles on the bounding box affect the whole object at one time.

Reference Window | Transforming an Object Using the Free Transform Tool

- In the Tools panel, click the Free Transform tool.
- Select the object to transform.
- In the Tools panel, click a modifier.
- Drag the bounding box handles to modify the object.

As you move the pointer near a bounding box handle, the pointer changes to indicate how the object will be modified when you drag that handle. For example, when you point just outside a corner handle, the pointer changes to ↻, indicating that you can rotate the object by dragging the corner. The Free Transform tool also has several modifiers in the Tools panel, which are described in Figure 2-31.

Figure 2-31 **Free Transform tool modifiers**

Button	Modifier	Description
	Rotate and Skew	Freely rotates an object by dragging a corner handle or skews it to a different angle by dragging an edge handle
	Scale	Changes the size of an object by dragging a corner or edge handle
	Distort	Repositions the corner or edge of an object by dragging its handle
	Envelope	Displays a bounding box with points and tangent handles that you can adjust to warp or distort the object

Aly's banner sketch shows a wavy line for the top of the blue rectangle that represents the ocean. You'll use the Free Transform tool to modify the rectangle. Her sketch also shows a smaller fish swimming to the right of the larger fish you already drew. Instead of drawing the smaller fish from scratch, you'll copy the existing fish, and then use the Free Transform tool to resize and rotate the copied fish. You'll first change the Tools panel to display the tools in two columns, which will make it easier to access the Envelope modifier.

To modify the blue rectangle to resemble the ocean using the Free Transform tool:

1. At the top of the Tools panel, click the **double-arrow** icon. The tools in the Tools panel are arranged in two columns.
2. In the Tools panel, click the **Free Transform** tool, and then click the blue rectangle on the Stage. The ocean rectangle is selected and the bounding box and transformation handles appear around the edge of the rectangle.
3. In the Tools panel, click the **Envelope** modifier button. Tangent handles appear on the bounding box.
4. On the top of the rectangle, drag the leftmost tangent handle slightly down to create a curve. See Figure 2-32.

Tip

The transformation handles are squares and the tangent handles are circles.

Figure 2-32 Curve created by dragging a tangent handle

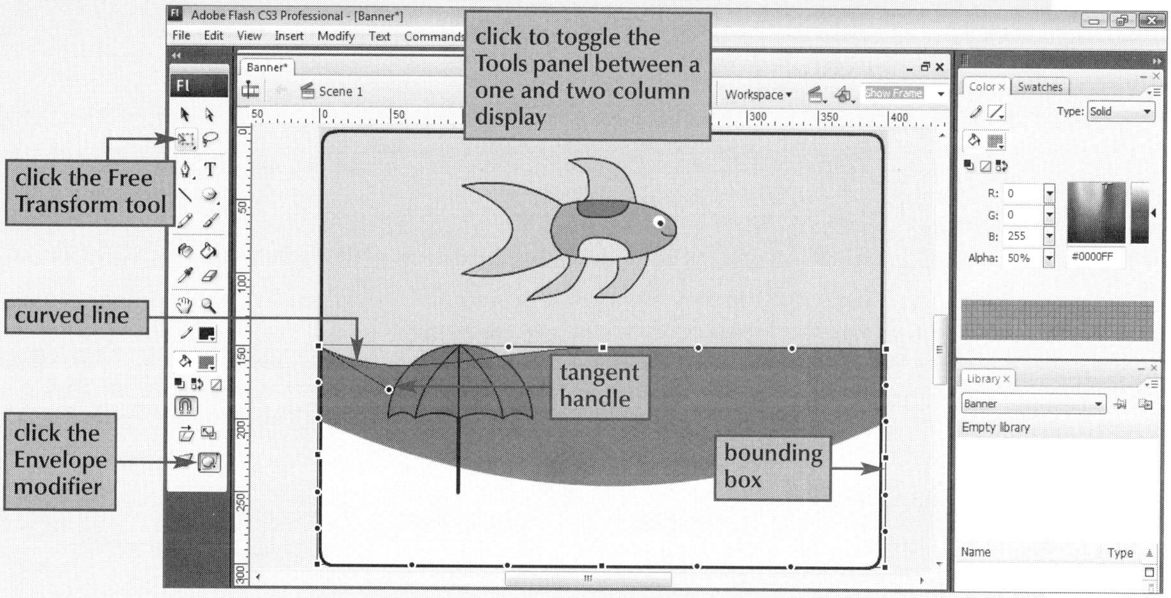

5. On the top of the rectangle, drag the rightmost tangent handle slightly down to create a curve. See Figure 2-33.

Figure 2-33 **Second curve created by dragging a second tangent handle**

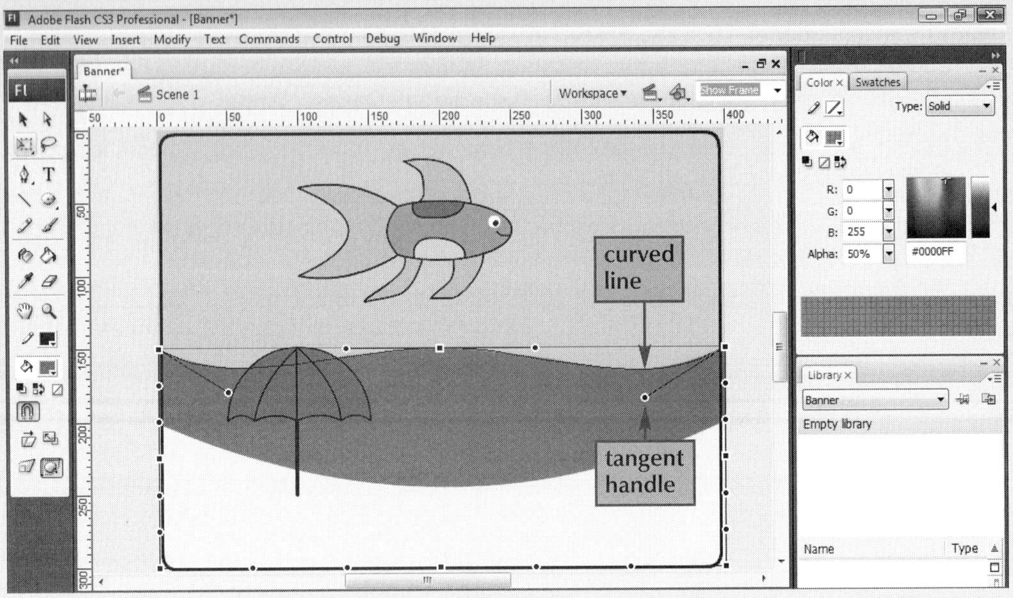

Next, you will copy the fish, and then reposition it. You will also reposition the first fish and the umbrella based on the sketch of the banner.

To make a copy of the fish and to reposition the fish and the umbrella:

1. In the Tools panel, click the **Selection** tool, and then click the fish. The grouped fish is selected.
2. Click **Edit** on the menu bar, and then click **Copy**. The fish is copied to the Windows Clipboard.
3. Click **Edit** on the menu bar, and then click **Paste in Center**. A copy of the fish is placed in the center of the Stage.

4. Drag the copy of the fish to the right side of the Stage so that half of it is below the ocean line, and then drag the first fish down toward the ocean. See Figure 2-34.

Figure 2-34 Repositioned fish

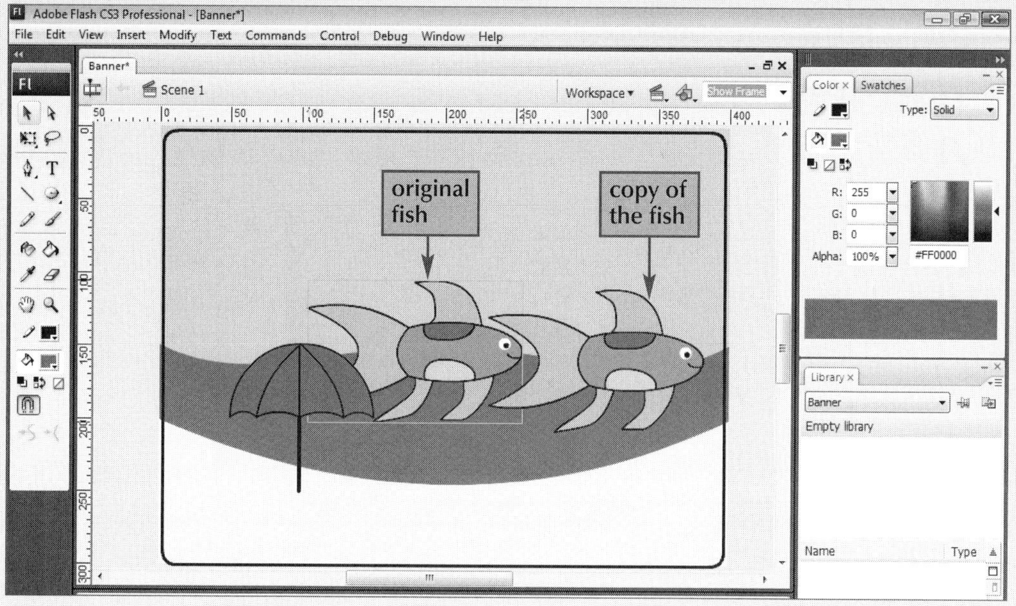

Next, you will use the Free Transform tool to rotate the copied fish and the umbrella based on the sketch of the banner.

To modify the copied fish and the umbrella with the Free Transform tool:

1. In the Tools panel, click the **Free Transform** tool, and then click the copied fish. A bounding box with transformation handles appears around the selected fish. You want to reduce the size of the copied fish.
2. In the Tools panel, click the **Scale** modifier button. When you drag a corner handle, the fish will resize.
3. Drag a corner handle to reduce the size of the fish to about half its original size.
4. In the Tools panel, click the **Rotate and Skew** modifier button, and then move the pointer near a corner handle. The pointer changes to a rotate pointer.
5. Drag the corner handle clockwise to rotate the fish so that it appears to be swimming downward. See Figure 2-35.

Figure 2-35 Scaled and rotated fish

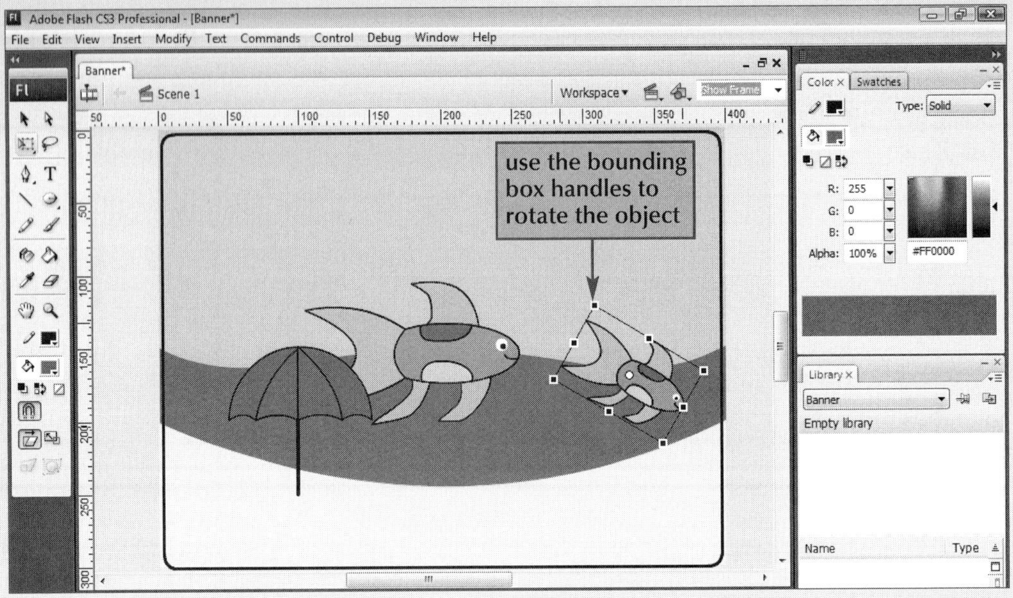

Trouble? If the fish in your banner are in a different location than shown in Figure 2-38, you need to reposition them. Drag the fish as needed to match the locations shown.

6. Click the umbrella to select it, drag a corner handle counterclockwise to tilt the umbrella to the left, and then drag the umbrella to position in the lower-left corner of the banner. See Figure 2-36.

Figure 2-36 Fish and umbrella rotated and positioned

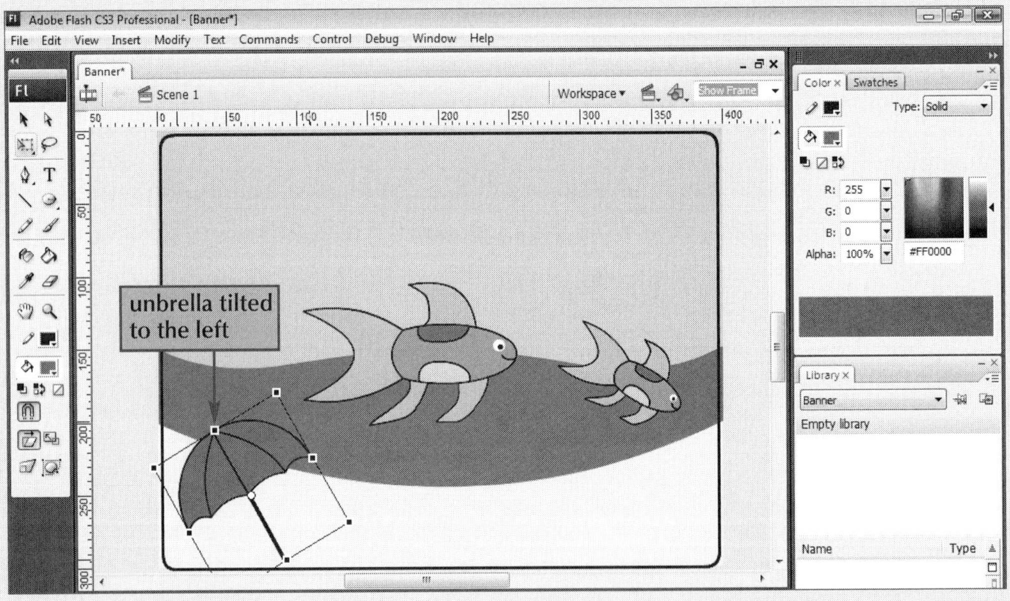

7. Save the banner.

Trasnforming Objects Precisely | InSight

Sometimes, you might want to make very specific transformations to an object. You can use the Transform panel to obtain more precise control when transforming objects. In the Transform panel, you can enter specific values in pixels to resize an object. You can also enter values in degrees to rotate an object or skew an object horizontally or vertically. Another option available in the Tranform panel is to make a copy of an object and to then apply a transformation to the copied object. This lets you try different transformations without affecting the original object.

In this session, you used the drawing tools to create and modify the graphics on the banner, including the fish, the umbrella, and the background. You modified their fill colors and the stroke colors, heights, and styles. You also scaled and rotated the fish and umbrella. Aly is pleased with the fish, the umbrella, and the background graphics. She suggests you turn your attention to the text at the top and bottom of the banner. You will add the text to the banner in the next session.

Session 2.1 Quick Check | Review

1. True or False? When drawing a shape with the Oval tool, you can draw a perfect circle when the Snap to Grid modifier is selected.
2. How can you draw a rectangle with rounded corners?
3. The ________________ tool can be used to draw pie shapes and half circles.
4. The ________________ modifier helps straighten lines you draw with the Pencil tool.
5. Describe how to use the Eyedropper tool to copy a stroke's attributes to another object.
6. Which tool can you use to add a fill to an enclosed area that has no fill?
7. Which modifier can be used with the Free Transform tool to resize a selected object?
8. True or False? The Free Transform tool is used to modify an object's gradient fill.

Session 2.2

Adding Text

As you have seen, Flash tools enable you to easily create graphic images. However, graphic images alone do not always communicate the message you are trying to convey. Many of the images and animations you create will also need to include text. In Flash, you can easily create text blocks in a variety of colors, sizes, and fonts. You use the Text tool to add static text blocks to a document. A **static text block** is an object that contains text that is entered when you create the document but does not change after you publish the document. You can also create dynamic text fields or input text fields. A **dynamic text field** is an advanced feature where the text is updated automatically with information from a Web server when the document is published and displayed in a Web browser. A **field** is a unit of data such as a person's age or phone number. An example of a dynamic text field is one that displays up-to-the-minute sports scores retrieved from a Web server. Dynamic text fields can also display the results of a calculation based on values entered into input text fields. An **input text field** allows the user to enter text in forms or surveys. You will only work with static text blocks in this tutorial.

Using the Text Tool

The **Text tool** is used to create text blocks for documents. Text can be created in a **fixed-width text block** that doesn't change as you type, or in a **single-line text block** that extends as you type. If the width of the text block is fixed, the text wraps to create new lines as needed. To create a fixed-width text block, you click the Text tool in the Tools panel, and then drag the text pointer on the Stage. The text block has a square handle in its upper-right corner, indicating that the width of the text block will remain fixed. As you type, the words wrap to the next line when you reach the right margin of the block. To create a single-line text block, click the Stage with the text pointer where you want the text to appear and begin typing. The text block has a round handle on the upper-right corner which indicates that the width of the text block extends as you type.

You can change a fixed-width text block to a single-line text block by double-clicking its square handle. The text block changes to one line and its handle becomes round. Similarly, if you drag the round handle of a single-line text block to adjust the width of the block, the handle becomes square indicating that the width of the block is now fixed.

After you create a text block, you can move it on the Stage using the Selection tool. You can also resize, rotate, and skew the text block using the Free Transform tool. The font, font size, text fill color, text styles, alignment, and other text properties are specified in the Property inspector. You can set these properties before you type the text, or you can select existing text and then change the properties.

You'll use the Text tool to add two text blocks to the banner—one at the top of the banner and one at the bottom. You will set the Property inspector options before you create each text block.

To add a single-line text block to the top of the banner:

1. If you took a break after the previous session, make sure the Banner document located in the Tutorial.02\Tutorial folder included with your Data Files is open, the Timeline is hidden, and the magnification is set to Show Frame.
2. In the Tools panel, click the **Text** tool [T]. The pointer changes to ┼T. Before you type the banner text, you'll set the text properties.
3. In the Property inspector, set the font to **Arial**, the font size to **28**, and the text fill color to **black** (#000000).
4. In the Property inspector, click the **Bold** button [B] to apply bold, and then click the **Italic** button [I] to apply italics.
5. In the Property inspector, click the **Align Center** button [≡] to apply the center style.
6. Click in the top area of the Stage to create a single-line text block, type **Jenny's Oyster Hut**, press the **Enter** key to move the insertion point the next line, and then type **10th Anniversary**.
7. In the Tools panel, click the **Selection** tool [▸], and then, if necessary, drag the text block to center it at the top of the Stage. See Figure 2-37.

Figure 2-37 Text block for the top of the banner

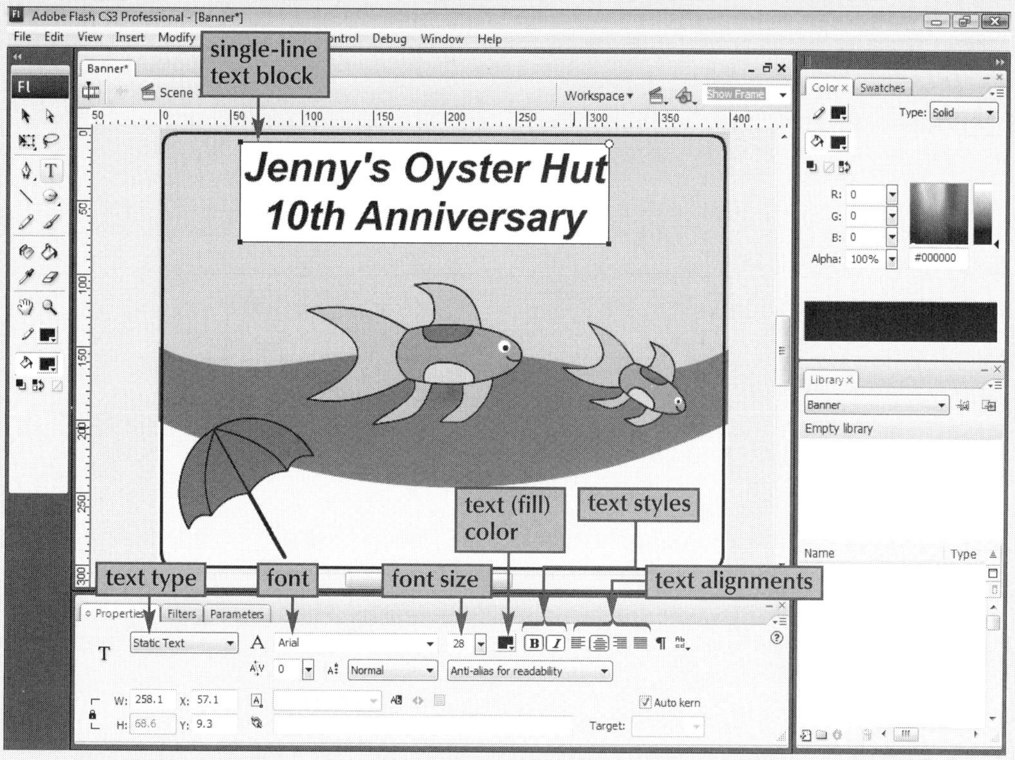

8. Click an empty area of the Stage to deselect the text block.

Before you create the second text block, you'll change the text properties in the Property inspector.

To add a single-line text block to bottom of the banner:

1. In the Tools panel, click the **Text** tool [T].
2. In the Property inspector, change the font to **Times New Roman**, the font size to **16**, and the text fill color to **maroon** (#660000) in fourteenth column, first row of the color palette.

   Trouble? If the first column of the color palette displays all black swatches, use the fifteenth column.
3. In the Property inspector, click the **Italic** button [I] to deselect italics. The bold style and the center alignment remain in place from the previous settings.
4. Click the bottom of the Stage in the light yellow beach area to create a single-line text block, and then type **Enjoy 10% off on Sundays this month!** in the text block.
5. If necessary, in the Tools panel, click the **Selection** tool, and then drag the text block to the right of the umbrella's pole.
6. Click the pasteboard to deselect the text block.
7. Save the banner. The banner matches the sketch Aly provided.

Tip

You can also press the V key to select the Selection tool in the Tools panel.

Checking the Spelling of Text

Flash can check the spelling of text you add to a document. The Check Spelling command verifies the spelling in each text block in the document. It can also check the spelling of text in other parts of the document, such as symbol names and layer names. Symbols are covered in the next session and layers are covered in Tutorial 3. Before you use the Check Spelling command, you can specify options in the Spelling Setup dialog box, as shown in Figure 2-38.

Figure 2-38 Spelling Setup dialog box

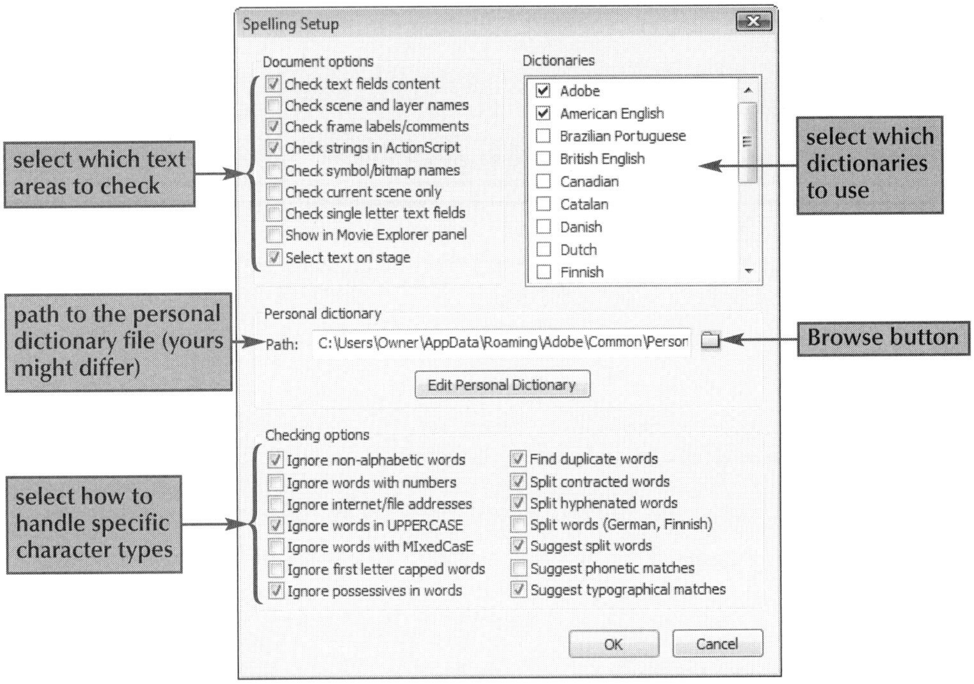

Under Document Options, you specify which text areas to check, such as the content of text fields and the names of layers. You also select which built-in dictionaries to use, such as the Adobe terms dictionary and a language dictionary such as American English. The Path for the Personal Dictionary specifies the location on your hard drive where you want Flash to create a file that will contain words and phrases you add yourself. You add words to your personal dictionary that are not in the Adobe or language dictionaries but are spelled correctly, such as a company name. You can also edit your personal dictionary after it is created. Finally, you select Checking Options that tell Flash whether to ignore or find specific character types such as words with numbers or words with all uppercase letters. You can also select options such as Suggest Phonetic Matches to have Flash provide a list of suggestions when it encounters a misspelled word. You can then choose one of the suggested words to replace the misspelled word.

Reference Window | Setting Options for the Spelling Checker

- Click Text on the menu bar, and then click Spelling Setup.
- In the Spelling Setup dialog box, select the desired spell-check options.
- Click the OK button.

When you check the spelling in a document, the Check Spelling dialog box opens if Flash finds a word that is misspelled or not in its dictionaries. Depending on the options you selected in the Spelling Setup dialog box, the Check Spelling dialog box might offer suggestions for replacing the word. You can choose to add the word to your personal dictionary, ignore the word, change it, or delete it. The Check Spelling dialog box also shows in what element of the document the word not found is located, such as in a text field, a scene name, or a layer name.

The Importance of Correct Spelling | InSight

You should always check the spelling of the text in your documents. Having a misspelled word in a Flash movie can detract from the message or idea you are trying to promote. Keep in mind that the spelling checker only compares words in your document with words that are contained in the selected dictionaries. If you use a word by mistake that is incorrect in that context but is spelled correctly, the spelling checker will not detect it. As a final check, it's a good idea to ask someone who isn't working on the document to proofread the text.

You will set the spell-check options and then check the spelling of the text in the banner.

To set the spelling checker options and to check the spelling of text in the banner:

1. Click **Text** on the menu bar, and then click **Spelling Setup**. The Spelling Setup dialog box opens.
2. Under Document options, click the **Check text fields content** check box to check it, if necessary.
3. Under Dictionaries, click the **American English** check box to check it, if necessary.
4. Under Checking options, make sure that the **Ignore words with numbers** check box is not selected.
5. Click the **OK** button. The Spelling Setup dialog box closes.
6. Click **Text** on the menu bar, and click **Check Spelling**. The Check Spelling dialog box opens, indicating the first word not found in the selected dictionaries. The word not found in the Check Spelling dialog box is *10th*. See Figure 2-39.

Figure 2-39 Check Spelling dialog box

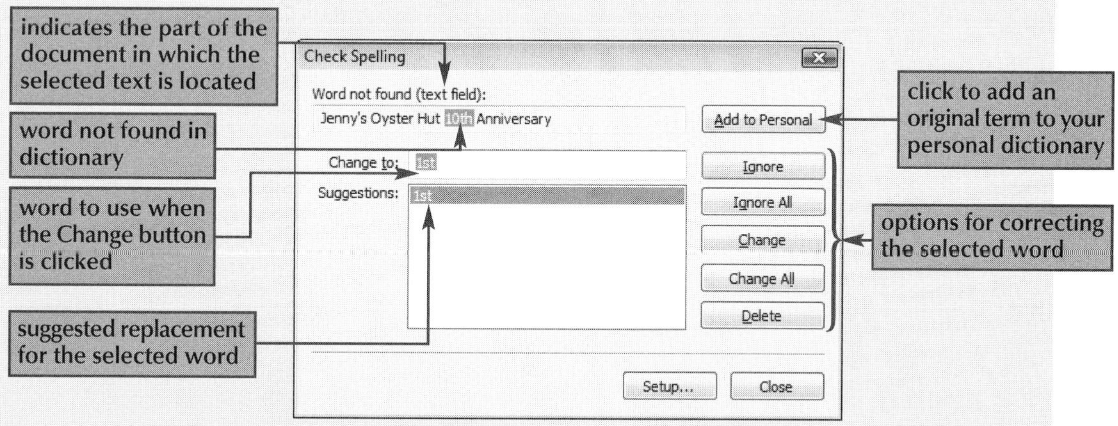

Trouble? If another word is found, you might have another word spelled incorrectly. If the word is spelled correctly, click the Ignore button. If the word is not spelled correctly, click the correct spelling in the Suggestions box or type the correct spelling in the Change to box, and then click the Change button. Repeat until *10th* is the word not found.

7. Click the **Ignore** button. A dialog box opens, indicating that the spelling check is complete.

   Trouble? If other words are not found, they are not in your selected dictionaries. Click the Ignore button to ignore the suggestion and leave the original spelling. Click the correct spelling in the Suggestions box or type the correct spelling in the Change to box, and then click the Change button to replace the word not found.

8. Click the **OK** button, and then save the banner.

Exporting a Graphic for Use on the Web

A document you create in Flash is saved in the FLA format. This format contains all of the different elements you create in Flash. To revise the document, you open the FLA file. To place the image in a Web page, however, it needs to be published or exported. Publishing a document will be covered in more detail in Tutorial 3 when you add animations to documents. A published document is in the SWF file format and is called a Flash movie. It requires the Flash Player plug-in to play in a Web browser. When you create a document such as Jenny's Oyster Hut banner that does not have animation, you can export it instead of publishing it. **Exporting** means that the program converts the document into another file format such as GIF or JPG, which does not require a plug-in to display in a Web page. Exporting also combines all of the individual elements of your document into one graphic. You cannot edit the individual elements of the image in an exported file. To edit the image's elements, you need to go back to the corresponding FLA file. Once you export the document into a GIF or JPG file format, it can be placed in a Web page.

Aly asks you to export the banner for use on the restaurant's Web site. Chris recommended that the Banner document be exported in the GIF file format.

To export the banner to the GIF file format:

1. Click **File** on the menu bar, point to **Export**, and then click **Export Image**. The Export Image dialog box opens.
2. Navigate the Save in box to the **Tutorial.02\Tutorial** folder included with your Data Files, and then type **Banner** in the File name box. The banner will be saved in that location with the name Banner.
3. Click the **Save as type** button to open a menu of file formats, and then click **GIF Image (*.gif)**. The banner will be saved in the GIF file format. See Figure 2-40.

Figure 2-40 Export Image dialog box

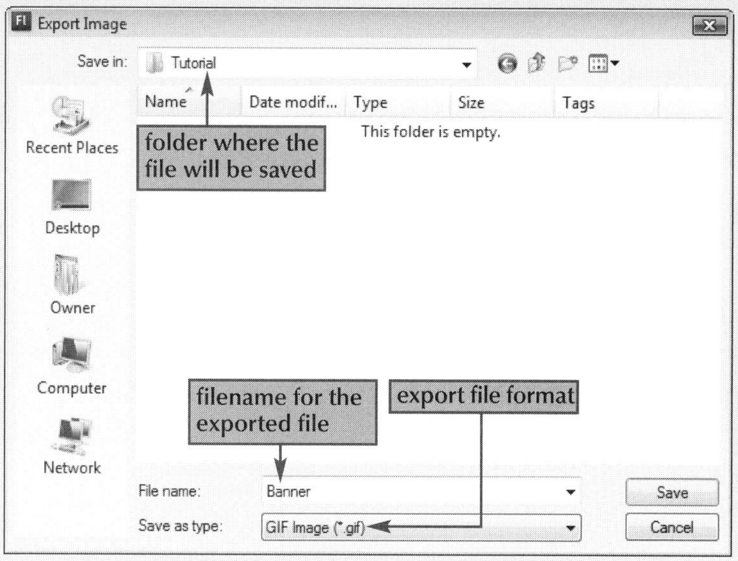

4. Click the **Save** button. The Export GIF dialog box opens with additional options and settings, including the document's dimensions, resolution, and colors.
5. Click the **Include** button, and then click **Full Document Size**, if necessary. This option makes the exported GIF image the same size as the Flash document. The Minimum Image Area option might reduce the size of the exported GIF image based on the content on the Stage.
6. Click the **OK** button. The banner is exported as a GIF file.
7. Click **File** on the menu bar, and then click **Close** to close the file. If a dialog box prompts you to save changes to the Flash document, click the **Yes** button.

Tip

You can quickly close a document by pressing the Ctrl+W keys.

Chris placed the GIF file with the exported banner in a Web page with the XHTML needed to display the Banner.gif image. You will preview this Web page in a Web browser.

To preview the Banner.gif file in a Web browser:

1. Start your Web browser.
2. Click **File** on the menu bar, and then click **Open**. The Open dialog box opens.
3. Click the **Browse** button, navigate to the **Tutorial.02\Tutorial** folder included with your Data Files, click the **Jennys.htm** file, and then click the **Open** button.
4. Click the **OK** button. The Web page opens in the browser and the Banner.gif file appears as part of the page. See Figure 2-41.

Figure 2-41 Web page with the exported Banner image

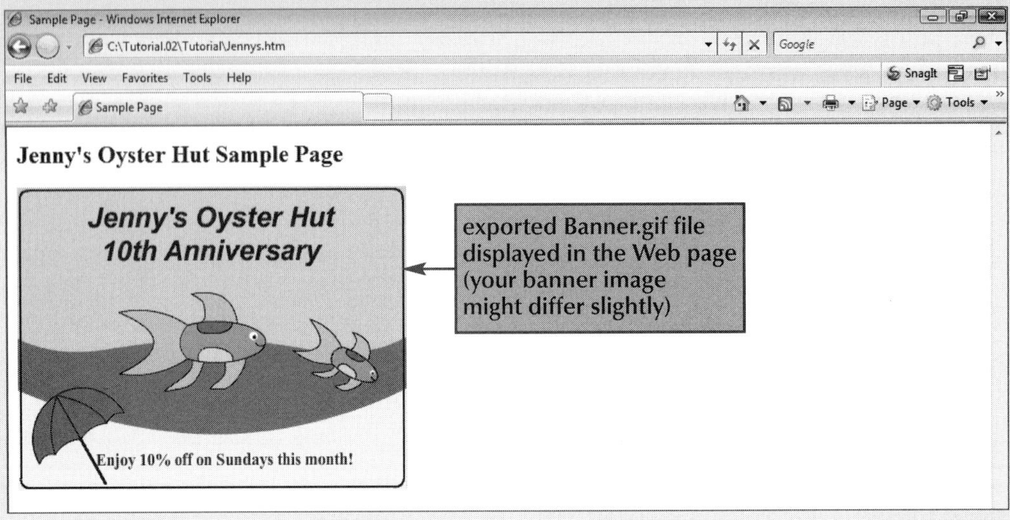

Trouble? If a dialog box opens, indicating that the browser needs to open a new window to display the Web page, click the OK button.

5. Close the browser.

Using the History Panel

The **History panel** is a record of the steps you have performed in the current document. After you open or create a document, each step is recorded and displayed in the History panel with an icon that reflects the particular step. The History panel displays only the steps for the current document. If you switch to another document, the History panel shows the steps taken in creating or editing that document. A document's history is maintained until you close the document or clear its history. You can also save selected steps by creating a command based on those steps. The command can then be used in the same document or in another document, and is available each time you use Flash. From the History panel, you can replay, undo, and save the recorded steps.

You'll use the History panel as you work with a document Aly created for another Admiral Web Design client, Jackson's Sports.

To use the History panel with the sports document:

1. On the Start page, in the Open a Recent Item list, click **Open**. The Open dialog box opens.
2. Navigate to the **Tutorial.02\Tutorial** folder included with your Data Files, and then double-click the **sports.fla** file. The Jackson's Sports banner opens.
3. Click **Window** on the menu bar, point to **Other Panels**, and then click **History**. The History panel opens.
4. If the History panel appears on top of the document, drag the History panel by its title bar to the right side of the screen.

   Before you can work with the document, you need to unlock the layers in the document. You do this using the Timeline.

Tip

You can also press the Ctrl+F10 keys to open and close the History panel.

5. In the Timeline, click the **Lock/Unlock All Layers** icon to unlock all the layers. A step labeled Lock Layers appears in the History panel.
6. Click the **Jackson's Sports** text block to select the block. The step appears in the History panel.
7. In the Property inspector, click the **Text (fill) color** control to open the color palette, and then click the **yellow** swatch (#FFFF00) in the first column, tenth row of the color palette. The letters in the text block change color, and this step appears in the History panel. See Figure 2-42.

Figure 2-42 History panel with the current session's steps

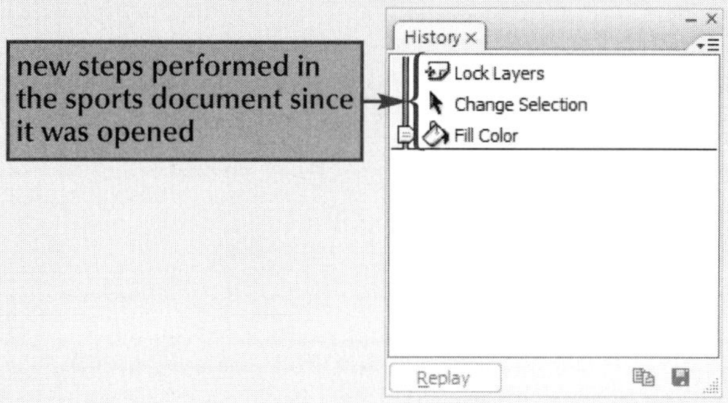

8. In the Tools panel, click the **Free Transform** tool, and then click the **Scale** modifier button to select it.
9. Drag the lower-right corner handle on the text block to make the text block slightly larger. The step appears in the History panel.

Replaying Steps

You can replay one or more selected steps in the History panel. For example, after you create a shape, you can select the steps in the History panel that you took to create the shape and then replay the steps to create a duplicate of the shape. If you select steps in the History panel that you used to format an object on the Stage, you can replay the steps to apply the same formatting to another object on the Stage. The steps you select in the History panel are applied to the selected object in the order shown in the panel. The replayed steps can be consecutive or nonconsecutive. Steps displayed with an icon that includes a small, red x cannot be replayed.

One or more steps taken in one document can also be selected and copied using the Copy selected steps to the clipboard button. The copied commands can then be applied using the Paste in Center command in another document.

You will replay the steps you performed previously from the History panel to further modify the sports document.

To replay steps from the History panel:

1. In the History panel, drag to select the **Fill Color** step and the **Scale** step. The two consecutive steps are selected. See Figure 2-43.

Figure 2-43 Steps selected in the History panel

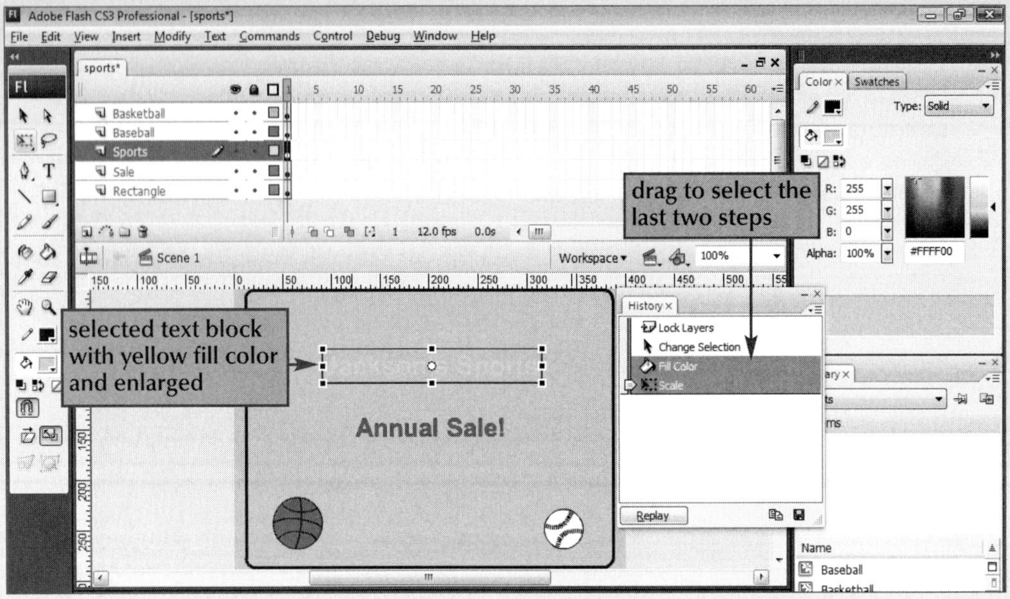

Trouble? If the last steps performed are undone, you probably dragged the slider on the left side of the History panel instead of the actual steps. Drag the slider down to the last step you performed, and then repeat Step 1, being careful to select the steps in the History panel and not the slider.

2. In the center of the Stage, click the **Annual Sale** text block to select it. The new step is added at the end of the History panel.
3. In the History panel, click the **Replay** button. The two selected steps are replayed; the Annula Sale text block increases in size and its text color changes to yellow. The History panel records the Replay Steps step.
4. In the Tools panel, click the **Selection** tool, and then drag the basketball to the upper-left corner of the Stage. The basketball is repositioned and the Change Selection and Move steps appears in the History panel.
5. Press and hold the **Ctrl** key, and then, in the History panel, click the **Move** step to select it and click the **Fill Color** step to deselect it. The nonconsecutive Scale and Move steps are selected in the History panel.
6. Release the **Ctrl** key.
7. On the Stage, click the baseball to select it, and then, in the History panel, click the **Replay** button. The nonconsecutive steps are replayed, and the baseball becomes slightly larger and moves to the top of the Stage. The History panel shows the last two steps you performed. See Figure 2-44.

Figure 2-44 Steps replayed and applied to baseball

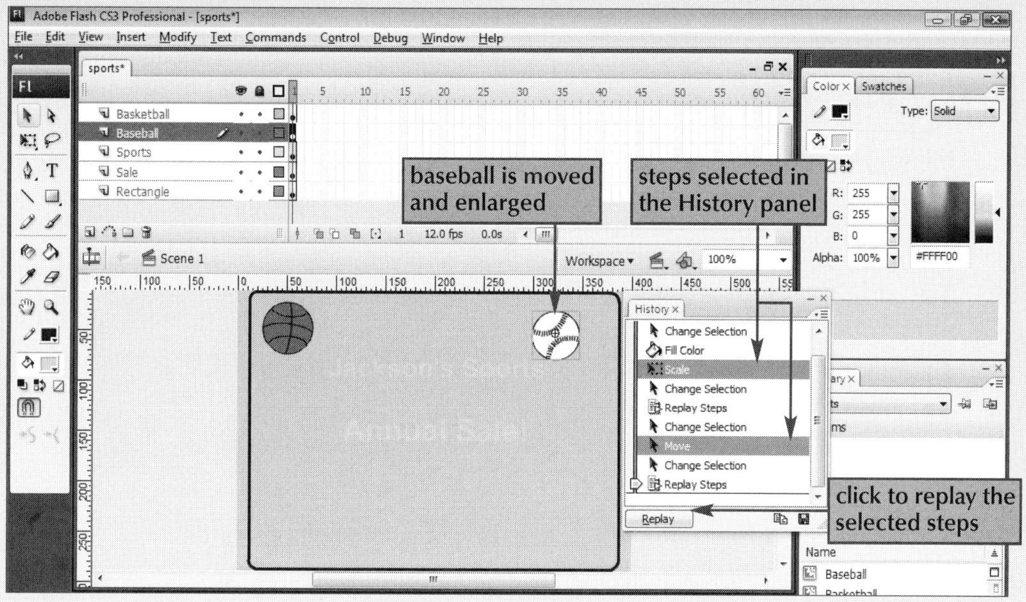

Undoing Steps

As you create and modify graphic images in Flash, you will often want to undo one or more steps within a document. This might occur if you make a mistake and you want to return to the previous step. You can undo one step or, by default, up to 100 steps. As a result, you can backtrack though a series of steps until the document returns to the particular state at which you want to start over. You can change the default maximum number of steps that can be undone in the Preferences dialog box.

Flash provides two types of undo. In **document-level undo**, the steps you undo affect the entire document. In **object-level undo**, you can undo steps performed on individual objects without affecting the steps performed on other objects. You change from one type of undo to another in the Preferences dialog box. When you change the type of undo, the steps currently recorded in the History panel are deleted. In this tutorial, you work with the default mode, document-level undo.

You can use the History panel to change the document back to how it was before you performed a series of steps,. The slider in the History panel initially points to the last step you performed. As you drag the slider to a previous step any subsequent step is undone and is reflected in the document on the Stage. Undone steps appear dimmed in the History panel.

You will use the History panel to undo some of the steps you have performed.

To undo steps in the sports document from the History panel:

1. In the History panel, drag the **slider** up to the Scale step. The steps below the Scale step are dimmed, indicating that they have been undone. The objects on the Stage also change to reflect that the steps were undone. See Figure 2-45.

Tip

You can also undo one step at a time by pressing the Ctrl+Z keys.

Figure 2-45 Steps in the History panel that were undone

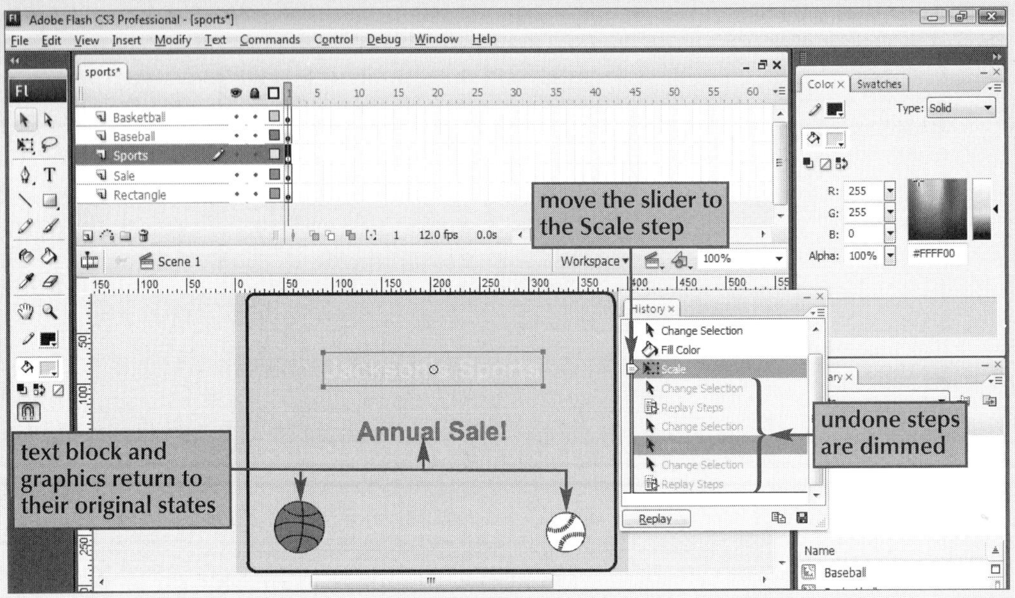

2. Close the History panel, and then close the sports document without saving the changes you made.

In this session, you learned how to create text blocks, how to set the properties for the text, and how to check for spelling errors. You added text blocks to the banner for Jenny's Oyster Hut and exported the finished banner as a GIF file, which was previewed in a Web page. Finally, you used the History panel to review, undo, and replay steps.

Review | Session 2.2 Quick Check

1. What is the difference between a static text block and a dynamic text field?
2. How do you create a fixed-width text block?
3. Which panel is used to set text attributes such as the font and size?
4. How can you change a single-line text block into a fixed-width text block?
5. If a text block displays a square handle in its upper-right corner, what type of text block is it?
6. What is the purpose of the personal dictionary in the Spelling Setup dialog box?
7. What does the History panel record?
8. How can you undo a series of steps using the History panel?

Session 2.3

Creating and Editing Symbols

Symbols are elements such as graphics and buttons that can be used more than once in a document. You can create a symbol from an existing object or you can create a new symbol. You can also use symbols from other Flash documents in the current document.

Comparing Symbol Behavior Types

Symbols can have one of three types of behavior. The default behavior, **movie clip**, contains its own Timeline and operates independently of the Timeline of the movie in which it appears. For example, a movie clip used in a document contains an animation sequence that spans 10 frames within its own Timeline. The movie clip occupies only one frame within the document's Timeline, yet it still plays its own 10-frame animation. Most of the symbols you create will be movie clips. A **graphic symbol** is a static image or an animated image that operates in sync with the Timeline of the movie in which it appears. For example, a graphic symbol with a 10-frame animation sequence occupies 10 frames in the document's Timeline. A **button symbol** has its own four-frame Timeline, which you use when you want to make a symbol into an interactive button. You will learn more about buttons in Tutorial 5. You can easily change a symbol's behavior at any time.

Creating Symbols

To create a symbol, you can either convert an existing graphic into a symbol or create a new symbol. For each symbol you create, you specify its name and its behavior type. When converting an existing graphic into a symbol, you can also specify its registration point, which can be used to control how the symbol is animated.

Creating a Symbol | Reference Window

- Select an existing graphic, click Modify on the menu bar, and then click Convert to Symbol.
- Type a symbol name in the Name box, click the appropriate behavior option button, and then click the OK button.

or

- Click Insert on the menu bar, and then click New Symbol.
- Type a symbol name in the Name box, click the appropriate behavior option button, and then click the OK button.
- In symbol-editing mode, create the graphic(s) for the symbol.
- Click Insert on the menu bar, and then click Edit Document.

Aly wants you to modify the banner you created for Jenny's Oyster Hut Web site. You will convert the fish graphic you created into a symbol.

To create a symbol from the fish in the banner:

1. Open the **Banner.fla** file located in the **Tutorial.02\Tutorial** folder included with your Data Files.
2. In the Tools panel, click the **Selection** tool, if necessary, and then click the larger fish on the center of the Stage. The larger fish graphic is selected. You will ungroup this graphic before converting it to a symbol.

   Trouble? If you the ocean graphic is selected instead of the fish graphic, you probably didn't click the fish graphic. Click the top part of the fish again to select the fish.
3. Click **Modify** on the menu bar, and then click **Ungroup**. The fish is no longer grouped, but all of its parts are still selected.
4. Click **Modify** on the menu bar, and then click **Convert to Symbol**. The Convert to Symbol dialog box opens. In this dialog box, you can specify a name for the symbol and select a behavior type.

Tip

You can also ungroup a grouped object by pressing the Ctrl+Shift+G keys.

5. Type **Fish1** in the Name box, and then click the **Movie clip** option button, if it is not already selected. See Figure 2-46.

Figure 2-46 Convert to Symbol dialog box

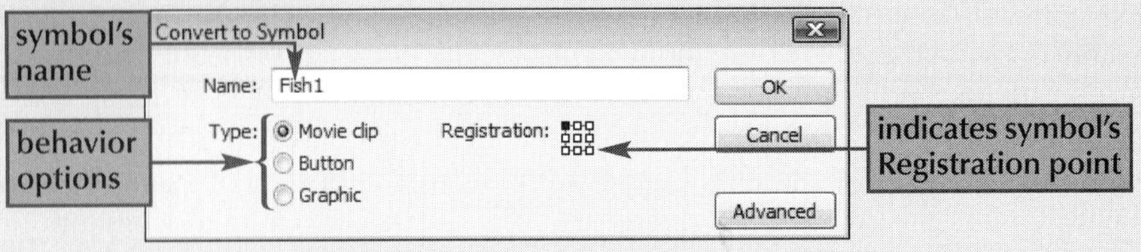

6. Click the **OK** button. The dialog box closes. The symbol is created and added to the library for this document.

InSight | Assigning Meaningful Names to Symbols

When creating symbols, you should assign meaningful names to them, especially if you plan to have many symbols in a document. Meaningful names make it easier to find the symbol you want in the document's Library panel without having to preview each symbol. If the number of symbols is small, such as is the case with the Banner document, you can use simpler names such as Fish1 and Fish2.

Using the Library

Symbols you create for a document are stored in the **library**. You view, organize, and edit symbols stored in the library from the Library panel. When you create a symbol for a document, you assign a name to it, and then specify its properties. These properties are stored with the symbol in the library. Symbols created within a document are saved with that document. However, you can share symbols with other documents by making them part of a shared library. You can modify a symbol's properties using the Library panel. The Library panel, shown in Figure 2-47, displays a list with the names of all the symbols in the library for a document. Each symbol in the Library panel has an icon to the left of its name to show what type of symbol it is. A symbol's type is the same as its behavior.

Figure 2-47 Library panel

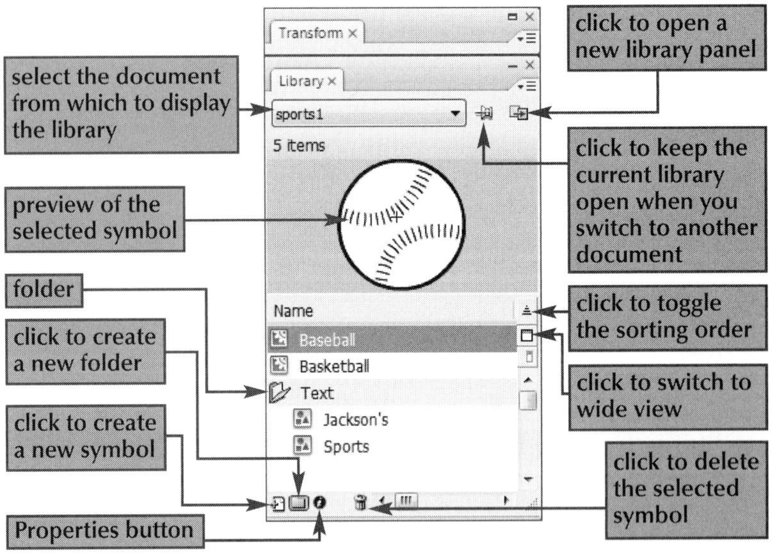

The Library panel can also be expanded to show several columns of information about each symbol, including the symbol's behavior (Type column), the number of times the symbol is used in the document (Use Count column), whether the symbol is shared with other documents (Linkage column), and the date it was last modified (Date Modified column). You can sort the symbols according to a column by clicking the column's header. For example, to sort the symbols by date, click the Date Modified header. The dates range from most recent to oldest. This order can be reversed by clicking the Toggle Sorting Order button.

Additional Library panel options can be accessed using the Library panel's options menu. This menu includes options to create new symbols, rename, edit, or delete symbols, as well as to create duplicates of a symbol.

Organizing Symbols in the Library | InSight

As you work with a document, you will often create many symbols. Some of these symbols may be related to a particular graphic in the document. For example, you may have multiple symbols that make up a button on the Stage. As your document gets more complex, the number of symbols in the library can increase significantly and become unmanageable. To make it easier to manage and organize the symbols in the Library panel, you can create folders that can group and hold related symbols. You create a folder by clicking the New Folder button in the Library panel. Any symbols inside a folder are indented under the folder name. You can double-click a folder's icon to collapse it, hiding its contents, and you can double-click a collapsed folder icon to expand the folder, displaying its contents.

You will explore the Banner document's library to see how symbols are stored.

To explore the Banner document's library:

1. If the Library panel is not open, click **Window** on the menu bar, and then click **Library**. The Library panel displays the symbols for this document.
2. In the Name column of the Library panel, click the **Fish1** symbol. A thumbnail of the fish appears in the preview window at the top of the Library panel.

   Next you'll change the view of the Library panel.
3. In the Library panel, click the **Wide Library View** button ☐. The Library panel expands to wide view, showing additional information about the symbol. See Figure 2-48.

Tip

You can also press the Ctrl+L keys to open and close the Library panel.

Figure 2-48 Library panel in wide view

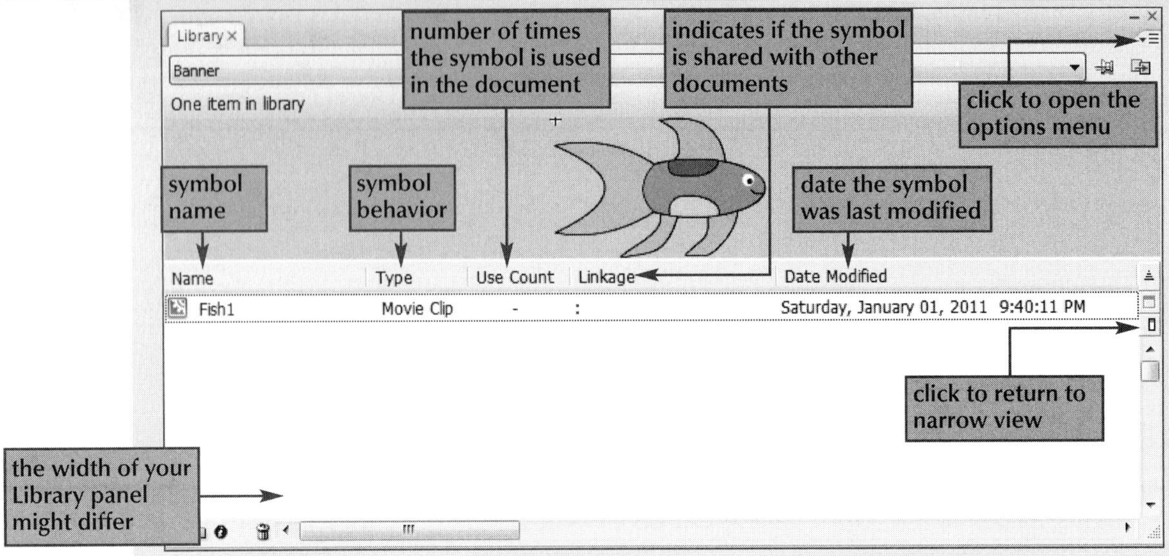

4. In the Library panel, click the **Properties** button . The Symbol Properties dialog box opens for the Fish1 symbol. You'll change this symbol's type.

5. Click the **Graphic** option button, and then click the **OK** button. The Properties dialog box closes, and the Fish1 symbol's icon and type reflect the new behavior. See Figure 2-49.

Figure 2-49 Changed symbol in the Library panel

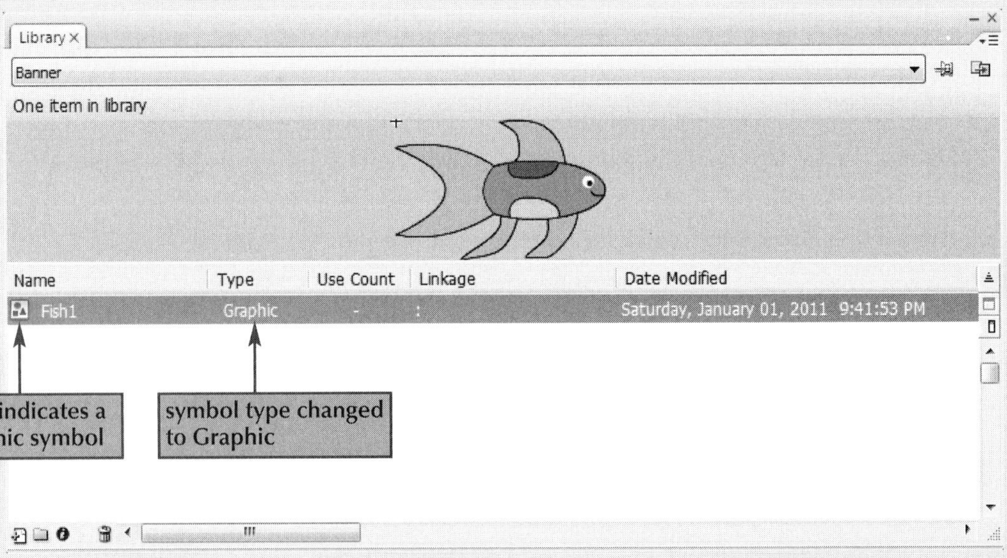

6. In the Library panel, click the **Properties** button , click the **Movie clip** option button, and then click the **OK** button. The symbol's icon and type change to reflect the movie clip behavior.

7. In the Library panel, click the **Narrow Library View** button . The Library panel returns to its default narrow view.

After a symbol is added to a document's library, you can create a duplicate of it. The duplicate symbol must have a different name.

You'll create a duplicate symbol of the Fish1 symbol that you can then edit to create a second, different fish symbol.

To create a duplicate of the Fish1 symbol:

1. In the Library panel, click the **options menu** button to open the options menu, and then click **Duplicate**. The Duplicate Symbol dialog box opens.
2. In the Name box, type **Fish2**. This is the name for the duplicated movie clip symbol. The movie clip type is already selected.
3. Click the **OK** button. The Fish2 symbol is added to the library.

Tip

You can also right-click the symbol's name in the Library panel, and then click Duplicate on the context menu to open the Duplicate Symbol dialog box.

Editing a Symbol

You can modify a symbol by placing it in symbol-editing mode. A symbol can be edited by itself in symbol-editing mode or it can be edited in place with the rest of the graphics on the Stage dimmed. When a symbol is in symbol-editing mode, the name of the symbol appears on the Edit bar next to the scene name. Flash documents can be divided into multiple scenes, but every document has at least one scene.

Editing a Symbol | Reference Window

- Select a symbol instance on the Stage, click Edit on the menu bar, and then click Edit Symbols, Edit Selected, or Edit in Place (or double-click a symbol instance on the Stage or select the symbol in the Library panel, click the Library panel's options menu button, and then click Edit).
- Modify the symbol in symbol-editing mode.
- Click the Scene 1 link on the Edit bar (or double-click an empty area of the Stage or click Edit on the menu bar, and then click Edit Document).

Aly wants you to edit the Fish2 symbol in the document's library so that it unique from the Fish1 symbol.

To edit the Fish2 symbol:

1. In the Library panel, select the **Fish2** symbol, if necessary.
2. In the Library panel, click the **options menu** button, and then click **Edit**. The symbol opens in symbol-editing mode, and Fish2 appears on the Edit bar.
3. Click an empty area of the Stage to deselect the fish.

   You will apply a different color to the Fish2 symbol.
4. In the Tools panel, click the **Paint Bucket** tool.
5. In the Property inspector, click the **Fill color** control, and then click the **pink** swatch (#FF99FF) in the third column from the right, bottom row of the color palette.

6. On the Stage, click the orange body of the fish to change it pink.

   You'll make the fish graphic smaller.

7. Click **Edit** on the menu bar, and then click **Select All**. All of the fish is selected.
8. Click **Window** on the menu bar, and then click **Transform**. The Transform panel opens.
9. In the Transform panel, click the **Constrain** check box to insert a check mark, if necessary. Constrain keeps the width and height proportional when either one is changed.
10. Double-click the **width** value in the upper-left box to select it, type **50,** and then press the **Enter** key. The height value also changes to 50%, and the fish becomes smaller.
11. In the Property inspector, type **0** in the X box, type **0** in the Y box, and then press the **Enter** key. The fish is repositioned toward the center. See Figure 2-50.

Tip

You can also press the Ctrl+A keys to select all of the objects on the Stage at one time.

Figure 2-50 **Revised Fish2 symbol**

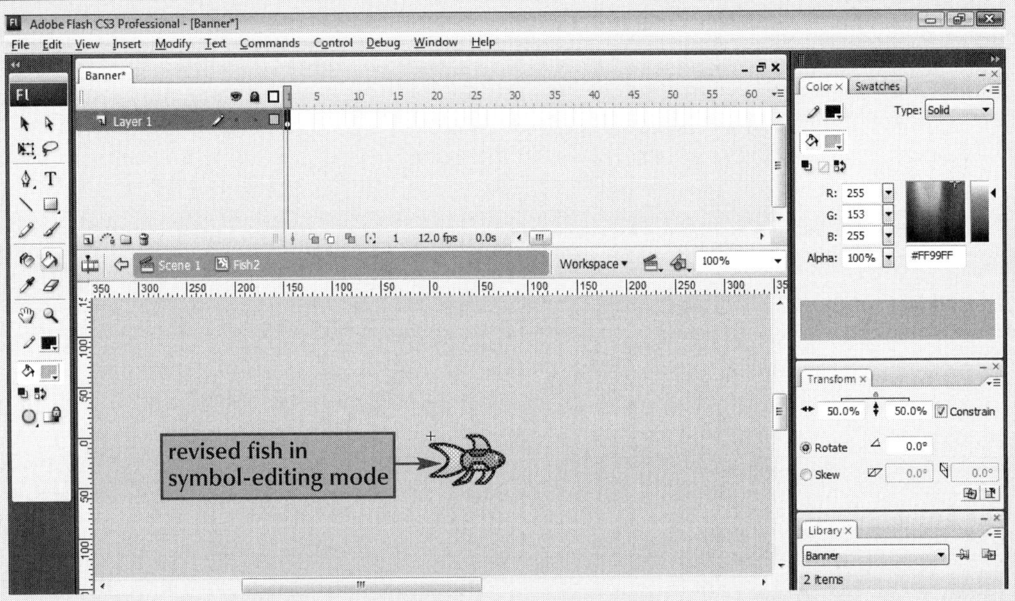

You are done editing the Fish2 symbol, so you'll exit symbol-editing mode.

12. On the Edit bar, click the **Scene 1** link to close the symbol-editing window. The banner appears on the Stage.

Creating and Editing Instances of Symbols

Every symbol you create is automatically stored in the document's library. To use the symbols in the document, you create instances. An **instance** is a copy of a symbol. Each time you drag a symbol from the Library panel onto the Stage, you create an instance of the symbol in the document. No matter how many instances of a symbol you create, the symbol is stored in the document only once.

Using Instances of Symbols

InSight

If you want to use a graphic multiple times in a document, convert it into a symbol. Then you can insert instances of the symbol wherever that graphic is needed in the document instead of creating the same graphic multiple times. Using instances of a symbol also makes it easier to modify all instances at the same time by just modifying the symbol. In addition, any graphic you convert into a symbol can be copied from one document's library to another. Also, using instances of a symbol minimizes the size of the document and, as a result, reduces the download time of the published SWF file.

Each instance in a document can be edited without changing the symbol in the document's library. For example, consider a document that includes several instances of the same symbol. You can make one instance smaller than the others. You can rotate each instance to a different angle. Any changes you make to one instance do not affect the other instances or the symbol. If you modify the symbol, however, all the instances of that symbol are also changed.

You will place an instance of the Fish2 symbol on the banner.

To create an instance of the Fish2 symbol in the banner:

1. In the Tools panel, click the **Selection** tool.
2. Drag the **Fish2** symbol from the Library panel to the Stage to create an instance of the symbol.
3. On the Stage, place the **Fish2** instance on the water to the left side of the Fish1 instance. See Figure 2-51.

Figure 2-51

Instance of the Fish2 symbol added to the Stage

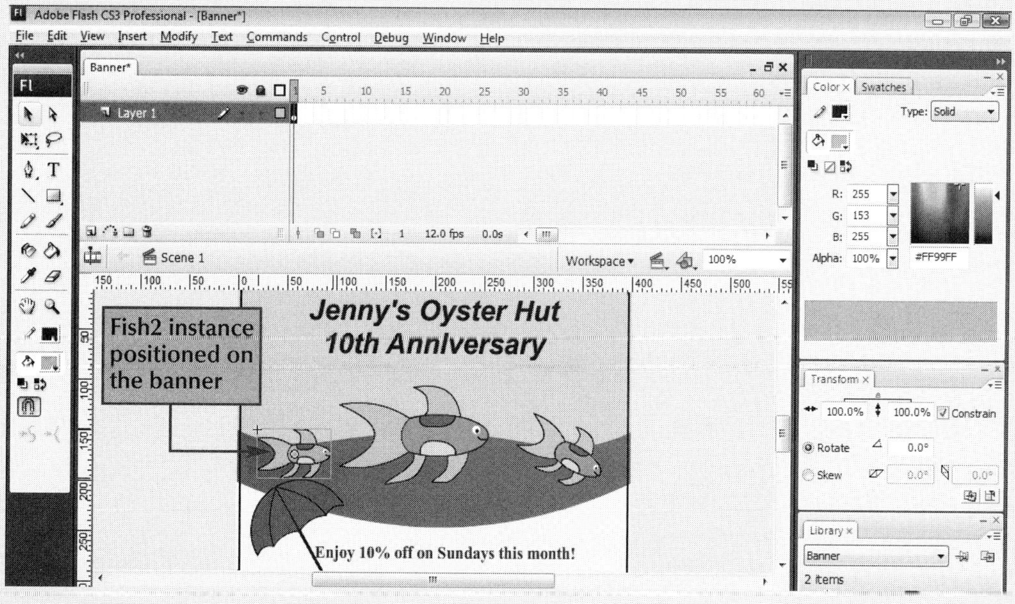

4. Save the document, and then close it.

In this session, you learned about symbols and used the Library panel to work with the symbols in the Banner document's library. In the next tutorial, you will learn how to create animations with the symbols in Jenny's Oyster Hut banner.

Review | Session 2.3 Quick Check

1. What are the three behavior types for symbols?
2. What is the purpose of the Library panel?
3. What are the two different views for the Library panel?
4. Why should you convert a graphic you want to use multiple times in a document into a symbol?
5. What is the difference between a symbol and an instance of a symbol?
6. True or False? When you modify a symbol, the instances created from that symbol are not affected.

Review | Tutorial Summary

In this tutorial, you learned how to use the main drawing tools in Flash. You drew lines, curves, ovals, and rectangles to create graphic elements, and then you applied and changed the colors of strokes and fills, and applied the properties of one object to another object. You used the Text tool to create different types of text boxes. Then you exported a graphic for use in a Web page. You used the History panel to review the steps you performed while working in the document, and then to undo and replay the steps. Finally, you created and edit symbols and instances of symbols.

Key Terms

button symbol
document-level undo
dynamic text field
export
Eyedropper tool
field
fixed-width text block
Free Transform tool
graphic symbol
History panel
input text field
instance
library
movie clip
object-level undo
Oval Primitive tool
Paint Bucket tool
Pencil tool
Rectangle Primitive tool
single-line text block
static text block
symbol
Text tool

Practice | Review Assignments

Practice the skills you learned in the tutorial.

Data File needed for the Review Assignments: JennysBanner.fla

Aly is pleased with the banner you created for Jenny's Oyster Hut Web site. She asks you to modify another version of the banner by changing the color of the umbrella, adding a second umbrella, adding a second fish, and adding a text block. She also wants you to change the color and style of the rectangle and to draw lines as underlines for text.

1. Open the **JennysBanner.fla** file located in the Tutorial.02\Review folder, set the workspace to its default layout, and then hide the Timeline.
2. Save the document as **JennysBannerRevised** in the Tutorial.02\Review folder included with your Data Files.
3. Select the umbrella on the Stage and convert it to a movie clip symbol named **Umbrella**.
4. Edit the Umbrella symbol in the library. Use the Paint Bucket tool to change the color of two of the panels in the umbrella to blue (#0000FF) so that the panels alternate between yellow and blue. Use the Transform panel to decrease the width and height of the symbol to 75% and then exit symbol-editing mode.
5. Drag the Umbrella symbol from the Library panel onto the Stage to create an instance of it. Place the instance on the lower-right corner of the banner and rotate it so that it is leaning to the right.
6. Drag the Fish symbol from the Library panel onto the Stage to create an instance of it. Place the instance on the water in the center of the banner.
7. Create another instance of the Fish symbol and place it to the right of the first instance. Rotate the second instance so that it appears to be swimming in the water in a downward direction.
8. Add a new single-line text block that reads **Free Drink with a Dinner Entree!**. Use Arial Narrow for the font, 22 for the text size, and brown (#663300) for the text color. Center the new text block on the beach at the bottom of the banner.
9. Use the Line tool to draw horizontal lines under each of the two lines of text on the top of the banner. The lines should be blue (#0000FF), have a height of 2, a stroke style of solid, and appear as underlines for the text.
10. Edit the rectangle that is framing the banner. Change its color to maroon (#660000), set the stroke height to 3, and choose a stroke style other than Solid in the Property inspector.
11. Export the image to the Tutorial.02\Review folder with the name **JennysBanner** and in the GIF file format, using the default settings in the Export GIF dialog box.
12. Submit the finished file to your instructor, either in printed or electronic form, as requested.

Apply | Case Problem 1

Create a grand opening banner for a store using shapes and text.

There are no Data Files needed for this Case Problem.

Sandy's Scrapbook Store Sandy's Scrapbook Store is preparing for its grand opening celebration and sale. Sandy Rodriguez, owner of the store, meets with John Rossini to discuss the development of the store's Web site. John suggests that a banner be developed first that will set the tone for the rest of the Web site. Sandy asks John to develop the banner. She wants the banner to help promote the grand opening celebration and sale, by including graphics that depict a celebration and text about the grand opening. You will create the banner shown in Figure 2-52.

Figure 2-52 Sandy's Scrapbook Store banner

1. Create a new document. Change the document properties so that the width is 500 pixels and the height is 150 pixels. Change the background color to light yellow (#FFFF99).
2. Save the document as **sssbanner** in the Tutorial.02\Case1 folder included with your Data Files.
3. Create a square with sides of about 45 pixels in length. Use light orange (#FFCC33) for the fill color and a dashed black stroke of two pixels in height. Place the square near the upper-left side of the stage.
4. Add a text block inside the square with the uppercase letter **S**. Use a font such as Comic Sans MS, a font size of 32, bold style, and black text.
5. Group the square and the text, being sure to select both the fill and the stroke for the square.
6. Make a copy of the group and edit the copy to change the letter to **A**. Move the copy to the right of the square with the letter S.
7. Repeat Step 6 to make four more copies of the group. Change the letters in the copies to **N**, **D**, **Y**, and **'S**, respectively. Move the copies so that the text blocks and squares spell SANDY'S.
8. Edit the squares to change the fill colors so that each square has a different color. Use the Free Transform tool to rotate and position each letter block, as shown in Figure 2-52.
9. Add a text block in the center of the Stage. Use the same font as in Step 4 with a font size of 36, dark blue (#000066) text, center align the text and use bold and italic styles. Type **Scrapbook Store** in the text block.
10. Add a second text block with a font size of 18, black text, and center alignment. Type **Grand Opening this Saturday!**, and then on a separate line in the same text block type **Come celebrate with us!**.
11. Draw three balloons on the left side of the Stage using the Oval tool with different colors for each balloon. Do not include a stroke for the balloons. Draw a string for each balloon using the Pencil tool with a light gray (#999999) color for the stroke.
12. Repeat Step 11 to draw three more balloons on the right side of the Stage with different colors.

EXPLORE

13. Use the Brush tool to draw multicolored confetti on the Stage. Select a small brush size from the Brush Size modifier in the Tools panel. Select a brush color of your choice using the Fill color control in the Tools panel, and then click dots with the tool on the banner to create the confetti. Repeat to create different colored dots throughout the Stage using at least three different colors.
14. Create a rectangle as a border around all of the objects on the Stage. The rectangle should have slightly rounded corners, a maroon (#660000) stroke, no fill, a stroke height of 3, and a solid style. Draw the rectangle so that it is just inside the edges of the Stage.

15. Export the image to the Tutorial.02\Case1 folder with the name **sssbanner** and in the GIF file format, using the default settings in the Export Image dialog box.
16. Submit the finished files to your instructor, either in printed or electronic form, as requested.

Apply | Case Problem 2

Create a banner advertising a zoo with text, shapes, and symbols.

There are no Data Files needed for this Case Problem.

Alamo City Zoo Janet Meyers, director of Alamo City Zoo, asks Alex Smith to develop a new banner for the zoo's Web site. The new banner will advertise an open house celebration event promoting a new bear exhibit. The banner will contain text with the zoo's name and event information as well as graphic elements depicting bear paws. You'll create the banner shown in Figure 2-53.

Figure 2-53 **Alamo City Zoo banner**

1. Create a new document. Change the document properties so that the width is 300 pixels and the height is 200 pixels. Change the background color to light green (#99CC66).
2. Save the document as **aczbanner** in the Tutorial.02\Case2 folder included with your Data Files.
3. Create a single-line text block on the top part of the Stage for the name of the zoo. Use the Monotype Corsiva font or a font of your choice, a font size of 36, black text color, center aligned, and bold and italic styles. Type **Alamo City Zoo** in the text block.
4. EXPLORE Create a fixed-width text block on the lower part of the Stage. Use the Arial font, a font size of 22, black text color, bold style, and center alignment. Type **Come Visit the New BEAR Exhibit!** in the text block.
5. Create a single line text block on the center of the Stage. Use the Arial font, a font size of 16, maroon text color (#990000), and center aligned. Deselect bold style. Type **Special Open House!** in the text block.
6. Use the Free Transform tool to rotate the text block so that it is in a vertical position on the left side of the Stage, as shown in Figure 2-53.
7. EXPLORE Create a new movie clip symbol named **bear_paw**. (*Hint*: Click Insert on the menu bar, and then click New Symbol.) In symbol-editing mode, on the center of the Stage draw a small circle about 40 pixels wide and 40 pixels high. Use brown (#663300) for the fill color, black (#000000) for the stroke color, solid for the stroke style, and 1 for the stroke height.

8. Zoom in to the circle and use the Selection tool to move the top part of the circle's stroke down to give the circle a slightly flattened appearance. Using the same stroke and fill colors as the circle, draw four small ovals equally spaced above the flattened part of the circle, as shown in Figure 2-53, and then exit symbol-editing mode.
9. Drag four instances of the bear_paw symbol from the Library panel to the Stage. Place two instances below the top text block, place one instance to the left of the bottom text block, and place one instance to the right of the bottom text block.
10. Use the Free Transform tool to resize two of the bear_paw instances to make them slightly smaller. Also, rotate the lower-left instance on the Stage slightly to the left, and then rotate the lower-right instance on the Stage slightly to the right.
11. Draw a rectangle along the inside edges of the Stage as a border around all of the objects on the Stage. Use a black stroke, a stroke height of 3, the fifth stroke style on the drop-down list, square corners, and no fill color.
12. Export the image to the Tutorial.02\Case2 folder with the name **aczbanner** and in the GIF file format, accepting the default settings in the Export Image dialog box.
13. Submit the finished files to your instructor, either in printed or electronic form, as requested.

Challenge | Case Problem 3

Extend your skills by using gradients and the Oval Primitive tool as you create a logo for a nursery.

There are no Data Files needed for this Case Problem.

Westcreek Nursery Alice Washington, owner of Westcreek Nursery, meets with Amanda Lester, who was contracted to update the company's Web site. Alice requests that a new logo be developed for her business. The logo should contain the business name, phone number, and an appropriate slogan, along with some graphics. You'll create the completed logo shown in Figure 2-54.

Figure 2-54 **Westcreek Nursery logo**

1. Create a new document. Change the document properties so that the width is 300 pixels and the height is 200 pixels.
2. Save the document as **wclogo** in the Tutorial.02\Case3 folder included with your Data Files.
3. Draw a rectangle about 280 pixels wide and about 50 pixels high across the top of the Stage. Use the Rectangle tool and the Merge Drawing model with a black stroke, a height of 1, a solid style, and no fill color. Place the rectangle about 10 pixels from the left of the Stage and 10 pixels from the top.

4. Create a single-line text block inside the rectangle. Use Verdana or a similar font of your choice, a font size of 22, black text, left aligned, and bold style. Type **Westcreek** in the text block, and then position the text block on the left side of the rectangle.
5. Draw a straight vertical line to the right of the text block to split the rectangle into two sections. One end of the line should snap to the top of the rectangle and the other end should snap to the bottom of the rectangle. Use a black (#000000) stroke, a stroke height of 1, and a solid style.

EXPLORE

6. Apply the green radial gradient fill (fourth gradient from the left on the color palette) to the right section of the rectangle.
7. Create a single-line text block on the inside of the rectangle over the gradient. Use Verdana or a similar font of your choice, a font size of 22, white text, left aligned, and bold and italic styles. Type **Nursery** in the text block, and then position the text block in the center of the right side of the rectangle.
8. Create a single-line text block below the center of the larger rectangle. Change the font size to 16, change the text color to black, and remove the bold and italic styles. Type **We deliver!** in the text block.

EXPLORE

9. Create a single-line text block in the center of the Stage. Change the font size to 42, the text color to dark green (#006600), and the style to bold. Type **FLOWERS** in the text block. Using the Free Transform tool, skew the text block so that the letters are slanted to the right.
10. Draw four straight horizontal lines, each about 40 pixels in length, to the left of the letter F in the center text block. Position the lines equally spaced and approximately the same distance from the letter F.
11. Use the Oval Primitive tool to draw a circle with a black fill and no stroke about 30 pixels in diameter on the bottom part of the Stage. If necessary, reset the values for the controls in the Property inspector before drawing the circle.

EXPLORE

12. Change the Inner radius value for the circle to 40 to create the image of a car tire.
13. Convert the circle to a movie clip symbol named **Tire**. Add a second instance of the Tire symbol from the Library panel to the Stage. Move the two Tire instances right below the text block in the center of the Stage. Place one tire right below the L on the FLOWERS text, and place the other tire right below the R.
14. Add a single-line text block below the tire graphics. Change the font size to 10 and the text color to black, and then remove the bold and italic styles, if necessary. Type **Find the freshest flowers in the city at Westcreek!** in the text block, and then center the text block on the Stage.
15. Draw a rectangle that has a light gray (#999999) stroke, a height of 1, no fill color, and rounded corners around the text block.
16. Below the text block you just created, create another single-line text block with the same attributes. Type **For fast deliveries call 555-5555** in the text block, and then center the text block on the Stage.
17. Draw a rectangle along the inside edges of the Stage to frame all of the graphic elements for the logo. Use a black stroke, a stroke height of 3, a solid stroke style, and no fill color. Do not round the corners.
18. Export the image to the Tutorial.02\Case3 folder with the name **wclogo** and in GIF file format, accepting the default settings in the Export Image dialog box.
19. Submit the finished files to your instructor, either in printed or electronic form, as requested.

Challenge | Case Problem 4

Extend your skills by using symbols and text blocks to create a banner for an association.

There are no Data Files needed for this Case Problem.

Regional Dietetic Association Richard Perez, president of the Regional Dietetic Association, meets with Katie Ellison to discuss improving the association's Web site. They decide to start by developing a new banner for the site's home page, which will include the association's name as well as keywords highlighting the services available to the association's members. You'll create the completed banner is shown in Figure 2-55.

Figure 2-55 **Regional Dietetic Association banner**

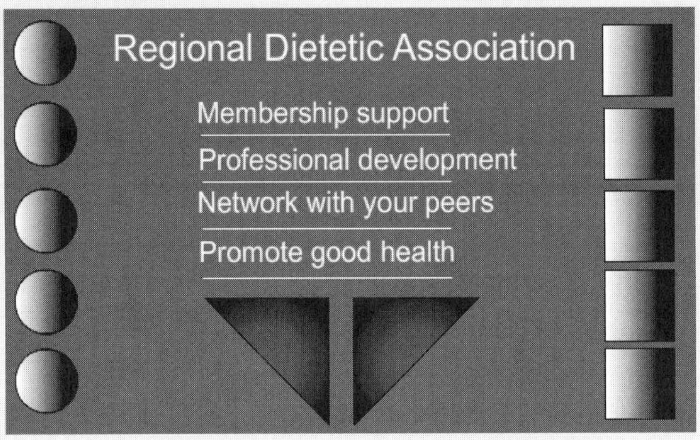

EXPLORE

1. Create a new document. Change the document properties so that the width is 500 pixels and the height is 300 pixels. Change the background color to a light blue by typing **#336699** in the color palette's hexadecimal box.
2. Save the document as **rdabanner** in the Tutorial.02\Case4 folder included with your Data Files.

EXPLORE

3. Draw a circle about 45 pixels in diameter in the upper-left corner of the Stage. Use the gray linear gradient fill located in the color palette, a black stroke, a stroke height of 1, and a solid stroke style.
4. Convert the circle to a movie clip symbol named **circle**.
5. Place a vertical guide about 30 pixels from the left side of the Stage, and then create four instances of the circle symbol lining up their centers on the guide.
6. Draw a square that is about 90 pixels on each side. Use the blue radial gradient fill located in the color palette and a black stroke with a stroke height of 1 and a solid style.

EXPLORE

7. Convert the square into a triangle by moving one of its corner anchor points to the center of the square until the two lines adjacent to the corner point merge.
8. Convert the triangle into a movie clip symbol named **triangle**. Create another instance of the triangle symbol, and then center both instances at the bottom of the Stage.

EXPLORE

9. Use the Transform submenu located on the Modify menu to rotate and arrange the triangles as shown in Figure 2-55.
10. On the right side of the Stage, draw a square that is about 50 pixels on each side. Use the gray linear gradient fill and a black stroke with a stroke height of 1,and a solid style.
11. Convert the square into a movie clip symbol named **square**.
12. Place a vertical guide about 460 pixels from the left side of the Stage, and then create four instances of the square symbol, lining up their centers on the guide.

13. Create a single-line text block at the top of the Stage. Use Arial or a similar font of your choice, a font size of 26, center aligned and white text. Do not apply bold or italic styles to the text. Type **Regional Dietetic Association** in the text block, and then center the text block on the Stage.
14. Create four more single-line text blocks below the first text block, changing the font size to 20. Type **Membership support** in the first text block, type **Professional development** in the second text block, type **Network with your peers** in the third text block, and type **Promote good health** in the fourth text block. Position the text blocks as shown in Figure 2-55.
15. Below the Membership Support text block, draw a straight horizontal line that is about 180 pixels in length. Copy the line three times, and then move the copies below each of the three other text blocks in the center of the Stage.
16. Export the image to the Tutorial.02\Case4 folder with the name **rdabanner** and in GIF file format, accepting the default settings in the Export Image dialog box.
17. Submit the finished files to your instructor, either in printed or electronic form, as requested.

Review | Quick Check Answers

Session 2.1

1. False. You must select the Snap to Objects modifier to draw a perfect circle.
2. Click the Set Corner Radius button, and enter a point value in the Rectangle Settings dialog box.
3. Oval Primitive
4. Pencil Mode
5. Click an object's stroke with the Eyedropper tool, and then click the other object to apply the stroke's attributes.
6. the Paint Bucket tool
7. the Scale modifier
8. False. The Fill Transform tool is used to modify an object's gradient fill.

Session 2.2

1. A static text block has text that does not change once the document is published, whereas a dynamic text field's content may be changed as it is updated from a Web server.
2. Click and drag on the Stage to set the desired width.
3. the Property inspector
4. Drag the single-line text block's round corner handle.
5. a fixed-width text block
6. enables the user to add words not found in the Adobe or language dictionaries but which are spelled correctly, such as a company name
7. steps performed in the current document
8. Drag the slider up to a previous step; steps that are dimmed in the History panel are undone.

Session 2.3

1. Movie Clip, Graphic, and Button
2. to store and organize the symbols contained in a document

3. the Wide Library View and the Narrow Library View
4. No matter how many instances of a symbol you create, the symbol is stored only once in the document.
5. Symbols are reusable elements such as graphics, buttons, and sound files that can be used more than once in a document. An instance is a single use of a symbol.
6. False. Modifying a symbol also changes the instances created from that symbol.

Ending Data Files

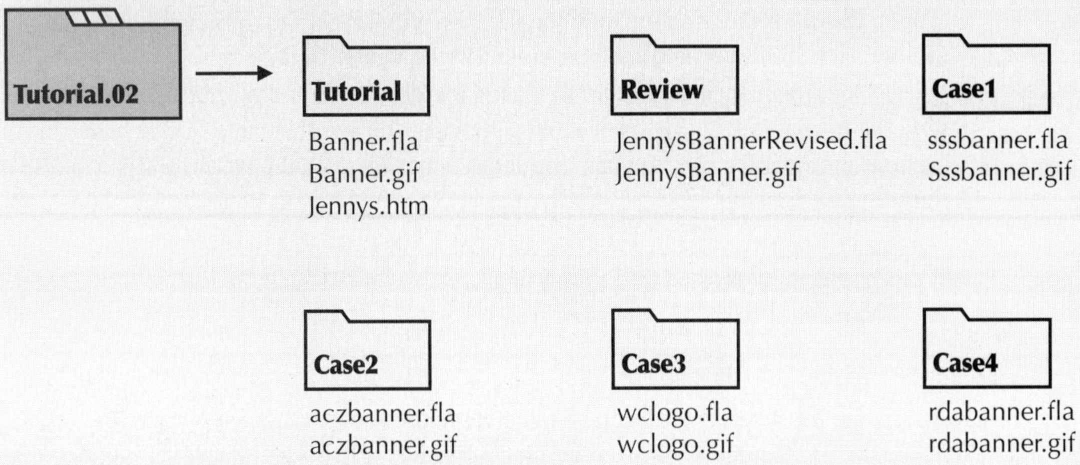

Objectives

Session 3.1
- Learn the different elements of animation
- Create frames and layers
- Organize frames and layers using the Timeline
- Work with scenes

Session 3.2
- Create Timeline effects
- Create frame-by-frame animations

Session 3.3
- Create tweened animations
- Create a graphic symbol animation

Creating Animations

Developing Frame-by-Frame, Tweened, and Graphic Symbol Animations

Case | Admiral Web Design

Aly Garcia, graphic designer for Admiral Web Design, met with Jenny Emerson, owner of Jenny's Oyster Hut, to show her the banner. Jenny expressed interest in adding animation to the banner to attract more attention to the anniversary specials the banner promotes. After this meeting, Aly revised the banner you created for Jenny's Oyster Hut to create a partially completed banner, which will be the basis for the new animated banner. The new banner will have an initial animation of a fish pulling a shrimp specials sign while the words "Fried Shrimp" and "Shrimp Scampi" display one after the other. The banner will also include an animated fish swimming as well as a sea plant with moving leaves. Before you complete the animation for the Jenny's Oyster Hut banner, Aly asks you to review and modify a document she recently created for another client, Jackson's Sports.

In this tutorial, you will learn the basics of creating Flash animations and how to coordinate these animations in the Timeline using frames and layers. You will also learn how to extend a document using scenes. You will learn how to create animations using Timeline effects, and how to create frame-by-frame, motion tweened, and shape tweened animations. Finally, you will learn how to create animations using graphic symbols.

Starting Data Files

Tutorial.03 →	Tutorial	Review	Case1	Case2	Case3	Case4
	bannerDraft.fla Jacksons.fla	JennysAd.fla	sssbanner.fla	aczbanner.fla	wclogo.fla	rdabanner.fla

Session 3.1

Elements of Animation

One of the most powerful features of Flash is its ability to create animation. Animation, which creates the perception of movement, is achieved by changing the location or appearance of an object from one moment in time to the next. Before you create an animation, you need to review some basic elements of a Flash document. A document is made up of layers, frames, and the graphic objects such as symbols that display on the Stage. You coordinate these elements from the document's Timeline.

The Timeline

The Timeline, which appears above the Stage, is used to control and coordinate the timing of the animation by determining how and when the frames for each layer are displayed. The Timeline is also a means of creating, modifying, and organizing layers and frames. Figure 3-1 shows the Timeline for an animation Aly created for Jackson's Sports.

Figure 3-1 Timeline of a sample document

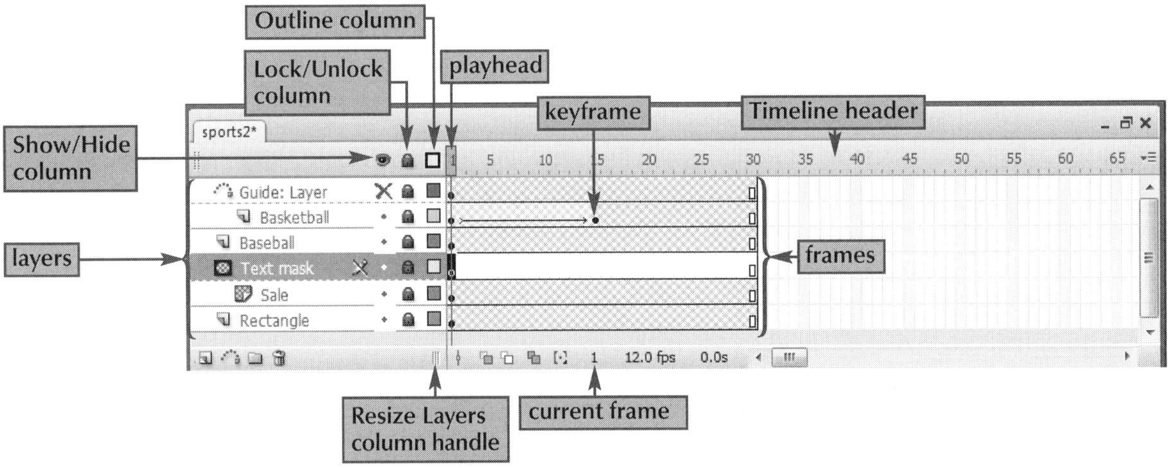

Layers

Layers organize the content of a document. A Flash document starts with one layer. You can insert additional layers in a document and then place the graphic objects in the document on different layers. When using the Merge Drawing model, any object you draw or move on top of other objects will split or merge with those objects. Placing objects on separate layers prevents this and allows you to overlap the objects on the Stage. Objects on different layers can be moved in front or in back of each other by changing the order in which the layers are organized. Layers are especially useful when you are animating more than one object at the same time. For example, you can have an object on one layer move in one direction at the same time as an object on another layer moves in a different direction. The animations occur simultaneously, but do not impact one another in any way.

A guide layer is a special type of layer that can be used to align objects on other layers to the objects on the guide layer. The contents of the guide layer do not appear in the published SWF file. For example, you can use a line you draw on a guide layer to align all the objects of the document. The line appears on the Stage but not in the published SWF file. Any layer can be converted to a guide layer. A guide layer that provides a path for an animated object to follow is called a motion guide layer. The layer below a motion guide layer is called a guided layer.

Another special type of layer is a mask layer. A mask layer contains a graphic object through which the content of the masked layer shows. The masked layer is the layer below the mask layer. The object of a mask layer becomes transparent to reveal the contents of the layer beneath it. The rest of the contents of the masked layer are hidden. The object on the mask layer can be a filled shape such as an oval or it can be text. You can convert any layer into a mask layer.

Frames

Frames contain the content for an animation and represent a particular instant in time. For example, at the default frame rate of 12 frames per second (fps), each frame appears for 1/12 of a second during the animation. Placing different content on each frame or slightly modifying the content from one frame to the next creates the perception of movement that is animation. Initially, a document contains just one frame that is a keyframe. A **keyframe** is a frame that represents a change in the content from the previous frame. To create an animation, you need to add more frames to a layer. The frames you add are used to create new content, to keep the content the same, or to change the content from previous frames. If you want the content to remain the same in the new frame, you add a regular frame. If you want the content to change, you add a keyframe. As you add more frames, you are increasing the length of the animation.

The frames for a layer appear in the Timeline in a row to the right of the layer. Regular frames are white when empty and shaded gray or another color when they have content. Keyframes contain a white dot when they are empty and a black dot when they have content. The layer icon to the left of a layer's name indicates the type of layer it is. For example, regular layers have a page icon and a mask layer has a mask icon.

Working with the Timeline

The layer controls are on the left side of the Timeline. Each row represents one layer. Next to the layer names are three columns: the Show/Hide column, Lock/Unlock column and Outline column. The Show/Hide column is used to show or hide a layer's content. A dot in this column means the layer's content is shown, whereas a red x means the layer's content is temporarily hidden. The Lock/Unlock column is used to lock or unlock a layer. A dot in this column indicates the layer is unlocked and editable, whereas a lock icon indicates the layer is locked and cannot be edited. The Outline column is used to show the content of a layer in Outline view, which changes the Stage to show an outline of each object in the layer's outline color. You display a layer in Outline view by clicking its colored square. Outline view is useful when you are working with a complex animation and you want to see how the objects from the various layers overlap each other. You can control the column settings for all layers at one time by clicking the column's corresponding icon above the list of layers.

InSight | Locking Completed Layers

If you have multiple objects in different layers, it might become difficult to select an object on one layer without accidentally selecting another object on a different layer. A good practice when working with objects on multiple layers is to lock a layer after you finish editing its content. Objects in a locked layer are not selectable.

You'll explore the Timeline of the Jackson's Sports banner that Aly has been developing.

To explore the Timeline of the Jackson's Sports banner:

1. Open the **Jacksons.fla** file located in the **Tutorial.03\Tutorial** folder included with your Data Files.
2. Save the document as **JacksonsRevised** in the **Tutorial.03\Tutorial** folder included with your Data Files.
3. On the document's title bar, click the **Maximize** button, if necessary, to maximize the document window.
4. On the Edit bar, click the **Workspace** button, and then click **Default**. The panels return to their default positions. See Figure 3-2.

Figure 3-2 Jackson's Sports banner

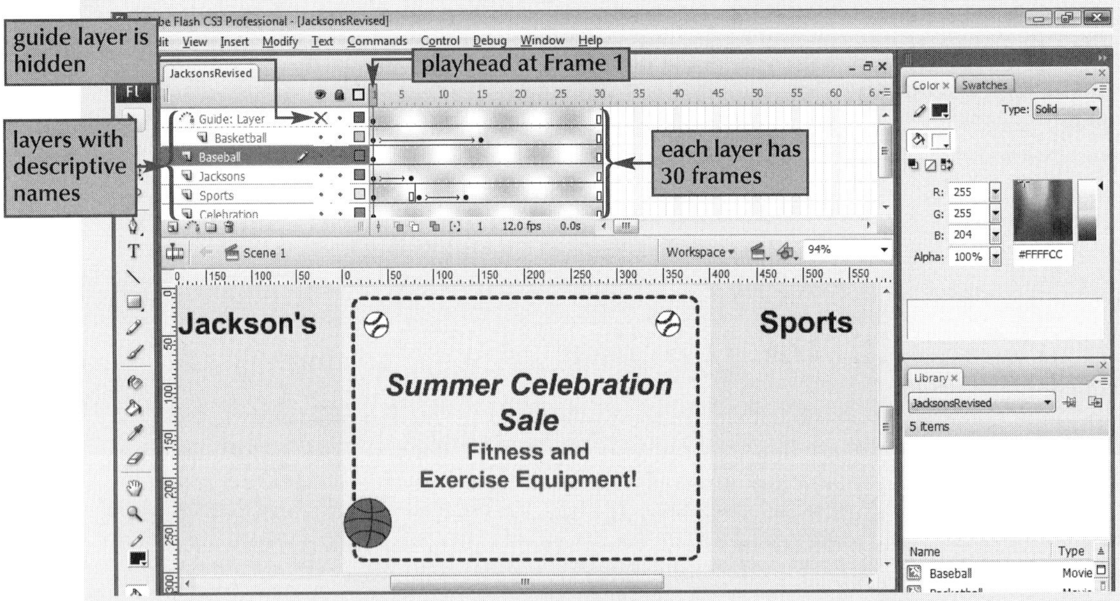

The Timeline for the Sports banner contains several layers. The layers include animations of a baseball, a basketball, and text as well a guide layer. Each layer has a name descriptive of its contents and contains 30 frames. You'll play the animation and watch the Timeline as it displays the elements of the document.

> **Tip**
> You can also press the Enter key to play the Timeline.

5. Click **Control** on the menu bar, and then click **Play**. As the playhead moves from Frame 1 to Frame 30 in the Timeline, the basketball moves across the Stage and the text moves in from the sides of the Stage.
6. Locate the playhead, and then review the current frame (30), frame rate (12.0 fps), and elapsed time (2.4s) at the bottom of the Timeline. See Figure 3-3.

Playhead on Frame 30 — Figure 3-3

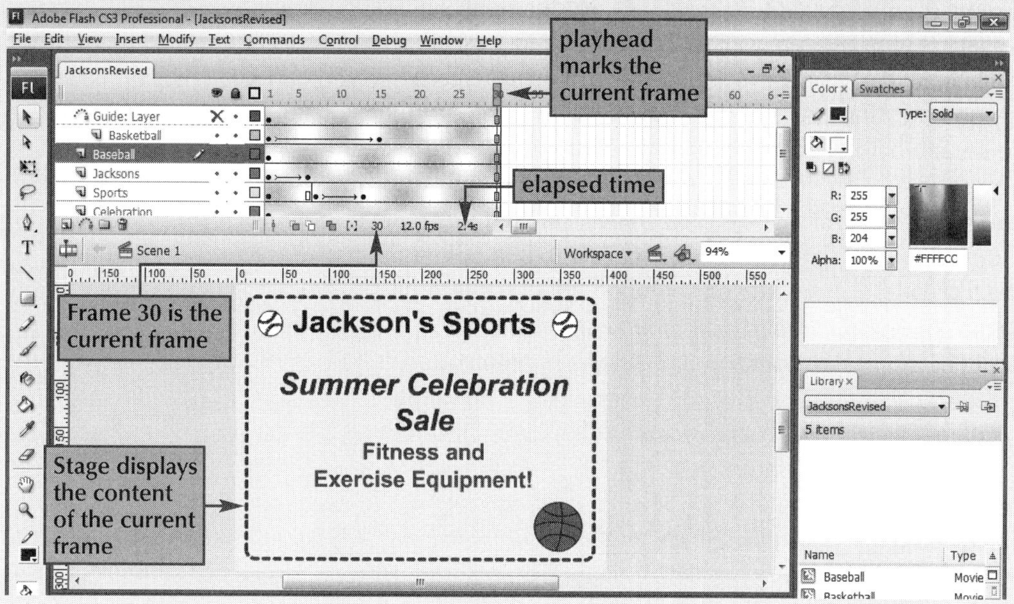

The Timeline displays useful information that you might review as you test an animation. The Elapsed Time control displays the time that has elapsed from Frame 1 to the frame that the playhead is currently on. The elapsed time depends on the frame rate, which is also shown at the bottom of the Timeline. By default, the frame rate is 12 frames per second, which means that an animation that spans 12 frames takes one second to play. The length of the Jackson's Sports banner animation you just viewed can be determined by looking at the elapsed time when the playhead is in the last frame. In this case, the length of the animation is 2.4 seconds.

Checking the Frame Number Before Modifying Content | InSight

A document can have a large number of frames, and the contents of the frames may look very similar from one frame to the next. As you work with content on the Stage, be aware of which frame is being displayed, because that is the frame whose content you are working with. Because the Stage and its contents might look very similar from one frame to the next, it is easy to get confused. If you are not careful, you can change or create the content for the wrong frame. To determine which frame you are working with, check the location of the playhead in the Timeline header.

Changing the View of the Timeline

As you develop an animation, the number of frames can grow very rapidly, as can the number of layers. At some point, you might need to change the view of the Timeline so you can work more efficiently with the elements of your animation. The Timeline can be modified in several ways. You can extend the Timeline to show more frames by closing the panels in the Flash program window. You can place the Timeline above, below, to the left, or to the right of the document window. You can also undock the Timeline and display it as a floating panel.

You can also modify the dimensions of the frames. You change the width of the frames from Normal to Tiny or Small to see more frames within the Timeline window or to Medium or Large to see more of the frame's contents. The change is visible when you are working with sounds. (Sounds will be covered in Tutorial 5.) A sound's waveform, which is a representation of the sound, appears in a frame when you add it to a document. Making the frames wider enables you to see more of the waveform. The Preview view shows a thumbnail of the frame's content that is scaled to fit the Timeline's frame. The Preview in Context view shows a preview of the entire frame's contents, including white or empty space. The Short option reduces the height of the layers. This can be useful when you have many layers and you need to fit more of them into the Timeline window.

By default, the frames are tinted different colors depending on the type of content they contain. For example, the frames of a motion tweened animation are tinted blue. You will learn about motion tweened animations later in this tutorial. You can deselect the Tinted Frames option to remove the color tints on the frames.

Because you will be working extensively with the Timeline, you will practice changing the view of its frames and layers.

To change the view of the Timeline:

1. Press the **F4** key. The panels disappear and the Timeline and Stage windows expand across the width of the program window. You'll resize the Timeline window so that all the layers for the sports banner are visible.

2. Position the pointer on the bottom border of the Timeline until the pointer changes to , and then drag the bottom border until the Rectangle layer is visible. See Figure 3-4.

Figure 3-4 **Timeline window resized**

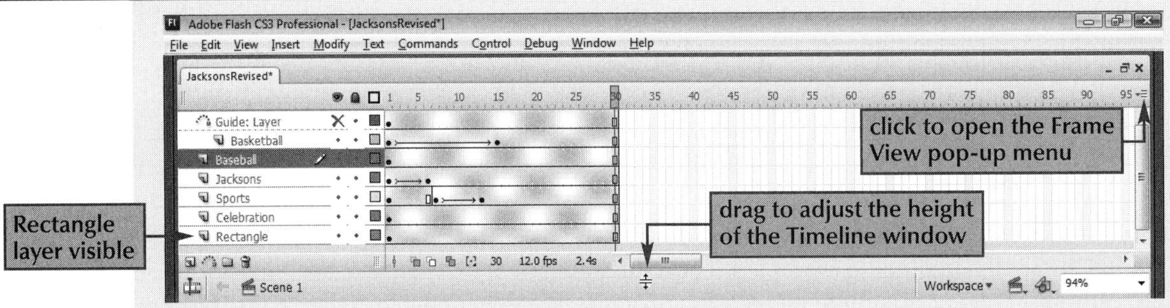

Next, you want to increase the size of the frames.

3. Click the Timeline's **Frame View** button to open the Frame View pop-up menu, and then click **Medium**. The size of the frames increases.

4. Click the **Frame View** button and then click **Preview**. The frames increase in size to show the content of each keyframe. You might need to scroll the Timeline window to see all of the frames. See Figure 3-5.

Figure 3-5 Frames in Preview view

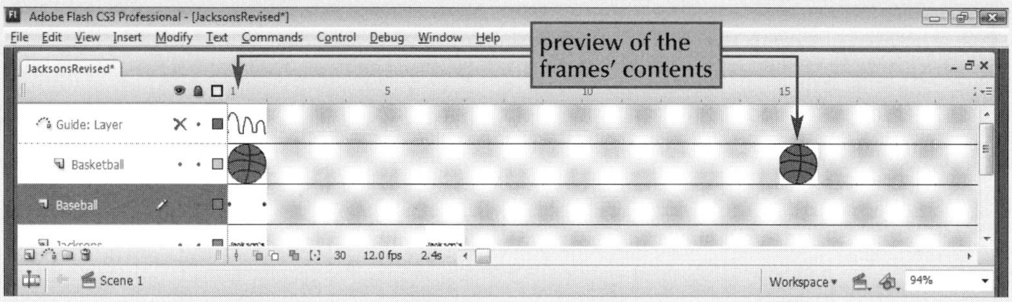

5. Click the **Frame View** button, and then click **Normal**. The frames return to their default, or Normal, view.
6. Press the **F4** key. The hidden panels reappear.

Organizing Layers Using the Timeline

A new document in Flash contains one layer and one frame within that layer. As you create an animation, you add more layers to the document. A lengthy or complex animation could have a large number of layers, which can become difficult to manage. The Timeline is a useful tool for working with the different layers and frames in your document most efficiently.

You select a layer to edit its content. The selected layer is highlighted and a pencil icon appears to the right of the layer's name. You can also delete layers and add new layers as needed. As you add more layers to the Timeline, it's a good idea to name each one according to the content it contains. This helps keep the content organized as the complexity of the animation increases. Layers can also be renamed as needed.

Tip

To see all of a layer's selected properties, double-click its layer icon in the Timeline to open the Layer Properties dialog box.

Organizing Content in Layers | InSight

The number of layers in a document can quickly increase as you add more content or animation to the document. In fact, it is best to insert new layers as you add new content to a document. This helps you work with and organize the document's contents more easily. For complex documents with many layers, you can temporarily hide some layers as you work with the content of other layers. Additional layers don't add to the overall size of the finished file. Keep in mind that you want to keep the size of the final published SWF file as small as possible so it will download quickly from the Web server to the viewer's computer.

You should assign layers meaningful names that correspond to their content. Then you or someone else who needs to edit the document can easily locate a layer based on its name. Although layer names can include spaces and punctuation marks, you can omit them for simplicity.

Adding Layer Folders

When you have multiple layers in the document's Timeline, you can create layer folders to help you work more efficiently. A **layer folder** is a container in the Timeline in which you can place layers. The names of layers in a layer folder are indented under the layer folder in the Timeline, as shown in Figure 3-6.

Figure 3-6 **Layer folder**

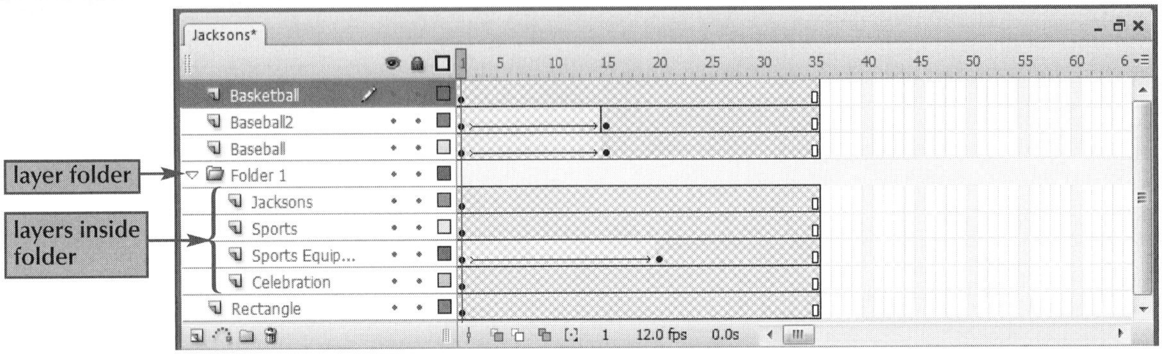

Using layer folders is similar to how you use a folder on your computer's hard drive—you place related files into the folder to make the files easier to find and manage. You can use a layer folder to keep related layers together. For example, you can create a folder to place all of the layers that contain text. Then you can quickly find the text layers when you need to edit them. You can also name a layer folder with a descriptive name the same way you name a layer, making it easier to know what each folder contains. You can collapse the layer folders so that the layers in the folders are not visible. This makes the Timeline less cluttered and makes it easier to work with the other layers in the document. Collapsing the folder's layers does not affect the view of the layers' content on the Stage.

You'll add a layer folder in the Jackson's Sports document.

To insert a layer folder in the Jackson's Sports banner:

1. In the Timeline, click the **Jacksons** layer. The layer is selected.
2. In the Timeline, click the **Insert Layer Folder** button. A layer folder named Folder 1 is inserted above the Jacksons layer.
3. Double-click **Folder 1** to select the folder name, type **Text layers** as the new name, and then press the **Enter** key. The name of the folder changes.
4. After a folder is created, you can move the related layers into it.
5. Drag the **Jacksons** layer to the Text layers folder, releasing the mouse when a dark line appears below the Text layers folder. The Jacksons layer is indented underneath the Text layers folder, as shown in Figure 3-7.

Figure 3-7 **Jacksons layer inside the Text layers folder**

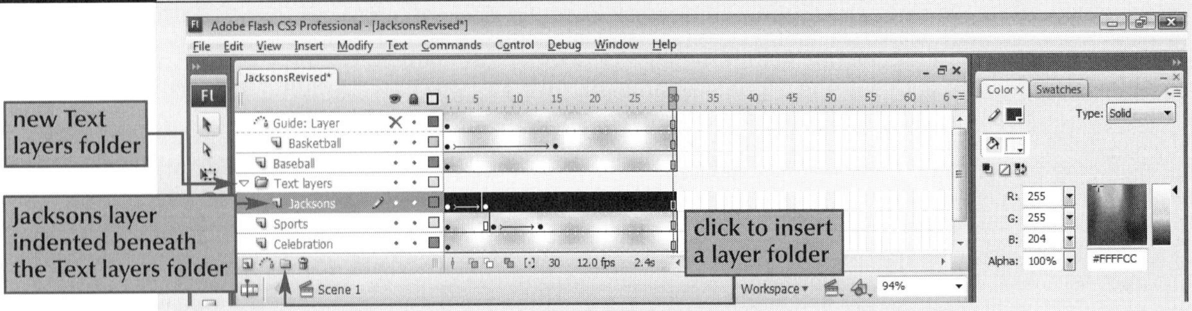

6. Drag the **Sports** and **Celebration** layers into the Text layers folder. Each of the text layers appears indented underneath the Text layers folder. The order of the text layers is not important because the text blocks do not overlap one another.
7. Click the Text layers folder's **Collapse arrow** ▽ The folder's icon changes to a closed folder and the text layers are no longer visible.

Tip

To expand the folder's contents and display the layers, click the folder's Expand arrow.

Selecting, Copying, and Moving Frames

A document's frames can be copied or moved within the same layer or from one layer to another. To copy or move frames, you must first select them. You can select individual or multiple frames in the Timeline You can select frames within one layer or across multiple layers.

You'll select and copy frames in the Jackson's Sports banner.

To select, copy, and paste frames:

1. In the Timeline, click the **Baseball** layer. The layer is selected.
2. In the Timeline, click the **Insert Layer** button. A new layer is inserted above the Baseball layer.
3. Double-click the new layer's name, type **Baseball 2**, and then press the **Enter** key. The layer is renamed.
4. Click the name of the **Baseball** layer. All of the frames for the Baseball layer are selected.

   You'll copy the selected frames to the new Baseball 2 layer.
5. Right-click the selected frames to open the context menu, and then click **Copy Frames**.
6. Click the name of the **Baseball 2** layer to select all of its frames.
7. Right-click the selected frames to open the context menu, and then click **Paste Frames**. The layer's frames are replaced with the copied frames from the Baseball layer.
8. In the Tools panel, click the **Selection** tool, if necessary. The two copied Baseball instances remain selected.
9. Drag the left Baseball instance to the lower-left corner of the Stage. Both instances move at the same time. The Baseball instance on the right is behind the Basketball. See Figure 3-8.

Figure 3-8 Copied Baseball instances moved to bottom of Stage

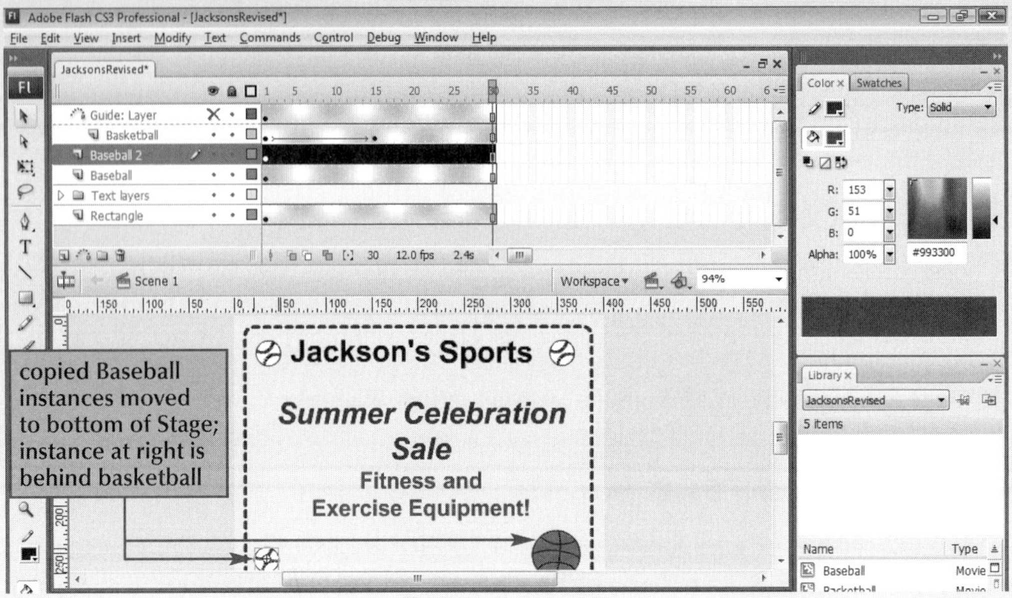

Using Scenes and Multiple Timelines

Scenes provide a way to break up a long or complex document into smaller sections that are more manageable. Every Flash document starts with one scene that contains a Timeline. For more complex animations, a document can have more than one scene, and each scene has its own Timeline, as shown in Figure 3-9. A document's scenes are similar to those of a motion picture. In the same way that the scenes in a motion picture are played in order, the scenes in a document are played one after the other. The content of all layers is displayed one frame at a time within a scene's Timeline. When you add new scenes to a document, you are essentially adding new Timelines that contain their own frames with new content.

Multiple scenes in one document **Figure 3-9**

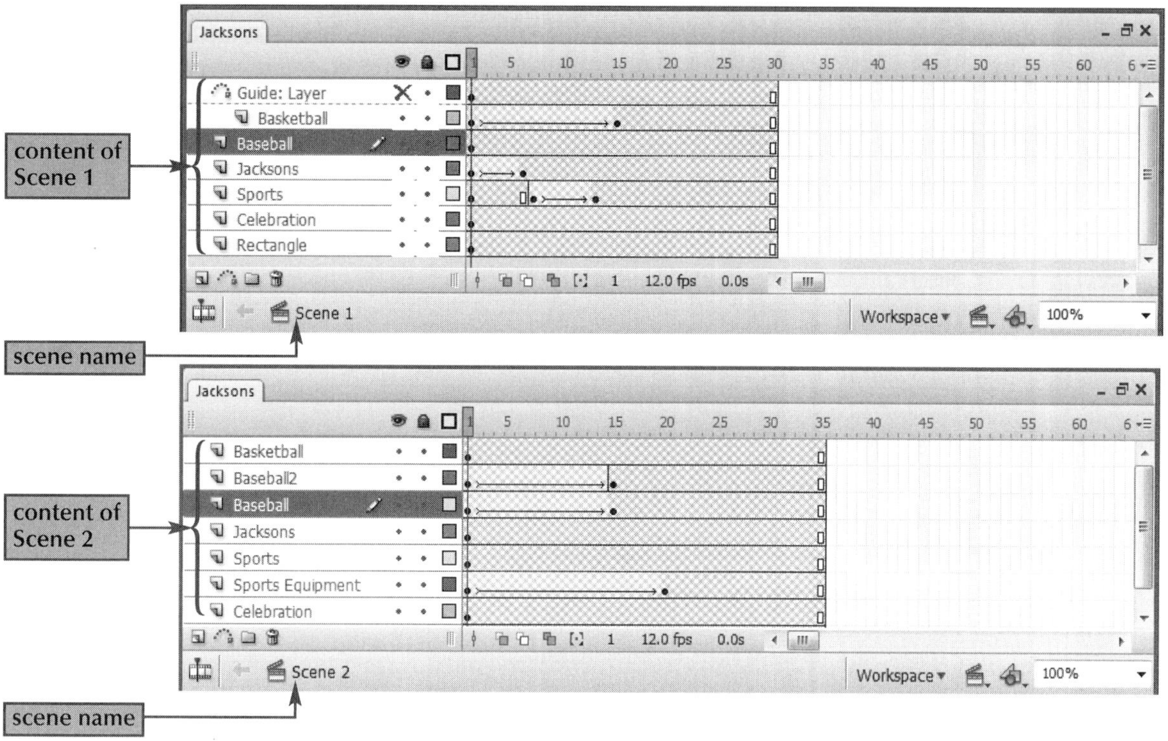

Once a document with multiple scenes is published, the SWF file plays in a Web page using the Flash Player. The player treats all of the scenes in a SWF file as one long Timeline. So, for example, if a Flash document has two scenes and each scene has 30 frames, Flash Player treats this as one long Timeline with 60 consecutive frames and play them according to the order of the scenes in the Scene panel.

Using the Scene Panel

The Scene panel lists the scenes in the current document in the order in which they will play. From the Scenes panel, you can change the order the scenes will play as well as duplicate, add, and delete scenes. A duplicate scene has the same name as the original with the word "copy" added to its name and it has the same contents as the original. Any new scene you add has the name Scene followed by a number that is one higher than the previous scene.

Naming Scenes | InSight

When a document has only a few scenes, using the default scene names such as Scene 1, Scene 2, and Scene 3 might be okay. When a document has many scenes, it is better to assign more meaningful names to each scene to make it simpler to manage the document. If you have 10 scenes, for example, you might not remember the content of each of the 10 scenes. You would then have to search through several scenes to find the one containing the content you want to work with. By giving each scene a meaningful name, you can more easily remember what each scene contains. Scene names can include spaces, symbols, and punctuation marks.

When you add a new scene or create a duplicate of a scene, the Stage automatically displays the new scene. You can tell which scene is currently displayed by the scene number in the upper-left corner of the Stage window or by looking at the Scene panel to see which scene is currently selected. You can switch between scenes at any time.

Aly wants you to rename and reorder the scenes in the Jackson's Sports document.

To work with scenes in the Jackson's Sports banner:

1. Click **Window** on the menu bar, point to **Other Panels**, and then click **Scene**. The Scene panel opens, showing two scenes named Scene 1 and Scene 2. You will rename these scenes with more meaningful names. See Figure 3-10.

Figure 3-10 Scenes displayed in the Scene panel

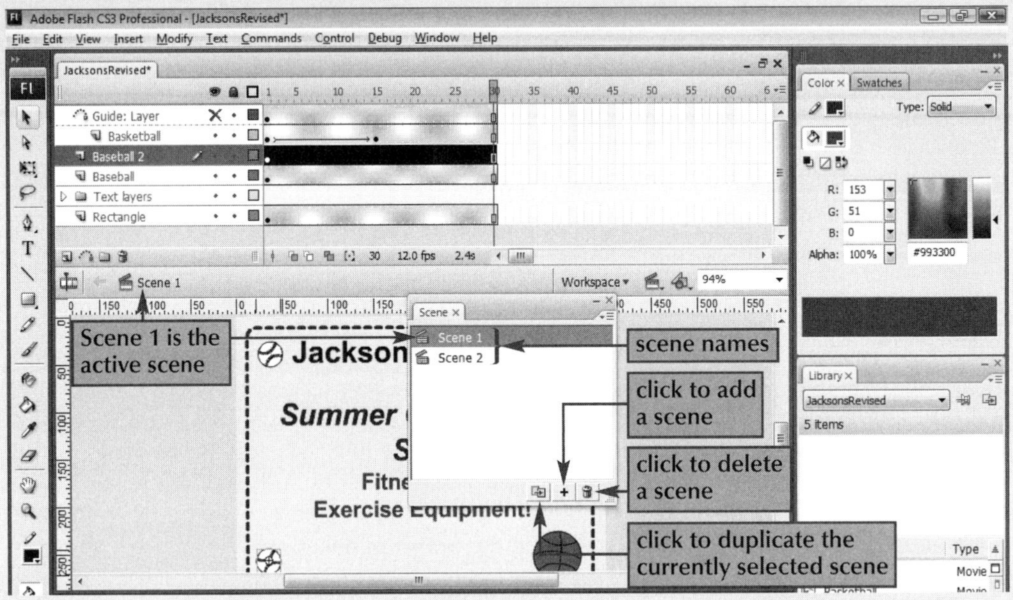

2. In the Scene panel, double-click **Scene 1** to select the name, type **Fitness and Exercise** as the new name, and then press the **Enter** key to rename the scene.
3. In the Scene panel, click **Scene 2**. The Scene 2 scene name appears on the Edit bar, the contents of the Timeline change to that scene, and the view of the Stage switches to the first frame of that scene.
4. In the Scene panel, double-click **Scene 2**, type **Sports Equipment**, and then press the **Enter** key. The scene is renamed and the Sports Equipment scene name appears on the Edit bar. See Figure 3-11.

Figure 3-11 Renamed scenes

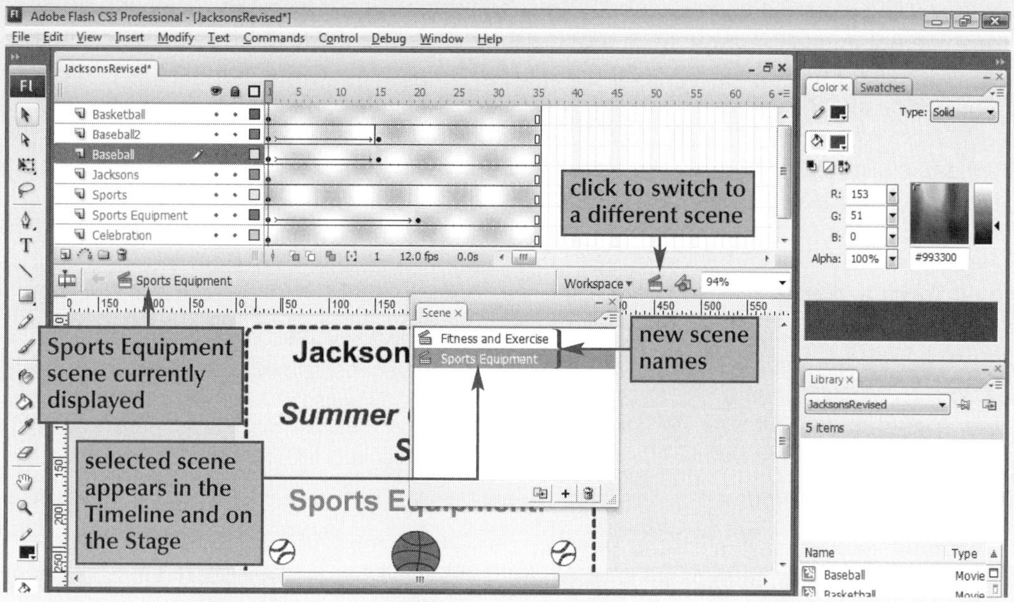

5. Drag the Scene panel to the right of the Stage, click **Control** on the menu bar, and then click **Play**. The animation for the Sports Equipment scene plays, showing the Sports Equipment text rotating and the baseballs moving.

   You'll test the animation to see how both scenes play one after the other.

6. Click **Control** on the menu bar, and then click **Test Movie**. A new window opens, showing the SWF file as it plays the animation of the Fitness and Exercise scene followed by the animation of the Sports Equipment scene.

7. On the JacksonsRevised window title bar, click the **Close** button. The new window closes and you to return to the document.

   You can use the Scene panel to reorder the scenes in a document.

8. In the Scene panel, click and drag the **Fitness and Exercise** scene so that it follows the Sports Equipment scene.

9. Click **Control** on the menu bar, and then click **Test Movie**. The movie plays, but the sequence of the animations changes based on the order of the scenes in the Scene panel. The Sports Equipment rotating text and baseballs' animation plays first, followed by the animation in the Fitness and Exercise scene.

10. On the JacksonsRevised window title bar, click the **Close** button to return to the document.

11. On the Edit bar, click the **Edit Scene** button to open a menu that lists all the scenes in the document, and then click **Sports Equipment**. The Timeline and Stage for the Sports Equipment scene appear.

12. On the Edit bar, click the **Edit Scene** button, and then click **Fitness and Exercise** to return to the Fitness and Exercise scene.

13. Save and close the JacksonsRevised document.

Adding a Duplicate Scene

Based on the planning instructions Aly provided, the Jenny's Oyster Hut banner will have two different animation sequences. The first sequence will show a fish swimming across the Stage with a sign advertising shrimp specials along with an animation of phrases displaying one after the other. The second animation sequence will show a fish swimming back and forth in the ocean and plant leaves moving. To make it easier to manage the two animation sequences, Aly suggests you create each in a separate scene. You'll add a new scene to the banner she has started by duplicating the initial scene.

To create a duplicate scene in the Jenny's Oyster Hut banner:

1. Open the **bannerDraft.fla** file located in the **Tutorial.03\Tutorial** folder included with your Data Files. The Scene panel shows one scene named Scene 1.
2. Save the document as **banner** in the **Tutorial.03\Tutorial** folder included with your Data Files.

   You need to create a duplicate of Scene 1.
3. In the Scene panel, click the **Duplicate scene** button. The duplicate scene appears in the Scene panel with the name Scene 1 copy.

   You'll rename the scenes with more meaningful names.
4. In the Scene panel, double-click **Scene 1**, type **Shrimp specials** as the new name, and then press the **Enter** key to rename the scene.
5. In the Scene panel, double-click **Scene 1 copy**, type **Fish and plant**, and then press the **Enter** key. The new scene name appears in the Scene panel.
6. Save the document.

Now that you have added a new scene to the Jenny's Oyster Hut banner document, you are ready to create the animations. In this session, you learned about the basic elements of Flash that are used in creating animations—layers and frames. You learned how to work with these elements using the Timeline. You also learned how scenes can help you manage a longer or more complex document. In the next session, you will learn how to create animations that are based on a series of frames that contain graphics.

Review | Session 3.1 Quick Check

1. What is the purpose of the Timeline?
2. How can you tell which is the current frame in the Timeline?
3. What is the default frame rate for a Flash document?
4. What is the difference between frames and layers?
5. What is a layer folder and what is its purpose?
6. What is a scene?
7. When you have more than one scene, how can you tell in what order the scenes will play?
8. Why would you rename a scene from its default name?

Session 3.2

Creating Animation

Animation is accomplished by displaying the content of different frames one after another. Each frame contains some graphic element that is displayed for a short instant in time. As the content of each frame is displayed in succession, the graphic elements appear to be moving. There are several ways to create animations in Flash. The simplest way is to use one of the prebuilt Timeline effects. **Timeline effects** allow you to quickly and easily create animations by selecting from various options in a dialog box. Based on the options selected, Flash creates the animation for you.

To create the animation yourself, there are basically two methods. You can create a **frame-by-frame animation** in which you create the content for each individual frame. Or, you can create a **tweened animation** in which you create the content for the beginning and ending frames, and Flash creates the content for the in-between frames. A tweened animation is quicker and easier to create than a frame-by-frame animation because you need to create only the content for two frames, the one at the beginning of the animation and the one at the end. Each of these two frames is a keyframe. Frame-by-frame animations take more time to create because you need to create all of the content for each frame in the animation. Frame-by-frame animations are usually used to build more detailed animations where you need to control the content of each step in the animation.

Avoiding Frame-by-Frame Animations | InSight

Avoid creating frame-by-frame animations when possible because frame-by-frame animations produce larger file sizes. A frame-by-frame animation usually has more keyframes than a tweened animation, and Flash stores the contents of every keyframe. In a tweened animation, only the contents of the start and end keyframes are stored.

Based on Aly's instructions and her sketch shown in Figure 3-12 of the new animated banner for Jenny's Oyster Hut, the banner has an initial animation sequence where a fish pulls a shrimp specials sign across the Stage. This animation will be created with a Timeline effect. In the second animation sequence, the plant leaves will be animated so that the leaves' tips appear to be moving. This will be done with a frame-by-frame animation because you need to specify the positions of the leaves at different moments in time. The fish in the banner will be animated using tweened animations in the next session.

Figure 3-12 Jenny's Oyster Hut partially completed banner

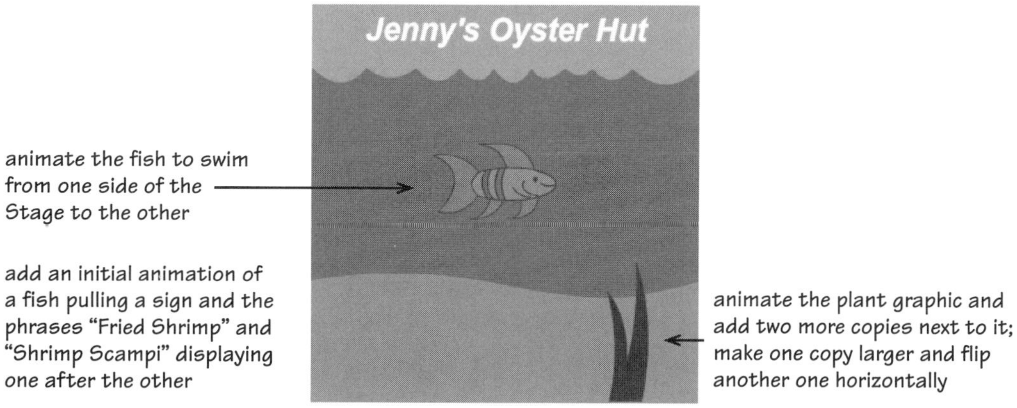

Creating Timeline Effects

Timeline effects allow you to create an animation or a special effect by selecting options in a dialog box. You can apply Timeline effects to objects on the Stage and Flash will create the necessary elements for the animation. This saves you time and does not require that you understand how the animation works. Each Timeline effect is created on its own layer and the layer name indicates the type of effect created. To create a Timeline effect, you select the object on the Stage to which you want to apply the effect, and then you select a Timeline effect from one of the following categories: Assistants, Effects, and Transform/Transition. Figure 3-13 describes the Timeline effects by category.

Figure 3-13 **Timeline effects**

Category	Timeline Effect	Description
Assistants	Copy to Grid	Duplicates the selected object across a grid; you specify the number of rows and columns in the grid plus the spacing between rows and columns
	Distributed Duplicate	Creates duplicates of an object and distributes them according to settings such as offset distance, rotation, and color
Effects	Blur	Animates an object by duplicating it and increasingly blurring each duplicate; you set the number of duplicates to create and the direction in which to display them throughout the animation
	Drop Shadow	Creates a drop shadow of an object; you select the color of the shadow, how much transparency to apply to it, and what distance to offset it from the object
	Expand	Creates an animation where an object, such as a text block, expands and/or contracts; includes settings to specify the number of frames to use for the animation as well as whether to expand or contract the object and in what direction to move the object
	Explode	Breaks an object into pieces simulating an explosion of the object; you can specify the direction, arc, and rotation the exploded pieces will move in, the size of the pieces, and the amount of transparency to apply to the pieces
Transform/ Transition	Transform	Creates an animation where an object is transformed; you can also specify that the object change position, rotate, scale in size, change color, or change its degree of transparency; you can control how slow it starts or ends the animation
	Transition	Creates a fade or wipe transition for an object; you specify what direction to fade or wipe and you can control how slowly it starts or ends the animation

After you select a Timeline effect, a dialog box displays a preview of the effect along with default settings specific to the effect. Figure 3-14 shows an example of the Blur Timeline effect.

Blur Timeline effect dialog box **Figure 3-14**

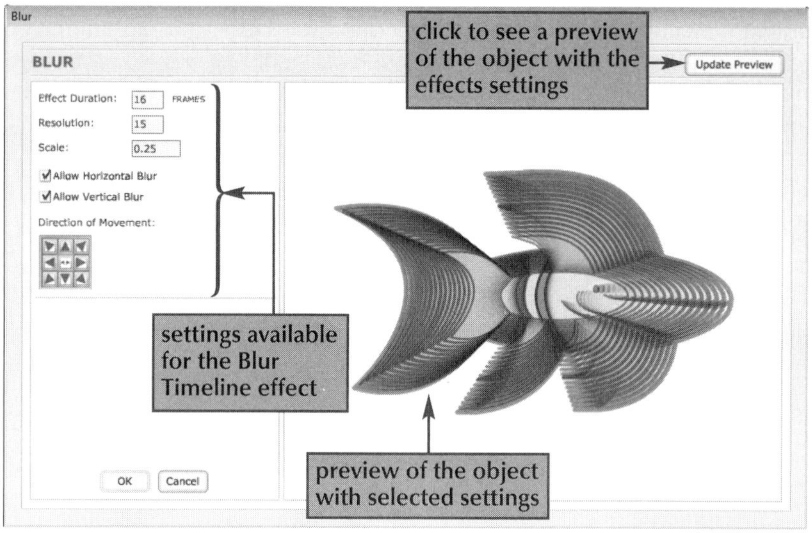

In the dialog box, you change the settings you want to apply. You can then update the preview to see the effect within the dialog box. When you are satisfied with the settings in the dialog box, Flash then creates a new layer in the Timeline and creates frames with the appropriate content for the animation, as shown in Figure 3-15. Flash also creates a new symbol for the Timeline effect. The symbol is added to the document's library in a new folder named Effects Folder, which holds the graphic symbols used to create the animation.

Timeline effect layer **Figure 3-15**

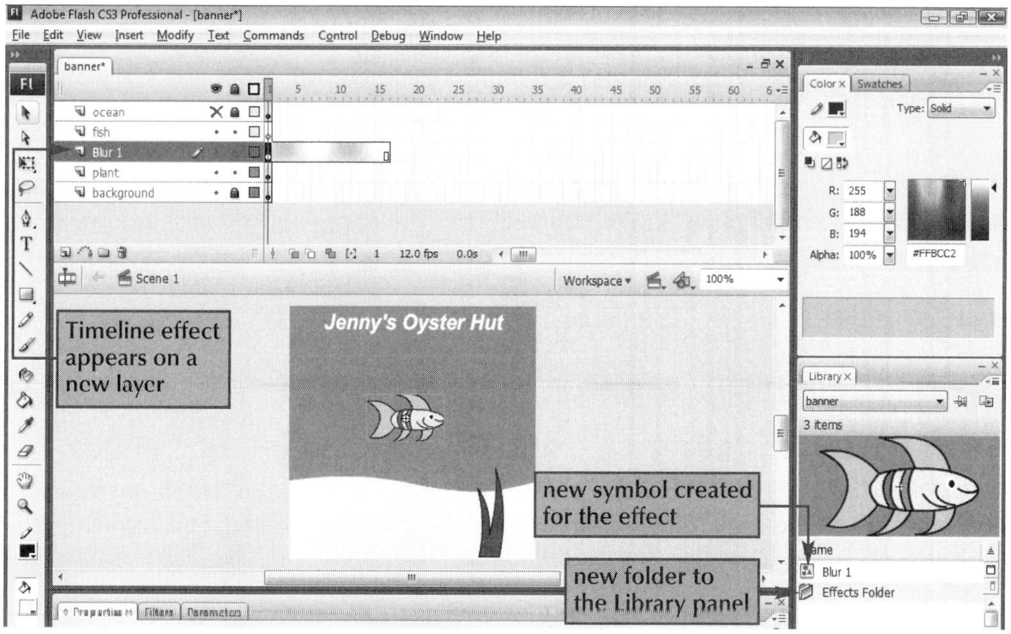

Adding a Transform Timeline Effect

The first animation sequence for the Jenny's Oyster Hut banner has an animation where a fish moves across the Stage pulling a shrimp specials sign. Aly wants you to create this animation in the first scene using the Transform Timeline effect. Before you create the Timeline effect, you'll draw the sign graphic.

To draw the graphics for the animation:

1. If you took a break after the previous session, make sure that the banner.fla file is open and the Scene panel is open and positioned on the right side of the Stage so that the Stage contents are visible.
2. In the Scene panel, click the **Shrimp specials** scene to make it the current scene.

   Because the plant leaves will not be used in this scene, you'll delete the plant layer.
3. In the Timeline, click the **plant** layer to select it, and then click the **Delete Layer** button . The layer is deleted.

   To make it easier to draw the sign, you will hide the ocean layer and create guides.
4. In the Timeline, in the Show/Hide column for the ocean layer, click the dot to hide the layer temporarily.
5. Display the rulers, and then drag a horizontal guide to approximately 150 pixels from the top of the Stage, and then drag a vertical guide to approximately 80 pixels from the left of the Stage.

   You'll draw the rectangle for the sign next.
6. In the Tools panel, click the **Rectangle** tool , click the **Black and white** button to change the stroke color to black and the fill color to white, and then, if necessary, click the **Object Drawing** button to deselect it.
7. In the Property inspector, if necessary, set the corner radius to **0**, the stroke height to **1**, and the stroke style to **Solid**.
8. In the Timeline, select the **fish** layer, and then, on the Stage, draw a rectangle that is approximately 75 pixels wide and 40 pixels high below the fish starting at the upper-left corner where the guides intersect. The rectangle will be the sign the fish pulls across the banner. You'll add the words to the sign next.
9. In the Tools panel, click the **Text** tool T, and then, in the Property inspector, if necessary, change the font to **Arial**, the font size to **14**, the text (fill) color to **black** (#000000), the font style to **bold**, and the alignment to **Align Center**.
10. Create a text block inside the rectangle you drew in Step 8, type **Shrimp** in the text block, press the **Enter** key, and then type **Specials!**.
11. If necessary, in the Tools panel, click the **Selection** tool , on the Stage, reposition the text block so it is centered within the rectangle, and then click an empty area of the Stage to deselect the text block.

Now you'll clear the guides and skew the rectangle.

12. Click **View** on the menu bar, point to **Guides**, and click **Clear Guides**. The guides are cleared from the Stage.

13. In the Tools panel, click the **Free Transform** tool, and then draw a marquee around the rectangle. Both the rectangle and the text are selected.

Trouble? If the fish is selected, the marquee you drew probably encompassed the fish. Click the pasteboard, and then draw the marquee again, being sure to select only the rectangle and the text block.

Tip

You can also press the Q key to select the Free Transform tool.

14. In the Tools panel, click the **Rotate and Skew** button, move the pointer over the top side of the rectangle until it changes to ⇌, and then drag the top side of the rectangle slightly to the right to skew it. See Figure 3-16.

Skewed rectangle for the sign — **Figure 3-16**

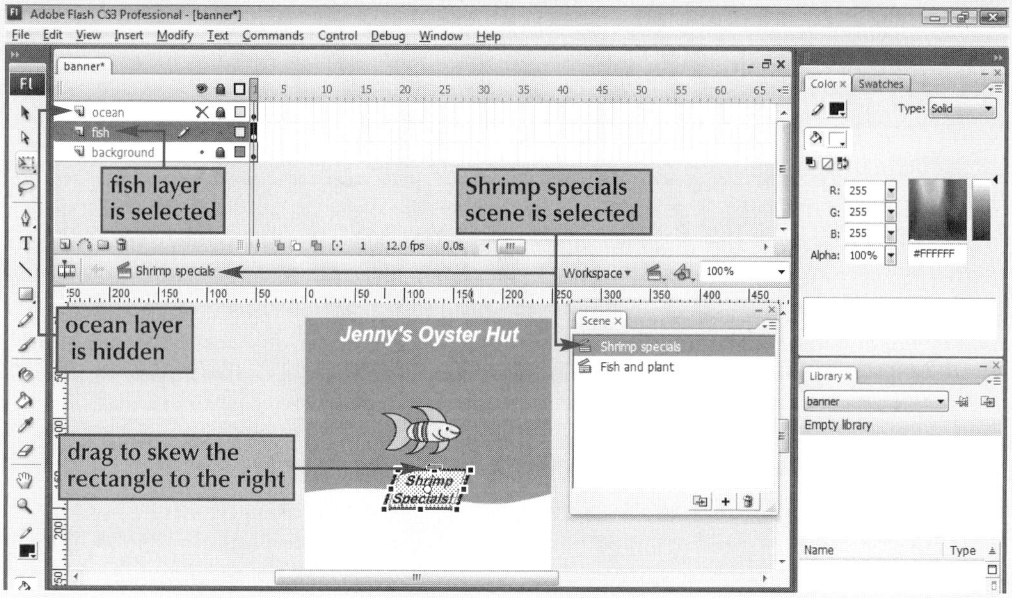

You now need to draw two lines to connect the sign to the fish.

15. In the Tools panel, click the **Line** tool, and then, if necessary, click the **Snap to Objects** button to select it.

16. In the Property inspector, set the stroke color to **black** (#000000), the stroke height to **1**, and the stroke style to **Solid**.

17. On the Stage, draw a line from the fish's lower-left fin to the top of the rectangle, and then draw a line from the fish's lower-right fin to the top of the rectangle. See Figure 3-17.

Figure 3-17 **Sign attached to fish**

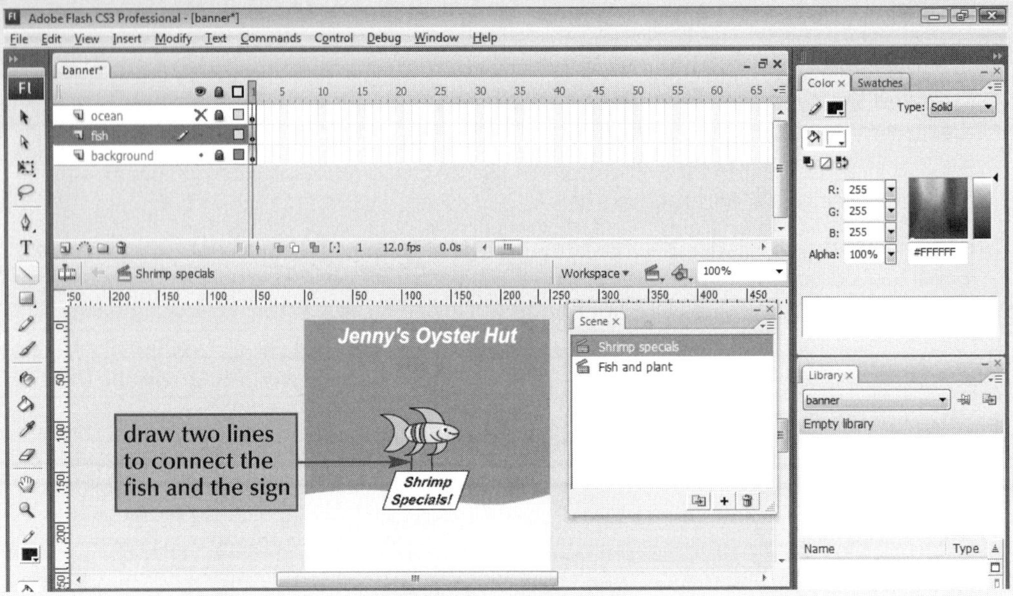

The graphic of the fish pulling the sign is complete. You are ready to animate it using the Transform Timeline effect. You must first select the sign, the lines, and the fish. Then you'll apply the Timeline effect and move the resulting symbol instance off the left side of the Stage. The animation of the fish and sign will start in the pasteboard to the left of the Stage, go across the Stage, and end in the pasteboard to the right of the Stage.

To add the Transform Timeline effect to the Jenny's Oyster Hut banner:

1. In the Tools panel, click the **Selection** tool, and then draw a marquee around the sign, lines, and fish graphic to select all of the objects at one time.
2. Click **Insert** on the menu bar, point to **Timeline Effects**, point to **Transform/ Transition**, and then click **Transform**. The Transform dialog box opens.
3. In the Transform dialog box, type **50** in the Effect Duration box to set the number of frames, select the **Change Position By** option in the Position box, if necessary, and then type **400** in the X box. These settings make the animation occupy 50 frames in the Timeline and move horizontally 400 pixels during the animation.
4. Type **–80** in the Motion Ease box. The motion ease value determines whether the animation starts slowly and goes faster at the end or starts quickly and goes slower at the end. This gives the movement a more natural look, more so than if the object moves at the same rate throughout the entire animation sequence. In this case, the animation movement starts slow and speeds up at the end of the movement. See Figure 3-18.

Figure 3-18 Settings for Transform Timeline effect

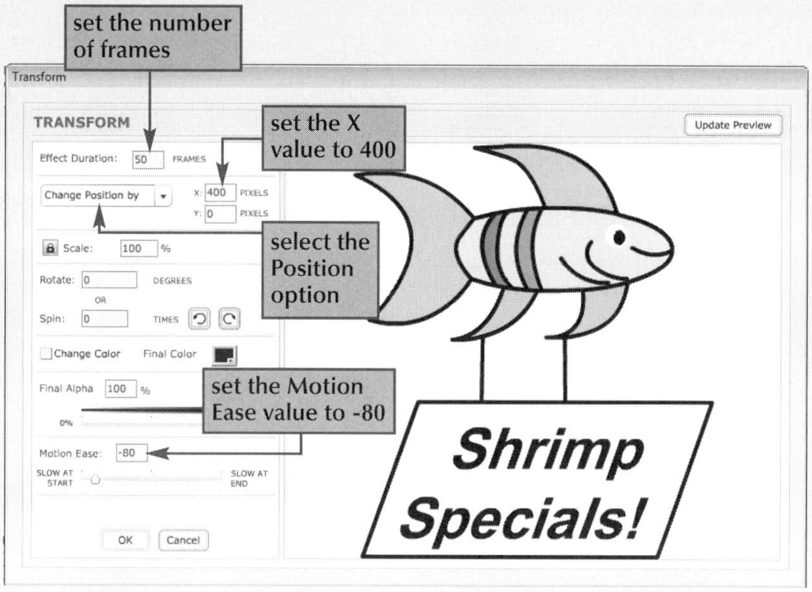

5. Click the **Update Preview** button to see how the animation will work, and then click the **OK** button to close the dialog box and create the effect in the Timeline. A new layer named Transform 1 is created in the Timeline and the selected objects on the Stage are converted into a symbol.

6. In the Timeline, if necessary, click **Frame 1** of the Transform 1 layer, and then use the **Selection** tool in the Tools panel to drag the symbol instance onto the pasteboard so that its center is about 100 pixels to the left of the Stage and about 90 pixels from the top of the Stage. See Figure 3-19.

Figure 3-19 Fish and sign positioned on the Stage

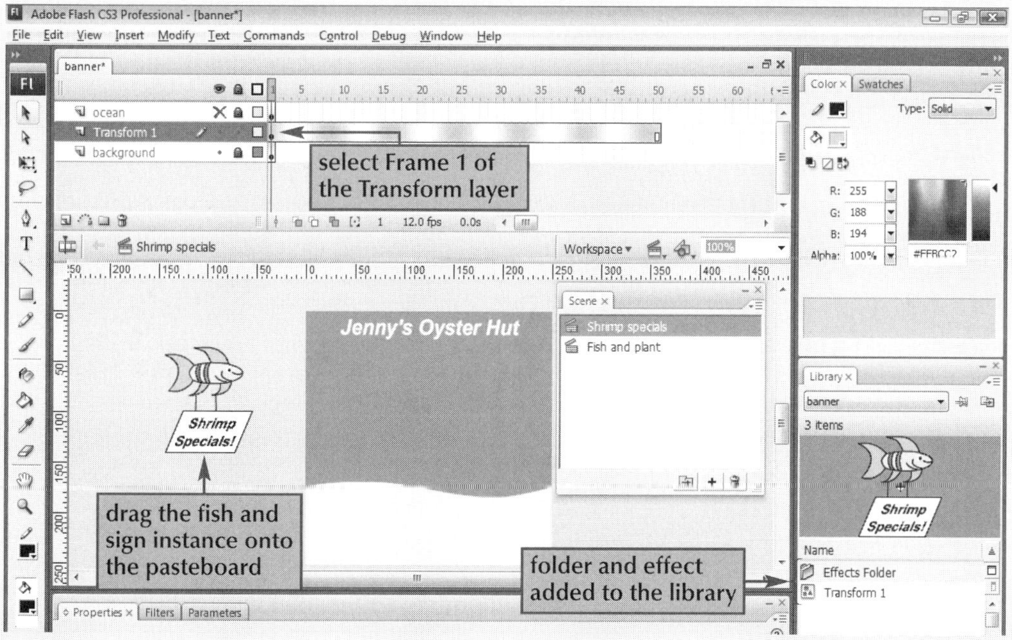

To complete the animation, you'll unhide the ocean layer and extend the layers so that they exist for 50 frames.

7. In the Timeline, in the Show/Hide column for the ocean layer, click the **Hide layer** button [X] to unhide it. The ocean layer content reappears on the Stage.
8. In the Timeline, click **Frame 50** of the ocean layer to select it, click **Insert** on the menu bar, point to **Timeline**, and then click **Frame** to insert a regular frame. The graphics in the ocean layer are displayed through Frame 50.
9. Repeat Step 8 for the background layer to display its graphics through Frame 50.
10. Click **Control** on the menu bar, and then click **Play** to test the animation. The fish and sign move across the Stage from the left to the right, starting slowly and speeding up slightly when they reach the end of the animation.

Tip

You can also press the F5 key to insert a regular frame in the selected location.

Modifying or Deleting a Timeline Effect

After a Timeline effect is created, you might need to modify or remove it. The Edit Effect command opens the same dialog box that was used to create the effect, allowing you to change the settings. The Remove Effect command removes the effect from the Timeline and also removes the effect's symbols. If the document contains no other Timeline effects, the Effects Folder is also removed from the document's library.

Aly wants you to modify the Transform Timeline effect so that the fish and sign graphic starts quickly and slows down at the end of the animation.

To edit the Transform Timeline effect:

1. In the Timeline, click the **Transform 1** layer. You'll edit the transform effect in this layer.
2. On the menu bar, click **Modify**, point to **Timeline Effects**, and click **Edit Effect**. The Transform dialog box opens.
3. Type **100** in the Motion Ease box. This changes the start and end of the animation movement.
4. Click the **Update Preview** button. The animation starts quickly and ends slowly.
5. Click the **OK** button to close the dialog box.
6. Click **Control** on the menu bar, and then click **Play** to test the animation. The fish and sign move across the Stage from the left to the right, slowing down slightly when they reach the end of the animation.

The Timeline effect for the first scene of the banner is complete. Next, you will continue your work with the banner by adding the animation to the second scene. You will animate the plant leaves using frame-by-frame animation.

Creating Frame-by-Frame Animations

To create a frame-by-frame animation, you need to create the graphic elements of the animation for each of its individual frames. If, for example, your animation will have 15 frames, then you need to create the content for each of the 15 frames. Some of the content can be the same from one frame to the next, but other content can be slightly modified. As the frames are displayed one after another, the perception of movement is achieved. To create a frame-by-frame animation, you start with a graphic object in the initial frame. Then, for each place in the animation where you need the object to change, you add a keyframe. Recall that a keyframe is any frame that has different content from the previous frame. Depending on the animation, every frame can be a keyframe or you can have intervening frames where the graphic objects do not change. As you add keyframes, you change the position of the graphic object. After you have created all of the keyframes, you test the animation.

The Fish and plant scene of the Jenny's Oyster Hut banner contains a graphic element that looks like a plant. You will convert this plant graphic into a symbol with a movie clip behavior, and then animate the plant's leaves so that they appear to be moving in the ocean. You will do this by creating a frame-by-frame animation. The plant's leaves will be animated within the Timeline of the plant symbol and not in the main Timeline of the document. Recall that a movie clip symbol has its own Timeline that is independent of the document's Timeline. By adding the animation in the symbol's Timeline, every instance of the symbol automatically includes the animation. This means that each plant instance you create on the document's Stage will have the same animation built in as part of the instance.

To create the animation of the plant leaves, Aly wants you add keyframes to every other frame of the plant leaves layer from Frame 1 through Frame 9. This will be sufficient to create the movement of the leaves. In each keyframe, she wants you to move the tips of the leaves slightly, first in one direction and then in the opposite direction.

Before you can create the frame-by-frame animation of the plant leaves, you need to convert these objects to symbols.

To convert the objects in the Fish and plant scene to symbols:

1. In the Scene panel, click the **Fish and plant** scene to make it the current scene, and then close the Scene panel. You will create symbols of the plant and fish graphics.
2. In the Timeline, in the Show/Hide column for the ocean layer, click the dot to hide the layer temporarily.
3. In the Tools panel, click the **Selection** tool, if necessary, and then, on the Stage, select the plant graphic, including both its stroke and its fill.
4. Click **Modify** on the menu bar, and then click **Convert to Symbol**. The Convert to Symbol dialog box opens.
5. Type **Plant** in the Name box, click the **Movie clip** option button, if necessary, and then click the **OK** button. The dialog box closes and the plant graphic is converted to a movie clip symbol.
6. On the Stage, select the entire fish graphic, including all of its strokes and fills, and then repeat Steps 4 and 5 to convert the graphic to a movie clip symbol named **Fish1**.

You are ready to animate the plant symbol. You first need to select the Plant symbol from the Library panel so you can edit it to create an animation within its Timeline.

To create a frame-by-frame animation of the plant symbol:

1. In the Library panel, double-click the **Plant** symbol icon. The symbol opens in symbol-editing mode.
2. In the symbol's Timeline, click **Frame 3**. This is the frame where you want to change the animation. See Figure 3-20.

Figure 3-20 **Plant symbol in symbol-editing mode**

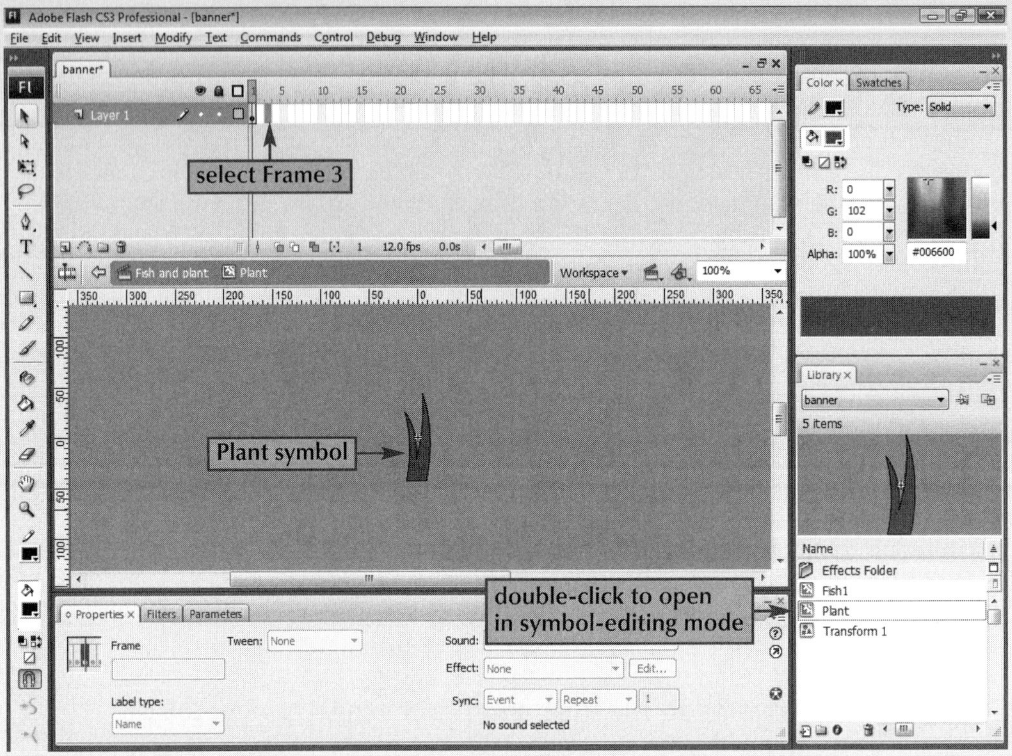

> **Tip**
>
> You can also press the F6 key on the keyboard to insert a keyframe at the selected location.

3. Click **Insert** on the menu bar, point to **Timeline**, and then click **Keyframe**. A keyframe is inserted in Frame 3 and a regular frame is added in Frame 2. When you add any kind of frame to a layer, Flash adds regular frames to fill the empty intervening frames. In this case, when you added a keyframe in Frame 3, Flash added a regular frame, not a keyframe, in Frame 2. The plant graphic is also automatically copied to all of the new frames. See Figure 3-21.

Figure 3-21 **Keyframe added to the Plant symbol in the Timeline**

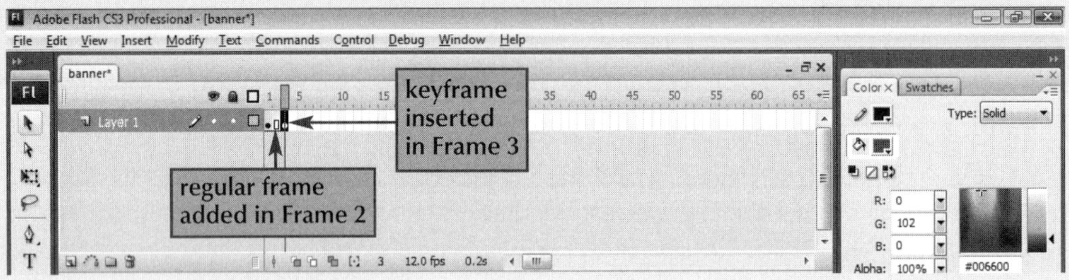

In this frame, you'll move the tips of the leaves slightly to the right.

4. In the Tools panel, make sure the **Selection** tool is selected, click another area of the Stage to deselect the plant, move the pointer over the tip of one of the leaves until it changes to , and then click and drag the tip of the leaf slightly to the right.

5. Repeat Step 4 to reposition the other leaf's tip slightly to the right. See Figure 3-22.

Figure 3-22 Tips of plant leaves modified

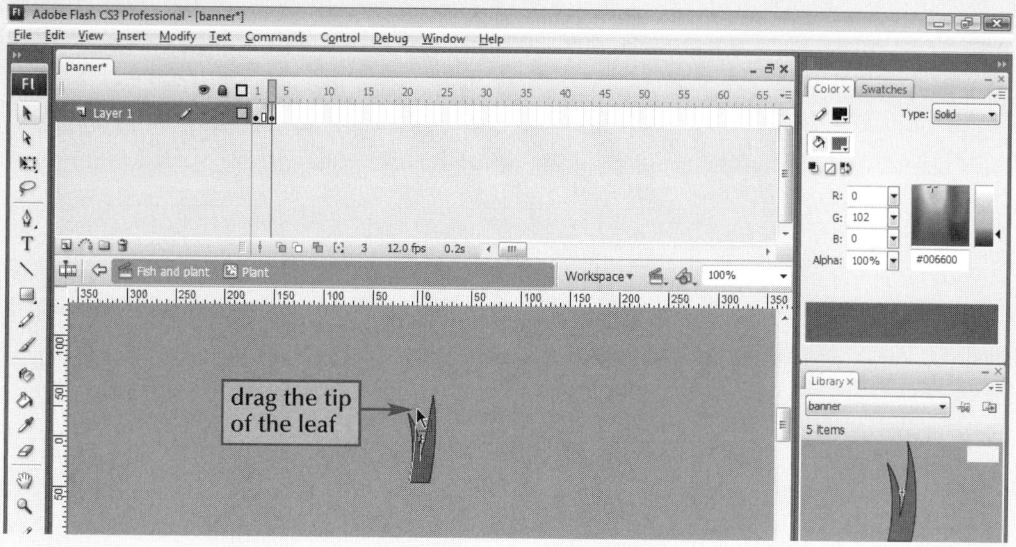

You will repeat this process to add keyframes in every other frame and reposition the leaves' tips farther right, then back left, and finally back to their starting positions.

6. Click **Frame 5**, insert a keyframe, and then repeat Steps 4 and 5 to reposition both of the leaves' tips slightly more to the right.
7. Click **Frame 7**, insert a keyframe, and then repeat Steps 4 and 5 to reposition the leaves' tips back slightly to the left.
8. Click **Frame 9**, insert a keyframe, and then repeat Steps 4 and 5 to move the leaves' tips slightly more to the left to almost the same positions where they started in Frame 1.
9. Drag the playhead back and forth through these frames to get a sense of what the animation looks like. This frame-by-frame animation is complete.
10. On the Edit bar, click the **Fish and plant** link to exit symbol-editing mode.

You have created a frame-by-frame animation within the Plant symbol. Because the animation was created within the symbol's Timeline, each instance of the symbol has the same animation. You can, therefore, place several instances of the Plant symbol in the document and all of the instances will be animated.

Recall from Aly's instructions that the banner should have three animated plants in the lower-right corner of the Stage. Because one instance of the animated plant leaves is already on the Stage, you need to add two more instances. The second instance needs to be modified to make it larger than the first, and the third instance needs to be modified so its leaves point to the right.

To create and modify two instances of the animated plant symbol:

1. On the Edit bar, click the **Zoom** control, and then click **Show All**. All of the contents fit on the Stage.

2. In the Timeline, select the **plant** layer, if necessary, and then drag an instance of the **Plant** symbol from the Library panel to the Stage and place it to the left of the existing instance.
3. In the Tools panel, click the **Free Transform** tool, and then click the **Scale** button.
4. On the Stage, drag one corner of the bounding box around the plant to make this plant instance slightly larger than the other instance. See Figure 3-23.

Figure 3-23 **Enlarged plant instance**

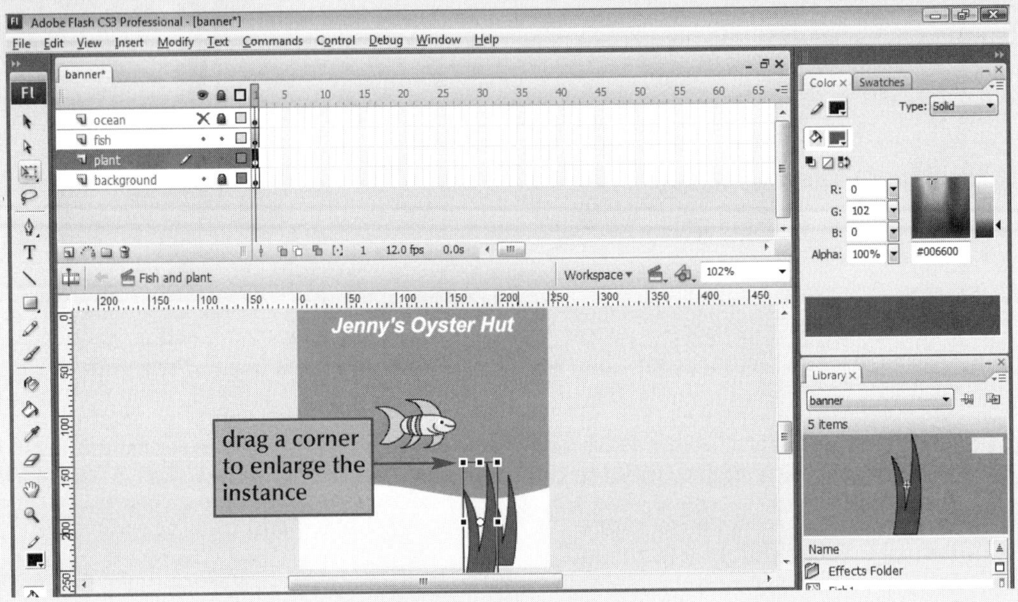

5. In the Tools panel, click the **Selection** tool, and then reposition this instance as needed to align it with the bottom edge of the other plant instance.
6. Drag another instance of the **Plant** symbol from the Library panel to the Stage and place it to the left of the larger plant instance.
7. With the third plant instance still selected on the Stage, click **Modify** on the menu bar, point to **Transform**, and then click **Flip Horizontal**. The leaves of the plant instance now face to the right.
8. If necessary, line up the bottoms of the plants with the bottom part of the Stage. See Figure 3-24.

Figure 3-24 Three plant instances arranged on the Stage

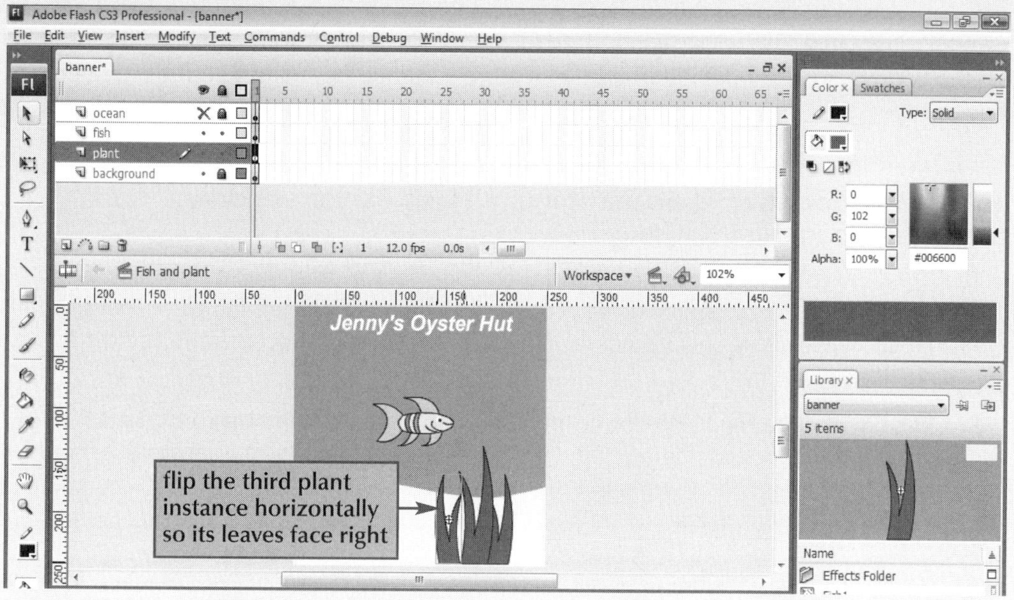

9. In the Timeline, in the Show/Hide column of the ocean layer, click the **Hide layer** button [X]. The contents of the ocean layer reappear on the Stage.
10. Save the banner.

Testing an Animation

After you create a document with animation, you need to test it to make sure it works correctly. To test the document's animation, you have several options. You can play the full animation on the Stage. You can test some or all of the animation by scrubbing the playhead back and forth through the frames, which is useful for testing a short animation sequence. Another way to test a document's animation is to create an SWF file from the document, and then play the file using the Flash Player plug-in. Finally, you can test an animation in a Web page. Flash publishes the document as an SWF file and also creates a Web page. The Web page with the SWF file is displayed in your computer's default browser. The SWF files created when testing the animation are saved in the same folder as the FLA file.

Testing a Document's Animation | Reference Window

- To test an animation on the Stage, click Control on the menu bar, and then click Play.
- To test a few frames of animation, scrub by dragging the playhead along the Timeline header.
- To test the animation in a Flash Player window, click Control on the menu bar, and then click Test Movie.
- To test the animation in a Web page, click File on the menu bar, point to Publish Preview, and click Default - (HTML).

Because the plant symbol's animation is within its own Timeline, you need to test the animation as an SWF file. The movie will appear in a Flash Player window. If you test the animation on the Stage, the plant symbol's animation will not play. To view the plant symbol's animation, however, you will need to stop the movie from repeating by turning off the Loop feature. By default, the Loop feature is turned on, causing a movie's animation to repeat.

To test the document's animation in a Flash Player window and a Web page:

1. Click **Control** on the menu bar, and then click **Test Movie**. The movie plays in a Flash Player window starting with the Shrimp specials scene. The plant leaves animation, however, is only visible for a fraction of a second because the second scene only has one frame.
2. Click **Control** on the Flash Player menu bar, and then click **Loop** to turn off the loop feature and stop the animation from repeating. The animation stops at the second scene, which contains the plant leaves. The leaves display their animation, as shown in Figure 3-25.

Figure 3-25 Flash Player window with the plant animation

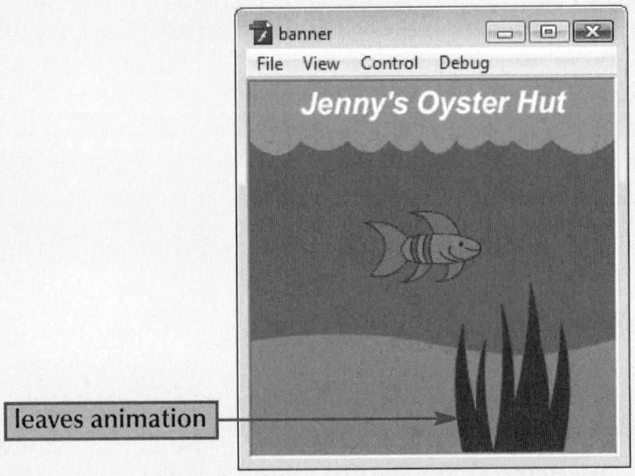

3. Click **File** on the Flash Player menu bar, and then click **Close**. The Flash Player window closes.
4. Click **File** on the menu bar, point to **Publish Preview**, and then click **Default - (HTML)**. Your computer's default browser opens and the animation plays in a Web page.
5. Close the browser window when you are finished viewing the animation.

Tip

You can also press the F12 key to preview the animation in a Web page in your computer's default browser.

You have completed two of the three animations for the Jenny's Oyster Hut banner using Timeline effects and frame-by-frame animation. In the next session, you will create the third animation Aly asked for in her planning sketch.

Session 3.2 Quick Check | Review

1. What is a Timeline effect?
2. True or False? Each Timeline effect is created in its own layer.
3. After you create a Timeline effect in your document, how can you change its settings?
4. In a frame-by-frame animation, what kind of frame do you need to have in the Timeline when the content changes on the Stage?
5. True or False? To create a frame-by-frame animation, the object being animated must first be converted to a symbol.
6. Can you include regular frames in a frame-by-frame animation? Why or why not?
7. Why is it important to test an animation after you create it?

Session 3.3

Creating Tweened Animation

In the previous session, you created a frame-by-frame animation by creating the content for each frame yourself. However, this process can be tedious and time consuming if you have many objects that need to be animated. For most animations where you want an object to move, resize, rotate, or change certain properties over a period of time, it is best to create a tweened animation. Recall that tweened animation is where you create the contents of the beginning frame and the ending frame and then Flash creates the in-between frames, varying the content evenly in each frame to achieve the animation. The beginning frame and the ending frame for a tweened animation must be keyframes. Many of the prebuilt Timeline effects are also created with tweened animations; however, you do not have as much control over the animation as you do when you create the tweened animation yourself.

The two types of tweened animations are motion tweening and shape tweening. **Motion tweening** creates an animation where an object changes its position, rotates, scales in size, or even changes in color. It can also make an object fade in or out. **Shape tweening** changes a shape into another shape over time. For example, you can create an animation where a circle shape is changed into a square shape.

Creating a Motion Tween

The process for creating a motion tweened animation is relatively simple. You create an object in the beginning keyframe of the animation and convert the object to a symbol. In order for an object to be animated using motion tweening, the object must be a symbol. Also, you can only have one object in the layer in which you create the motion tween. If you have more than one object, Flash groups the objects and tries to animate them together. So, be sure to place any object that you don't want to be part of the motion tween on a separate layer. After the object to be animated is a symbol, you create a keyframe in the frame where the animation will end. In this keyframe you move the object to a different position or you change its properties, such as its size, color tint, or color brightness. When you create the motion tween, Flash creates tweened frames between the keyframes varying the content in each frame to change the object's position or properties slightly from one frame to the next.

After you create a motion tween, the Property inspector provides additional settings, as shown in Figure 3-26. The Ease value makes an object accelerate or decelerate to create a more natural appearance of movement. The Rotate button allows you to specify whether the object should also rotate during the motion tween. Selecting CW causes the object to rotate in a clockwise direction. Selecting CCW rotates the object in a counterclockwise direction. You then specify how many times to rotate the object throughout the motion tween in the times box.

Figure 3-26 **Property inspector with motion tween options**

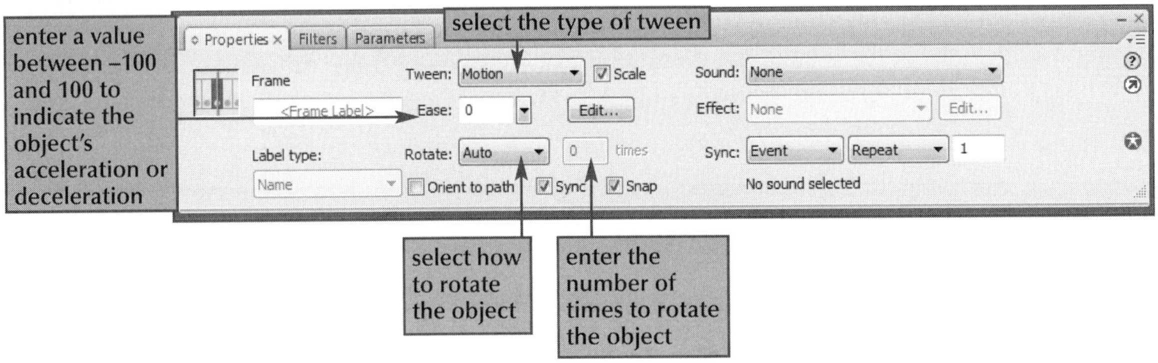

InSight | Controlling an Object's Speed in an Animation

Objects don't usually move at a constant rate of speed. They might start slowly and then accelerate, or they might start quickly and then decelerate. For example, a kicked ball starts moving quickly but then slows down toward the end of its movement. To simulate this natural movement, you can adjust a motion tween's Ease value in the Property inspector. A negative value causes the object to begin slowly and accelerate toward the end of the animation. A positive value causes the object to begin rapidly and decelerate toward the end of the animation. For more control over a motion tween, you can use the Custom Ease In/Ease Out dialog box, which displays an adjustable graph representing an object's degree of motion over time.

Frames with a motion tween have a light blue background as well as a solid line across the frames. If a dashed line appears instead of the solid line, the tween is broken or incomplete, such as when it is missing the ending keyframe or the object to be animated is not a symbol.

You will add a motion tweened animation of the fish graphic in the second scene of Jenny's Oyster Hut banner. The fish will swim from one side of the Stage, turn around, and swim back. Aly suggests making the animation approximately 4 seconds in length, which, at the frame rate of 12 frames per second, will take 48 frames. So, the fish will swim to the right side of the Stage and back in 48 frames. The fish should arrive at the right side at Frame 24 so that it can turn around and return to the other side during the second half of the animation.

To create a motion tween with the fish graphic:

1. If you took a break after the previous session, make sure that the banner.fla file is open.
2. In the Timeline, click the **fish** layer to select it, and then, on the Stage, drag the **Fish1** instance to the pasteboard at the left of the Stage so that its center is about 60 pixels from the top of the Stage. The fish will swim in from the left of the Stage. See Figure 3-27.

Figure 3-27 Repositioned Fish1 instance

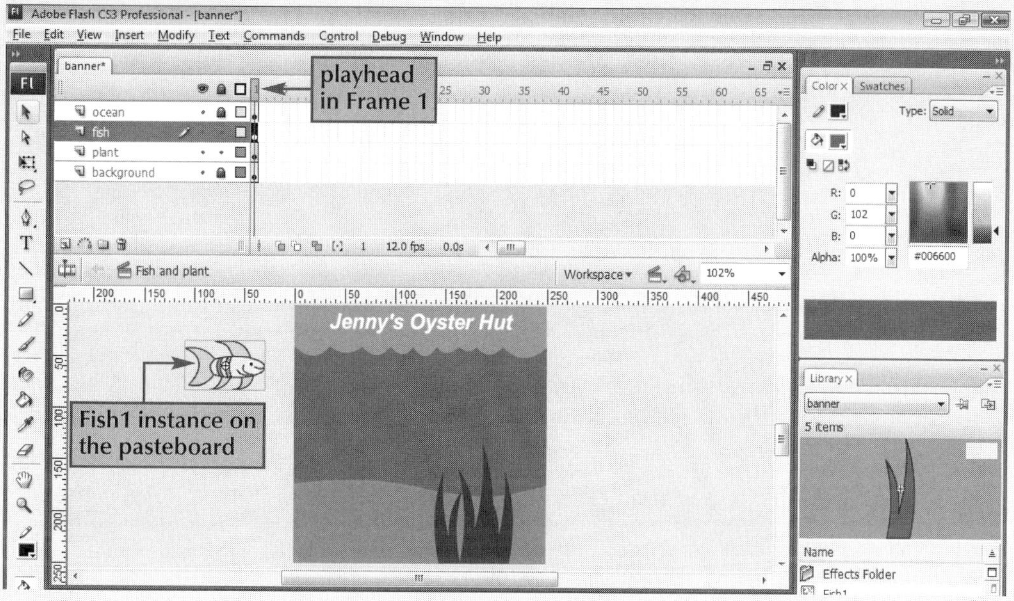

3. In the Timeline, click **Frame 48** of the ocean layer, click **Insert** on the menu bar, point to **Timeline**, and then click **Frame**. A regular frame is added at Frame 48. Regular frames are also automatically added between Frames 1 and 48. The ocean layer graphics from Frame 1 are copied to Frame 48.

   The fish, plant, and background graphics disappeared when you added the frame in Frame 48 because these graphics exist only in Frame 1. For these graphics to exist through Frame 48, you need to add frames to their respective layers.
4. Click **Frame 48** of the plant layer, insert a regular frame to extend the layer through Frame 48, click **Frame 48** of the background layer, and then insert a regular frame to extend the layer to Frame 48.
5. Click **Frame 24** of the fish layer, click **Insert** on the menu bar, point to **Timeline**, and then click **Keyframe**. A keyframe is added at Frame 24, which is where the fish will arrive at the right side of the Stage, and regular frames are automatically added between Frames 1 and 24. The Fish1 graphic is copied to Frame 24.
6. While Frame 24 is still selected, drag the **Fish1** instance from the left side of the Stage to the right side of the Stage, being sure to stay within the Stage. See Figure 3-28.

Figure 3-28 Fish1 instance repositioned for Frame 24

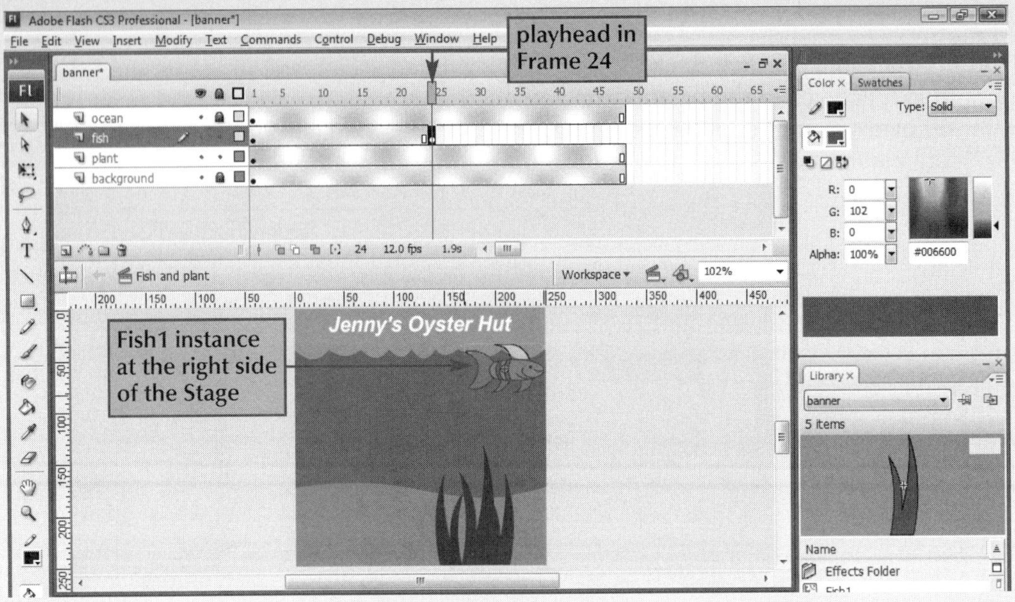

7. Click **Frame 25** of the fish layer, and then insert a keyframe. In this frame, you will flip the fish to turn it around.
8. On the Stage, click the **fish** to select it, if necessary, click **Modify** on the menu bar, point to **Transform**, and then click **Flip Horizontal**. The fish flips to face in the opposite direction.
9. Click **Frame 48** of the fish layer, insert a keyframe, and then drag the **Fish1** instance back to its original position in the pasteboard at the left of the Stage. The keyframe is at the end of the animation for the fish layer.
10. Click **Frame 1** of the fish layer, click **Insert** on the menu bar, point to **Timeline**, and then click **Create Motion Tween**. A motion tween is created as evidenced by the line and light blue background on Frames 1 through 24 in the Timeline.
11. Click **Frame 25** of the fish layer, and then, in the Property inspector, click the **Tween** button, and click **Motion**. A second motion tween is created for the second part of the animation.

Now that you have created the motion tweens, you should test them. Testing ensures that the motion tweened animation works as you expect. You can test the animation on the Stage because it occurs only in one scene and you are not testing the entire movie.

Tip

You can also press the Ctrl+Alt+R to rewind the movie to frame 1.

To test the motion tweened animations:

1. Click **Control** on the menu bar, and then click **Rewind**. The playhead moves to Frame 1.
2. Click **Control** on the menu bar, and then click **Play**. The fish moves from the left side of the Stage to the right and then back again to the left.
3. Save the banner.

Creating a Shape Tween

Shape tweens are created similarly to motion tweened animations. Recall that a shape tween takes one shape and transforms it into another shape. To create a shape tween, you create the graphic content in the beginning and ending frames of the animation and Flash creates the tweened frames to complete the animation. The object in a shape tween must *not* be a symbol or a grouped object. This is different from a motion tween where the object must be converted into a symbol. A shape tween is indicated in the Timeline by a line and a light green color for the frames. You can also control the shape tween's acceleration and deceleration by changing the Ease value in the Property inspector. The Jenny's Oyster Hut banner does not require a shape tween.

Creating Graphic Symbol Animations

Both movie clip and graphic symbols have their own Timelines. With a movie clip symbol, the frames in its Timeline play independently of the document's main Timeline. However, with a graphic symbol, the frames in its Timeline are synchronized with the document's main Timeline. For example, suppose you insert a movie clip instance that contains an animation with ten frames into a document whose main Timeline has only one frame. Even though the main Timeline contains only one frame, the movie clip's ten frames will still play in their entirety. However, if you insert a graphic instance that contains an animation with ten frames into a document whose main Timeline has only one frame, then only one frame of the graphic instance will play. If you want all ten frames of the graphic instance to play you must extend the length of the document's main Timeline to at least ten frames. Graphic symbols are useful when you want to synchronize the animations in the symbol to that of the main Timeline.

Another difference between graphic symbols and movie clips is that movie clip instances always start playing from their first frame. With a graphic instance, however, you can specify which of its frames to play first. As a result, if you create a graphic symbol animation and then create several instances of the symbol, each instance can have a different starting frame. For example, one instance can start playing at Frame 1 of its Timeline while another instance can start playing at Frame 20. Using this technique, you can create multiple instances of one graphic symbol in the same scene and have each instance exhibit a different behavior.

Also, graphic symbol instances display their animation when you scrub the playhead in the document's main Timeline or play the main Timeline's animation on the Stage. You do not need to test the document in the Flash Player to see the animations contained in instances of graphic symbols as you do with animations contained in instances of movie clips, which appear as static objects when played on the Stage. This occurs because the frames of graphic symbols are synchronized with the document's main Timeline, while the frames of a movie clip symbol are independent of the document's main Timeline.

Creating Graphic Symbol Animations

You create a graphic symbol animation the same way you create a movie clip animation. When you create a new symbol, you just specify Graphic as the symbol's behavior. The symbol displays a different icon in the document's Library panel to indicate its behavior type. After you create a graphic symbol animation, you can create instances of the symbol on the Stage in the same way you create instances of movie clip symbols. However, when you select an instance of a graphic symbol on the Stage, you can use the Property inspector to indicate in which frame you want the instance's animation to begin. You do this by entering a value in the First box, as shown in Figure 3-29.

Figure 3-29 Graphic instance properties in the Property inspector

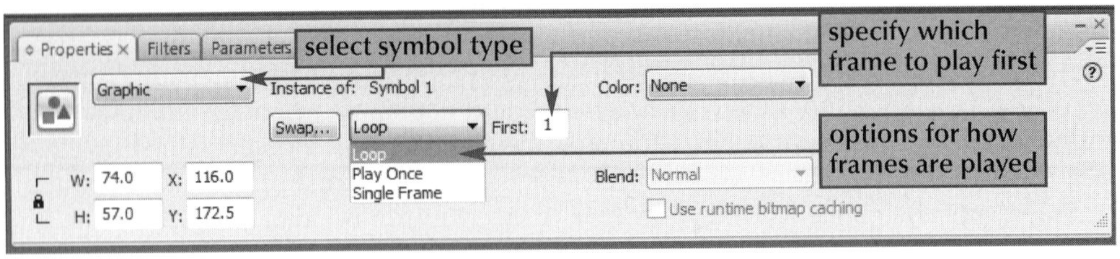

You can also specify how you want the instance's animation to play. The Loop option plays the animation continuously. The Play Once option plays the animation only one time starting with the frame specified in the First box. The Single Frame option plays only the frame specified in the First box.

The Jenny's Oyster Hut Web site banner should contain an animation that displays the phrases "Fried Shrimp" and "Shrimp Scampi" on the Stage. These phrases will appear one at a time and continuously change from one phrase to another. The animation will be placed in several places in the document. Aly suggests that you create the animation only once, as a graphic symbol animation, and then create several instances of this symbol in the Shrimp specials scene, specifying each instance to begin its animation in a different frame.

To create the graphic symbol animation in the Shrimp specials scene:

1. On the Edit bar, click the **Edit Scene** button, and then click **Shrimp specials** to switch to this scene.
2. Click **Insert** on the menu bar, click **New Symbol** to open the Create New Symbol dialog box, type **Phrases** in the Name box, click the **Graphic** option button, and then click the **OK** button. The graphic symbol named Phrases appears in symbol-editing mode.
3. In the Tools panel, click the **Text** tool, and then, in the Property inspector, set the font to **Monotype Corsiva**, the font size to **24**, the text (fill) color to **white** (#FFFFFF), and the alignment to **Align Center**.
4. On the center of the Stage, create a single-line text block, and then type **Fried Shrimp**.
5. In the Tools panel, click the **Selection** tool to select the text block.

   The registration point of a symbol is usually at the center of the symbol, and it can be used to control how the symbol is animated. To align several symbols in an animation, make each symbol's registration point the same. You can set the registration point when you create the symbol in symbol-editing mode by setting the symbol's X and Y coordinates for its registration point. Zero X and Y coordinates center the symbol on the Stage. You set the symbol's coordinates in the Info panel, which displays the registration point coordinates when the Registration/Transformation button displays a small circle in its lower-right corner.
6. Click **Window** on the menu bar, click **Info** to open the Info panel, click the **Registration/Transformation** button so that it displays a small circle in its lower-right corner, if necessary, and then type **0** in the X and Y boxes. The text block is centered on the Stage. See Figure 3-30.

Tip

After you click the Font arrow in the Property inspector, you can type the first letter of the font name to scroll the list to that name.

Settings in the Info panel **Figure 3-30**

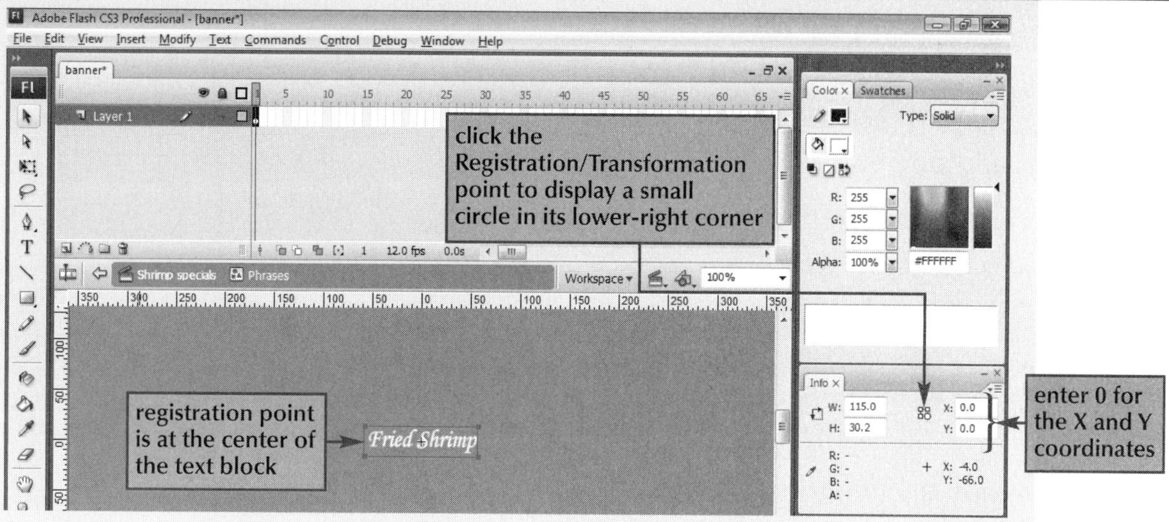

Next, you will convert the text block to a movie clip and duplicate it. To animate the text block using a motion tween, the text block must be a symbol.

7. With the text block still selected, click **Modify** on the menu bar, click **Convert to Symbol** to open the Convert to Symbol dialog box, type **Fried Shrimp text** in the Name box, click the **Movie clip** option button, click the **center** registration point, and then click the **OK** button. The movie clip symbol is created inside the graphic symbol.
8. Click the title bar of the panel group containing the Color panel. The panel group collapses and the contents of the Library panel are visible.
9. In the Library panel, right-click the **Fried Shrimp text** symbol to open the context menu, and then click **Duplicate**. The Duplicate Symbol dialog box opens.
10. Type **Shrimp Scampi text** in the Name box, make sure the **Movie clip** option button is selected, and then click the **OK** button. The dialog box closes. You will change the text in the duplicate symbol.
11. On the Edit bar, click the **Edit Symbols** button, and then click **Shrimp Scampi text**. The symbol opens in symbol-editing mode.
12. In the Tools panel, if necessary, click the **Selection** tool, double-click the text block, change the text to **Shrimp Scampi**, and then, in the Info panel, set the X and Y values to **0**, if necessary. See Figure 3-31.

Figure 3-31 Edited Shrimp Scampi text symbol

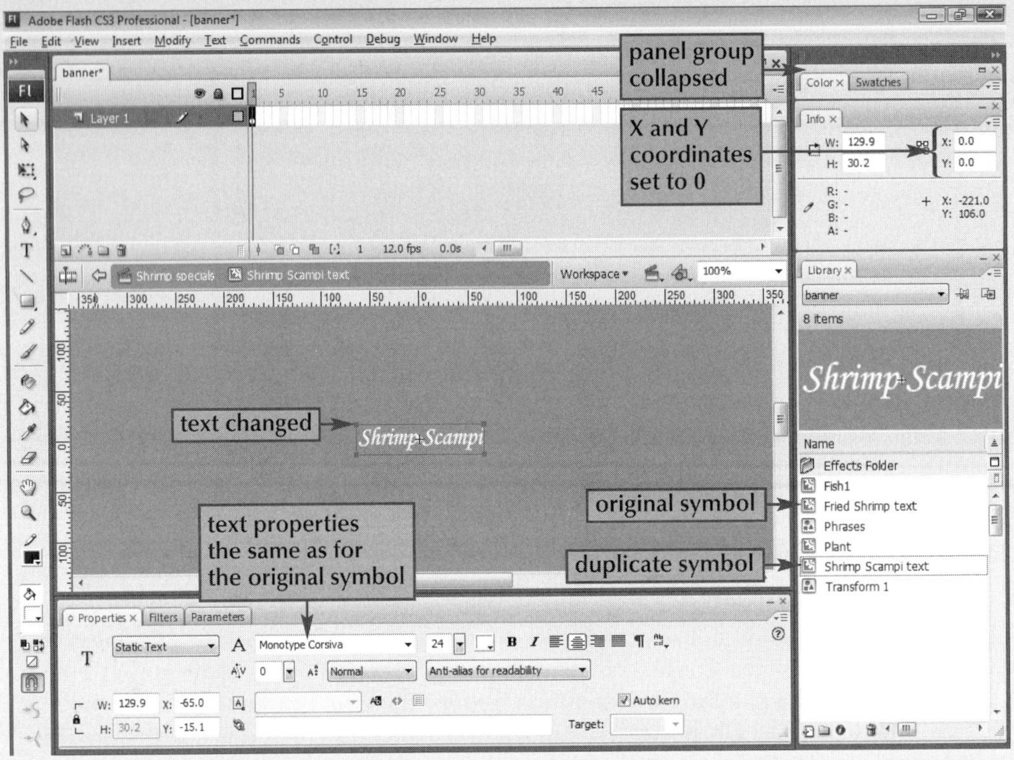

13. On the Edit bar, click the **Edit Symbols** button, and then click **Phrases**. The Phrases symbol opens in symbol-editing mode. You will create the Fried Shrimp text animation next.
14. In the Timeline, rename Layer 1 to **Fried Shrimp**, click **Frame 15**, and then insert a keyframe. Regular frames are added in Frames 2 through 14.
15. In the Tools panel, click the **Selection** tool, if necessary, and then select the **Fried Shrimp text** instance.
16. In the Property inspector, click the **Color** button, click **Alpha**, and then, if necessary, type **0** in the Alpha Amount box. The Fried Shrimp text disappears because an alpha amount of 0% makes an object completely transparent.
17. Right-click **Frame 1** to open the context menu, and then click **Create Motion Tween**. The motion tween is created between Frames 1 and 15.
18. Press the **Enter** key to test the animation. The Fried Shrimp text instance fades out throughout the animation.

You need to create a similar animation for the next phrase. Instead of repeating all of these steps in a new layer, you can copy the frames in the Fried Shrimp layer and paste them into a new layer. Then, you can swap the instances of the Fried Shrimp text symbol with instances of the Shrimp Scampi text symbol. Recall that a motion tween has a beginning keyframe and an ending keyframe and that each keyframe has an instance of a symbol. When swapping instances of a symbol in a motion tween, you need to swap the instances in both the beginning and ending keyframes. Finally, you will reposition the frames that contain the motion tween so that the animation for the second phrase starts later than the animation for the first phrase.

To create an animation for the Shrimp Scampi text symbol in a new layer:

1. In the Timeline, click the **Fried Shrimp** layer name to select all of its frames.
2. Click **Edit** on the menu bar, point to **Timeline**, and then click **Copy Frames**. The frames are copied to the Windows Clipboard.
3. In the Timeline, click the **Insert Layer** button to insert a new layer, rename Layer 2 to **Shrimp Scampi**, and then click the **Shrimp Scampi** layer name to select all of its frames.
4. Click **Edit** on the menu bar, point to **Timeline**, and then click **Paste Frames**. The frames containing the Fried Shrimp text animation are pasted into the Shrimp Scampi layer.

   You need to swap the Fried Shrimp text symbol with the Shrimp Scampi text symbol.
5. In the Timeline, click **Frame 1** of the Shrimp Scampi layer, and then click the instance of the Fried Shrimp text symbol at the center of the Stage. You can tell the instance is selected because the Property inspector shows "Instance of: Fried Shrimp text."
6. In the Property inspector, click the **Swap** button to open the Swap Symbol dialog box, and then click **Shrimp Scampi text**. See Figure 3-32.

Tip

You can use the Duplicate Symbol button in the Swap Symbol dialog box to make a copy of a symbol that is stored in the document's library.

Figure 3-32 Swap Symbol dialog box

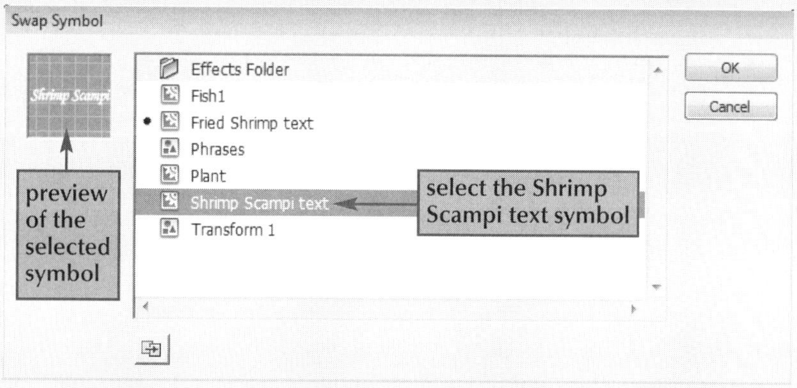

7. Click the **OK** button. The Fried Shrimp text instance is replaced with the Shrimp Scampi text instance. The text blocks for the two layers overlap on the Stage, so one word appears on top of the other. You will fix this in the next set of steps.

   Next, you'll swap the instance in the second keyframe.
8. In the Timeline, click **Frame 15** of the Shrimp Scampi layer, and then click blue outline of the **Fried Shrimp text** instance at the center of the Stage. The words are not visible because you set the alpha amount to 0% at this keyframe.
9. In the Property inspector, click the **Swap** button to open the Swap Symbol dialog box, click **Shrimp Scampi text**, and then click the **OK** button. The Fried Shrimp text instance is replaced with the Shrimp Scampi text instance.

The animation in the Shrimp Scampi layer works the same as the one in the Fried Shrimp layer, except that the symbol being animated is the Shrimp Scampi text symbol and not the Fried Shrimp text symbol. Instead of having to repeat the steps to create an animation in the new layer, you copied an existing animation and swapped the instances in the keyframes.

Now that both animations are complete, you need to reposition the Shrimp Scampi text animation so that the two animations do not occur at the same time. You want the Fried Shrimp text animation to start first, followed by the Shrimp Scampi text animation. This means that the Shrimp Scampi text animation will begin at Frame 16 after the Fried Shrimp text animation ends. The Shrimp Scampi text animation's 15 frames will end at Frame 30. You can easily change the location of frames within a layer.

To reposition the frames within the Shrimp Scampi layer:

1. In the Timeline of the Shrimp Scampi layer, drag the pointer from **Frame 1** to **Frame 15**, and then release the mouse button. The frames that make up the Shrimp Scampi text animation are selected.

   Trouble? If the keyframe in Frame 1 moves when you drag the pointer, you released the mouse button after clicking the first keyframe, and then started dragging from that same keyframe. This moved the keyframe instead of selecting the series of frames. Click Edit on the menu bar, click Undo, and then repeat Step 1.

2. Drag the selected frames to the right so that the first keyframe starts on **Frame 16** of the same layer. See Figure 3-33.

Figure 3-33 Selected frames being moved

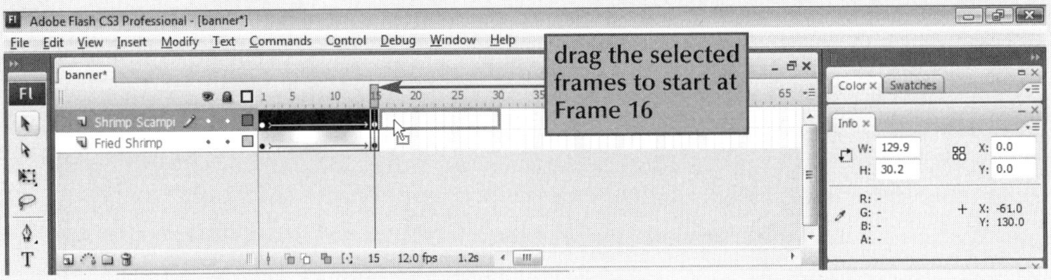

3. Release the mouse button. The selected frames start on Frame 16 and end on Frame 30.
4. Drag the playhead to Frame 1, and then press the **Enter** key. The phrases appear and fade out in turn. The Phrases graphic animation is now complete.
5. On the Edit bar, click the **Shrimp Specials** scene to exit symbol-editing mode and return to the Shrimp Specials scene.

You want to insert two instances of the Phrases symbol onto the Stage for the Shrimp Specials scene. You will then change the starting frame for one of the instances. The instances will each start off displaying a different phrase and display the subsequent phrase in turn.

To insert the Phrases graphic symbol instances and change their starting frames:

1. In the Timeline of the Shrimp Specials scene, insert a new layer above the ocean layer, name the layer **Phrases**, and then click **Frame 1** of the Phrases layer.
2. Drag two instances of the Phrases symbol from the Library panel to the bottom part of the Stage, as shown in Figure 3-34.

Figure 3-34 Phrases graphic symbol instances

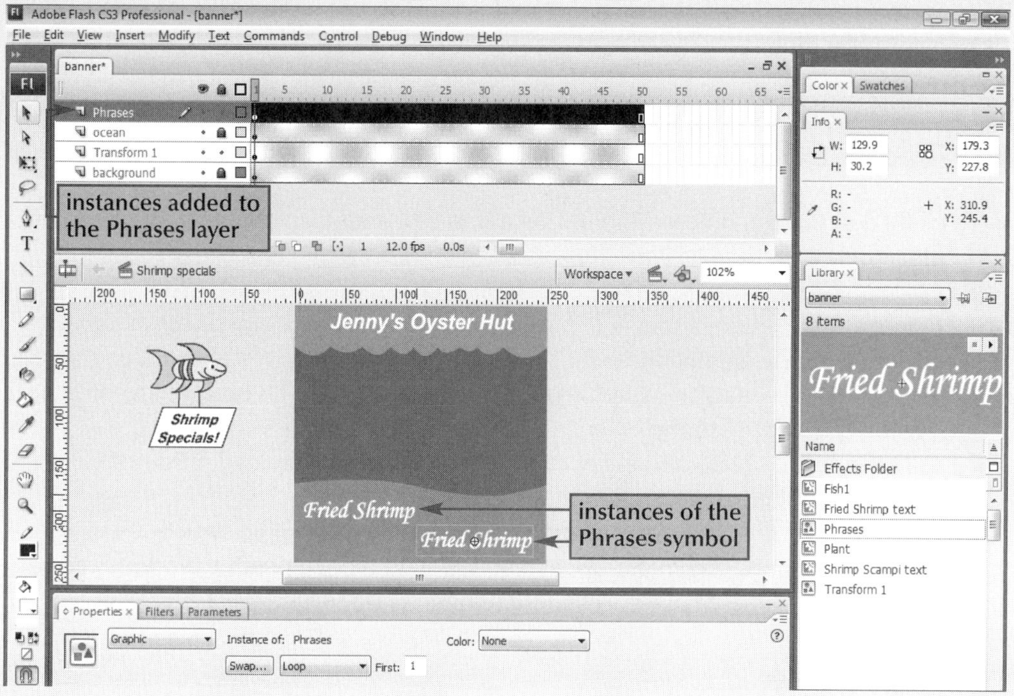

3. Select the **Phrases** symbol instance on the right side of the Stage, if necessary, and then, in the Property inspector, type **10** in the First box. This instance will start after the first motion tween begins, but before the second motion tween begins in the Phrases animation.
4. In the Property inspector, make sure the instance's option is set to **Loop**. The Fried Shrimp text displays slightly faded.
5. Click the pasteboard, and then press the **Enter** key to test the animation. The Phrases instances each start at a different frame as they fade in and out.
6. Save the banner.

Now that you have completed the animation for the Shrimp Specials scene, you will test the banner to see how its various animations work. When you test the document's animation on the Stage, Flash plays only the current scene. To see how all of the scenes work together, you need to test the movie in the Flash Player window. Each scene then plays in sequence with the animation repeating until you close the Flash Player window. You will test the completed document next.

To test the entire banner document's scenes in Flash Player:

1. Click **Control** on the menu bar, and then click **Test Movie**. A Flash Player window opens and each scene plays in sequence.
2. When you are finished viewing the animation, click **File** on the Flash Player menu bar, and then click **Close**. The Flash Player window closes and you return to the Flash document.
3. Close the banner.

Tip

You can also press the Ctrl+Enter keys to test the movie.

In this session, you created animations using motion tweens and you learned how to create shape tweens. You also learned how to create animations using graphic symbols. Aly is pleased with the completed banner and is looking forward to showing it to Jenny of Jenny's Oyster Hut.

Review | Session 3.3 Quick Check

1. Briefly describe the difference between a frame-by-frame animation and a tweened animation.
2. How many objects can you have on a layer with a motion tween?
3. How can you animate a movie clip symbol so that each of its instances automatically contains the animation?
4. What type of tweened animation would you create to have an object move from one side of the Stage to the other?
5. True or False? To create a shape tween, the object being animated must first be converted to a symbol.
6. List two differences between a movie clip symbol and a graphic symbol.
7. Why do animations within graphic symbols play in a document's main Timeline without the document having to be tested in the Flash Player?

Review | Tutorial Summary

In this tutorial, you learned about the different elements that make up a Flash animation. You explored the Timeline and worked with layers and frames with multiple scenes. You also created animations in Flash using the Timeline effects, frame-by-frame animations, tweened animations, and graphic symbol animations. When you created tweened animations, you learned how to create both motion tweened and shape tweened animations. You also learned the different ways to test an animation.

Key Terms

frame
frame-by-frame animation
keyframe
layer
layer folder
motion guide layer
motion tweening
scene
shape tweening
Timeline effect
tweened animation

Practice | Review Assignments

Practice the skills you learned in the tutorial.

Data File needed for the Review Assignments: JennysAd.fla

After reviewing an animated ad banner, Aly asks you to modify the banner so that the text animation in the first scene includes the word "Anytime!". She also wants you to animate the title text block in the first scene to fade in as the fish pulls the sign. Finally, she asks you to add another animated fish in the second scene that swims in a direction opposite the current fish.

1. Open the **JennysAd.fla** file located in the Tutorial.03\Review folder included with your Data Files, save the file in the same folder as **JennysAdComplete.fla**, and then set the workspace to its default layout.
2. In the Daily specials scene, unlock the background layer and select the Jenny's Oyster Hut text block. Use the Edit menu to cut the text block and place it in the Windows Clipboard. Insert a new layer above the background layer and name it **Title**. Use the Paste in Place command on the Edit menu to paste the text block in the layer. Change the text color to light yellow (#FFFF66). Insert a Transition Timeline effect. Set the Effect Duration to 40 frames and select only the Fade In effect so the text will fade in throughout the Daily specials scene.
3. In the Library panel, make a duplicate of the Lunch text symbol and name it **Anytime text**. Edit the Anytime text symbol by changing the Lunch text to read **Anytime!**.
4. Edit the Text animation symbol by inserting a new layer in its Timeline. Name the layer **Anytime**. Select all of the Dinner layer's frames and copy them to the Clipboard. Select all of the Anytime layer's frames and paste the copied frames. Select Frames 11 through 21 of the Anytime layer, and then move them so they start on Frame 22 of the same layer.
5. Select Frame 22 of the Anytime layer and swap the Dinner text instance on the Stage with an instance of the Anytime text symbol. Select Frame 32 and also swap this Dinner text instance with an instance of the Anytime text symbol. Exit symbol-editing mode.
6. In the Daily specials scene, select the Text layer, and then add two more instances of the Text animation symbol to the Stage. Place one on the center-left of the Stage and start its animation in Frame 5. Place the other on the center-right of the Stage and start its animation in Frame 15.
7. In the Library panel, make a duplicate of the Fish1 symbol and name it **Fish2**, and then edit the Fish2 symbol by changing the color of each of its fins to yellow (#FFFF00). Exit symbol-editing mode.
8. In the Swimming fish scene, insert a new layer above the fish layer and name it **fish2**. In this layer, drag an instance of the Fish2 symbol to the pasteboard next to the lower-right corner of the Stage. Create two motion tweens for this Fish2 instance similar to the motion tweens in the fish layer. You want the Fish2 instance to start from the pasteboard on the right side of the Stage, swim left across the Stage, stop just before the left side of the Stage, and then turn around and swim back to its starting point.
9. Submit the finished document to your instructor, either in printed or electronic form, as requested.

Apply | Case Problem 1

Create a new Flash document with tween animations and Timeline effects.

Data File needed for this Case Problem: sssbanner.fla

Sandy's Scrapbook Store Planning is well underway at Sandy's Scrapbook Store for the grand opening celebration. Sandy Rodriguez, the store's owner, is expecting a good turnout for the celebration. Sandy meets with John Rossini to discuss the development of the banner for the new Web site. Sandy asks John to make the banner more festive by adding animation to it. John has started developing the revised banner shown in Figure 3-35 and wants you to help him complete the task by adding animations for block graphics and balloon graphics. The balloons will float up as the block graphics rotate. You will also add a drop shadow effect to the Grand Opening text.

Figure 3-35 **Initial version of the revised Sandy's Scrapbook Store banner**

1. Open the **sssbanner.fla** file located in the Tutorial.03\Case1 folder included with your Data Files, and then save the banner in the same folder as **sssbannerRevised.fla**. The document contains some of the graphic elements that will be used to create the animated banner.
2. Select the grouped object in the lower-left corner of the Stage with the yellow square and the word "Sandy's." Convert the object to a graphic symbol named **square**.
3. Convert the balloon into a movie clip symbol named **balloon1**. Be sure to include both the balloon and the string.
4. Delete the square and balloon graphics from the Stage.
5. Change the name of Layer 1 to **background** and the name of Layer 2 to **text**. Insert regular frames to extend both layers through Frame 30.
6. Create a duplicate of the balloon1 symbol and name it **balloon2**. Edit the balloon2 symbol to change the color of the balloon to red. Create another duplicate of the balloon1 symbol and name it **balloon3**. Edit the balloon3 symbol to change its color to pink.
7. Insert a new layer above the background layer and name it **balloon1**. On this layer, drag an instance of the balloon1 symbol to the lower-left corner of the Stage. Create a motion tween so that the balloon moves up to the top of the banner throughout the layer's 30 frames.
8. Insert a new layer and name it **balloon2**. On this layer, drag an instance of the balloon2 symbol to the middle of the Stage. Create a motion tween so that the balloon moves up to the top of the banner throughout the layer's 30 frames.
9. Insert a new layer and name it **balloon3**. On this layer, drag an instance of the balloon3 symbol to the lower-right corner of the Stage. Create a motion tween so that the balloon moves up to the top of the banner throughout the layer's 30 frames.
10. Double-click the square symbol in the Library panel to open it in symbol-editing mode. Select the square graphic and convert it to a movie clip symbol named **square_mc**.

EXPLORE 11. Create a motion tween that spans 10 frames and has the square_mc symbol rotate clockwise one time throughout the animation. Return to Scene 1.

12. Insert a new layer and name it **squares**. Insert an instance of the square symbol and place it to the left of the bottom text block. Insert another instance of the square symbol and place it to the right of the bottom text block. The second instance should start its animation in Frame 5 of its Timeline.

EXPLORE 13. Select the bottom text block and insert a Drop Shadow Timeline effect. Use the default settings for the effect. Select the top text block and insert a Transform Timeline effect that changes the color of the text to red.

14. Test the animation.

15. Submit the finished document to your instructor, either in printed or electronic form, as requested.

Apply | Case Problem 2

Create a frame-by-frame animation of a movie clip symbol and two Timeline effect animations with text.

Data File needed for this Case Problem: aczbanner.fla

Alamo City Zoo Janet Meyers, zoo director, meets with Alex Smith to review the banner that Alex has developed promoting the new bear exhibit. They agree to make the banner more interesting by adding animation to it. Alex has started developing a revised banner, as shown in Figure 3-36, and he wants you to help him complete the task by adding two text blocks that will be animated and by animating the bear paw graphic.

Figure 3-36 **Initial version of the Alamo City Zoo banner**

1. Open the **aczbanner.fla** file located in the Tutorial.03\Case2 folder included with your Data Files, and then save the banner in the same folder as **aczbannerComplete.fla**. The document contains some of the graphic elements that will be used to create the animated banner.
2. Select the bear paw instance on the Stage and delete it.
3. Create a new movie clip symbol named **bear tracks**. In symbol-editing mode, add a horizontal guide at the center of the Stage. Line up the guide with the 0 mark on the left vertical ruler. Add another horizontal guide approximately 40 pixels above the first guide.
4. Drag an instance of the bear paw symbol from the Library panel to the center of the Stage. If necessary, select the instance and set both the X and Y values in the Property inspector to 0 so that the center of the instance is exactly centered on the Stage.

5. Insert a keyframe at Frame 5, and then drag another instance of the bear paw symbol so that its center is on the top guide and approximately 30 pixels to the right of the first instance. Insert a keyframe at Frame 10, and then drag an instance of the bear paw symbol so that its center is on the bottom guide and approximately 30 pixels to the right of the second bear paw instance.
6. Insert a keyframe at Frame 15, and then drag an instance of the bear paw symbol so that its center is on the top guide and approximately 30 pixels to the right of the third instance. Insert a keyframe at Frame 20, and then drag an instance of the bear paw symbol so that its center is on the bottom guide and approximately 30 pixels to the right of the fourth bear paw instance. Insert a keyframe at Frame 25, and then drag an instance of the bear paw symbol so that it is positioned on the top guide approximately 30 pixels from the fifth bear paw.
7. Insert a regular frame at Frame 40 of the Timeline to extend the end of the animation, and then test the animation. The bear paws should display one at a time.
8. In the main Timeline, rename Layer 1 as **bear layer**. Drag an instance of the bear tracks symbol from the Library panel to the Stage. Position the instance so that it is on the left side of the Stage and aligned with the bear graphic on the right side of the Stage. Insert a regular frame at Frame 40.
9. Insert a new layer and name it **title**. In Frame 1 of this layer, create a text block with the text **Alamo City Zoo**. Use a fancy font such as Monotype Corsiva and use a text font size such as 20. Select white for the font color and turn on the bold and italics styles. Center the text block on the banner above the bear tracks and bear.
10. Select the text block and insert a Transform Timeline effect. Enter 40 for the effect duration, change the scale percentage value to 200, check the Change Color check box, select black for the final color, and then set the motion ease to 80. Preview the effect to see the text increase in size and change in color. After you create the effect, test the animation in your document. The text block should start out small, grow in size, and change color.
11. Insert a new layer and name it **exhibit**. Create a text block in Frame 1 of the exhibit layer with the text **Visit the Bear Exhibit!** using the same font and font size as the title text. Use black for the font color. Center the text block below the bear tracks and bear. Select this text block and insert an Expand Timeline effect. Enter 40 for the effect duration, select the Both option, and then set the fragment offset to 1. Preview the effect to see the text expand and contract. After you create the effect, test the animation in your document. The text block should expand and contract throughout the animation.
12. Test the animation.
13. Submit the finished document to your instructor, either in printed or electronic form, as requested.

Challenge | Case Problem 3

Add a new scene, create shape tweens, add a Timeline effect, and create a frame-by-frame animation.

Data File needed for this Case Problem: wclogo.fla

Westcreek Nursery Alice Washington, owner of Westcreek Nursery, meets with Amanda Lester, who was contracted to update the company's Web site. Amanda shows Alice the logo she developed and they both agree that the logo could be enhanced by adding some animation. Amanda decides to revise the logo by adding shape tweens to the company name and a masking effect on the word Flowers. You will animate the Westcreek Nursery text and the FLOWERS text. Each should be on a separate layer. The banner will look similar to the one shown in Figure 3-37.

Figure 3-37 **Westcreek Nursery logo**

1. Open the **wclogo.fla** file located in the Tutorial.03\Case3 folder included with your Data Files, and then save the file in the same folder as **wclogoEnhanced.fla**.
2. Rename Layer 1 to **Background**, and then insert regular frames so that the layer extends to Frame 30.
3. Insert a layer and name it **Westcreek**. Insert another layer and name it **Flowers**. Insert one more layer and name it **Nursery**.
4. Select the Westcreek text block. Use the Cut command on the Edit menu to cut the text block. Then, on Frame 1 of the Westcreek layer, use the Paste in Place command on the Edit menu to place the text in the same relative position as it was in the Background layer. Select the Nursery text block. Use the Cut command to cut the text. Insert a keyframe on Frame 15 of the Nursery layer. In this frame, use the Paste in Place command to place the text in the same relative position as it was in the Background layer.
5. Select the FLOWERS text block in the center of the Stage. Make sure you do not select any other graphics besides the text. Use the Cut command to cut the text block. Then, on Frame 1 of the Flowers layer, use the Paste in Place command to place the text in the same relative position as it was on the Background layer.
6. Use the Scene panel to create a duplicate of Scene 1. Rename Scene 1 copy to **Wheel animation** and rename Scene 1 to **Flowers animation**.

EXPLORE

7. In the Flowers animation scene, select the Westcreek text and use the Break Apart command to break the text apart into individual letters. Use the command a second time to break the letters into filled shapes.
8. Insert a keyframe in Frame 15 of the Westcreek layer. In the Frame 1, draw a rectangle over the Westcreek text block. Use green (#009900) for the rectangle's fill and do not include a stroke. If necessary, turn off Snap to Objects to make it easier to draw the rectangle. The size of the rectangle should be just slightly larger than the text block itself. Insert a shape tween in Frame 1. Test the animation. The rectangle should transform into the text Westcreek.

EXPLORE

9. In Frame 15 of the Nursery layer, select the Nursery text and apply the Break Apart command twice to break the text into filled shapes. Insert a keyframe in Frame 25 of the Nursery layer.
10. In Frame 15 of the Nursery layer, draw a rectangle with a green (#009900) fill and no stroke. The rectangle should be slightly larger than the text block. Insert a shape tween in Frame 15. Test the animation. The rectangle should transform into the text "Nursery."
11. In the same scene, select the FLOWERS text in Frame 1 of the Flowers layer and insert a Transform Timeline effect. Enter 30 for the effect duration, select Change Position By, set the value in the X box to 5, and enter 25 in the Final Alpha box. Preview the effect to see the text block move slightly to the right and fade out gradually. Once you create the effect, test the animation in your document. The text block should move slightly from left to right and fade out.

EXPLORE

12. Switch to the Wheel animation scene. Select the left wheel graphic below the FLOWERS text and convert it to a graphic symbol named **Wheel**. Open the Wheel symbol in symbol-editing mode. Zoom in on the wheel graphic, and then apply the Break Apart command twice to ungroup the two circles that make up this graphic.
13. Draw a short horizontal line across the middle of the white area of the wheel graphic to represent a wheel spoke. Use black as the color and 2 for the stroke height. Draw a short vertical line across the white area of the wheel graphic to represent another wheel spoke.

EXPLORE

14. To create a frame-by-frame animation to rotate the wheel, first open the Transform panel. Insert a keyframe in Frame 2. Select the wheel graphic, if necessary, and in the Transform panel enter a value of 30 for the number of degrees to rotate the wheel. (Be sure to press the Enter key to apply the Rotate value.) Insert another keyframe at Frame 3 and enter 30 for the rotate value in the Transform panel to rotate the wheel again. Continue this process of inserting a keyframe and entering 30 for the rotate value in the Transform panel until you reach Frame 12 and the wheel has been rotated 360 degrees. Exit symbol-editing mode and return to the Wheel animation scene.
15. Delete the original wheel under the R of FLOWERS on the Stage and add an instance of the Wheel graphic symbol in the same position. Test the animation to see the wheels rotate.
16. Submit the finished document to your instructor, either in printed or electronic form, as requested.

Apply | Case Problem 4

Create tween animations, shape animations, and a frame-by-frame animation.

Data File needed for this Case Problem: rdabanner.fla

Regional Dietetic Association Richard Perez, president of the Regional Dietetic Association, meets with Katie Ellison who has been hired to improve the association's Web site to discuss the progress in the development of a new banner. They decide that adding animation to the banner will enhance its appearance. Katie has started to develop the banner and instructs you to complete it by adding animation using the shapes she has created. You will also create an animation of key phrases to be displayed on the banner. The banner will look similar to that shown in Figure 3-38.

Figure 3-38 Regional Dietetic Association banner

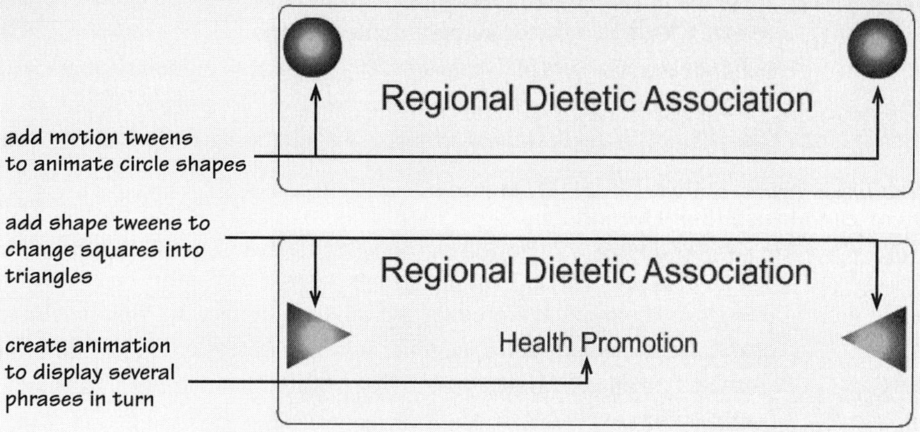

1. Open the **rdabanner.fla** file located in the Tutorial.03\Case4 folder included with your Data Files, and then save the banner in the same folder as **rdabannerRevised.fla**. The document contains some of the graphic elements that will be used to create the animated banner.
2. Draw a rectangle with no fill, a black solid stroke with a stroke height of 1, and rounded corners to frame all of the contents on the Stage. The sides of the rectangle should be close to the edges of the Stage and all of the contents on the Stage should be inside the rectangle.
3. Select the circle graphic on the Stage and convert it to a movie clip symbol named **circle**. Select the square graphic and convert it to a movie clip symbol named **square**. Delete the circle and square symbol instances from the Stage.
4. Change the name of Layer 1 to **background** and then insert regular frames to extend it to Frame 45.
5. Insert a new layer and name it **circle1**. Add an instance of the circle symbol and place it on the upper-left corner of the Stage inside the rectangle. Insert a keyframe at Frame 20. In Frame 20, move the circle instance to the lower-right corner of the Stage inside the rectangle. Create a motion tween at Frame 1. The circle should move from the upper-left corner of the Stage to the lower-right corner.
6. Insert a keyframe at Frame 40 of the circle1 layer. In Frame 40, move the circle instance to the upper-right corner of the Stage. Add a motion tween at Frame 20 so that the circle instance moves from the lower-right corner of the Stage to the upper-right corner.
7. Insert a new layer and name it **circle2**. In Frame 1 of the circle2 layer, add an instance of the circle symbol to the upper-right corner of the Stage inside the rectangle. Insert a keyframe at Frame 20. In Frame 20, move the circle instance to the lower-left corner of the Stage inside the rectangle. Create a motion tween at Frame 1. The circle should move from the upper-right corner of the Stage to the lower-left corner.
8. Insert a keyframe at Frame 40 of the circle2 layer. In Frame 40, move the circle instance to the upper-left corner of the Stage. Add a motion tween at Frame 20 so that the circle instance moves from the lower-left corner of the Stage to the upper-left corner.
9. Use the Scene panel to create a duplicate of Scene 1. Rename Scene 1 to **Intro** and rename Scene 1 copy to **Words animation**. In the Words animation scene, delete the circle1 layer and the circle2 layer. Move the text block to the top of the Stage just below the top side of the rectangle.

10. Create a new text block with the words **Peer Networking** on the center of the Stage. Use Arial for the font, black for the font color, and 20 for the font size. Convert the text block to a graphic symbol named **words**.
11. Edit the words symbol to create a frame-by-frame animation that changes the text block to a different phrase periodically. In symbol-editing mode, select the text block and, if necessary, in the Info panel click the Registration/Transformation button to display the registration coordinates, and change the X and Y values to 0 to center the text.
12. Insert a keyframe at Frame 9 and change the text block to read **Professional Development**. Set the X and Y values in the Info panel to 0 to center the text. Insert a keyframe at Frame 17 and change the text to **Health Promotion**. Center the text. Insert a keyframe at Frame 25 and change the text to **Member Benefits**. Center the text. Insert a keyframe at Frame 33 and change the text to **Join Now!** Center the text. Insert a regular frame at Frame 45 to extend the symbol's Timeline. Exit symbol-editing mode.

EXPLORE

13. Insert a new layer and name it **square1**. In Frame 1 of the square1 layer, add an instance of the square symbol so that it is centered on the left side of the Stage. Use the Break Apart command to convert the instance to a filled shape. Insert a keyframe at Frame 20 of the square1 layer. At Frame 20, use the Selection tool to change the square shape to a triangle shape. Do this by first deselecting the square shape and then moving the upper-right corner of the square down to the center of the square's right side. Then move the lower-right corner of the square up to the center of the square's right side. Insert a shape tween at Frame 1. Test the animation. The square shape should change to a triangle shape during the animation.

EXPLORE

14. Insert a new layer and name it **square2**. Add an instance of the square symbol to the right side of the Stage and break it apart. Create another shape tween in Frames 1 through 20 in this layer to have the square shape change to a triangle shape. At Frame 20, deselect the square shape, and then change it to a triangle shape by changing the corners on the left side of the square. Test the animation in your Web browser.
15. Submit the finished document to your instructor, either in printed or electronic form, as requested.

Review | Quick Check Answers

Session 3.1

1. to coordinate and control the frames that make up an animation and to organize the layers that contain the different elements of a document
2. by looking at the location of the playhead on the Timeline header or the current frame number displayed at the bottom of the Timeline
3. 12 fps
4. Frames contain content that is displayed for an instant in time and are displayed one after another to create the perception of movement. Layers are made up of one or more frames and are used to organize the graphic elements of a document.
5. a container in the Timeline in which you can place layers; allows you to work more efficiently when you have a lot of layers
6. a way to break up a Flash document into separate mini-movies, each with its own Timeline
7. by the order they are listed in the Scene panel or by the order they appear in the Edit Scene button on the Edit bar

8. If you have multiple scenes in a document, the default names might not be descriptive of the content in each scene. To make it easier to know what a scene contains, you should rename it.

Session 3.2

1. a way to create an animation or a special effect by selecting from options in a dialog box without having to know how to create the animation yourself
2. True
3. Click Modify on the menu bar, point to Timeline Effects, and then click Edit Effect to open the same dialog box used to create the effect.
4. a keyframe
5. False; the object being animated in a frame-by-frame animation does not need to be a symbol.
6. Yes, you include regular frames in a frame-by-frame animation to indicate that the content has not changed from the previous keyframe.
7. to ensure the animation works the way you intended and meets the project's requirements

Session 3.3

1. A frame-by-frame animation requires that you create the content for each of the frames. With a tweened animation, Flash creates the frames between the beginning and ending keyframes.
2. only one object
3. Create the animation in the symbol's Timeline instead of in the document's Timeline. Each instance of the movie clip symbol then automatically contains the animation.
4. a motion tweened animation
5. False; an object used in a shape tween must not be converted to a symbol.
6. A movie clip symbol's Timeline is independent from the document's main Timeline, whereas a graphic symbol's Timeline is synchronized with the main document's Timeline. Also, when you test the document's animation within Flash, movie clip animations do not play, while graphic symbol animations do play. And you can also specify from which frame a graphic instance's animation should start. A movie clip animation always starts from the first frame of its Timeline.
7. The frames of a graphic symbol are synchronized with the document's main Timeline.

Ending Data Files

Tutorial.03 →

Tutorial
AC_RunActiveContent.js
banner.fla
banner.html
banner.swf
JacksonsRevised.fla
JacksonsRevised.swf

Review
JennysAdComplete.fla

Case1
sssbannerRevised.fla

Case2
aczbannerComplete.fla

Case3
wclogoEnhanced.fla

Case4
rdabannerRevised.fla

Tutorial 4

Objectives

Session 4.1
- Create an animation using a motion guide layer
- Create an animation using a mask layer

Session 4.2
- Animate text blocks
- Animate individual letters within a text block

Session 4.3
- Test animations using onion skinning
- Create nested movie clips
- Learn how to use the Movie Explorer

Creating Special Animations

Creating Animations with Motion Guides, Masks, Text Blocks, and Onion Skinning

Case | Admiral Web Design

Graphic designer Aly Garcia wants to develop a second banner for the Jenny's Oyster Hut Web site so that Jenny can have more than one to choose from. The second banner, which Aly has already started, will consist of three scenes. The first scene will include an animation of the company name. This will be a complex animation where the individual letters of the name rotate one after another onto the screen and into place to form the word Jenny's. As each letter moves into place, it will fade in and decrease in size. The second scene will have a fish swimming across the banner. Aly started the second scene, but you need change it so that the fish swims along a curved path and not just in a straight line. You will also create a second animated fish that exhibits more natural movements of its fins and tail. The third scene will be a new animation sequence that consists of several text blocks with the restaurant's name and a message promoting the seafood specials. You will also create an animation showing a spotlight effect on the Jenny's Oyster Hut name.

In this tutorial, you will create animations using a motion guide layer and a mask layer. You will work with text to create animations of text blocks and individual letters. You will also test an animation using onion skinning and work with nested movie clip symbols to create complex animations. Finally, you will use the Movie Explorer to review all of the document's elements.

Starting Data Files

Tutorial.04 →

Tutorial
AltBanner.fla
SportsLetters.fla
SportsMask.fla

Review
ReviewBanner.fla

Case1
sssAdDraft.fla

Case2
azcAdDraft.fla

Case3
(none)

Case4
(none)

Session 4.1

Creating an Animation Using Special Layers

Aly has begun working on one scene of the banner. The plan for this scene is shown in Figure 4-1. The scene requires two special types of layers: guide layers and mask layers. A **guide layer** contains graphic elements that serve as a guide when creating content on other layers. A **mask layer** contains a graphic element that hides the contents of the layer below it, which is called the **masked layer**. Both of these types of layers can also be used with animations. For example, you can create a guide layer that contains a path for an object on another layer to follow. You can also create an animation in a mask layer to show different areas of a masked layer throughout the animation. Both types of layers can be used with frame-by-frame and tweened animations.

Figure 4-1 **Animation plan for one scene of Jenny's Oyster Hut banner**

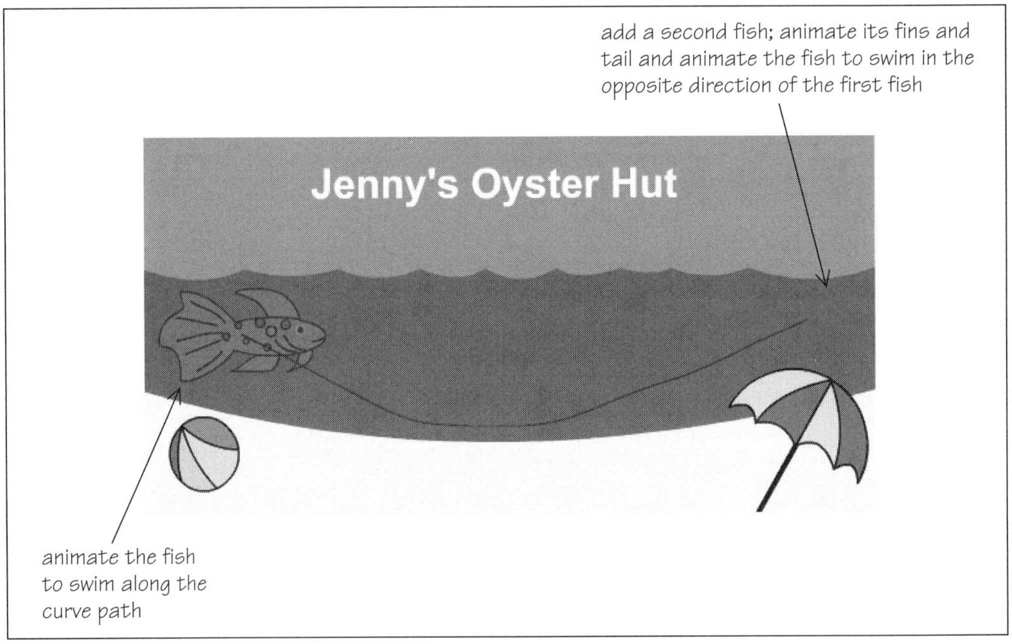

Using a Motion Guide Layer to Create Animation

When a guide layer is used to control the movement of an object in a motion tween, it is called a **motion guide layer**. A motion guide layer provides a path for an object in the guided layer to follow throughout the motion tween. The **guided layer** is the layer below a motion guide layer. This technique enables you to animate objects to move in a more natural way. Instead of having objects move only in straight lines, you can use a motion guide layer to have an object move along a curved path. For example, you can make a ball appear to be bouncing up and down while gradually coming to a stop, you can have a car move along a curved road, or you can have a bird fly in a circular pattern. Whatever path you draw on the guide layer, you can attach an object to follow that path.

To create a motion guide layer, you create the motion tween on one layer, and then insert a motion guide layer above that layer. The layer with the motion tween is indented and the motion guide layer has a motion guide icon to the left of its name.

To draw a path for the animated object to follow, you use a tool such as the Pencil, Pen, Line, or Brush tool to draw the path on the motion guide layer. To make the object on the guided layer follow the path, you need to attach it to the path. In the first frame of the guided layer that contains the motion tween, you move the object to the beginning of the path. In the last frame of the animation, you move the object to the end of the path. In both places, the registration point of the object must snap to the path. The registration point of a symbol is usually the center of the symbol.

Drawing the Path in a Motion Guide Layer | InSight

The line you draw for the path in a motion guide layer affects where on the Stage the animated object in the guided layer moves. Before you draw a line for the path, consider how the animated object will move in relation to other objects on the Stage. For example, to prevent the animated object from moving behind or in front of other objects, you should draw the line away from those objects. Also, consider the size of the animated object as you draw the line for the path. The larger the animated object, the farther away you should draw the line from other objects on the Stage.

Creating a Motion Guide Layer

The alternate banner for Jenny's Oyster Hut that Aly started includes a fish swimming across the banner in a straight line. Aly's notes, shown in Figure 4-1, indicate this fish needs to swim along a curved path. You will create this animation using a motion guide layer with a path for the animated fish to follow. The motion guide layer will guide the fish along a curved path from the left side of the banner, down towards the bottom, and then back up to the right side of the banner.

Creating a Motion Guide Layer | Reference Window

- Create a motion tween animation.
- In the Timeline, select the layer with the motion tween, and then click the Add Motion Guide button (or click Insert on the menu bar, point to Timeline, and then click Motion Guide).
- Use the Pen, Pencil, Line, Circle, Rectangle, or Brush tool to draw a path in the Motion Guide layer.
- Click first frame of the motion tween, and then, if necessary, in the Property inspector, click Orient to path and Snap check boxes to insert check marks.
- In the first frame of the motion tween, snap the registration point of the animated object to the beginning of the path.
- In the last frame of the motion tween, snap the registration point of the animated object to the end of the path.

You'll use a motion guide layer to create the path that the fish swims along.

To animate the fish along a path using a motion guide layer:

1. Open the **AltBanner.fla** file located in the **Tutorial.04\Tutorial** folder included with your Data Files, save the file as **NewBanner.fla** in the same folder, and then set the workspace to the default layout.
2. In the Timeline, click the **Fish1** layer to select it. This layer contains the motion tween for which you want to create a motion guide layer.
3. In the Timeline, click the **Add Motion Guide** button to insert a motion guide layer, and then scroll down to show the Fish1 layer. The Guide: Fish1 layer appears above the Fish1 layer. See Figure 4-2.

Figure 4-2 Motion guide layer added to Timeline

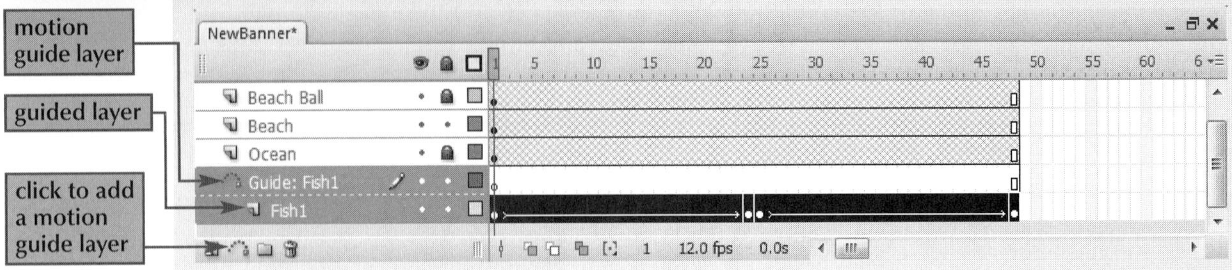

4. In the Tools panel, click the **Snap to Objects** button to select it, if necessary. In the Timeline, click **Frame 1** of the Guide: Fish1 layer. You will use the Pencil tool to draw the path the fish will follow.
5. In the Tools panel, click the **Pencil** tool, click the **Pencil Mode** button, and then click **Smooth**.
6. In the Property inspector, if necessary, set the stroke color to **black** (#000000), the stroke height to **1**, and the stroke style to **Solid**.
7. In the Property inspector, set the Smoothing value to **100**. The Smoothing value, which ranges from 0 to 100, specifies the degree of smoothness applied to the line you draw. The larger the value, the smoother the line.
8. On the left side of the Stage, starting at the center of the fish, draw a line that curves down slightly toward the top of the beach and then back up to the right side of the Stage. See Figure 4-3.

Figure 4-3 Line drawn with Pencil tool

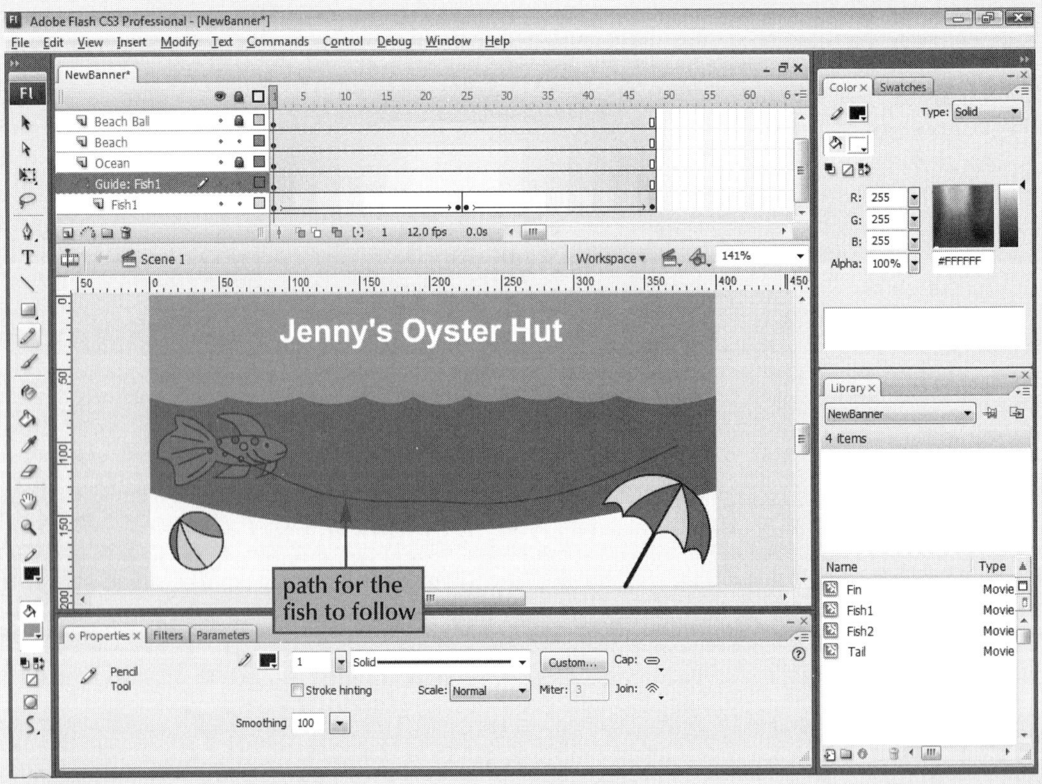

You'll attach the fish to the starting and ending points of the line.

9. In the Tools panel, click the **Selection** tool.

10. In the Timeline, click **Frame 1** of the Fish1 layer, and then, on the Stage, make sure the registration point of the fish is snapped to the beginning of the line, repositioning it as needed.

11. In the Timeline, click **Frame 24** of the Fish1 layer, and then, on the Stage, drag the fish so that it snaps to the right endpoint of the line. See Figure 4-4.

Figure 4-4 Registration point of fish snaps to endpoint of line

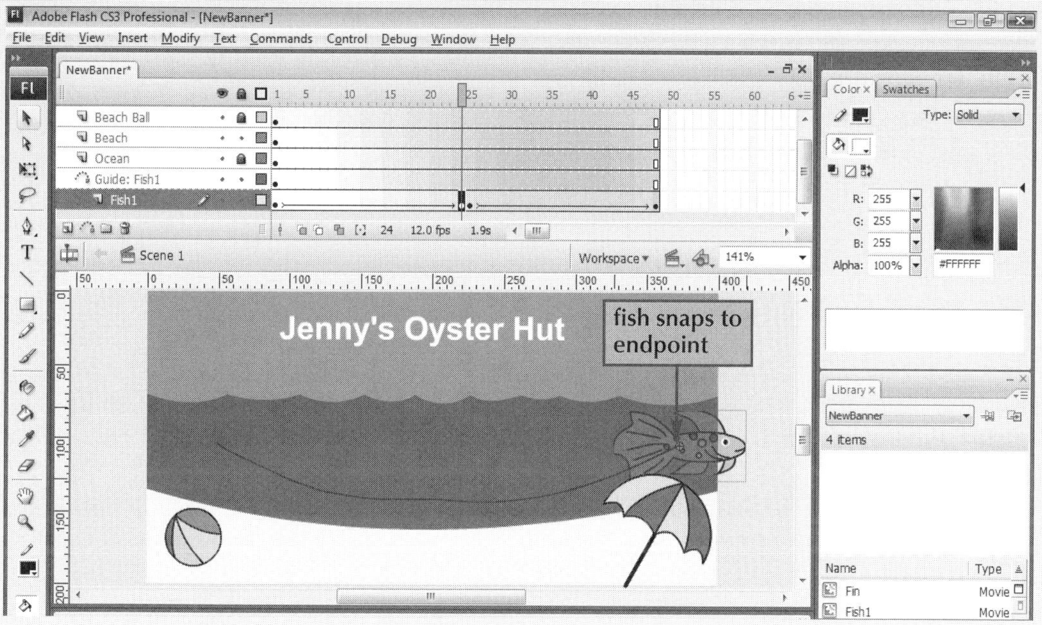

Trouble? If you move the endpoint of the line by mistake, click Edit on the menu bar, click Undo, and then try moving the fish again.

12. In the Timeline, click **Frame 25** of the Fish1 layer, and then, on the Stage, drag the fish so that it snaps to the right endpoint of the line. This is where the fish starts a new motion tween to swim to the left side of the banner.

13. In the Timeline, click **Frame 48** of the Fish1 layer, and then, on the Stage, drag the fish so that it snaps to the left endpoint of the line. This is the location where the fish is positioned at the end of the motion tween.

When you animate an object to follow a curved path, the object stays in a horizontal position as it moves along the path. You'll usually want the object to move in a more natural way. The Orient to path option in the Property inspector causes the object to align itself with the direction of the path, making the movement appear more natural. This works best with curves that have gentle slopes.

You'll test the animation with the motion guide layer to make sure the fish follows the path you drew in the guide layer. When you are sure that the fish is animated along the line correctly, you'll orient the fish to the line.

To test the motion guide layer and orient the fish to the path:

1. Press the **Enter** key to test the motion guide tween. As the animation plays on the Stage, the fish follows the path you drew in the guide layer.

   Trouble? If the fish does not follow the path, its registration point may not be snapped to the endpoints of the line. Check Frames 1, 24, 25, and 48 of the Fish1 layer to make sure the registration point of the fish is snapped to the endpoints of the line. If necessary, move the fish to snap it to the endpoints.

   You'll orient the fish to follow the slope of the path. You set the Orient to path option in any frame within the motion tween.

2. In the Timeline, click **Frame 1** of the Fish1 layer, and then, in the Property inspector, click the **Orient to path** check box to check it. The fish will have a more natural movement during the animation.
3. In the Timeline, click **Frame 25** of the Fish1 layer, and then, in the Property inspector, click the **Orient to path** check box to check it.

   Before testing the animation again, you'll hide the Guide layer so that the path is not visible.

4. In the Timeline, in the Show/Hide column of the Guide: Fish1 layer, click the dot to hide its contents. The line you drew no longer appears on the Stage.
5. Press the **Enter** key to test the animation again. This time the fish orients itself to the slope of the motion guide.
6. Save the banner.

Using a Mask Layer to Create Animation

You can also create animations that incorporate a mask layer to create special effects. To create an animation using a mask layer, you create the object to be masked on one layer and add a new layer above it that will contain the mask. When you change the top layer to a mask layer, the bottom layer becomes the masked layer. The masked layer is indented below the mask layer in the Timeline.

Reference Window | Creating a Mask Layer Animation

- Select the layer whose content will be masked.
- In the Timeline, click the Insert Layer button.
- Add content to the new layer that will be used as the mask.
- Right-click the new layer's name, and then click Mask.
- Unlock the layers and create an animation in either the mask layer or the masked layer.
- Lock the layers, and then test the animation.

The object on the mask layer can be a filled shape, such as an oval or a rectangle. It can also be text or an instance of a symbol. The fill of the shape on the mask layer will reveal the content in the underlying masked layer. This shape determines what part of the masked layer's content is visible. The color of the shape is insignificant because its color is not displayed. You can animate either the object on the mask layer or the object on the masked layer. For example, you can animate an oval shape on the mask layer so that it moves over some stationary text on the masked layer. This technique creates a spotlight effect, as shown in Figure 4-5.

Figure 4-5 Masked layer example

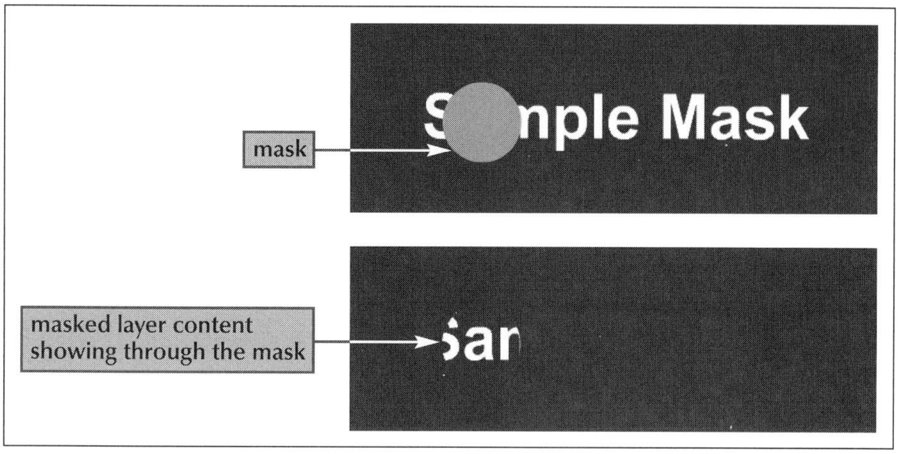

If you animate the object on the masked layer while the object on the mask layer remains stationary, you can create a different type of effect. For example, you can create a scrolling text effect by drawing a rectangle on the mask layer and then animating a block of text on the masked layer. As the text block moves across the mask, only the portion of the text behind the rectangle is visible, as shown in Figure 4-6.

Figure 4-6 Masked layer with scrolling text effect

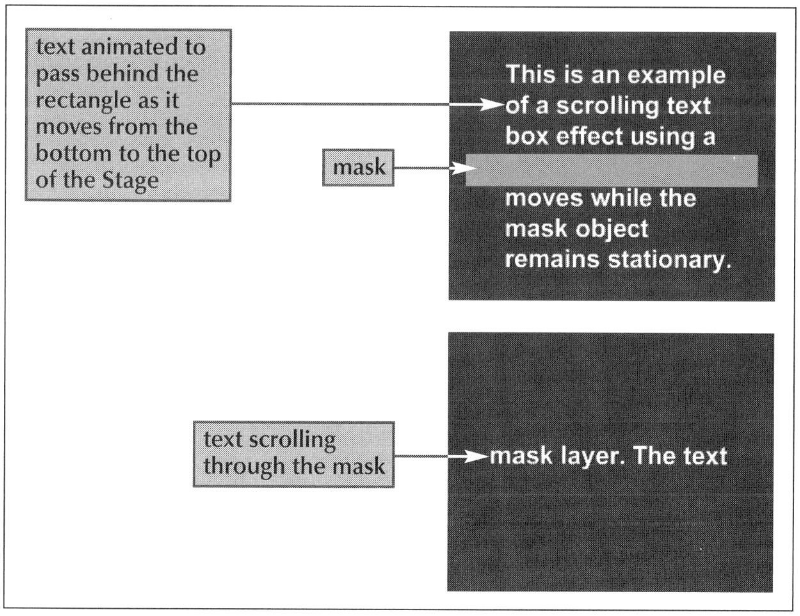

Creating an Animated Picture Masked with Text | InSight

An interesting effect you can create with mask layers is to use text for the mask object and have another object such as a picture show through the text. With this technique, the text acts like a window for the content behind it. For example, if you animate a picture on the masked layer, as the picture moves, only the parts of the picture that are behind the text will be visible.

When you first create a mask layer, Flash locks both the mask and the masked layers. These layers must be locked to preview the effects of the mask on the Stage. When the layers are locked, the mask layer object is not visible, and only the content in the masked layer that is behind the mask layer object becomes visible. You need to unlock the layers to work with the objects on both layers, and then lock the layers again to test the animation.

You'll explore a mask layer animation Aly has created for another Admiral client, Jackson's Sports.

To explore the mask layer animation in the Jackson's Sports banner:

1. Open the **SportsMask.fla** file located in the **Tutorial.04\Tutorial** folder included with your Data Files. The SportsMask document opens.

   Before you can view the mask layer's contents, you must first unlock it.

2. In the Timeline, in the Lock/Unlock column of the Text Mask layer, click the **lock** icon. The layer is unlocked, and you can see the contents of the Text Mask layer. See Figure 4-7.

Figure 4-7 Mask layer animation

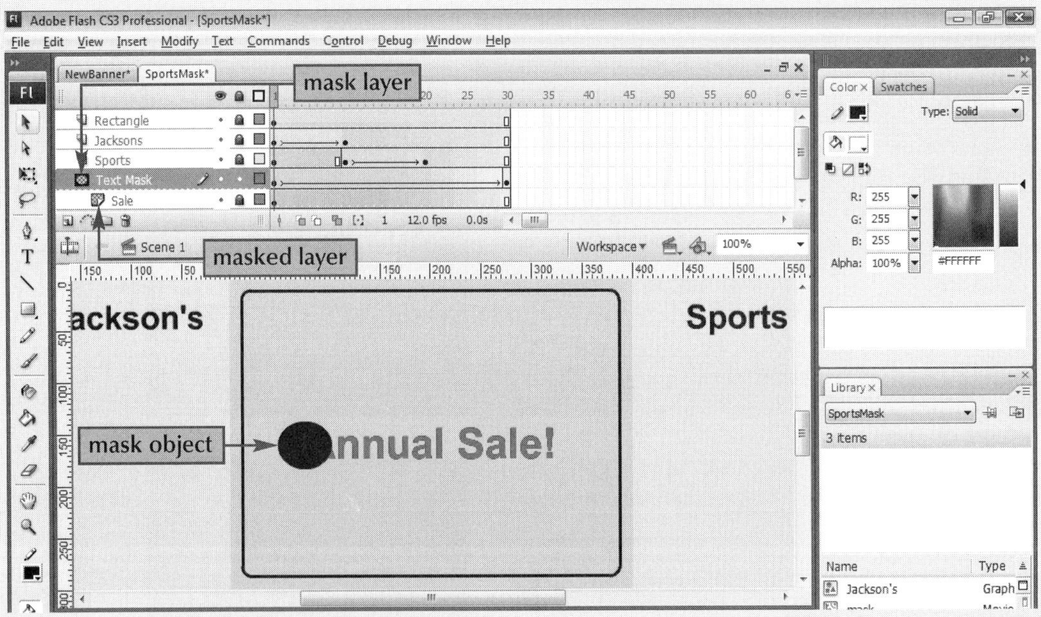

The content of the Text Mask layer is just a motion tween animation of an oval shape. As the oval moves from left to right, different parts of the underlying Annual Sale text become visible. You'll lock the mask layer again so that you can test the animation. When a mask layer is locked, the masking effect is visible on the Stage.

3. In the Timeline, in the Lock/Unlock column of the Text Mask layer, click the dot. The layer is locked, as indicated by the padlock icon.

4. Press the **Enter** key to test the animation. The part of the text under the oval becomes visible as the oval moves across the Stage.

5. Close the SportsMask document without saving any changes.

Creating a Mask Layer

As shown in Figure 4-8, Aly's notes for the Jenny's Oyster Hut banner indicate that in the last scene, the Jenny's Oyster Hut text block should have a spotlight effect. To create this, you will first add a duplicate of the current scene in the file, and then you will modify it by creating a spotlight effect where the spotlight moves across the Jenny's Oyster Hut text block.

Animation plan for spotlight effect **Figure 4-8**

You'll create the mask layer animation in a new scene.

To create a new scene for the mask layer animation:

1. Click **Window** on the menu bar, point to **Other Panels**, and then click **Scene**. The Scene panel opens.
2. In the Scene panel, click the **Duplicate scene** button. A copy of Scene 1 is added to the document. You'll rename the scenes.
3. In the Scene panel, double-click **Scene 1**, type **Fish Swimming**, and then press the **Enter** key to rename the scene.
4. In the Scene panel, double-click **Scene 1 copy**, type **Animated Text**, press the **Enter** key to rename the scene, and then close the Scene panel. The Animated Text scene is the current scene.
5. In the Timeline, select the **Fish1** layer, click the **Delete Layer** button, select the **Guide: Fish1** layer, and then click the **Delete Layer** button. The unneeded layers in the Animated Text scene are deleted.

   You need to create a duplicate of the title text block.

6. In the Tools panel, click the **Selection** tool, if necessary, and then click the text block on the Stage to select it. You need to create a duplicate of this text box.
7. Click **Edit** on the menu bar, and then click **Copy**. The text is copied to the Clipboard.
8. In the Timeline, select the **Beach Ball** layer, click the **Insert Layer** button to insert a new layer above the Beach Ball layer, and then rename the new layer **Gray text**.

Tip

You can also press the Shift+F2 keys to open and close the Scene panel.

Tip

You can also press the Ctrl+C keys to copy the selected object and press the Ctrl+Shift+V keys to paste it in place.

9. Click **Edit** on the menu bar, and then click **Paste in Place** to paste the text block in the new Gray text layer in the same relative position as it is in the Title layer.
10. In the Timeline, in the Show/Hide column of the Title layer, click the dot to hide the layer's content.
11. On the Stage, click the text block to select it, and then, in the Property inspector, change the text fill color of the text block to **dark gray** (#666666).
12. In the Timeline, lock the Gray text layer, and then show the Title layer. The gray text will provide a background for the title as part of the spotlight effect.

You'll add a mask layer above the Title layer. The mask layer will contain a motion tween of a circle. You will create a highlight effect by moving the circle back and forth across the title text.

To create the mask layer animation:

1. In the Timeline, click **Frame 1** of the Title layer, click the **Insert Layer** button, to insert a new layer above the Title layer, and then rename the new layer as **Mask**. The Mask layer's type needs to be changed to Mask.
2. Right-click the **Mask** layer name, and then click **Mask** on the context menu. The layer changes to a mask layer and the Title layer changes to a masked layer indented below the Mask layer. Both layers are locked. See Figure 4-9.

Figure 4-9 Locked mask and masked layers

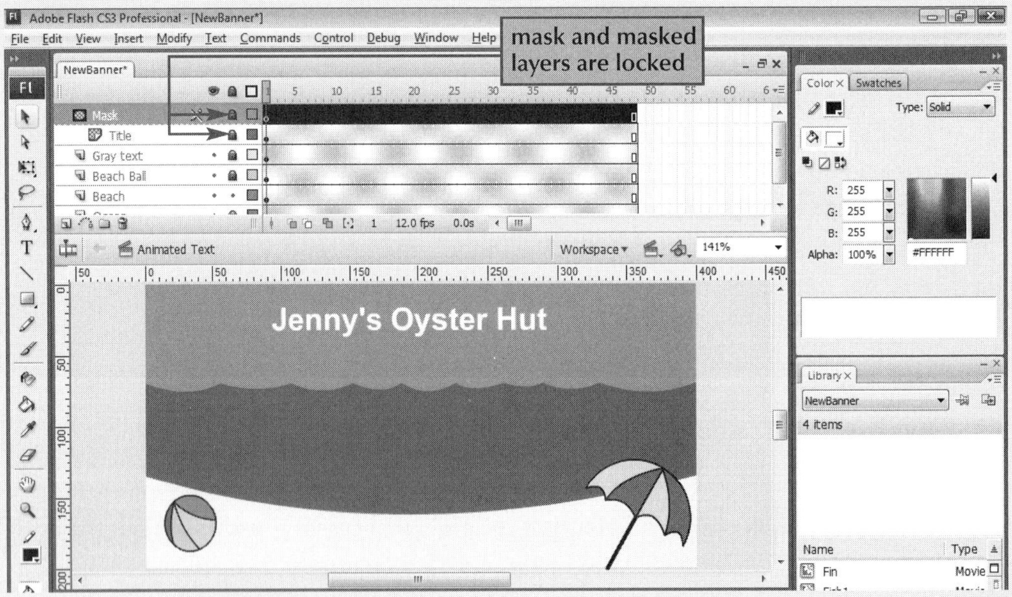

3. Unlock the Mask layer, and then click **Frame 1** of the Mask layer. You will draw a circle on the Mask layer to represent the spotlight.
4. In the Tools panel, click the **Oval** tool, and then set the fill color to **white** (#FFFFFF) and the stroke color to **no color**.
5. On the Stage, draw a small circle to the left of the letter "J" in the Jenny's Oyster Hut text block. See Figure 4-10.

Figure 4-10 Circle drawn in the Mask layer

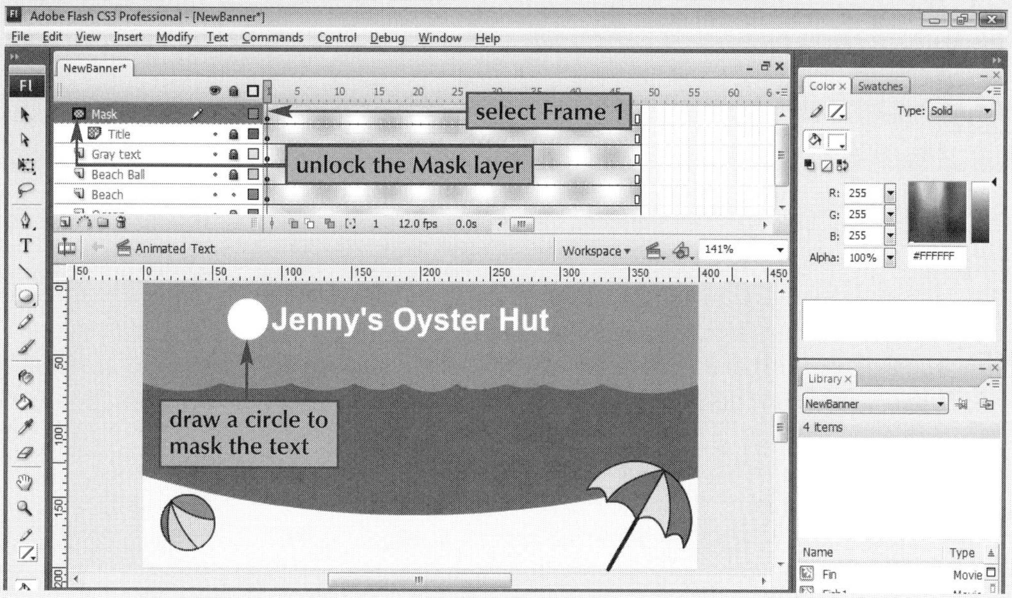

6. In the Tools panel, click the **Selection** tool, and then, on the Stage, select the circle.
7. Click **Modify** on the menu bar, click **Convert to Symbol** to open the Convert to Symbol dialog box, name the symbol **Circle**, select **Movie clip** as the behavior type, and then click the **OK** button.

   You'll create two motion tweens for the circle so that it moves to the end of the title text block and then back to its starting point.
8. In the Timeline, right-click **Frame 48** of the Mask layer, and then click **Insert Keyframe** on the context menu. A keyframe is inserted at the end of the animation sequence. The circle will be back to this starting point at this frame.

   You need to insert additional keyframes to complete the motion tweens.
9. Insert a keyframe at **Frame 24** of the Mask layer, and then drag the circle to the right of last letter of the text block.
10. Insert a keyframe at **Frame 25** of the Mask layer. Frame 24 represents the end of the first motion tween and Frame 25 represents the beginning of the second motion tween where the circle moves back to its starting point.
11. Right-click between Frames 1 and 24 and click **Create Motion Tween** on the context menu, and then right-click between Frames 25 and 48 and click **Create Motion Tween**. The first motion tween is created between Frames 1 and 24, and the second motion tween is created between Frames 25 and 48.

   You'll test the animation next. Before you can test the animation, you must lock the mask layer.
12. In the Timeline, lock the Mask layer, move the playhead to **Frame 1**, and then press the **Enter** key to test the animation. The circle creates a spotlight effect as it moves across and back over the title text.
13. Save the document.

Tip

You can also click the Tween button in the Property inspector, and then click Motion to create a motion tween.

In this session, you created a motion guide layer to have the fish instance swim along a curved path. You also added a duplicate scene where you created a mask layer animation to create a spotlight effect. In the next session, you will continue your work on the banner by creating text animations.

Review | Session 4.1 Quick Check

1. List two ways to insert a motion guide layer.
2. Name two tools you can use to create a path on a motion guide layer.
3. How can you see the effect that a mask layer has on a masked layer when testing an animation within the Flash workspace?
4. True or False? Text cannot be used as a mask in a mask layer.
5. When a guide layer is used together with a motion tween it is called a(n) ________________ layer.
6. What is the purpose of the Orient to path option in the Property inspector?
7. True or False? In a mask layer animation, the contents of the mask layer are revealed when the object in the masked layer moves over it.

Session 4.2

Animating Text Blocks

You can animate text to create special effects. For example, you can have text move onto the Stage in a fly-in effect. Or in a more complex animation, you can make the individual letters of a text block rotate, fade in, and change in size as they appear one at a time on the Stage to form a word or phrase. You can also animate text so that it increases and decreases in size to create a pulsating effect.

You can animate text blocks using frame-by-frame or tweened animations. For example, you can have a text block move from one side of the Stage to the other using a frame-by-frame animation by changing the location of the text in each keyframe. Using a motion tween, you can animate a text block so that it rotates as the animation is played, or you can even have the text block change in size or color. Before you can create a motion tween with a text block, you need to convert the text block to a symbol. You then create the keyframes for the beginning and the ending of the animation and move the text block to its starting position in the first frame and to its ending position in the last frame. Finally, you create the motion tween.

You can also apply a shape tween to text. However, you must first convert the text to fills by using the Break Apart command. When you apply the Break Apart command to a text block, each character in the text block becomes an individual text block. You can apply the command again to the individual letters to convert them to fills. Once the text blocks are converted to fills, you can apply a shape tween to them. For example, you can make the letters change into an oval shape, as shown in Figure 4-11. Be aware that once you convert the text to fills, you can no longer edit the fills as text.

Sample shape tween **Figure 4-11**

Creating Text Animations | Reference Window

- For a shape tween, select the text block in the first frame of the animation.
- Click Modify in the menu bar, and then click Break Apart to break the text into individual letters.
- Click Modify in the menu bar, and then click Break Apart a second time to convert the text to fills.
- Create a keyframe in the last frame of the animation and change the shape of the text fills.
- Select the first frame of the animation, and then, in the Property inspector, click the Tween button and click Shape (or right-click the frame, and then click Create Shape Tween on the context menu).

or

- For a motion tween, select the text block in the first frame of the animation, and then convert the text block into a symbol.
- Create a keyframe in the last frame of the animation and change the position, size, orientation, or tint of the text instance.
- Select the first frame of the animation, and then, in the Property inspector, click the Tween button and click Motion (or right-click the frame, and then click Create Motion Tween on the context menu).

Adding Animated Text

Based on Aly's notes for completing the banner, shown in Figure 4-12, you need to add four text blocks to the banner for the third scene. The Seafood text block and the Specials text block will move from the pasteboard to the center of the Stage. The during our text block will not be animated but will only appear after the first two text blocks. The 10th Anniversary text block will appear during the second half of the animation and will increase in size. Each text block will be on its own layer so you can animate each individually.

Figure 4-12 **Animation plan for text blocks**

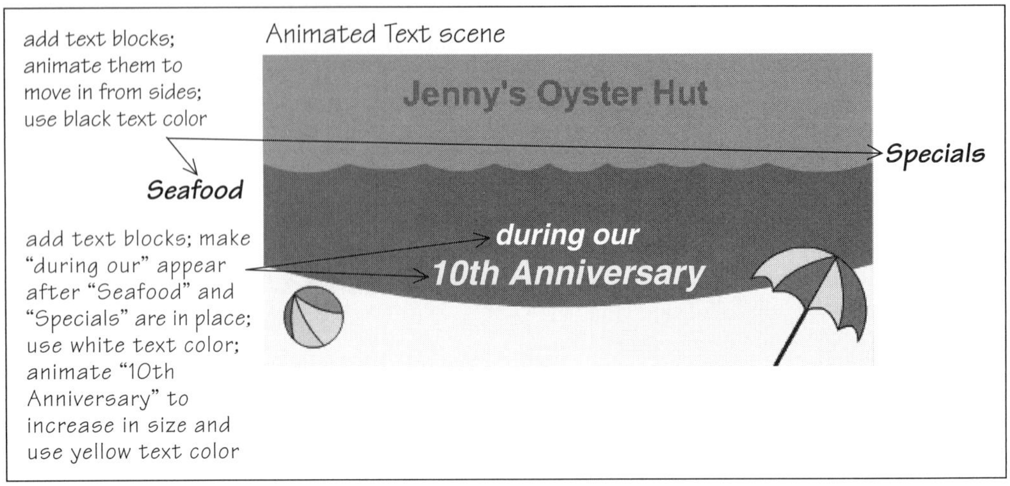

You will start by adding four new layers, one for each text block, to the Animated Text scene.

To add layers and animate the Seafood text block:

1. If you took a break after the previous session, make sure the NewBanner.fla file is open, the Animated Text scene is the current scene, and the workspace is set to its default layout.
2. In the Timeline, select the **Mask** layer of the Animated Text Scene, and then insert four new layers named **Seafood**, **Specials**, **During**, and **Anniversary**. The new layers appear above the Mask layer.
3. On the Edit bar, click the **Zoom control arrow**, and then click **100%** to change the view of the Document window.
4. If necessary, display the rulers, and then drag a horizontal guide to approximately 70 pixels from the top of the Stage and drag a vertical guide to approximately 200 pixels from the left of the Stage. The guides will help you align the text.

   You will create the Seafood text block next.
5. In the Tools panel, click the **Text** tool [T], and then, in the Property inspector, set the font to **Arial**, the font size to **26**, the text fill color to **black** (#000000), the font style to **Bold** and **Italic**, and the alignment to **Align Left**. You will use these text properties for the first text block you will create in Frame 1 of the Seafood layer.
6. In the Timeline, click **Frame 1** of the Seafood layer.
7. In the pasteboard to the left of the Stage, click the horizontal guide to create a text block, and then type **Seafood**. The formatted text is entered in the text block.
8. In the Tools panel, click the **Selection** tool, and then drag the text block to the position shown in Figure 4-13.

Figure 4-13 **Start position for the Seafood text block**

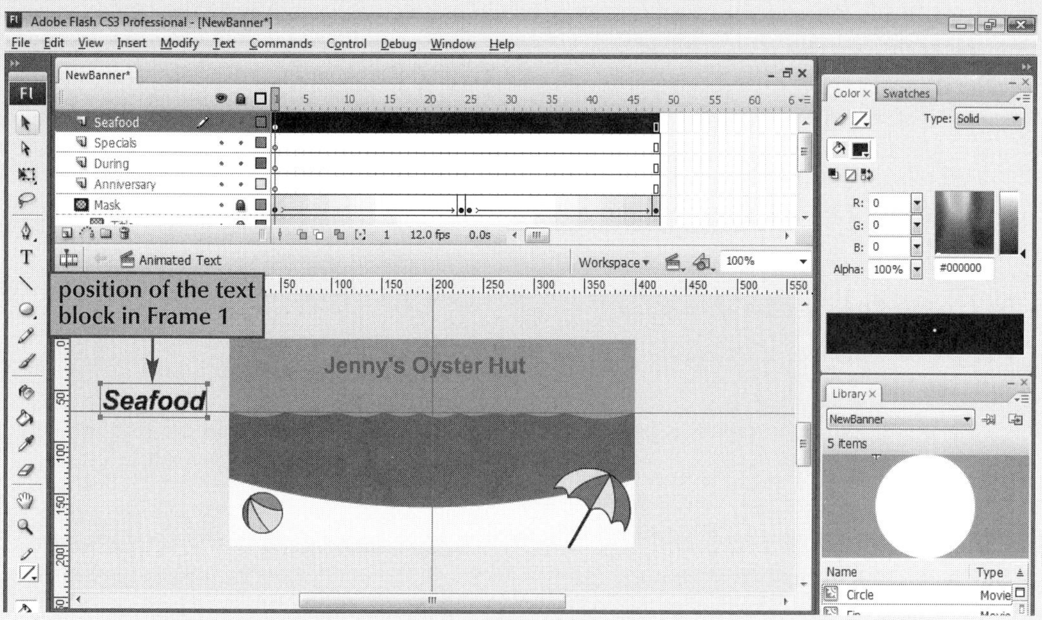

Before you can create a motion tween of this text block, it needs to be converted to a symbol.

9. Convert the **Seafood** text block to a symbol named **Seafood text** with the **Movie clip** behavior type.

10. In the Timeline, click **Frame 7** of the Seafood layer, insert a keyframe, and then drag the **Seafood** text block to the center of the Stage so its right side touches the vertical guide and its bottom is aligned with the horizontal guide. See Figure 4-14.

> **Tip**
>
> To open the Convert to Symbol dialog box, you can also press the F8 key.

Figure 4-14 **End position for the Seafood text block**

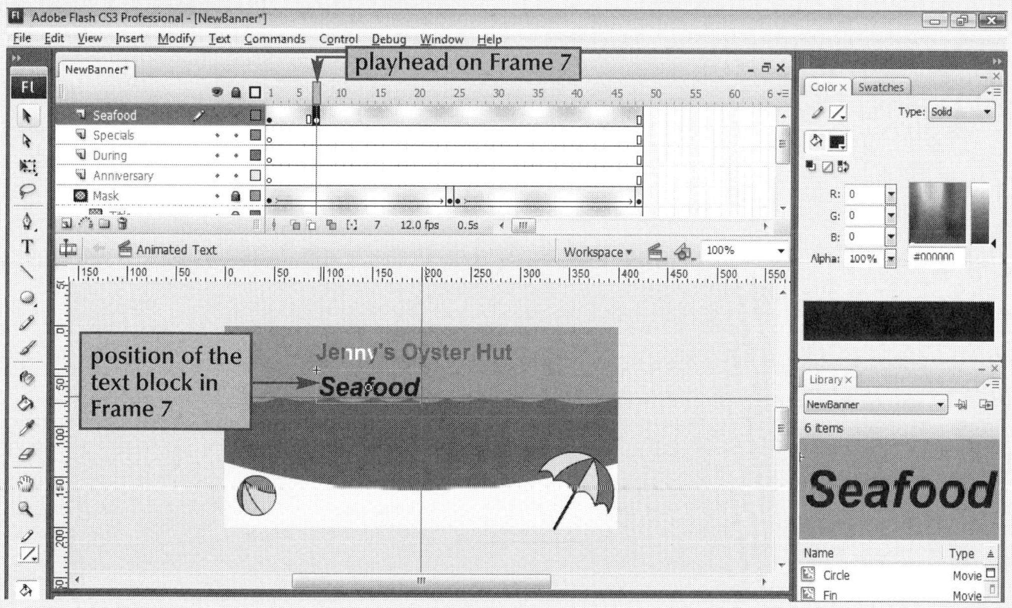

11. In the Timeline, right-click between Frames 1 and 7 of the Seafood layer and click **Create Motion Tween** on the context menu. A motion tween is created between Frames 1 and 7 so that the text moves from the left of the Stage to the center of the Stage.

The Seafood text block uses a motion tween to animate it. You will repeat this process to create additional text blocks in the other layers. Recall that to animate more than one symbol instance at a time, each instance must be in its own layer. You will start by creating the Specials text block animation.

To create the Specials text animation for the banner:

1. In the Timeline, click **Frame 7** of the Specials layer, and then insert a keyframe. The Specials text block animation will begin at Frame 7.
2. In the Tools panel, click the **Text** tool T, click the horizontal guide in the pasteboard to the right of the Stage to create a new text block, and then type **Specials**. The new text block has the same properties as the Seafood text block.
3. In the Tools panel, click the **Selection** tool, and then drag the **Specials** text block to the position shown in Figure 4-15.

Tip

You can also press the T key to select the Text tool.

Figure 4-15 Start position for the Specials text block

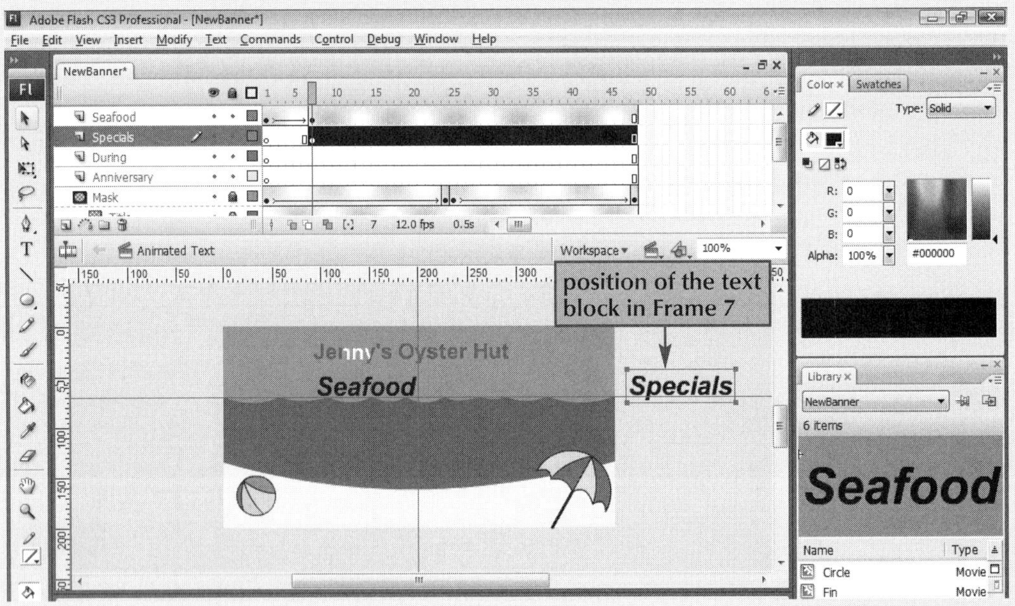

4. Convert the Specials text block to a symbol named **Specials text** with the **Movie clip** behavior type.
5. In the Timeline, click **Frame 14** of the Specials layer, insert a **keyframe**, and then drag the **Specials** text block to the right of the Seafood text block aligned with the horizontal guide. See Figure 4-16.

Specials text aligned with Seafood text — **Figure 4-16**

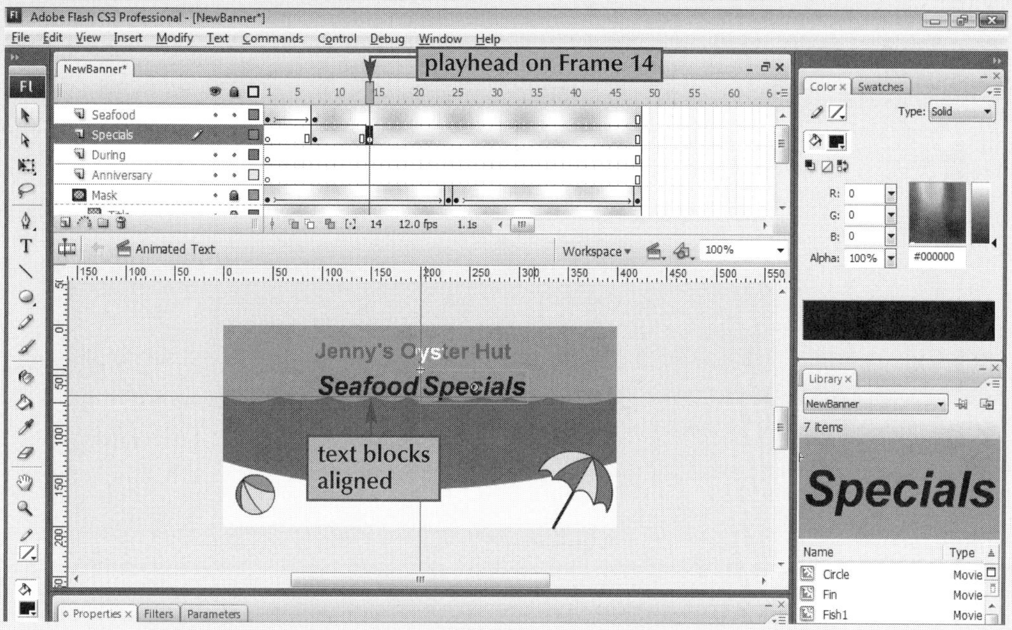

6. In the Timeline, right-click between Frames 7 and 14 of the Specials layer, and then click **Create Motion Tween** on the context menu. A motion tween is created so that the Specials text moves from the right of the Stage to the right of the Seafood text.

The next text block, for the During layer, will not have a motion tween because it will not be animated. Instead, the During text will only appear starting with Frame 20. This means that from Frame 1 through Frame 19, the text is not displayed. The text is only displayed from Frame 20 through Frame 48.

To add the during our text block:

1. In the Timeline, click **Frame 20** of the During layer, and then insert a keyframe. The during our text block will appear in Frame 20.
2. In the Tools panel, click the **Text** tool [T], and then, in the Property inspector, change the font color to **white** (#FFFFFF), the font size to **18**, and the alignment to **Align Center**. You'll use these properties for the new text block.
3. On the Stage, create a text block centered below the Seafood Specials text blocks, and then type **during our**. The formatted text is entered in the text block.
4. In the Tools panel, click the **Selection** tool, and then drag the text block so that it is centered on the Stage. See Figure 4-17.

Figure 4-17 The during our text block centered on the Stage

The last text block, 10th Anniversary, will be animated with a motion tween. Although the text block will not move, it will change in size throughout the animation. The text block will not be visible until Frame 30, at which point the motion tween will start.

To create and animate the 10th Anniversary text block:

1. In the Timeline, click **Frame 30** of the Anniversary layer, and then insert a keyframe. The motion tween for the 10th Anniversary text will begin at Frame 30.
2. In the Tools panel, click the **Text** tool [T], and then, in the Property inspector, change the font size to **12** and the font color to **yellow** (#FFFF00).
3. On the Stage, create a text block below the during our text block, and then type **10th Anniversary**. The formatted text is entered in the text block.
4. In the Tools panel, click the **Selection** tool, and then, on the Stage, drag the **10th Anniversary** text block so that it is centered about 130 pixels from the top of the Stage.
5. Convert the text block to a symbol named **Anniversary text** with the **Movie clip** behavior type.
6. In the Timeline, click **Frame 40** of the Anniversary layer, and then insert a keyframe. This is the keyframe for the end of the animation.
7. Click **Window** on the menu bar, and then click **Transform** to open the Transform panel.
8. On the Stage, make sure that the **10th Anniversary** text block is still selected.
9. In the Transform panel, click the **Constrain** check box to check it if necessary, type **230%** in the width box, and then press the **Enter** key. The size of the text in the 10th Anniversary text block increases. See Figure 4-18.

Tip

You can also press the Ctrl+T keys to open and close the Transform panel.

Transform panel **Figure 4-18**

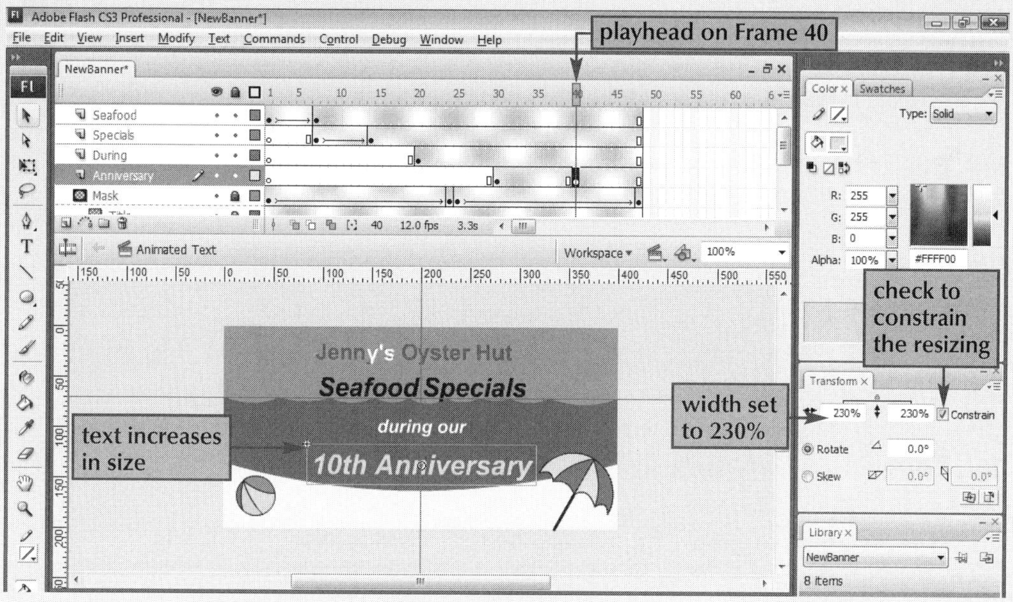

▶ **10.** In the Timeline, right-click between Frames 30 and 40 of the Anniversary layer, and then click **Create Motion Tween**. A motion tween is created so that the text increases in size throughout the animation.

▶ **11.** In the Timeline, drag the playhead to Frame 1, and then press the **Enter** key to test the animation. The Seafood and Specials text blocks move in from the sides of the Stage to the middle of the Stage. Then the during our text appears followed by the 10th Anniversary text which appears below the during our text and increases in size.

▶ **12.** On the menu bar, click **View**, point to **Guides**, and then click **Clear Guides**. The guides are removed.

▶ **13.** Close the Transform panel, and then save the document. The text animations for the Animated Text scene are complete.

Animating Individual Letters

You can animate individual letters in a word or phrase to create interesting text effects. For example, you can animate the letters of a word to fall into place on the Stage one at a time. Or you can have a word explode with the individual letters flying off the Stage in different directions. Another example is to have the individual letters of a word increase and decrease in size to create a pulsating effect. To create most of these text effects, you first need to break a word into its individual letters and then animate each letter separately. The easiest way to animate each letter is to create motion tweens. This means that each letter must be converted to a symbol and must reside on its own layer. Recall that you cannot have motion tweens on a layer with more than one symbol.

InSight | Having Flash Create Symbols Automatically

When you apply a motion tween to a grouped object such as a text block that was not first converted to a symbol, Flash automatically converts the objects into symbols and assigns names to them such as Tween 1, Tween 2, and so on. Letting Flash generate the symbols automatically can save you time, especially when creating animations of words or phrases with many letters. If these symbols are not used in any other part of the document's animation, the names of the symbols are not important. However, if these symbols will be used with other animations, you should assign meaningful names to them. This will make it easier to select the correct symbols when creating the animations.

Aly wants you to look at a banner that includes individual letter text animation that she has been working on for Jackson's Sports. In this banner, each letter has the same motion tweens applied to it to create a pulsating effect.

To explore the Jackson's Sports document with individual letters text effect:

1. Open the **SportsLetters.fla** file located in the **Tutorial.04\Tutorial** folder included with your Data Files.
2. Press the **Enter** key to play the animation. The text animation plays, showing each letter increase and decrease in size one after the other. Notice that each letter resides on its own layer.
3. In the Timeline, click **Frame 1** of the J layer, and then look at the size of the letter J on the Stage.
4. In the Timeline, click **Frame 5** of the J layer, and then look at how the letter J increases in size on the Stage.
5. In the Timeline, click **Frame 10** of the J layer, and then look at the letters J and A on the Stage. In this frame, the letter J returns to its original size. At the same time, the next letter, A, increases in size. See Figure 4-19.

Figure 4-19 Sample letters animation

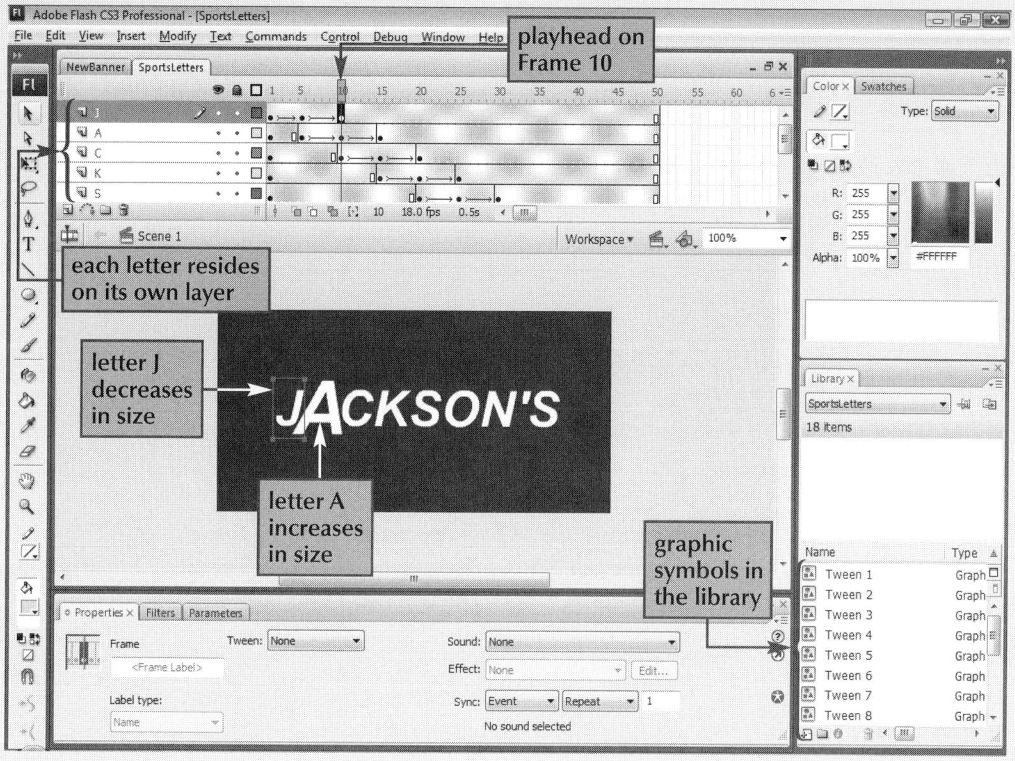

6. Review the document's library to see the symbols in this animation. The library contains a series of symbols named Tween 1, Tween 2, and so on.
7. In the Library panel, click the **Tween 3** symbol. The letter A appears in the Library's preview pane. The Tween 3 symbol was automatically created when a motion tween was applied to the letter A.
8. Close the document without saving any changes.

Creating a Complex Text Animation

The next animation you will create for the Jenny's Oyster Hut banner consists of individual letters rotating into place one after the other to form the word Jenny's, as described in Aly's notes shown in Figure 4-20. Each letter will fade in and decrease in size as it falls into place. This effect involves animating the individual letters of the word in a similar way to the animated text in the banner Aly created for Jackson's Sports. To create the animations for the individual letters, you will first create the Jenny's text block, convert each letter in that text block into its own individual text block, and then distribute these individual letter text blocks onto their own layers. This animation will appear in the first scene.

Figure 4-20 Animation plan for title text

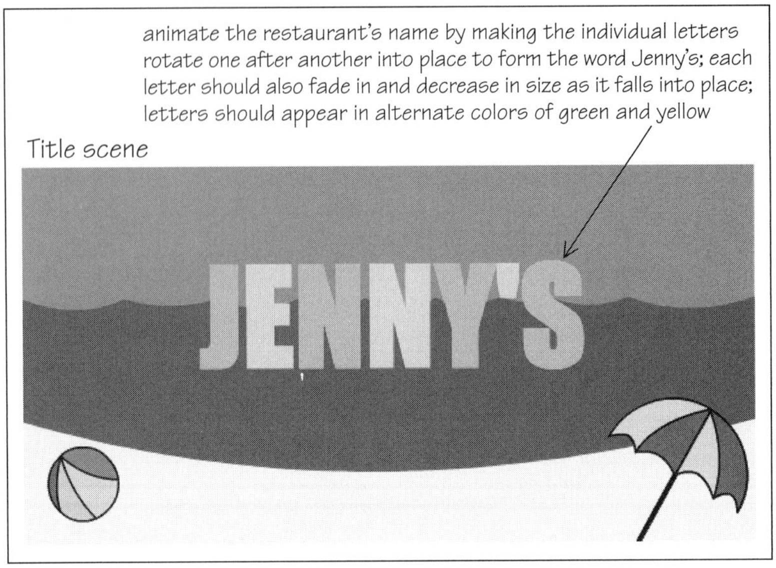

Reference Window | Animating Individual Letters

- On the Stage, select the text block containing the letters to be animated.
- Click Modify on the menu bar, and then click Break Apart.
- Click Modify on the menu bar, point to Timeline, and then click Distribute to Layers.
- Delete the original layer, which is now empty.
- Convert each letter that will be animated to a symbol with an appropriate name.
- Create a motion tween for each letter.

Before animating the letters, you'll change the colors of the letters in the Jenny's text block to alternate between yellow and green to enhance the special effect. You will initially create the Jenny's text block in a new layer folder. Then, when you distribute the letters to individual layers, all of the new layers will be inside the folder. This new animation will reside in its own scene, which will play before the other two scenes in the document.

To create the JENNY'S text block for the animation in the first scene:

1. Click **Window** on the menu bar, point to **Other Panels**, and click **Scene** to open the Scene panel.
2. In the Scene panel, click the **Fish Swimming** scene to select it, and then click the **Duplicate scene** button. A duplicate scene named Fish Swimming copy is created.
3. In the Scene panel, rename the Fish Swimming copy scene to **Title**, drag the **Title** scene above the Fish Swimming scene, and then close the Scene panel. The Title scene is the first scene in the document.
4. In the Timeline of the Title scene, delete the **Guide: Fish1** layer, delete the **Fish1** layer, and then, in the Title layer, delete the text block.

   Next, you'll create a new layer folder for the new text block.

5. In the Timeline, select the **Title** layer, if necessary, and, then click the **Insert Layer Folder** button . A new layer folder is created above the Title layer.
6. Rename the layer folder **Letters**, drag the **Title** layer into the Letters folder, and then click **Frame 1** of the Title layer.
7. In the Tools panel, click the **Text** tool , and then, in the Property inspector, set the font to **Impact**, the font size to **70**, the text fill color to **yellow** (#FFFF00), the font style to **bold**, and the alignment to **Align Center**.
8. On the Stage, create a text block, and then type **JENNY'S**.
9. In the Tools panel, click the **Selection** tool , and then, on the Stage, drag the **JENNY'S** text block to center it about 50 pixels from the top of the Stage. See Figure 4-21.

Figure 4-21 JENNY'S text block

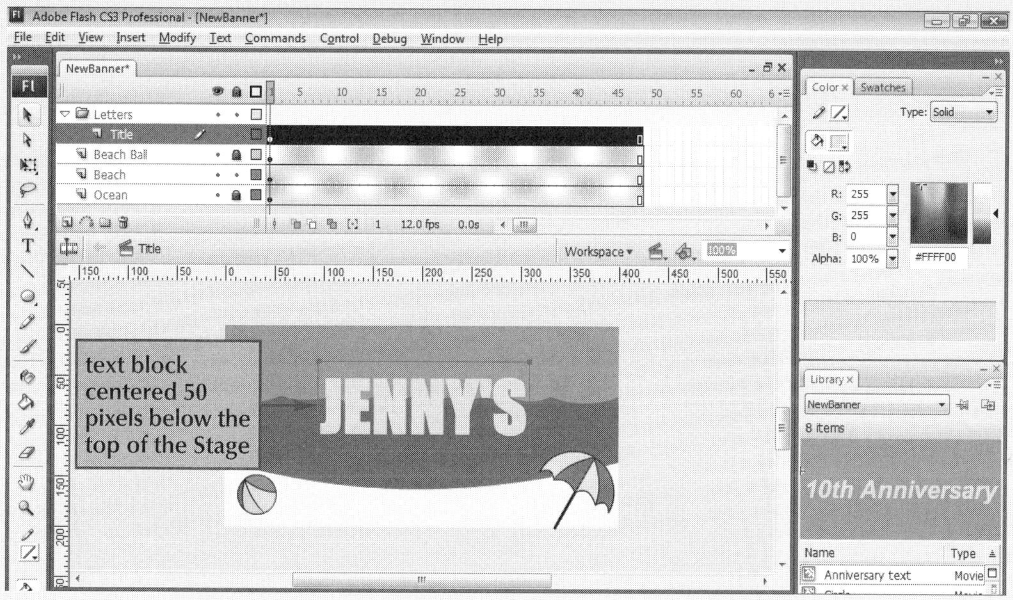

You'll change the color of the letters next.

10. On the Stage, double-click the **JENNY'S** text block, click and drag in the text block to select the letter **J**, and then change the letter's text fill color to **green** (#00FF00).
11. Repeat Step 10 to change the color of the first letter **N**, the letter **Y**, and the letter **S** to the same color green. The letters in the word JENNY'S alternate between green and yellow.
12. In the Tools panel, click the **Selection** tool . The Jenny's text block remains selected.

Distributing Objects to Individual Layers

Animating a word's individual letters as in the Jackson's Sports banner requires that each letter be placed on its own layer. A quick way to place each letter into its own layer is to use the Distribute to Layers command. This command takes a group of selected objects and places each individual object onto its own layer. Each new layer is named based on its content. For example, if the objects distributed are text blocks, then the names of the new layers are the same as the text in the text blocks. If the objects are symbols, the names of the new layers are the same as the names of the symbols. Other layers are named "Layer" followed by a number. This helps you to identify which layers the selected objects have been distributed to. The layer that originally contained the grouped objects will be empty after you apply the Distribute to Layers command and can be deleted. Before you apply the Distribute to Layers command, be sure to select all of the objects you want distributed.

InSight | Organizing Distributed Layers in a Layer Folder

Before distributing a group of objects to layers, create a new layer folder and move the layer containing the objects into the layer folder. After the objects are distributed to layers, all of the new layers will reside inside the layer folder. You can then collapse the layer folder to hide the individual layers when you are not working with them. This makes it easier to work with the document's Timeline and any other layers in your document.

To convert the Jenny's text block into individual letters so they can be distributed to individual layers, you need to use the Break Apart command. This command breaks a text block into separate text blocks, one for each letter. When you apply the Distribute to Layers command to the selected text blocks, each letter is placed on its own layer. You then can create the necessary motion tween animations for each of the letters.

You will start by separating the letters into individual text blocks and distributing the text blocks into individual layers.

To create the individual letters from the word JENNY'S for the animation:

1. Click **Modify** on the menu bar, and then click **Break Apart**. Each letter is placed in its own text block, and all the text blocks are selected. See Figure 4-22.

Figure 4-22 Individual letter text blocks

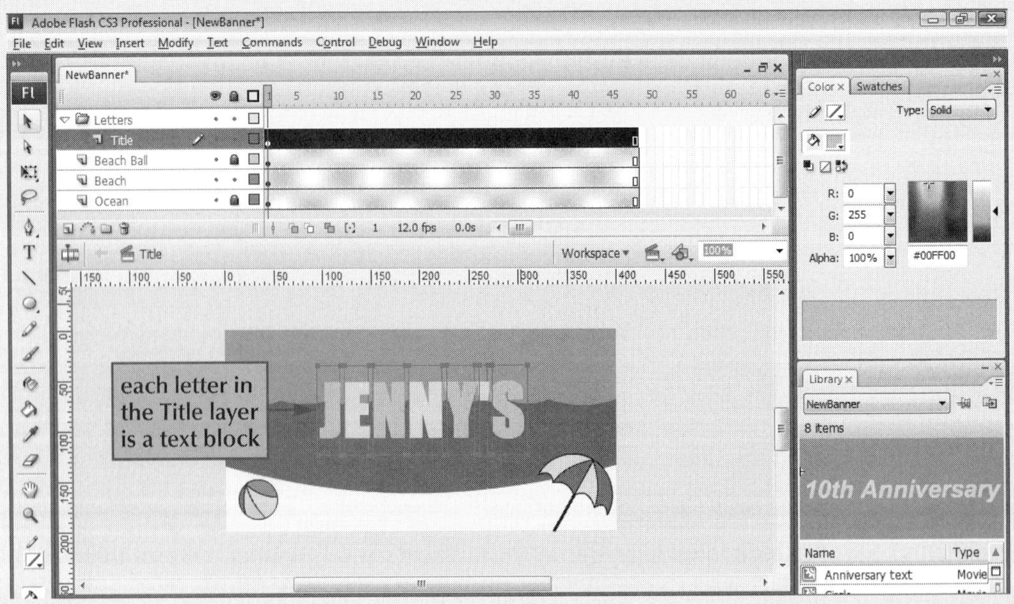

Tip

You can also press the Ctrl+B keys to break apart letters into individual text blocks and you can press the Ctrl+Shift+D keys to distribute selected objects to individual layers.

2. With all of the letters still selected, click **Modify** on the menu bar, point to **Timeline**, and then click **Distribute to Layers**. Each letter is placed on its own layer that is named with the letter it contains. The Title layer is empty and is no longer needed.
3. In the Timeline, delete the **Title** layer. The empty Title layer is deleted from the Timeline.

Now that the letters have been split into individual text blocks and onto separate layers, you can animate each one of them to create the Jenny's letters animation. You will convert each letter into a symbol and create a motion tween to cover 15 frames. Each letter should start its animation a few frames after the previous letter. This means that the starting keyframe for each subsequent letter needs to be moved to a later frame in the Timeline. Aly wants a motion tween to start every three frames. The first letter, J, starts in Frame 1 of the J layer. The second letter, E, starts in Frame 3 of its layer. The letter, N, starts in Frame 6 of its layer. The next letter, N, starts in Frame 9 of its layer, and so on. This animation creates the effect of the letters dropping in one after the other. You will create the motion tween animations for the letters. First you will extend all of the layers by adding regular frames to Frame 60 so that the animation plays for five seconds.

To animate the letters:

1. In the Timeline, drag from Frame 60 of the J layer down to Frame 60 of the Ocean layer. Frame 60 is selected in all the layers.
2. Click **Insert** on the menu bar, point to **Timeline**, and then click **Frame**. Each layer extends to Frame 60.
3. In the Timeline, click **Frame 1** of the J layer, select the letter **J** on the Stage if necessary, and then convert the letter to a symbol named **J** with the **Movie clip** behavior type. The symbol is added to the document's library.

   You'll convert the rest of the letters to symbols.
4. Repeat Step 3 for each of the remaining letters, naming each symbol for its letter it represents using **N1** as the symbol name the first letter N, **N2** as the symbol name for the second letter N, and **Apostrophe** as the symbol name for the apostrophe.

   Next, you will move the starting keyframes for each of the letters except J. The letter J is the first letter and will start in Frame 1.
5. In the Timeline, click **Frame 1** of the E layer, and then drag the keyframe to **Frame 3** of the same layer. The animation for the letter E will start in third frame of the animation. See Figure 4-23.

Figure 4-23 Repositioned keyframe for the E layer

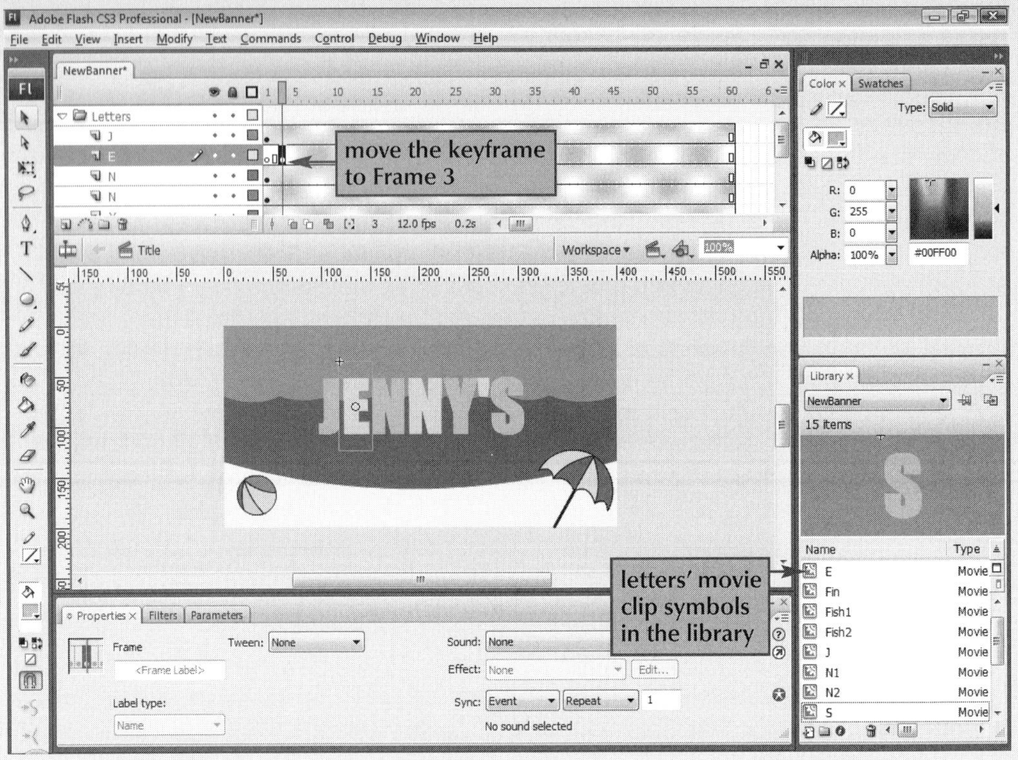

6. Repeat Step 5 to move the first keyframes for each of the following layers as follows: layer for the first letter N to **Frame 6**, layer for the second letter N to **Frame 9**, layer Y to **Frame 12**, layer for the apostrophe to **Frame 15**, and layer S to **Frame 18**.

   The motion tween for each letter will occupy 15 frames in their respective layers. To accomplish this, each layer should have another keyframe added 15 frames after its first one. You will add the ending keyframes to each layer, and then create the motion tweens.

7. Insert a keyframe at **Frame 15** of the J layer. This is the ending keyframe for the J layer, which is where the motion tween for the J will end.

8. Insert ending keyframes for each of the other layers as follows: layer E at **Frame 18**, layer for the first letter N at **Frame 21**, layer for the second letter N at **Frame 24**, layer Y at **Frame 27**, layer for the apostrophe at **Frame 30**, and layer S at **Frame 33**.

9. In the Timeline, right-click between Frame 1 and Frame 15 of the J layer, and then click **Create Motion Tween** on the context menu. The motion tween is created for the letter J.

10. Repeat Step 9 for each of the other layers between their respective keyframes. Each layer has a motion tween. See Figure 4-24.

Motion tweens created for each layer

Figure 4-24

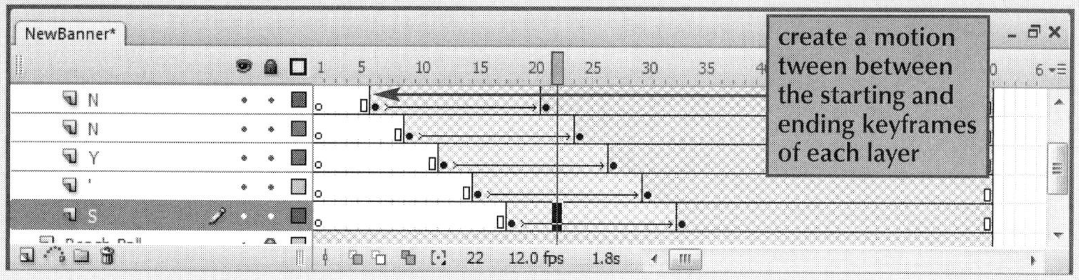

Now that each layer has a motion tween, you need to change the starting instance of the letter in each layer so that it is different from the ending instance. The instance at the end of each layer does not need to change. You will change the starting instance by making it twice as large as its ending size, rotating it to the left at a −45 degree angle, and making it slightly transparent. Then each letter will rotate into its upright position, while fading in, and reducing in size. This will create the effect of the letters falling into place to spell the word Jenny's.

To change the starting instance of the motion tweens in each layer:

1. In the Timeline, click **Frame 1** of the J layer. The letter J instance is selected on the Stage.
2. Click **Window** on the menu bar, and then click **Transform**. The Transform panel opens.
3. In the Transform panel, click the **Constrain** check box to insert a check mark if necessary, type **200** in the width box, type **−45** in the Rotate box, and then press the **Enter** key. The width and height values change to 200, enlarging the letter, and the letter J rotates counterclockwise to a −45 degree orientation.
4. On the Stage, click the **J** instance to select it, and then, in the Property inspector, click the **Color** button, click **Alpha**, type **20** in the Alpha Amount box and then press the **Enter** key. The letter becomes slightly transparent. See Figure 4-25.

Figure 4-25 J instance modified in Frame 1

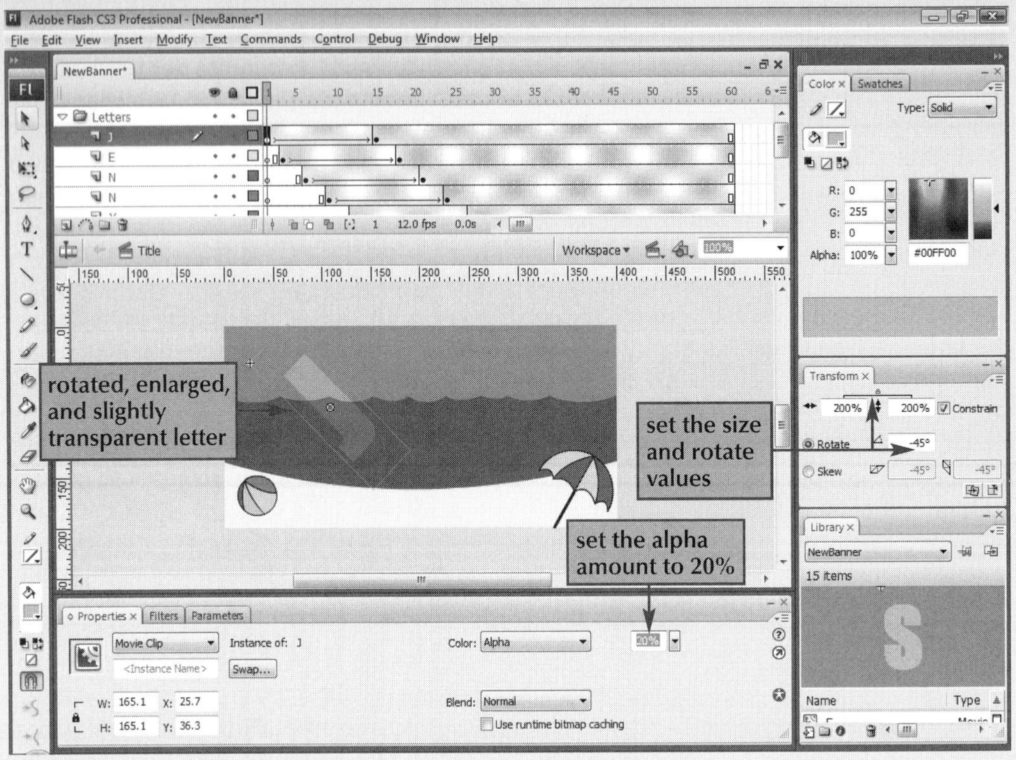

5. Scrub the playhead between Frames 1 and 15 of the J layer to test the animation for the letter J. The J starts out large, slightly transparent, and tilted to the left, and then moves into place as it fades in and decreases in size.
6. Select each letter in its starting keyframe, and then repeat Steps 3 and 4 to create the same animation effect as you did for the letter J. The starting instances for all of the letters are changed.
7. Drag the playhead to Frame 1, and then press the **Enter** key to test the animation. The special effect for the Jenny's text is complete. See Figure 4-26.

Figure 4-26 Individual letters animation

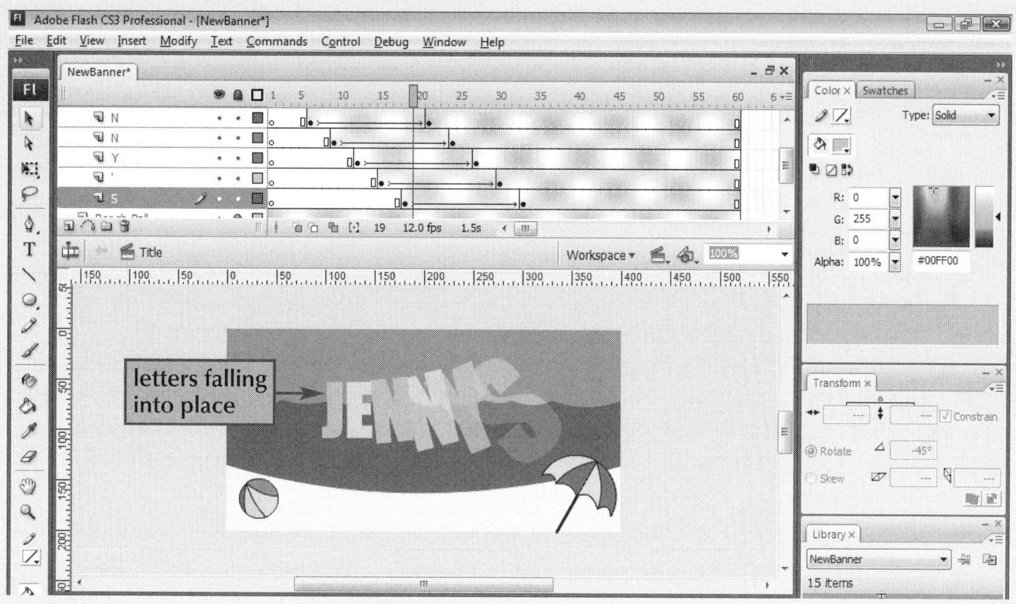

8. Close the Transform panel, and then save the banner.

In this session, you animated several text blocks in the last scene of the banner. You also created a new scene with an animation of the individual letters of the Jenny's name. In the next session, you will complete the banner by adding a complex animation to the second scene.

Session 4.2 Quick Check | Review

1. List two examples of how text can be animated.
2. To apply a shape tween to a text block, what must you do first to the text?
3. If you apply the Distribute to Layers command to a group of selected text blocks, how will the new layers be named in the Timeline?
4. Why must each letter to be animated be on its own layer?
5. Why is it a good idea to place all of the individual letter layers in a layer folder?
6. True or False? A layer whose contents are distributed to separate layers with the Distribute to Layers command retains a copy of its original contents.

Session 4.3

Creating Complex Animation with Nested Symbols

As you have seen, complex animations can be created by animating objects on separate layers. For example, you can animate one object to move across the Stage on one layer while at the same time another object on another layer rotates and increases in size. As a result, you can create complex animation effects just by adding more layers to the document's main

Timeline. Sometimes, however, you cannot achieve the desired special effect by just adding layers with more animations. For example, the Jenny's banner has a fish swimming across the Stage. Its fins and tail, however, remain stationary in relation to the fish. A better design would be to create animations for the fins and the tail so that the fish moves more realistically. You could separate the fins and the tail from the body of the fish, convert them to movie clip symbols, and then create animations for each one on separate layers. Then you could animate the fish body, fins, and tail to move across the Stage at the same time as one object to achieve a more natural look. This is difficult to do, however, because it requires that you synchronize all of the animations to work together. A simpler way to do this is to create a nested symbol.

A **nested symbol** is a symbol that contains instances of other symbols within its Timeline. Recall that each symbol has its own Timeline. In the case of movie clip symbols, their Timelines are independent of the document's main Timeline. Within the Timeline of a movie clip symbol, you can insert instances of other symbols that in turn can contain their own animations within their own Timelines. The nested movie clip instances are referred to as the **child movie clips** and the movie clip they are nested within is referred to as the **parent movie clip**. Instances of the parent movie clip can then be inserted into the document's main Timeline, and can be modified and animated just like any other symbol instance. When you modify or animate the parent movie clip, the child movie clips are also affected. In the case of the fish, the parent movie clip can consist of the fish body plus nested instances of the fins and the tail, as shown in Figure 4-27.

Figure 4-27 **Example of a nested movie clip**

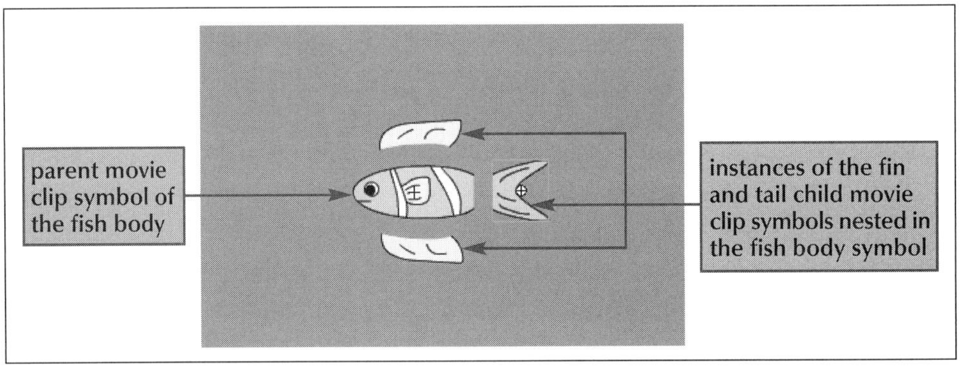

The fins and tail movie clip instances can contain their own animations to make them change slightly to simulate the movement of a real fish. These animations are independent of the fish body. The whole fish, which is the parent movie clip, can then be inserted in the document's main Timeline and animated to move across the Stage. When you apply a motion tween to the whole fish to make it move across the Stage, the motion tween is also applied to its nested instances. As a result, the fish body, fins, and tail all move across the Stage as one object while at the same time the fins and tail exhibit their own animations.

Creating a Nested Movie Clip

Because the second scene of the banner requires a fish that has its fins and tail animated to appear more natural, Aly wants you to create a fish using separate fin and tail symbols that contain their own animations. You will create a nested movie clip symbol using symbols she has already created for the fish body, fin, and tail. You will create frame-by-frame animations for the fin and the tail. Then, you will add two instances of the fin movie clip and one instance of the tail movie clip to the fish body. The resulting nested movie clip symbol will then be inserted into the Fish Swimming scene of the restaurant's banner and will be animated to move across the Stage.

You will start by creating a frame-by-frame animation for the fin. To create the animation for the fin, you'll add keyframes at every other frame of the fin Timeline starting at Frame 3. You will then change the shape of the fin slightly at each keyframe for a total of nine frames.

To insert frames for the fin frame-by-frame animation:

1. If you took a break after the previous session, make sure the NewBanner.fla file is open.
2. On the Edit bar, click the **Edit Symbols** button, and then click **Fin**. The Fin symbol opens in symbol-editing mode.
3. On the Edit bar, click the **Zoom control arrow**, and then click **200%**. The magnification of the Stage increases, making it easier to see the Fin symbol on the Stage.
4. In the Timeline, insert keyframes in the Layer 1 layer at **Frame 3**, **Frame 5**, **Frame 7**, and **Frame 9**. The fin is copied to each of the new frames.

Creating and Testing Animations Using Onion Skinning

When working with complex animations, it is often helpful to turn on onion skinning. **Onion skinning** displays more than one frame at a time on the Stage. This can be especially helpful when creating a frame-by-frame animation where you need to compare the current frame's contents to the previous frame's contents. Usually, you see only the current frame's contents on the Stage. With onion skinning, the current frame plus two or more frames appear on the Stage at once. The content of the current frame, indicated by the position of the playhead, appears in full color as usual. The contents of the frames before and after the current frame appear dimmed.

When you activate onion skinning, the Start Onion Skin marker and End Onion Skin marker appear on the Timeline header on either side of the playhead. The content displayed on the Stage is determined by the frames that are within the onion skin markers. You can also choose to display only the outlines of the content on the Stage, which can be helpful when working with complex animations, by clicking the Onion Skin Outlines button. The Edit Multiple Frames button makes the content of all the frames in a frame-by-frame animation that are within the onion skin markers available for editing.

Locking Layers While Onion Skinning | InSight

When using onion skinning with a complex document, a confusing array of images might be displayed on the Stage. Because the content of locked layers is not affected when onion skinning is turned on, lock those layers you aren't editing. You can then focus on the content of the layers you are editing. Also, be sure to turn off onion skinning when you are finished using it so as not to display multiple frames at one time.

You will turn onion skinning on to help you as you create the fin frame-by-frame animation.

To create the fin frame-by-frame animation:

1. In the Timeline, click the **Onion Skin** button. The onion skin markers appear in the Timeline header.
2. In the Timeline, click the **Modify Onion Markers** button, and then click **Onion 2** if necessary. The two frames before and after the current frame appear on the Stage.
3. In the Timeline, click **Frame 3** of the Layer 1 layer. This is the frame where you will first modify the fin.
4. In the Tools panel, click the **Selection** tool if necessary, click an empty area of the Stage to deselect the fin, and then use to drag the right side of the fin slightly to the left. The onion skinned frames provide a reference on the changing fin. See Figure 4-28.

> **Tip**
>
> You can also drag the onion skin markers on the Timeline header to increase or decrease the number of frames displayed on the Stage.

Figure 4-28 **Frame 3 of the Fin movie clip modified**

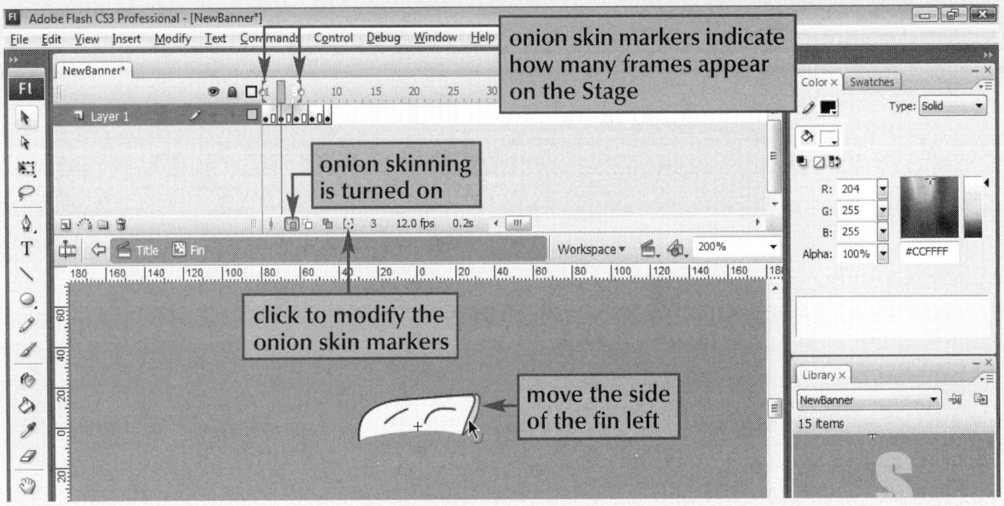

You'll repeat this process to modify other parts of the fin in Frames 5 and 7. In Frame 9, the fin returns to its original state so you will not make any changes in this frame.

5. In the Timeline, click **Frame 5**, deselect the fin on the Stage, and then drag the top edge of the fin slightly up. See Figure 4-29.

Figure 4-29 **Frame 5 of the Fin movie clip modified**

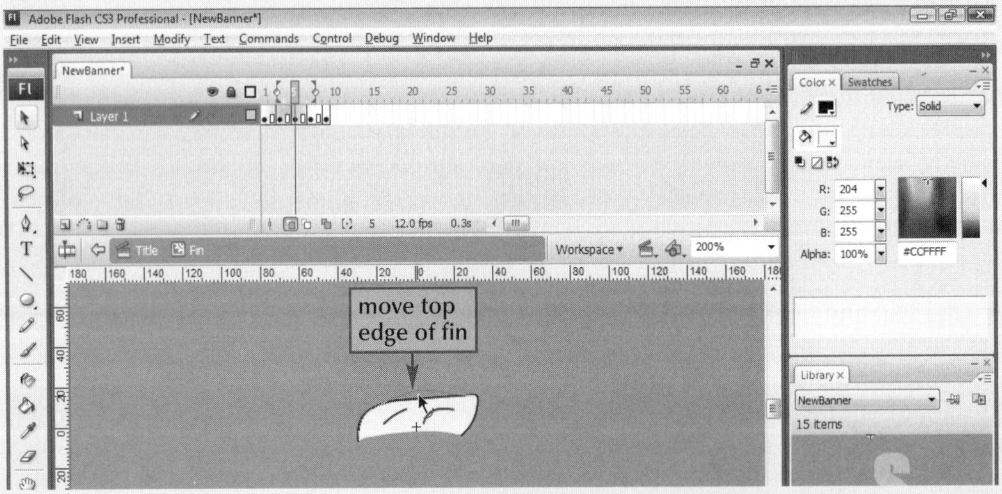

6. In the Timeline, click **Frame 7**, deselect the fin on the Stage, and then drag the upper-right tip of the fin slightly to the right. The fin animation is complete.
7. Drag the playhead to Frame 1, and then press the **Enter** key to test the frame-by-frame animation. The fin changes slightly at each keyframe throughout the animation.

The frame-by-frame animation for the fin is complete. You will create a similar frame-by-frame animation for the Tail symbol. You'll use the same number of keyframes for the Tail symbol as you did for the Fin symbol and change the shape of the tail slightly at each keyframe.

To create the tail frame-by-frame animation:

1. On the Edit bar, click the **Edit Symbols** button, and then click **Tail**. The Tail symbol opens in symbol-editing mode.
2. In the Timeline, insert keyframes in the Layer 1 layer at **Frame 3**, **Frame 5**, **Frame 7**, and **Frame 9**. The tail is copied to each of the new frames. Onion skinning is still on and stays on until you click the Onion Skin button.
3. In the Timeline, click **Frame 3** of the Layer 1 layer, and then click an empty area of the Stage to deselect the tail.
4. On the Stage, use to drag the two tips on the right side of the tail slightly inward. The dimmed tail from the previous frame provides a reference as you change the shape of the tail. See in Figure 4-30.

Figure 4-30 Frame 3 of the Tail movie clip symbol modified

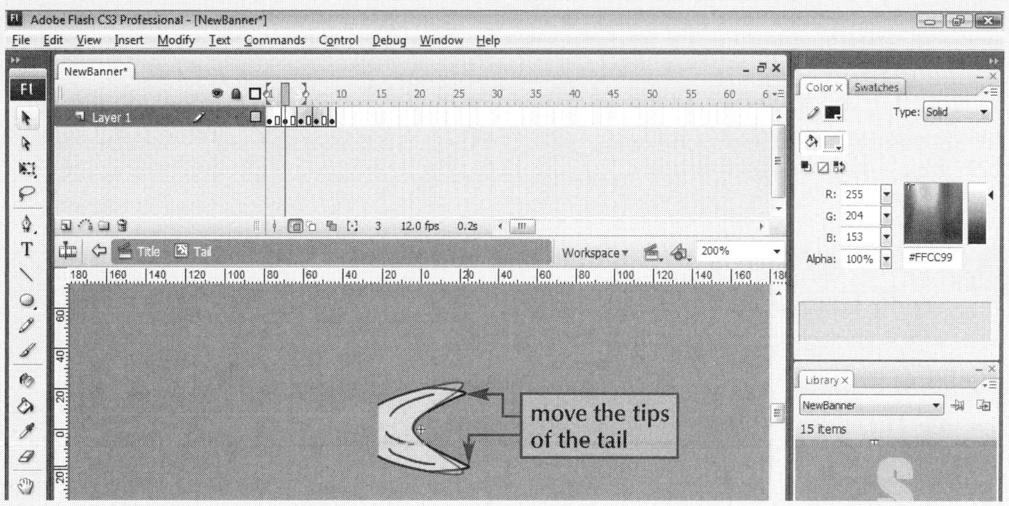

5. In the Timeline, click **Frame 5**, deselect the tail on the Stage, and then drag the tail's top edge near the left side of the tail slightly down. See Figure 4-31.

Figure 4-35 **Movie Explorer**

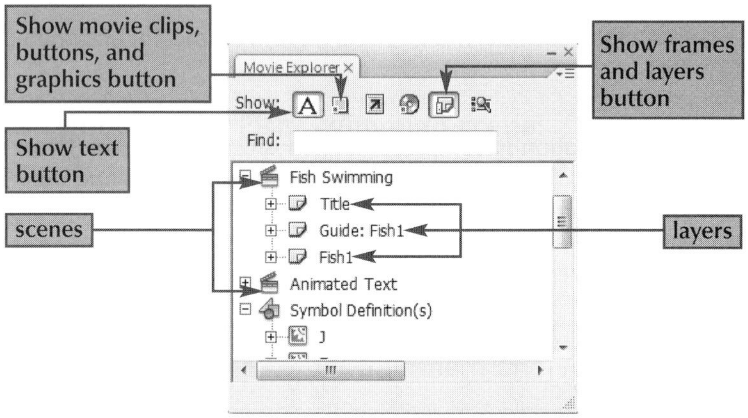

The display options in the Movie Explorer enable you to select which elements to display in the Movie Explorer panel. For example, if you want to see only the text blocks used in the document, you can click the Show text button but not the other buttons in the Movie Explorer. The panel displays each text block with information about the font and font size used in the text block. If you want to see each instance of the symbols used in the document, click the Show movie clips, buttons, and graphics button. If you select an instance in the Movie Explorer, information about where the instance is located in the document appears at the bottom of the panel.

You can select additional options from the Movie Explorer's options menu. For example, you can specify whether to show the document's elements or the symbol definitions or both. The document's elements include the layers, frames, and instances used in the document. The symbol definitions display below the document's elements along with each symbol and its elements. Other options available on the Movie Explorer's options menu include:

- Go to Symbol Definition, which selects the symbol definition for the symbol selected in the Movie Explorer.
- Find in Library, which displays the selected symbol in the Library panel.
- Show Movie Elements, which displays the document's elements such as its layers, frames, and symbol instances.
- Show Symbol Definitions, which displays all elements associated with a symbol.
- Show All Scenes, which displays the elements and symbols for all scenes in the document, not just the current scene.

InSight | Using the Movie Explorer to Troubleshoot Problems

If you are working with a Flash document developed by someone else, use the Movie Explorer to become familiar with the way the scenes, symbols, and other elements of the document are organized. You can explore how and where each of the document's symbols is used and how it is constructed. You can then more easily make changes to the document. Also, when working with a complex animation, you can use the Movie Explorer to troubleshoot problems. For example, if an animation is not working correctly, you can check the symbol instances that are part of the animation and determine whether they are in the correct scene, layer, and frame.

Because the banner you created for the Jenny's Oyster Hut Web site has multiple scenes, layers, and symbols, you can use the Movie Explorer to review all of its elements and view how all the various symbol instances throughout the document are organized.

To use the Movie Explorer to examine the banner's elements:

1. Click **Window** on the menu bar, and then click **Movie Explorer**. The Movie Explorer opens.
2. If necessary, click the **Show text** button [A] to select it, and click the other Show buttons to deselect them.
3. Click the **Movie Explorer options menu control** to open the options menu, click **Show Movie Elements** to select it, if necessary, and then repeat this step to also select **Show Symbol Definitions** and **Show All Scenes**. The panel displays the scenes that contain text blocks as well as the symbols that contain text. This display can make it easier to locate text blocks within the document.
4. Drag the bottom edge of the Movie Explorer window down to increase its size so you can see more of the elements in the window.
5. If necessary, click the **plus sign** next to the Animated Text scene name to expand its contents. The Movie Explorer displays all of the text blocks for the scene, including the text properties. You can compare the text properties of all the text blocks in the scene. This information can be useful if you need to maintain consistency across all of the text blocks within a scene. See Figure 4-36.

Tip

If a text block does not reside in a locked layer, you can double-click the text block in the Movie Explorer to change its contents.

Figure 4-36 Movie Explorer displaying text blocks

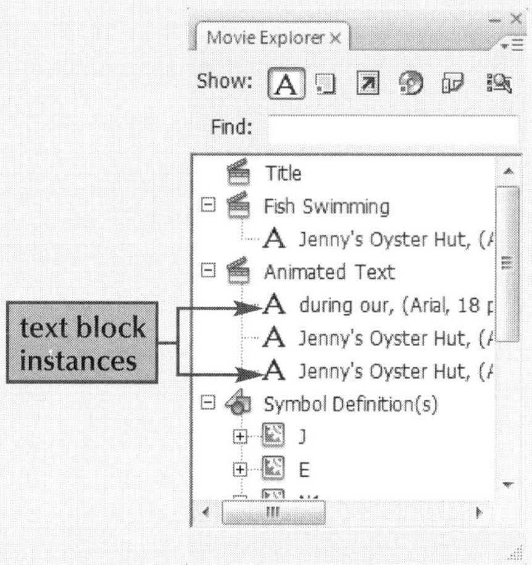

6. Click the **Show frames and layers** button to select it, and then, if necessary, click the **minus sign** next to the Title scene to collapse its display and click the **plus sign** next to the Fish Swimming scene to expand its display. Each layer of the Fish Swimming scene is displayed in the panel. Selecting a layer name in the panel also selects the layer in the document, enabling you to find specific layers in a complex document.
7. In the Movie Explorer, scroll down the panel, click the **Fish2** layer name under the Fish Swimming scene, and then, if necessary, click the **plus sign** next to it. Each keyframe within the Fish2 layer is displayed. See Figure 4-37.

Figure 4-37 **Movie Explorer displaying Fish2 layer and its keyframes**

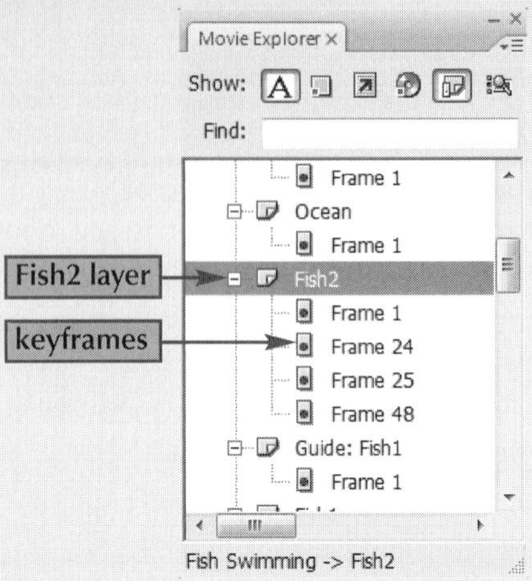

Selecting a keyframe in the Movie Explorer panel also selects that keyframe in the Timeline.

8. In the Movie Explorer, click the **Show movie clips, buttons, and graphics** button to select it, scroll down the panel, and then select the **Fish2** instance in Frame 1 of the Fish2 layer. The path of the instance is displayed at the bottom of the panel. This path indicates where the instance is located within the document. See Figure 4-38.

Figure 4-38 **Fish2 instance in Frame 1 of Fish2 layer**

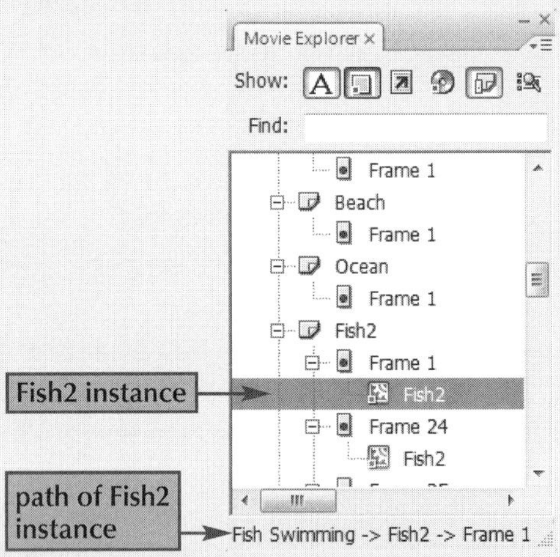

9. In the Movie Explorer, click the **Movie Explorer options menu control**, and then click **Go to Symbol Definition**. The Movie Explorer shows the Fish2 symbol under the Symbol Definitions area. The Symbol Definitions area shows all the elements associated with the selected symbol.

10. In the Movie Explorer, right-click the **Layer 1** name under the Fish2 symbol, and then click **Expand Branch** on the context menu. All the elements that make up the Fish2 symbol are displayed. See Figure 4-39.

Fish2 symbol definition | **Figure 4-39**

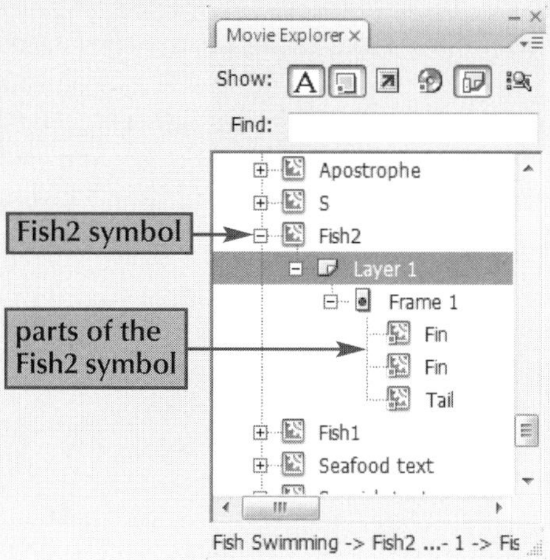

11. Close the Movie Explorer, and then close the NewBanner file.

Tip

You can also press the Alt+F3 keys to open and close the Movie Explorer.

Aly thinks the document elements look great and is ready to show to Jenny.

In this session, you used onion skinning to display the contents of multiple frames on the Stage. You also created nested movie clips, which contain instances of other movie clips within their Timelines. Finally, you used the Movie Explorer to review the elements of a complex document.

Session 4.3 Quick Check | Review

1. How can you change the position of the onion skin markers in the Timeline header?
2. How can onion skinning help you when working with a complex animation?
3. What is a nested movie clip?
4. What is a movie clip that has other movie clips nested within it called?
5. Why will the animations of movie clips embedded in a nested movie clip not play when you test them within the Flash Program window?
6. How can you use the Movie Explorer to find the definition of a particular symbol?

Tutorial Summary | Review

In this tutorial, you created animations using motion guide layers and mask layers. You used these techniques to modify an animation, and create a spotlight effect animation with text. You also created various types of text animations, including an animation of the individual letters of a word. You created a complex movie clip animation with symbols nested inside another movie clip symbol. You also used onion skinning to create and test complex animations. Finally, you used the Movie Explorer to examine all the elements of a Flash document.

Key Terms

child movie clip
guide layer
guided layer
mask layer
masked layer
motion guide layer
Movie Explorer
nested symbol
onion skinning
parent movie clip

Practice | Review Assignments

Practice the skills you learned in the tutorial.

Data File needed for the Review Assignments: Banner2.fla

Aly showed Jenny the two banners you created for the restaurant's Web site. Jenny asks for a third banner similar to the one you created. Aly asks you to have two fish swimming along curved paths. In the same scene, you will add a mask effect to the Jenny's Oyster Hut title that makes the text block appear gradually from left to right. You will also create a new animation of a small circular sign that contains rotating text inside. Two instances of the sign will be animated to move in the scene.

1. Open the **ReviewBanner.fla** document located in the Tutorial.04\Review folder included with your Data Files, and then save the file as **ThirdBanner.fla** in same folder.
2. Add a guide layer above the Fish1 layer. Draw a path that starts at the left side of the Stage where the Fish1 instance is initially located. It should curve up to the center of the Stage slightly above the top of the ocean graphic and then back down to the right side of the Stage. Attach the Fish1 instance at Frame 1 to the left endpoint of the path. Then attach the Fish1 instance at Frames 24, 25, and 48 so that it swims along the path as it goes from the left to the right and back. Orient the fish to the path. Hide the contents of the guide layer.
3. Insert a new layer above the Guide: Fish1 layer and name it **Fish2**. Add an instance of the Fish2 symbol to the right side of the Stage slightly below the top edge of the ocean. Insert a keyframe to the Fish2 layer at Frame 24 and move the fish to the left side of the Stage. Insert a keyframe at Frame 25 and flip the Fish2 instance to face to the right. Insert a keyframe at Frame 48 and move the Fish2 instance back to its starting point on the right side of the Stage. Create a motion tweens between Frames 1 and 24 and between Frames 25 and 48.
4. Add a new motion guide layer above the Fish2 layer and draw a path. The path should start at the right side of the Stage where the Fish2 instance is initially located. It should curve down to the center of the Stage slightly above the top side of the beach graphic and then back up to the left side of the Stage. Attach the Fish2 instance at Frame 1 to the right endpoint of the path. Then attach the Fish2 instance at Frames 24, 25, and 48 so that it swims along the path as it goes from the right to the left and back. Orient the fish to the path. Hide the contents of the guide layer.
5. Insert a new layer above the Title layer, name it **Mask**, and then change its type to Mask. Make sure the Title layer's type is changed to Masked and that it is indented below the Mask layer.
6. Unlock the Mask layer and draw a rectangle that covers the entire Jenny's Oyster Hut text block. The rectangle's width should be the same width as the text block and its height should only be as high as the text block. Do not include a stroke with the rectangle. The fill can be any color. Convert this rectangle to a movie clip symbol named **Rectangle**.
7. Insert a keyframe at Frame 24 of the Mask layer. Select Frame 1 and move the rectangle to the left of the text block to reveal the entire text block. Create a motion tween between Frames 1 and 24. The rectangle should move from left to right to gradually cover the text block. Lock the Mask layer and test the mask animation effect. The text block should appear gradually from left to right.

8. Create a new movie clip symbol named **Rotating text**. In symbol-editing mode, add a text block to the center of the symbol's Stage. Use Arial for the font, 12 for the font size, and white for the text color. Also apply the bold and italic styles to the text and select Align Center for alignment. Type **Shrimp** in the text block. In the Property inspector, set the text block's X and Y coordinates to 0. Convert the text block into a movie clip symbol named **Shrimp text**.
9. Insert a keyframe at Frame 10 and create a motion tween between Frames 1 and 10. In the Property inspector, set the text to rotate clockwise one time.
10. Insert a keyframe at Frame 15, delete the Shrimp text instance on the Stage and create a new text block. Type **Catfish** in the text block, and use the same properties as the Shrimp text. Set the text block's X and Y coordinates to 0. Convert the text block into a movie clip symbol named **Catfish text**. Insert another keyframe at Frame 25 and create a motion tween between Frames 15 and 25. Set this text block to rotate counterclockwise one time.
11. Insert a keyframe at Frame 30, delete the Catfish text instance on the Stage and create a new text block. Type **Oysters** in the text block, and use the same properties as the Shrimp text. Set the text block's X and Y coordinates to 0. Convert the text block into a movie clip symbol named **Oyster text**. Insert another keyframe at Frame 40 and create a motion tween between Frames 30 and 40. Set this text block to rotate clockwise one time. Insert a regular frame at Frame 45. Exit symbol-editing mode.
12. Create a new movie clip symbol named **Rotating sign**. In symbol-editing mode, add a small circle to the center of the symbol's Stage. Use dark blue (#003366) for the fill of the circle and do not add a stroke. Use the Property inspector to make the circle 60 pixels wide and 60 pixels high. Also, set its X and Y coordinates to 0. Drag an instance of the Rotating text symbol to the center of the circle. Exit symbol-editing mode.
13. Insert a new layer above the Mask layer, and name it **Rotating sign**. On this layer, drag an instance of the Rotating sign symbol to the lower-left side of the pasteboard just to the left of the Stage. Insert a keyframe at Frame 20 and create a motion tween between Frames 1 and 20 so that the Rotating sign instance moves from the pasteboard to the center of the beach graphic at the bottom of the Stage.
14. Test the new animations for the document using the Test Movie command.
15. Submit the finished file to your instructor, either in printed or electronic form, as requested.

Apply | Case Problem 1

Animate the letters in a text block, add several motion tweens for text, and create motion guide layers to set a path for animated graphics.

Data File needed for this Case Problem: ssAdDraft.fla

Sandy's Scrapbook Store Sandy Rodriguez, owner of Sandy's Scrapbook Store, is pleased about the banner developed for the store's Web site. She asks John Rossini about creating a new Flash document that will serve as an advertisement on the store's Web site. In particular, she would like text information promoting the store's services. John asks you to create the advertisement by starting with a document he has developed. You'll add new text messages promoting the grand opening sale and the services provided by the store. The store's name will be animated so that it displays one letter at a time. After the store's name appears, the next text message will fade in. Another text message will appear and will increase in size and change in color. Also, you'll add several instances of the balloon and confetti symbols.

1. Open the **sssAdDraft.fla** file located in the Tutorial.04\Case1 folder included with your Data Files, and then save the document as **sssAd.fla** in the same folder.
2. Extend the layers in the Timeline so that they each have 60 frames.
3. Select the text block in Frame 1 of the Title layer. Create a new layer folder and move the Title layer inside the folder. Convert the text block to individual text blocks, one for each character. Distribute the characters to individual layers inside the layer folder and delete the empty Title layer. Move the keyframes for each of the letters and apostrophe so that each starts one frame after the previous character. The first letter, S, starts in Frame 1. The second letter, a, starts in Frame 2. The third letter, n, starts in Frame 3, and so on. The characters will appear one at a time to form the complete store name.
4. Insert a new layer above the layer folder and name it **Sale**. Insert a keyframe at Frame 15 of this layer and in this frame, drag an instance of the Sale symbol from the Library panel to the center of the Stage. Animate the text block instance to fade in over the next 10 frames. To do this, insert a keyframe at Frame 25 on the same layer. Create a motion tween between Frames 15 and 25 and then at Frame 15, change the alpha amount of the Sale instance to 0%. This will cause the text block to fade in throughout the animation.

EXPLORE

5. To further animate the Sale text block, insert a keyframe at Frame 35 and also at Frame 45. Create motion tweens between Frames 25 and 35 and between Frames 35 and 45. At Frame 35, change the tint of the Sale text instance to 100% blue (#0000FF). The text will change from red to blue between Frames 25 and 35 and then change back to red between Frames 35 and 45.
6. Insert a new layer named **Supplies**. On this layer, insert a keyframe at Frame 25 and drag an instance of the Supplies symbol to the lower part of the Stage. Insert keyframes at Frames 35 and 45. Create a motion tween between Frames 25 and 35. Select Frame 25 and then use the Transform panel to reduce the size of the Supplies instance to 50% of its original size. Also in Frame 25, change the alpha amount of the instance to 0%. The text block will fade in as it increases in size from Frame 25 to 35.
7. Insert another keyframe at Frame 40 of the Supplies layer and reduce the size of the Supplies instance in this frame to 80% of its original size. Create motion tweens between Frames 35 and 40 and between Frames 40 and 45. The text block will decrease in size slightly in the first motion tween and increase back to its original size in the second motion tween.
8. Insert a new layer above the Background layer and name it **Balloon1**. Drag an instance of the Balloon symbol to the lower-left side of the Stage. Insert a keyframe at Frame 30 and create a motion tween between Frames 1 and 30. Add a motion guide layer above the Balloon1 layer and make sure the Balloon1 layer becomes the guided layer. In the Guide: Balloon1 layer draw a smooth wavy line from the lower-left side of the Stage to the upper-right side for the balloon to follow. Attach the balloon to the line so that it follows the path. Hide the Guide: Balloon1 layer.
9. Insert another layer above the Background layer and name it **Balloon2**. Drag an instance of the Balloon symbol to the lower-right corner of the Stage. Insert a keyframe at Frame 30 and create a motion tween between Frames 1 and 30. Add a motion guide layer above the Balloon2 layer and make sure the Balloon2 layer becomes the guided layer. In the Guide: Balloon2 layer, draw a smooth wavy line from the lower-right corner to the upper-left corner of the Stage. Attach the balloon to the line so that it follows the path. Hide the Guide: Balloon2 layer.
10. Add several instances of the confetti symbol to the Background layer.

11. Test the animation.
12. Submit the finished file to your instructor, either in printed or electronic form, as requested.

Apply | Case Problem 2

Add a mask layer effect, animations of individual letters, and text block animations to an advertising banner.

Data File needed for this Case Problem: acdAdDraft.fla

Alamo City Zoo Janet Meyers, zoo director for Alamo City Zoo, meets with Alex Smith and asks that a new advertising banner be developed for the zoo's Web site. In particular, she wants to see some new animations that highlight the Alamo City Zoo name. She also wants several text messages displayed on the banner promoting the zoo's attractions including the new bear exhibit. Alex asks you to create the new advertisement based on a banner that he started to develop. You'll add a spotlight effect where the spotlight starts small at the center of the banner and increases to reveal the banner. You'll also develop a special text effect for the store name where the letters increase in size one after the other to give it a pulsating effect. Finally, you will add the text messages promoting the company.

1. Open the **aczAdDraft.fla** file located in the Tutorial.04\Case2 folder included with your Data Files, and then save the document as **aczAd.fla** in the same folder.
2. Create a new movie clip symbol named **Circle**. In symbol-editing mode, draw a circle at the center of the Stage. The circle should have a white fill, no stroke, and dimensions of 40 pixels wide and 40 pixels high. In the Info panel, set the X and Y registration point coordinates to 0. Exit symbol-editing mode.
3. Extend the Company Name layer to 20 frames. Insert a new layer above the Company Name layer and name it **Mask**. Select Frame 1 of the Mask layer and drag an instance of the Circle symbol from the Library panel to the center of the Stage. In the Property inspector, set the instance's X and Y coordinates to 150 each to center it on the Stage.
4. Insert a keyframe at Frame 20 of the Mask layer. Select the Circle instance at Frame 20 and change its size to 300 pixels wide by 300 pixels high. Create a motion tween between Frames 1 and 20.
5. Select all of the frames on the Mask layer, and then copy the frames to the Clipboard. Insert a new layer above the Mask layer and select all of its frames. Paste the copied frames to the new layer named **Circle**.
6. Temporarily hide the contents of the Mask layer to work with the contents of the Circle layer. Click Frame 1 of the Circle layer, select the Circle instance on the Stage, and then change its alpha amount to 40%. Click Frame 20 of the Circle layer, select the Circle instance, and then change its alpha amount to 40%. Move the Circle layer so that it is below the Company Name layer.
7. Show the Mask layer, right-click the layer, and then change its type to Mask. Make sure the Company Name layer is masked. Test the animation. The mask gradually reveals the company name. The motion tween on the Circle layer displays the dimmed circle to coincide with the circle on the Mask layer to create the special effect.
8. Hide the Mask layer temporarily, unlock the Company Name layer, select the company name text block, and then copy the text block. Insert a new layer above the Mask layer and name it **Name**. Use the Paste in Place command to paste the company name text block in the Name layer in the same relative position as in the Company Name layer.
9. Insert a layer folder above the Name layer, move the Name layer inside the new layer folder named **Letters**.

10. Select the text block in the Name layer, convert the text to individual letters, and then distribute the letters to individual layers. Delete the empty Name layer. Move all the letter keyframes to Frame 20 by selecting all the Frame 1s of the individual letter layers and dragging them all to start in Frame 20. This is where the individual letters animation will begin.
11. Extend all of the layers except the Mask and Company layers by inserting regular frames at Frame 100 of each layer.
12. To make each letter change in size for a brief moment, you will insert two keyframes to each layer where the size of the letter is increased slightly in the first of the two new keyframes. So for the A layer, add a keyframe at Frame 22 and another at Frame 24. Then use the Transform panel to change the size of the instance in Frame 22 to be 130% larger. For the next letter in layer l, insert a keyframe at Frame 26 and another at Frame 28. Increase the size of the instance in Frame 26 to 130%. For the letter a in layer a, insert a keyframe at Frame 30 and another at Frame 32. Then increase the size of the letter in Frame 30 to 130%.
13. Repeat Step 12 for each letter, starting two frames after the previous letter. The last layer (for the second o in Zoo) will have keyframes added at Frames 66 and 68. Show the Mask layer, lock the Company Name layer, and then test the animation. The individual letters should increase in size one at a time after the mask effect.
14. Drag a horizontal guide from the top ruler and place it about 50 pixels from the top of the Stage. Drag two more horizontal guides, placing one about 100 pixels from the top of the Stage and the other about 200 pixels from the top of the Stage.
15. Insert three new layers above the Letters folder and name them **Text1**, **Text2**, and **Text3**. Insert a keyframe at Frame 20 of the Text1 layer. Create a new text block centered just below the guide 50 pixels from the top of the Stage. Use the Monotype Corsiva font, a font size of 20, and the text fill color of black. Use bold and italic styles. Type **Monkeys and Gorillas!** in the text block.
16. Convert the text block to a symbol named **Text1**. Insert a keyframe at Frame 25 of the Text1 layer and create a motion tween between Frames 20 and 25. At Frame 20, use the Transform panel to reduce the size of the Text1 instance to 50% of its original size. The text will increase in size throughout the motion tween.
17. Insert a keyframe of Frame 25 of the Text2 layer. Create a new text block in the pasteboard to the left of the Stage just below the guide 100 pixels from the top. Use the same text settings as in Step 15 and type **Elephants and Tigers!** in this text block.
18. Convert the text block to a symbol named **Text2**. Insert a keyframe at Frame 30 of the Text2 layer and create a motion tween between Frames 25 and 30. At Frame 30, move the text instance to the Stage about 100 pixels from the top and centered on the banner. The text will fly in from the left of the Stage throughout the motion tween.
19. Create one more text motion tween in the Text3 layer between Frames 30 and 35. Create a text block with the words **New Bear Exhibit!** in the pasteboard to the right of the Stage just below the guide 200 pixels from the top. This text block should fly in from the right of the Stage to the center of the banner about 200 pixels from the top. Clear the guides.
20. Insert a new layer above the Text3 layer and name it **Paw1**. Insert a keyframe at Frame 35. Drag an instance of the bear paw symbol to the upper-left corner of the banner, staying within the large circle. Insert another keyframe at Frame 40 and move the bear paw instance toward the bottom so that it is below the letters "Ne" in the New Bear Exhibit! text. Create a motion tween between Frames 35 and 40 and have the bear paw instance rotate clockwise twice as it moves from the top to the bottom.

21. Insert a new layer above the Paw1 layer and name it **Bear**. Insert a keyframe at Frame 40. Drag an instance of the bear symbol to the right of the bear paw instance below the New Bear Exhibit! text. Insert another keyframe at Frame 45. At Frame 40 change the bear instance's alpha amount to 0%. Create a motion tween between Frames 40 and 45 so that the bear instance fades in throughout the tween.
22. Insert a new layer above the Bear layer and name it **Paw2**. Insert a keyframe at Frame 45. Drag an instance of the bear paw symbol to the upper-right side of the banner, staying within the large circle. Insert another keyframe at Frame 50 and move the bear paw instance toward the bottom so that it is below the New Bear Exhibit! text and to the right of the bear instance. Create a motion tween between Frames 45 and 50 and have the bear paw instance rotate counterclockwise twice as it moves from the top to the bottom.
23. Test the banner's animation to see all the animations play.
24. Submit the finished file to your instructor, either in printed or electronic form, as requested.

Create | Case Problem 3

Create an ad with animations of individual letters, text block animations, a nested movie clip, and a motion guide layer.

There are no Data Files needed for this Case Problem.

Westcreek Nursery Westcreek Nursery is expanding and opening a new store at a new location. To advertise the new location and promote her business, Alice has started a new marketing campaign. As part of this campaign, she wants to place an ad on the local newspaper's Web site. She asks Amanda Lester to develop the new ad. To help Amanda, you will create several animations, including one where the letters in the word "Westcreek" fall into place followed by an animation of the word "Nursery" to create the title for the ad. Then several animated text blocks will move into place on the ad, followed by a graphic of the word "Flowers" that will move across the ad banner simulating a truck. The graphic will have animated tires.

1. Create a new document that is 400 by 400 pixels in size and has a green (#006633) background. Save the file as **westcreekAd.fla** in the Tutorial.04\Case3 folder included with your Data Files.
2. Draw a rectangle to create a border around the inside of the Stage. Do not include a fill and use yellow (#FFFF66) for the stroke. Set the stroke height to 3 and use a dashed line for the stroke style. Use the Property inspector to set the width and height to 365 and the X and Y values to 18. Then name Layer 1 as **Background**, extend this layer to Frame 120, and lock the layer.
3. Create horizontal guides at 50 pixels and at 150 pixels from the top of the Stage.
4. Insert a new layer and name it **Title1**, and then create a text block with the word **Westcreek**. Use white for the text color, Impact for the font, 40 for the font size, and apply bold and italic styles. Center the word on the guide 150 pixels from the top of the Stage.
5. Insert a layer folder above the Title1 layer and name it **Westcreek text**. Move the Title1 layer to the new layer folder. Then select the Title1 text block, break it apart, and distribute the individual letters to separate layers. The new layers for the letters should be inside the layer folder. Delete the Title1 layer.

EXPLORE

6. Convert each of the letters into symbols with movie clip behavior. Use the following names for the symbols to match the letters they represent: **W**, **E1**, **S**, **T**, **C**, **R**, **E2**, **E3**, and **K**. Create a new folder in the Library, name it **Westcreek**, and then move all the letter symbols inside the folder.

7. Each letter will be animated to drop in from the top part of the Stage to its current location 150 pixels from the top. The letters will move one at a time, rotating, and fading in as they move to form the word Westcreek. The first letter will start in Frame 1 and every other letter will start every 10 frames. Move each of the letters' keyframes that are in Frame 1 of their respective layers to start every 10 frames. The keyframes should be moved to the following frames: W – Frame 1; e – Frame 11; s – Frame 21; t – Frame 31; c – Frame 41; r – Frame 51; e – Frame 61; e – Frame 71; k – Frame 81. Be sure to keep each letter in its own layer.
8. Insert ending keyframes for each letter in its corresponding layer as follows: W – Frame 10; e – Frame 20; s – Frame 30; t – Frame 40; c – Frame 50; r – Frame 60; e – Frame 70; e – Frame 80; k – Frame 90. Then create motion tweens between the two keyframes on each layer.
9. For each letter, select its first keyframe and move the letter to the guide 50 pixels from the top of the Stage. This is where the letters will start. Each letter will drop in one at a time to form the word Westcreek at the center of the Stage. At the beginning keyframe for each letter, also change the alpha amount to 0% for the letter instance and use the Property inspector to add a clockwise rotation in each motion tween. Each letter should rotate twice. Test the animations. The letters for the word Westcreek drop into place one at a time. They fade in and rotate as they fall. Collapse the Westcreek text folder to make it easier to work with the other layers in the Timeline.
10. Insert a layer above the Westcreek text layer folder and name it **Title2**. Insert a keyframe at Frame 71. Create a text block using the same type settings as in Step 4. Type **Nursery** in the text block. Center this text block on the guide 50 pixels from the top of the Stage.
11. Convert the Nursery text block to a movie clip symbol named **Title2**. Insert a keyframe at Frame 80 of the Title2 layer. Create a motion tween on this layer between Frames 71 and 80. Select the Title2 instance at Frame 71 and change its alpha amount to 0%. Select Frame 80 of the layer and move the Title2 instance so that it is centered below the Westcreek text. The Nursery text should move from its initial position to below the Westcreek text and should fade in as it moves into position.
12. Insert a new layer and name it **Text1**. Insert a keyframe at Frame 80 of this layer and then create a text block in this frame. The text should be white, use Impact for the font, use 30 for the font size, and be styled with bold but not italic. Place the text block on the pasteboard to the left of the Stage about 50 pixels from the top. Type **Always Fresh!** in this text block. Convert the text block to a symbol named **Text1**.
13. Insert a keyframe at Frame 85 of the Text1 layer and move the text block to the center of the Stage, keeping it about 50 pixels from the top. Create a motion tween between Frames 80 and 85 so that the Text1 instance moves in from the left of the Stage.
14. Insert a new layer and name it **Text2**. Insert a keyframe at Frame 85 and create a text block using the same settings used in Step 12. Place the text block in the pasteboard to the right of the Stage about 370 pixels from the top. Type **Delivered on Time!** in this text block. Convert the text block to a symbol named **Text2**.
15. Insert a keyframe at Frame 90 of the Text2 layer and move the text block to the center of the Stage, keeping it about 370 pixels from the top. Create a motion tween between Frames 85 and 90 so that the Text2 instance moves in from the right of the Stage.

16. To create a graphic that will simulate a truck moving across the Stage you will start by creating a rotating wheel symbol. This symbol will then be embedded in the truck graphic. Create a new movie clip symbol named **Rotating wheel**. In symbol-editing mode, use the Oval tool to draw a circle at the center of the Stage. The circle should be about 22 pixels in diameter. Use a black solid stroke color with a stroke height of 2 and a white fill color. If necessary, set the circle's X and Y coordinates to 0.
17. Use the Line tool to draw a line horizontally across the center of the circle and another vertically across the center. Keep the lines inside the circle. These lines represent the spokes for the wheel. Select both the circle and the lines at the same time and convert them to a movie clip symbol. Name this symbol **Wheel**.
18. While still in symbol-editing mode for the Rotating wheel symbol, insert a keyframe at Frame 12 and then create a motion tween between Frames 1 and 12. In Frame 1, set the Wheel instance to rotate clockwise one time. The Rotating Wheel symbol is complete. Exit symbol-editing mode.
19. Create a new movie clip symbol named **Truck**. In symbol-editing mode, create a text block at the center of the Stage using Impact for the font, 42 for the font size, and green (#66FFCC) for the font color. Make the text bold and italic. Type the word **FLOWERs** in all uppercase, except for the letter *s*. Select the letter s and reduce its font size to 34. Use the Info panel to set the X and Y registration point coordinates to 0 to center the text on the Stage.
20. Use the Line tool to draw a short horizontal line about 30 pixels wide using a stroke color of yellow (#FFFF00) and a stroke height of 1. Draw the line about 5 pixels to the left of the letter F. Create three copies of this line and place the lines to the left of the letter F. Each line should be about the same distance from the letter F and they should be equally spaced from each other. The lines will add to the effect of the FLOWERs text moving.
21. Drag an instance of the Rotating Wheel instance to the Stage and place it right below the letter L in FLOWERs. Drag another instance and place it below the letter R. These instances will be the wheels for the truck. The Truck symbol is complete. Exit symbol-editing mode.
22. Insert a new layer above the Text2 layer and name it **Truck**. Insert a keyframe at Frame 70 and drag an instance of the Truck symbol in the pasteboard to the upper-left side of the Stage. Insert another keyframe at Frame 100, and then create a motion tween between Frames 70 and 100.
23. Insert a motion guide layer above the Truck layer. Make sure the Truck layer becomes the guided layer. On the Guide: Truck layer, insert a keyframe at Frame 70. Use the Pencil tool to draw a smooth line starting from where the Truck instance is located and ending at the center of the Stage below the Nursery text about 300 pixels from the top of the Stage. This is the path the Truck graphic will follow. Make sure the Truck instance is attached to the beginning of the line at Frame 70 and to the end of the line at Frame 100. Click the Orient to path option in the Property inspector at the beginning of the motion tween. Hide the Guide: Truck layer.
24. Test the animation.
25. Submit the finished file to your instructor, either in printed or electronic form, as requested.

Create | Case Problem 4

Create an ad banner with a motion guide layer, a mask, text block animations, and a nested movie clip.

There are no Data Files needed for this Case Problem.

Regional Dietetic Association Richard Perez, president of the Regional Dietetic Association, meets with Web designer Katie Ellison to discuss the development of a new advertisement banner they can use to place in various Web sites promoting the association. The ad will contain the association's name, an animation of a star going around the name, and several graphics containing text messages. Katie asks you to create the new ad, following her instructions.

1. Create a new document 250 by 250 pixels in size with a yellow (#FFFF00) background. Save this file as **rdaAd.fla** in the Tutorial.04\Case4 folder included with your Data Files.
2. Create a text block at the center of the Stage. Use Garamond for the font, 34 for the font size, dark brown (#663300) for the text color, and make the text bold. Type **Regional Dietetic Association** in the text block where each word is in a separate line and all three lines are centered within the text block. Change the name of Layer 1 to **Dark text** and extend the layer to Frame 60.
3. Insert a new layer and name it **Mask**. On this layer, create a rectangle with a black fill and no stroke. Make the rectangle the same size as the text block and draw it so that it completely covers the text block. Select the rectangle on the Stage and convert it to a movie clip symbol named **Mask rectangle**.
4. Insert a keyframe at Frame 30 of the Mask layer and create a motion tween between Frames 1 and 30. At Frame 1 move the rectangle above the text block. The rectangle will move from above the text block down to cover the text block. The rectangle mask will reveal the text block as it moves over it.
5. Change the Mask layer's type to Mask. Make sure the Dark text layer becomes a masked layer. Test the mask animation to see the text block revealed as the mask goes over it.
6. Unlock the Dark text layer and select the text block in Frame 1. Copy the text block to the Clipboard. Lock the Dark text layer again. Insert a new layer and name it **Light text**. If necessary, move the Light text layer to below the Dark text layer. The Light text layer should not be masked. At Frame 1 of the Light text layer, use the Paste in Place command to place the text block in the same relative position as the original in the Dark text layer.
7. Select the text block in the Light text layer and change its color to light cyan (#99CCCC). The light cyan text will show first and will then be replaced by the dark brown text as the rectangle mask moves over the dark brown text.
8. Insert a new layer above the Mask layer and name it **Border**. Draw a rectangle using black (#000000) for the stroke color, no fill, and rounded corners. Use 20 for the rectangle corner radius. Make the rectangle 190 pixels in width and 160 pixels in height. Position the rectangle so that the text block is completely inside the rectangle.
9. Insert a new layer above the Border layer and name it **Star**. In Frame 1 of the Star layer, create a star shape at the bottom of the Stage using the PolyStar tool. Use 5 for the number of sides and 0.5 for the point size. Use beige (#FFCC99) for the fill and black for the stroke. Use a solid stroke with a height of 1. Make the star shape approximately 40 pixels wide and 40 pixels high. Select the star shape and convert it to a movie clip symbol named **Star**. Insert a keyframe at Frame 60 of the Star layer and create a motion tween between Frames 1 and 60.

10. Animate the Star instance to move around the text block following the rectangle as a path. First copy the existing rectangle in Frame 1 of the Border layer. Then insert a motion guide layer above the Star layer. Make sure the Star layer becomes the guided layer. In Frame 1 of the Guide: Star layer, use the Paste in Place command to paste the copy of the rectangle in the same relative position as the original rectangle.

EXPLORE

11. Hide the contents of the Border layer to work with the copied rectangle in the guide layer. Use the Eraser tool with a small eraser size to erase a small section of the rectangle in the middle of its bottom side.
12. In Frame 1 of the Star layer, attach the Star instance to the bottom of the rectangle at the left endpoint that was created by the eraser. At Frame 60 of the Star layer, attach the Star instance to the bottom of the rectangle at the right endpoint.
13. Hide the contents of the Guide: Star layer and show the contents of the Border layer. Test the animation to see the Star instance move around the banner following the rectangle path.
14. Create a new movie clip symbol named **Text animation**. In symbol-editing mode, create a text block using Arial as the font, 12 for the font size, blue (#0000FF) for the text color, and no bold or italic styles. Center align the text within the text block. Type **Develop Professionally** in the text block and then center the text block on the Stage by setting its X and Y registration point coordinates to 0 in the Info panel.
15. Insert a keyframe at Frame 11 and change the text in the text block to **Network with Peers**. Insert another keyframe at Frame 21 and change the text to **Promote Health Awareness**. Insert another keyframe at Frame 31 and change the text to **Join Now!**. Insert a regular frame at Frame 40 to extend the layer. The text block will change every 10 frames. Exit symbol-editing mode.
16. Create a new movie clip symbol named **Text rectangle**. In symbol-editing mode, create a rectangle with rounded corners at the center of the Stage. Use black (#FFFFFF) for the stroke color and green (#66FF00) for the fill color. Set the stroke height to 1 and the corner radius points to 10. The size of the rectangle should be 160 pixels wide and 25 pixels high. Select all of the rectangle and, in the Info panel, set its X and Y registration point coordinates to 0 to center it on the Stage. Drag an instance of the Text animation symbol to the center of the rectangle. Use the Info panel to set the Text animation instance X and Y registration point coordinates to 0. Exit symbol-editing mode.
17. Insert a new layer above the Guide: Star layer and name it **Text rectangle**. In Frame 1 of this layer, drag an instance of the Text rectangle symbol to the top of the Stage. Place its left edge about 45 pixels from the left of the Stage. Insert a keyframe at Frame 30 of the Text rectangle layer and create a motion tween between Frames 1 and 30. At Frame 30, move the Text rectangle instance so that it is at the bottom of the Stage and so that its left edge is still about 45 pixels from the left of the Stage. The Text rectangle instance will move from the top to the bottom of the Stage.
18. Test the document's animation in a separate Flash player window to see the Text animation that is nested inside the Text rectangle movie clip.
19. Submit the finished file to your instructor, either in printed or electronic form, as requested.

Review | Quick Check Answers

Session 4.1

1. use the Motion Guide command on the Insert menu; click the Motion Guide button in the Timeline
2. any two of the following tools: Pencil, Pen, Oval, Rectangle, or Brush
3. Lock both layers.
4. False. Text can be used as a mask in a mask layer.
5. motion guide
6. to make a motion tweened object orient itself to the slope of the path it is following
7. False. The contents of the masked layer are revealed when the object in the mask layer moves over it.

Session 4.2

1. Text can be animated to move from one part of the Stage to another. Text can be animated to rotate, fade in or fade out, and increase or decrease in size. Individual letters of a text block can be animated to create special effects.
2. break it apart twice
3. The new layers are named according to the text in each text block.
4. because you cannot have more than one object or symbol on a layer with a motion tween
5. To make the letter layers easier to work with and organize in the Timeline. A layer folder can be collapsed to hide its layers, which makes it easier to work with the other layers.
6. False. The original layer content is moved to the new, separate layers.

Session 4.3

1. Drag the onion skin markers left or right or use the Modify Onion Markers menu to change how many frames are onion skinned.
2. It enables you to see the contents of the frames before and after the current frame, which helps you compare what the current frame contents should be in comparison to the other frames.
3. A nested movie clip contains other movie clips in its Timeline that might have their own animations in their respective Timelines. Any change you apply to a nested movie clip in the main Timeline also affects the movie clips it contains.
4. parent movie clip
5. because each nested movie clip has its own Timeline that is independent of the document's main Timeline
6. In the Movie Explorer, select an instance of a symbol, and then use the Go to Symbol Definition command on the options menu.

Ending Data Files

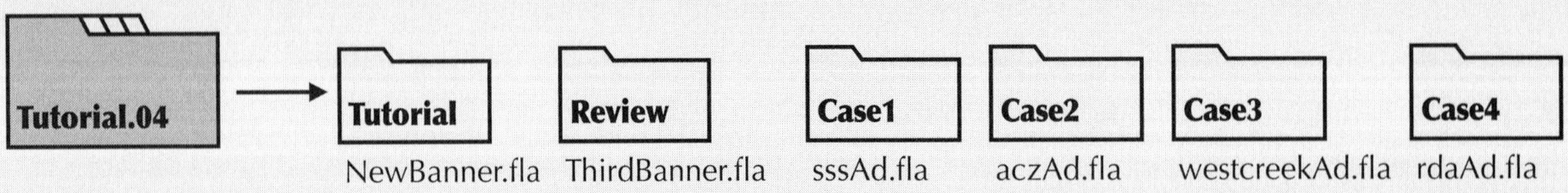

Objectives

Session 5.1
- Explore the different button states
- Add a button from the Button library
- Create a button

Session 5.2
- Learn about actions
- Add actions to buttons
- Add actions to frames

Session 5.3
- Compare different types of sound effects
- Learn how to acquire sounds for your documents
- Add sound effects to buttons
- Add a background sound to a document

Making a Document Interactive

Adding Buttons, Actions, and Sounds

Case | Admiral Web Design

Admiral Web Design is designing a lunch specials page for the Jenny's Oyster Hut Web site. Jenny Emerson wants the new banner design for the lunch specials page to be similar to the site's other banners and to include a background sound as well as animation. Aly suggests that visitors have the option to turn off the animation and the background sound, which some visitors might find distracting while they view the page. She suggests adding several buttons to the banner to control the animation and to mute the sound. She also suggests that the buttons include their own sound effects to help the visitor know when the button has been clicked. Jenny agrees to Aly's suggestions and approves the development of the new banner.

In this tutorial, you will create buttons, including buttons that change in response to the pointer. You will add buttons to a document and then add actions to the buttons so they can be used to control the animation. You will also learn how to change the way the animation plays by using frame actions. Finally, you will add sound effects to the buttons and a background sound to the animation.

Starting Data Files

Tutorial.05 →

Tutorial
Bubbles.wav
jennysbanner.fla
Stamp.wav

Review
Ding.wav
specialsbanner.fla

Case1
Door.wav
Party.wav
sssbanner.fla

Case2
PianoLoop.wav
Ping.wav
zoobanner.fla

Case3
AutoLoop.wav
Carhorn.wav
westcreeklogo.fla

Case4
rdabanner.fla

Session 5.1

Exploring the Different Button States

Published Flash SWF files, also called movies, can include interactive elements. **Interactive** means that the user has some control over the movie, such as being able to stop or play its animation. Adding interaction to a movie draws the viewer in because the viewer is able to do more than passively watch the animation. One of the easiest ways to include interactivity is to add buttons that perform an action. Buttons are symbols that contain a Timeline with only four frames. Buttons can take many forms, can include sound effects, and can even change appearance or behavior when the user places the pointer over them. Each of the button's frames represents a different state of the button and can contain different content, as shown in Figure 5-1.

Figure 5-1 **Sample button states for each frame**

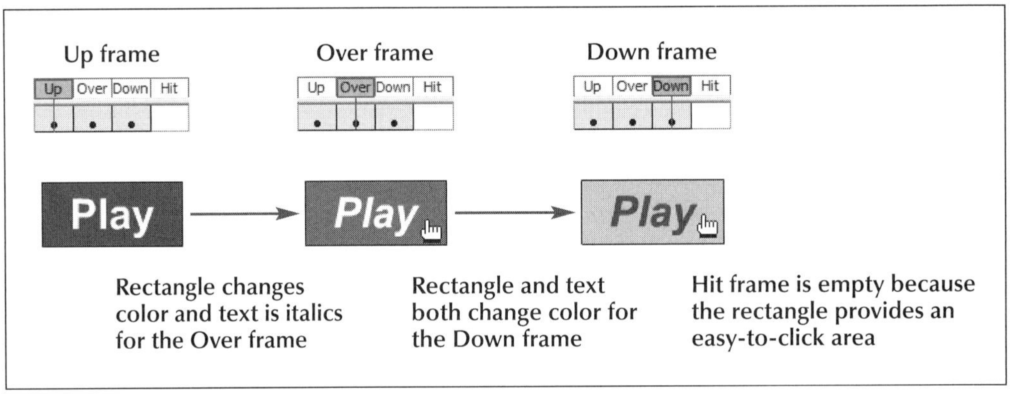

The content in each frame appears in response to the pointer's action. The **Up frame** contains the button's default state. This is what the button looks like to the user before the user has used the button to take an action. When the pointer is over the button, the content in the **Over frame** is displayed. If you make the content of the Over frame different from the content in the Up frame, you create a **rollover effect**—that is, when the user moves the pointer over the button, the button changes to show what is in the Over frame. The contents of the **Down frame** show what the button looks like when the user clicks it. You can make the contents of the Down frame different from the other frames to give the user a visual clue that the button has been clicked. The **Hit frame** does not change the appearance of the button. Instead, it represents the clickable or active area of the button. This is the area of the button that responds to a mouse click and displays the hand pointer when the pointer is over it. In Figure 5-1, the rectangle changes color and its text becomes italic for the Over frame, the rectangle changes color and its text changes color and remains italic for the Down frame. The Hit frame is empty because the rectangle provides an easy-to-click area. You will make the banner for Jenny's Oyster Hut lunch specials page interactive by adding buttons with these different states to control the animation and mute the background sound.

Choosing When to Include a Button's Hit Frame | InSight

The Hit frame is the area of the button the user can rollover or click to perform an action. When a button is a solid shape, such as a rectangle or oval, the button area is easy to click and you can leave the Hit frame empty. When a button consists of text, the user must click the letters in the text to activate the button. This can be difficult, especially if the text is small. To make it easier to click the button, draw a filled shape such as a rectangle to cover the text in the Hit frame. The shape is not visible in the published movie, but it represents the area the user can click to activate the button.

Adding a Button from the Buttons Library

A quick way to add a button to a document is by using one of the predesigned buttons in the Buttons library. The Buttons library is one of the Common Libraries, which store symbols that install with Flash and can be copied to your documents. The library's button symbols can be copied to your document's library and used within your document. Recall that symbols are stored in a document's library, and that you can add copies of the symbol, called instances, to the Stage.

Aly has included a background sound in the new banner design, which is shown in Figure 5-2. You will add a button from the Buttons library that allows the user to mute the background sound that you will add later. This enables users to decide whether they want to listen to background sounds when visiting the Web site.

Initial banner design **Figure 5-2**

You will add the first button to the banner design that Aly started.

To add the flat blue stop button from the Buttons library:

1. Open the **jennysbanner.fla** file located in the **Tutorial.05\Tutorial** folder included with your Data Files, and then save the file as **jennysbanner2.fla** in the same folder.
2. Change the workspace to its default layout, and then display the rulers if necessary. All of the banner contents are visible.

3. In the Timeline, click the **title** layer to select it, click the **Insert Layer** button to add a new layer, and then rename the new layer **buttons**. You'll place all of the buttons for the banner on the buttons layer.

4. Click **Window** on the menu bar, point to **Common Libraries**, and then click **Buttons**. The Buttons Library panel opens in the middle of the program window. The library contains 277 items organized into folders that represent categories of buttons such as Buttons Oval and Classic Buttons. See Figure 5-3.

Figure 5-3 Buttons Library panel

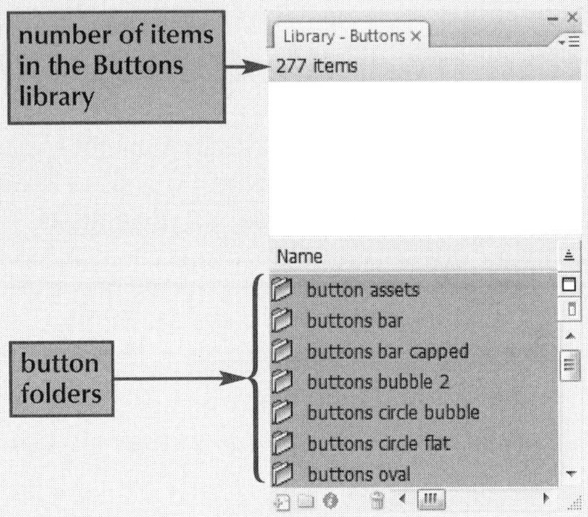

5. In the Buttons Library panel, scroll down and then double-click the **playback flat** folder icon . The list of buttons in that folder appear.

6. In the Buttons Library panel, scroll down and then click the **flat blue stop** button to select it. A preview of the button appears at the top of the panel. You want to copy the flat blue stop button into the buttons layer of the document.

7. In the Timeline, make sure that the buttons layer is still selected, and then drag the **flat blue stop** button from the Buttons Library panel to the lower-left corner of the Stage to create an instance of the button. The flat blue stop button is added as a symbol with a Button behavior type to the document's library. The library now contains five items.

8. On the Stage, drag the button instance approximately **10** pixels from the left edge of the Stage and approximately **210** pixels from the top of the Stage.

   You don't need the Buttons library anymore, so you'll close it.

9. On the Buttons Library panel tab, click the **Close** button to close the panel. See Figure 5-4.

Button symbol added to the banner **Figure 5-4**

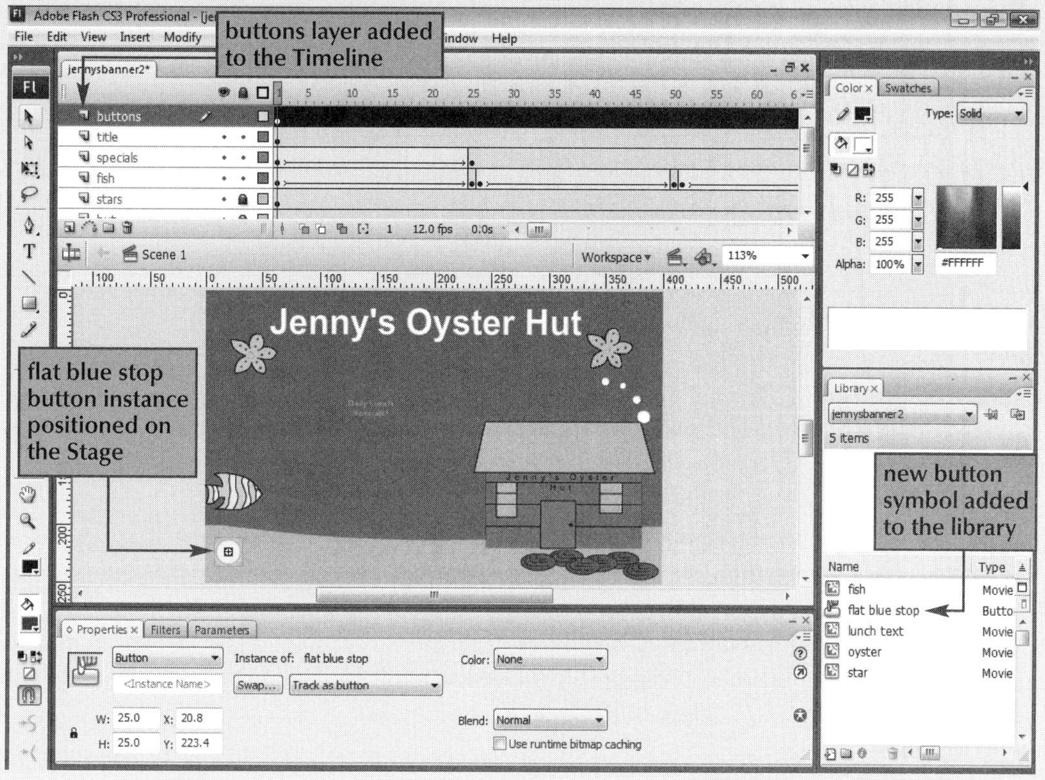

After you have added a button instance to a document, you should test it to be sure that it works as expected. You can do this within the Flash program window by turning on the Enable Simple Buttons command. When you turn this command on, the button exhibits its behavior on the Stage. When you move the pointer over the button, the pointer changes to a hand pointer and the button displays any rollover effects that are part of the button. This feature allows you to ensure that the button works properly. After you have reviewed the button's behavior, you need to turn off the Enable Simple Buttons command to select the button instance on the Stage and continue to modify it. You cannot select a button with the hand pointer.

You'll use the Enable Simple Buttons command to test the new button instance.

To view the flat blue stop button's behaviors:

1. Click **Control** on the menu bar, and then click **Enable Simple Buttons**. The command is turned on and you can test the button.
2. On the Stage, click an empty area away from the button to deselect the button.
3. On the Stage, position the pointer over the flat blue stop button instance. The pointer changes to a hand, indicating that an action will occur after the button is clicked.
4. Click the **flat blue stop** button. When you click the button, the button changes color to indicate that it was pressed.

Editing a Button Instance

You can edit any button you add from the Buttons library. For example, you can change the contents of the Over frame to change the button's rollover effect or you can change the contents of the Down frame to change the effect exhibited when the button is clicked. You can also change the colors or graphics in a predesigned button to match the design of the document and to make it look less like a standard button. You can even delete the contents in one of the button's frames if you don't want the button to exhibit a certain behavior such as a rollover effect.

Aly's instructions are to modify the flat blue stop button so that it uses a different color for its Down frame. This frame is displayed when the button is clicked, giving the user visual feedback that the button has been clicked. Because the button is a symbol, you must be in symbol-editing mode to modify it.

To edit the flat blue stop button to change its Down frame color:

1. In the Library panel, double-click the **flat blue stop** button icon. The button opens in symbol-editing mode and its four-frame Timeline appears.
2. Increase the magnification level to **400%** to get a better view of the button. See Figure 5-5.

Figure 5-5 Flat blue stop button in symbol-editing mode

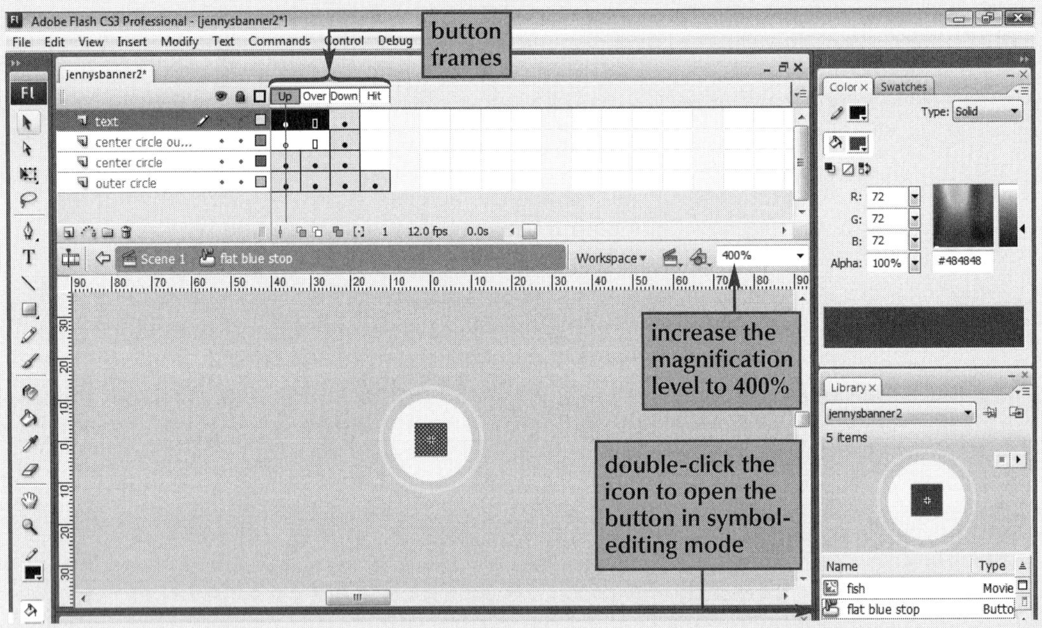

3. In the Timeline, drag the playhead back and forth between the Up frame and the Down frame to see how the button changes.
4. In the Timeline, click the **Down** frame of the text layer. The small white square in the center of the button is selected, which is indicated by the fine dot pattern.
5. In the Tools panel, use the Fill color palette to change the square's color to **green** (#00FF00). See Figure 5-6.

Tip

You can also press the comma and period keys to move the playhead backward and forward, respectively, one frame at a time.

Figure 5-6

Color changed in the button's Down frame

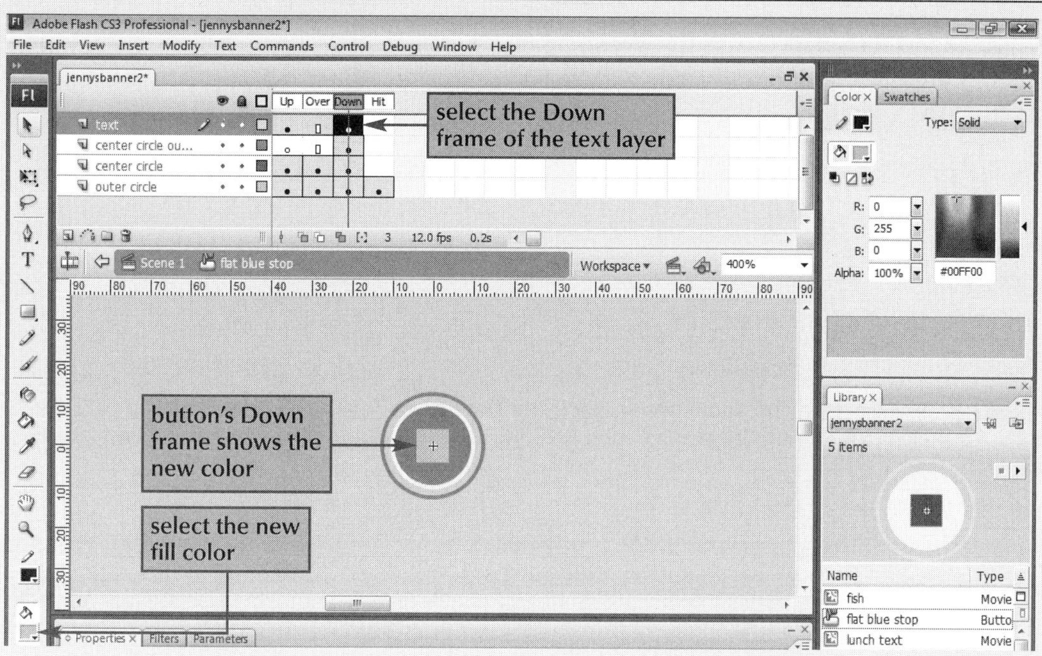

6. On the Edit bar, click the **Scene 1** link to exit symbol-editing mode and return to the document.

   Now you can see how the button works with the change you made.

7. On the Stage, click the **flat blue stop** button instance. The small gray square in the center of the button turns green when you click the button instance.

8. Click **Control** on the menu bar, and then click **Enable Simple Buttons**. The Enable Simple Buttons command is turned off, so you can select the button instance on the Stage.

Anti-aliasing Text | InSight

To improve readability, Flash uses a rendering engine that provides high-quality, clear text in Flash documents. **Anti-aliasing**, which is part of the rendering process, smoothes the edges of text displayed on the computer screen. Anti-aliasing is especially effective when using small font sizes. When text is selected on the Stage, you can choose a font rendering method in the Property inspector. Two of the methods available are Anti-alias for animation and Anti-alias for readability. Select Anti-alias for animation when the text will be animated such as when you apply a motion tween to a text object. This results in a smoother animation. If the text will not be animated, select Anti-alias for readability. This improves the legibility of the text.

Labels often identify the purpose of each button so that it is clear to the user what will happen when a button is clicked. You should add a label either within the button's frames or to an instance of a button on the Stage. You will add text below the flat blue stop button instance on the Stage to label it as the Mute button. This tells the user what happens when the button is clicked. Otherwise, the user may not know what purpose the button serves.

To add text to identify the Mute button instance:

1. Increase the magnification level to **200%**.
2. In the Tools panel, click the **Hand** tool, and then drag the document so that the button instance is centered on the Stage.

   You will set the text properties and add a text block below the button.
3. In the Tools panel, click the **Text** tool, set the font to **Arial**, set the font size to **10**, set the text color to **black** (#000000), and then apply the **bold** style.
4. In the Property inspector, if necessary, click the **Font rendering method** button, and then click **Anti-alias for readability**.
5. On the Stage, add a text block below the button with the text **Mute**, and then deselect the text block.
6. If necessary, in the Tools panel, click the **Selection** tool, reposition the text block as shown in Figure 5-7, and then deselect the text block.

> **Tip**
>
> You can also hold down the Spacebar to change the pointer to a hand pointer, drag the document to change its view on the Stage, and then release the Spacebar to return to the previous pointer.

Figure 5-7 Label added below the button

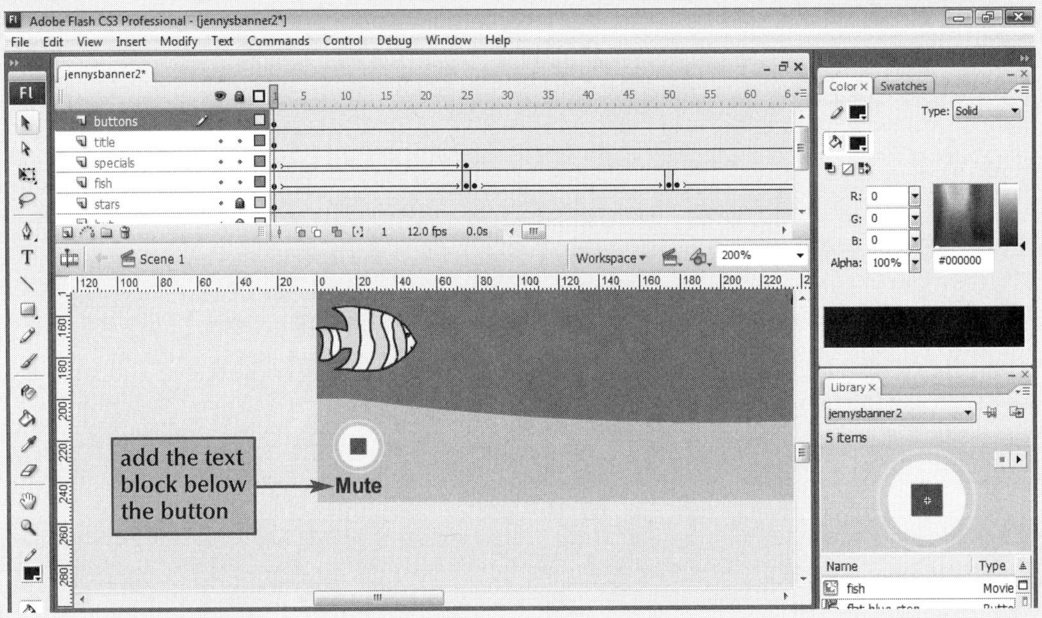

7. Save the document.

Creating a Custom Button

The buttons in the Common Buttons Library provide many choices to use in documents. For a more professional look, you will often want to create unique buttons that match your project's design. Flash has the tools to create almost any kind of button you need. Buttons can be any shape such as rectangles and ovals or even in the form of text.

You can convert an existing object on the Stage, such as a rectangle, into a button symbol and then edit the button in symbol-editing mode, creating or modifying the content for each of the button's four frames as needed. The object on the Stage becomes an instance of the button symbol and the symbol is added to the library. You can also create a new symbol with a button behavior and then draw the button shape in symbol-editing mode as well as create or modify the content for each of the button's four frames. Thebutton you created is stored in the document's library, but no instances appear on the Stage. To use the button in your document, you must create instances of the button.

Creating a Custom Button

| Reference Window

- Create the button's shape on the Stage, and then select the shape.
- Click Modify on the menu bar, and then click Convert to Symbol.
- Type a name in the Name box, click the Button option button, and then click the OK button.
- Switch to symbol-editing mode, and then modify the content for each of the button's four frames as needed.

or

- Click Insert on the menu bar, and then click New Symbol.
- Type a name in the Name box, click the Button option button, and then click the OK button.
- Create the button's shape on the Stage.
- Switch to symbol-editing mode, and then modify the content for each of the button's four frames as needed.

Based on Aly's instructions, you need to create two new buttons for the banner. These buttons are both rectangles with rounded corners. However, one button is a Stop button, which the user clicks to stop the animation while it is playing. The second button is a Play button, which the user clicks to start the animation playing at any time. Because these two buttons have a similar appearance, you can create the Stop button, and then modify a copy of the Stop button to create the Play button. You will then add instances of these buttons to the banner.

To create the Stop button:

1. In the Tools panel, click the **Rectangle** tool. The rectangle should have rounded corners, so you need to specify how much rounding to apply.
2. In the Property inspector, click the **unlock** icon to change it to its locked state if necessary, type **10** in the Rectangle corner radius box, and then press the **Enter** key. Each corner radius is set to 10.
3. In the Property inspector, set the stroke color to **black** (#000000), set the fill color to **red** (#FF0000), set the stroke height to **2**, and then set the stroke style to **Solid**.
4. In the Timeline, select the **buttons** layer, if necessary.
5. On the Stage to the right of the Mute button, draw a rectangle that is approximately 60 pixels wide and 20 pixels high. See Figure 5-8.

Tip

In the Property inspector, click the Reset button to set the corner radius values to zero and lock the values.

Figure 5-8 Rectangle button shape

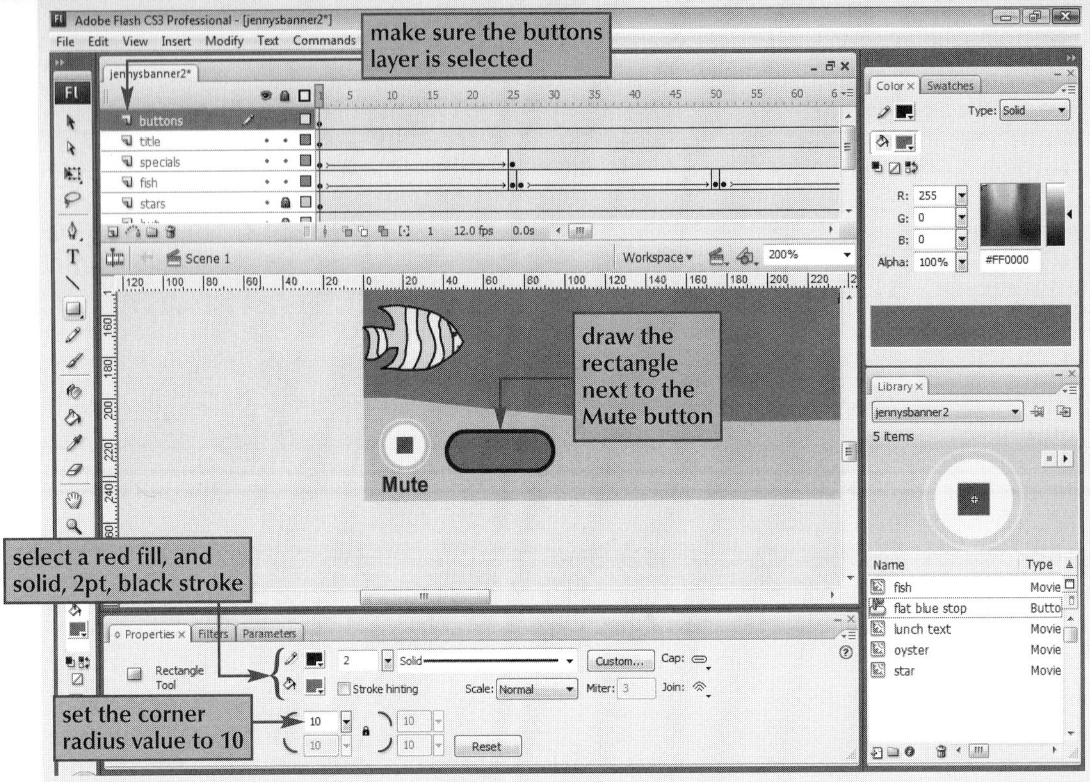

6. In the Tools panel, click the **Selection** tool, and then, on the Stage, double-click the **rectangle** to select both its fill and its stroke. You'll convert the selected button shape to a symbol.
7. Click **Modify** on the menu bar, and then click **Convert to Symbol**. The Convert to Symbol dialog box opens.
8. Type **Stop button** in the Name box, click the **Button** option button to select the behavior type, and then click the **OK** button. The new button is added to the document's library, and then selected button instance remains on the Stage.

You'll edit this button to add a text label and to create the different states of the button. The Stop button will have a rollover effect. When you roll the pointer over the button, the button should change from a red fill to a red radial gradient fill. This provides a visual clue to the user that something will happen if the button is clicked. The button should also move when it is clicked, providing visual feedback that reinforces the user's action. There are four frames in the Timeline for the button. The Up frame has a keyframe and contains the rectangle you created, which represents the default state of the button. You will add text to the button and then add keyframes to the Over and Down frames to create the different states of the button.

To add text to the Stop button and create the different states of the button:

1. In the Library panel, double-click the **Stop button** icon to open it in symbol-editing mode, and then increase the magnification level to **200%**. See Figure 5-9.

Figure 5-9 Stop button in symbol-editing mode

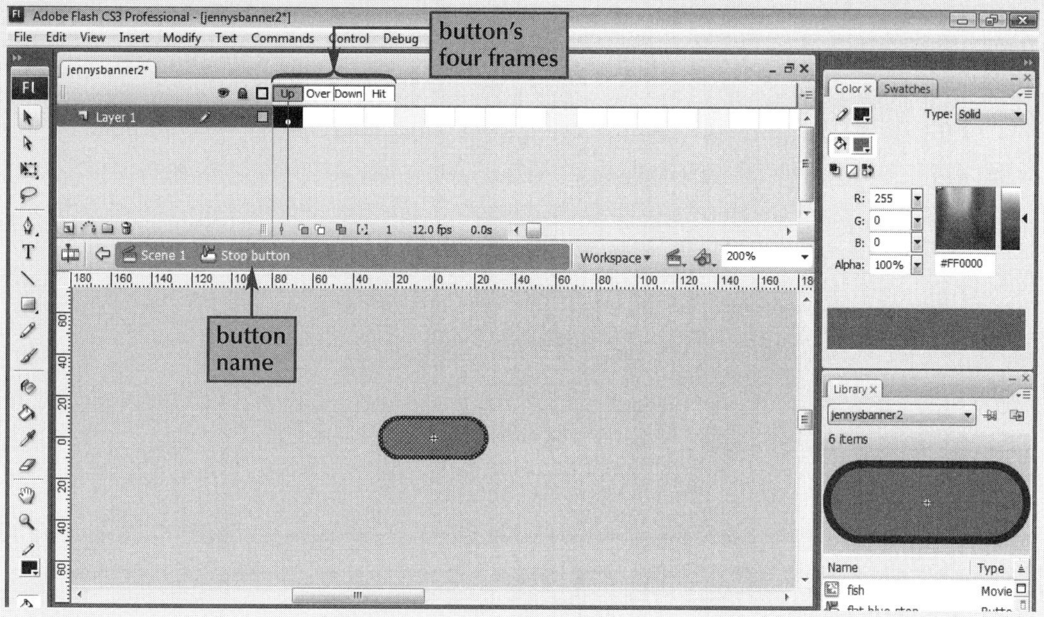

2. In the Tools panel, click the **Text** tool [T] to select it, and then, in the Property inspector, if necessary, set the font to **Arial**, set the font size to **10**, set the text color to **white** (#FFFFFF), and apply the **bold** style.
3. Inside the rectangle, create a text block, and then type **Stop**. You want the text block to be centered inside the rectangle.
4. In the Tools panel, click the **Selection** tool to select it, and then click the **Snap to Objects** button to deselect it.
5. On the Stage, drag the text block so that it is centered inside the rectangle. See Figure 5-10.

Figure 5-10 Label added to the Stop button

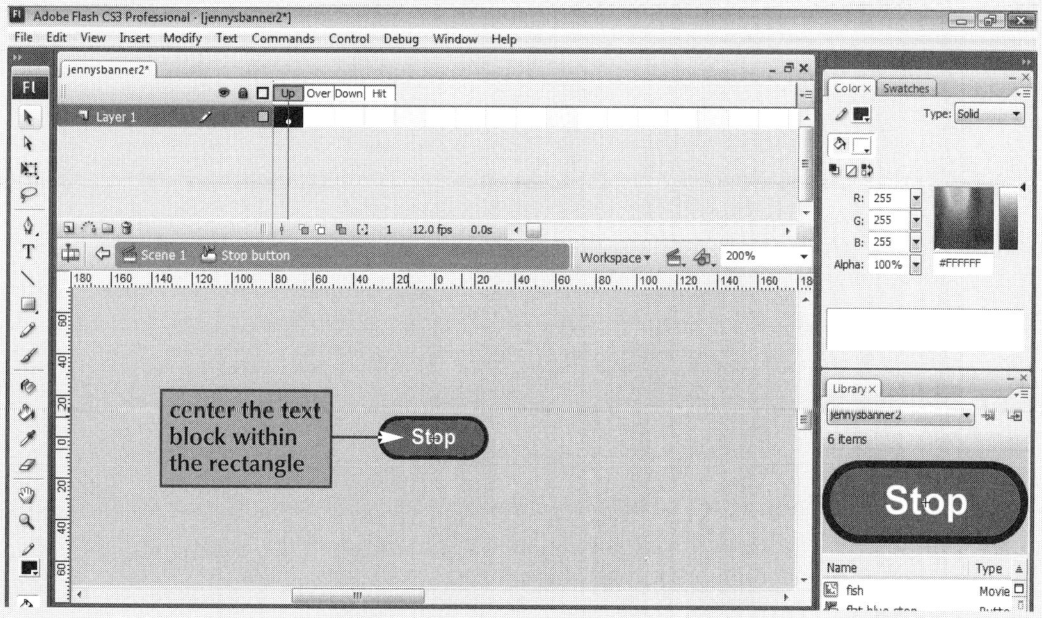

Next, you will create the contents for the Over frame.

6. In the Timeline, click the **Over** frame to select it, and then insert a keyframe. The contents of the Up frame are automatically copied to the Over frame.

   You want the button's appearance to change from the default state to the Over state, so that the button's color changes when the user moves the pointer over the Stop button. To accomplish this, you will change the button's fill color in the Over frame.

7. In the Tools panel, click the **Fill color** control, and then click the **red radial gradient** button, which is the third swatch in the bottom row of the color palette. The red radial gradient replaces the rectangle's red fill. See Figure 5-11.

Figure 5-11 **Rectangle's fill changed in Over frame**

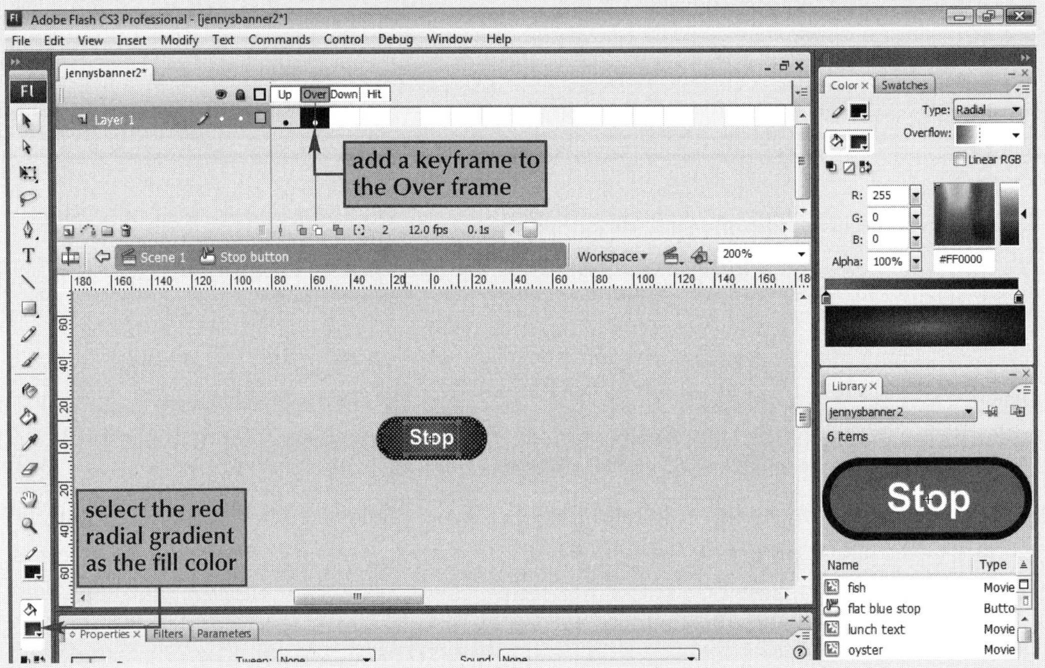

When the user clicks the Stop button, you want the button to appear as if it has been pressed and released. To create this effect, you need to change the button's position in the Down frame.

8. In the Timeline, click the **Down** frame, and then insert a keyframe. The contents of the Over frame are copied to the Down frame.

9. With the rectangle and text box still selected, press the **Down Arrow** key three times, and then press the **Right Arrow** key three times. The rectangle moves three pixels down and three pixels to the right, which will make the button appear to shift when the user clicks it.

   You don't need to add anything to the Hit frame because the rectangle shape provides the clickable or active area for the button.

10. On the Edit bar, click the **Scene 1** link to exit symbol-editing mode and return to the document.

The button and its different states are complete. You'll preview the button instance's behavior on the Stage to make sure the different effects you created appear correctly. You use the Enable Simple Buttons command to preview the effects.

To test the Stop button instance's rollover effects:

1. Click **Control** on the menu bar, and then click **Enable Simple Buttons**. The command is turned on.
2. On the Stage, click a blank area to deselect the button, and then move the pointer over the **Stop button** instance. Because of the rollover effect, the button changes color. See Figure 5-12.

Figure 5-12 Stop button's rollover effect

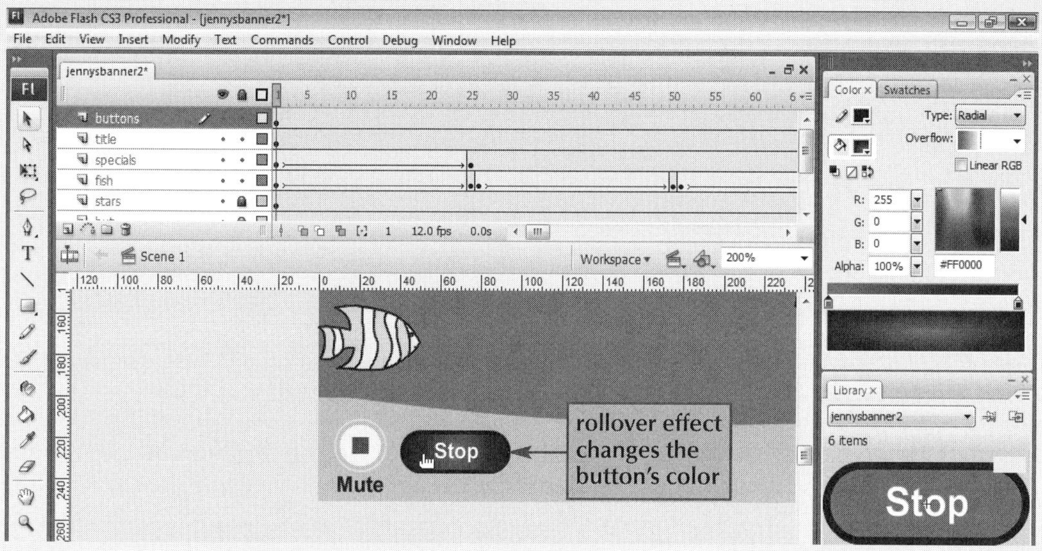

3. Click the **Stop** button instance. The button shifts down and right, providing a visual cue that the button was clicked. You are done testing the visual effects of the Stop button.
4. Click **Control** on the menu bar, and then click **Enable Simple Buttons**. The command is turned off and you can select the button instances on the Stage.

Copying and Editing a Custom Button

Many times, a Flash document will require two or more buttons that are similar. Rather than creating each button individually, you can create the first button and then copy and modify the button for each of the remaining buttons. This method is faster and helps to ensure consistency in the design of the buttons.

The lunch specials page requires one more button—the Play button. The Play button looks very similar to the Stop button. Instead of creating a new button, you will make a copy of the Stop button you just created, and then modify it to create the Play button.

To create a copy of the Stop button:

1. In the Library panel, click the **Stop button** to select it.
2. In the Library panel, click the **options menu** control, and then click **Duplicate**. The Duplicate Symbol dialog box opens with the duplicate button's name, Stop button copy, selected. You will rename the button.

3. Type **Play button** in the Name box, and then click the **OK** button. The Duplicate Symbol dialog box closes, and the new Play button symbol is added to the document's library. See Figure 5-13.

Figure 5-13 Play button symbol in the library

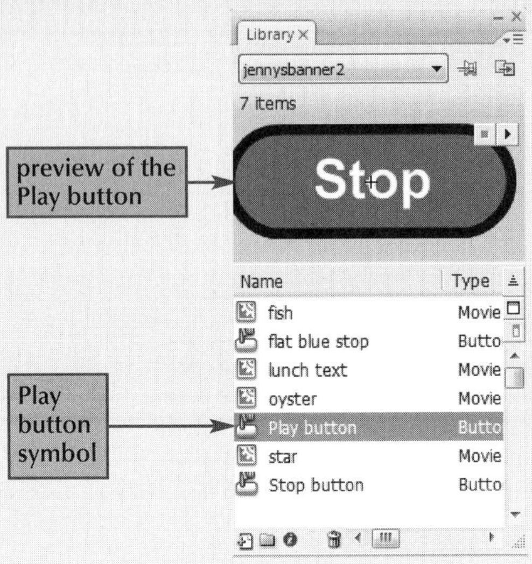

You need to modify the Play button so it is not an exact copy of the Stop button. You will modify the Play button to be green in its default state and change to a green radial gradient color when the user positions the pointer over the button. As you change the button's colors, check that you have selected the appropriate frame. Also, make sure that you don't change the text block. For example, in the Up frame, you only want to change the color of the rectangle's fill to green. So the Up frame must be selected and the text block must be deselected. After you modify the Play button in the document's library, you need to create an instance of the button symbol in the document.

To edit the Play button and add an instance of the button to the Stage:

1. In the Library panel, double-click the **Play button** icon. The button opens in symbol-editing mode.
2. Increase the magnification level to **200%**. The close up view of the button makes the button easier to edit.

   For the Up frame you only want to change the color of the rectangle's fill to green, so you need to make sure the Up frame is selected and the text block is deselected.
3. In the Timeline, click the **Up** frame, click a blank area of the Stage to deselect the rectangle and the text block, and then click the rectangle's fill to select it. Only the rectangle's fill in the Up frame is selected. You'll apply a different color to the button.
4. In the Tools panel, click the **Fill color** control, and then click **dark green** (#006600). The Play button's fill becomes green, replacing the red color. See Figure 5-14.

Figure 5-14 Play button's fill changed

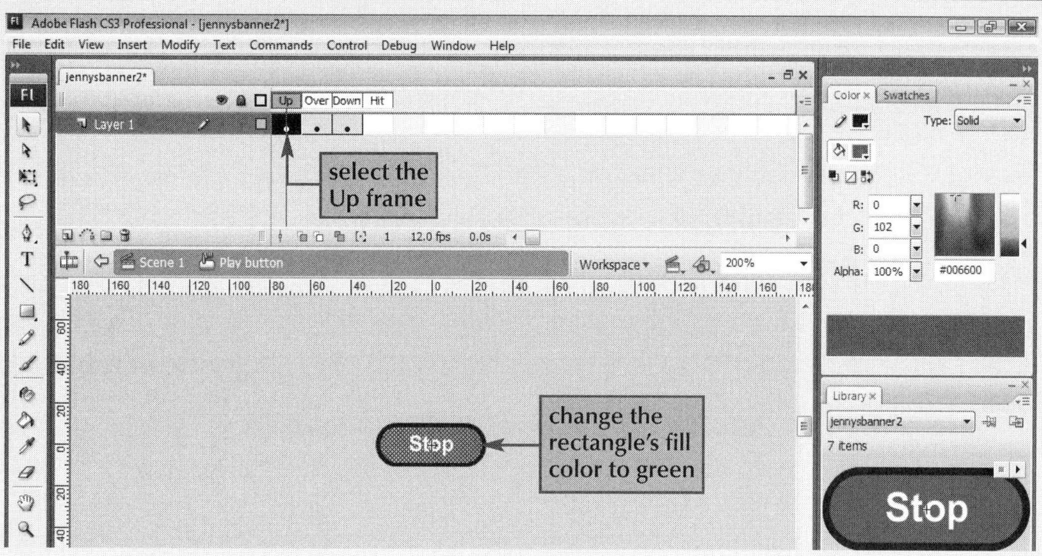

5. In the Tools panel, click the **Text** tool [T], and then make sure the font is **Arial**, the font size is **10**, the text color is **white**, and the text style is **bold**.
6. On the Stage, click the **Stop** text block, and then change the text to **Play**. The button text reflects the button's purpose.

   So far, you changed the color and text of the Up frame. The Over and Down frames still contain the red fill and the Stop text. You will modify those frames next.
7. In the Timeline, click the **Over** frame to select the button.
8. In the Tools panel, click the **Fill color** control, and then click the **green radial gradient**, the fourth gradient swatch in the bottom row of the color palette. The button's fill color changes color. You'll change the button's text next.
9. In the Tools panel, click the **Text** tool [T], and then, on the Stage, click the **Stop** text block and change the text to **Play**. The Over frame is edited for the Play button. See Figure 5-15.

Figure 5-15 Over frame changed

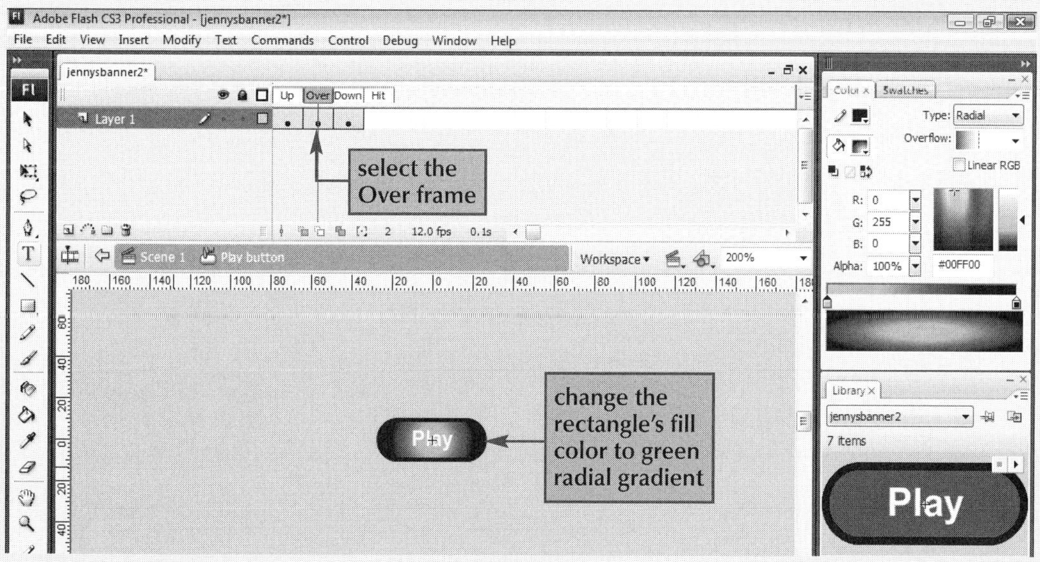

10. In the Timeline, click the **Down** frame, and then repeat Steps 8 and 9. The button changes in the Down frame to the green radial gradient fill and the button text is updated to Play.
11. On the Edit bar, click the **Scene 1** link to exit symbol-editing mode.

    Although the Play button is complete, you still need to add an instance of the button to the Stage.
12. Drag the **Play** button from the Library panel to the Stage, placing the instance to the right of the Stop button instance. See Figure 5-16.

Figure 5-16 **Play button instance added to the document**

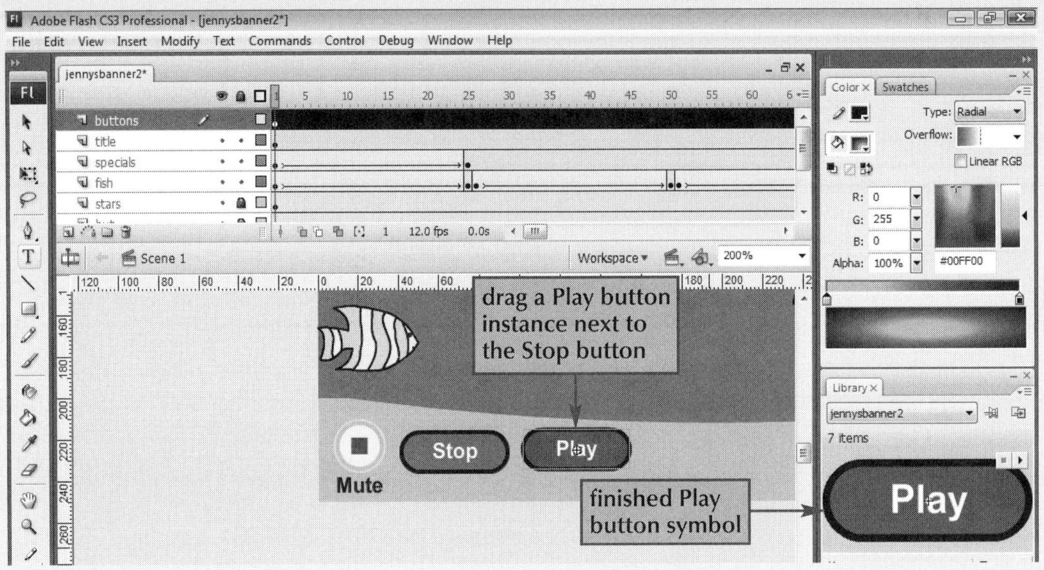

Aligning Objects on the Stage

When a document includes multiple objects similar in design, you should align them with each other. If several objects are placed vertically, then align them by their left or right sides. If the objects are placed horizontally, then align then by their top or bottom sides. You should also make the space between the objects the same. Taking the time to align and space the objects evenly will give a document a more professional appearance. The Align panel, shown in Figure 5-17, includes different options to arrange a group of selected objects on the Stage. You can line up selected objects by their edges or centers and you can also distribute them so that they are evenly spaced. Objects will align with the leftmost or rightmost selected object when aligned by their left edges or right edges, respectively. They will align with the topmost or bottommost selected object when aligned by their top edges or bottom edges, respectively.

Figure 5-17 **Align panel**

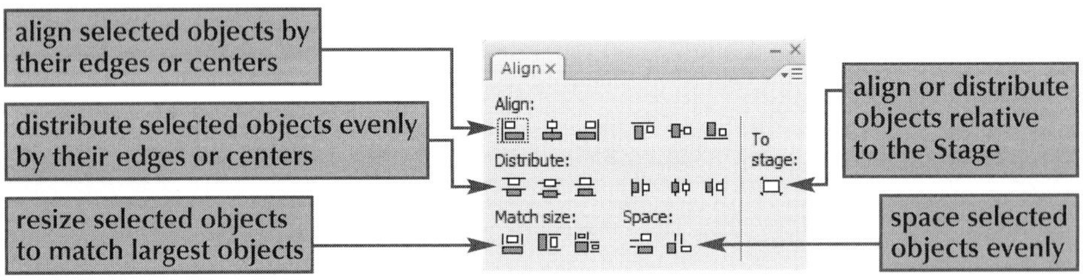

Aly wants you to align the Mute, Stop, and Play buttons by their bottom edges. She also wants you to make sure that they are positioned with an equal amount of space between them.

To align the Mute, Stop, and Play buttons using the Align panel:

1. Click **Window** on the menu bar, and then click **Align**. The Align panel opens.
2. In the Tools panel, click the **Selection** tool to select it.
3. On the Stage, click the **Mute** button instance, press and hold the **Shift** key, click the **Stop** button instance, click the **Play** button instance, and then release the Shift key. All three buttons instances are selected on the Stage.
4. In the Align panel, click the **Align/Distribute to stage** button to deselect it, if necessary. The selected objects will align relative to each other and not relative to the Stage.
5. In the Align group of the Align panel, click the **Align bottom edge** button. The three button instances align along their bottom edges.
6. In the Space group of the Align panel, click the **Space evenly horizontally** button. The button instances now have an equal amount of space between them. See Figure 5-18.

Tip

You can also press the Ctrl+K keys to open and close the Align panel.

Figure 5-18 Three buttons aligned and evenly spaced

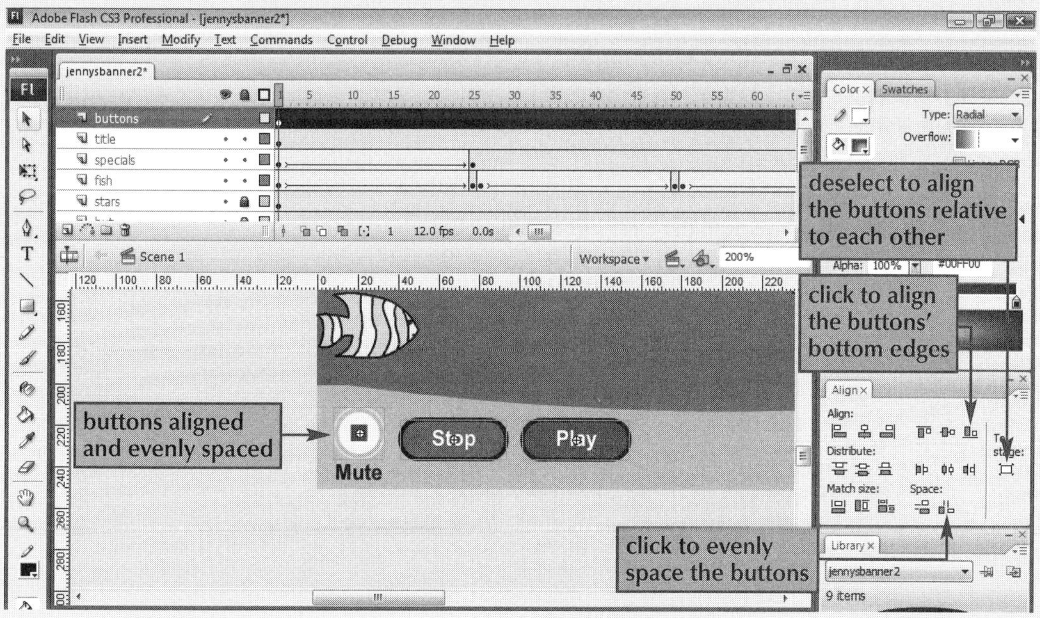

7. Click a blank area of the Stage to deselect the buttons, and then save the document.

In this session, you added a button from the Buttons library to the banner, and then modified it. You also created your own buttons. You then aligned the buttons along their bottom edges and spaced the buttons evenly. The buttons, though attractive and professional looking, do not control anything yet. You will modify them in the next session to control the banner's animation.

Review | Session 5.1 Quick Check

1. What is a button?
2. Why would you add buttons to a document?
3. How can you add a button from the Buttons library to your document's library?
4. How many frames are in a button's Timeline? List their names.
5. How do you create a rollover effect for a button?
6. How can you test a button in your document while in Flash?
7. Which Flash tool can help you to easily align several objects on the Stage?

Session 5.2

Understanding Actions

The buttons you added to the banner do not yet allow the user to control the document's animation. When the button is clicked, the animation does not change. The document still plays sequentially one frame after another until it reaches the end of the animation. According to Aly's instructions, the buttons should allow the user to stop and play the animation. To make the buttons fully functional and interactive, you need to add **actions**, which are instructions that are used to control a document while its animation is playing. Actions are part of the programming language used in Flash called **ActionScript**. The ActionScript language is very similar to the Web language **JavaScript**, which is used to add interactive elements to Web pages. Many of the actions in ActionScript are simple and can be used to create basic navigation controls to manage a document's animation. For example, you can add actions that stop or play an animation. You use ActionScript to create scripts that tell Flash what action to take when a certain event occurs. A **script** is a set of one or more actions that perform some function. An **event** is a situation where the user is interacting with a button, such as clicking a button with the mouse and then releasing it. The Flash Player listens for these events, which can be used to trigger or start the actions in a script.

The sample script shown in Figure 5-19 contains three lines of code. The first line has the mouse event handler `on` followed by the event `release` in parentheses. Release is an event that occurs when the user clicks and then releases the mouse button. An **event handler** tells Flash how to respond to an event. The second line has the action. In this script, the event handler is triggered when the user clicks and then releases the button, causing the `stop` action to execute. The movie then stops playing. You will add this script to the Stop button instance in the banner.

Figure 5-19 Sample script

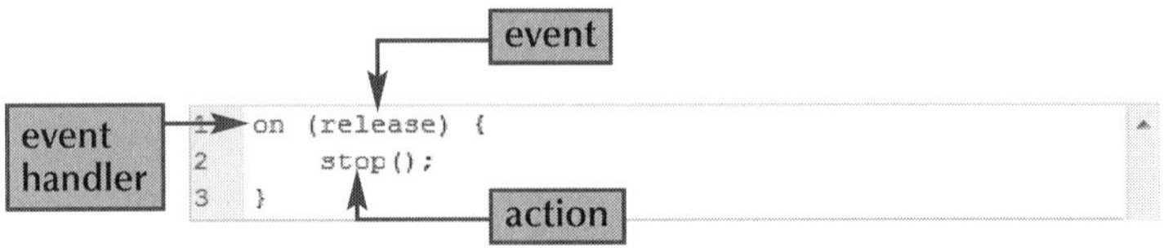

Adding Actions Using the Actions Panel

You do not need to fully understand ActionScript to use its basic actions. Also, you don't need to manually write the scripts yourself. Instead, Flash can create the scripts for you when you select actions in the Actions panel, which is shown in Figure 5-20. Flash creates the scripts needed for these actions to work in your document.

Actions panel **Figure 5-20**

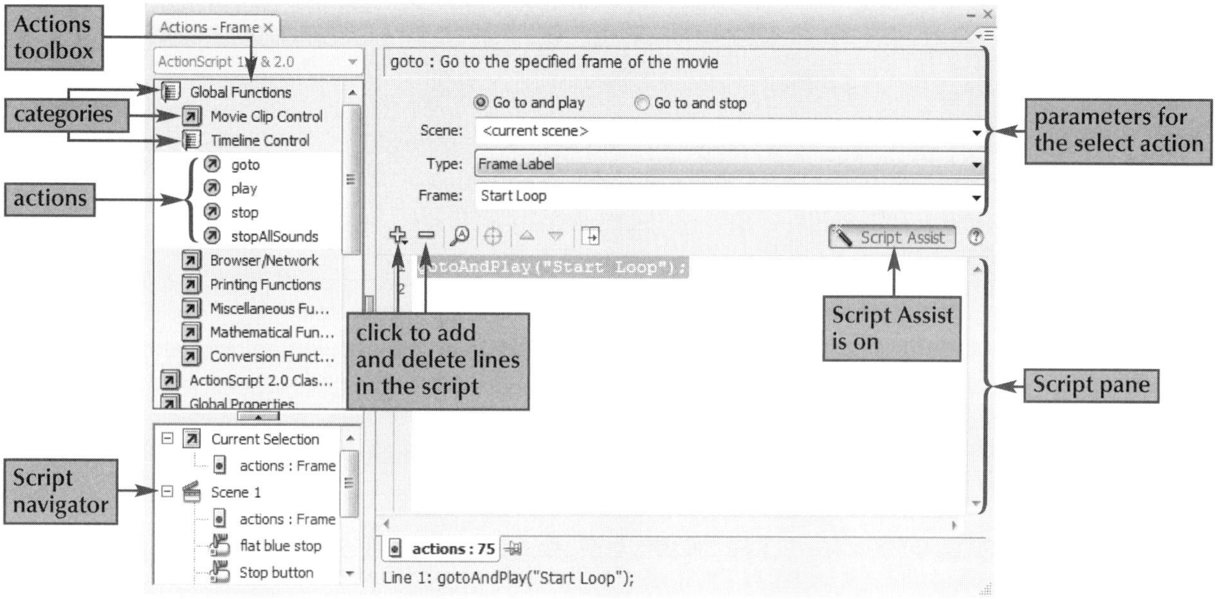

ActionScript 3.0 is the default version for Flash CS3 Professional. Version 3.0 is conceptually different from the earlier versions 1.0 and 2.0 and supports more complex programming structures. You will work with Version 3.0 in Tutorial 8. In Tutorials 5 through 7, you will use ActionScript 2.0, which is easier to use when adding basic navigation actions to buttons.

ActionScript Versions | InSight

ActionScript 3.0, the latest version of the Flash programming language, has been significantly revised and improved. The language is now compliant with industry standards and is based on an international standardized programming language known as ECMAScript. Programs written in ActionScript 3.0 can run up to 10 times faster than those written in previous versions and require Flash Player version 9 or higher to run. Using ActionScript 3.0 also makes developing highly complex applications easier. For a novice, learning ActionScript 3.0 can be a challenging task. However, if you only need to add simple actions to a document, you can still use previous versions of the language such as ActionScript 2.0.

In ActionScript 2.0, you can use the Actions panel in normal mode or Script Assist mode. In normal mode, you write the scripts yourself. This requires a deeper understanding of the ActionScript language. In Script Assist mode, Flash provides actions you select from the Actions toolbox, located on the left side of the Actions panel. The Actions toolbox organizes the available actions into categories. For example, the Global Functions category contains the Timeline Control category, which contains a list of actions that control the timeline. The Script pane, located on the right side of the Actions panel, is where the script is created. When you select an action, Flash automatically adds the appropriate statements to the script, depending on the action and the object to which the action is applied. Some actions require additional settings called **parameters**, which can be selected or entered in the parameters area of the Actions panel.

Reference Window | Using the Actions panel

- Click Window on the menu bar, and then click Actions to open the Actions panel.
- Click the Script Assist button to turn on Script Assist mode.
- If necessary, click the Show/Hide Toolbox button to show the Actions toolbox.
- Click a category in the Actions toolbox to display additional categories or actions.
- Double-click or drag an action to add it to the Script pane.
- To delete an action from the Script pane, select it and then click the Delete (–) button.
- Select or enter values in the parameters section.

When you plan how and where the user needs to interact with a document, you also need to plan what interactions will be part of the document and where these interactions will be placed. You can add actions to buttons or to frames in the timeline.

Adding Actions to Buttons

Buttons are one way to give the user control over the animation. If you want to use buttons, then you need to plan what actions are required to make the buttons functional. You then add the appropriate actions to the button instances on the Stage, and not to the button symbol in the library. A button symbol cannot have actions applied to it, only instances of the button. Different instances of the same button symbol can have different actions.

You will add the stop action to the Stop button and the play action to the Play button.

To add actions to the Stop and Play buttons:

1. If you took a break after the previous session, make sure the jennysbanner2.fla file is open, the workspace is set to its default layout, and no elements are selected on the banner.
2. On the Stage, click the **Stop** button instance to select it. You will add the stop action to this button instance.
3. Click **Window** on the menu bar, and then click **Actions**. The Actions panel opens.
4. In the Actions panel, click the **Script Assist** button to select it, if necessary. The parameters area appears in the upper-right corner of the Actions panel and the Action toolbox displays a list of action categories. The stop action is located in the Global Functions category.
5. In the Actions toolbox, click the **Global Functions book** icon, if necessary, to display its subcategories. The stop action controls the Timeline, so it is located in the Timeline Control category.
6. In the Actions toolbox, click the **Timeline Control book** icon to expand it, if necessary. A list of the available Timeline control actions appears.

7. Double-click **stop**. The stop action is added to the Stop button instance, and the action and its script are visible in the Script pane. See Figure 5-21.

Figure 5-21 Stop script

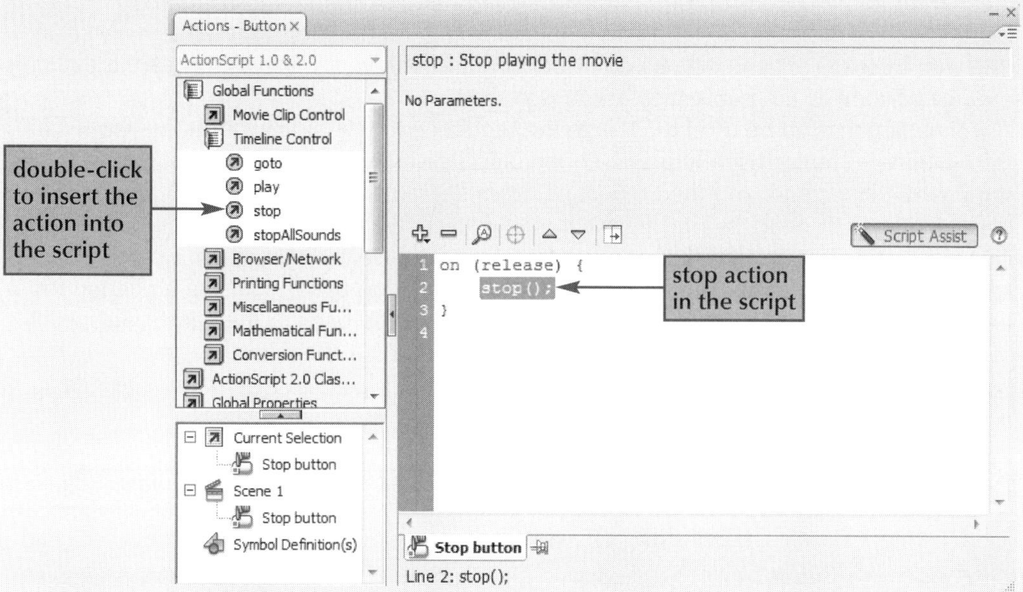

Now you can add the play action to the Play button. To do so, you first need to select the button instance.

8. Click the **Actions panel title bar** to collapse the panel so that you can see the Stage, and then click the **Play** button instance on the Stage to select it.

9. Click the **Actions panel title bar** to expand the Actions panel, and then double-click **play** in the Timeline Control category of the Actions toolbox. The play action and its script are added to the Play button instance.

10. Click the **Actions panel title bar** to collapse the Actions panel.

Tip

To delete an action from the script, select the action and then click the Delete (–) button above the Script pane.

Now that you have added the appropriate actions to the Stop and Play buttons, you should test them to make sure they work correctly.

To test the Stop and Play button actions:

1. Click **Control** on the menu bar, and then click **Test Movie**. The animation plays in the Flash Player, and the fish swims across the banner.

2. In the Flash Player, click the **Stop** button to stop the animation, and then click the **Play** button to restart the animation. The buttons work in Flash Player.

3. Click **File** on the Flash Player menu bar, and then click **Close**.

4. Save the document.

Adding Actions to Frames

Actions that have been added to buttons are executed when certain events occur, such as when the user clicks the button. Another place where you can add actions is in individual frames. Actions in a frame execute when that particular frame is played. Scripts created for frame actions do not require an event handler, unlike those created forbuttons. For example, if you add a stop action to a frame, the script contains only one line with `stop();`. Frame actions do not depend on an event to occur. Instead, they execute as soon as the frame they are in is played.

Frame actions can be used to change the sequence in which the frames are played in the Timeline. A movie usually plays sequentially, starting with Frame 1, continuing through the last frame, and then repeating again at Frame 1. However, you can create a special animation effect by playing the frames in a different order. For example, you can create an animation in which a group of frames plays repeatedly by having the playhead return to an earlier frame. This is called a **loop**. You can do this by placing an action in the last frame of the group that causes the animation to go back to the frame you specify, as shown in Figure 5-22. The frame action is indicated by a small **a** in the frame—in this case, Frame 50. Every time the last frame is played, the playhead in the Timeline jumps back to Frame 25.

Figure 5-22 **Loop created with frame action**

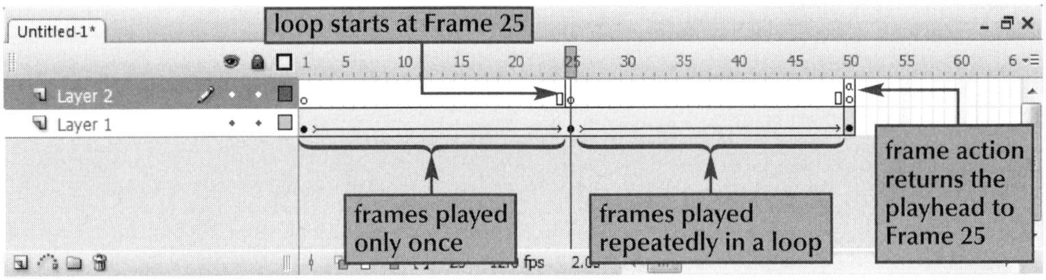

When you need to refer to specific frames in an action, you should use frame labels instead of the frame numbers. A frame label is a name you assign to a keyframe that appears in the Timeline, as shown in Figure 5-23. Remember, anytime a change occurs in a frame, including adding a label, a keyframe needs to be inserted at that frame. You refer to the frame label in an action the same way you refer to a frame number. If you use frame numbers in an action and then later add or delete frames from the Timeline, the action might reference the wrong frames. This is because adding or deleting frames causes the subsequent frames to be renumbered. You would then have to update each action that refers to the renumbered frame. However, if you use frame labels, adding or deleting frames does not affect the labels. For example, if you add a frame label to Frame 25, and then delete Frame 14, the label stills exists but in Frame 24. The renumbered frames still have the appropriate labels attached to them. Any actions that refer to the frames by their labels work correctly and, therefore, do not have to be changed.

Figure 5-23 Frame label

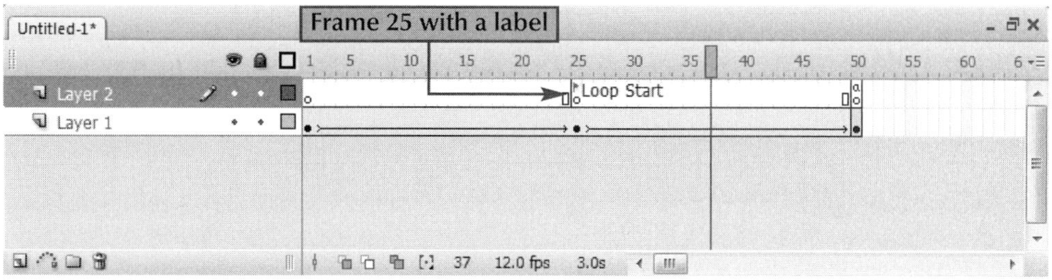

Organizing Documents Using Layers | InSight

To keep a document organized, you should place frame actions and frame labels on separate layers. Although not required, the separate layers make it easier to keep track of the actions and frames, especially when a document contains more than one. If you later need to modify other parts of the document, the actions and frame labels are not affected. As a Flash document gets more complex, placing the different elements on separate layers makes it easier to keep track of them.

The lunch specials banner contains three motion tweens to make the fish swim back and forth. It also contains a motion tween that animates the Daily Lunch Specials text block. When the banner is published, the text and fish motion tweens repeat continuously because the movie plays from Frame 1 to Frame 75 and then restarts again at Frame 1. Aly wants you to change the animation sequence so that the text animates only once and then remains stationary as the fish continues to swim. This means that the text motion tween should not be repeated. To accomplish this, you need to change the animation sequence so that the animation returns to Frame 25 where the text animation ends instead of Frame 1 and then continues to loop from Frame 25 to Frame 75. You will add a frame action to the last frame in the document that moves the playhead to Frame 25. The playhead then continues from Frame 25 to Frame 75 again. As a result, the playhead does not replay the text block's animation, but instead continues with the last two fish motion tweens. Because frames might be added or deleted from the banner at a later date, the frame action in the last frame should refer to a frame label and not to a frame number. You'll add a frame label at Frame 25 that can be referred to by the frame action in Frame 75.

To add an action to a frame:

1. In the Timeline, insert a new layer above the buttons layer and name it **actions**, and then insert a new layer above the actions layer and name it **labels**. The labels layer is the current layer.

   Before adding a label at Frame 25, you need to make Frame 25 a keyframe. Without a keyframe at Frame 25, the label would be added to Frame 1.

2. On the labels layer in the Timeline, click **Frame 25**, and then insert a keyframe. The keyframe in Frame 25 of the labels layer is selected.

3. In the Property inspector, type **Start Loop** in the Frame box, and then press the **Enter** key. The frame label is added to Frame 25 of the labels layer. See Figure 5-24.

Figure 5-24 Frame label added

You will add a frame action to the last frame of the actions layer. This frame action directs the animation to go back to the Start Loop frame. This last frame also needs to be a keyframe.

4. On the actions layer in the Timeline, scroll horizontally to display Frame 75, click **Frame 75**, and then insert a keyframe. You'll add the frame action to this frame.

5. Click the **Actions panel title bar** to expand the Actions panel to list the action categories, and then, if necessary, click **Timeline Control** to list its available actions.

6. In the Actions toolbox, under the Global Functions category and Timeline Control subcategory, double-click the **goto** action. The action is added to the Script pane.

   The script in the Script pane reads `gotoAndPlay(1);`. This means that the action causes the playhead to go back to Frame 1. You want to change the action so that the playhead goes back to Frame 25 instead of Frame 1, which is where the text block motion tween ends. Rather than referring to a frame number in the script, you will refer to the frame label you added to Frame 25.

Tip

You can also click the Add a new item to the script button above the Script pane, point to an action category, and then click an action to add it to the Script pane.

7. In the parameters area of the Actions panel, click the **Type** button to display the available types, and then click **Frame Label**.

8. Click the **Frame** arrow to display the available labels, and then click **Start Loop** to insert it into the script. The Script pane displays `gotoAndPlay("Start Loop");`. The frame action is indicated by a small **a** in Frame 75 of the actions layer in the Timeline. See Figure 5-25.

Figure 5-25 Frame action

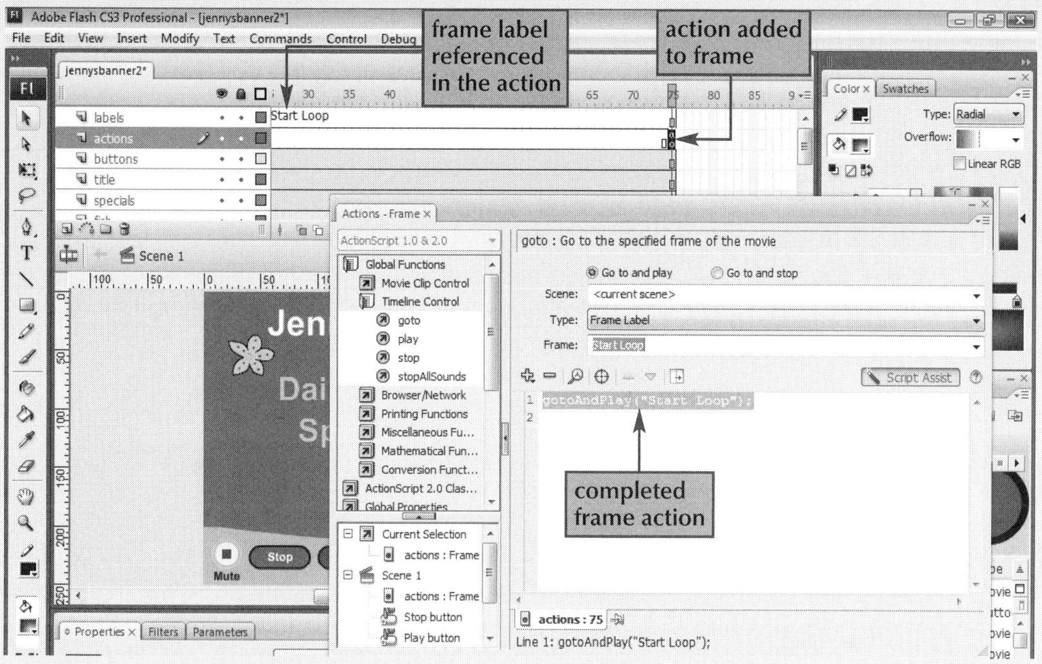

9. Close the Actions panel.

You should test the frame action you added to make sure the animation plays properly. You can do this within the Flash program window by turning on the Enable Simple Frame Actions command. When you turn this command on, frame actions will play when you press the Enter key or use the Play command to test the movie. Testing the frame actions within the Flash program window is another way to test the movie in the Flash Player.

To test the frame action:

1. Click **Control** on the menu bar, and then click **Enable Simple Frame Actions**. The command is turned on and the frame action will play.
2. Click **Control** on the menu bar, and then click **Play**. The animation plays on the Stage. When the playhead reaches Frame 75, it goes back and starts again at the frame labeled Start Loop, which is Frame 25. This makes the fish swim back and forth continuously while the text remains stationary.
3. Click **Control** on the menu bar, and then click **Stop**. The animation stops.
4. Click **Control** on the menu bar, and then click **Enable Simple Frame Actions**. The command is turned off.
5. Save the document.

In this session, you added actions—which are part of ActionScript language—to button instances and to frames on the banner to control the animation. Then, you tested the actions. In the next session, you'll add sounds to the banner.

Review | Session 5.2 Quick Check

1. What is ActionScript?
2. True or False? To use ActionScript, you must know JavaScript.
3. What are actions?
4. Why do scripts created for frame actions not require an event handler?
5. True or False? Actions are added to a button symbol and not to an instance of the symbol.
6. What is an example of an event that triggers an action on a button to execute?
7. Why is it better to refer to a frame label in an action instead of a frame number?
8. What is the difference between a frame action and a button action?

Session 5.3

Using Sounds in a Flash Animation

Flash offers several ways to use sounds. You can add sounds to a document that play continuously and that are independent of the Timeline, such as a background sound. You can add sound effects to instances of buttons to make them more interactive. For example, you can add a sound that plays when a user clicks a button. You can add sounds that are synchronized with the animation, such as a sound simulating a clap of thunder that coincides with an animation of a lightning bolt. You can also add sounds in the form of a voice narration to supplement the information being displayed in the Web page as text or graphics.

Finding Sounds for Animations

Adding sound to an animation can have a very powerful effect, bringing another level of excitement to a well-designed document. The sound you use can be subtle or loud. You can create sounds with a separate sound-editing program and then import the sounds, or you can acquire prerecorded sounds from other sources. Most vendors offer a wide variety of sound effects and music that can be purchased on CDs or DVDs. Sounds are also available for purchase on the Web. You can even download sounds for free from Web sites such as Flash Kit (*www.flashkit.com*). Flash Kit provides a wealth of resources for Flash developers. At its site, shown in Figure 5-26, you can find sounds under Sound FX and under Sound Loops. You can search for sounds using keywords or browse for sounds by category. Sounds listed at the site can also be previewed before being downloaded. Note that the Flash Kit Web site may have been updated or modified since this tutorial was published.

Tip

Sound files you download may be in a compressed format; decompress the file with a utility program such as WinZip before using the sounds.

Flash Kit Web site | Figure 5-26

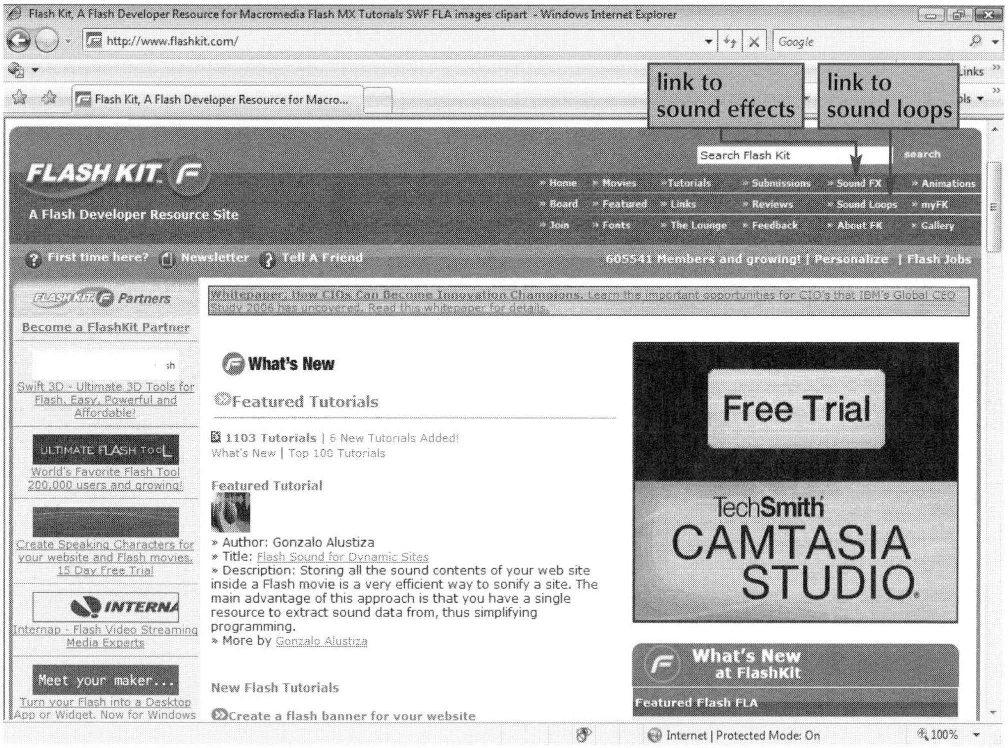

Other Web sites offer sounds for purchase. These Web sites have preproduced sounds from which you can select. They will even create customized sounds for a fee. Two such sites are killersound (*www.killersound.com*) and SoundShopper (*www.soundshopper.com*). These sites also have a few sounds that you can download for free to use in personal projects such as a family or hobby Web site.

Licensing Issues When Using Sounds | InSight

When acquiring sound files, carefully examine the license agreement that determines how you can use the sounds. Even though a sound file can be downloaded for free, restrictions may apply on how you can use it, especially if you plan to distribute the sound with a document. Look for sounds that are **royalty-free**, which means that no additional usage fees apply when you distribute the sounds with your projects. An alternative to downloading free sounds or purchasing sounds is to record your own. This may not always be possible, but if you record a sound file yourself, you don't have to worry about licensing issues.

Adding Sounds to a Document

Because you cannot create sounds in Flash, the sound files you use in documents must first be imported into Flash. The sounds you import must be in a file format that is compatible with Flash, which include Windows Waveform (WAV), Audio Interchange File Format (AIFF) used with Macintosh computers, and MPEG-3 (MP3) used with both

Windows and Macintosh operating systems. The WAV and AIFF formats are not compressed and tend to be larger than MP3 files, which are compressed. Compressed files are smaller because the parts of the sound data that listeners are not likely to notice have been removed. Compressing a sound file basically means that its size has been reduced-without sacrificing too much of the sound quality. You need to pay attention to the size of sound files you add to Flash documents, because they can significantly increase the overall size of the published files, affecting their download time. You can import a WAV file into your document and then compress it to MP3 format within Flash.

Tip

Use MP3 sound files in Flash movies; this format produces very small sound files, retains very good sound quality, and is compatible with Windows and Macintosh computers.

Sound files you import are placed in the document's library along with any symbols and buttons already in the library. In the library, a sound is preceded by a sound icon. Also, when you select a sound in the library, its waveform appears in the Library panel's preview box, as shown in Figure 5-27. A **waveform** is a graphical representation of a sound. After you have a sound file in the document's library, you can use it as many times as you need in the document. The additional uses do not further increase the document's file size, because only one copy of the sound is stored.

Figure 5-27 **Sample sound in the Library panel**

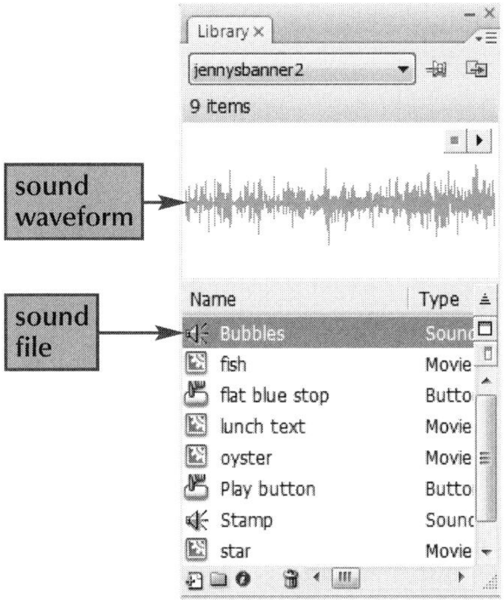

Before you add a sound to a document, you should create a separate layer for each sound and name each layer for the sound contained in the layer. This makes it easier to identify the sound in the Timeline. Also, sounds can be added only to keyframes in the main Timeline or keyframes in a button's Timeline. After you add a sound to a keyframe, it plays when the playhead reaches the keyframe.

Adding Sound to a Button

You can add sounds to buttons to make a button more interactive, such as a sound that plays when the user clicks the button or even when the user moves the pointer over the button. To add a sound to a button, you add it to either its Over frame or its Down frame. A sound added to the Over frame plays when the pointer is moved over the button. A sound placed in the Down frame plays when the button is clicked.

Adding a Sound to a Button

| Reference Window

- Import the sound to the document's library.
- Open the button in symbol-editing mode.
- In the button's Timeline, create a new layer.
- Create a keyframe in the frame where the sound will be placed.
- Select the keyframe.
- In the Property inspector, select the sound from the Sound box.

Based on the banner plan, Aly wants you to add sound effects to the Stop and Play buttons. You'll add the sound to the Down frame, so that it plays when the user clicks the button, providing an audio cue that the button was clicked.

To import the Stamp sound and add it as a sound effect to the Stop button:

1. If you took a break after the previous session, make sure the jennysbanner2.fla file is open and the workspace is set to its default layout.
2. Click **File** on the menu bar, point to **Import**, and then click **Import to Library**. The Import to Library dialog box opens.
3. Navigate to the **Tutorial.05\Tutorial** folder included with your Data Files, click the **Stamp.wav** sound file, and then click the **Open** button. The Stamp file is added to the document's library.
4. In the Library panel, click the **Stamp** sound. The preview box shows the sound's waveform.
5. On the Stage, double-click the **Stop** button instance. The Stop button opens in symbol-editing mode.
6. In the Timeline, insert a new layer and name the layer **Sound**. You will add the Stamp sound to the Sound layer.
7. On the Sound layer in the Timeline, click the **Down** frame to select it, and then insert a keyframe. You will add the Stamp sound to this keyframe.
8. In the Property inspector, click the **Sound** button to display the available sounds, and then click **Stamp**. The Stamp sound is added to the Down frame. See Figure 5-28.

Tip

You can also add a sound to a document by selecting the keyframe where the sound starts and then dragging the sound from the Library panel to the Stage.

Figure 5-28 Sound added to the Down frame

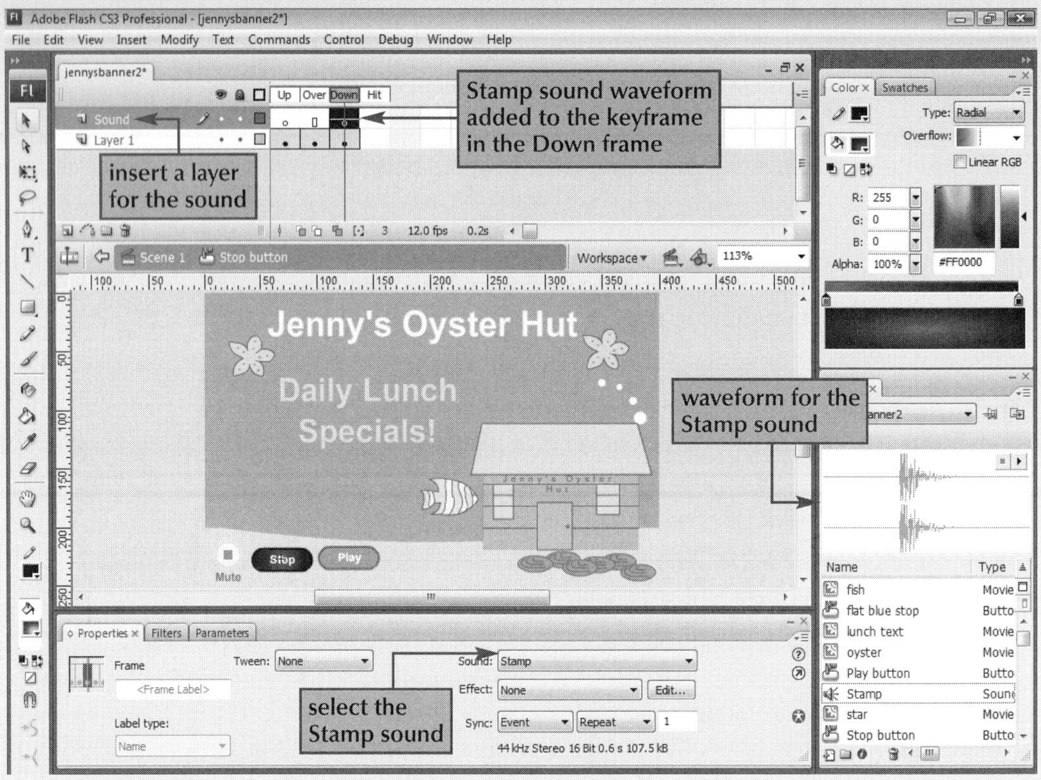

9. On the Edit bar, click the **Scene 1** link to return to the document and exit symbol-editing mode.

You should test the sound you added to the Stop button to make sure it works correctly. You can test the sound within the Flash program window after you turn on the Enable Simple Buttons command. When clicked, the button should exhibit its rollover effect and play the Stamp sound.

To test the sound effect added to the Stop button:

1. Click **Control** on the menu bar, and then click **Enable Simple Buttons**. The command is selected, so clicking the Stop button tests the button rather than selects it.
2. On the Stage, click the **Stop** button. The Stamp sound plays.

   Trouble? If you don't hear a sound when you click the Stop button, your computer's speakers might be off or at a soft volume. Make sure that the speakers are turned on and the volume control is turned up.
3. Click **Control** on the menu bar, and then click **Enable Simple Buttons**. The command is turned off.

The Play button uses the same Stamp sound effect. Because the Stamp sound file is already part of the document's library, you don't need to import another copy to the library. You'll add the sound to the Play button the same way you added it to the Stop button.

To add the Stamp sound effect to the Play button and test it:

1. In the Library panel, double-click the **Play button** icon. The button opens in symbol-editing mode.
2. In the Timeline, insert a new layer and name it **Sound**. You'll add the sound to this new layer.
3. On the Sound layer in the Timeline, click the **Down** frame, and then insert a keyframe.
4. In the Property inspector, click the **Sound** button, and then click **Stamp**. The sound is added to the Down frame.
5. On the Edit bar, click the **Scene 1** link to return to the document.
6. Click **Control** on the menu bar, and then click **Enable Simple Buttons**. You can now test the button by clicking it.
7. Click the **Play** button on the Stage to hear the sound.
8. Click **Control** on the menu bar, and then click **Enable Simple Buttons**. The command is off, and you can select the button on the Stage.

Adding a Background Sound

The user's experience with a Flash movie can be enhanced by playing a background sound. You add a background sound in a separate layer and in the keyframe where you want the sound to start playing.

Aly recorded a bubbling sound that she wants you to use as the background sound for the banner. This sound file is in the WAV format. You will import the sound into your document's library, and then add it as a background sound.

To add the Bubbles background sound to the banner and test it:

1. Click **File** on the menu bar, point to **Import**, and then click **Import to Library**. The Import to Library dialog box opens.
2. Navigate to the **Tutorial.05\Tutorial** folder included with your Data Files if necessary, click the **Bubbles.wav** sound file, and then click the **Open** button. The Bubbles.wav sound file is added to the document's library.
3. In the Timeline, insert a new layer above the labels layer, and then name the new layer **sound**. You will add the bubbles sound to this layer.
4. In the Timeline, click **Frame 1** of the sound layer.
5. In the Property inspector, click the **Sound** button to view the available sounds, and then click **Bubbles**. The Bubbles sound is added to the sound layer. See Figure 5-29.

Figure 5-29 Bubbles sound waveform in layer

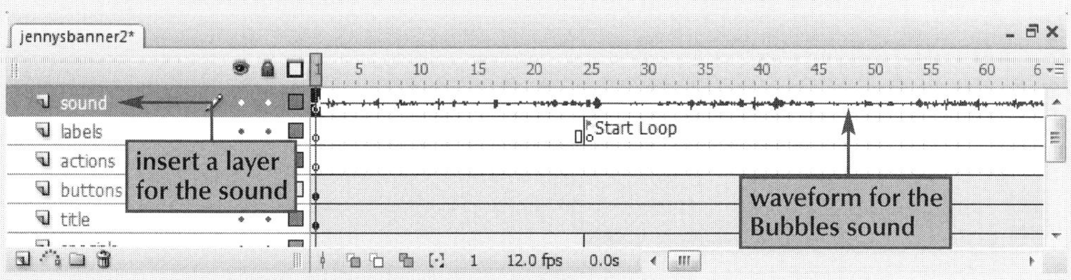

Changing the Sound Sync Settings

After you have added a sound to a document, you can control the way the sound plays by using the sound settings in the Property inspector. The Sync setting lets you set the sound as an event sound or as a stream sound, the two main types of sounds used in Flash. An **event sound** does not play until the entire sound has downloaded completely. Event sounds are not synchronized with the Timeline, which means that after an event sound is started, it continues to play regardless of the Timeline until all of the sound is played or until the user takes an action to stop it. A **stream sound** is synchronized with the Timeline and begins playing as soon as enough data has downloaded. Stream sounds are useful when you need the animation in your movie to coincide with the sound.

InSight | Using Stream Sounds

Before adding a stream sound to a Flash document, consider your target audience. When a movie has a stream sound, Flash forces the animation to keep pace with the sound. If a user has a slow computer, the Flash Player might skip frames to play the sound. This can result in a less than ideal viewing experience for the user. Unless there is a need to synchronize a sound to the Timeline, use the event sound setting.

After an event sound starts, the sound continues to play until it is stopped by the user or until it finishes. As a result, several instances of the same sound might play at one time. Because event sounds play independently of the Timeline, an event sound starts to play when the playhead reaches the sound's keyframe and continues to play until it is completely finished. If the playhead returns to the keyframe with the sound before the sound has finished playing, another instance of the sound starts playing at the same time. This means that one sound instance overlaps the other. To prevent this, you can change the Sync setting of the sound to Start instead of Event. With the Start Sync setting, a new instance of the sound does not start if the first instance of the sound is still playing, preventing the overlap of multiple instances of the same sound. Finally, the Stop Sync setting ends a sound that is playing. For example, you might want a sound that starts playing in Frame 1 to stop playing in Frame 10. You add the same sound to Frame 10 but use the Sync setting of Stop. When the playhead reaches Frame 10, the sound stops playing.

The Loop and Repeat sound settings let you set how many times a sound replays. If you want a sound to play continuously for a period of time, select Repeat and then specify how many times the sound should play. For example, if you want a sound to play for 2 minutes and the sound is 10 seconds long, enter 12 as the number of times to repeat; the sound will play 12 times for a total of 120 seconds or 2 minutes. If you want the sound to repeat continuously, select Loop.

The banner's background sound should be an event sound. You'll make this change now.

To change the Sync setting for the background sound and then test it:

1. In the Property inspector, click the **Sync** button, and then click **Event**, if necessary. Event is the default setting and is used when you don't need the sound synchronized with the Timeline.
2. In the Property inspector, type **10** in the Repeat box to set how many times the sound should repeat. See Figure 5-30.

Sound settings in Property inspector **Figure 5-30**

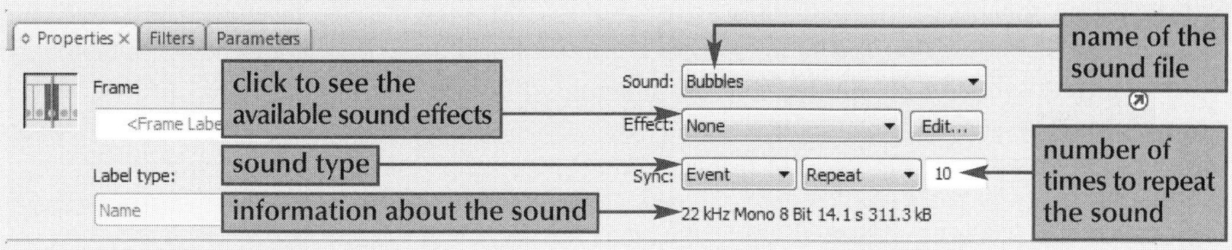

The information below the Sync box indicates that the Bubbles sound is 14.1 seconds long. If you leave the Repeat setting at 0, the sound ends if the user views the animation for more then 14.1 seconds. By changing the Repeat setting to 10, the sound continues playing for 141 seconds—more than 2 minutes.

3. Click **Control** on the menu bar, and then click **Test Movie**. The movie opens in a Flash Player window. The bubbling background sound plays.
4. Close the Flash Player window to return to the document.

Tip

You can test a sound by playing the movie in a Flash Player window or in a Web page.

Adding Sound Effects

The Effect setting changes the way a sound plays. The Left channel effect plays the sound only in the left speaker, whereas the Right channel effect plays the sound only in the right speaker. The Fade left to right effect starts the sound in the left speaker and gradually moves the sound to the right speaker. The Fade right to left effect starts the sound in the right speaker and gradually moves the sound to the left speaker. The Fade in effect gradually increases the sound whereas the Fade out effect gradually decreases the sound. Finally, the Custom setting allows you to create your own sound effects by adjusting the sound's starting point and controlling its volume.

Aly wants you to explore the various Effect settings to see how they impact the banner's background sound.

To explore the Effect settings with the Bubbles background sound:

1. In the Timeline, click **Frame 1** of the sound layer to select it, if necessary.

   You'll try different Effect settings for the sound in this layer.
2. In the Property inspector, click the **Effect** button to display the list of effects, and then click **Fade left to right**. The effect is applied to the Bubbles background sound.
3. Click **Control** on the menu bar, click **Test Movie** to play the movie and hear the background sound, and then close the Flash Player window to return to the document.
4. Repeat Steps 2 and 3 to apply and test at least four other Effect settings.

   Aly decides that the Fade in effect fits well with the overall design and purpose of the banner and instructs you to apply that setting.
5. In the Property inspector, click the **Effect** button, and then click **Fade in**. The Fade in effect is applied to the background sound. Even though the background sound is set to repeat 10 times, the fade in effect will not be repeated. The effect is applied only when the sound starts playing.

Although some users may enjoy the background sound, other users may not want to hear it. You want to give the user the option to turn off the sound. You already added a Mute button for this purpose, but you still need to add an action to the button instance to turn off the sound. Using the Actions panel, you will add an action to the Mute button instance that will stop all sounds that are playing when the button is clicked. Subsequent sounds that are played, such as the sound effects you added to the Stop and Play buttons, are not affected because they will not be playing when the Mute button is clicked.

To add an action to mute the background sound and then test it:

1. On the Stage, click the **Mute button** to select it. Be sure to select the button and not the Mute text block.
2. Click **Window** on the menu bar, and then click **Actions**. The Actions panel opens. You'll display the basic Timeline control actions.
3. If necessary, in the Actions toolbox, click **Global Functions**, and then click **Timeline Control**. The action to stop the background sound is in this list.
4. Double-click **stopAllSounds**. The action is selected and its script is added to the button instance and appears in the Script pane. See Figure 5-31.

Figure 5-31 **Stop all sounds script**

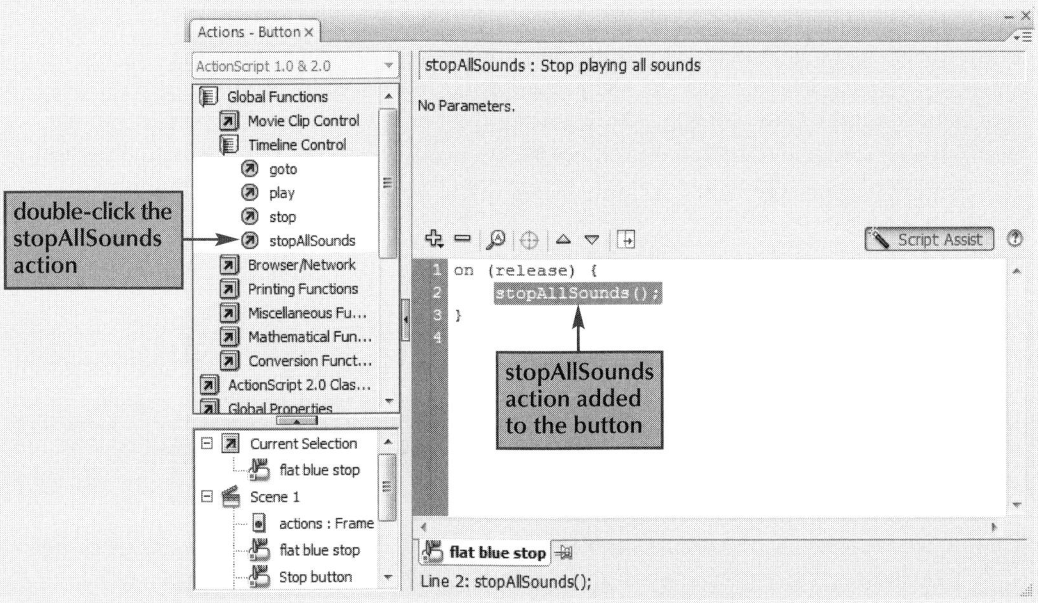

You'll close the Actions panel, and then test the completed document in a Flash Player window.

5. Close the Actions panel and then save the document.
6. Click **Control** on the menu bar, and click **Test Movie**. The animation and the background sound play in the Flash Player.
7. In the Flash Player window, click the **Mute** button. The sound stops, but the animation continues to play.
8. Close the Flash Player window to return to the document.

You have completed the banner by adding buttons, actions, and sounds. Jenny is pleased with the progress you made on the banner. In this session, you learned how to acquire sounds, what types of sounds Flash uses, and the different sound file formats that can be imported into documents. You imported sounds to the document's library, and then added the sounds to buttons and as a background sound to the document. You also changed the sound effect settings. Finally, you added an action to a button to stop all sounds from playing.

Session 5.3 Quick Check | Review

1. List two Web sites from which you can download sounds to use with your documents.
2. Describe the two main types of sounds used in a Flash document.
3. What three sound file formats may be imported into Flash?
4. Where is sound that you import into a document stored?
5. True or False? Sounds can only be added to keyframes.
6. List three simple effects you can add to a sound in a document.
7. Why would you assign the Start Sync setting to a sound?

Tutorial Summary | Review

In this tutorial, you added a button from a library of existing buttons that are included with Flash and created a custom button with a rollover effect. You aligned the buttons using the Align panel. You used the Actions panel to add actions to the buttons you created. You also added an action to a frame and then you tested these actions in your browser. You learned about the different sound file formats and how to adjust the various sounds you added to your document. You added sound effects to the buttons you created, and you added a background sound to the document. You also changed the sound settings, making the sound repeat and adding an effect.

Key Terms

action
ActionScript
anti-aliasing
Down frame
event
event handler
event sound
Hit frame
interactive
JavaScript
loop
Over frame
parameter
rollover effect
royalty-free
script
stream sound
Up frame
waveform

Practice | Review Assignments

Practice the skills you learned in the tutorial.

Data Files needed for the Review Assignments: specialsbanner.fla, Ding.wav

Aly asks you to make some changes to another interactive banner she has started for a fish and shrimp specials page. She wants you to modify the Mute button and add an action to stop all sounds when the button is clicked. She also asks you to add actions to the Play and Stop buttons to control the animation of the fish and to change the animation for the Fish and Shrimp Specials text block to only play one time. Finally, she wants you to select a different sound effect for the Stop and Play buttons and to change the text on the Play button to Start.

1. Open the **specialsbanner.fla** file located in the Tutorial.05\Review folder included with your Data Files, save the document as **newspecials.fla** in the same folder, and then set the workspace to its default layout.
2. Open the MuteButton symbol in symbol-editing mode, select the Down frame in Layer 2, change the color of the small black square in the middle of the button to green (#00FF00), and then exit symbol-editing mode.
3. Use the Actions panel in Script Assist mode to add a stopAllSounds action to the MuteButton instance, add an action to the PlayButton instance to play the animation when the button is clicked, and then add an action to the StopButton instance to stop the animation when the button is clicked.
4. In the Timeline, insert a new layer above the Buttons layer and name it **Actions**. Insert a new layer above the Actions layer and name it **Labels**. Create a frame label in Frame 20 of the Labels layer with the name **Loop**.
5. Use the Actions panel in Script Assist mode to add a gotoAndPlay action to Frame 60 of the Actions layer. In the parameters area, select Frame Label from the Type list and select Loop from the Frame list.
6. Import the **Ding.wav** file located in the Tutorial.05\Review folder to the document's library.
7. Open the StopButton symbol in symbol-editing mode, insert a new layer and name it **Sound**, and then add the Ding sound to the Down frame so that the sound plays when the button is clicked.
8. Open the PlayButton symbol in symbol-editing mode, insert a new layer and name it **Sound**, and add the Ding sound to the button's Down frame. Also, change the text block in the PlayButton to from Play to **Start**. (*Hint*: Be sure to change the text in each of the button's frames.)
9. Test the banner in the Flash Player to make sure each of the buttons works properly and that the Fish and Shrimp Specials! text block animation plays only one time.
10. Submit the finished file to your instructor, either in printed or electronic form, as requested.

Apply | Case Problem 1

Create an interactive banner with sounds for a store's Web site.

Data Files needed for this Case Problem: sssbanner.fla, Door.wav, Party.wav

Sandy's Scrapbook Store Sandy Rodriguez, owner of Sandy's Scrapbook Store, is excited about the graphics developed for the store's Web site. She asks John Rossini to create an interactive banner similar to one developed earlier to generate more interest from visitors to the Web site. Sandy wants sounds added to the banner. You will revise an animated banner that John created. The banner contains two sets of text animations. The first set displays text blocks with the store's name and a grand opening announcement. The second set of animations displays after the first set is finished and contains several text blocks with services provided by the store. You'll add two buttons from the Buttons library: a Repeat button and a Play Song button. The buttons should be similar in design and should appear after the first set of animations is finished. You also need to add a short sound effect that plays when the buttons are clicked. Then, you'll add an action to the Repeat button so that it plays the first set of animations and add an action to the Play Song button so that it plays the second set of animations plus a background sound that John has provided. Finally, you will add a frame action on the last frame that moves the playhead to the start of the second set of animations.

1. Open the **sssbanner.fla** file located in the Tutorial.05\Case1 folder included with your Data Files, and then save the document as **sssbannerRev.fla** in the same folder.
2. Insert a new layer above the Stickers layer, name it **Buttons**, and then insert a keyframe at Frame 40 of the Buttons layer.
3. In the Buttons library, open the classic buttons folder, and then open the Circle Buttons folder. Make sure the Buttons layer is selected, and then drag the circle button – previous button to the lower-left corner of the banner and drag the circle button – next button to the right of the first button.
4. Open the circle button – previous button in symbol-editing mode, insert a new layer and name it **Sound**, import the **Door.wav** sound located in the Tutorial.05\Case1 folder included with your Data Files, and then add it to the Down frame of the Sound layer.
5. Open the circle button – next button in symbol-editing mode, insert a new layer and name it **Sound**, add the Door sound to this button in its Down frame of the Sound layer, and then exit symbol-editing mode.
6. Insert a new layer and name it **Labels**, create a label in Frame 1 and name it **Start**, and then create a label in Frame 40 and name it **Part2**.
7. Insert a new layer and name it **Actions**, and then add a stop action at Frame 40 of the Actions layer.
8. Add the gotoAndPlay action to the circle button – previous button instance. The action should move the playhead to the Start frame, repeating the first set of animations.
9. Add the play action to the circle button – next button instance. This causes the second set of animations to play.
10. Add a gotoAndStop action at Frame 100 of the Actions layer. The action moves the playhead to the Part2 frame. (*Hint:* The gotoAndStop action is in the Timeline Control category within the Global Functions category in the Actions panel in normal mode.)
11. Insert a new layer and name it **Background Sound**.
12. Import the **Party.wav** sound file located in the Tutorial.05\Case1 folder included with your Data Files, add sound to start at Frame 41 of the Background Sound layer, make its Sync setting Start, and then set the number of times to Repeat to 1.
13. Test the revisions to the banner. Make sure the buttons work properly and that the sounds play.
14. Submit the finished file to your instructor, either in printed or electronic form, as requested.

Apply | Case Problem 2

Add sound and interactivity to an animated banner for a zoo.

Data Files needed for this Case Problem: zoobanner.fla, PianoLoop.wav, Ping.wav

Alamo City Zoo Janet Meyers, director for Alamo City Zoo, asks Alex Smith to develop a new banner with some enhancements for the zoo's Web site. In particular, she wants sound added to the banner to make it interesting. Alex also suggests adding some interactivity to the banner. You will complete the banner Alex created by adding an action that repeats the movement of the bear and bear paws without repeating the text animations. You will add a button that resembles a bears paw that users can click to start the animation from the beginning. You will also add a background sound to the banner and a sound effect to the button.

1. Open the **zoobanner.fla** file located in the Tutorial.05\Case2 folder included with your Data Files, and then save the document as **zoobannerRev.fla** in the same folder.
2. In the Timeline, insert a new layer above the title layer and name it **labels**. In Frame 1 of the labels layer, insert the label name **Start**. In Frame 20, insert the label name **Loop**. This is where the motion tweens for the bear paws begin.
3. Insert a new layer and name it **actions**. Add a gotoAndPlay action to the last frame, Frame 40, of the actions layer. The action should make the playhead go to the Loop frame to repeat the last group of frames that keep the animated bear and bear paws moving.
4. Insert a new layer and name it **music**. Import the **PianoLoop.wav** sound located in the Tutorial.05\Case2 folder included with your Data Files. Add the PianoLoop sound to Frame 18 of the music layer, change its Sync setting to Start, and have it play one time.
5. Create a duplicate of the bear paw symbol in the library, name the copy **bear paw button**, and make sure its behavior type is set to Button. Open the bear paw button in symbol-editing mode. Use the Transform panel to set the bear paw's Rotate value to –90 and its width and height to 60%.
6. Add a keyframe in the Over frame, and then change the color of the bear paw's fill to the green color of your choice.
7. Add a keyframe in the Down frame, and then use the arrow keys to move the bear paw three pixels down and three pixels to the right.
8. **EXPLORE** Add a keyframe in the Hit frame, and then draw a rectangle that covers the bear paw for the clickable area of the button.
9. Insert a new layer into the button's Timeline and name it **sound**. Import the **Ping.wav** sound located in the Tutorial.05\Case2 folder included with your Data Files. Add the Ping sound to the Down frame of the sound layer, and then exit symbol-editing mode.
10. Insert a new layer and name it **button**. Add an instance of the bear paw button symbol to the banner in the Button layer. Place the instance in the lower-left corner of the banner.
11. Select the bear paw button instance, and then, in the Actions panel, add the gotoAndPlay action. Change the action parameters so that the action refers to the Start frame. When the button is clicked, the playhead goes to the Start frame and repeats all of the animation.
12. Add a text block above the bear paw button with the text **Replay**. Use a small font size and black text.
13. Test the animation to make sure the background music plays and that the button works.
14. Submit the finished file to your instructor, either in printed or electronic form, as requested.

Apply | Case Problem 3

Add sounds and interactive components to an animated logo for a nursery.

Data Files needed for this Case Problem: westcreeklogo.fla, AutoLoop.wav, Carhorn.wav

Westcreek Nursery Amanda Lester shows Alice Washington and several of her employees a new animated logo for the nursery's Web site. They have several suggestions, including adding sound and some interactive components to the logo. Amanda asks you to complete the revisions by adding a background sound to the logo as well as adding a Stop button and a Go button, each with a sound effect. You also will add a frame action to control how the animation plays. The wheels should continue to rotate after the Westcreek text shape animation has finished. The Stop button will stop the wheel animations, and the Go button will start the wheel animations.

1. Open the **westcreeklogo.fla** file located in the Tutorial.05\Case3 folder included with your Data Files, and then save this file as **westcreeklogoRev.fla** in the same folder.
2. Insert three layers above the Flowers layer, and name the layers **Actions**, **StopLabel**, and **LoopLabel**, respectively.
3. In Frame 19 of the StopLabel layer, add the frame label **Stop**. In Frame 20 of the LoopLabel layer, add the frame label **Loop**.
4. In the last frame of the Actions layer, add an action that makes the playhead go to the frame with the Loop label and continues playing the animation from that frame. The shape tween animation plays one time and the tire animations play repeatedly.
5. Import the **AutoLoop.wav** sound located in the Tutorial.05\Case3 folder included with your Data Files to the document's library. Insert a new layer and name it **Sound**. Add the AutoLoop sound to Frame 20 of the new layer, and set it to play several times without overlapping itself.
6. Create a new button and name it **Stop button**. This button shape is a circle that is about 20 pixels in diameter with a red fill and black stroke to represent a red stop light. Import the **Carhorn.wav** sound located in the Tutorial.05\Case3 folder included with your Data Files, and then add the sound to the button's Down frame.
7. Duplicate the Stop button, name the duplicate **Go button**, and then change its fill to green.
8. Insert a new layer in Scene 1 and name it **Buttons**.
9. In the Buttons layer at Frame 19, insert a keyframe, add an instance of the Stop button in the lower-right corner of the Stage to the right of the word "today," and then add an instance of the Go button to the right of the Stop button instance.
10. Add an action to the Stop button instance that causes the playhead to go to the frame with the Stop label at which point the animation should stop.
11. Add an action to the Go button instance that causes the playhead to go to the frame with the Loop label and continue to play the animation.
12. Test the logo animation, making sure the sounds play and that the buttons work properly.
13. Submit the finished file to your instructor, either in printed or electronic form, as requested.

Challenge | Case Problem 4

Download sounds, add actions to control an animation, and create a button to replay the animation.

Data File needed for this Case Problem: rdabanner.fla

Regional Dietetic Association Richard Perez wants Webmaster Katie Ellison to add some interaction with appropriate sounds to enhance the impact that the banner can have when viewers visit the Regional Dietetic Association Web site. Katie asks you to modify the banner so that the animation stops when it reaches the last frame. She also instructs you to add a button that will repeat the animation. The button should resemble the circles that are part of the banner's design. She asks you to search the Web to find a background sound for the banner and a sound effect to be added to the button.

1. Open the **rdabanner.fla** file located in the Tutorial.05\Case4 folder included with your Data Files, and then save the document as **rdabannerRev.fla** in the same folder.
2. Go to the Flash Kit Web site (*www.flashkit.com*) or another site of your choice that has sound files you can download and use for free. Find two sound files appropriate for your banner. One sound should be short and will be used as a sound effect on a button. The other should be a sound loop that will be used as a background sound. Download the sounds to the Tutorial.05\Case4 folder.
3. Insert a new layer above the circle2 layer and name it **sound**, and then insert another layer and name it **actions**.
4. Add a stop action to Frame 55 of the Actions layer. This action should stop the animation and keep it from repeating.
5. Import the sound loop you downloaded into the document's library, and then add the sound to Frame 1 of the sound layer. Set it to play three times without overlapping itself.
6. EXPLORE — Duplicate the circle symbol in the library. Change the behavior type to Button and name the button **repeat**. The circle shape will be the normal state for this button.
7. Add an Over frame to the button and change the circle shape in the Over frame so that it has a green fill. Change the shape in the Down frame so that it is offset by a few pixels. Import the sound effect you downloaded and add it to the Down frame.
8. EXPLORE — Insert a new layer in Scene 1 and name it **buttons**. In Frame 55 of the buttons layer, add a repeat button instance that covers the circle symbol in the lower-right corner of the banner. When the animation stops at Frame 55, the button instance should completely cover the circle symbol. It will look the same as the circle symbol until the pointer is moved over it. Then the rollover effect changes the way it looks.
9. Add a play action to the button instance so that the animation will start to play.
10. Test the banner animation, making sure the sounds play and that the button works properly.
11. Submit the finished file to your instructor, either in printed or electronic form, as requested.

Review | Quick Check Answers

Session 5.1

1. a special symbol that contains its own four-frame Timeline
2. To provide an interactive element to a Flash document so users can control how they watch the published movie.
3. Click Windows on the menu bar, point to Common Libraries, and then click Buttons to open the Buttons library. Drag a button from the Buttons library to the Stage, which automatically adds the button to the document's library. Or, drag a button from the Buttons library to the document's library.
4. four: Up, Over, Down, and Hit frames
5. Make the Over frame's content different from the Up frame's content. When the pointer is over the button, the content in the Over frame is displayed in place of the content in the Up frame.
6. Turn on the Enable Simple Buttons command on the Control menu.
7. the Align panel

Session 5.2

1. the scripting language used in Flash to create scripts to control how a movie plays
2. False. You do not need to know JavaScript or any other scripting language.
3. instructions that are used to control how a movie plays
4. Scripts created for frame actions are executed when the frame is played and do not depend on an event to occur.
5. False. Actions are added to a button instance and not to the symbol.
6. The user clicks and releases a button.
7. If you later add or delete frames, the scripts do not have to be changed.
8. You add a frame action to a keyframe, whereas you add a button action to a button's instance.

Session 5.3

1. *www.flashkit.com*, *www.killersound.com*, and/or *www.soundshopper.com*
2. An event sound does not play until the entire sound has downloaded completely and is not synchronized with the Timeline. A stream sound is synchronized with the Timeline and begins playing as soon as enough data has downloaded.
3. WAV, AIFF, and MP3
4. the document's library
5. True.
6. Left channel, Right channel, Fade left to right, Fade right to left, Fade in, and Fade out.
7. to prevent several instances of the sound from playing at the same time

Ending Data Files

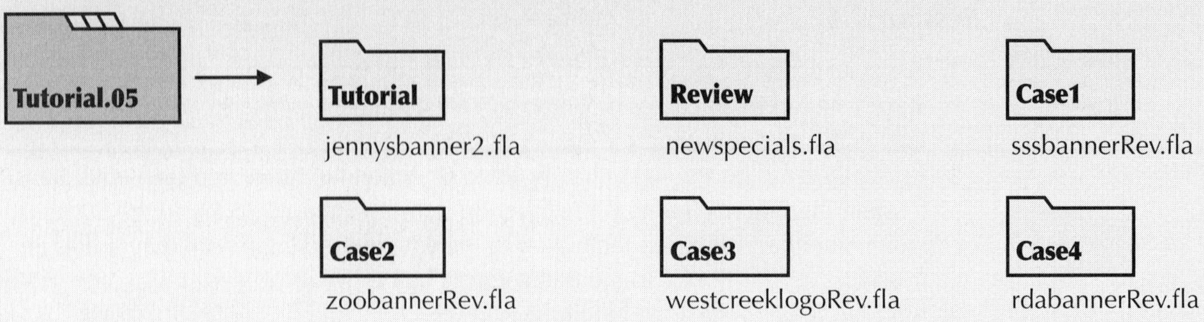

Objectives

Session 6.1
- Import bitmap graphics into a document
- Change a bitmap graphic's properties
- Convert a bitmap graphic to a vector graphic
- Create a fade effect animation using bitmaps

Session 6.2
- Learn about gradients
- Create and save a new gradient
- Use and transform a gradient

Session 6.3
- Explore the Flash publish settings
- Publish a Flash movie
- Create a publish profile
- Export a Flash graphic
- Insert a Flash movie into an existing Web page

Working with Bitmaps and Gradients, and Publishing Flash Files

Creating Special Effects with Graphics and Gradients

Case | Admiral Web Design

Jenny Emerson wants to create a new banner for the home page of the Jenny's Oyster Hut Web site. She also wants to develop a new logo to use on the Web site. Jenny wants photos of sample seafood items included in the banner and logo designs. During the planning meeting, Aly suggests using the photos as part of an animation. Chris suggests using a gradient for the banner's background to create a professional-looking design. As you complete the banner and create the logo, you will be adding bitmaps, creating gradients, and preparing the final movies for use on the restaurant's Web site.

In this tutorial, you will import bitmap graphics into a Flash document, change the bitmaps' properties, convert a bitmap into a vector graphic, and create animations using bitmaps. You will also create, modify, and use gradients to add a special effect to the banner. Finally, you will explore the various export and publishing options available with Flash, and then incorporate the banner and logo into an existing Web page.

Starting Data Files

Tutorial.06 →

Tutorial	Review	Case1	Case2	Case3	Case4
jennys.fla	jennysAlt.fla	ssslogo.fla	aczlogo.fla	wclogo.fla	rdabanner.fla
sample.htm	jennysbanner.jpg	store1.jpg	giraffe.jpg	flower1.jpg	pasta.jpg
crablegs.jpg	salmon.jpg	store2.jpg		flower2.jpg	
tunasteaks.jpg	sampleAlt.htm			flower3.jpg	
lobster.jpg					
logo.jpg					
jennysbanner.jpg					

Session 6.1

Working with Bitmaps

The banner and logo you will create for Jenny's Oyster Hut use photographs. A photograph is a bitmap graphic. Recall that a bitmap graphic is stored as a row-by-row list of every pixel in the graphic, along with each pixel's color. The most common bitmap file formats for Web graphics are JPEG and GIF. Bitmap graphics are different from vector graphics, which are stored as mathematical instructions that describe the color, outline, and position of all the shapes in the graphic. Bitmap graphics do not resize well and their file sizes tend to be larger than the vector graphics created in Flash. As a result, using bitmaps in a Flash movie increases the movie's download time. However, file size and download time alone should not keep you from using bitmap graphics in Flash documents. Just make sure that the graphic is really needed in the document's design.

InSight | Using Bitmaps in Flash

You cannot easily edit bitmap graphics within Flash, so you should use an image-editing program such as Adobe Photoshop or Adobe Fireworks to edit and resize the bitmaps before importing them into a Flash document. Before using a bitmap graphic in Flash, optimize it by reducing its size while maintaining its quality. Reducing the file size of the bitmap minimizes its impact on the download time of the Flash document. If possible, you should also consider the target audience and the type of Internet connections they have. Flash documents targeted at users with slower Internet connections should include few, if any, bitmap graphics although bitmap graphics can greatly enhance a document's design.

Importing Bitmaps

You cannot create bitmap graphics in Flash, so you need to import them into the Flash documents. After you have imported a bitmap into Flash, you can change properties such as compression settings, use it in animations, and even change it into a vector graphic. Importing a bitmap into a Flash document places the bitmap in the document's library. After the bitmap is in the document's library, you can create multiple instances of it on the Stage. No matter how many instances you create, only one copy of the bitmap is stored with the file. A bitmap in the document's library is not a symbol, although the copies you drag onto the Stage are called instances. An instance of a bitmap on the Stage can be converted into a symbol that can then be used in a motion tween animation. This symbol is then stored in the document's library separately from the original bitmap.

Reference Window | Importing a Bitmap

- Click File on the menu bar, point to Import, and then click Import to Stage or Import to Library.
- In the Import or Import to Library dialog box, navigate to the location of the bitmap file, and then select the bitmap file in the file list.
- Click the Open button to import the bitmap into the document's library.

The new Jenny's Oyster Hut banner, shown in the sketch provided by Aly in Figure 6-1, uses an animation that includes two photos of seafood. Aly edited the pictures in a seperate image-editing program so that they are both the same size. You need to import these photos into the library of the partially completed banner that Aly has created. You will combine these pictures into one animation where each picture is displayed in turn within a mask, fading in and then fading out. For the banner's background, you will create a radial gradient that will be a blend of a light blue color that transitions into a dark gray color. The gradient's light blue center will be positioned behind the seafood photos animation, giving the photos a highlighted effect.

Figure 6-1 Sketch for the new Jenny's Oyster Hut banner

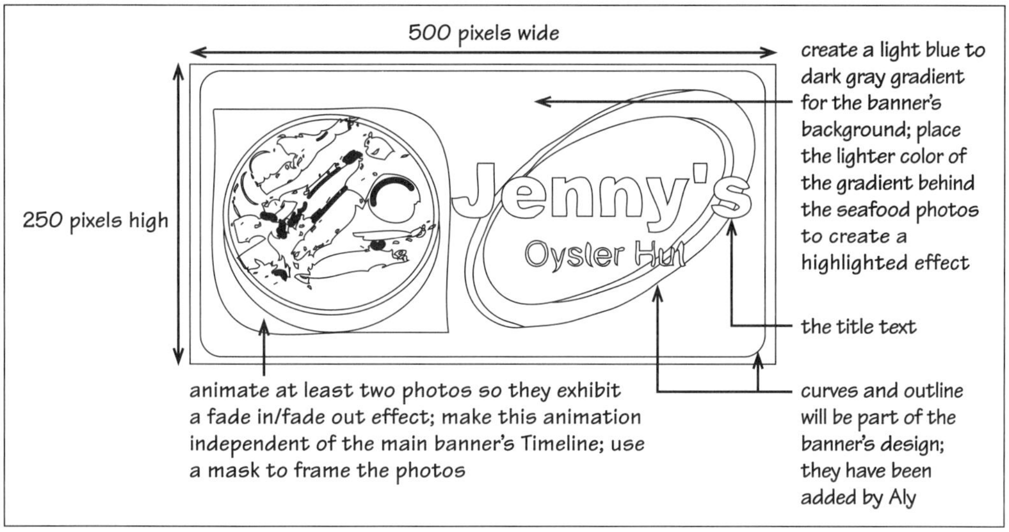

You'll import the photos into the banner.

To import the seafood bitmap images into the banner document:

1. Open the **jennys.fla** file located in the **Tutorial.06\Tutorial** folder included with your Data Files, save the file as **jennys2.fla** in the same folder, and then change the workspace to its default layout.

   Next, you will import a bitmap into the document's library.

2. Click **File** on the menu bar, point to **Import**, and then click **Import to Library**. The Import to Library dialog box opens.
3. Click the **Formats** button, click **All Image Formats**, and then navigate to the **Tutorial.06\Tutorial** folder included with your Data Files.
4. Click the **crablegs.jpg** file, press and hold the **Ctrl** key, click the **tunasteaks.jpg** file, and then release the Ctrl key. The two files are selected.
5. Click the **Open** button. The two bitmap files are imported into the document's library and appear in the Library panel.
6. In the Library panel, click the **crablegs** bitmap. The crablegs picture appears the preview area. See Figure 6-2.

Tip

You can use the Import to Stage command to simultaneously place a bitmap in the document's library and create an instance on the Stage.

Figure 6-2 **Bitmaps in the Library panel**

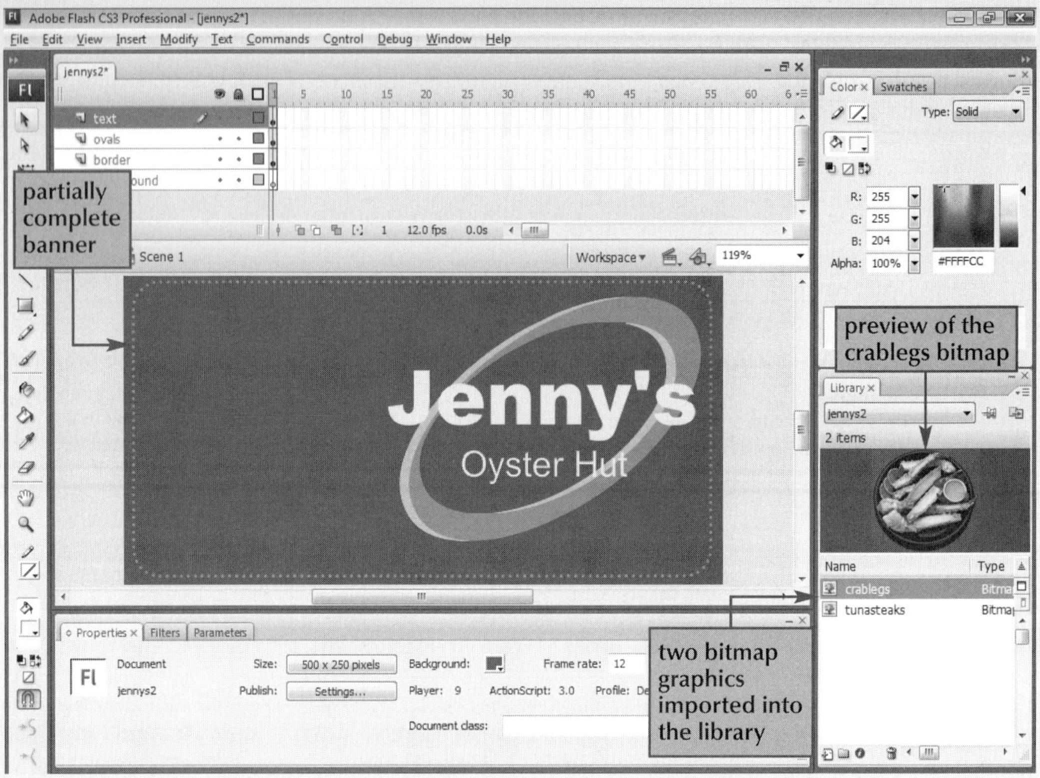

7. In the Library panel, click the **tunasteaks** bitmap. The tunasteaks picture appears in the preview area.

Setting a Bitmap's Properties

You can modify a bitmap's properties by changing the bitmap's name, updating the bitmap if the original file has been modified, and even changing its compression settings. **Compression** means taking away some of the file's data to reduce its size. You can compress a bitmap yet maintain its quality. **Lossy compression** removes some of the original data in the image to achieve a smaller file size. **Lossless compression** retains all the original data in the image, but is limited to 256 colors. JPEG is a lossy compression method designed for compressing full-color images such as photographs. Although JPEG removes some of the image data, it stores full color information, resulting in very good image quality. The GIF and PNG formats are better for images with solid areas of color such as logos and drawn shapes. The PNG format is not as widely used as the GIF format, but is supported by most current Web browsers.

Finding the Right Compression for a Bitmap | InSight

A bitmap file in the JPEG file format is already compressed. Compressing it further in Flash can degrade the quality of the picture, so you need to balance how much compression to apply to a bitmap with the picture's quality. Keep in mind that pictures in a Flash movie don't always have to be of the highest quality, especially if they are small and are used as part of a larger graphic. Applying additional compression to bitmaps in Flash reduces the overall size of the final movie.

Experiment with several quality values to compare how the quality of the picture is affected. Select the value that maintains the quality of the picture needed for the particular design while still compressing the bitmap as much as possible.

The bitmap properties available depend on the bitmap's file type. Figure 6-3 describes the different properties, which are available in the Bitmap Properties dialog box.

Bitmap Properties — Figure 6-3

Property	Description
Name	The name of the bitmap in the document's library.
Smoothing	The option to smooth the edges of the bitmap so they do not appear jagged.
Compression	The type of compression. Choose Lossless (PNG/GIF) for bitmaps in the PNG or GIF file format or that have large areas of single colors. Choose Photo (JPEG) for bitmaps with many colors or many color transitions such as photographs.
Quality	The amount of compression to apply to the bitmap, ranging from 0 (most compression) to 100 (least compression). The more compression that is applied, the more data that is lost. You can also keep the quality setting of the original bitmap for JPEGs or use the quality value set for the whole document for PNGs or GIFs.

Before placing the bitmaps in the banner, Aly wants you to minimize the size of the final movie by changing the compression settings for each bitmap. You will reduce the JPEG quality to decrease the overall size of the final movie, and then check what effect the new JPEG quality value has on the pictures.

To change the crablegs and tunasteaks bitmap properties:

1. In the Library panel, click the **crablegs** bitmap, and then click the **Properties** button. The Bitmap Properties dialog box opens.
2. Right-click the **bitmap preview** in the upper-left corner, and then click **Zoom In** on the context menu. The preview image is larger, so you can more easily see the effects of changes to the bitmap's properties.
3. Click the **Use imported JPEG data** check box to remove the check. You deselected this option because you want to adjust the bitmap's compression rather than use its imported compression data. The Quality box appears, showing the default value of 50.
4. Double-click **50** in the Quality box, type **20**, and then click the **Test** button. The preview shows the bitmap with then new compression settings. With the lower quality value, the picture quality is poor. Some of its colors have changed significantly and it has less detail as evidenced by the small blocks that appear throughout the picture. See Figure 6-4.

Tip

You can drag the image in the preview in the Bitmap Properties dialog box to see other areas of the bitmap.

Figure 6-4 **Bitmap with a lower compression value**

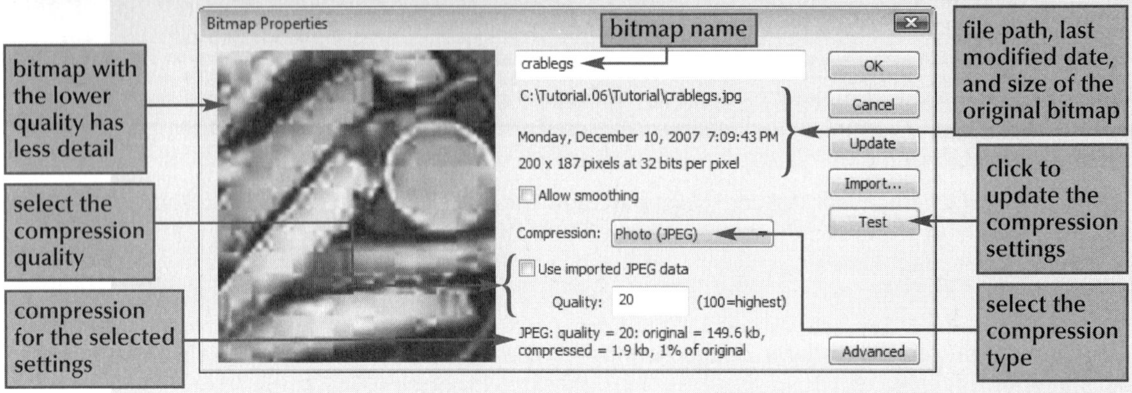

You want to find a quality value that maintains the photo's quality while reducing its file size.

5. Enter **80** in the Quality box, and then click the **Test** button. The compressed bitmap is smaller than the original and the picture quality is not adversely affected.
6. Click the **OK** button to accept the compression value.

   You need to adjust the quality for the other bitmap.
7. In the Library panel, click the **tunasteaks** bitmap, and then click the **Properties** button. The Bitmap Properties dialog box opens.
8. Click the **Use imported JPEG data** check box to remove the check mark, enter **80** in the Quality box, and then click the **Test** button to preview the tunasteaks picture. The tunasteaks picture looks fine with this setting.
9. Click the **OK** button to accept the compression value.

Tip

You can also double-click the bitmap's icon in the Library panel to open the Bitmap Properties dialog box.

Animating Bitmaps

You animate an imported bitmap the same way you animate any other object. For instance, you can create a motion tween that causes the bitmap to move, rotate, change in size (scale), or fade in or out. To animate a bitmap in a motion tween, you first need to convert the bitmap instance on the Stage to a symbol.

Aly's instructions for the new banner indicate that the crablegs and tunasteaks bitmaps are part of an animation where one bitmap appears and then fades away while the second bitmap fades in over the first. To accomplish the fade effect, you change the alpha amount for each instance. The **alpha amount** controls the transparency of an image. The alpha amount is a percentage from 0 to 100. An alpha amount of 0% makes the object completely transparent. An alpha amount of 100% makes the object completely opaque, which means it has no transparency. A motion tween that starts the object at an alpha amount of 100% and changes it at the end of the tween to 0% makes the object appear to fade out of view. You reverse the amounts to make the object appear to fade into view. Because this animation should be independent of any other animation that may be added to the banner, you will create a movie clip symbol that contains the seafood pictures animation within its own Timeline, independent of the main document's Timeline. (Recall that symbols with the movie clip behavior have independent Timelines.)

To create a new movie clip symbol and convert the crablegs bitmap into a symbol:

1. Click **Insert** on the menu bar, and then click **New Symbol**. The Create New Symbol dialog box opens.
2. Type **seafood animation** in the Name box, click the **Movie clip** option button if necessary, and then click the **OK** button. The new movie clip symbol opens in symbol-editing mode.
3. Drag an instance of the **crablegs bitmap** from the Library panel to the center of the Stage.
4. Click **Window** on the menu bar, and then click **Info**. The Info panel opens, and you can specify the exact location for the bitmap.
5. In the Info panel, enter **0** in both the X and Y boxes, and then make sure the center registration point is selected in the Registration icon. The selected bitmap instance is centered within the editing window. See Figure 6-5.

Tip

You can also press the Ctrl+I keys to open or close the Info panel.

Figure 6-5 Crablegs bitmap instance centered

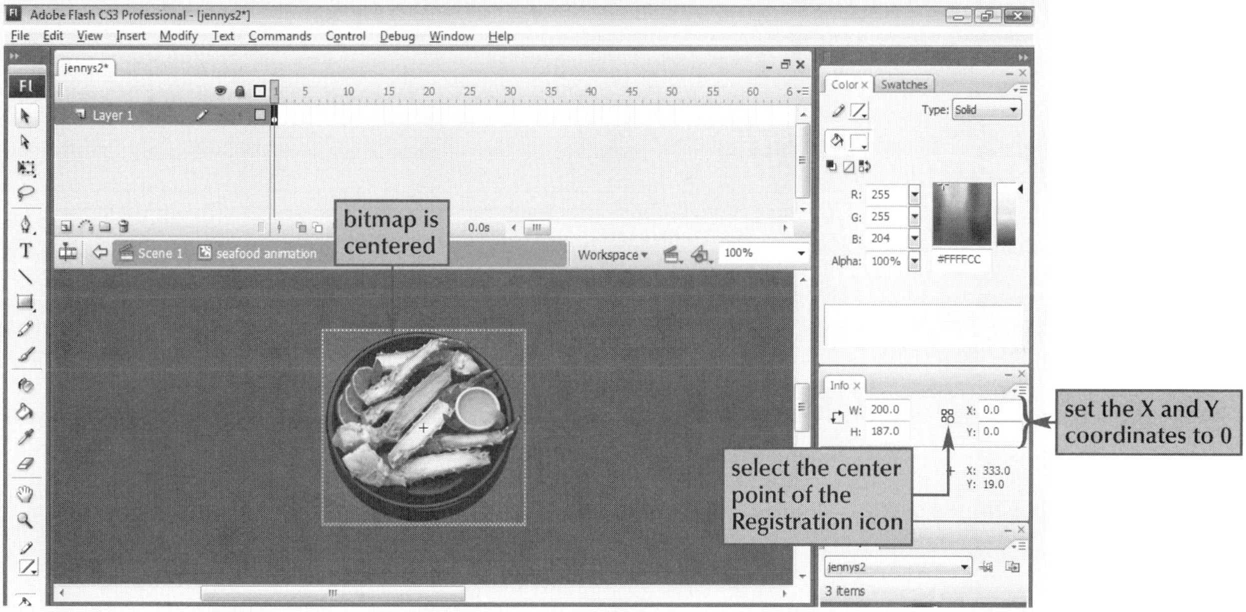

You will convert the crablegs bitmap instance on the Stage into a symbol so that you can use it in a motion tween animation.

6. Click **Modify** on the menu bar, and then click **Convert to Symbol**. The Convert to Symbol dialog box opens.
7. Type **crablegs symbol** in the Name box, click the **Movie clip** option button if necessary, and then click the center registration point in the Registration icon. The registration point specifies what part of the symbol is used for alignment. Because the two crablegs and the tunasteaks images need to be in the same position on the Stage, you specified a point in the crablegs image to use for alignment when you position the tunasteaks image. See Figure 6-6.

Figure 6-6 Convert to Symbol dialog box

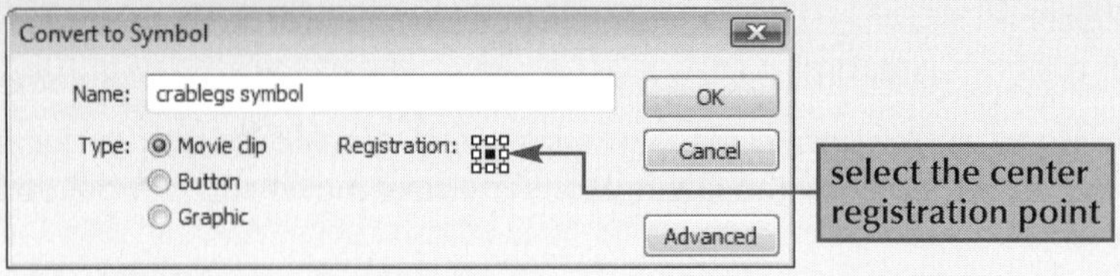

▶ **8.** Click the **OK** button. The crablegs symbol is created.

In the animation, the crablegs bitmap fades out of view after a period of time and then the tunasteaks bitmap fades in. Aly provides a sketch that outlines how the animation occurs, as shown in Figure 6-7. Based on the sketch, the animation of the pictures takes place over six seconds. During the first two seconds, the crablegs picture is displayed. During the third second, the crablegs picture fades out as the tunasteaks picture fades in. Then, during the next two seconds, the tunasteaks picture is displayed. Finally, during the last second, the tunasteaks picture fades out and the crablegs picture fades back in. Because the frame rate is 12 frames per second, each second requires 12 frames. Converting these time specifications to frame numbers means that you need keyframes at Frames 1, 24, 36, 60, and 72. These are the frames where a change occurs from the previous frames.

Figure 6-7 Fade animation

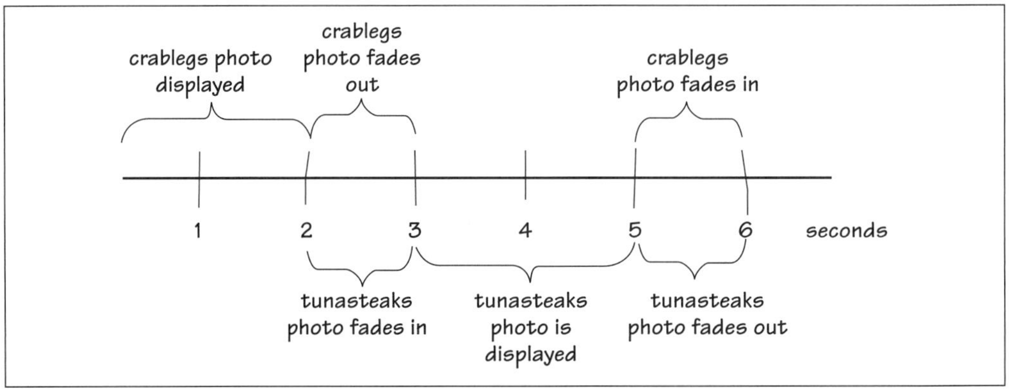

You'll create the crablegs animation.

To create the crablegs animation:

▶ **1.** In the Timeline, rename Layer 1 to **crablegs layer**. Next you'll insert keyframes for the animation.

▶ **2.** In the crablegs layer, insert keyframes at **Frame 24** and **Frame 36**. You'll set the alpha amounts for the crablegs instance in these two frames to control the transparency of the crablegs, which creates the fade in and fade out effect.

▶ **3.** In the Timeline, click **Frame 36**, if necessary, and then, on the Stage, click the **crablegs symbol** instance to select it.

▶ **4.** In the Property inspector, click the **Color** button, click **Alpha**, type **0** in the Alpha Amount box, and then press the **Enter** key. The crablegs symbol instance becomes transparent. See Figure 6-8.

Figure 6-8 Transparent crablegs symbol instance

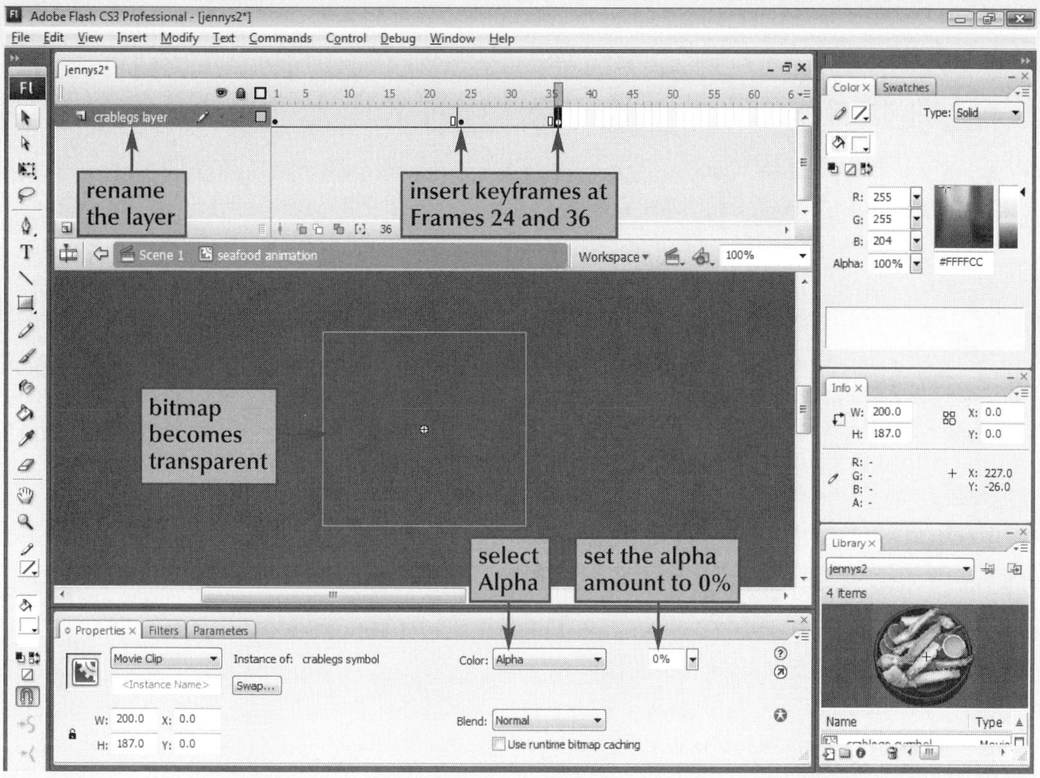

5. In the Timeline, click **Frame 24**, and then, in the Property inspector, click the **Tween** button and click **Motion**. A motion tween is created between Frame 24 and Frame 36.

6. Move the playhead to Frame 1, and then press the **Enter** key. In the preview of the motion tween, the crablegs symbol instance is displayed and then fades out throughout the motion tween. See Figure 6-9.

Figure 6-9 Crablegs bitmap animation

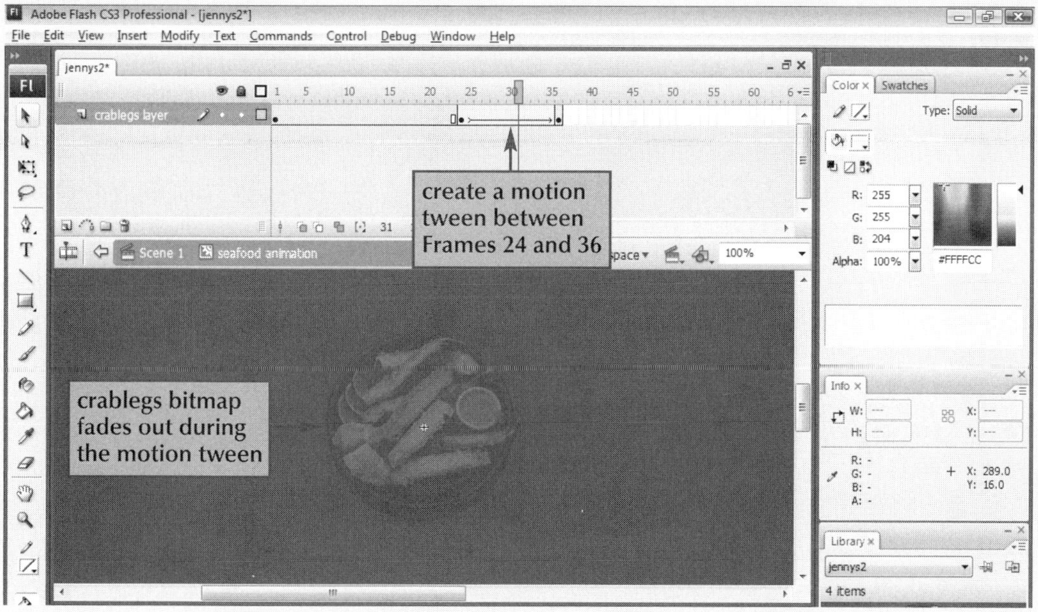

The crablegs photo is supposed to fade out and then fade back into view at the end of the animation. You will create another motion tween to fade in the crablegs.

7. In the Timeline, insert keyframes at **Frame 60** and **Frame 72**.
8. In the Timeline, click **Frame 72** if necessary, click the **crablegs symbol** instance on the Stage to select it, and then, in the Property inspector, set its alpha amount to **100%**. The crablegs symbol instance becomes fully visible.
9. In the Timeline, click **Frame 60**, and then, in the Property inspector, click the **Tween** button and click **Motion**. The motion tween is created to fade in the crablegs symbol instance.
10. Move the playhead to **Frame 1**, and then press the **Enter** key. The crablegs symbol instance is displayed, fades out, and then fades back in at the end of the animation.

You will follow a similar process to make the tunasteaks bitmap fade in as the crablegs bitmap fades out. The tunasteaks bitmap will then fade out as the crablegs bitmap fades back in. You'll place the tunasteaks animation on a separate layer.

To add the tunasteaks bitmap to the animation:

1. In the Timeline, insert a new layer, name the layer **tunasteaks layer**, and then insert a keyframe at **Frame 24**.
2. Click the Info panel's **title bar** to collapse the panel, and then drag an instance of the **tunasteaks bitmap** from the Library panel to the center of the Stage. You want to center the tunasteaks bitmap instance.

   Trouble? If the Library panel collapsed or closed, your screen resolution is probably too small to display all the panels at once. Click Window on the menu bar, and then click Library to open the Library panel.
3. Click the Info panel's **title bar** to expand the panel, enter **0** in the X and Y boxes, and then click the center Registration point if necessary. See Figure 6-10.

Figure 6-10 Tunasteaks bitmap added to the tunasteaks layer

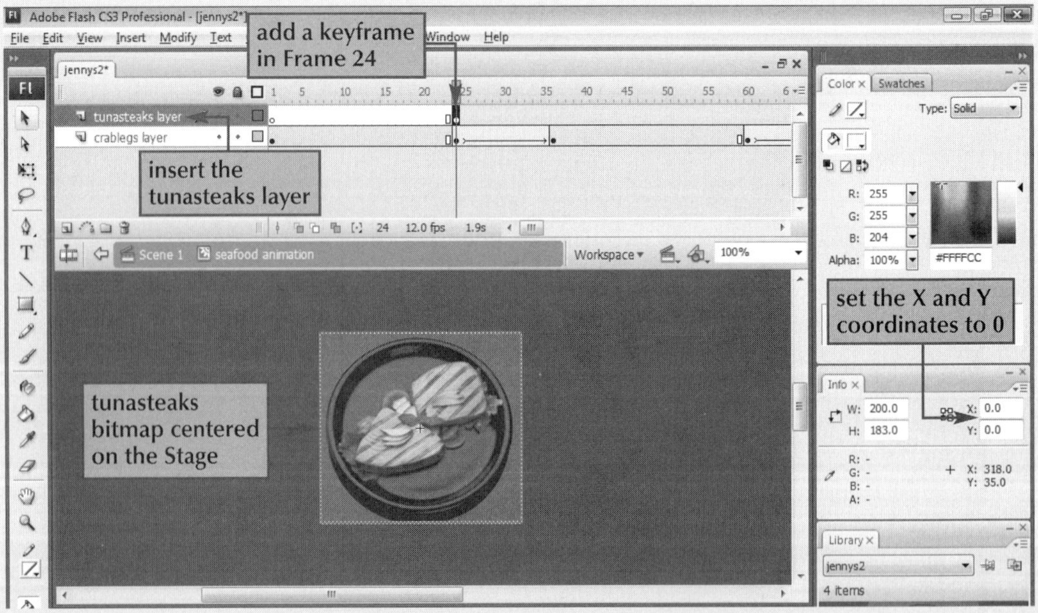

Next, you'll convert the tunasteaks bitmap to a symbol.

4. Convert the tunasteaks bitmap on the Stage to a symbol, using **tunasteaks symbol** as the name, **Movie clip** as the behavior, and the center registration point in the Registration icon.
5. In the tunasteaks layer on the Timeline, insert a keyframe at **Frame 36**. The tunasteaks symbol will become fully visible in this frame.
6. In the tunasteaks layer, click **Frame 24**, select the **tunasteaks symbol** instance on the Stage, and then, in the Property inspector, click the **Color** button, click **Alpha**, type **0** in the Alpha Amount box, and press the **Enter** key. The tunasteaks symbol instance becomes transparent, allowing the crablegs symbol instance to show through.
7. In the tunasteaks layer, click **Frame 24**, create a motion tween, and then drag the playhead between Frame 24 and Frame 36 to preview how the tunasteaks picture fades in while the crablegs picture fades out. See Figure 6-11.

Figure 6-11 Motion tweens complete

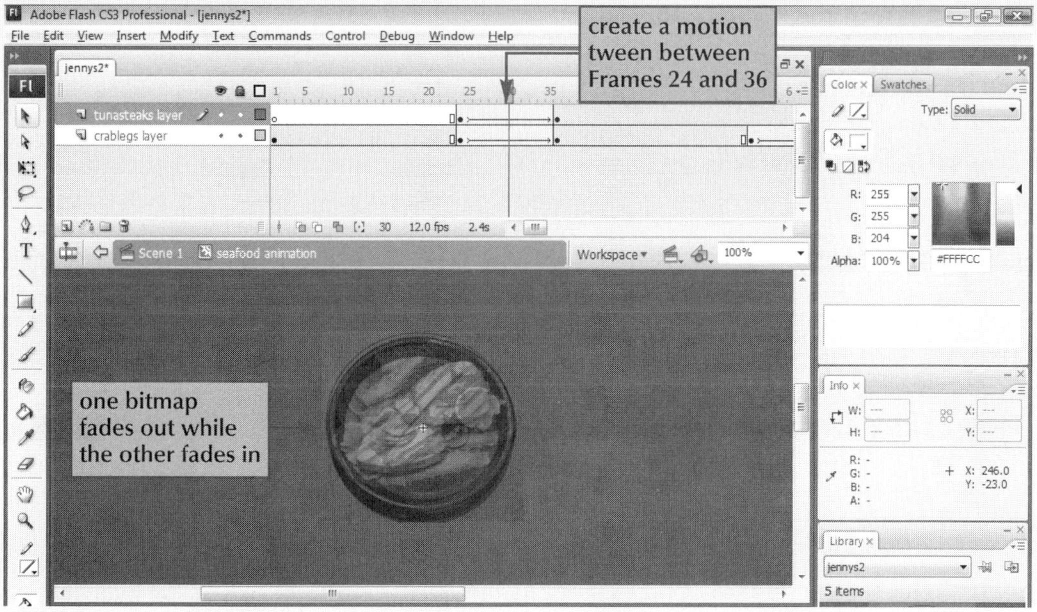

You'll create the motion tween for the tunasteaks to fade out of view and the crablegs to fade back in to view.

8. In the tunasteaks layer, insert keyframes at **Frame 60** and **Frame 72**, and then click **Frame 72**.
9. On the Stage, click the **tunasteaks symbol** instance to select it, and then, in the Property inspector, set the alpha amount to **0%**.
10. In the tunasteaks layer, click **Frame 60**, and then create a motion tween.
11. In the Timeline, move the playhead to **Frame 1**, and then press the **Enter** key. The crablegs picture is displayed and then fades out when the tunasteaks picture fades in. Then the crablegs picture fades back in while the tunasteaks picture fades out. The seafood animation is complete.

Based on Aly's instructions, you need to add a mask. Recall that a mask is created on a separate mask layer. The layer below the mask layer becomes the masked layer. The contents of the masked layer that are covered by the filled shape in the mask layer appear when the movie is played. In this case, you need to create a mask layer, draw a filled shape that covers the seafood animation, and then make both the crablegs layer and the tunasteaks layer masked layers. The filled shape determines how much of the seafood animation shows through.

To create the mask layer for the seafood animation:

1. In the Timeline, select the **tunasteaks layer**, if necessary, and then insert a new layer named **mask**. This new layer will be the mask layer.
2. Right-click the **mask** layer, and then click **Mask** on the context menu. The mask layer's icon changes to represent the layer's property. The tunasteaks layer is indented, and its icon changes to indicate it is a masked layer.

   You need to change the crablegs layer's properties so that it, too, is masked.
3. Right-click the **crablegs layer**, and then click **Properties** on the context menu. The Layer Properties dialog box opens.
4. Click the **Masked** option button, and then click the **OK** button. The dialog box closes. The crablegs layer in the Timeline is indented and its icon changes to indicate that it is a masked layer. See Figure 6-12.

Tip

You can also double-click a layer's icon to open its Properties dialog box.

Figure 6-12 Layers converted to masked layers

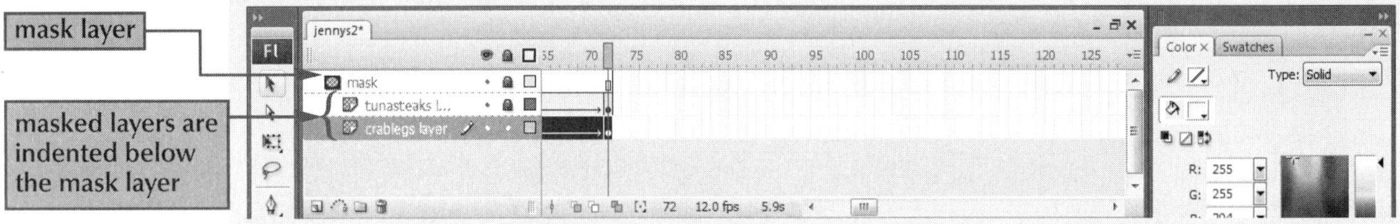

To draw the shape, you need to unlock the mask layer, which starts out locked to display its effect.

5. In the Timeline, click the **mask** layer, and then click the **lock** icon to unlock the layer.

   You'll draw the shape for the mask, which can be any shape that contains a fill. The area covered by the shape's fill determines what part of the masked layers' contents are displayed.
6. In the Tools panel, click and hold the **Rectangle** tool, and then click the **Rectangle Primitive** tool. You need to draw a rectangle shape with two rounded corners so that the seafood animation appears as though it is framed by the shape.
7. In the Tools panel, use the **Fill Color** control to set the fill to **yellow** (#FFFF00). Although you set the shape's fill to yellow, the shape's fill can be any color because it is not displayed.
8. On the Stage, drag the crosshair pointer from the upper-left corner of the crablegs symbol instance to its lower-right corner. The yellow rectangle covers the entire picture.

9. In the Info panel, set the rectangle's width to **200**, its height to **185**, and its X and Y coordinates to **0**, if necessary.
10. In the Property Inspector, click the **lock** icon for the corner radius boxes to unlock the values, enter **50** in the lower-left corner radius value box, and then enter **50** in the upper-right corner radius value. See Figure 6-13.

Figure 6-13 Mask covers the bitmaps

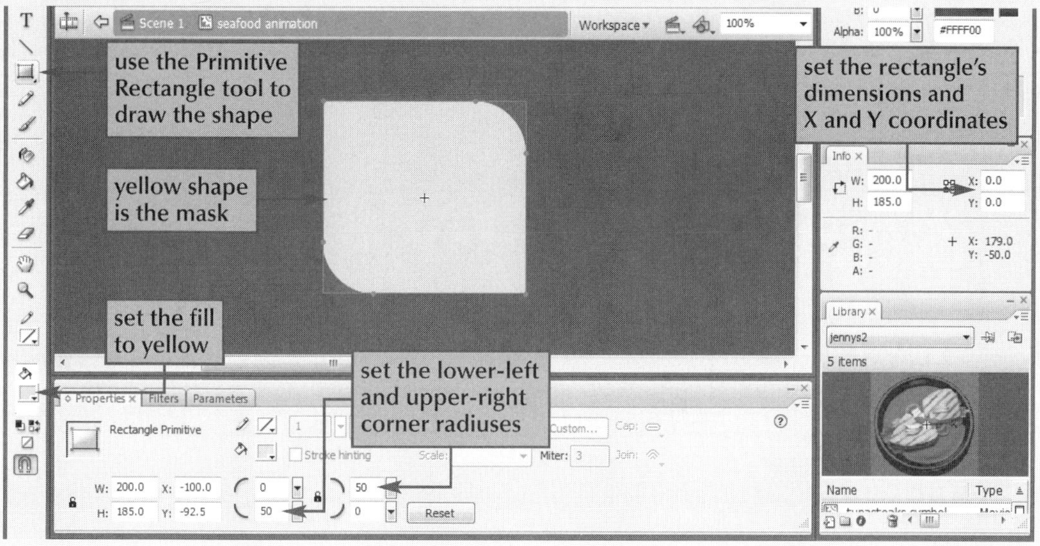

11. In the Timeline, click the **Lock/Unlock All Layers** icon to lock all of the layers and display the result of the mask. The crablegs picture shows through the mask. The mask for the seafood animation is now complete.
12. Close the Info panel, click the **Scene 1** link on the Edit bar to exit symbol-editing mode and return to the document's main Timeline, and then save the document.

You need to add the completed seafood animation movie clip to the banner. Based on the specifications for this banner that Aly provided, the seafood animation is to be placed on the left side of the banner.

To add the seafood animation to the banner and preview it:

1. In the Timeline, insert a new layer above the text layer and name it **bitmaps**. You'll add the seafood animation to the banner in this layer.
2. Drag the **seafood animation** symbol from the Library panel to the left side of the Stage. The animation is added to the banner.
3. In the Property inspector, enter **118** for the X coordinate and **125** for the Y coordinate. The animation is positioned attractively in the banner. See Figure 6-14.

Figure 6-14 Seafood animation in the banner

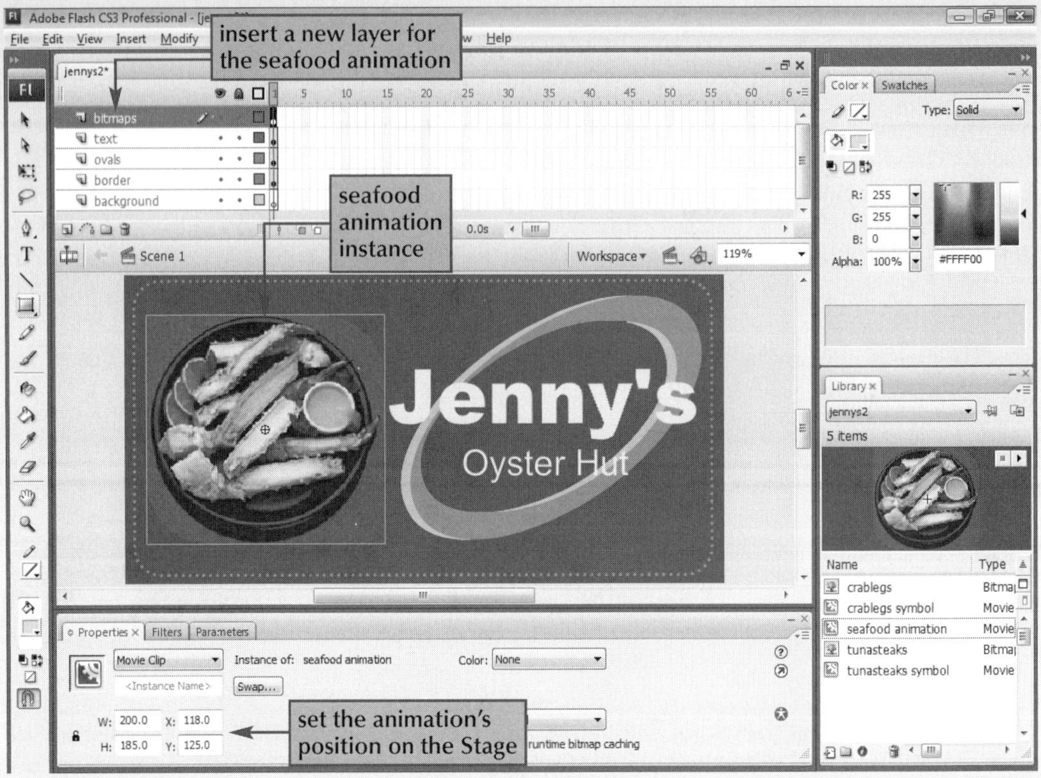

Because the animation was created inside the movie clip's Timeline, you cannot preview it within the main document's Timeline. To preview the seafood animation with the banner, you need to create an SWF file and play it in a separate window or in a Web page.

4. Save the banner.
5. Click **Control** on the menu bar, and then click **Test Movie**. A Flash Player window opens with the banner and the seafood animation.
6. View the animation in the banner, and then close the Flash Player window.

Converting a Bitmap to a Vector Graphic

A bitmap instance on the Stage can also be converted to a vector graphic. You can modify the converted graphic just like any other vector graphic created in Flash. The converted graphic is no longer linked to the imported bitmap in the document's library. So, any changes you make the vector graphic do not affect the original bitmap in the library, which can still be used to create instances of the bitmap on the Stage.

Converting a bitmap to a vector graphic has several benefits. If the imported bitmap is geometric, converting it to a vector graphic enables you to use the Flash editing tools to edit the graphic. You might also want to convert a bitmap to a vector graphic so you can create a visual effect with the image. Finally, converting a bitmap instance to a vector graphic can reduce the file size of the final movie.

The Trace Bitmap command converts a bitmap instance on the Stage into a vector graphic by comparing each pixel in the graphic to assign it a color. Pixels with similar colors are converted into areas of one color, essentially reducing the number of colors in the picture. Also, areas of contrasting color are converted to lines and curves. You specify how Flash should do this conversion through the settings in the Trace Bitmap dialog box, which are described in Figure 6-15.

Figure 6-15 Trace Bitmap dialog box settings

Setting	Description
Color threshold	Determines how pixels are compared to assign colors to them. The value ranges from 1 to 500. Higher values create fewer distinct colors because adjacent pixels must vary more before they are considered a different color. Smaller values result in more distinct colors.
Minimum area	Specifies the number of surrounding pixels to average when assigning a color to assign to each pixel. The value ranges from 1 to 1000. A smaller minimum area compares fewer surrounding pixels, creating more colors. A larger area compares more surrounding pixels, creating fewer colors.
Curve fit	Specifies how smoothly the outlines are drawn. The value ranges from Pixels, which results in more detail, to Very Smooth, which results in less detail.
Corner threshold	Specifies whether sharp edges are retained or smoothed out. The Many Corners setting results in more detail whereas the Few Corners setting results in less detail.

Selecting different values for the settings in the Trace Bitmap dialog box creates different effects in the converted graphic. For example, a bitmap that is converted to a vector graphic using a color threshold of 50, a minimum area of 50, a normal curve fit, and a normal corner threshold creates the special effect shown in Figure 6-16.

Figure 6-16 Bitmap converted to a vector

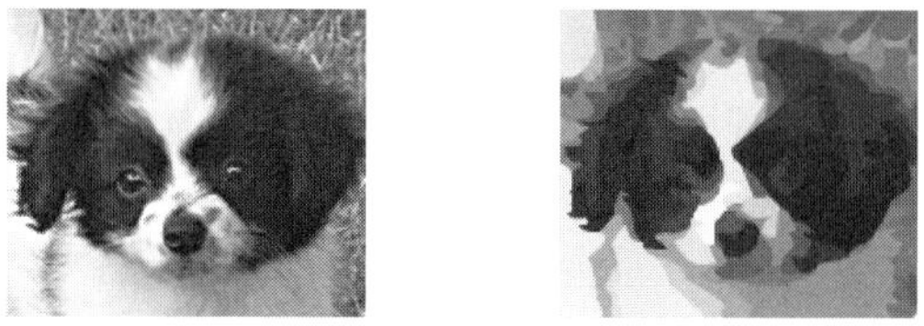

original bitmap   converted vector

Jenny wants the new company logo to include a photo of a lobster as shown in the sketch of the logo in Figure 6-17. Aly provides a lobster photo to use as the logo's background. You will convert the bitmap to a vector graphic to create a special effect using the Trace Bitmap command.

Figure 6-17 Sketch for new Jenny's Oyster Hut logo

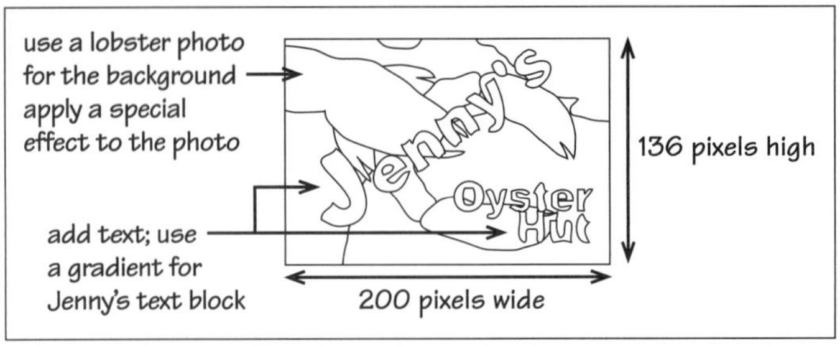

You'll convert the bitmap.

To convert the lobster bitmap to a vector:

1. Click **File** on the menu bar, and then click **New** to open the New Document dialog box, click **Flash File (ActionScript 3.0)** in the Type box on the General tab, and then click the **OK** button. A new Flash file opens.
2. Click **Modify** on the menu bar, and then click **Document**. The Document Properties dialog box opens
3. Type **200** in the Width box, type **136** in the Height box, and then click the **OK** button. The document's dimensions are set to match the logo dimensions provided by Aly.
4. Save the file as **jennyslogo.fla** in the **Tutorial.06\Tutorial** folder included with your Data Files, and then set the workspace to its default layout.
5. Click **File** on the menu bar, point to **Import**, and then click **Import to Library**. The Import to Library dialog box opens.
6. Click the **Formats** button and click **All Image Formats** if necessary, navigate to the **Tutorial.06\Tutorial** folder included with your Data Files, click the **lobster.jpg** file, and then click the **Open** button. The lobster bitmap is imported into the document's library.
7. Drag a copy of the **lobster** bitmap from the Library panel to the Stage, and then, in the Property Inspector, set the X and Y coordinates to **0**. The lobster bitmap instance is centered on the Stage.

   Now you will convert the bitmap to a vector graphic.
8. With the lobster instance selected on the Stage, click **Modify** on the menu bar, point to **Bitmap**, and then click **Trace Bitmap**. The Trace Bitmap dialog box opens. See Figure 6-18.

Figure 6-18 Trace Bitmap dialog box

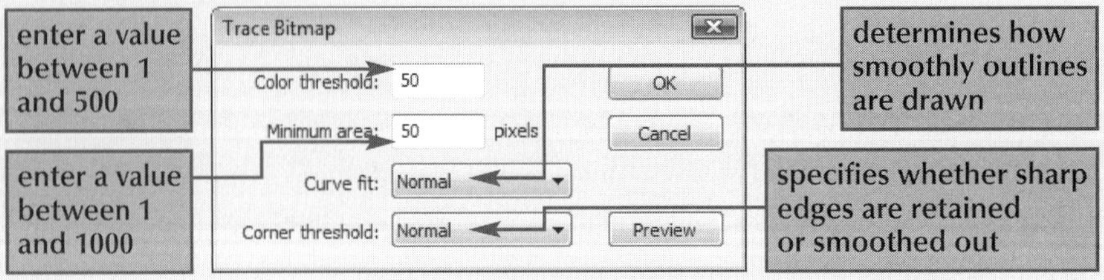

9. Type **60** in the Color threshold box, and then type **10** in the Minimum area box. The color threshold setting determines how pixels are compared to assign colors to them. The minimum area setting specifies how many surrounding pixels to average when assigning a color to each pixel.

10. Click the **Curve fit** button, and then click **Very Smooth**. This setting affects how the outlines are drawn. Very Smooth will result in less detail.
11. Click the **Corner threshold** button, and then click **Many corners**. This setting determines whether sharp edges are retained or smoothed out. Many Corners will result in more detail.
12. Click the **OK** button. The lobster bitmap converts to a vector graphic based on the settings you entered in the Trace Bitmap dialog box. The lobster vector graphic contains less detail, larger areas of solid color, and smoother outlines than the original bitmap.
13. In the Tools panel, click the **Selection** tool, and then click the pasteboard to deselect the graphic. The changes to the graphic are visible.
14. In the Timeline, lock Layer 1 to prevent accidentally changing its contents. See Figure 6-19.

Figure 6-19 Lobster picture as a vector graphic

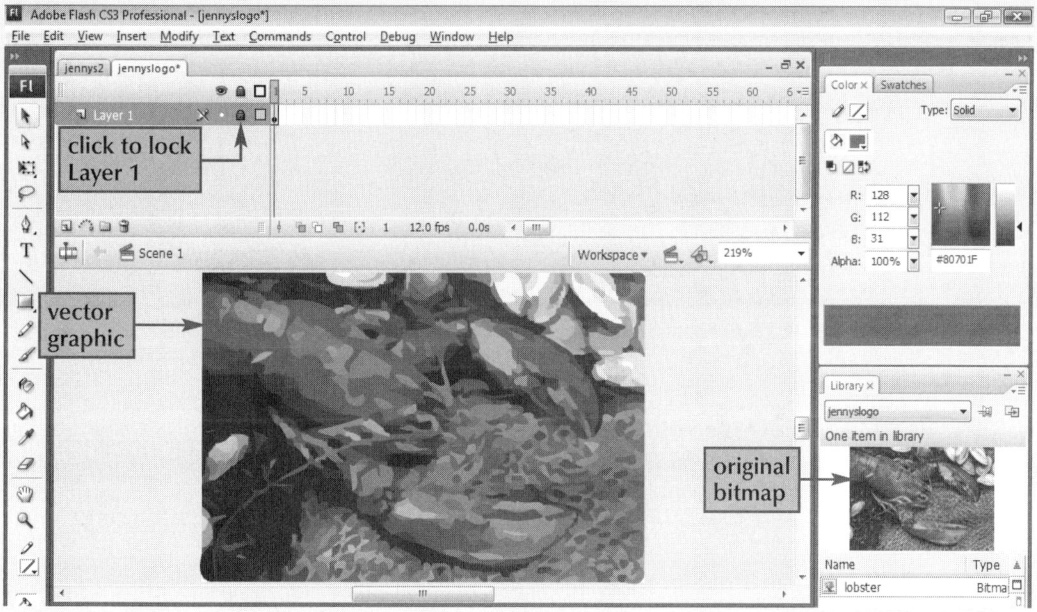

You will complete the logo by adding text on top of the graphic, as shown in Aly's planning sketch. The graphic is the background for the logo. You will add the text on a separate layer.

To complete the logo by adding text:

1. In the Timeline, insert a new layer and name it **jennys**. You will create the text for the logo in this layer.
2. In the Tools panel, click the **Text** tool, and then, in the Property inspector, change the font to **Arial Black**, change the font size to **30**, change the text color to **green** (#00FF00), make sure the Bold and Italic styles are not selected, and set the alignment to **Align Left**.
3. Click the left-center area of the lobster, type **Jenny's**, select the letter **J**, and then, in the Property inspector, change the font size to **58**. The first letter is larger than the rest of the name.

4. In the Tools panel, click the **Free Transform** tool, and then click the **Rotate and Skew** button. A bounding box appears around the text block.
5. Drag a corner handle on the bounding box around the text to rotate the text block counterclockwise, and then reposition the text block as needed so that it is centered on the picture. See Figure 6-20.

Figure 6-20 Rotated and centered text block

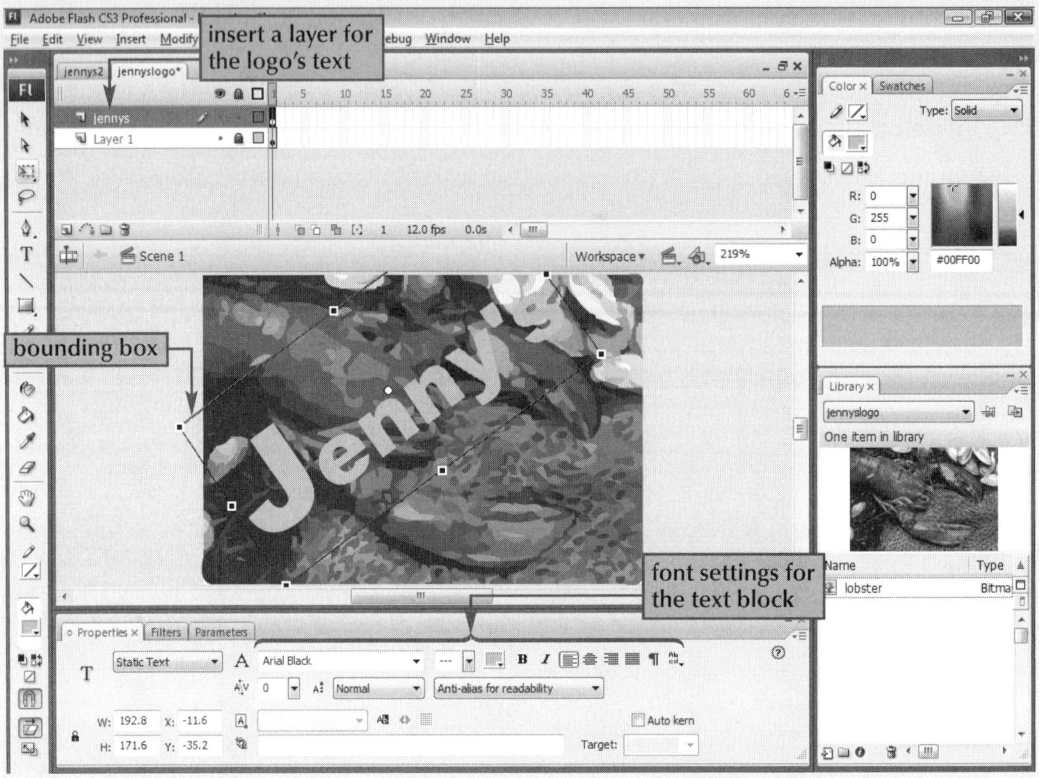

You need to create two more text blocks for the other words in the restaurant name. Each word will have a slightly different color.

6. Click the pasteboard to deselect the Jenny's text block.
7. In the Tools panel, click the **Text** tool, and then, in the Property inspector, change the font size to **24** and change the text color to **light yellow** (#FFFF99).
8. On the lower-right corner of the Stage, create a text block, type **Oyster**, and then click the pasteboard to deselect the text block.
9. In the Property inspector, change the text color to a **lighter yellow** (#FFFFCC), create another text block below the Oyster text, and then type **Hut**.
10. In the Tools panel, click the **Selection** tool, and then reposition the two text blocks so that they are in the lower-right corner of the Stage and their right edges are aligned. See Figure 6-21.

Figure 6-21 Logo with text

11. Save the logo.

In this session, you added bitmaps to the lunch specials banner. You imported the bitmaps into the document's library and then created instances on the Stage. You created an animation with two bitmaps, changing the alpha amount to create a fade effect. You also converted a bitmap to a vector graphic to create the new logo. In the next session, you'll modify the logo with gradients.

Session 6.1 Quick Check | Review

1. What is a bitmap?
2. What is the difference between the Import to Stage and the Import to Library commands?
3. How do you access a bitmap's properties within Flash?
4. For what type of bitmaps should you use the Photo (JPEG) compression setting?
5. What alpha amount makes an object transparent?
6. What command do you use to convert a bitmap to a vector graphic?
7. When converting a bitmap to a vector graphic, how does the color threshold value affect the resulting graphic?

Session 6.2

Using Gradients

A **gradient** is a gradual blend or transition from one color to another. Gradients can help you create special effects and add a professional touch to documents. For example, you can use a gradient for a banner's background, create a gradient to simulate a sunset or a rainbow, or use a gradient as part of an animation. Gradients can be added as fills to any object the same way you add solid color fills.

The two types of gradients you can create in Flash are linear and radial. A **linear gradient** blends the colors from one point to another in a straight line. A **radial gradient** blends the colors from one point outward in a circular pattern. Figure 6-22 shows examples of linear and radial gradients.

Figure 6-22 Gradient examples

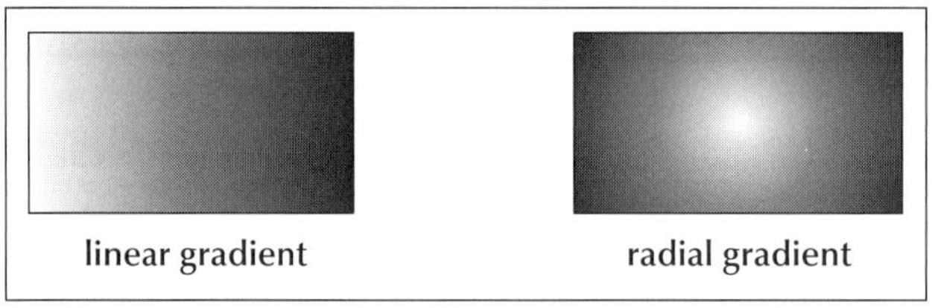

Flash includes several preset gradients in the color palette and in the Swatches panel. You can use these gradients as fills for any closed shape. You can also create custom gradients using the Color panel.

InSight | Gradients Impact Performance

Although gradients are easy to create and add to a Flash document, they increase the processing requirements of the computer displaying the SWF movie. Because of the greater number of colors in a gradient, a computer's processor might have to work harder to display a gradient compared to displaying solid colors. If you have concerns about a movie's performance when displayed on a user's computer, you can reduce the number of gradients used in the movie or omit them altogether if the SWF movie contains complex graphics or animations. You should always test the movie to ensure its quality is acceptable.

Creating and Saving a Custom Gradient

You create a new gradient in the Color panel. First you specify whether to use a linear or radial gradient as the fill style, and then you add **color pointers** to the gradient definition bar for each time you want to change the color in the gradient. A gradient can have anywhere from 2 to 15 color pointers. Each color pointer creates a **fall off point**, which is the spot where the gradient shifts or transitions from one color to another. A gradient's colors are displayed in the color space at the bottom of the Color panel. You can add a new gradient to the document's color swatches that appear in the color palette and in the Swatches panel. The gradient is stored only with the current document.

Creating, Editing, and Saving a Gradient | Reference Window

- To create a gradient, open the Color panel, click the Type button, and then click Linear or Radial (or click a preset gradient in the color palette or the Swatches panel).
- To edit a gradient, add or delete a color pointer.
- To specify a color for a color pointer, select the color pointer, and then enter the color's RGB values, hexadecimal value, or click the color picker in the Color panel.
- To add a color pointer, click a spot on the gradient definition bar.
- To remove a color pointer, drag it down, away from the gradient definition bar.
- To reposition a color pointer, drag it to the left or right on the gradient definition bar.
- To save a gradient with the current document, click the Color panel options menu, and then click Add Swatch.

The background of the new banner for the Jenny's Oyster Hut should be a radial gradient using a blend of a light blue color that transitions into a dark gray color. You will create the radial gradient to use as the fill for the banner's background.

To create a custom radial gradient for the banner:

1. If you took a break after the previous session, make sure both the jennys2.fla and the jennyslogo.fla files are open, and set both workspaces to the default layout.
2. Click the **jennys2** tab to make the document active, and then click the **Swatches** tab to display the Swatches panel. The preset gradients appear at the bottom of the Swatches panel.
3. In the Swatches panel, click the **gray radial gradient** (the second gradient from the left) with the eyedropper pointer. You'll use modify this gradient to create the custom gradient. See Figure 6-23.

Tip

You can also press the Ctrl+F9 keys to open and close the Swatches panel, and press the Shift+F9 keys to open and close the Color panel.

Figure 6-23 Swatches panel

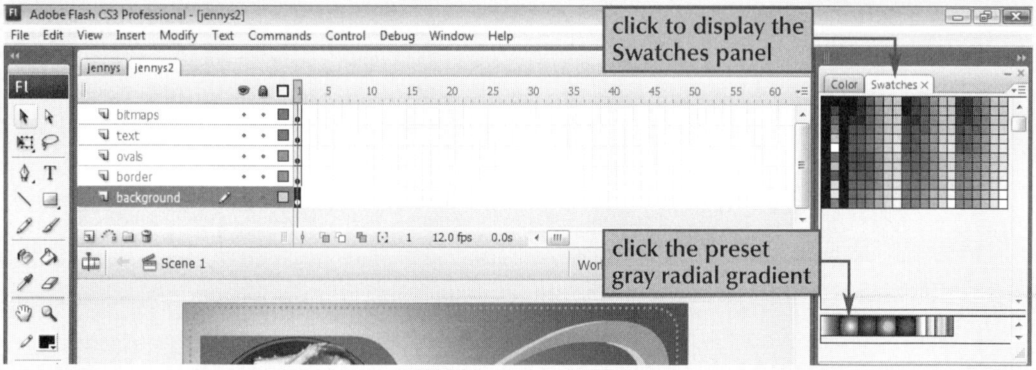

4. Click the **Color** tab to display the Color panel. The Color panel displays the preset gray radial gradient and its two color pointers. You'll change these color pointers to create the new gradient based on the colors specified in the planning sketch.
5. In the Color panel, click the **left color pointer** below the gradient definition bar to select it. The small triangle for the color pointer changes to black to indicate it is selected.
6. Type **#99FFFF** in the Hex value box, and then press the **Enter** key. The left color point for the gradient is set to a light blue color.

7. Click the **right color pointer** below the gradient definition bar, type **#333333** in the Hex value box, and then press the **Enter** key. The right color pointer is set to a dark gray color, and the color space in the Color panel shows the new gradient based on the colors you entered. See Figure 6-24.

Figure 6-24 Color space with new gradient

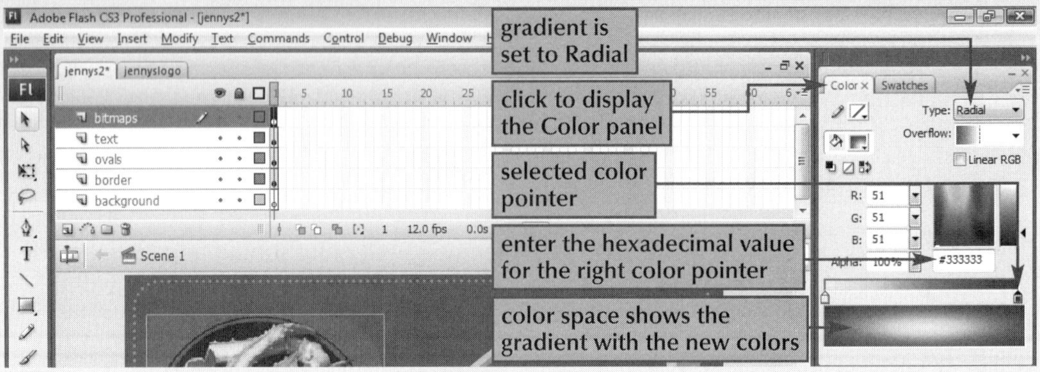

You'll save this gradient as a swatch in the Swatches panel for the document. If you don't save the gradient, it is discarded when you close the document.

8. In the Color panel, click the **options menu** control, and then click **Add Swatch**. The gradient is saved with the document.

9. Click the **Swatches** tab to display the Swatches panel. The custom gradient appears at the end of the preset gradients. See Figure 6-25.

Figure 6-25 New gradient in Swatches panel

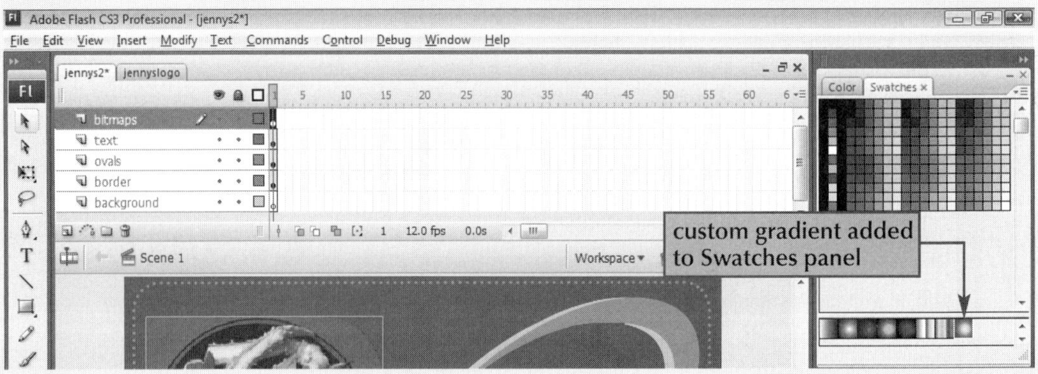

Tip

To delete a swatch, click the Swatches panel options menu button and then click Delete Swatch.

Applying a Gradient Fill

Gradient fills can be applied to both shapes such as circles, rectangles, and triangles as well as to text. You apply a gradient fill to an object the same way as you apply a solid fill. You can select the gradient for the fill color before you draw a shape such as a rectangle, or you can use the Paint Bucket tool to apply a gradient to an existing shape. When using the Paint Bucket tool to apply a radial gradient, you specify the gradient's center point, which is where the first color begins. The point you click becomes the gradient's center point, as shown in Figure 6-26. When using the Paint Bucket tool to apply a linear gradient, you drawing a straight line with the Paint Bucket pointer. The line you draw determines the direction of the gradient.

Figure 6-26 Applying a radial gradient with the Paint Bucket tool

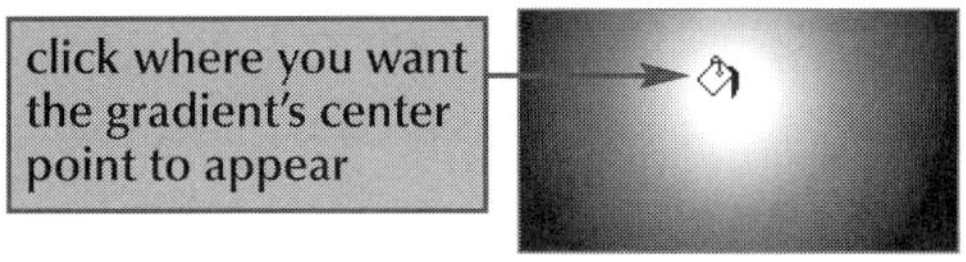

You can also use the Lock Fill modifier, which appears in the Tools panel when the Paint Bucket tool is selected, when applying gradients. With the Lock Fill modifier selected, the Paint Bucket tool paints one gradient across several objects on the Stage rather than one gradient for each object, as shown in Figure 6-27.

Figure 6-27 Effect of Lock Fill modifier on gradients

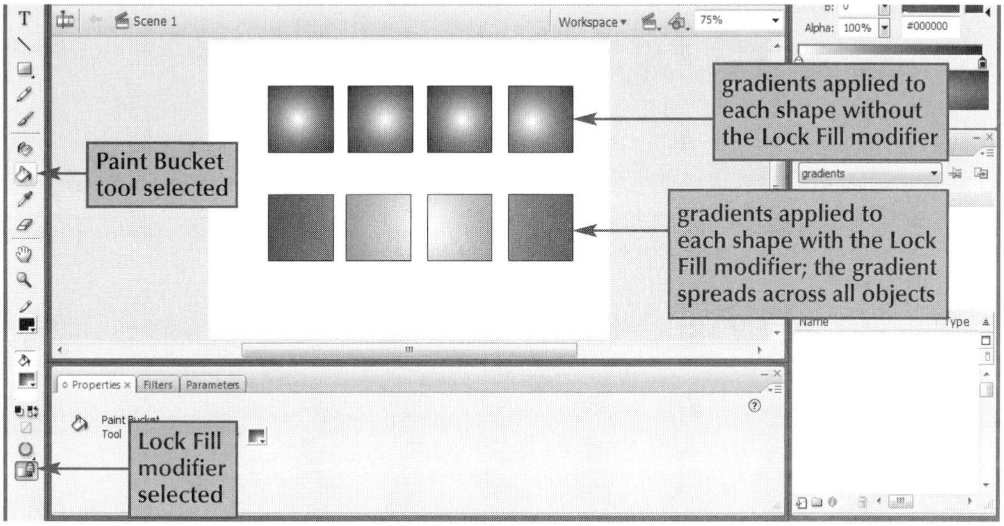

You will use the custom gradient as the fill for a rectangle that will serve as the banner's background.

To add a rectangle with the custom gradient to the background layer:

1. In the Timeline, select the **background** layer. You'll draw the rectangle for the banner's background in this layer.
2. In the Tools panel, click and hold the **Rectangle Primitive** tool, and then click the **Rectangle** tool to select it.
3. In the Tools panel, click the **Fill color** control, and then click the gradient you created in the bottom row of the color palette to confirm that it is selected. The rectangle you draw will use the gradient you created as its fill.
4. In the Tools panel, click the **Stroke color** control, and then click **no color**. The rectangle you draw will not have a visible stroke.
5. On the Stage, draw a large rectangle that is the same size as the Stage. The rectangle covers the entire Stage but does not obscure the text and images because the rectangle is in the bottommost layer. See Figure 6-28.

Tip

You can toggle between the Rectangle Primitive tool and the Rectangle tool in the Tools panel by pressing the R key once to select the tool and again to switch the tool.

Figure 6-28 Gradient background added to the banner

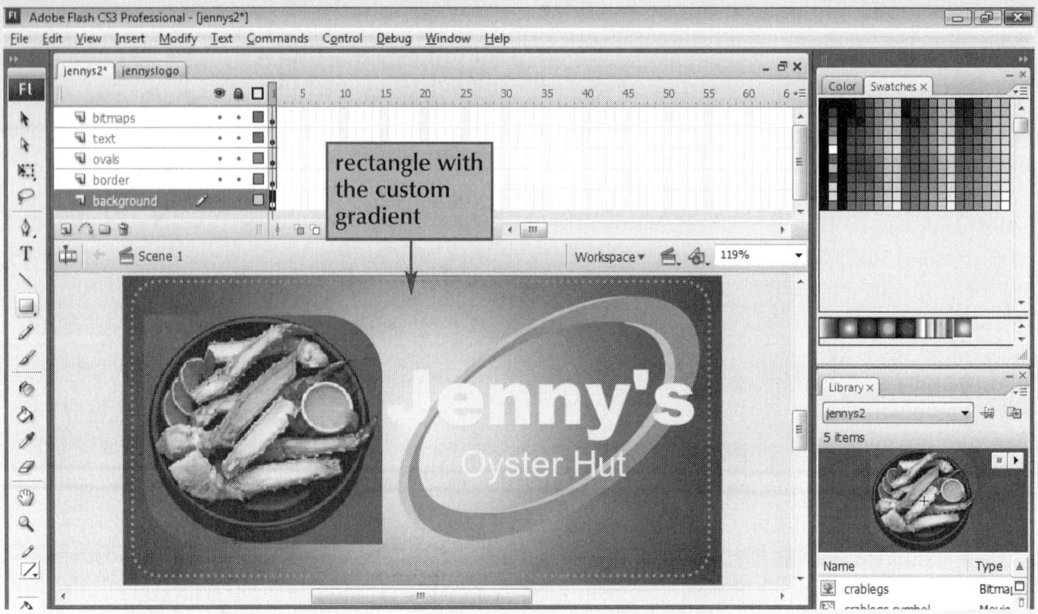

6. Save the document.

Filling Text with a Gradient

You can also apply a gradient fill to text. Before you can apply a gradient to text, you must first convert the text to a fill with the Break Apart command. If the text block has multiple letters, the first time you apply the Break Apart command to a text block, the text block is broken into smaller text blocks consisting of the individual letters. When you apply the Break Apart command a second time, the letter text blocks are converted into fills. Then, you can apply a gradient to the individual letters the same way you do any other shape. If the text block only has one letter, the Break Apart command needs to be applied only once to convert the letter into a fill.

The Jenny's text block in the logo should have a gradient fill applied to it. You will convert the text block to fills, apply a preset gradient, and then modify the colors to create a custom gradient.

To apply a gradient fill to the Jenny's text block:

1. Click the **jennyslogo** tab to make the logo document active.
2. In the Tools panel, click the **Selection** tool, and then select the **Jenny's** text block on the Stage. You'll break apart text block so you can apply a gradient fill.

3. Click **Modify** on the menu bar, and then click **Break Apart**. The text block breaks into individual blocks for each letter. See Figure 6-29.

Figure 6-29 **Jenny's text block broken apart**

4. Click **Modify** on the menu bar, and then click **Break Apart**. The individual text blocks are converted to fills. The text fills are selected and ready for you to apply a gradient fill.

5. Click the **Color** tab, if necessary, to display the Color panel, click the **Type** button, and then click **Linear**. A linear gradient is applied to the text fills.

   You will modify the gradient used in the selected text fills.

6. Click the **left color pointer** below the gradient definition bar to select it, type **#FFFFFF** in the Hex value box, and then press the **Enter** key. The starting color for the linear gradient is set.

7. Click the **right color pointer** to select it, type **#FFFF00** in the Hex value box, and then press the **Enter** key. The ending color for the linear gradient is set, and the text gradient fill color changes. See Figure 6-30.

Figure 6-30 Gradient applied to text fills

8. Save the document.

Transforming Gradient Fills

A gradient fill in an object can be modified by using the Gradient Transform tool. You can move a gradient's center, change its size, or change its direction. When you select a linear gradient with the Gradient Transform tool, a bounding box surrounds it. When you select a radial gradient, a bounding circle surrounds it. The gradient's center point also appears along with editing handles, as shown in Figure 6-31. You drag these handles to transform the gradient.

Figure 6-31 Editing handles

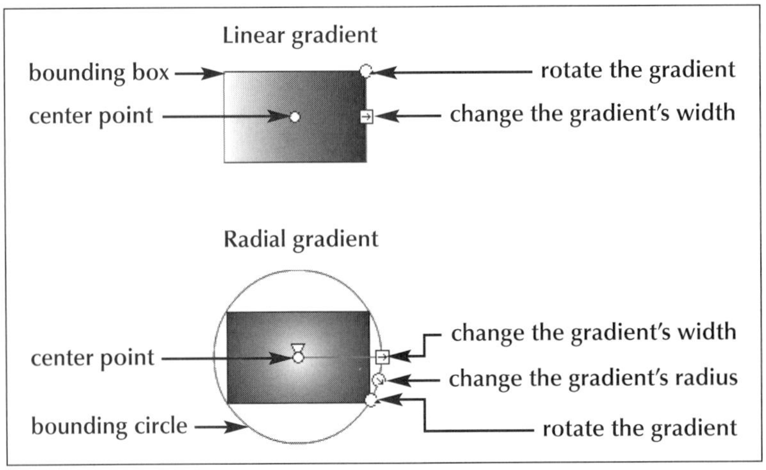

You drag a gradient's center point to reposition it. The linear gradient has a circular handle to rotate the gradient and a square handle to change the gradient's width. The radial gradient has two circular handles. The middle circular handle changes the gradient's radius and the bottom circular handle rotates the gradient. It also has a square handle, which changes the gradient's width. A radial gradient also has a focal point, indicated by a small triangle, which is initially in the same position as the center point. You can drag the small triangle to change the gradient's focal point.

Aly wants you to modify the gradient in the banner background so that the lighter color of the gradient is behind the animation of the seafood pictures. To do this, you will move the gradient's center point to the left side of the banner over the seafood animation and increase its radius slightly to spread more of the lighter color to the rest of the banner.

To modify the gradient in the banner background:

1. Click the **jennys2** tab to make the document active. The banner appears on the Stage.
2. In the Tools panel, click and hold the **Free Transform** tool, and then click the **Gradient Transform** tool. The Gradient Transform tool is selected.
3. Click the **rectangle** with the gradient fill. The gradient's bounding circle and editing handles appear.
4. Reduce the magnification level of the Stage to **50%**. The entire bounding circle is visible, making the rectangle easier to work with. See Figure 6-32.

Figure 6-32 Gradient selected for transformation

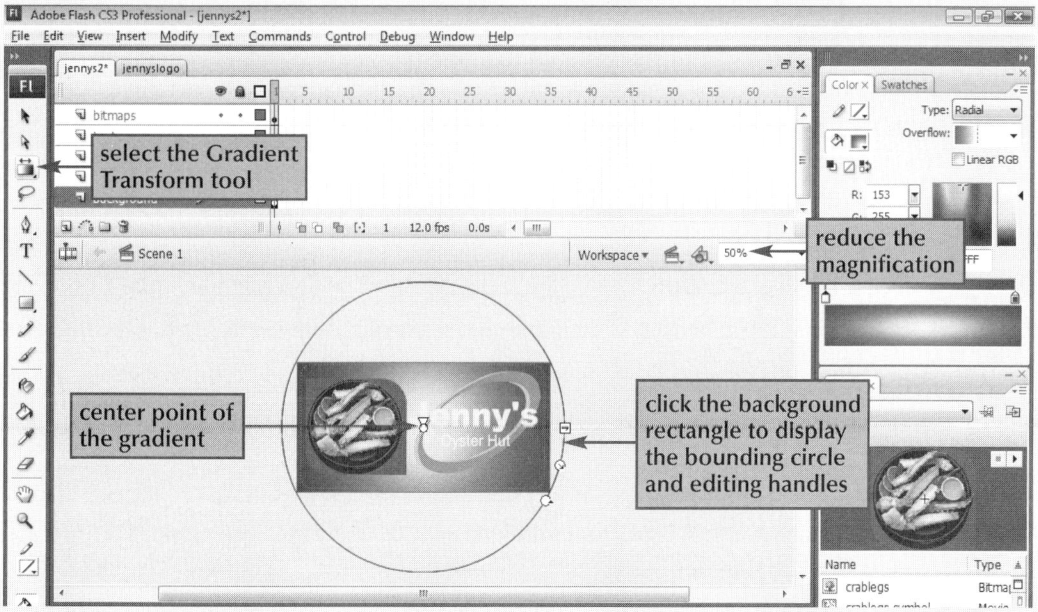

5. Move the pointer over the center point of the gradient until the pointer changes to a center-point pointer to indicate it is over the center point, and then drag the **center point** of the gradient to the left until it is positioned over the center of the seafood animation instance. The entire bounding circle moves as you reposition the center point of the gradient.

6. Drag the **radius handle** outward until the right side of the bounding circle touches the right of the letter "s" in the Jenny's text. See Figure 6-33. The gradient's radius increases so that the light blue color extends more than halfway across the banner.

Figure 6-33 **Gradient's radius increased**

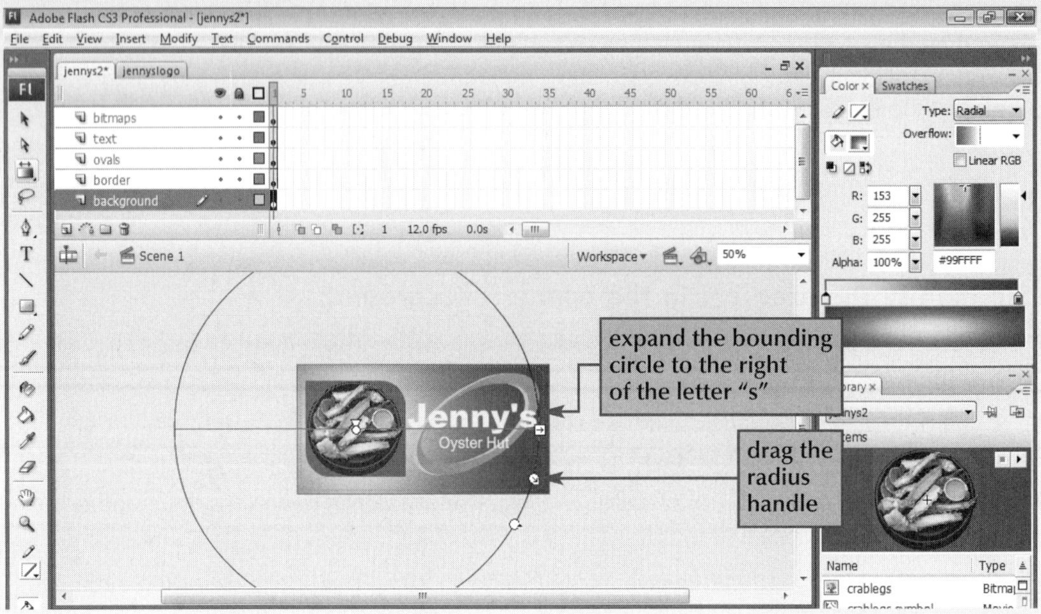

7. Save the jennys2 banner.

The banner is complete. Aly is pleased with your work and thinks the banner will look great on the Jenny's Oyster Hut Web site. In this session, you worked with gradients. You created a custom gradient for the banner and used it in the background rectangle you drew. You also modified the gradient's position, size, and width using the Gradient Transform tool. In addition, you applied a gradient to existing text in the logo, and then modified the colors in the gradient. In the next session, you will publish the banner you created.

Review | Session 6.2 Quick Check

1. What is a gradient?
2. Describe the two different kinds of gradients available in Flash.
3. How do you save a gradient?
4. True or False? A gradient is saved only within the current document.
5. How do you add another color to a gradient with two colors?
6. True or False? You can apply a gradient to an existing object using the Gradient Transform tool.
7. When using the Paint Bucket tool to apply a linear gradient, how do you specify the direction of the gradient?
8. What are two changes you can make to a radial gradient with the Gradient Transform tool?

Session 6.3

Comparing Publishing Options

FLA documents created in Flash are usually made available for use on the Web. To do so, the document must be published or exported into a format that is readable by a Web browser. You have done this when you published FLA documents as SWF movie files in previous tutorials to test or preview the movie. You have used the Test Movie command, which creates an SWF file that plays in a separate Flash Player window. You have also used the Default – (HTML) command, which creates both an SWF file and an HTML file to play the movie. The browser uses the Flash Player plug-in to play the movie. In most cases, when you create movies for the Web, you want to publish an SWF file. However, sometimes you need to publish or export the document in a different file format. Flash allows you to publish Flash documents in such file formats as JPEG, GIF, and PNG.

Creating a Projector File | InSight

A Flash file can be published as a projector file, which is a standalone application with the .exe extension. A projector file has Flash Player incorporated into it and plays the movie in its own window rather than in a Web browser. This is a useful option if you want to distribute a Flash movie on a platform other than the Web. The advantage to distributing a Flash projector file is that it can be viewed on a computer that does not have the Flash Player plug-in installed. The disadvantage is that the file size will be larger than a SWF file because the Flash Player is embedded in the projector file.

You can also save the publishing settings as a profile that you can use with other documents.

Selecting a Document's Publish Settings

You specify how you want an FLA document published in the Publish Settings dialog box. The Formats tab lists the many file formats in which you can publish a Flash document. Most of the time, you will use only the Flash (.swf) and HTML (.html) file types because the documents you create are meant to be played in a Web page. However, you can choose to publish a document in a different format such as the JPEG Image (.jpg) file format. Each file format selected on the Formats tab has a corresponding tab in the Publish Settings dialog box with additional options and settings for that file type.

InSight | Choosing a Flash Player Version

When publishing Flash movies, you can specify that they run on the latest version of the Flash Player. If you are certain that all members of the target audience have the latest player installed on their computers, then publishing to the latest format is not a problem. Publishing to the latest format ensures that all features of the Flash CS3 program work in the Flash Player. If you are unsure which version of Flash Player the audience has, it's a good idea to publish to a player that is two or three versions earlier. For example, if the current version of the Flash Player is version 9, you can set the version in the Publish Settings dialog box to version 6 or 7 to ensure that most members of your target audience can see the Flash movies. If you publish to version 6 of the Flash Player, for example, then anyone with Flash Player 6 or later can see the Flash movie. Publishing the Flash movie to the latest version may limit the number of people who are able to see the movie.

The banner you just completed will be added to the home page of the Jenny's Oyster Hut Web site. Because the Web page already exists, you need to publish the banner only as an SWF file. When publishing in the Flash (.swf) format, the Flash tab in the Publish Settings dialog box contains options to specify the Version, the Load order, and the ActionScript version, as well as other settings. Version specifies the oldest version of the Flash Player in which the published movie will play. The published banner SWF file should be compatible with all Flash Player plug-ins starting with version 6, so you will select Flash Player 6. Load order specifies whether the layers are played from the top down or the bottom up. You'll use the default setting of Bottom Up because this movie contains a small number of layers so the order in which they are loaded is insignificant. ActionScript version specifies which version of the Flash programming language will be used by the published movie. The banner does not use ActionScript so there is no need to change the default setting. The JPEG quality and audio settings can also be changed in this dialog box. However, the bitmap properties you set as you worked with the photos override these JPEG settings. Also, this movie includes no sounds so the audio settings are not used. Aly wants you to generate a size report, which shows the size of the different parts of the movie. The report is created as a text file using the FLA file's name plus the word Report followed by the extension .txt. The report also appears in the Output panel after the file is published.

Tip

A file published with the compressed movie option only plays in Flash Player 6 or later. Compression is especially useful for a text-intensive Flash document.

To publish the jennys2 file as an SWF file:

1. If you took a break after the previous session, make sure the jennys2.fla and jennyslogo.fla files are open, the workspace for each document is set to the default layout, and the jennys2 document is active.
2. Click **File** on the menu bar, and then click **Publish Settings**. The Publish Settings dialog box opens.
3. If necessary, click the **Formats** tab to display its settings. See Figure 6-34.

Figure 6-34

Formats tab in the Publish settings dialog box

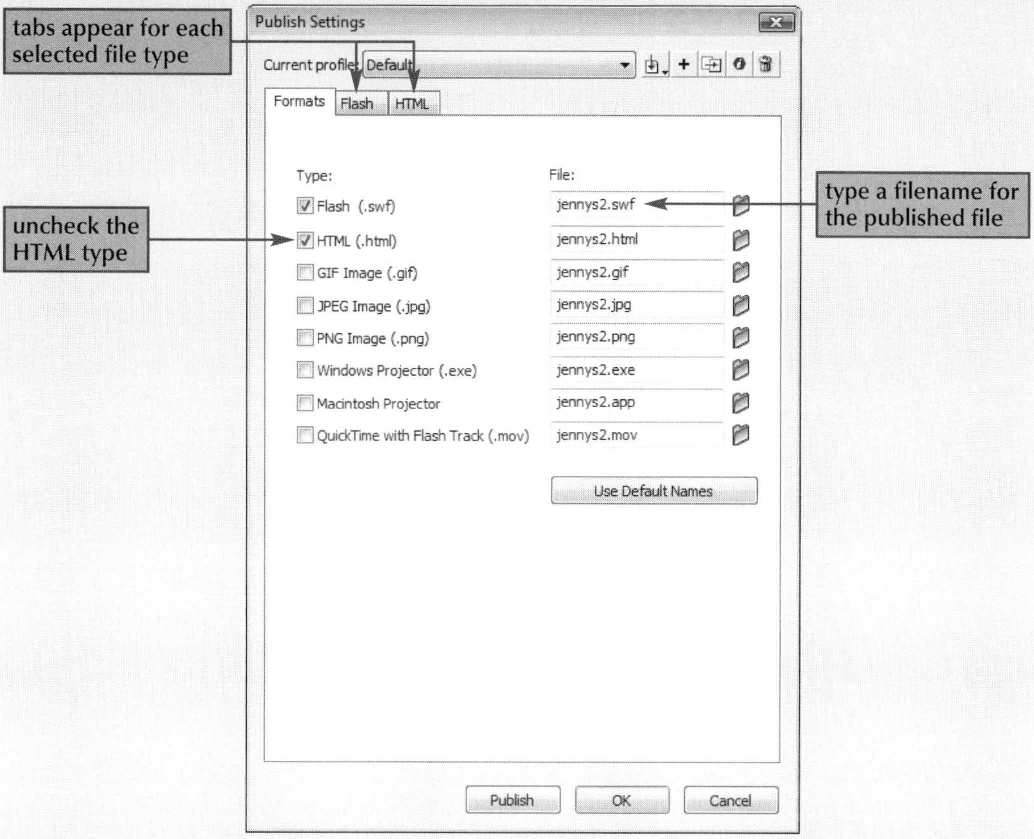

4. On the Formats tab, click the **HTML (.html)** check box to remove the check mark, and then make sure that the **Flash (.swf)** check box is checked. You want to publish the banner only in the Flash format.

5. Type **banner.swf** in the File box to the right of Flash (.swf) to specify the name for the published SWF file.

6. Click the **Select Publish Destination** button to the right of Flash (.swf) to open the Select Publish Destination dialog box, navigate to the **Tutorial.06\Tutorial** folder included with your Data Files, if necessary, and then click the **Save** button to specify the folder in which to save the published SWF file.

7. Click the **Flash** tab to display the settings for this format. You will set the publishing options for the published movie on this tab.

8. Click the **Version** button, and then click **Flash Player 6**. You selected the earlier version so that the movie can be played on all computers with Flash Player 6 or later. You'll leave the load order set to bottom up because the order won't affect the movie. You'll leave the ActionScript 2.0 as the version because the banner does not use ActionScript.

9. In the Options area, click the **Generate size report** check box to insert a check mark. The report will specify how big each part of the movie is.

10. Click the **Compress movie** check box to remove the check mark. You don't need to compress the movie because it is not a large document.

11. Click the **Export hidden layers** check box to remove the check mark. The movie doesn't have any hidden layers, so you don't need this option. See Figure 6-35.

Figure 6-35 Flash publish settings

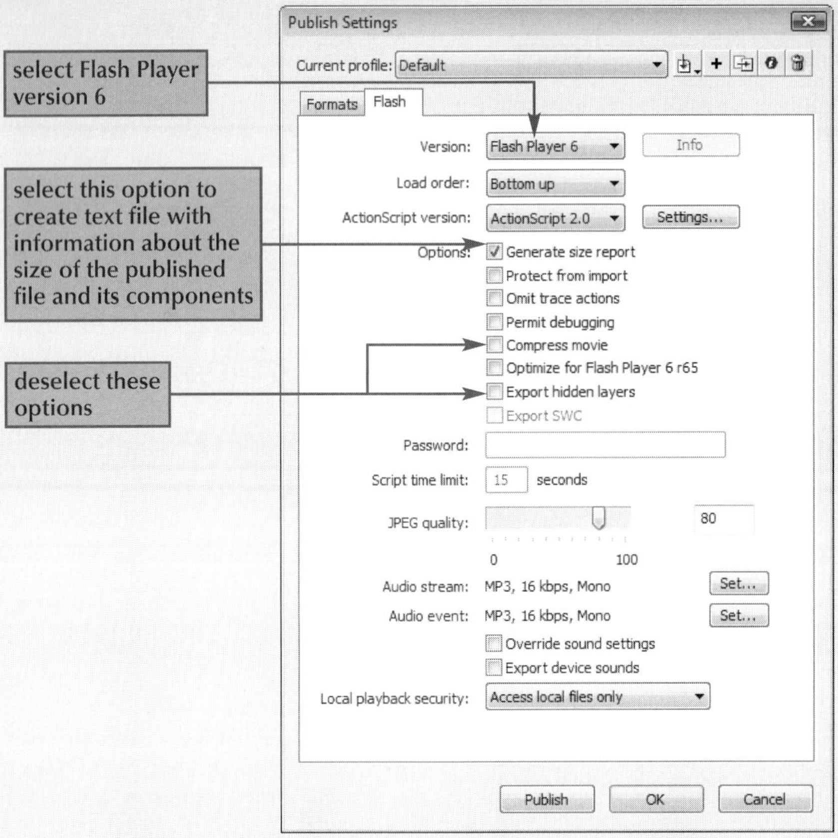

12. Click the **Publish** button. The Publish Settings dialog box remains open, and the SWF file and the size report file are created in the same folder as the FLA file. The report also appears in the Output panel. You will view its contents later in this session.

You can save your preferred publish settings for a document, including the Flash and HTML settings, as a **publish profile**. The settings in the publish profile are available to any document you create in Flash on the same computer. After you save a publish profile, the Publish command publishes the files according to the settings saved in the profile. A profile can be deleted in the Publish Settings dialog box. Also, if you remove HTML (.html) as a format for a file, the Publish Preview command will default to the first format selected in the Formats tab of the Publish Settings dialog box. You'll create a publish profile for all of the Jenny's Oyster Hut documents.

To create a publish profile for the Jenny's Oyster Hut documents:

1. In the Publish Settings dialog box, click the **Create new profile** button [+]. The Create New Profile dialog box opens.
2. Type **Oyster Hut** in the Profile name box, and then click the **OK** button. The Oyster Hut profile is created and appears as the current profile in the Publish Settings dialog box. All the settings revert to the defaults. See Figure 6-36.

Publish Settings dialog box with a publish profile **Figure 6-36**

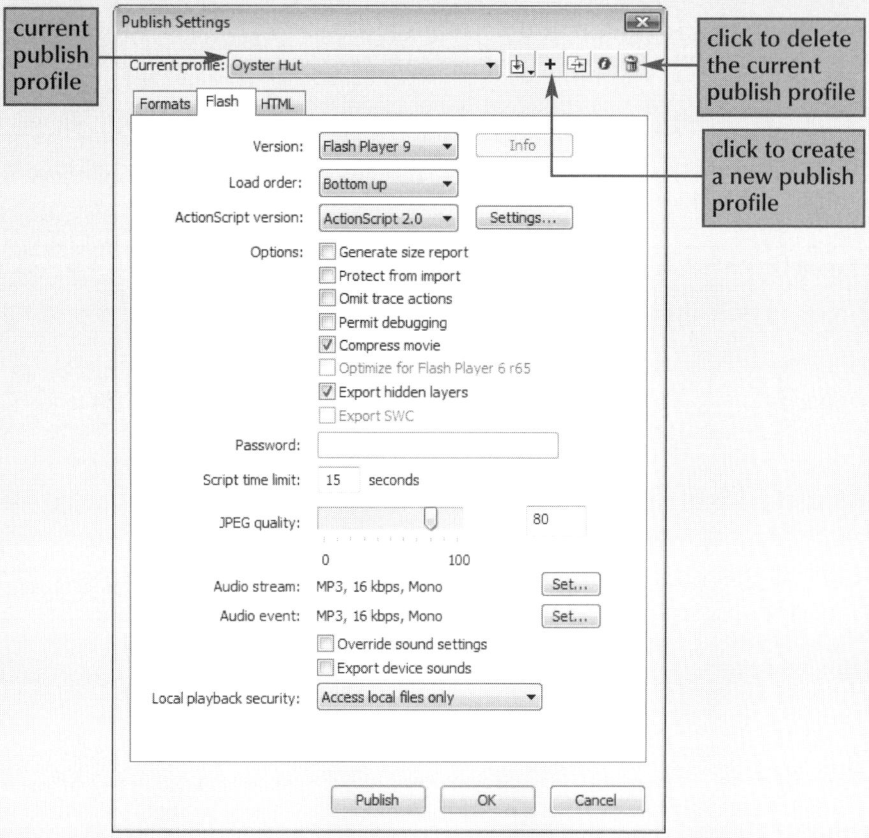

3. Click the **Version** button, and then click **Flash Player 8** to select this version.
4. In the Options area, click the **Compress movie** check box to remove the check mark.
5. Click the **Publish button** to publish the SWF and HTML files.

   Aly wants to check on some statistics about the target user and the version of Flash they might have on their computers. So you will delete this publish profile.

6. In the Publish Settings dialog box, click the **Delete profile** button, and then click the **OK** button in the dialog box that opens to confirm the deletion. The Oyster Hut profile is not saved, but you can easily create a new publish profile at any time.
7. Click the **OK** button to close the Publish Settings dialog box.
8. Save and close the jennys2 document.

You'll review the size report text file generated by Flash when you published the banner. The file opens in the Output panel, but you can also open it in Notepad, which is part of Windows. The report file shows information about the movie, including its number of frames, the total size of the movie in bytes, a list of the symbols in the movie, and a list of the bitmaps. This information can be useful when optimizing a larger, more complex movie to find ways to reduce its size. You will view the report in the Output panel.

To view the size report file in the Output panel:

1. Drag the Output panel to the center of the Stage.

   Trouble? If the Output panel did not open, you need to open it manually. Click Window on the menu bar, and then click Output.

2. Drag the lower edge of the Output panel to enlarge the panel as needed, and then scroll to the top of the panel to view the report. The report shows that the movie is 29980 bytes in size, has three symbols with a total size of 61 bytes, and has two bitmaps, each of which is compressed. See Figure 6-37.

Figure 6-37 Output panel with movie report

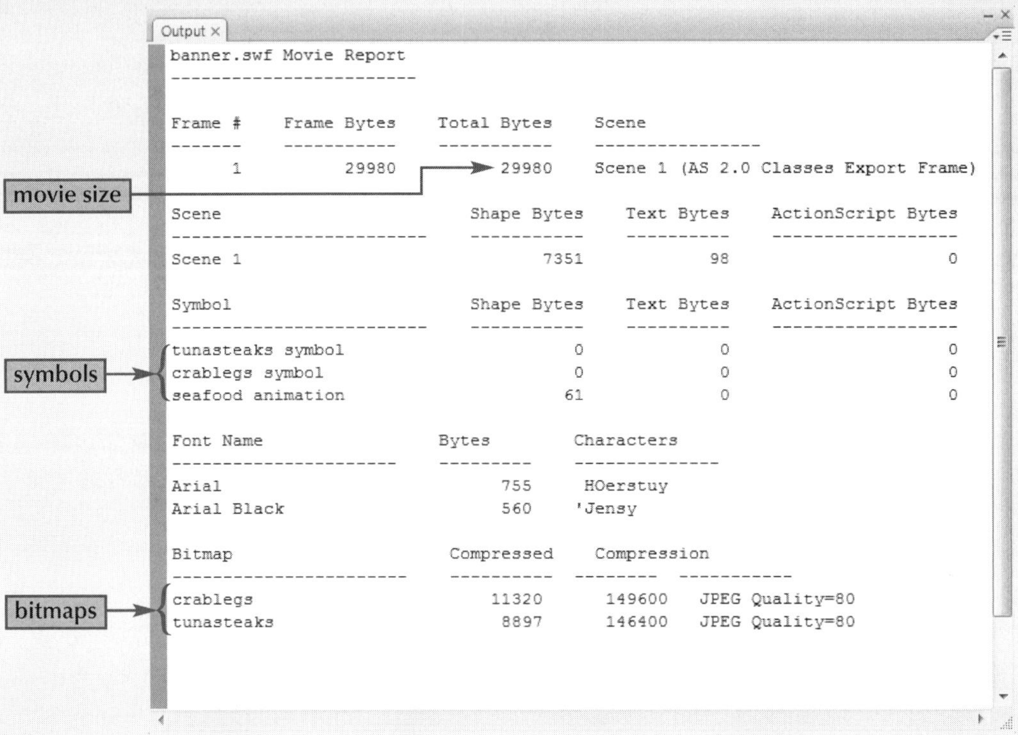

3. Click the **Close** icon ☒ on the Output panel's tab to close the panel.

Tip

You can also press the F2 key to open or close the Output panel.

Exporting an Image

The JPEG and GIF file formats are the most common file formats used for images in Web pages. JPEG format is best for images that include many colors, such as the original photograph of the lobster. GIF format is best for images with fewer colors, such as the lobster bitmap you converted to a vector for the logo. You can use the Publish Settings dialog box to select JPEG or GIF as the format in which to publish. You can also use the Export Image command on the File menu, which allows you to specify the type of format you want to export to and then displays settings you can change based on the selected file format. Some of the formats you can export to include JPEG image (*.jpg), GIF image (*.gif), and PNG image (*.png).

Because the logo you created is static, includes only a picture and some text, and contains mostly solid areas of color, you can export it as a GIF image. Some of the GIF settings include the dimensions and resolution of the exported GIF image, the area of the image to export and the number of colors to export. If the document has empty space, the Minimum Image Area setting will not export the empty space. The standard number of colors in a GIF image is 256, but if an image uses fewer colors, you can reduce the number of colors to export, shrinking the size of the file.

Tip

The Publish command saves the export settings you select with the document, whereas the Export Image command does not store the settings.

To export the logo as a GIF image:

1. Click **File** on the menu bar, point to **Export**, and then click **Export Image**. The Export Image dialog box opens.
2. If necessary, navigate to the **Tutorial.06\Tutorial** folder included with your Data Files, type **jennyslogo** in the File name box, click the **Save as type** button, and then click **GIF Image (*.gif)**.
3. Click the **Save** button. The Export GIF dialog box opens. See Figure 6-38.

Figure 6-38 Export GIF dialog box

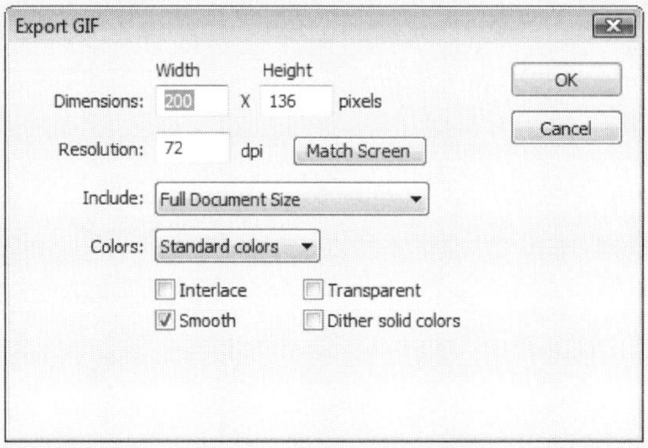

4. If necessary, click the **Match Screen** button to change the dimensions to 200 by 136 pixels and the resolution to 72 dpi.
5. If necessary, select **Full Document Size** in the Include list; select **Standard colors** in the Colors list, check the **Smooth** check box, and then uncheck the **Interlace**, **Transparent**, and **Dither solid colors** check boxes.
6. Click the **OK** button. The dialog box closes, and the logo is saved as a GIF image.
7. Close the jennyslogo document.

Adding Flash Graphics to a Web Page

The final output of creating movies with Flash is a Web page that displays the movies along with text, hyperlinks, and other graphics. After you complete a Flash graphic, such as a banner or a logo, you need to incorporate its file information into the Web page's HTML. When you publish a movie with the HTML format option, Flash creates a simple Web page to display the movie. More often, you'll want to add the SWF file to an existing Web page, which requires you to edit the actual Web page. You can do this with a Web page editing program such as Adobe Dreamweaver. You can also edit the HTML in a text editor such as Notepad.

The published banner and exported logo are ready to be placed in a Web page that Chris has created. The Web page has a simple banner and logo that you will replace. You will edit the Web page using Notepad.

To add the banner and logo to a sample Web page:

1. Click the **Start** button on the taskbar, click **All Programs**, click **Accessories**, and then click **Notepad**. The Notepad program starts.
2. Click **File** on the Notepad menu bar, and then click **Open**. The Open File dialog box opens.
3. Click the **Files of Type** button, click **All Files**, navigate to the **Tutorial.06\Tutorial** folder included with your Data Files, click **sample.htm** in the file list, and then click the **Open** button. The HTML for the sample Web page opens in the Notepad window.
4. Click the **Maximize** button on the title bar to maximize the program window. See Figure 6-39.

Figure 6-39 Sample Web page HTML

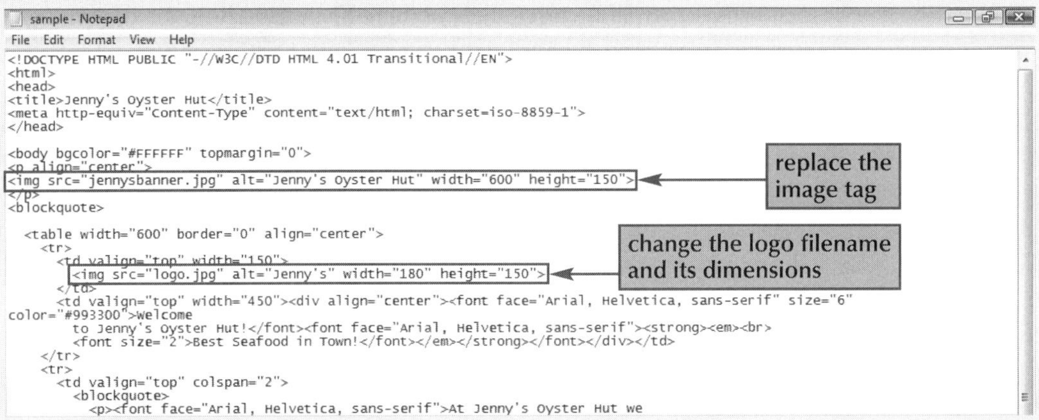

```
<!DOCTYPE HTML PUBLIC "-//W3C//DTD HTML 4.01 Transitional//EN">
<html>
<head>
<title>Jenny's Oyster Hut</title>
<meta http-equiv="Content-Type" content="text/html; charset=iso-8859-1">
</head>

<body bgcolor="#FFFFFF" topmargin="0">
<p align="center">
<img src="jennysbanner.jpg" alt="Jenny's Oyster Hut" width="600" height="150">
</p>
<blockquote>

  <table width="600" border="0" align="center">
    <tr>
      <td valign="top" width="150">
        <img src="logo.jpg" alt="Jenny's" width="180" height="150">
      </td>
      <td valign="top" width="450"><div align="center"><font face="Arial, Helvetica, sans-serif" size="6"
color="#993300">Welcome
        to Jenny's Oyster Hut!</font><font face="Arial, Helvetica, sans-serif"><strong><em><br>
        <font size="2">Best Seafood in Town!</font></em></strong></font></div></td>
    </tr>
    <tr>
      <td valign="top" colspan="2">
        <blockquote>
          <p><font face="Arial, Helvetica, sans-serif">At Jenny's Oyster Hut we
```


The tenth line contains the image tag <img src= "jennysbanner.jpg" alt="Jenny's Oyster Hut" width="600" height="150" > that places the current banner at the top of the Web page. You need to replace this tag with a special EMBED tag for the SWF file. EMBED is not a standard HTML tag, but is used to load external media such as an SWF movie that requires the use of a plug-in.

> **Tip**
>
> When possible, use an HTML editor such as Adobe Dreamweaver to insert Flash graphics into a Web page. Dreamweaver inserts code in addition to the embed tag so that Flash movies display properly in most browsers.

5. In line 10, replace the image tag, including the two angle brackets, with the following code: **<embed src="banner.swf" width="500" height="250">**

   You need to replace the reference for the current logo with a reference for the new logo file, jennyslogo.gif, and then update the logo's dimensions.

6. On line 17, replace logo.jpg with **jennyslogo.gif**. The code references the logo you created.
7. On line 17, replace width="180" height="150" with **width="200" height="136"**. The code includes the correct dimensions for the logo.

8. Save and close the file, and then exit Notepad. The Web page is updated with the new banner and logo.

You have changed the HTML of the sample Web page so that the page will display the animated banner and logo that you created for Jenny's Oyster Hut. You will test the Web page by opening the page in your browser.

To preview the sample.htm Web page:

1. Start your Web browser.
2. Click **File** on the menu bar, and then click **Open**. The Open dialog box opens.
3. Click the **Browse** button, navigate to the **Tutorial.06\Tutorial** folder included with your Data Files, click **sample.htm** in the file list, and then click the **Open** button. The file path to the sample Web page appears in the Open box.
4. Click the **OK** button. The sample Web page opens in the browser window. The banner at the top of the page plays the animation and the logo appears below the banner. See Figure 6-40.

Figure 6-40 Sample Web page with Flash graphics

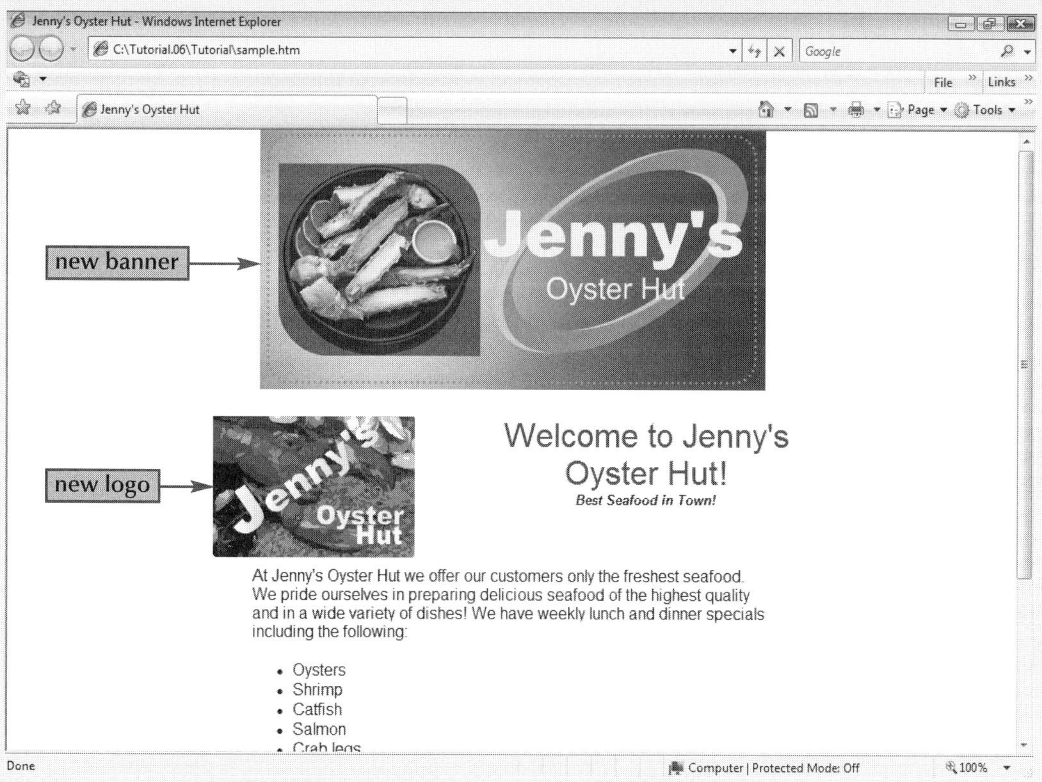

Trouble? If a dialog box opens, indicating that Internet Explorer needs to open a new window to display the webpage, click the OK button. The page opens a new window.

Trouble? If a security warning appears in the Information Bar, you need to allow blocked content to view the page. Click the Information Bar, click Allow Blocked Content, and then click the Yes button in the Security Warning dialog box.

5. Close the browser window when you are done previewing the Web page.

Aly likes the look of the new banner and logo in the Web page and will present the finished pieces to Jenny at their next meeting. In this session, you published the Jenny's Oyster Hut banner and you exported a logo for the restaurant's Web site. You also edited a sample Web page to incorporate references for the new banner and logo.

Review | Session 6.3 Quick Check

1. What is the purpose of the Version setting in the Flash tab of the Publish Settings dialog box?
2. What is the purpose of the Load order setting in the Flash tab of the Publish Settings dialog box?
3. How do you display the GIF tab in the Publish Settings dialog box?
4. How can you use the information generated by a size report when publishing a file?
5. Why would you save a document's publish settings in a publish profile?
6. What is the purpose of the EMBED tag?
7. True or False? To add an SWF file to an existing Web page, you must use Notepad.

Review | Tutorial Summary

In this tutorial, you worked with bitmaps. You imported bitmap graphics into a Flash document, changed the bitmap properties, and then created a movie clip animation using the bitmaps. You also converted a bitmap graphic to a vector graphic and used the resulting graphic to create a logo. Next, you used preset gradients. You created a new gradient using the Color panel, saved the new gradient within a document, and then applied the gradient to an object on the Stage. You also applied a gradient to text and then modified the applied gradient. Finally, you learned about the publishing options in Flash. You explored the publishing settings, and then you published a document as an SWF file and exported a document as a GIF file. You also incorporated the published files into an existing Web page.

Key Terms

alpha amount
color pointer
compression
fall off point
gradient
linear gradient
lossless compression
lossy compression
publish profile
radial gradient

Practice | Review Assignments

Practice the skills you learned in the tutorial.

Data Files needed for the Review Assignments: jennysAlt.fla, jennysbanner.jpg, salmon.jpg, sampleAlt.htm

Aly asks you to make some changes to another version of the Jenny's Oyster Hut banner before she shows it to Jenny. She wants you to add a new seafood bitmap of salmon in the seafood animation. The new bitmap will appear after the fish bitmap, display for two seconds, and then fade out while the salmon bitmap fades in. This will extend the animation by three seconds. She also asks you to change the letters in the Jenny's text block to a gradient fill.

1. Open the **jennysAlt.fla** file located in the Tutorial.06\Review folder included with your Data Files, and then save the banner as **jennysRev.fla** in the same folder.
2. Import the **salmon.jpg** bitmap located in the Tutorial.06\Review folder included with your Data Files into the document's library. Modify the salmon bitmap's properties so that the quality value is 80.
3. Open the seafood animation movie clip in symbol-editing mode, insert a new layer above the shrimp layer and name it **salmon layer**. Make sure the salmon layer is indented under the mask layer. Temporarily hide the contents of the fish layer, the shrimp layer, and the mask layer while you work with the salmon layer.
4. At Frame 60 of the salmon layer, insert a keyframe, and then drag a copy of the salmon bitmap to the Stage. In the Info panel, set the X and Y values to 0 and make sure the center registration point is selected. Convert the salmon bitmap into a movie clip symbol named **salmon symbol**, selecting the center registration point in the Convert to Symbol dialog box.
5. At Frame 72 of the salmon layer, insert a keyframe. At Frame 60, change the alpha amount of the salmon symbol to 0%. At Frame 72, make sure the alpha amount is 100%. Create a motion tween at Frame 60.
6. At Frame 108 of all the layers, add regular frames to extend the layers.
7. In the salmon layer, insert a keyframe at Frame 96 and at Frame 108. At Frame 108, change the alpha amount of the salmon symbol to 0%. Create a motion tween at Frame 96.
8. Temporarily hide the contents of the salmon layer and unhide the contents of the fish layer. Select Frames 60 through 72 of the fish layer, and then drag the selected frames to the right, placing them in Frames 96 through 108 of the fish layer.
9. Unhide all the layers, lock the salmon layer, test the animation, and then exit symbol-editing mode.
10. On the Stage, select the Jenny's text block, and then apply the Break Apart command twice to convert the text to fills.
11. With the text still selected, in the Color panel to select the white-to-black linear gradient, change the color of the left color pointer to #FF6600 and leave the right color pointer at #000000.
12. Publish the banner as an SWF file with the name **newbanner.swf**, and then change the Flash publish settings so that you do not generate a size report.
13. In Notepad, open the **sampleAlt.htm** Web page located in the Tutorial.06\Review folder included with your Data Files, replace the image tag that has the jennysbanner.jpg reference to an EMBED tag with the newbanner.swf reference using the following statement, **<embed src="newbanner.swf" width="500" height="250">** so that the Web page will display the new banner, and then save and close the sampleAlt.htm file.

14. Preview sampleAlt.htm in a Web browser.
15. Submit the finished files to your instructor, either in printed or electronic form, as requested.

Apply | Case Problem 1

Create and then export a logo with a bitmap fade animation and a gradient fill for the letter.

Data Files needed for this Case Problem: ssslogo.fla, store1.jpg, store2.jpg

Sandy's Scrapbook Store Sandy Rodriguez, owner of Sandy's Scrapbook Store, asks John Rossini to develop a new logo for her store's Web site. She wants the logo to include two pictures of the store that each displays for a few seconds at a time. John asks you to create an animation of the pictures where one fades out while the other fades in to use as the background for the logo. He also wants you to create a gradient to use as a fill for the letters in the logo.

1. Open the **ssslogo.fla** file located in the Tutorial.06\Case1 folder included with your Data Files, and then save the document as **ssslogo2.fla** in the same folder.
2. Import the **store1.jpg** and **store2.jpg** bitmaps located in the Tutorial.06\Case1 folder included with your Data Files directly into the document's library. Do not place copies of the bitmaps on the Stage.
3. Modify each bitmap's properties by changing the compression quality to 80%.
4. Create a new movie clip symbol named **store animation**. In symbol-editing mode, drag an instance of the store1 bitmap to the center of the Stage. In the Info panel, set its X and Y coordinates to 0 and, if necessary, select the center registration point. Convert the bitmap instance to a movie clip symbol named **store1 symbol**. Rename Layer 1 to **store1 layer**.
5. In the store1 layer, insert keyframes at Frames 36 and 48. At Frame 48, change the alpha amount for the store1 symbol instance to 0%. Create a motion tween at Frame 36 so that the store1 symbol instance fades out between Frames 36 and 48.
6. In the store1 layer, insert keyframes at Frames 84 and 96. At Frame 96, change the alpha amount for the store1 symbol instance to 100%. Create a motion tween at Frame 84 so that the store1 symbol instance fades in between Frames 84 and 96.
7. In the Timeline, add a new layer and name it **store2 layer**. In Frame 36, insert a keyframe add an instance of the store2 bitmap to the Stage. In the Info panel, center the bitmap on the Stage and select its center registration point. Convert the store2 bitmap instance to a movie clip symbol named **store2 symbol**.
8. In the store2 layer, insert a keyframe at Frame 48. In Frame 36, change the alpha amount of the store2 symbol to 0%. Create a motion tween at Frame 36 so that the store2 symbol instance fades in between Frames 36 and 48.
9. In the store2 layer, insert keyframes at Frames 84 and 96. At Frame 96, change the alpha amount for the store2 symbol instance to 0%. Create a motion tween at Frame 84 so that the store2 symbol instance fades out between Frames 84 and 96. Exit symbol-editing mode.
10. In the Timeline, select the background layer, and then drag a copy of the store animation from the library to the center of the Stage. In the Align panel, align the bitmap to the left edge and the top edge of the Stage. Lock the background layer.
11. In the scrapbooks layer, change the text to fills by applying the Break Apart command twice.

12. In the Swatches panel, select the gray radial gradient swatch (bottom row, second from the left). In the Color panel, change the color of the right color pointer to #0000FF. The text now has a white to blue gradient. Deselect the text, and then lock the scrapbooks layer.
13. Publish the logo as an SWF file and a JPEG file. Also, let Flash create an HTML file. Use the default names for the published files and the default Flash, HTML, and JPEG settings.
14. Preview the logo in a Web browser using the HTML file created by Flash.
15. Submit the finished files to your instructor, either in printed or electronic form, as requested.

Apply | Case Problem 2

Create and then publish a logo with a background that includes an imported bitmap and a custom gradient with transparency.

Data Files needed for this Case Problem: aczlogo.fla, giraffe.jpg

Alamo City Zoo Janet Meyers, director of Alamo City Zoo, asks Alex Smith to create a new logo that can be used as an ad on other Web sites to promote the zoo's new giraffe exhibit. She wants the logo to include a picture of a giraffe. Alex suggests using a gradient in the background. You'll help Alex complete the logo. You need to import a bitmap of a giraffe and then add the bitmap as a background for the logo. You will also add a rectangle with a radial gradient over the bitmap to enhance the logo. The gradient should start with white, end with a light yellow color, and be partially transparent.

1. Open the **aczlogo.fla** file located in the Tutorial.06\Case2 folder included with your Data Files, and then save the document as **aczlogo2.fla** in the same folder.
2. Import the **giraffe.jpg** bitmap located in the Tutorial.06\Case2 folder included with your Data Files to the document's library, and then change the bitmap's compression quality to 80%.
3. In the background layer, drag a copy of the giraffe bitmap from the library to the center of the Stage. In the Property inspector, set the X and Y coordinates to 0. Lock the background layer.
4. In the Timeline, insert a new layer above the background layer and name it **gradient layer**. In the Swatches panel, select the gray radial gradient. In the Color panel, change Hex value of the right color pointer to #FFFF99.
5. EXPLORE In the Color panel, set the alpha amount to 10% to make the gradient partially transparent.
6. In the gradient layer, draw a rectangle with no stroke and the new gradient as its fill that covers the entire Stage. If necessary, in the Property inspector, set the X and Y coordinates to 0, set the width to 300, and set the height to 225.
7. With the rectangle still selected, use the Gradient Transform tool to display the gradient's bounding circle. Drag the middle editing handle on the lower-right side of the bounding circle to reduce the gradient's radius to about half its original size.
8. Drag the gradient's center point to the upper-left corner of the Stage between the letters "A" and "l" in the Alamo text.
9. In the Publish Settings dialog box, create a new profile and name it **zooprofile**. Set the zooprofile to publish a Flash file using the default name, an HTML file named **zoologo.html**, and a JPEG image named **zoologo.jpg**.
10. In the Flash publish settings, change the player version to Flash Player 6 and do not export hidden layers. In the HTML publish settings, do not display the menu and do not loop. In the JPEG publish settings, change the quality value to 90. Publish the files.

11. Preview the logo in a browser using the HTML file created by Flash.
12. Submit the finished file to your instructor, either in printed or electronic form, as requested.

Apply | Case Problem 3

Create and publish a logo that includes imported bitmaps in an animation with a mask and an animated gradient that highlights the title text.

Data Files needed for this Case Problem: wclogo.fla, flower1.jpg, flower2.jpg, flower3.jpg

Westcreek Nursery Alice Washington and her staff are excited about the interactive logo developed for the Web site. Alice tells Amanda Lester that she wants to use pictures of flowers in an animation as part of a new logo. Amanda suggests adding some sample pictures of flowers so that Alice can see how the logo will look. Amanda also suggests changing the title of the logo to make it more dynamic. You'll help Amanda revise the logo by creating an animation with the flower bitmaps and adding a new, more dynamic title.

1. Open the **wclogo.fla** file located in the Tutorial.06\Case3 folder included with your Data Files, and then save the document as **wclogo2.fla** in the same folder.
2. Import the **flower1.jpg**, **flower2.jpg**, and **flower3.jpg** bitmaps located in the Tutorial.06\Case3 folder included with your Data Files to the document's library.
3. Modify the properties of each bitmap to have a compression quality of 80%.
4. Create a new movie clip symbol named **flower animation**. In symbol-editing mode, extend Layer 1 to Frame 90, rename Layer 1 to **flower1**, drag an instance of the flower1 bitmap to the center of the Stage, and then use the Info panel to center it on the Stage.
5. Convert the flower1 bitmap instance to a movie clip symbol named **flower1 symbol**. Insert keyframes at Frames 10 and 20. In Frame 20, change the alpha amount of the flower1 symbol instance to 0%. Create a motion tween between Frames 10 and 20 to fade out the flower1 symbol.
6. Insert keyframes at Frames 80 and 90. In Frame 90, change the flower1 symbol instance's alpha amount to 100%. Create a motion tween between Frames 80 and 90 to fade in the flower1 symbol.
7. Insert a new layer and name it **flower2**. In this layer, insert a keyframe at Frame 20 and drag an instance of the flower2 bitmap to the center of the Stage, using the Info panel to center it.
8. Convert the flower2 bitmap instance to a movie clip symbol named **flower2 symbol**. Insert a keyframe at Frame 30. In Frame 20, change the flower2 symbol instance's alpha amount to 0%. Create a motion tween between Frames 20 and 30 to fade in the flower2 symbol.
9. In the flower2 layer, insert keyframes at Frames 40 and 50. In Frame 50, change the flower2 symbol instance's alpha amount to 0%. Create a motion tween between frames 40 and 50 to fade out the flower2 symbol.
10. Insert a new layer and name it **flower3**. In Frame 50, insert a keyframe and then drag an instance of the flower3 bitmap to the center of the Stage, using the Info panel to center it on the Stage.
11. Convert the flower3 bitmap instance to a movie clip symbol named **flower3 symbol**. In Frame 60, insert a keyframe. In Frame 50, change the flower3 symbol instance's alpha amount to 0%. Create a motion tween between Frames 50 and 60 to fade in the flower3 symbol.

12. In the flower3 layer, insert keyframes at Frames 70 and 80. In Frame 80, change the flower3 symbol instance's alpha amount to 0%. Create a motion tween between frames 70 and 80 to fade out the flower3 symbol.
13. Insert a new layer above the flower3 layer and name it **mask**. Change it to a mask layer, and then change all of the flower layers into masked layers. The flower layers should all be indented under the mask layer.
14. Unlock the mask layer, if necessary. Draw a five-sided star shape with a point size of 0.50, no stroke, and a fill color of your choice. In the Info panel, set the star shape's width to 200, its height to 195, and its X and Y coordinates to 0. Lock all of the layers. Exit symbol-editing mode.
15. Insert a new layer and name it **star**. Move the star layer below the content layer. In the star layer, add an instance of the flower animation symbol to the center of the Stage.
16. Open the Title symbol in symbol-editing mode. Copy the text block in the title text layer. Add a new layer and name it **title mask**. In this layer, use the Paste in Place command to paste a copy of the text in the same relative position as in the title text layer. If necessary, deselect the text.

EXPLORE

17. Create a new gradient. Make the gradient linear and select the gray linear gradient from the Swatches panel as a starting point. In the Color panel, add two more color pointers close together in the center of the gradient definition bar. Make these two new gradient colors white (#FFFFFF). Make the far left gradient color black (#000000). The middle of the gradient has a narrow white band.
18. Insert a new layer below the title mask layer and name it **gradient**. In the gradient layer, draw a rectangle with the gradient you created as the fill and with no stroke that covers the letters "West" in Westcreek and is about 150 pixels wide and 55 pixels high.
19. Convert the rectangle to a movie clip symbol name **gradient symbol**. Extend all the layers to Frame 20. Insert keyframes in the gradient layer at Frames 10 and 20. In Frame 10 of the gradient layer, move the gradient instance to the right so that it covers the last four letters ("reek") of Westcreek. Create motion tweens at Frames 1 and 10.
20. Change the title mask layer to a mask layer, and make sure the gradient layer becomes the masked layer. The letters mask the gradient, giving the text a moving highlight effect. Exit symbol-editing mode.
21. Publish the logo as an SWF file and an HTML file. Use the default names for the published files, and in the Flash settings, change the Version to Flash Player 8. Use the defaults for the rest of the Flash and HTML settings.
22. Preview the logo in a browser using the HTML file created by Flash. Make sure the flowers within the star fade in and out and the Westcreek text has the gradient moving through its letters.
23. Submit the finished file to your instructor, either in printed or electronic form, as requested.

Challenge | Case Problem 4

Create and publish a banner that uses a bitmap background and custom gradients applied to graphics.

Data Files needed for this Case Problem: rdabanner.fla, pasta.jpg

Regional Dietetic Association Richard asks Webmaster Katie to create a new banner that can be used on the Regional Dietetic Association Web site to promote the association and the benefits to its members. He also asks Katie to add highlighting effects to the banner. Katie tells him that gradients can be used to provide highlight effects. Katie asks you to complete the new banner by adding a bitmap as a background and by applying various gradients on the different banner elements.

1. Open the **rdabanner.fla** file located in the Tutorial.06\Case4 folder included with your Data Files, and then save the document as **rdabanner2.fla** in the same folder.
2. Import the **pasta.jpg** bitmap located in the Tutorial.06\Case4 folder included with your Data Files to the document's library.
3. Modify the properties of the bitmap to allow smoothing and to have a quality setting of 80%.
4. In the background layer, drag an instance of the pasta bitmap to the center of the Stage, and then, in the Property inspector, set its X and Y values to 0.
5. Convert the pasta bitmap to a movie clip symbol named **pasta symbol**. In the Property inspector, set the symbol's alpha amount to 50%. Lock the background layer.
6. Edit the circle symbol. Replace its fill color with the gray radial gradient (second gradient from the left) in the color palette. Change the gradient's right color pointer to dark blue (#000066), and then move the gradient's center point to the upper-left part of the circle.
7. **EXPLORE** Edit the triangle1 symbol. Replace its gray fill with a new linear gradient. Use white (#FFFFFF) for the gradient's left color pointer and use dark blue (#000066) for the gradient's right color pointer. Move the left color pointer slightly to its right to increase the amount of white in the gradient. Add this gradient to the Swatches panel.
8. Edit the triangle2 symbol. Replace its gray fill with a new linear gradient. Use white (#FFFFFF) for the gradient's left color pointer and use dark blue (#000066) for the gradient's right color pointer.
9. **EXPLORE** In the gradient's definition bar, add two more color pointers. Use dark blue (#000066) for the new center-left color pointer and use white (#FFFFFF) for the new center-right color pointer. The white and dark blue colors alternate in the gradient.
10. In the Publish Settings dialog box, create a new profile and name it **rdaProfile**. Set the rdaProfile to publish a Flash file, an HTML file, a GIF file, and a PNG file using the default filenames.
11. In the Flash publish settings, select the Protect from import, Compress movie, and Export hidden layers options. In the HTML publish settings, select the Display menu option. In the GIF publish settings, select the Optimize colors, Interlace, Smooth, and Dither solids options. In the PNG publish settings, set the Bit depth to 24-bit. Publish the files.
12. **EXPLORE** Export the new profile and save it with its default name in the Tutorial.06\Case4 folder included with your Data Files.
13. Preview the logo in a browser using the HTML file created by Flash.
14. Submit the finished files to your instructor, either in printed or electronic form, as requested.

Review | Quick Check Answers

Session 6.1

1. a graphic that is stored as a row-by-row list of pixels, along with each pixel's color information
2. Both commands place the imported bitmap into the library. The Import to Stage command also places an instance of the bitmap on the Stage.
3. Select the bitmap in the library and then double-click the bitmap icon in the Library panel, or click the Properties button.
4. for bitmaps with many colors or many color transitions, such as photographs
5. 0%
6. the Trace Bitmap command
7. The color threshold value determines how many colors are used. A smaller value results in more colors.

Session 6.2

1. a gradual blend or transition from one color to another
2. A linear gradient blends the colors from one point to another in a straight line. A radial gradient blends the colors from one point outward in a circular pattern.
3. Click Add Swatch from the options menu in the Color Mixer panel.
4. True
5. add another color pointer by clicking on or below the gradient definition bar
6. False. The Gradient Transform tool is used to modify an existing gradient.
7. Draw a straight line with the Paint Bucket pointer. The line you draw determines the direction of the gradient.
8. change the gradient's radius and rotate the gradient

Session 6.3

1. to specify the oldest version of the Flash Player in which the published movie will play
2. to specify the order in which the layers are played—from the top down or the bottom up
3. click the GIF Image (.gif) check box
4. The size report includes the total size of the movie and the size of the movie's elements, such as its symbols and bitmaps, which can be used to reduce the size of the movie.
5. so that you can apply the same settings to another document created on the same computer
6. to load external media such as an SWF movie that requires the use of a plug-in
7. False. You can also add an SWF file to an existing Web page using Adobe Dreamweaver or other Web page editing tools.

Ending Data Files

Tutorial.06 →

Tutorial
- AC_RunActiveContent.js
- banner.swf
- banner Report.txt
- jennys2.fla
- jennyslogo.fla
- jennyslogo.gif

Review
- jennysRev.fla
- newbanner.swf
- sampleAlt.htm

Case1
- AC_RunActiveContent.js
- ssslogo2.fla
- ssslogo2.swf
- ssslogo2.jpg
- ssslogo2.html

Case2
- AC_RunActiveContent.js
- aczlogo2.fla
- aczlogo2.swf
- zoologo.htm
- zoologo.jpg

Case3
- AC_RunActiveContent.js
- wclogo2.fla
- wclogo2.html
- wclogo2.swf

Case4
- AC_RunActiveContent.js
- rdabanner2.fla
- rdabanner.gif
- rdabanner2.html
- rdabanner2.png
- rdabanner2.swf
- rdaProfile.xml

Tutorial 7

Planning and Creating a Flash Web Site

Building a Site with a Template, a Navigation Bar, and ActionScript

Objectives

Session 7.1
- Review the structure of a Flash Web site
- Plan and create a Flash Web site

Session 7.2
- Create a Flash template and use the template to create Flash documents
- Work with external libraries
- Create a navigation bar with complex buttons

Session 7.3
- Load external SWF files into the Flash Player using levels
- Learn basic ActionScript 2.0 commands
- Use the Actions panel
- Load external image files into the Flash Player using a movie clip
- Use the Behaviors panel

Case | Admiral Web Design

Jackson's Sports, a local sports equipment and supply company, provides discounted equipment, team uniforms, and player trophies to youth basketball, baseball, softball, volleyball, and soccer teams. Dan Jackson, owner of the company, wants Admiral Web Design to develop a new Jackson's Youth Sports Web site that is accessible through links provided on the existing site and that focuses on services the company provides to local youth sports. The Web site will have a home page with appropriate graphic elements and a navigation scheme that will lead to the other key areas of the site. Site developer Chris Johnson suggests using Flash to develop the entire site—not just the graphic elements of the site. With Flash, the site can be more visually interesting and include multimedia elements such as the team photos that change regularly to showcase different teams and players. You will work with Chris and graphic designer Aly Garcia to plan and create the Web site.

In this tutorial, you will plan and create a Flash Web site based on the client's requirements. The Web site will include a navigation bar. You will use levels to load one SWF file on top of another in the Flash Player and use ActionScript commands to control how an SWF file is loaded. You will create a Flash template to create additional documents. You will also load external image files into a movie clip.

Starting Data Files

Tutorial.07 →

Tutorial	Review	Case1	Case2	Case3	Case4
JSports.fla	JSPhotosDraft.fla	Sandys.fla	Music.fla	flower1.jpg	background.jpg
leslie.fla	MainPageDraft.fla	Welcome.fla		flower2.jpg	
lesliehome.fla	picture1.jpg			ivy1.jpg	
lesliehome.swf	picture2.jpg			WCstart.fla	
location.fla	SpecialsDraft.fla				
location.swf					
photo1.jpg					
photo2.jpg					
Soccer.jpg					
specialties.fla					
specialties.swf					

Session 7.1

Understanding the Structure of a Flash Web Site

Many of the Web sites you see on the Internet consist mainly of HTML or XHTML documents. **XHTML** is the latest version of HTML. These documents, often called Web pages, can contain text, graphics, hyperlinks, and multimedia elements such as those created with Flash. The animations and graphic elements you have created so far with Flash are all meant to be part of an HTML document. However, Flash can also be used to create a complete Web site that consists primarily of Flash SWF files and not HTML documents. A Flash Web site includes a navigation system using buttons or other graphic elements that can be clicked to navigate to the various parts of one or more SWF files. In some cases, a Web site is built in two versions, one using mostly HTML and one using mostly Flash. An organization might build an HTML version of the Web site in addition to the Flash version to accommodate users who do not have a fast Internet connection or users who do not have the latest version of the Flash Player installed on their computers. An example of a Flash Web site is shown in Figure 7-1.

Figure 7-1 NASA Mars 2004 Flash Web site

The SWF files that make up the Web site are referenced from an HTML document. The HTML document is usually created by the site developer using a program such as Adobe Dreamweaver. It can also be created in Flash by selecting the HTML format in the publish settings for the document. Notice that the URL of the Flash site shown does not reference an SWF file. Instead, the URL shows frameset.html as the name of the document. The HTML document appears in the Web browser and then calls or references the SWF file that activates the Flash Player. Recall that the Flash Player is a plug-in that enables the Web browser to play SWF files. Within the HTML document, the Flash Player plays the SWF file and initially displays the home or main page of the Web site. In the Web site shown in Figure 7-1, when the user clicks the Challenges button on the Mars 2004 page, another SWF file containing the Challenges of Getting to Mars page loads into the Flash Player using the same HTML document, as shown in Figure 7-2.

Challenges of Getting to Mars page **Figure 7-2**

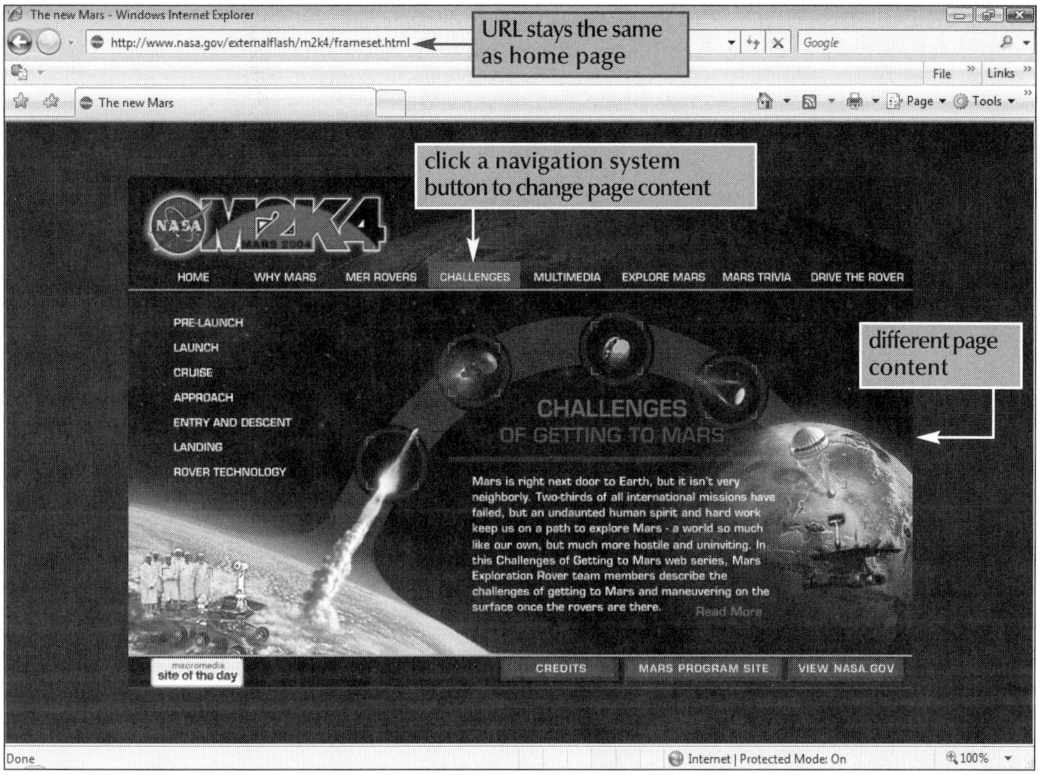

Comparing Navigations Systems for Flash Web Sites and HTML Web Sites | InSight

Because a Flash Web site uses only one HTML document rather than of a series of HTML documents, the Back and Forward buttons on the Web browser toolbar do not provide the same functionality as they do when for an HTML Web site. With a traditional HTML Web site, each time you navigate to a different Web page within the Web site, the browser tracks which Web pages you visited in its history and the URL in the Address bar changes based on the filename of the current Web page. In a Flash Web site, however, only one HTML document might be displayed, so the URL does not change even though the frames or SWF files being displayed in the Flash Player within the HTML document change. The HTML document displayed in the Web browser acts only as a container for the Flash content. After a user has navigated to several parts of the Flash Web site, the browser's Back button does not display the most recently visited SWF file. Instead, it returns to the most recently visited URL. As a result, it is vitally important to provide a clear and intuitive navigational system within the Flash Web site so that users can easily understand how to navigate within the site without using the browser navigation buttons.

Creating a Navigation System

The navigation system for a Flash Web site is simply a set of buttons that the user clicks. A navigation system can work in two ways. In one system, the buttons cause the playhead to go to different frames in the same Timeline. The content for each part of the Web site is placed in separate frames and actions are added to the frames to control the playhead. In another system, the buttons load a different SWF file using levels. **Levels** are like different planes in which the Flash Player can load SWF files or other content such as images. You can load an SWF file into the Flash Player so that it replaces the currently playing SWF file or so that it loads on top of the currently playing SWF file. The first SWF file is usually loaded into the Flash Player at level 0 and is considered the home or main page of the Flash Web site. Other SWF files can then be loaded at higher levels. For example, an SWF file specified to load at level 1 plays on top of the SWF file that is already playing at level 0, and the content of the SWF file at level 0 shows through any empty areas of the SWF file at level 1, as shown in Figure 7-3.

Figure 7-3 **SWF files loaded at different levels**

If an SWF file loads at a level already occupied by another SWF file, the newly loaded SWF file replaces the file currently playing. The properties of the SWF file at level 0 take precedence over those of the SWF files loaded at higher levels. For example, if the SWF file at level 0 has a green background and an SWF file with a blue background is loaded at level 1, then the level 1 SWF file also has a green background. The same applies to the dimensions of the Stage. The dimensions of the SWF file at level 0 take precedence over the dimensions of the SWF files that load at higher levels. It is important, therefore, to make certain the contents of the loaded SWF files do not interfere with those of the SWF file loaded at level 0.

Exploring a Sample Flash Web Site

The Jackson's Youth Sports Web site will use levels in its navigation system. To get a better idea of how a Flash Web site that uses levels works, Aly instructs you explore a sample site she and Chris have been working on for another client, Leslie's Bakery Shop. The site is organized with a home page, a location page, and a specialties page. The SWF file that contains the title, background picture, large rectangle, and buttons is loaded at level 0 of the Flash Player. Each button, when clicked, will load a different SWF file at level 1 to replace the content within the rectangle.

To explore the Leslie's Bakery Flash Web site:

1. Open the **leslie.fla** file located in the **Tutorial.07\Tutorial** folder included with your Data Files, and then set the workspace to its default layout.
2. Click **File** on the menu bar, point to **Publish Preview**, and then click **Default – (HTML)**. Your browser opens and displays the leslie.html file with the leslie.swf file playing in the Flash Player plug-in.
3. Click the **Location** button. The location information appears in the Flash Player window although the URL in the Address bar does not change. It still shows leslie.html as the last part of the URL. See Figure 7-4.

Figure 7-4 Leslie's Bakery Shop Flash Web site

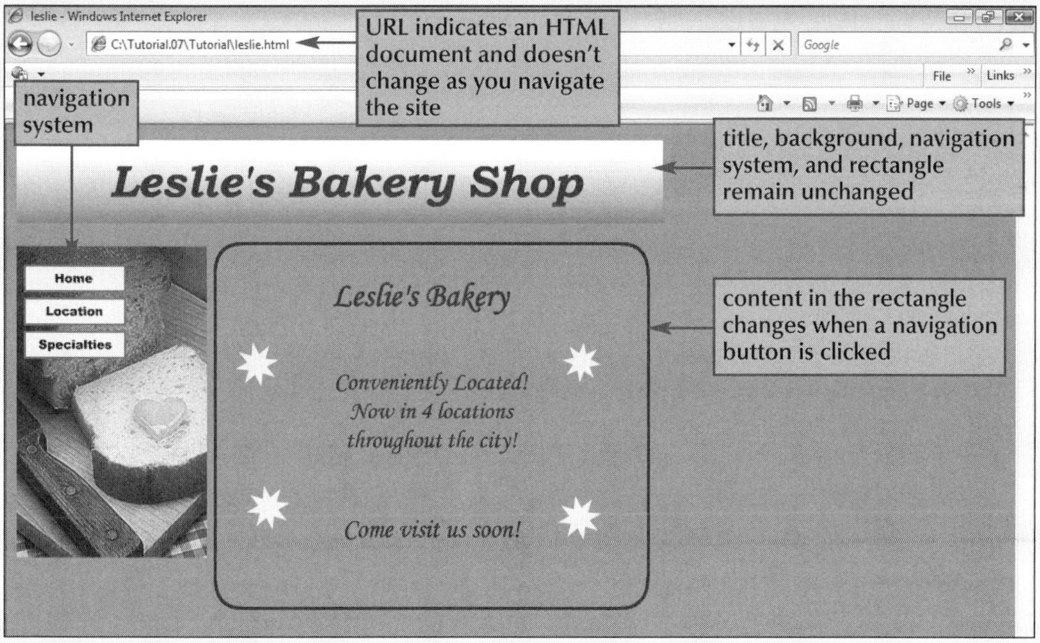

4. Click the **Specialties** button. The specialties information appears, although, again, the URL does not change.
5. Click the **Home** button to return to the Home page. The Home page appears, although the URL remains unchanged.
6. Close the browser to return to Flash.

You will view one of the other documents used in this Web site.

7. Open the **specialties.fla** file located in the **Tutorial.07\Tutorial** folder included with your Data Files. The specialties document contains only the information about the specialty items. It does not contain the navigation buttons or any of the graphic elements of the Web site such as the background and title banner. Those elements are contained only in the leslie.fla file.
8. Click **File** on the menu bar, and then click **Close All** to close the leslie.fla and specialties.fla files without saving any changes.

Tip

You can also press the Ctrl+Alt+W keys to close all documents at once.

Planning a Flash Web Site

The first and most crucial step for creating a Flash Web site is to plan the content and structure for the site. As discussed, a Flash Web site might consist of a series of Flash SWF files that work together to present the desired information. The basic process for developing a Web site requires the following planning. First, identify the goals and objectives for the Web site based on the needs of the client. Based on the goals and objectives, develop the content of the site. The content then leads to the design of the Web pages including the navigation system. Finally, you build the site and test it to make sure all parts of the site work as designed.

Reference Window | **Developing a Flash Web Site**

- Identify the site's goals and objectives.
- Determine the target audience.
- Develop the site's contents.
- Create a storyboard, and design the navigation system and the site pages.
- Build the site and test it.

Identifying the Site Goals and Objectives

The first step in the development process is to identify the goals of the site. **Goals** represent what the Web site is intended to accomplish. A Web site can have one goal or many goals, but initially you should define only three to five goals to ensure that the developed site can effectively accomplish these goals. It is essential that the goals be clearly defined. Otherwise, the developed site might not meet the needs of the client. You start defining the goals of the site by meeting with the client and discussing what he or she wants the site to accomplish.

Consider these examples. The client might want the site to help the company sell a product or to provide information about the services offered by the company. The client might want the site to increase brand awareness for the company's products or to provide information for the company's employees, such as company policies and procedures. Or, the client might want to disseminate information to customers about how to use certain products. Each of these goals requires a different approach and results in a different type of Web site. The success of the site depends on how well it meets the goals that have been developed and agreed to by the client. The goals identified for a Web site impact the overall design of the Web site and determine how the site is developed.

To develop goals for the Jackson's Youth Sports Flash Web site:

1. Write down three goals for the Jackson's Youth Sports Youth Sports Web site.

2. Review the list of goals to make sure they are clearly defined.

3. Compare your goals to those identified by Aly and Chris after their meeting with Dan Jackson. See Figure 7-5.

Jackson's Youth Sports Web site goals **Figure 7-5**

Goals for Jackson's Youth Sports Web Site

- Promote the Jackson's Sports name.
- Increase sales to local youth sports teams.
- Provide a site dedicated to serving local youth sports.

Based on the goals, develop a list of objectives. The site **objectives** more clearly define the information that the Web site will contain, the types of media that are required, and the number of Web pages that are needed to provide the information and fulfill the needs of the client. The objectives also help determine how the Web site pages are organized and what types of pages to develop. For example, one type of site might require pages with many pictures and little text, whereas another type of site might require pages with a lot of text and only a few pictures. Other sites might require pages that display animations or even videos.

The objectives must be clear and measurable so that after the site is complete, you can determine whether each objective has been met. For example, if one site goal is to enhance a company's brand awareness, then one objective might be to include a list of the benefits of using the company's products and another objective might be to highlight the company's logo that appears on all of its products. These objectives are focused and quantifiable. You can easily develop a page that has a list of the benefits of using the company's products. You can also include the company's logo on all of the pages of the Web site, increasing the company's brand awareness.

To develop objectives for the Jackson's Youth Sports Flash Web site:

1. Review the Jackson's Youth Sports Web site goals.

2. Determine four objectives based on the site's goals.

3. Compare your objectives to those developed by Aly. See Figure 7-6.

Jackson's Youth Sports Web site objectives **Figure 7-6**

Objectives for Jackson's Youth Sports Web Site

- Include the message that Jackson's Sports supports local youth sports.
- Provide a list of products and services offered by Jackson's Sports.
- Provide the names of the local teams doing business with Jackson's Sports.
- Include pictures of the teams; these pictures will change every few weeks.

Determining the Target Audience

As part of the planning process, you must consider the **target audience**, which is the group of people intended to use the site. The characteristics of the people who will be using the site impact how the information is presented on the Web site. The characteristics could be based on demographic information such as the age group, education level, or economic level of the audience. A young audience might indicate that more engaging animations need to be included, whereas a more mature audience might indicate that the site include less animation and perhaps a more conservative color scheme. You can also try to determine the expectations of the target audience. Do they expect to be entertained or do they expect to obtain detailed information about a product? This determines whether to include interactive games and graphics or detailed information in the form of text. The target audience for the Jackson's Youth Sports Web site consists of team coaches, players, and players' parents. The site, therefore, should appeal to both young sports participants and the adults involved with the teams.

The goals, objectives, and the target audience guide the rest of the Web site planning process. They determine which Flash documents need to be developed, what information each document should contain, and how the documents should be organized.

Developing the Web Site Content

The next step is to determine what content the site's pages will contain. The content is determined in large part by what the client wants the site to accomplish, which you identified with the goals and objectives and partly the target audience. The goals and objectives help determine the required pages and required media to include on the Web site. For example, each objective for the Jackson's Youth Sport site will result in one or more separate Web pages designed to meet that specific objective. One page will display pictures that need to change regularly, so that capability has to be designed as part of the page.

One way to determine the site's contents is to develop an outline with categories and subcategories. Each category might correspond to one objective or a stated objective may have more than one category. The categories in the outline can correspond to the pages that will be developed for the site and also help determine the navigation system for the site.

You'll develop an outline for the Jackson's Youth Sports Web site.

To develop an outline for the Jackson's Youth Sports Web site content:

1. Review the Jackson's Youth Sports Web site objectives.
2. Develop an outline with categories that correspond to the objectives.
3. Compare your outline with the one developed by Aly and Chris, which has one page for each objective. See Figure 7-7.

Figure 7-7 Jackson's Youth Sports Web site outline

Outline for Jackson's Youth Sports Web Site

1. Home page
   a. Banner
   b. Message about Jackson's Sports' support to local youth sports
   c. Navigation bar with buttons exhibiting rollover effects and animation
2. Services
   a. List products and services
3. Teams
   a. Names of local teams
4. Photos
   a. Pictures of local teams

After the outline is complete, you can start to gather and organize the required information, bitmaps, videos, and other graphics to include on the site. The client often provides much of the information for a site, such as the products and services available. Graphic elements, such as bitmap files of pictures or video files, often need to be prepared by the site developer or someone else such as a graphic designer.

Developing a Storyboard and Designing the Navigation System and Site Pages

After the main areas of content to include on the Web site are outlined, you create a **storyboard**, which is a diagram that shows how all of the site's pages are organized. The storyboard shows a sketch of each page with lines indicating how the page links to the other pages. The way the pages link to each other determines the navigation system for the site. As you develop the navigation system, you should keep in mind the characteristics of the target audience. For example, if a large segment of the target audience has limited Internet skills, you should keep the navigation simple and easy to understand.

Based on the content outline for the Jackson's Youth Sports Web site, Aly and Chris have developed a storyboard for the site, as shown in Figure 7-8. The storyboard shows the site's main page as well as each other page that will be developed and the basic design of each page. The home page will be loaded at level 0 in the Flash Player. The other pages, which will be loaded at level 1, include the Teams' Names page, the Services page, and the Photos page. In addition, the Welcome page will appear when the main page is first displayed. The Welcome page will be replaced when another page is loaded at level 1. When the site visitor clicks the Home button, the Welcome page will load again, replacing the page currently at level 1.

Figure 7-8 Jackson's Youth Sports Web site storyboard

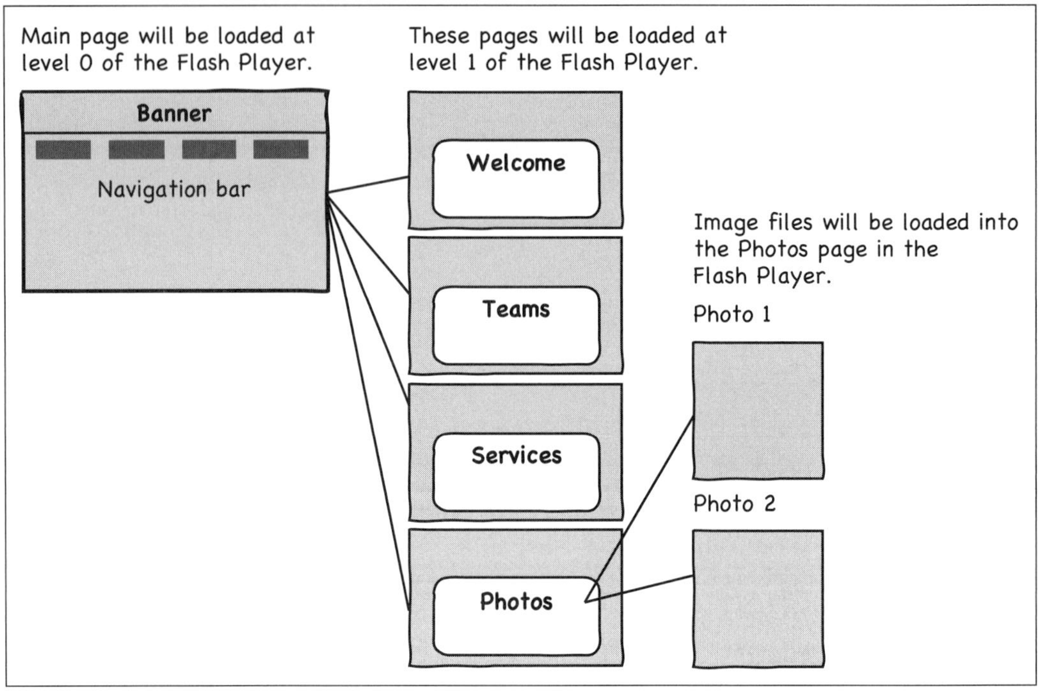

InSight | Documenting Web Site Specifications

After you develop the goals, objectives, outline, and storyboard for a Web site, be sure to compile all of this information in a written report. Then, meet with the client, and have the client review and sign the report to indicate that he or she is in agreement. It's very important to have the client sign off on the Web site specifications before you start creating the Flash files for the Web site. Otherwise, the client may request changes to the Web site specifications during the development of the Flash files, forcing you to revise or recreate files you have already completed. After you start creating the Web site files, any changes requested by the client should also be in writing. After the Web site is complete, the documentation is proof that the site you developed meets the agreed upon specifications.

So far, you have reviewed the process for the development of a Flash Web site. During the planning of the Jackson's Youth Sports We site, you determined the site's goals and objectives, you developed an outline of the site's contents, and you created a storyboard to show the site's pages and navigation system. The planning for Jackson's Youth Sports Web site is complete. In the next session, you will create the pages for the Jackson's Youth Sports Web site and the navigation bar.

Review | Session 7.1 Quick Check

1. The SWF files that make up a Flash Web site are referenced from a(n) ________________ document.
2. The Flash Player uses ________________ to load more than one SWF file at one time.
3. True or False? When an SWF file is loaded at the same level already occupied by another SWF file, the new SWF file is automatically loaded at a higher level.

4. List the steps in the planning process for developing a Web site.
5. How can you start to define the goals of the site?
6. What is a storyboard?

Session 7.2

Creating the Web Site's Contents

To create the site's contents, you start by creating a Flash document that will be the main page that is displayed when the user first enters the Web site. You create the document in the same way you have created other Flash documents, but you also include a navigation system that works with other Flash documents. Because you want the site's documents to work together and to provide a consistent viewing experience, each of the documents should be the same size and have the same background. As in the Leslie's Bakery Shop Web site, the main document will contain the background, banner, and navigation system. The other documents in the Web site will contain only the elements specific to the particular component of the Web site. These documents can have any number of graphic elements, including animations. Because these documents will play on top of the main document, you need to make certain that the elements on one document do not hide or overlap the elements of the main document.

Creating the Web Site's Main Document

Based on Aly's instructions, the main page of the Jackson's Youth Sports Web site will have a banner with an animation of the store's name and a background picture that she has prepared. It will also contain a navigation bar consisting of a set of buttons. You start to create the Web site's main document by creating the banner.

To create the Jackson's Youth Sports Web site's banner:

1. Click **File** on the menu bar, click **New** to open the New Document dialog box, and then click the **General** tab, if necessary.
2. In the Type box, click **Flash File (ActionScript 2.0)**, and then click the **OK** button. The new document opens in the program window.
3. Click **Modify** on the menu bar, and then click **Document**. The Document Properties dialog box opens.
4. Click in the Title box and type **Jackson's Youth Sports Web Site**, click in the Description box and type **Youth sports equipment and supplies**, set the width to **700 px**, set the height to **500 px**, set the background color to **gray** (#666666), and then click the **OK** button. The document's properties are set.
5. Save the document as **Main.fla** in the **Tutorial.07\Tutorial** folder included with your Data Files, and then set the workspace to its default layout.

   Next, you'll create the banner.

6. Click **Insert** on the menu bar, click **New Symbol** to open the Create New Symbol dialog box, type **Banner** in the Name box, click the **Movie clip** option button, and then click the **OK** button. The banner will be a movie clip symbol.

Tip

You can also create the new document by clicking Flash File (ActionScript 2.0) in the Create New section of the Start page.

7. In the Tools panel, click the **Rectangle** tool, and then, in the Property inspector, set the corner radius to **0**, set the fill color to **light blue** (#6699CC), and don't include a stroke.
8. On the center of the Stage, draw a rectangle, click the **Selection** tool in the Tools panel, and then select the rectangle on the Stage.
9. Click **Window** on the menu bar, click **Info** to open the Info panel, make sure the center registration point is selected, set the rectangle's width to **700 pixels**, set its height to **80 pixels**, set its X and Y coordinates to **0**, and then close the Info panel. The rectangle is resized and centered on the Stage.
10. Click **File** on the menu bar, point to **Import**, click **Import to Library** to open the Import to Library dialog box, and then double-click the **Soccer.jpg** bitmap located in the **Tutorial.07\Tutorial** folder included with your Data Files. The Soccer photo is added to the document's library.
11. Drag an instance of the **Soccer.jpg** bitmap from the Library panel to the left edge of the rectangle on the Stage. The bitmap picture is included as part of the banner.
12. Click **Edit** on the menu bar and then click **Select All**. Both the bitmap and the rectangle are selected.
13. Open the Align panel, click the **To Stage** button to deselect it if necessary, click the **Align left edge** button, click the **Align top edge** button, click an empty area of the Stage to deselect the objects, and then close the Align panel. The left and top sides of the two objects on the Stage are aligned. See Figure 7-9.

Tip

You can also press the Ctrl+Alt+1 keys to align the left edges of the selected objects and you can press the Ctrl+Alt+4 keys to align the top edges of the selected objects.

Figure 7-9 **Bitmap and rectangle aligned**

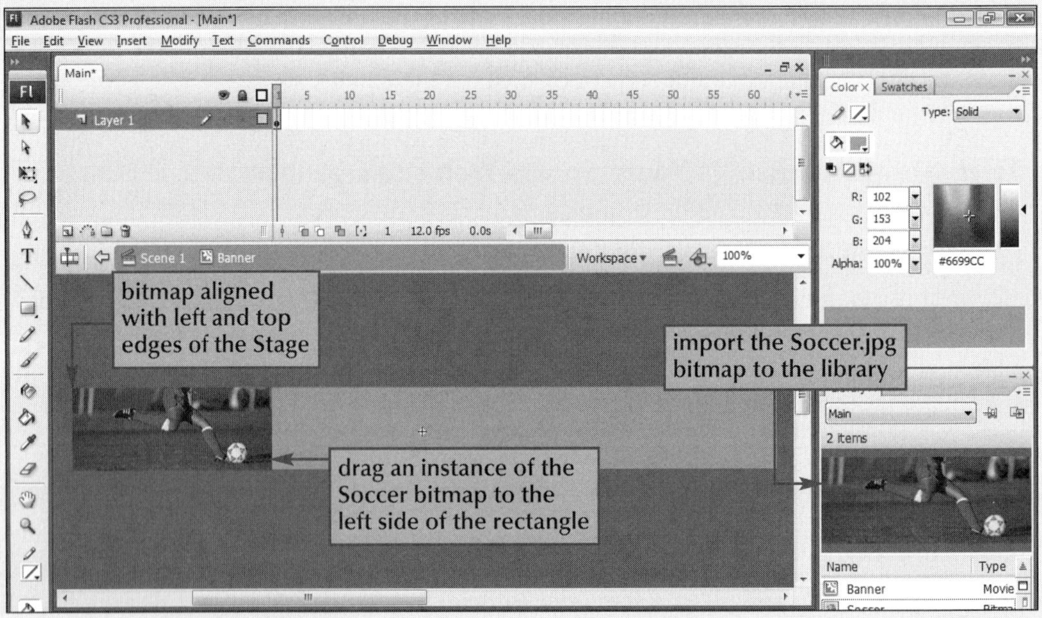

14. Rename Layer 1 as **Background**, and then lock the layer to prevent its objects from being moved accidentally.
15. In the Timeline, insert a new layer and name it **Text1**. You'll add text to the banner in this layer.

16. In the Tools panel, select the **Text** tool [T], and then, in the Property inspector, set the font to **Verdana**, set the font size to **26**, set the text color to **white** (#FFFFFF), select the **Bold** and **Italic** attributes, and select **Align Left**.
17. In the Text1 layer, click the left side of the picture to create a text block, type **Jackson's**, and then change the font size for the letter J to **35**.
18. Create a text block below the Jackson's text using the same attributes you set in Step 16, type **Sports**, and then change the font size for the letter S to **35**.
19. In the Tools panel, select the **Selection** tool, position the two text blocks as shown in Figure 7-10, and then deselect the text blocks.

Figure 7-10 Text blocks added to banner

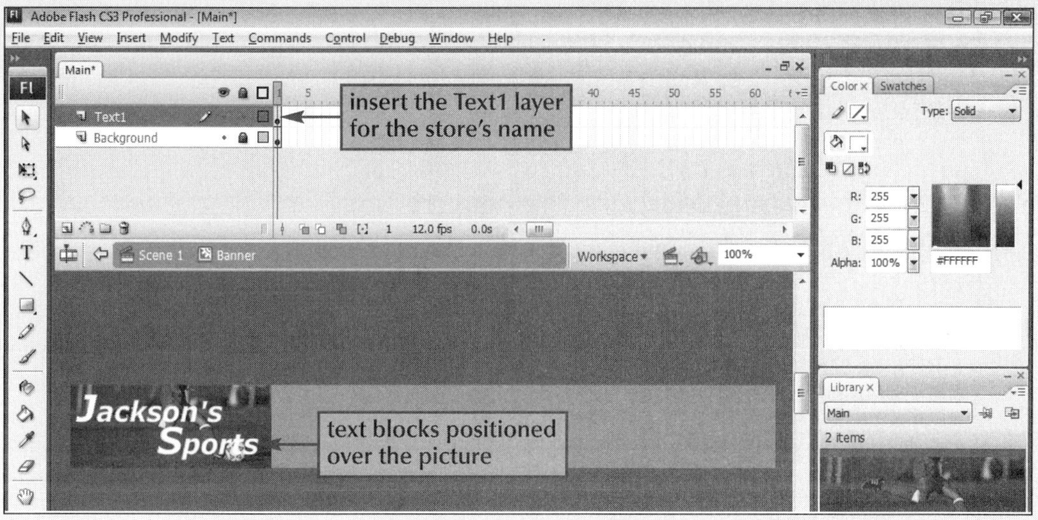

Aly instructs you to create an animation using the text you created over the picture. The text will be animated to increase in size over a short period of time and then decrease. Aly wants the animation to be 2.5 seconds long. You will create a motion tween in which the text starts out 50% smaller than its original size and then increases to its original size. After a short pause, the text will decrease back to 50% of its original size.

To animate the Jackson's Sports text:

1. On the Stage, select the **Jackson's** text block, press and hold the **Shift** key, select the **Sports** text block, and then release the **Shift** key. Both text blocks are selected.
2. Convert the selected text blocks to a symbol named **JS Title** with the **Movie clip** behavior type.
3. In the Background layer, insert a regular frame at **Frame 30** to extend the layer.
4. In the Text1 layer, insert keyframes at **Frame 10**, **Frame 25**, and **Frame 30**. The text will start small at Frame 1, be full size at Frame 10, start to decrease in size at Frame 25, and then be back to its original size at Frame 30.
5. Create a motion tween between **Frames 1** and **10**, and then create a motion tween between **Frames 25** and **30**.

   You'll change the size of the symbol next.
6. Click **Window** on the menu bar, and then click **Transform** to open the Transform panel.

7. In the Timeline, select **Frame 1** of the Text1 layer, and then, in the Transform panel, click the **Constrain** check box to check it; if necessary, type **50** in the Width box, and press the **Enter** key. The JS Title instance decreases to half its size in Frame 1.
8. In the Timeline, select **Frame 30** of the Text1 layer, and then, in the Transform panel, type **50** in the Width box, and press the **Enter** key. The JS Title instance decreases to half its size at Frame 30.
9. In the Timeline, drag the playhead to **Frame 1**, and then press the **Enter** key to test the animation. The JS Title instance starts small, increases in size, and then decreases to its original size. The text animation is complete.
10. Close the Transform panel.

The final part of the banner is a text block over the rectangle with a message about Jackson's Sports' support of youth sports. This text block uses a smaller font than the title text. The banner will also be aligned along the left and top edges of the Stage.

To create another text block for the banner:

1. In the Timeline, insert a new layer above the Text1 layer and name it **Text2**.
2. On the Text2 layer, create a text block on the rectangle to the right of the picture, set the font to **Verdana** for the font, set the font size to **32**, set the text color to **white** (#FFFFFF), select the **Bold**, **Italic**, and **Align Left** attributes, and then type **Supporting Youth Sports!** in the text block.
3. In the Tools panel, click the **Selection** tool, and then resize the text block to one line, if necessary, and center the text block over the blue area of the rectangle. See Figure 7-11.

Figure 7-11 Title text block added to banner

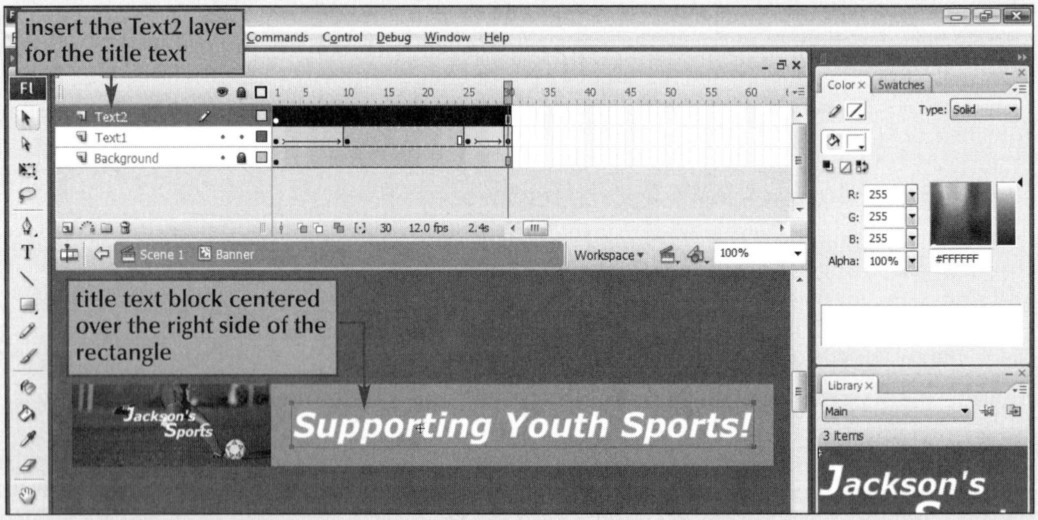

4. On the Edit bar, click the **Scene 1** link to exit symbol-editing mode and return to the main document.
5. Drag an instance of the **Banner symbol** from the Library panel to the top of the Stage.
6. In the Timeline, change the name of Layer 1 to **Banner**.

The banner needs to be aligned with the left and top edges of the Stage.

7. On the Stage, select the Banner instance.
8. Open the Align panel, click the **To Stage** button to select it, click the **Align left edge** button, click the **Align top edge** button, click an empty area of the Stage to deselect the objects, and then close the Align panel. The banner aligns with the left and top sides of the Stage.
9. Lock the Banner layer. The banner instance now cannot be repositioned accidentally.

The Web site's main page uses a background to enhance the appearance of the content that will appear for each document in the Web site. Aly wants you create a rectangle with a gradient fill that covers the Stage area below the banner. Because the Stage is 700 pixels wide, the rectangle should also be 700 pixels wide. Because the Stage is 500 pixels high and the banner is covering the top 80 pixels, the rectangle should be 420 pixels high. You'll also align the rectangle to the bottom-left edge of the Stage.

To add a background rectangle to the main page:

1. In the Timeline, insert a new layer and name it **Background**. You will add the rectangle to this layer.
2. In the Tools panel, select the **Rectangle** tool, set the fill color to the **gray radial gradient**, and do not include a stroke.
3. On the Stage, draw a rectangle on the Background layer that covers all of the Stage below the banner.
4. In the Tools panel, click the **Selection** tool, and then, on the Stage, select the rectangle.
5. In the Property inspector, set the dimensions of the rectangle to **700 pixels** wide by **420 pixels** high.
6. Open the Align panel, click the **Align left edge** button, click the **Align bottom edge** button, click an empty area of the Stage to deselect the objects, and then close the Align panel. The rectangle is aligned with the left and bottom sides of the Stage. See Figure 7-12.

Figure 7-12 Rectangle aligned with the Stage

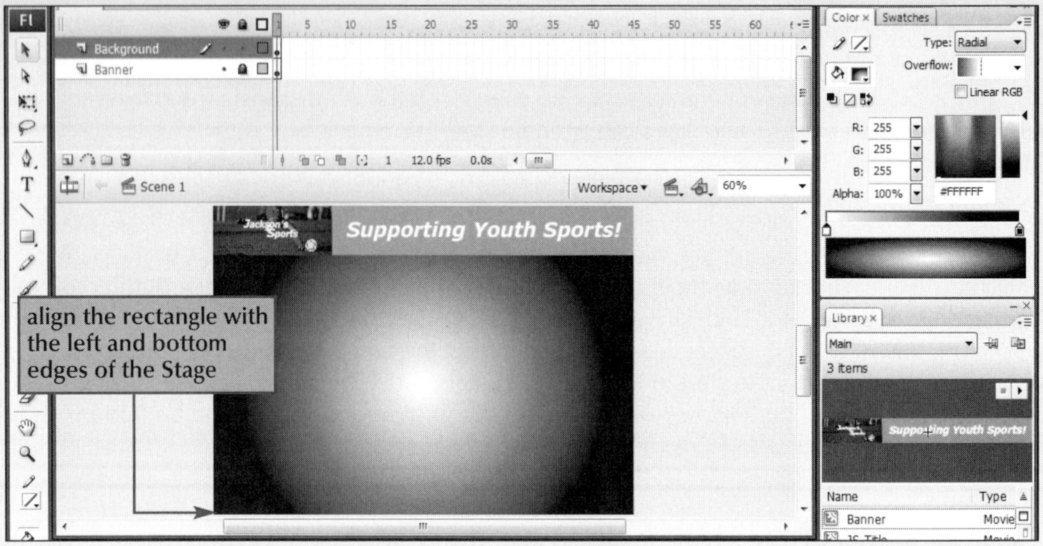

7. Save the Main document.

The graphics for the Main document are complete. The only item missing is the navigation bar with the buttons to control how the Web site pages are loaded. Before creating the navigation bar, you will create the additional pages for the Web site using a template.

Using a Flash Template to Create Additional Web Pages

The additional documents for the Web site will load on top of the main document. The main document will be at level 0 and its contents will remain visible on the Stage as other documents are loaded at higher levels. These additional documents, therefore, don't need to include the banner or other background graphics that are contained in the main document. They include only the content to be displayed. These documents will have the same dimensions as the main page to ensure that the additional text appears consistently in the correct location. The background color of the loaded documents does not matter because they automatically use the gray background of the main document. To ensure that all the additional documents have the same dimensions as the main document and to make it simpler to create new documents for this Web site, you can create a Flash template. A **template** is a prebuilt document that can be used as a starting point for a Flash project. Flash installs with several templates, and you can also create your own Flash templates.

InSight | Creating Documents Quickly with Templates

The pre-installed templates available in Flash enable you to quickly create professional documents such as advertisements, photo slideshows, or documents that play on mobile devices. You can then customize the templates to produce a document with the look and feel you want. Additional templates are available through the Flash Exchange, which is accessible through the Help menu. The **Flash Exchange** is an Adobe Web site with many templates created by the Flash developer community. If the pre-installed templates don't meet your needs, then explore those available on the Flash Exchange.

You can create custom templates based on existing documents. Based on the custom template, you can then create new documents, saving development time. For example, you can create a template that contains the basic graphic elements, background, and animations you want to include in other documents. Then, each time you create a new document based on the template, the graphic elements, background, and animations are already included with the new document. You can save any Flash document as a template within an existing template category or a new category. You can also include a description of the template that appears when the template is selected in the New from Template dialog box.

Creating a Flash Template | Reference Window

- Create a Flash document.
- Click File on the menu bar, and then click Save as Template.
- Type a name for the template.
- Select an existing template category or create a new category.
- Type a description for the template.
- Click the Save button.

Because you need to create several documents for the Jackson's Youth Sports Web site and because each document will have the same dimensions as well as other similar elements, Aly asks you to create a template. First, you will create the document with the basic graphic elements. Then you will save the document as a template, which you will use to create the other documents.

The banner of the main document occupies the top 80 pixels of the main document. The navigation bar, consisting of buttons arranged horizontally, will be placed right below the banner. Therefore, the content of the new documents must be placed below the navigation bar so it will not interfere with the content on the main document. You will place a horizontal guide 150 pixels from the top edge of the Stage, and then add the new content below the horizontal guide.

To create a Flash template for the Jackson's Youth Sports Web pages:

1. Create a new **Flash File (ActionScript 2.0)** document, click the **Size** button in the Property inspector to open the Document Properties dialog box, enter **JS Template** for the title, enter **Template file for Jackson's Youth Sports Web site.** for the description, set the dimensions to **700 px** × **500 px**, set the background color to **white** (#FFFFFF), and then click the **OK** button.
2. On the Edit bar, click the **Zoom control arrow**, and then click **Show Frame** to display all of the Stage.
3. Display the rulers, and then drag a horizontal guide to 150 pixels from the top edge of the Stage. The content for each document based on this template will be added below the horizontal guide.
4. In the Tools panel, click the **Rectangle** tool, and then, if necessary, click the **Object Drawing** button to deselect it.
5. In the Property inspector, set the stroke color to **none**, set the fill color to **light blue** (#6699FF) and then set the rectangle corner radius to **10** points. The rectangle you draw will be light blue with rounded corners.
6. On the Stage, draw a rectangle with its top edge aligned with the horizontal guide.

7. In the Tools panel, click the **Selection** tool, and then select the rectangle on the Stage.
8. In the Property inspector, set the rectangle's width to **600** pixels, set its height to **320** pixels, and then center the rectangle horizontally on the Stage. See Figure 7-13.

Figure 7-13 Rectangle aligned with horizontal guide

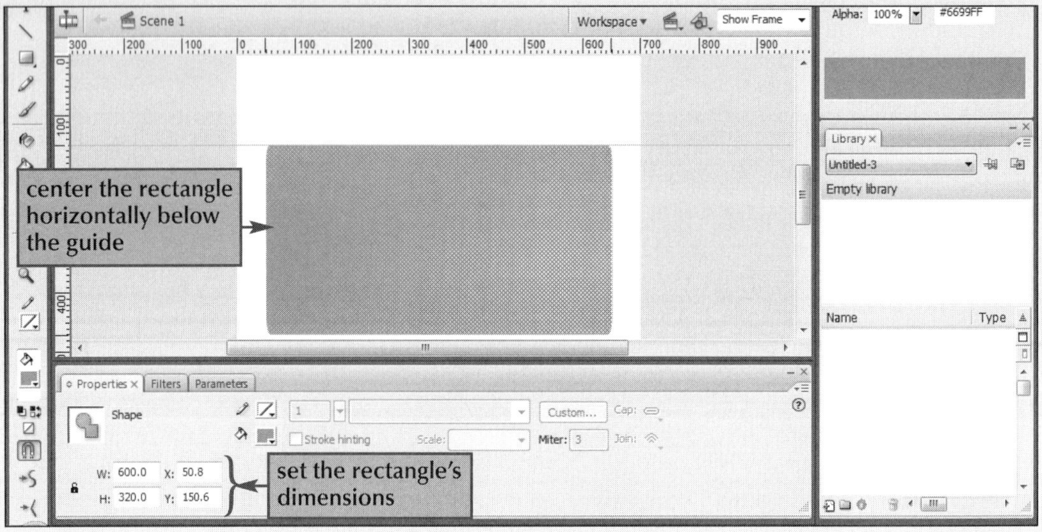

9. In the Timeline, change the name of Layer 1 to **Rectangle**, and then insert a new layer and name it **Contents**. The Contents layer will remain empty in the template, but be used to create the content of each new Web site document.

   The document is ready to save as a template.

10. Click **File** on the menu bar, and then click **Save as Template**. The Save as Template dialog box opens.
11. Type **JSDocument** in the Name box, type **Jackson's Sports** in the Category box, and then type **Use this template to create the Jackson's Youth Sports Web site pages.** in the Description box. See Figure 7-14.

Figure 7-14 Save as Template dialog box

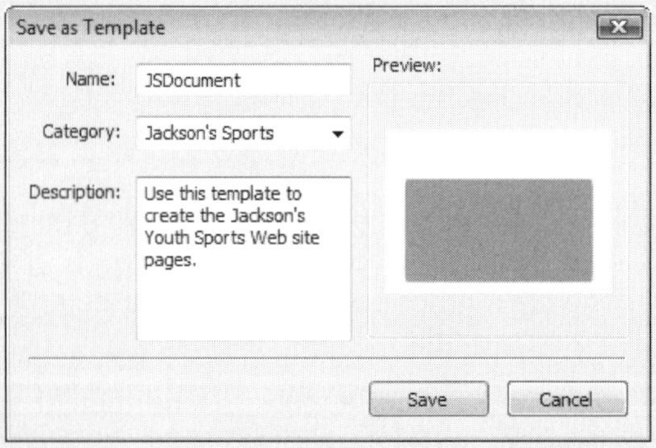

12. Click the **Save** button to save the template.

Using External Libraries

The template will contain animations of a baseball and of a basketball. Rather than creating a new graphic object of each ball, you can copy them from existing symbols in another Flash document to the template document. Both symbols will then be available to every document created from the template. To copy symbols from an existing document, you open the document's library as an external library. An **external library** contains the symbols for a stored document and makes these symbols available to the currently active document. An external library opens in a Library panel separate from the Library panel for the current document. You can drag instances of the symbols from the external library's Library panel to the Library panel for the current document or to the Stage.

Copying Symbols from an External Library | Reference Window

- Click File on the menu bar, point to Import, and then click Open External Library.
- Select the file with the symbols you want to copy, and then click the Open button.
- Drag an instance of a symbol from the external library's panel to the current document's Library panel or to the Stage.
- Close the external library.

Aly created a sample document for Jackson's Youth Sports that contains a basketball symbol and a baseball symbol. You will copy these symbols to the template document.

To copy symbols from an external library:

1. Click **File** on the menu bar, point to **Import**, and then click **Open External Library**. The Open as Library dialog box opens.
2. Click the **JSports.fla** document located in the **Tutorial.07\Tutorial** folder included with your Data Files, and then click the **Open** button. The JSports Library panel opens as an external library. See Figure 7-15.

Figure 7-15 JSports external library

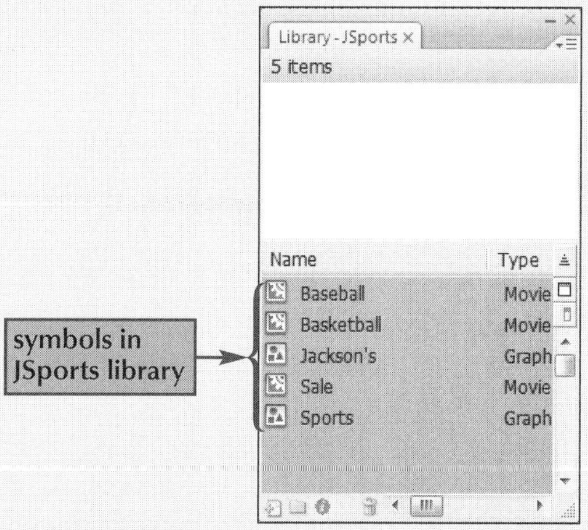

You will copy symbols from the external library to the JSDocument's library.

3. Drag the **Baseball** symbol from the JSports Library panel to the JSDocument Library panel, and then drag the **Basketball** symbol from the JSports Library panel to the JSDocument Library panel. Both symbols are copied to the current document's library, so you can close the external library.

   Trouble? If the symbols do not copy to the JSDocument's Library panel, you are probably dragging the symbol to the preview area. Drag the symbol from the JSports Library panel to the lower pane of the JSDocument Library panel.

4. Click the **Close** button on the JSports Library panel's title bar. The external library closes.

Both the basketball and the baseball symbols are stored in the current document's library. You will use the baseball in an animation you will create next as part of the JSDocument template. You will use the basketball symbol in an animation you create later in this tutorial.

To create an animation with the baseball symbol:

1. In the Timeline, insert a new layer above the Contents layer and name it **Animation**.
2. Drag an instance of the **Baseball** symbol from the Library panel to the lower-left corner of the blue rectangle on the Stage.
3. In the Timeline, insert a regular frame at **Frame 30** of the Rectangle layer, and then insert a regular frame at **Frame 30** of the Contents layer. Both layers extend to Frame 30.
4. On the Animation layer, insert keyframes at **Frame 15** and **Frame 30**, and then use the Selection tool to move the baseball to the lower-right corner of the rectangle in Frame 15.
5. Create a motion tween between **Frames 1** and **15**, and then create a motion tween between **Frames 15** and **30**. The baseball will move from the left side of the rectangle to the right side and back.
6. Next, you will add a rotation effect.
7. In the Timeline, select **Frame 1** of the Animation layer, and then, in the Property inspector, click the **Rotate** button and click **CW**. The baseball will rotate clockwise one time as it moves to the right side of the rectangle.
8. In the Timeline, select **Frame 15** of the Animation layer, and then, in the Property inspector, click the **Rotate** button and click **CCW**. The baseball will rotate counterclockwise one time as it returns to the left side.
9. Move the playhead to **Frame 1**, and then press the **Enter** key. The baseball moves back and forth as it rotates. The animation is complete.
10. Save and close the JSDocument file. The Main document remains open.

Tip

You can move an object in a straight horizontal or vertical line by holding down the Shift key as you drag the object with the Selection tool.

The template for the Jackson's Youth Sports Web site's pages is complete. You are ready to create the additional pages according to Aly's instructions. The first page you will create will load initially with the main document. This page's content will display the first time the Web site is visited and each time the Home button is clicked. The Home button will be created later in this session.

To create the Home page from the JSDocument template:

1. Click **File** on the menu bar, click **New** to open the New Document dialog box, and then click the **Templates** tab. The template you created is added to the category you specified—Jackson's Sports.
2. Click **Jackson's Sports** in the Category box, and then, if necessary, click **JSDocument** in the Templates box. The template is selected. See Figure 7-16.

Figure 7-16 New from Template dialog box

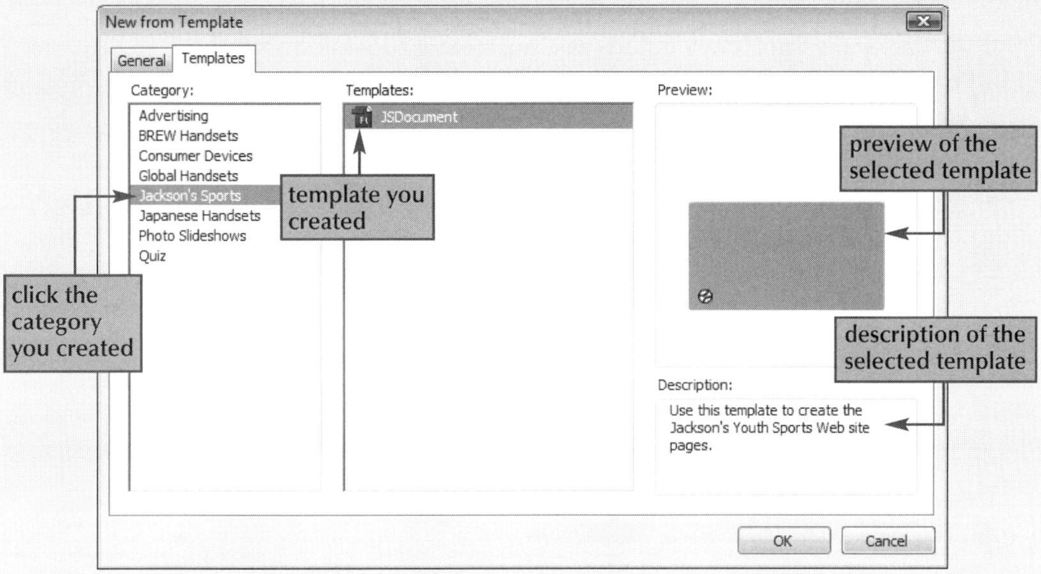

3. Click the **OK** button. A new untitled document based on the JSDocument template opens.
4. Save the document as **Home.fla** in the **Tutorial.07\Tutorial** folder included with your Data Files.
5. On the Edit bar, click the **Zoom control arrow**, and then click **Show All** to display all of the contents on the Stage.

The home page includes all of the content contained in the JSDocument template. You'll add the specific content needed for the Home page.

To add content to the Home page:

1. In the Timeline, select the **Contents** layer.
2. In the Tools panel, click the **Text** tool T, and then, in the Property inspector, set the font to **Arial**, set the font size to **24**, set the text color to **black** (#000000), select the **Bold** attribute, deselect the **Italic** attribute, and select the **Align Left** attribute.
3. On the Stage, create a text block at the top of the blue rectangle about 150 pixels from the left edge of the Stage and about 200 pixels from the top of the Stage, type **Welcome to Jackson's Youth Sports!** as the page title, and then deselect the title text block.

4. In the Property inspector, set the font size to **14**, and then deselect the **Bold** style.
5. On the Stage, click the **Text** tool pointer ┼T about 150 pixels from the left edge of the Stage and about 250 pixels from the top of the Stage, and then drag to the right to about 550 pixels from the left edge of the Stage. A fixed-width text block with a width of about 400 pixels appears on the Stage. The text you type will wrap onto separate lines within the text block as opposed to appearing on one long line.
6. In the text block, type the following paragraphs of text, allowing the text to wrap around to the next line when it reaches then right side of the text block, and pressing the **Enter** key twice after the first paragraph:

   At Jackson's Sports we value your business and we'll do our best to provide you the best sports equipment and supplies at the best prices.

   We are proud to support our local youth sports teams. We have been supplying equipment and sports supplies to many of the local teams for over 15 years.
7. Click **Text** on the menu bar, click **Check Spelling**, make any corrections needed, continue checking from the start of the document if necessary, and then click the **OK** button in the dialog box that indicates the spelling check is completed. See Figure 7-17.

Figure 7-17 Text for the Home page

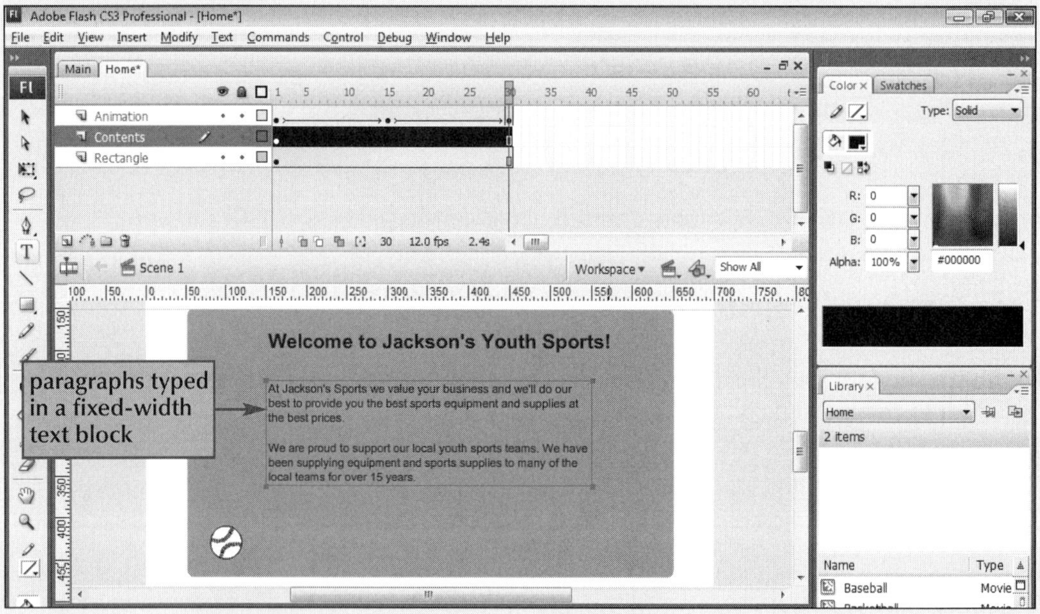

Trouble? If a dialog box opens indicating that, based on your settings, there is nothing to check, you need to set up the spelling options. Click Text on the menu bar, click Spelling Setup to open the Spelling Setup dialog box, select the Check Text Fields Content check box under Document Options, click the OK button, and then repeat Step 7.

8. Save the document.

Tip

You can also press the Ctrl+S keys to save the active document.

The Home page that appears on top of the Main document when the Main document is first displayed is complete. You need to create three other pages. One contains the names of local sports teams that have done business with Jackson's Sports. The second is a list of services offered by the store. The third contains pictures of local teams and players. You will create each of these pages using the JSDocument template as a starting point.

To create the Teams' Names page:

1. Create a new document based on the **JSDocument** template, save the document as **Teams.fla** in the **Tutorial.07\Tutorial** folder included with your Data Files, and the change the zoom to **Show All**. The entire contents on the Stage appear.
2. In the Timeline, if necessary, select the **Contents** layer.
3. On the Stage, create a text block centered at the top of the blue rectangle about 240 pixels from the left edge of the Stage and about 200 pixels from the top of the Stage, set the font to **Arial**, set the font size to **24**, set the text color to **black** (#000000), select the **Bold** and **Align Left** attributes, and then type **Local Sports Teams**. The title text block is complete.
4. Deselect the title text block, set the font size to **14**, deselect the **Bold** attribute, and then create a fixed-width text block about 150 pixels from the left edge of the Stage and about 250 pixels from the top of the Stage that is about 400 pixels wide.
5. Type the following paragraphs of text in the text block, pressing the **Enter** key twice after the first paragraph and once between the other paragraphs:

   Jackson's Sports is proud to support the following youth sports teams. For more information about these teams, contact our staff.

   The Stars Basketball Team
   The Sting Volleyball Team
   The Tigers Softball Team
   The Angels Baseball Team
6. Check the spelling and correct any misspelled words.

   You will change the color of the background rectangle to provide a visual cue that a different page has loaded.
7. In the Tools panel, click the **Selection** tool, select the **rectangle** on the Stage, and then, in the Property inspector, change the rectangle's fill color to **peach** (#FFCC99). See Figure 7-18.

Figure 7-18 Text for the Teams page

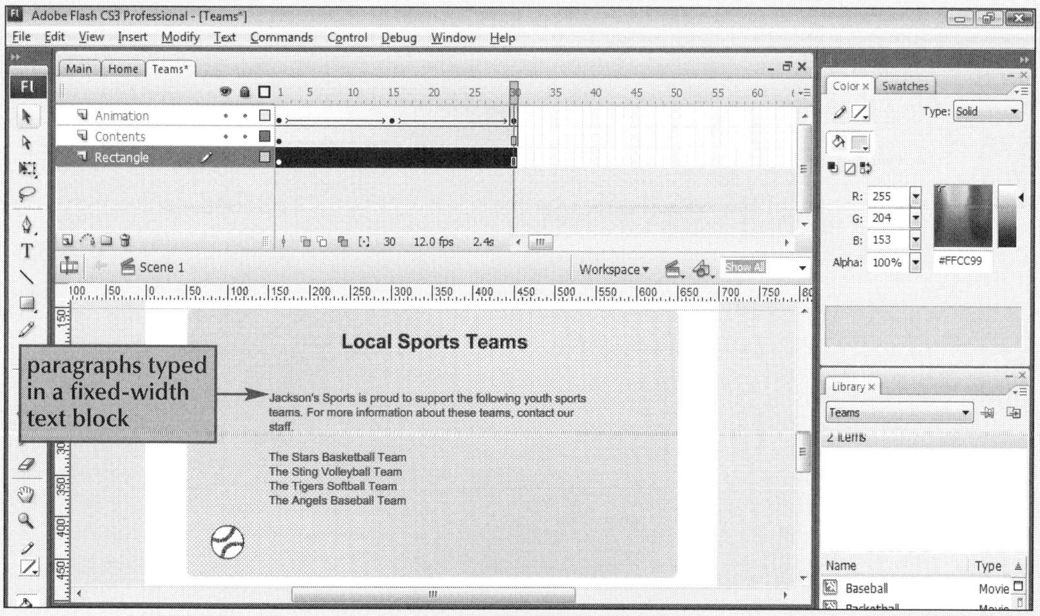

8. Save the document.

The Services page contains a list of the main services offered by Jackson's Sports. The document has a format similar to the Home and Teams documents, but will use the basketball graphic in the animation instead of the baseball.

To create the Services page:

1. Create a new document based on the **JSDocument** template, save the file as **Services.fla** in the **Tutorial.07\Tutorial** folder included with your Data Files, and change the zoom to **Show All**. The entire contents on the Stage appear.
2. In the **Contents** layer, create a text block centered at the top of the blue rectangle about 160 pixels from the left edge of the Stage and about 200 pixels from the top of the Stage, set the font to **Arial**, set the font size to **24**, set the text color to **black** (#000000), select the **Bold** and **Align Left** attributes, and then type **Jackson's Youth Sports Services** in the text block.
3. Deselect the title text block, set the font size to **14**, deselect the **Bold** attribute, and then create a fixed-width text block about 150 pixels from the left edge of the Stage and about 250 pixels from the top of the Stage that is 400 pixels wide.
4. Type the following paragraphs of text in the text block, pressing the **Enter** key between paragraphs, and then check the spelling, correcting any misspelled words.

   - Sale of equipment and supplies at a discount

   - Team and individual trophies, including engraving of players' names

   - Sponsorship of tournaments

   - Team and player pictures
5. In the Tools panel, click the **Selection** tool, select the **rectangle** on the Stage, and then, in the Property inspector, change the rectangle's fill color to **light green** (#99FFCC). The color of the rectangle provides a visual cue that a different page is loaded. See Figure 7-19.

Figure 7-19 Text for the Services page

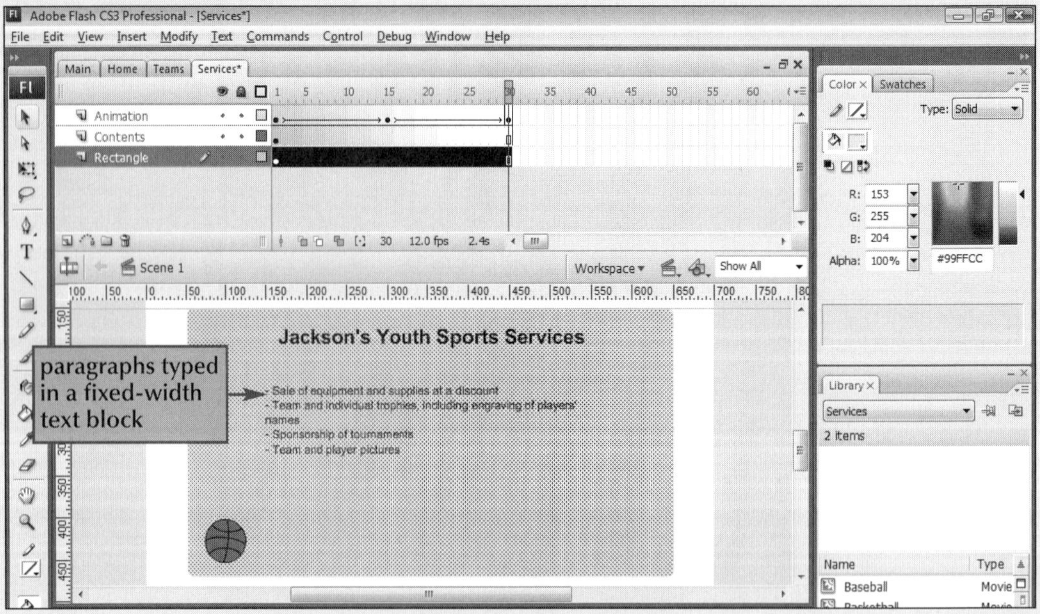

Next, you will change the animated graphic to the basketball symbol you copied from the external library earlier.

6. Select **Frame 1** of the Animation layer, click the **Baseball** instance on the Stage, and then in the Property inspector, click the **Swap** button. The Swap Symbol dialog box opens.
7. Click the **Basketball** symbol, and then click the **OK** button. The Baseball instance changes to a Basketball instance on the Stage.

   You'll swap the other Baseball instances in each keyframe of the motion tweens.
8. Repeat Steps 6 and 7 for **Frame 15** and **Frame 30** of the Animation layer.
9. Save the document, and then test the animation. The basketball rotates as it moves from the left of the rectangle to the right and then back.

The Photos page contains buttons that load pictures of local teams or players. This document will be similar in format to the previous documents, but it will not include the animation.

To create the Photos page:

1. Create a new document based on the **JSDocument** template, save the file as **Photos.fla** in the **Tutorial.07\Tutorial** folder included with your Data Files, and then change the zoom to **Show All**. The entire contents of the Stage are visible.
2. In the **Contents** layer, create a text block centered at the top of the blue rectangle about 230 pixels from the left edge of the Stage and about 200 pixels from the top of the Stage, set the font to **Arial**, set the font size to **24**, set the text color to **black** (#000000), select the **Bold** and **Align Left** attributes, and then type **Team and Player Photos** in the text block.
3. In the Timeline, select the **Animation** layer, and then click the **Delete Layer** button . The layer is deleted, removing the animation from the page because it is not used with this page.
4. Save the document. You will complete the Photos page later in this tutorial.

Tip

To delete a layer, you can also right-click the layer's name in the Timeline, and then click Delete Layer on the context menu.

Creating a Navigation Bar

A Web site needs a way for users to navigate from one Web page to another. In an HTML-based Web site, hyperlinks load another HTML document into the Web browser when clicked. In a Flash Web site, the hyperlinks are replaced with buttons that move the playhead to other frames or load other SWF files into the Flash Player when clicked. You create these buttons the same way as you created the buttons to control animations. When using levels to load SWF files, the buttons have ActionScript programming code that instructs the Flash Player which SWF file to load and how to load it. You will add this programming code in the next session. The buttons must include obvious visual clues that indicate how the buttons can be used to navigate the site. It is also helpful if some sort of animated effect occurs when the pointer is over the button, indicating that something will happen when you click the button.

Most Web sites include a **navigation bar**, which is simply a set of related buttons grouped together. The navigation bar buttons can be arranged horizontally or vertically. The buttons often look the same but have different text indicating what action will occur when clicked. For the Jackson's Youth Sports Web site, the navigation bar will appear below the banner of the Main document and include four buttons that are arranged horizontally. Each button will load a different SWF file when clicked. To make easier to create and place on the Stage, you will create the navigation bar as a symbol and add an instance of it to the Main document. The navigation bar will always appear as long as the Main document is played in the Flash Player.

To create the Home button for the navigation bar:

1. Click the **Main** tab to make the Main document active.
2. Click **Insert** on the menu bar, click **New Symbol** to open the Create New Symbol dialog box, type **Home button** in the Name box, click the **Button** option button, and then click the **OK** button. The Home button symbol opens in symbol-editing mode.
3. In the Tools panel, click the **Rectangle** tool, and then, in the Property inspector, set the stroke color to **white** (#FFFFFF), set the fill color to **light blue** (#0099FF), and set the corner radius value to **0**.
4. Draw a small rectangle centered in the editing window.
5. In the Tools panel, click the **Selection** tool, select both the stroke and the fill of the rectangle, and then, in the Property inspector, set the rectangle's width to **125 pixels** and its height to **25 pixels**.

   You will add a rollover effect to the button.
6. In the Timeline, insert a keyframe in the Over frame of Layer 1, select all of the rectangle if necessary, and then, in the Property inspector, change the fill color to **dark green** (#009900) and change the stroke color to **black** (#000000).
7. In the Timeline, rename Layer 1 to **Background**, lock the Background layer, insert a new layer, and then name it **Text**.

   You will add text to the button on the new layer.
8. Click the **Up** frame of the Text layer, create a text block, set the font to **Verdana**, set the font size to **16**, set the text color to **white** (#FFFFFF), deselect the **Bold** and **Italic** attributes, select the **Align Center** alignment, and then type **Home** in the text block.
9. In the Tools panel, click the **Selection** tool, and then position the text block at the center of the rectangle. The rollover effect is complete. See Figure 7-20.

Figure 7-20 Home button symbol

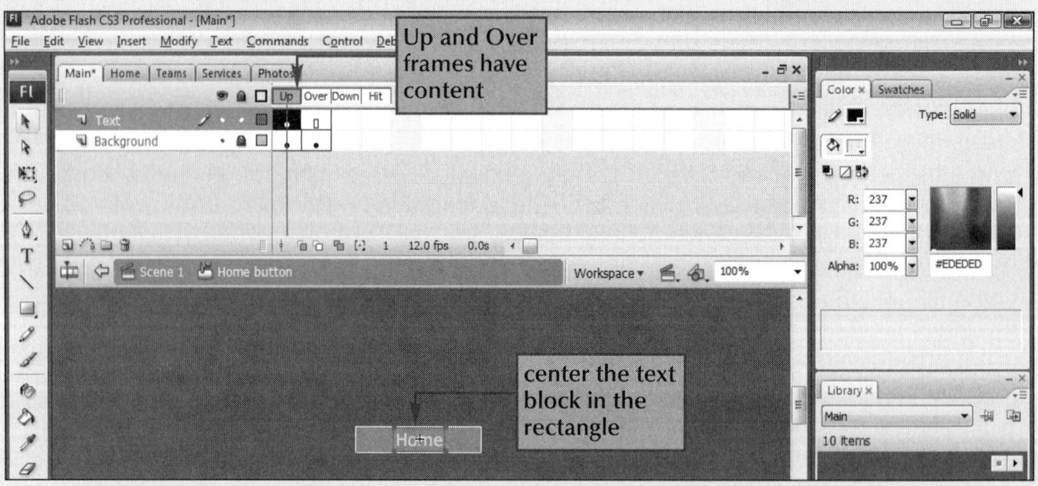

Adding an Animation to a Button Frame

A simple rollover effect reinforces the fact that clicking the button causes something to happen. You can also add animations to any of the Up, Over, or Down frames of the button's Timeline to provide visual cues. One common effect is an animation in the Over frame of the button that appears only when the pointer is over the button. When the pointer is not over the button, the animation does not appear. To create this effect, you need to create a separate movie clip symbol with an animation in its Timeline and then place an instance of the symbol in the Over frame of the button symbol. The animation of the movie clip appears only when the Over frame is active, which is when the pointer is over the button. This effect is similar to the nested movie clip animations you created that included an instance of a movie clip inside the Timeline of another symbol. In the case of buttons, you will place an instance of another symbol inside the button's Timeline.

Aly wants you to add an animation to the Home button that appears only when the pointer is over the button. You'll create the animation in a movie clip symbol. This animation will be a simple motion tween of a small circle with a pulsating effect.

To create the small circle animation:

1. Click **Insert** on the menu bar, click **New Symbol** to open the Create New Symbol dialog box, type **Button animation** in the Name box, click the **Movie clip** option button, and then click the **OK** button. The Button animation symbol opens in symbol-editing mode. You will create a small circle.
2. In the Tools panel, click the **Oval** tool, set the fill color to the **gray linear gradient**, set the stroke to none, and then draw a small circle in the center of the editing window.

   You'll position and set the size of the circle.
3. In the Tools panel, click the **Selection** tool, select the circle, set the width and height of the circle to **16 pixels** in the Property inspector, and then center the circle.
4. With the circle still selected, click **Modify** on the menu bar, click **Convert to Symbol** to open the Convert to Symbol dialog box, type **Circle** in the Name box, click the **Movie clip** option button if necessary, and then click the **OK** button. The circle is a symbol that you can animate with a motion tween.
5. In the Timeline, insert keyframes at **Frame 4** and **Frame 7** to add the keyframes for the animation, and then select **Frame 4**. You'll increase the size of the circle in the middle keyframe.
6. Click **Window** on the menu bar, and then click **Transform** to open the Transform panel.
7. In the Transform panel, click the **Constrain** check box to check it if necessary, type **120** in the width box, and then press the **Enter** key. The circle increases in size.
8. Close the Transform panel, create a motion tween between **Frames 1** and **4**, and then create another motion tween between **Frames 4** and **7**. See Figure 7-21.

Figure 7-21 **Animation of small circle**

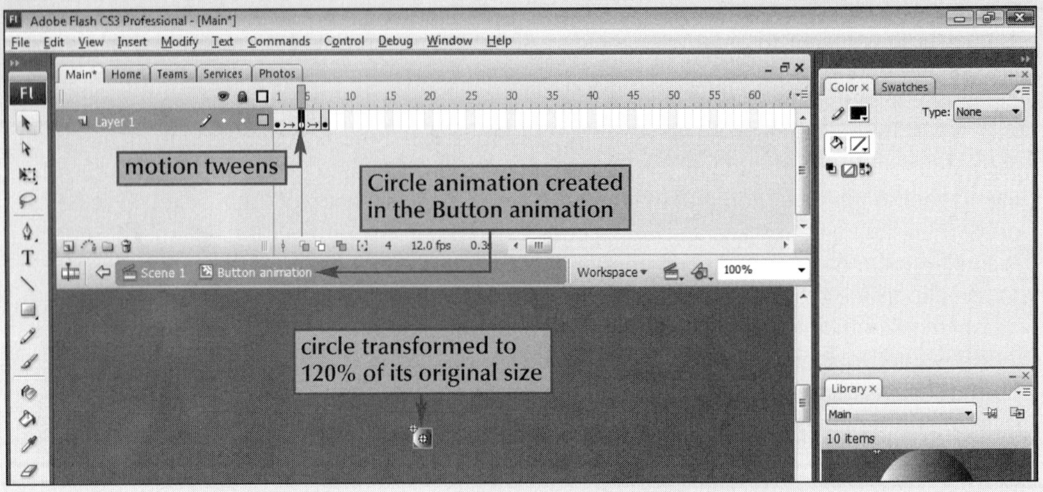

9. Move the playhead to **Frame 1**, and then press the **Enter** key. As the animation plays, the circle increases in size and returns to its original size in a pulsating effect.

The Circle animation is complete. Next, you'll add the animation to the Over frame of the button symbol so that the animation plays only when the pointer is over the button.

To add the Circle animation to the button:

1. On the Edit bar, click the **Edit Symbols** button, and then click **Home button**. The Home button opens in symbol-editing mode.
2. In the Timeline, insert a new layer above the Text layer and name it **Animation**. You'll create a movie clip animation on this layer.
3. Insert a keyframe in the Over frame of the Animation layer. You'll add the movie clip animation to this frame.
4. Drag an instance of the **Button animation** symbol from the Library panel to the left side of the button in the editing window. See Figure 7-22.

Figure 7-22 **Button animation instance added to the button's Over frame**

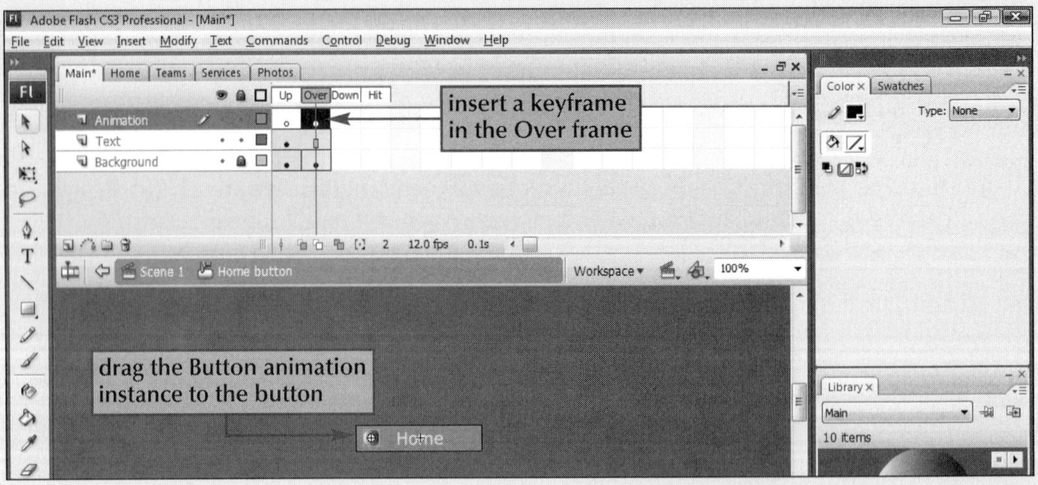

The Home button symbol is complete. The other three buttons for the navigation bar are similar to this button. The only difference will be the text that appears on the buttons. Rather than creating the other buttons from scratch, you will make duplicates of the Home button symbol and then change the text for the other buttons.

To create three additional buttons for the navigation bar:

1. In the Library panel, right-click the **Home button**, and then click **Duplicate** on the context menu. The Duplicate Symbol dialog box opens.
2. Type **Teams button** in the Name box, click the **Button** option button if necessary, and then click the **OK** button. The Teams button is added to the library.
3. Repeat Steps 1 and 2 to create a duplicate of the Home button named **Services button** and a duplicate of the Home button named **Photos button**. The four buttons are all exactly the same. You'll change the text of the buttons next.
4. On the Edit bar, click the **Edit Symbols** button, and then click **Teams button**. The Teams button symbol opens in symbol-editing mode.
5. In the Timeline, select the **Up frame** of the Text layer, click the **Text** tool T in the Tools panel, click the **Home** text block, select **Home**, and then type **Teams**.
6. Repeat Steps 4 and 5 to open the **Services button** in symbol-editing mode and change the Home text to **Services**.
7. Repeat Steps 4 and 5 to open the **Photos button** in symbol-editing mode and change the Home text to **Photos**.

Tip

When the Selection tool is selected, you can double-click the text to switch to the Text tool and make the text box active.

The additional buttons are complete. You will combine button instances in a movie clip symbol to create the navigation bar. The navigation bar will contain the Home, Teams, Services, and Photos buttons arranged horizontally. After you place the button instances in the symbol, you will add an instance of the navigation bar to the Stage of the Main document.

To create the navigation bar:

1. Click **Insert** on the menu bar, click **New Symbol** to open the Create New Symbol dialog box, type **Navbar** in the Name box, click the **Movie clip** option button if necessary, and then click the **OK** button. You will add instances of the buttons in symbol-editing mode.
2. Drag an instance of the **Home button** symbol from the Library panel to the left side of the editing window.
3. Drag an instance of the **Teams button** symbol from the Library panel to the right of the Home button instance.
4. Drag an instance of the **Services button** symbol from the Library panel to the right of the Teams button instance.
5. Drag an instance of the **Photos button** symbol from the Library panel to the right of the Services button instance.
6. Click **Edit** on the menu bar, and then click **Select All** to select all the button instances at one time.
7. Click **Modify** on the menu bar, point to **Align**, and then click **Vertical Center** to align the buttons.

8. Click **Modify** on the menu bar, point to **Align**, and then click **Distribute Widths** to space the buttons evenly.
9. If necessary, in the Tools panel, click the **Selection** tool, and then center all the button instances in the editing window. See Figure 7-23.

Figure 7-23 **Completed navigation bar**

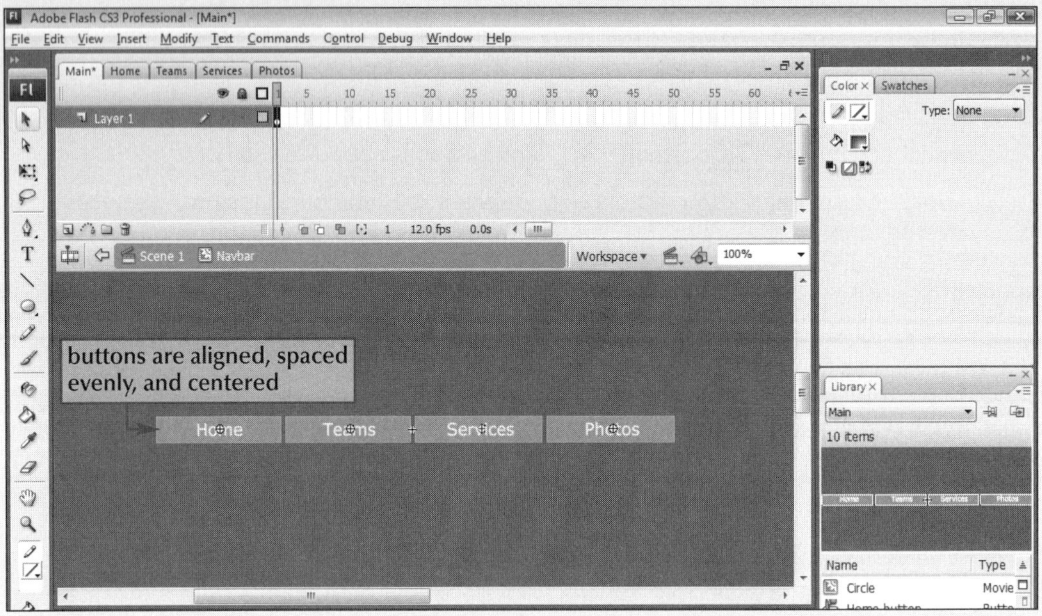

The navigation bar is complete. You will add an instance of the navigation bar below the banner in the Main document.

To add the navigation bar to the Main document:

1. On the Edit bar, click the **Scene 1** link to return to the Main document's Timeline, click the **Zoom control arrow**, and then click **Show All** to display all of the contents on the Stage.
2. In the Timeline, insert a new layer above the Background layer and name it **Navbar**.
3. Drag an instance of the **Navbar** symbol from the library to the Stage below the banner and then center the navigation bar horizontally. See Figure 7-24.

Navigation bar on Main document **Figure 7-24**

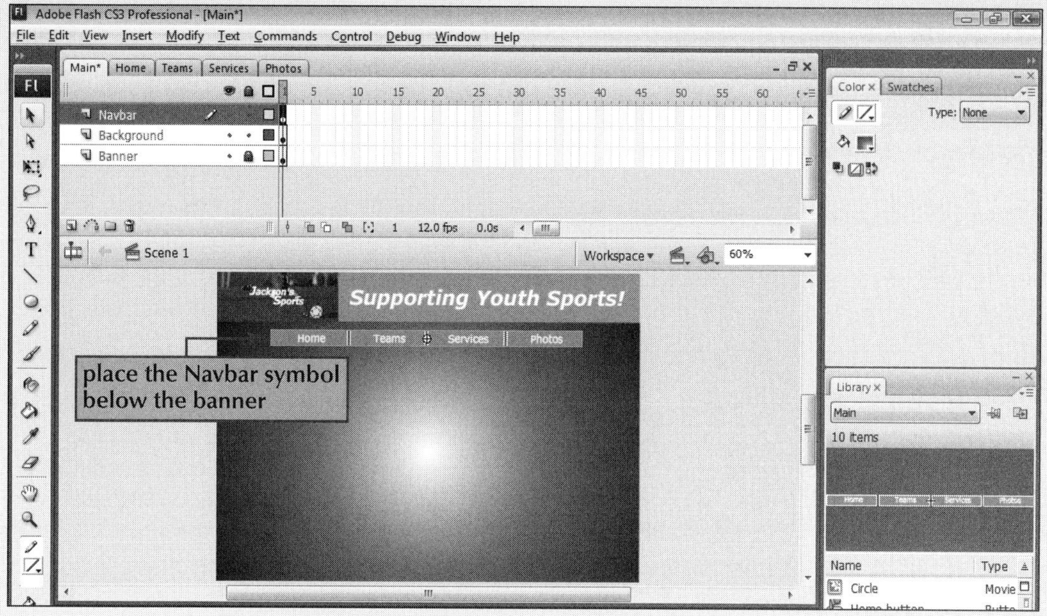

4. Save the Main document, click **Control** on the menu bar, and then click **Test Movie**. The SWF file opens in a separate window.
5. Move the pointer over each of the four buttons to test how the button changes color and plays the circle animation while the pointer is over it.
6. Click **File** on the menu bar, and then click **Close** to return to the Main document.

In this session, you created the documents that make up the Jackson's Youth Sports Web site. You created the site's main document, and then created a Flash template that you used to create the additional documents for the site. You also created the navigation bar with a set of buttons to navigate from one document to another in the Web site. The buttons include a movie clip animation that displays when the pointer is over the buttons. Although the navigation bar and its buttons are complete, they do not yet control anything. You will add the ActionScript code to these buttons in the next session.

Session 7.2 Quick Check | Review

1. What is a Flash template?
2. What is the purpose of opening a document's library as an external library in another document?
3. A(n) ________________ effect reinforces the fact that clicking a button causes something to happen.
4. True or False? An external library opens in a Library panel separate from the Library panel for the current document.
5. In a Flash Web site, ________________ are replaced with buttons that move the playhead to other frames or load other SWF files into the Flash Player when clicked.
6. Briefly explain how you add an animation to a button that displays when the pointer is over the button.

Session 7.3

Using ActionScript

A Flash Web site's navigation system consists of a set of buttons. When you click a button, the Flash Player loads a different SWF file at the specified level. The navigation bar you created for the Jackson's Youth Sports Web site has buttons, but the buttons don't yet control anything. To make the buttons operational, you need to add ActionScript instructions to them. ActionScript, the programming language used within Flash, allows you to add actions to objects or frames in a document. Actions are instructions that are used to control a document while its animation is playing. You have added actions to buttons to make the buttons control an animation. You can also add actions to buttons to control how a movie loads into the Flash Player. You will use the Actions panel to add actions in the form of scripts, which can contain one or more actions as well as other programming code to control how the actions are executed. The actions will be added to the button instances on the Navbar symbol. The two latest versions of ActionScript are versions 2.0 and 3.0, and you can use either version, depending on the complexity of the animation. Because you need to add only simple scripts to the buttons to control how the Web site's pages are loaded, you will use ActionScript 2.0. You will work with ActionScript 3.0 in Tutorial 8.

Using the loadMovieNum Action

In a Flash Web site, the main document loads into the Flash Player at level 0 and other SWF files can then be loaded at different levels. An SWF file loaded at a higher level will be on top of the SWF file at level 0. Using this method, you can load the Web site's main document with the banner, background, and navigation bar at level 0, and then load the other pages of the Web site at level 1 or higher. For example, you will load the Services page at level 1 so it will display on top of the main document loaded at level 0.

To load an SWF file into the Flash Player at a specific level, you need to create an ActionScript script with the `loadMovieNum` action. The format of this action is the following:

```
loadMovieNum("filename.swf", level)
```

Within the parentheses, you specify the parameters of the action. The parameters give the action the information it needs to execute properly. In the case of the `loadMovieNum` action, the two parameters are the name of the SWF file to be loaded and the level number at which the file will be loaded. The name of the SWF file must be enclosed in quotation marks and a comma must separate the filename and the level number. For example, the following is the action to load the Services page at level 1:

```
loadMovieNum("Services.swf", 1)
```

The `loadMovieNum` action is executed only when the button instance to which it is attached is clicked and released. For the action to work with the button, you must add an event handler that determines when to execute the action. Flash uses event handlers to check for events, such as when a button is clicked or when it is released. The event handler determines the action to take when a specific event occurs. Buttons use the on event handler, which has the following format:

```
on (mouseEvent)
```

The `mouseEvent` can be press or release. Press refers to a button being clicked. The event handler is followed by a pair of curly braces within which you place statements such as the `loadMovieNum` action. When the button is clicked with the mouse, the press event occurs. When the mouse button is released, the release event occurs. So, to execute an action after the button is released, the on event handler is:

```
on (release)
```

The event handler is then followed by the statement to be executed within curly braces. The complete script to load the Services page is as follows:

```
on (release)  {
      loadMovieNum("Services.swf", 1);
}
```

The curly braces can be placed on the same lines as other statements or on separate lines. The preceding format is recommended to make the script easier to read. It is also recommended practice to end ActionScript statements with a semicolon.

Tip

In the Script pane, you can format the code automatically by pressing the Ctrl+Shift+F keys.

Using the Actions Panel

You can use the Actions panel in either Script Assist mode or normal mode. In Script Assist mode, Flash helps you create the scripts when you select actions from the Actions toolbox. In normal mode, you write all or part of the scripts yourself. Aly wants you use normal mode to write the scripts so you gain a better understanding of ActionScript.

Adding ActionScript Code to a Button | Reference Window

- Select the button instance on the Stage.
- Open the Actions panel, select a category from the Actions toolbox, and then double-click an action to add its code to the Script pane.
- If necessary, type required code such as parameters that reference filenames.
- Click the Check syntax button to check the script for errors.

Because the navigation bar for the Jackson's Youth Sports Web site has buttons that are designed to load an SWF file when clicked, you will add the on event handler with the release parameter. So when the button is clicked and then released, the event handler executes the `loadMovieNum` action to load the specified movie at a particular level. This script will be added to each button instance with the corresponding name of the SWF file.

To add ActionScript to the Home button:

1. If you took a break after the previous session, make sure the Main.fla, Home.fla, Teams.fla, Services.fla, and Photos.fla documents are open, the Main.fla document is active, and the workspace is set to its default layout.
2. On the Edit bar, click the **Edit Symbols** button, click **Navbar** to open the symbol in symbol-editing mode, deselect the button instances, and then select only the **Home button** instance. This is the first button to which you will add ActionScript.
3. Click **Window** on the menu bar, click **Actions** to open the Actions panel, and then click the **Script Assist** button to deselect it.
4. If necessary, click the **ActionScript version** control located below the Actions – Button tab, and then click **ActionScript 1.0 & 2.0**. The Actions panel is set to write code for ActionScript 1.0 and 2.0.

Tip

You can also press the F9 key to open and close the Actions panel.

5. Click **Global Functions** in the Actions toolbox to expand this category, click **Movie Clip Control** to expand this category, and then double-click the **on** event handler. The on event handler is added to the Script pane along with parentheses and curly braces. Also, a code hints list of events opens so that you can quickly add the appropriate event to the script. See Figure 7-25.

Figure 7-25 Script pane with the event handler

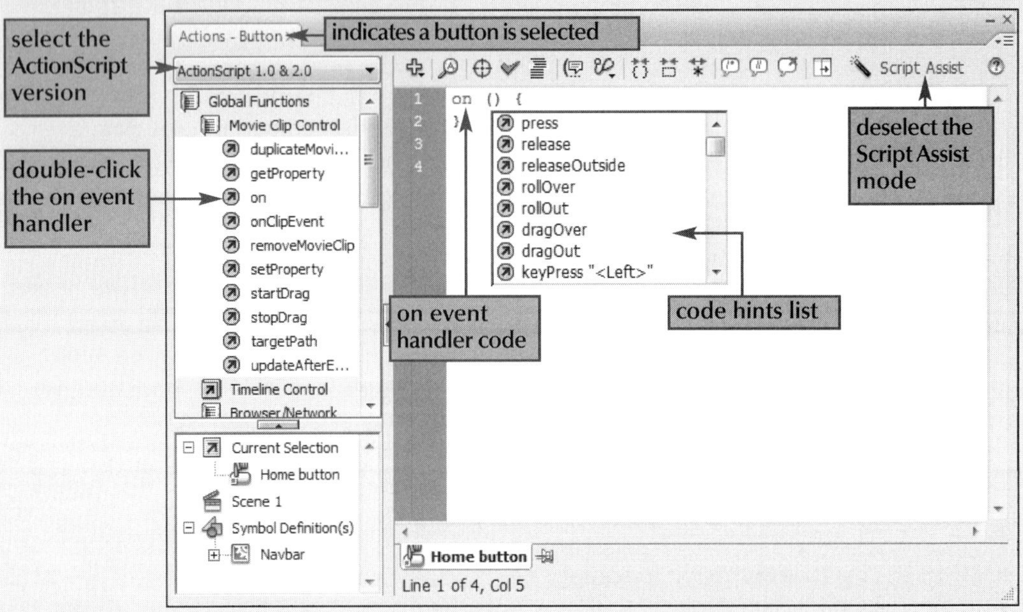

6. Double-click the **release** event. The word *release* is added between the parentheses.

   Trouble? If the list of events does not open, type **release** within the parentheses.

   The `loadMovieNum action` must now be added between the two curly braces.

7. Press the **Right Arrow** key until the insertion point is at the end of the first line after the opening curly brace in the Script pane, and then press the **Enter** key to add a new line between the curly braces.

8. In the Actions toolbox, scroll down as needed, and then click **Browser/Network** to expand this category. A list of actions opens.

9. Scroll down as needed, and then double-click the **`loadMovieNum`** action to add it to the script. A tooltip appears, prompting you to type the parameters for the file-name and the level number within the parentheses.

10. In the Script pane, within the parentheses of the `loadMovieNum` action, type **"Home.swf", 1** to complete the script. See Figure 7-26.

Completed script for the Home button **Figure 7-26**

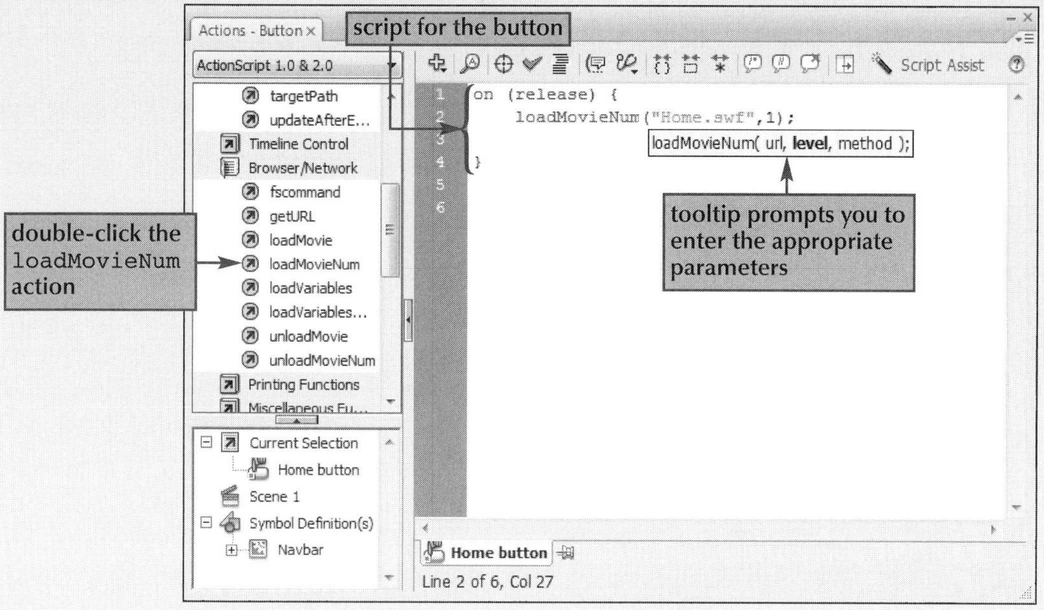

The Actions panel includes an option to check your script for errors. You will use this option to ensure the script does not contain errors.

11. In the Actions panel, click the **Check syntax** button. A dialog box opens stating "This script contains no errors."

    Trouble? If a dialog box opens stating "This script contains errors. The errors encountered are listed in the Compiler Errors Panel.", your script contains errors. The Compiler Errors panel opens at the bottom of the screen with a list of the errors. Close the Compiler Error panel, compare your script to the script shown in Figure 7-26, make the necessary corrections, and then repeat Step 11 until no more errors are encountered.

12. Click the **OK** button to close the dialog box.

The Home button is operational. When clicked, the button loads the Home.swf file into the Flash Player at level 1. The same script must be added to the rest of the buttons. The only difference is the name of the SWF file within the parentheses of the `loadMovieNum` action. You will add the scripts to the remaining buttons.

To add ActionScript to the remaining buttons:

1. Collapse the Actions panel, select the **Teams button** instance on the Stage, and then expand the Actions panel.
2. In the Actions toolbox, double-click the **on** event handler in the Movie Clip Control category to add it to the Script pane, and then double-click the **release** event from the list of events. The event handler and event are added to the Script pane.
3. Press the **Right Arrow** key until the insertion point in the Script pane is at the end of the first line after the opening curly brace, and then press the **Enter** key to add a new line.
4. In the Actions toolbox, double-click the **`loadMovieNum`** action in the Browser/Network category to add it to the script.

5. In the Script pane, within the parentheses of the `loadMovieNum` action, type **"Teams.swf", 1** to add the parameters for the filename and the level number and complete the script.
6. In the Actions panel, click the **Check syntax** button to check the script for errors, and then click the **OK** button to close the dialog box.

   Trouble? If the Compiler Errors panel opens, close the panel, make the necessary corrections, and then repeat Step 6 until no more errors are encountered.

   Next, you'll create the script for the Services and Photo buttons.
7. Collapse the Actions panel, select the **Services button** instance on the Stage, expand the Actions panel, and then repeat Steps 2 through 6, typing **"Services.swf"** for the filename parameter in the `loadMovieNum` action in Step 5 to create the script for this button.
8. Collapse the Actions panel, select the **Photos button** instance on the Stage, expand the Actions panel, and then repeat Steps 2 through 6, typing **"Photos.swf"** for the filename parameter in the `loadMovieNum` action in Step 5 to create the script for this button.
9. Close the Actions panel, and then, on the Edit bar, click the **Scene 1** link to return to the Main document.

The ActionScript scripts for the buttons are complete. You want to ensure that the buttons work as expected. To test the buttons, you must first publish each of the site's documents as SWF files. Remember, the `loadMovieNum` action will load the SWF files named in the parameter portion of the ActionScript code. You will publish the Flash documents you created and saved as FLA files using the Publish Settings command on the File menu. After the documents have been published, you will use the Test Movie command for the Main document to test the buttons in the navigation bar.

To test the buttons in the navigation bar:

1. Click the **Home** tab to make the Home document active.
2. Click **File** on the menu bar, and then click **Publish Settings**. The Publish Settings dialog box opens. This file needs to be published only as an SWF file.
3. Deselect the **HTML (.html)** check box so that only the **Flash (.swf)** check box is selected, and then click the **Publish** button to publish the SWF file. The Home.swf file is created and saved to the same folder as the Home.fla file.
4. Click the **OK** button to close the Publish Settings dialog box.
5. Switch to the **Teams** document, and then repeat Steps 2 through 4 to publish the Teams.swf file.
6. Switch to the **Services** document, and then repeat Steps 2 through 4 to publish the Services.swf file.
7. Switch to the **Photos** document, and then repeat Steps 2 through 4 to publish the Photos.swf file.
8. Switch to the **Main** document, click **Control** on the menu bar, and then click **Test Movie**. Flash creates the SWF file for the Main.fla document, and displays the Main.swf file in a separate window.
9. Click the **Home** button on the navigation bar to display the Home.swf file. See Figure 7-27.

Figure 7-27 Home page of the Jackson's Youth Sports Web site

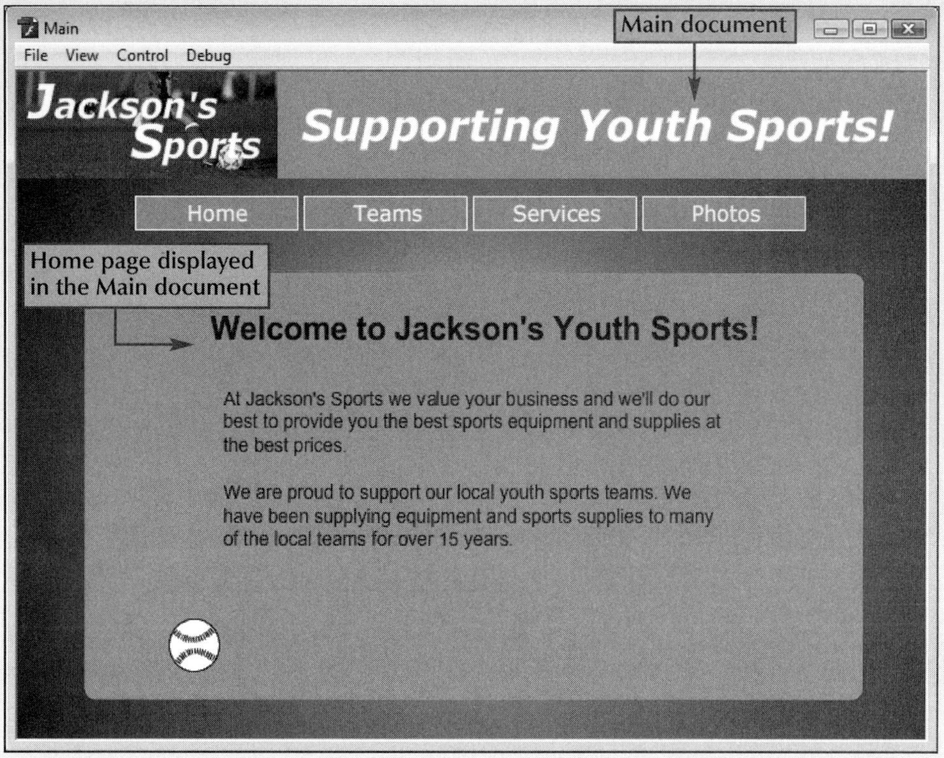

10. Click the **Teams**, **Services**, and **Photos** buttons to display their respective SWF files. The corresponding SWF file appears when each button is clicked.
11. Click **File** on the Flash Player menu bar, and then click **Close**. The Flash Player closes.

When the Main.swf file first displayed, the contents of the Home.swf file did not appear until you clicked the Home button. When someone visits the Jackson's Youth Sports Web site, you want the Home.swf file to load right away without requiring the site visitor to click the Home button. This requires another `loadMovieNum` action to tell the Flash Player to load the Home.swf file as soon as the Main.swf file is loaded. Because this action is not part of a button, it is not enclosed within an event handler. Instead, the action is added to Frame 1 of the Main.fla document's Timeline. Then, when the Main.swf file is loaded into the Flash Player and Frame 1 plays, the `loadMovieNum` action causes the Home.swf file to load right away. You will add this action next.

To add the loadMovieNum action to Frame 1 of the Main document:

1. In the Timeline of the Main document, insert a new layer, name it **Action**, and then select **Frame 1** of the Action layer. You'll add the action to this frame.
2. Open the Actions panel, and then, in the Actions toolbar, double-click the **`loadMovieNum`** action in the Browser/Network category to add it to the Script pane.
3. In the Script pane, within the parentheses of the `loadMovieNum` action, type **"Home.swf", 1** to enter the parameters for the filename and the level number and complete the action. See Figure 7-28.

Figure 7-28 Script in Frame 1

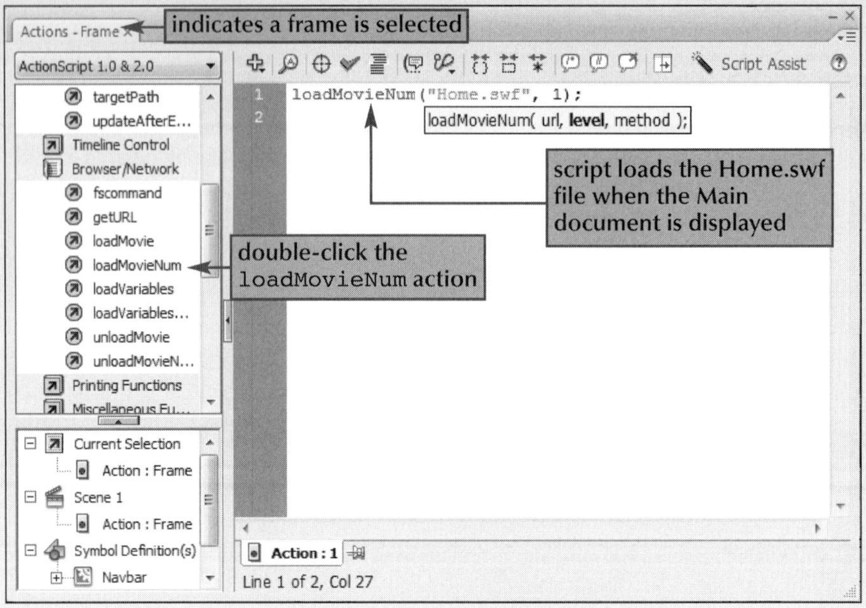

4. In the Actions panel, click the **Check syntax** button to check the script for errors, and then click the **OK** button to close the dialog box.

   Trouble? If the Compiler Errors panel opens, close the panel, make the necessary corrections, and then repeat Step 4 until no more errors are encountered.

5. Close the Actions panel.

6. Click **Control** on the menu bar, and then click **Test Movie**. The Main.swf file opens in a separate window with the contents of the Home.swf also displayed.

7. Click **File** on the Flash Player menu bar, and then click **Close** to return to the Main.fla document.

8. Save the Main document.

The ActionScript scripts you added make the navigation bar buttons operational and load the Home.swf file when the Main.swf file is first loaded into the Flash Player. The site is almost complete. You only need to complete the Photos page so that it displays several pictures of local youth sports teams and events.

Loading External Image Files

The Photos page will display bitmap pictures of sports teams and individual players. The pictures will change as different teams submit pictures to Jackson's Sports. Usually, a picture displayed in a Flash document is imported and becomes part of the document. However, because the pictures on the Photos page will change regularly, you would need to modify the document each time a different set of pictures is to be displayed. A better option is to leave the pictures as separate files and bring them into the Flash Player only when they are to be displayed. These external image files should reside in the same folder as the Photos.swf file, which will make it easier to reference the files from within the Photos page. All of the pictures will be displayed in the same area of the Photos page, so they should be no larger than the display area. The images should be assigned nonspecific filenames such as Photo1.jpg so that the replacement picture can be assigned the same name of Photo1.jpg and saved to the same folder. When the Photos.swf file loads the Photo1.jpg file, the new picture appears. The Flash document doesn't have to be modified each time the pictures are replaced.

Preparing Pictures for Flash Documents | InSight

When using pictures in a Flash document, determine the dimensions of the area in the Flash document where the pictures will be displayed. Then size the pictures in an image-editing program such as Adobe Photoshop so that the pictures fit within the specified dimensions. You should also optimize each picture by reducing its file size while maintaining its quality. This will help minimize the download time.

Using the loadMovie Action

Loading external image files into an SWF file in the Flash Player can be accomplished by using the `loadMovie` action. The `loadMovie` action is similar to the `loadMovieNum` action but can be used to load image files into a movie clip instance instead of a level. You create an empty movie clip symbol in a document such as the Photos document, add an instance of the symbol to the Stage, and then use the `loadMovie` action to load a picture into the movie clip instance. The format of the `loadMovie` action is as follows:

```
movieclip.loadMovie("filename")
```

In this action, `movieclip` represents the name of the movie clip instance. To use this action, you must assign a name to the movie clip instance on the Stage in addition to the name of the symbol in the library. If you have a movie clip instance named Picture_mc, the following action loads the picture file Photo1.jpg into the instance:

```
Picture_mc.loadMovie("Photo1.jpg")
```

You can create this `loadMovie` action along with the event handler code using the Actions panel similarly to how you created the `loadMovieNum` action. However, this action can also be added to a button using the Behaviors panel, which is easier than using the Actions panel.

When using the `loadMovie` action, the image files for the pictures need to be in the standard JPEG file format and not in the progressive JPEG format. The **progressive JPEG** format causes a picture that is downloading to a Web browser to appear to fade in by gradually downloading the data that makes up the picture.

Aly has prepared two pictures for the Jackson's Youth Sports Web site. You will use the Behaviors panel to add the `loadMovie` action to a new set of buttons you will create on the Photos page. You will add the movie clip, buttons, and behaviors to complete the Photos page. There will be two buttons, one for each picture. The buttons will be created as part of a navigation bar that will be placed at the bottom of the rectangle in the Photos page.

To create the navigation bar for the Photos page:

1. Click the **Photos** tab to make the document active.
2. Click **Insert** on the menu bar, click **New Symbol** to open the New Symbol dialog box, type **Photos Navbar** in the Name box, click the **Movie clip** option button if necessary, and then click the **OK** button. The symbol opens in symbol-editing mode.

3. In the Tools panel, click the **Oval** tool, and then, in the Property inspector, set the stroke color to **black** (#FFFFFF), set the stroke height to **1**, set the stroke style to **Solid**, and then set the fill color to **light green** (#66FF99).
4. Draw a small oval at the center of the editing window.
5. In the Tools panel, click the **Selection** tool, select the oval (both the stroke and the fill), type **50** in the W box and type **40** in the H box in the Property inspector to set the oval's dimensions, and then center the oval in the editing window.
6. Click **Modify** on the menu bar, click **Convert to Symbol** to open the Convert to Symbol dialog box, type **Button1** in the Name box, click the **Button** option button, and then click the **OK** button. The oval is converted to a button symbol.

   The oval's color will be different in the Over frame of the button.
7. On the Edit bar, click the **Edit Symbols** button, and then click **Button1**. The Button1 symbol opens in symbol-editing mode.
8. In the Timeline, insert a keyframe in the Over frame, and then, in the Tools panel, change the oval's fill color to **yellow** (#FFFF00).
9. Insert a new layer and name it **Text**, click the **Up** frame of the Text layer, create a text block inside the oval, set the font to **Verdana**, set the font size to **12**, set the text color to **black** (#000000), deselect the **Bold** and **Italic** attributes, select the **Align Left** alignment, and then type **Photo 1** in the text block.
10. In the Tools panel, click the **Selection** tool, and then drag the text block to center the text over the oval. See Figure 7-29.

Figure 7-29 Button1 symbol

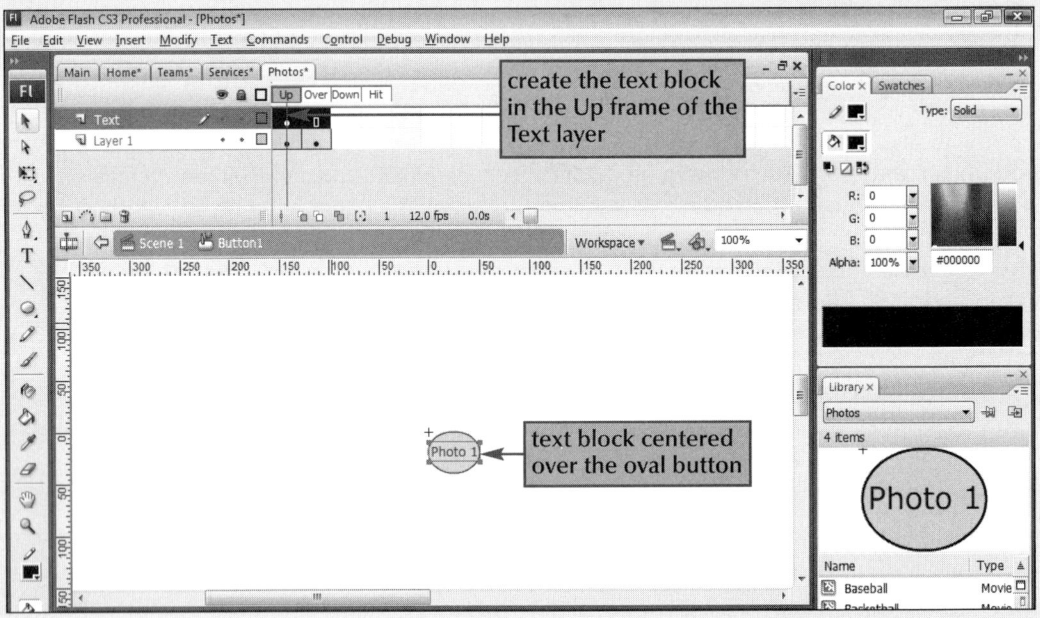

You will duplicate the button to create the second button for the Photos Navbar.

11. In the Library panel, right-click the **Button1** symbol, click **Duplicate** on the context menu to open the Duplicate Symbol dialog box, type **Button2** in the Name box, and then click the **OK** button. The new symbol is an exact copy of the Button1 symbol.

12. On the Edit bar, click the **Edit Symbols** button, click **Button2** to open the symbol in symbol-editing mode, double-click the text block, and then change the text to **Photo 2**.

13. On the Edit bar, click the **Edit Symbols** button, and then click **Photos Navbar** to open the navigation bar in symbol-editing mode.

14. Drag an instance of the **Button2** symbol from the library to the right of the Button1 instance.

15. Click **Edit** on the menu bar, and then click **Select All** to select both button instances at the same time.

16. Click **Modify** on the menu bar, point to **Align**, and then click **Vertical Center** to align the buttons to each other.

17. On the Edit bar, click the **Scene 1** link to return to the document's main Timeline.

18. In the Timeline, click the **Contents** layer to select it, and then drag an instance of the **Photos Navbar** from the Library panel to the lower-left side of the rectangle on the Stage, as shown in Figure 7-30.

Figure 7-30 Navigation bar added to the Photos page

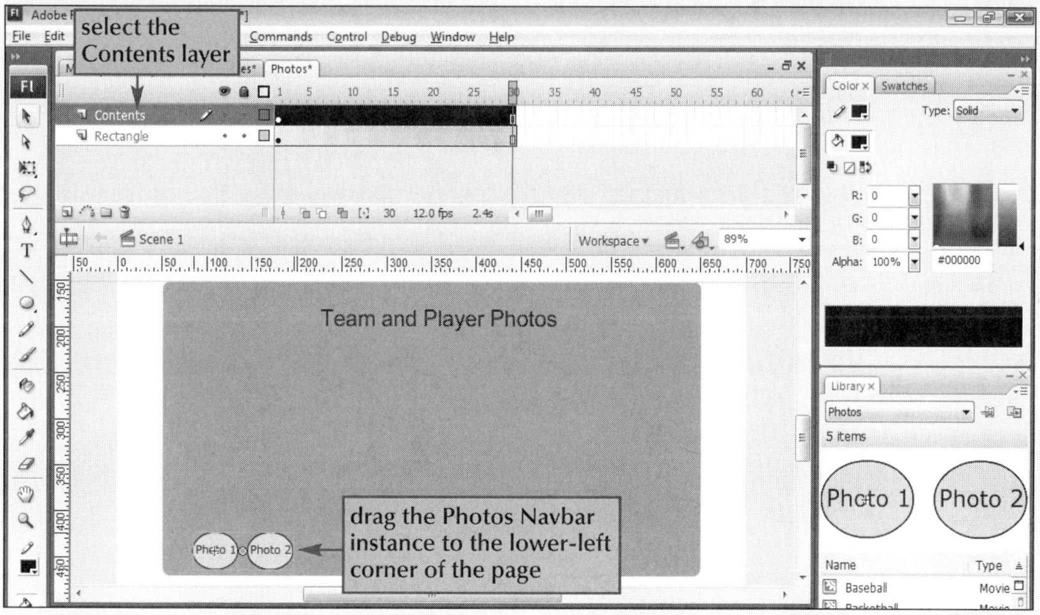

The buttons for the Photos page's navigation bar are complete. To make them operational, however, you need to add the `loadMovie` action to each button instance. Before you add the action, you will create an empty movie clip symbol and place an instance of it on the Stage. The instance will be indicated by a small circle on the Stage, which is the symbol's registration point. When a picture is loaded into the movie clip instance, the upper-left corner of the picture will be aligned with the registration point of the instance. Also, the instance must be named so that the `loadMovie` action can refer to it when it loads the pictures to the instance on the Stage. You will create the movie clip next.

To create the Picture movie clip:

1. Click **Insert** on the menu bar, click **New Symbol** to open the Create New Symbol dialog box, type **Picture movie clip** in the Name box, click the **Movie clip** option button, and then click the **OK** button. The Picture movie clip symbol opens in symbol-editing mode. Because the movie clip will be empty, you will exit symbol-editing mode.

2. On the Edit bar, click the **Scene 1** link to return to the document's main Timeline.
3. Drag an instance of the **Picture movie clip** symbol from the Library panel to the Stage under the title, and then place the instance approximately 220 pixels from the top of the Stage and 300 pixels from the left of the Stage. The instance is indicated by a small circle.
4. In the Property inspector, type **Picture_mc** in the Instance Name box, and then press the **Enter** key. The instance is named. See Figure 7-31.

Figure 7-31 Picture_mc movie clip instance

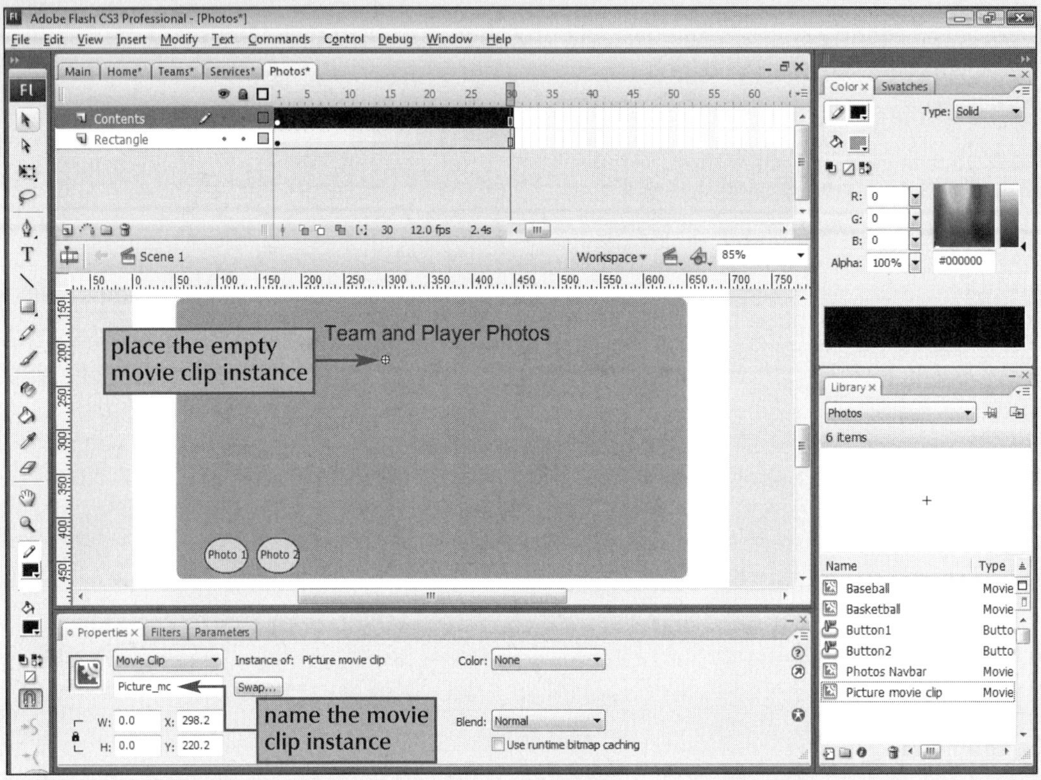

Using the Behaviors Panel

Instead of writing actions with the Actions panel, you can use precoded actions called behaviors. **Behaviors** are actions with prewritten ActionScript scripts that assign controls and transitions to an object on the Stage. You can use behaviors to control an object in a document without writing any ActionScript coding yourself. A variety of behaviors are available for Flash objects, including movie clips, video, and sound files. Behaviors are only available with ActionScript 1.0 and 2.0.

You'll use the Behaviors panel to add actions to the Photo1 button and the Photo2 button.

To add actions to the buttons using the Behaviors panel:

Tip

You can also press the Shift+F3 keys to open and close the Behaviors panel.

1. On the Edit bar, click the **Edit Symbols** button, click **Photos Navbar** to open the symbol in symbol-editing mode, and then select the **Button1** instance in the editing window.
2. Click **Window** on the menu bar, and then click **Behaviors**. The Behaviors panel opens.

3. In the Behaviors panel, click the **Add Behavior** button, point to **Movieclip**, and then click **Load Graphic**. The Load Graphic dialog box opens.

4. Type **photo1.jpg** in the Enter the URL to the .JPG to load box, click **Picture_mc** in the list of movie clips at the center of the dialog box, and then click the **Relative** option button if necessary. See Figure 7-32.

Figure 7-32 Load Graphic dialog box

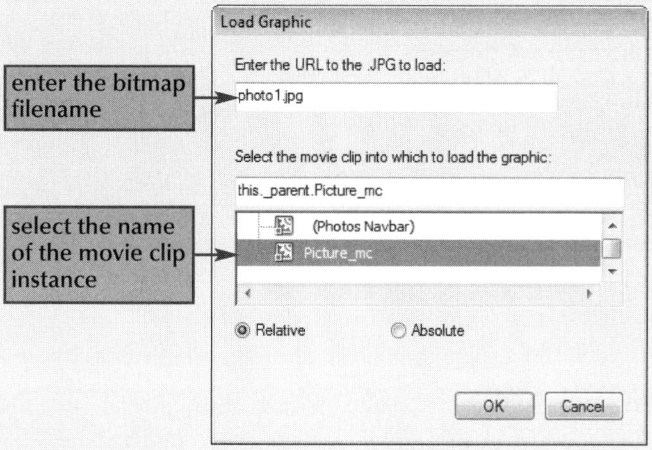

5. Click the **OK** button to create the behavior and close the Load Graphic dialog box.

   Next, you'll add the behavior to the other button.

6. Collapse the Behaviors panel, select the **Button2** instance on the Stage, expand the Behaviors panel, repeat Steps 3 through 5, typing **photo2.jpg** in the Enter the URL to the .JPG to load box in Step 4.

7. Close the Behaviors panel, and then, on the Edit bar, click the **Scene 1** link to return to the Photo document's main Timeline.

   The Photos document needs to be saved and published as an SWF file so that it will work with the Main document.

8. Save the Photos file, click **File** on the menu bar, and then click **Publish** to create the Photos.swf file.

Tip

You can also press the Shift+F12 keys to publish a document.

The photo buttons and the Photos page are complete. When the Photos page is loaded into the Flash Player, the buttons appear. The site visitor can click one of the photo buttons to load a picture into the Flash Player. You will test the completed Web site in a browser.

To save and publish the Main page:

1. Click the **Main** tab to make that document active. You need to set the publish settings.

2. Click **File** on the menu bar, and then click **Publish Settings**. The Publish Settings dialog box opens.

3. Make sure that the **Flash (.swf)** and the **HTML (.html)** check boxes are checked, and then click the **OK** button to close the dialog box.

4. Click **File** on the menu bar, point to **Publish Preview**, and then click **Default - (HTML)**. The Jackson's Youth Sports Web site opens in your Web browser.

5. Click the **Photos** button to display the Photos page, and then click the **Photo 1** button on the Photos page to display the first picture. See Figure 7-33.

Figure 7-33 **Photos page previewed in a Web browser**

6. On the Photos page, click the **Photo 2** button to display the second picture.
7. Close the browser, and then save and close all of the documents.

In this session, you used the Actions panel to add ActionScript scripts to the buttons in the navigation bar to make them operational. You also used the Behaviors panel to add actions to buttons on the Photos page to load external image files into the Flash Player. The site is ready to show to Dan and Gloria.

Review | Session 7.3 Quick Check

1. What is ActionScript?
2. Write the ActionScript statement to load the Staff.swf file to level 1 of the Flash Player.
3. What is the purpose of the on event handler?
4. What option in the Actions panel can be used to check for errors in your script?
5. What action can be used to load external image files into a movie clip instance?
6. When you use the Load Graphic behavior, you must assign a(n)__________________ to the movie clip instance where the picture will be loaded.

Tutorial Summary | Review

In this tutorial, you reviewed the process for developing a new Flash Web site and learned how a Flash Web site differs from a non-Flash Web site. In the process of planning a Flash Web site, you identified the site's purpose and objectives, and then developed a storyboard showing the major parts of the site and its navigation system. You then built a Flash Web site by creating the home page, creating a template that you used for additional pages, and creating a navigation bar for the site. You used the Actions panel to add ActionScript instructions to the navigation bar buttons you created. Finally, you created a page for the Web site with buttons to display pictures and appropriate ActionScript instructions to control how the pictures are loaded into a movie clip in the Flash Player.

Key Terms

behavior
external library
Flash Exchange
goal
levels
navigation bar
objective
progressive JPEG
storyboard
target audience
template
XHTML

Practice | Review Assignments

Practice the skills you learned in the tutorial.

Data Files needed for the Review Assignments: MainPageDraft.fla, JSPhotosDraft.fla, SpecialsDraft.fla, picture1.jpg, picture2.jpg

Aly developed an alternative Web site for Jackson's Sports. She wants you to add a new Specials page that includes information about the weekly sales promotion offered by Jackson's Sports. You need to add a button to the MainPage document's navigation bar to load the Specials page. You also will add the option to display a second photo in the Player Photos page.

1. Open the **SpecialsDraft.fla** file located in the Tutorial.07\Review folder included with your Data Files, and then save the file as **Specials.fla** in the same folder.
2. Select the Contents layer, and then add a text block near the top of the rectangle with the text **Specials of the Week!**, using Times New Roman for the font, 24 for the font size, black for the text color, bold for the style, and Align Center for the alignment. Position the text block on the rectangle about 215 pixels from the top and about 330 pixels from the left.
3. Add another text block in the center of the rectangle (approximately 280 pixels from the top and 330 pixels from the left), using Times New Roman for the font, 14 for the font size, and black for the text color, deselecting the bold style, setting the alignment to Align Center, and then entering the following text:
   The following items are on sale this week.
   Softball bats—as low as $89
   Softballs—$3.99 each
   Batting gloves—$12.99
4. Save and publish the document to create the Specials.swf file.
5. Open the **MainPageDraft.fla** file located in the Tutorial.07\Review folder included with your Data Files, and then save the file as **MainPage.fla** in the same folder.
6. In the Library panel, make a duplicate of the Home symbol, name the duplicate **Specials**, and then edit the Specials symbol by changing the text in the Up frame of the Text layer to **Specials**.
7. Add an instance of the Specials symbol to the bottom of the navigation bar in the JSNavbar symbol below the Photos button. In the Property inspector, set the Specials button's X coordinate to –75 to align its left edge with the other buttons. Select all of the buttons on the Stage simultaneously, and then use the Distribute Heights option in the Align submenu of the Modify menu to distribute the buttons evenly.
8. Add the `loadMovieNum` action to the Specials button instance, using the on event handler so that the action executes when the button is released after being clicked. The `loadMovieNum` action should load the Specials.swf file into level 1 of the Flash Player.
9. Save and publish the MainPage.fla file to create the MainPage.swf file.
10. Open the **JSPhotosDraft.fla** file located in the Tutorial.07\Review folder included with your Data Files, and then save the file as **JSPhotos.fla** in the same folder.
11. Make a duplicate of the Pic_button1 symbol, name the duplicate **Pic_button2**, edit the Pic_button2 symbol by changing the text to **Picture 2**.
12. Add an instance of the Pic_button2 symbol to the Stage below the Pic_button1 instance, and then align the two instances vertically.
13. Add the Load Graphic behavior to the Pic_button2 instance so that it loads the **picture2.jpg** file located in the Tutorial.07\Review folder included with your Data Files. The picture should be loaded to the Picture_mc movie clip instance.
14. Save and publish the JSPhotos.fla file to create the JSPhotos.swf file.

15. Test the Web site to make sure the Specials button loads the Specials page and the JSPhotos page displays a photo using the second button.
16. Submit the finished files to your instructor, either in printed or electronic form, as requested.

Apply | Case Problem 1

Create a new Flash Web site based on a template with a navigation bar and custom graphics.

Data Files needed for this Case Problem: Sandys.fla, Welcome.fla

Sandy's Scrapbook Store Sandy Rodriguez, owner of Sandy's Scrapbook Store, asks John Rossini to create a new Web site that will include information to promote some of the store's special services. She wants the site to be visually appealing and easy to use for anyone who wants help in creating scrapbooks. Based on John's meeting with Sandy, John develops the following list of goals for the Web site:

- Promote the Sandy's Scrapbook Store name.
- Increase awareness of its services.

Based on these goals, John puts together the following list of objectives:

- Provide a list of services.
- Highlight the scrapbook classes available.
- Highlight the monthly scrapbooking retreats.

John then prepares the outline for the site, which includes a home page with a banner at the top with the name of the store and a navigation bar on the left side. The navigation bar will have buttons in rectangular shapes that link to a Scrapbook Supplies page, a Scrapbook Classes page, and a Monthly Retreats page.

John asks you to create the Web site that will include the Main, Welcome, Supplies, Classes, and Retreats pages. You will create the Supplies, Classes, and Retreats pages based on the Welcome page that John has prepared. The banner and the navigation for the site will be in the site's Main page. John also created a document with several symbols that you will use in the site, including a rectangular symbol for the buttons in the navigation bar, a picture and various graphics for the banner, and an animation for some of the pages.

1. Create a new document 600 pixels wide by 400 pixels high. Use a light yellow (#FFFF99) for the background color. Save the document as **SSSmain.fla** in the Tutorial.07\Case1 folder included with your Data Files.
2. Create a new movie clip symbol named **Banner**. In the Banner symbol, create a rectangle 600 pixels wide by 100 pixels high. Use a purple color (#CC33CC) for the fill and do not include a stroke. Rename Layer 1 as **Background**.
3. Insert a new layer and name it **Graphics**. Open the **Sandys.fla** file located in the Tutorial.07\Case1 folder included with your Data Files as an external library. On the Graphics layer, add an instance of the store bitmap picture from the external library to the left side of the banner. Align the picture with the left and top edges of the rectangle. Also, add two instances each of the triangle, circle, and square symbols arranged over the area of the banner not covered by the store bitmap.
4. Insert a new layer above the Graphics layer and name it **Text**. On the Text layer, add a text block in the center of the rectangle. Use Comic Sans MS for the font, 46 for the font size, yellow (#FFFF00) for the text color, and bold for the font style. Type **Sandy's Scrapbook Store** in the text block. If necessary, center the text block within the banner. The banner is complete.

5. In Scene 1, insert an instance of the Banner symbol at the top of the Stage. Align the Banner instance with the top and left sides of the Stage. Rename Layer 1 as **Background**.
6. Create a new movie clip symbol named **Navbar**. In the Navbar symbol, create a rectangle 100 pixels wide by 300 pixels high. Use a pink color (#FF99FF) for the fill and do not include a stroke. Center the rectangle on the Stage. Rename Layer 1 as **Background** and lock it.
7. Insert a new layer and name it **Buttons**. On the Buttons layer, drag an instance of the square2 symbol from the external library to the upper-left side of the rectangle. With the square2 instance selected, use the Break Apart command on the Modify menu to break it into a regular graphic. Convert the square2 graphic into a button symbol named **Home button**.
8. Edit the Home button symbol. In the button's Timeline, insert a keyframe in the Over frame. In the Over frame, click the center of the Home button graphic to select the inside square area, and then change the fill color to gray (#CCCCCC).
9. Insert a new layer and name it **Text**. On the Text layer, add a text block with the words **SSS Home** on two lines. Use Comic Sans MS for the font, 12 for the font size, white for the text color, bold for the font style, and Align Center for the alignment. Place the text block at the center of the square.
10. Make three duplicates of the Home button, and then rename the duplicate buttons as **Supplies button**, **Classes button**, and **Retreats button**, respectively. Change the text in the Supplies button to **Supplies**. Change the text in the Classes button to **Classes**. Change the text in the Retreats button to **Retreats**.
11. Edit the Navbar symbol. Add an instance of the Supplies button below and to the right of the Home button instance, placing it close to the right edge of the rectangle. Add an instance of the Classes button, placing it below and to the left of the Supplies button instance, near the left edge of the rectangle. Add an instance of the Retreats button, placing it toward the lower-right side of the rectangle.
12. Select the Home button in the Navbar symbol, open the Actions panel, and add a `loadMovieNum` action so that when the button is clicked and then released, the Welcome.swf file loads at level 1 of the Flash Player. Add `loadMovieNum` actions to the other button instances to load SWF files at level 1. The Supplies button should load the Supplies.swf file. The Classes button should load the Classes.swf file. The Retreats button should load the Retreats.swf file.
13. Return to Scene 1, insert a new layer, and name it **Navbar**. On the Navbar layer, add an instance of the Navbar symbol to the left side of the Stage below the banner. Align the Navbar instance with the left and bottom edges of the Stage.
14. Insert a new layer and name it **Action**. Add a `loadMovieNum` action at Frame 1 of the Action layer that loads the Welcome.swf file at level 1 as soon as Frame 1 is played. This displays the Welcome.swf file as soon as the SSSmain.swf page plays in the Flash Player.
15. Open the **Welcome.fla** file located in the Tutorial.07\Case1 folder included with your Data Files. Insert a new layer and name it **Animation**. Add an instance of the animated_clip symbol from the external library so that it is to the left of the top text block.
16. Save the Welcome.fla file as a template named **SSSTemplate** in a new template category called **SSS** with the following description for the template: **Template for the Sandy's Scrapbook Store Web site pages**. Close the SSSTemplate.fla file. The Welcome.fla document remains unchanged.

17. Create a new document based on the SSSTemplate, and then save this document as **Supplies.fla** in the Tutorial.07\Case1 folder included with your Data Files. Change the top text block to **Sandy's Scrapbook Supplies!**, and then center the text block above the second text block. Change the second text block to the following text, and then spell check the text and make the necessary corrections:

    Sandy's has everything you could possibly need for scrapbook projects, including albums, stickers, ribbons, and colorful paper. We also have a variety of cutting tools, alphabets, charms, and scrapbooking kits for themes such as holidays, sports, family vacations, and more. Check back regularly as we are always adding to our scrapbook supplies inventory.
18. Create a new document based on the SSSTemplate, and then save this document as **Classes.fla** in the Tutorial.07\Case1 folder included with your Data Files. Change the top text block to **Sandy's Classes are Fun!**, center the text block above the second text block, and change the color of the text to blue (#0000FF). Change the second text block to the following text, spell check the text and make the necessary corrections, and then change the color of the text to red (#FF0000):

    Here at Sandy's, we can help you learn many techniques to make you an expert scrapper. We have beginning classes as well as classes for the more advanced scrapper. Classes include Scrapbook 101, Working with Albums, Layout Design, and Recipe Cards. We also offer special classes for different holidays. Make your reservations early as our classes fill up fast.
19. Create a new document based on the SSSTemplate, and then save this document as **Retreats.fla** in the Tutorial.07\Case1 folder included with your Data Files. Change the top text block to **Sandy's Monthly Retreats!**, center the text block above the second text block, and change the color of the text to dark green (#006600). Change the second text block to the following text:

    Ask about our regular monthly scrapbooking retreats. Every third weekend of each month we hold a retreat at our store. During each retreat you practice different techniques to improve your skills. Retreats are led by our expert staff. Lunch and dinner are served as well as coffee and desserts. The cost depends on the activities planned for the retreat. Ask one our staff members for more details.
20. Save and publish each of the documents to create the Supplies.swf, Classes.swf, and Retreats.swf files. Open the **Welcome.fla** file and publish it to create the Welcome.swf file. Return to the SSSmain.fla document and test the Web site by using the Test Movie command. Test each of the buttons and make certain the individual pages are loaded. Make any necessary corrections.
21. Submit the finished files to your instructor, either in printed or electronic form, as requested.

Apply | Case Problem 2

Create a new Flash Web site based on a custom template with a navigation bar and custom graphics for a music store.

Data File needed for this Case Problem: Music.fla

River City Music Janet Meyers, store manager for River City Music, meets with Alex Smith to discuss the development of a new Web site to showcase some special services available at her store. They agree on the following goal for the Web site:

- Promote some of the unique services available at River City Music.

Based on this goal, Alex puts together the following list of objectives:

- Highlight the store's large selection of sheet music.
- Highlight the recital hall available for rental.
- Promote the monthly specials on musical instruments.

You will help Alex create the new Web site based on these goals and objectives. Alex designs a background picture for the Web site as well as some of the graphics to be used. He provides these graphics in a Flash document. You'll develop the main page, and then create a template for the remaining pages. The navigation system will use a musical note graphic for the buttons with an animation effect that appears when the user moves the pointer over the buttons.

1. Create a new document 600 pixels wide by 400 pixels high with white for the background color, and then save the document as **RCMmain.fla** in the Tutorial.07\Case2 folder included with your Data Files.
2. Open the **Music.fla** document located in the Tutorial.07\Case2 folder included with your Data Files as an external library, drag an instance of the pianobk.jpg bitmap onto the Stage, align the picture to cover all of the Stage, and then rename Layer 1 as **Background**.
3. Create a new movie clip symbol named **Banner**. In the Banner symbol, create a rectangle 600 pixels wide by 70 pixels high. Use the Color panel to create a radial gradient with a blue (#0066FF) inner color (left gradient pointer) and a white outer color (right gradient pointer). Use this gradient for the fill of the rectangle. Use a stroke color of a dark blue (#006699) and a stroke height of 2. Center the rectangle on the Stage, and then rename Layer 1 as **Background**.
4. Insert a new layer and name it **Text**. Add a text block in the center of the rectangle. Use Monotype Corsiva for the font, 60 for the font size, black for the text color, bold and italic for the style attributes, and Align Center for the alignment. Type **River City Music** in the text block, and then center the text inside the rectangle. The banner is complete.
5. Return to Scene 1, add an instance of the Banner symbol to the top of the Stage, and then align the instance with the top and left edges of the Stage.
6. Create a new button symbol named **Home button**. In symbol-editing mode, drag an instance of the note1 symbol from the external library to the center of the Stage. Use the Property inspector to center the note1 symbol. Rename Layer 1 to **Note**. The note1 instance will be present only in the Up frame of the button's Timeline. Close the external library.
7. Insert a new layer and name it **Text**. Add a text block on the Text layer to the right of the note1 instance on the Stage. Use Monotype Corsiva for the font, 18 for the font size, and black for the text color. Deselect the bold and italic styles, and use Align Left for the alignment. Type **Home** in the text block. Insert a keyframe in the Over frame of the Text layer. In this frame, change the text color to blue (#0000FF).
8. Insert a new layer and name it **Animation**. Insert a keyframe in the Over frame of the Animation layer. Drag an instance of the note1 symbol to the center of the Stage and center it using the Property inspector. Convert the note1 instance to a movie clip symbol named **Note animation**. Edit the Note animation symbol, add a keyframe in Frame 10 of its Timeline, create a motion tween between Frames 1 and 10, and then rotate the note clockwise one time in the motion tween.

EXPLORE

9. Edit the Home button and insert a blank keyframe in the Hit frame of the Text layer. Turn on onion skinning and extend the onion skin markers to cover all four frames of the Timeline. In the Hit frame of the text layer, draw a small rectangle to cover the area for both the note and the text. The Home button is complete.
10. Make three duplicates of the Home button, and then name the duplicate buttons **Sheet button**, **Recital button**, and **Instruments button**, respectively.
11. Change the text in both the Up and Over frames of the Sheet button to **Sheet Music**, and then resize the rectangle in the Hit frame of the Text button to cover all of the text. Change the text in the Up and Over frames of the Recital button to **Recital Hall**, and then resize the rectangle in the Hit frame to cover all of the text. Change the text in the Up and Over frames of the Instruments button to **Musical Instruments**, and then resize the rectangle in the Hit frame to cover the text.
12. Create a new movie clip symbol named **Navbar**. In the Navbar symbol, drag an instance of the Home button to the left side of the Stage, and then drag an instance of the Sheet button, the Recital button, and the Instruments button to the right of the previous button instance. Align the instances by using the Property inspector to set each instance's X and Y coordinates as follows: Home button (X=–175, Y=0), Sheet button (X=–110, Y=0), Recital button (X=0, Y=0), Instruments button (X=110, Y=0).
13. Select the Home button in the Navbar, open the Actions panel, and add a `loadMovieNum` action so that when the button is clicked and then released, the Home.swf file loads at level 1 of the Flash Player. Add `loadMovieNum` actions to the other button instances to load SWF files at level 1. The Sheet button should load the Sheet.swf file. The Recital button should load the Recital.swf file. The Instruments button should load the Instruments.swf file. The Navbar is complete.
14. Return to Scene 1, insert a new layer and name it **Navbar**, and then drag an instance of the Navbar symbol to the Stage and center it right below the banner.
15. Insert a new layer and name it **Action**. Add a `loadMovieNum` action at Frame 1 of the Action layer that loads the Home.swf file at level 1 as soon as Frame 1 is played. This displays the Home.swf file as soon as the RCMmain.swf page plays in the Flash Player.
16. Create a new document to save as the Home page and as a template that is 600 pixels wide by 400 pixels high. Drag a horizontal guide to about 110 pixels from the top edge of the Stage, and then draw a rectangle below the guide to frame the contents of each page. Use a dark blue color (#006699) for the stroke, a stroke height of 2, and do not include a fill. Make the rectangle 500 pixels wide by 250 pixels high. Center the rectangle in the area below the guide. Rename Layer 1 as **Rectangle**.
17. Insert a new layer and name it **Text**. Add a text block inside the rectangle. Place it close to the top of the rectangle. Use Monotype Corsiva for the font, 32 for the font size, black for the text color, and the bold and Align Left attributes. Type **RCM - Serving Musicians** in the text block. Add a fixed-width text block below the first text block. Use Arial for the font, 14 for the font size, and black for the text color. Use the Align Left attribute and deselect the Bold style. Type the following in this text block:

    River City Music provides musical instruments and supplies to musicians of all ages in the local region. Some of the special services offered by RCM include a large selection of sheet music, a recital hall, and musical instruments of all types.
18. Center the two text blocks within the rectangle. Save this page as **Home.fla** in the Tutorial.07\Case2 folder included with your Data Files, and then save this same document as a template named **RCMTemplate** in a new template category called **RCM** with the description: **Template for the RCM Web site pages**. Close the RCMTemplate.fla file.

19. Create a new document based on the RCMTemplate, and save the document as **Sheet.fla** in the Tutorial.07\Cases2folder included with your Data Files. Change the top text block to **RCM's Sheet Music**, and then center the text block within the rectangle. Change the second text block to the following text:
    River City Music has one of the largest selections of sheet music in the local region. We have every type of sheet music from pop to classical, for everyone from beginners to professionals. Come visit our store and plan to spend some time browsing through our library.
20. Create a new document based on the RCMTemplate, and then save the document as **Recital.fla** in the Tutorial.07\Case2 folder included with your Data Files. Change the top text block to **RCM's Recital Hall**, and then center the text block within the rectangle. Change the second text block to the following text, and then change the text color in both text blocks to blue (#0000FF):
    River City Music has an intimate recital hall available for rental by small groups or music teachers. The hall seats 40 people and has a raised stage with a grand piano. Many local piano teachers use the hall to showcase their students' skills.

    Call 1-800-44-PIANO for more information about our recital hall and to check for available dates.
21. Create a new document based on the RCMTemplate, and then save the document as **Instruments.fla** in the Tutorial.07\Case2 folder included with your Data Files. Change the top text block to **Musical Instruments**, and center the text block within the rectangle. Change the second text block to the following text, and then change the text color in both text blocks to red (#FF0000):
    River City Music carries a wide variety of musical instruments. Here, you can find trumpets, clarinets, flutes, drums, trombones, guitars, violins, and much more. If we don't have it in stock, we will order it for you at no extra charge. We also service all musical instruments.
22. Save and publish each of the documents to create the Sheet.swf, Recital.swf, and Instruments.swf files. Open the **Home.fla** file and publish it to create the Home.swf file. Return to the RCMmain.fla document, and then test the Web site using the Test Movie command. Test each of the buttons and make certain the individual pages are loaded. Make any necessary corrections.
23. Submit the finished files to your instructor, either in printed or electronic form, as requested.

Challenge | Case Problem 3

Create a new Flash Web site based on a template with a navigation bar and custom graphics for a nursery.

Data Files needed for this Case Problem: flower1.jpg, flower2.jpg, ivy1.jpg, WCstart.fla

Westcreek Nursery Alice has been pleased with the work Amanda Lester has done in creating various graphics using Flash, and she asks her about creating a new Web site to showcase her nursery's weekly specials. This Web site will be separate from their current Web site. Amanda discusses Alice's request with her and she develops the following goals for the new Web site:

- Promote the Westcreek Nursery name.
- Showcase weekly specials available for delivery.

Based on these goals, Amanda develops the following list of objectives:

- Provide a welcome message with contact information.
- Showcase flowers and plants available for delivery.
- Display photos of flowers and plants.

You will help Amanda create the Web site. The outline Amanda has prepared for the site includes a home page with a banner at the top consisting of the Westcreek Nursery name with an animation. The navigation bar will have buttons in the shape of a car wheel, which rotate when the mouse pointer is over them. She wants a link to the Photos page, with buttons to display each of three pictures. You will start with a document Amanda has created and use the graphics and photos she has provided.

1. Open the **WCstart.fla** file located in the Tutorial.07\Case3 folder included with your Data Files and then save the document as **WCmain.fla** in the same folder.
2. Create a new movie clip symbol named **Banner**. In the Banner symbol, create a text block in the center of the Stage. Use Verdana for the font, 46 for the font size, and black for the text color. Apply the Bold and Italic attributes and use the Align Left alignment. Type **Westcreek Nursery** in the text block. Use the Property inspector to center the text block. Change the name of Layer 1 to **Text1**.
3. EXPLORE Insert a new layer and name it **Text2**. Copy the text block on the Text1 layer, and then use the Paste in Place command to paste the copy on the Text2 layer in the same position as the original text block.
4. Insert a new layer between the Text1 and Text2 layers and name it **Gradient**. Drag an instance of the Gradient symbol to Frame 1 of the Gradient layer, placing the gradient rectangle on the right side of the text block so that the rectangle's left side covers the letter y. Insert a keyframe at Frame 20 of the Gradient layer, and then insert regular frames at Frame 20 of both the Text1 and Text2 layers to extend them.
5. At Frame 20 of the Gradient layer, move the gradient rectangle to the left side of the text block so that the rectangle's right side covers only the letter W. Create a motion tween at Frame 1 of the Gradient layer. The gradient rectangle will move across the text from the right to the left side.
6. Change the Text2 layer to a mask layer and make certain that the Gradient layer becomes a masked layer. The banner is complete.
7. Return to Scene 1, insert a new layer and name it **Banner**. On the Banner layer, add an instance of the Banner symbol to the top of the Stage. Center the instance right below the top edge of the box created by the rectangle on the Stage.
8. Create a new button symbol named **Home button**. Drag an instance of the Wheel symbol from the library to the center of the Stage. Use the Property inspector to center the Wheel symbol. Add a text block to the right of the Wheel instance on the Stage. Use Verdana for the font, 16 for the font size, and black for the text color. Do not use the bold or italic styles. Type **Home** in the text block. In the Over frame, insert a keyframe, delete the Wheel instance, and then change the text color to red (#FF0000).
9. Insert a new layer and name it **Animation**. Insert a keyframe in the Over frame of the Animation layer. Drag an instance of the Rotating Wheel symbol to the center of the Stage and center it using the Property inspector.
10. EXPLORE Add a blank keyframe in the Hit frame of Layer 1. Turn on onion skinning and extend the onion skin markers to cover all four frames of the Timeline. In the Hit frame of Layer 1, draw a small rectangle to cover the area for both the wheel and the text. The Home button is complete.

11. Make a duplicate of the Home button and name it **Photos button**. Change the text in both the Up and Over frames of the Photos button to **Photos**, and then resize of the rectangle in the Hit frame of the Photos button to cover all of the text.
12. Create a new movie clip symbol named **Navbar**. In the Navbar symbol, drag an instance of the Home button to the left side of the crosshair on the Stage. Drag an instance of the Photos button to the right of the Home button. Align both symbol instances along their top edges.
13. Select the Home button in the Navbar, open the Actions panel, and add a `loadMovieNum` action so that when the button is clicked and then released, the Nursery.swf file loads at level 1 of the Flash Player. Add a `loadMovieNum` action to the Photos button instance to load the Photos.swf file at level 1. The Navbar is complete.
14. Return to Scene 1, insert a new layer, and name it **Navbar**. On the Navbar layer, drag an instance of the Navbar symbol to the Stage and center it right below the banner.
15. Insert a new layer and name it **Action**. Add a `loadMovieNum` action at Frame 1 of the Action layer that loads the Nursery.swf file at level 1 as soon as Frame 1 is played. This file displays as soon as the WCmain.swf page plays in the Flash Player.
16. Create a new document 600 pixels wide by 400 pixels high. Drag a horizontal guide to about 100 pixels from the top edge of the Stage. The content for the page will be below this guide.
17. Add a text block below the guide about 150 pixels from the top edge of the Stage. Use Verdana for the font, 16 for the font size, and black for the text color. Also use the bold and Align Left styles. Type **Westcreek's Specials of the Week!** in the text block. Add a fixed-width text block below the first text block. Use Verdana for the font, 14 for the font size, and black for the text color. Use Align Left but deselect the Bold attribute. Type the following in this text block:

    Welcome to Westcreek's specials of the week. Here, we bring you information about some great deals on flowers, plants, and trees. Each week, we highlight several items available for quick delivery.

    Please call our friendly staff for more information.
18. Center the two text blocks on the Stage, and then save the page as **Nursery.fla** in the Tutorial.07\Case3 folder included with your Data Files.
19. Create a new document 600 pixels wide by 400 pixels high. Drag a horizontal guide to about 100 pixels from the top edge of the Stage. The content for the page will be below this guide.
20. Create a new movie clip symbol named **Photo MC**. Exit the movie clip's symbol-editing mode and return to Scene 1. Drag an instance of the Photo MC symbol to the Stage. Use the Property inspector to place the movie clip instance at the X coordinate of 150 and the Y coordinate of 100. Also, assign the name **Picture** to the movie clip instance.
21. Create a new movie clip symbol named **Photos Navbar**. In the Photos Navbar, draw a star shape with a dark green (#006600) fill and a black stroke. Set the star's width and height at 45 pixels each. Convert the star to a button symbol named **Photo button**. Edit the Photo button symbol and add a keyframe in the Over frame. In the Over frame, change the color of the star's fill to light yellow (#FFFFCC).
22. Return to the Photos Navbar symbol, add two more instances of the Photo button to the Stage, and then arrange the instances vertically below the first instance. Add a text block above the buttons. Use Verdana as the font, 12 for the font size, and black for the text color. Do not use the Bold or Italic attributes. Type **Click below** in the text block.
23. Return to Scene 1, and then drag an instance of the Navbar to the left side of the Stage right below the guide and about 30 pixels from the left edge of the Stage.

EXPLORE

24. Return to the Photos Navbar symbol, select the top button instance in the Navbar, open the Behaviors panel, and add a Load Graphic behavior to the button instance. The behavior should load the flower1.jpg file into the Picture movie clip instance. The Behavior text box should display this._parent.Picture, indicating the graphic will load into the Picture instance on the Scene 1 Timeline. Also, add the Load Graphic behavior to the other two button instances on the Stage. One should load the flower2.jpg file and the other should load the ivy1.jpg file. Both photos should load in the Picture movie clip instance.
25. Return to Scene 1, and then save the page as **Photos.fla** in the Tutorial.07\Case3 folder included with your Data Files.
26. Publish each of the documents to create the **Nursery.swf** and **Photos.swf** files. Return to the WCmain.fla document and test the Web site using the Test Movie command. Test each of the buttons and verify that the individual pages and photos are loaded. Make any necessary corrections.
27. Submit the finished files to your instructor, either in printed or electronic form, as requested.

Create | Case Problem 4

Create a Flash Web site based on a template with a navigation bar and custom graphics for an association.

Data File needed for this Case Problem: background.jpg

Regional Dietetic Association Katie Ellison, Web designer for Regional Dietetic Association, is developing a preliminary version of a new Web site that will highlight special services available to the association's members. Based on discussions with Richard Perez, president of the association, the following goals are developed:

- Promote the association's main services.
- Promote the association's name.

Based on these goals, Katie and Richard develop the following list of objectives for the Web site:

- Provide information about professional development opportunities.
- Provide information about job opportunities.
- Provide information about health programs.
- Provide information about community involvement.
- Use a picture for the background of the content and allow for the picture to be changed periodically.

You will develop the Web site for Katie. The Web site will be a preliminary version and the content for each page is under development.

1. Create a new document 500 pixels wide by 300 pixels high, use a blue (#0099FF) for the background color, and then save the document as **RDAmain.fla** in the Tutorial.07\Case4 folder included with your Data Files.
2. Draw a rectangle to cover all of the Stage. Use the gray radial gradient for the rectangle's fill and do not include a stroke. Make the rectangle 500 pixels wide by 300 pixels high. Use the Align options to align it with the Stage. Rename Layer 1 as **Rectangle** and lock the layer.
3. Insert a new layer and name it **Title**. On the Title layer, create a text block centered at the top of the Stage. Use Arial for the font, 32 for the font size, and white for the text color. Apply the Bold attribute and use the Align Left alignment. Type **Regional Dietetic Association** in the text block.

4. Create a new button symbol named **Development button**. In the Up frame of the Development button, draw a small oval at the center of the Stage. Use a light blue color (#66FFFF) for the fill and use a black solid stroke with a height of 1. Make the oval 50 pixels wide by 30 pixels high. Convert the small oval into a movie clip symbol named **Oval**.
5. Create a new movie clip symbol named **Animated oval**. Add an instance of the Oval symbol to the center of the Stage for the Animated oval symbol. Insert a keyframe at Frame 5 and another one at Frame 10. Use the Transform panel to increase the width of the oval in Frame 5 by 120%. The height should remain the same. Create motion tweens at Frame 1 and at Frame 5. The oval's width increases through Frame 5, and then decreases back to its original size in Frame 10.
6. Edit the Development button, insert a blank keyframe in its Over frame, and then drag an instance of the Animated oval symbol in the Over frame and make certain it is centered on the Stage.
7. Insert a new layer in the Development button Timeline and name it **Text**. Add a text block in the Up frame of the Text layer that is centered over the oval. Use Garamond for the font, 14 for the font size, black for the text color, and Align Center for the alignment. Do not apply the bold attribute. Type **Development Opportunities** with each word on a separate line in the text block. The text will extend outside the outline of the oval.

EXPLORE

8. Insert a keyframe in the Over frame of the Text layer and then apply the bold attribute to the Development Opportunities text. Insert a blank keyframe in the Hit frame of the Text layer. Use onion skinning to see the contents of all the frames, and then draw a rectangle in the Hit frame to cover both the oval and the text.
9. Make three duplicates of the Development button, and name the duplicate buttons **Jobs button**, **Health button**, and **Community button**, respectively. Change the text in both the Up and Over frames of the Jobs button to **Job Opportunities**, keeping each word on separate lines. If necessary, change the size of the rectangle in the Hit frame of the Text button to cover all of the text.
10. Change the text in the Health button to **Health Programs**, placing each word on a separate line. Change the text in the Community button to **Community Involvement**, placing each word on a separate line. Be certain to change the text in the Up and Over frames for both buttons and, if necessary, resize the rectangle in the Hit frames of each button to cover both the text and the oval.
11. Create a new movie clip symbol named **Navbar**. In the Navbar symbol, drag an instance of the Development button to the left side of the Stage, and then drag instances of the Jobs button, Health button, and Community button to the Stage, placing each one to the right of the previous button instance. Align them by using the Property inspector to set each instance's X and Y coordinates as follows: Development button (X=–135, Y=25), Jobs button (X=–55, Y=–15), Health button (X=55, Y=–15), Community button (X=135, Y=25).
12. Select the Development button in the Navbar, open the Actions panel, and add a `loadMovieNum` action so that when the button is clicked and then released, the Development.swf file loads at level 1 of the Flash Player. Add `loadMovieNum` actions to the other button instances to load SWF files at level 1. The Jobs button should load the Jobs.swf file. The Health button should load the Health.swf file. The Community button should load the Community.swf file.
13. Return to Scene 1, drag an instance of the Navbar symbol to the Stage, and center it right below the text title.

14. Insert a new layer and name it **Action**. Add a `loadMovieNum` action at Frame 1 of the Action layer that loads the Development.swf file at level 1 as soon as Frame 1 is played.
15. Create a new document to save as a template. Make the document 500 pixels wide by 300 pixels high. Use a blue (#0099FF) for the background color.
16. Create a new movie clip symbol named **Picture**. Leave the movie clip symbol empty, and drag an instance of it to the Scene 1 Stage. Set its X and Y coordinates to 100 and assign the name **Picture_mc** to the instance. Rename Layer 1 as **Background picture**.
17. Insert a new layer and name it **Picture mask**. On this layer, draw an oval. Use black for the fill and do not include a stroke. Make the oval 300 pixels wide by 200 pixels high. Use the Info panel to select the center point for the oval's registration point. Then set its X coordinate to 250 and its Y coordinate to 200. The oval should be centered in the lower part of the Stage.
18. Change the Picture mask layer to a mask layer. Make certain the Background picture layer is masked. The oval disappears when the layers are locked.
19. Insert a new layer and name it **Action**. Add a Load Graphic behavior to Frame 1 of the Action layer. The behavior should load the background.jpg file into the Picture_mc movie clip. When the SWF file is played, the background picture loads into the Picture_mc movie clip. The area of the picture covered by the oval mask is displayed.
20. Insert a new layer and name it **Content**. Add a horizontal guide about 130 pixels from the top edge of the Stage, and a vertical guide at about 100 pixels from the left edge of the Stage, and then add another vertical guide about 400 pixels from the left edge of the Stage.
21. Save the document as a template with the name **RDATemplate** in a new template category called **RDA**, using the following description: **Template to be used for Regional Dietetic Association Web site**. Close the RDATemplate.fla file.
22. Create a new document based on the RDATemplate and save the document as **Development.fla** in the Tutorial.07\Case4 folder included with your Data Files. Add a text block on the Content layer, placing the text block on the Stage below the horizontal guide and between the vertical guides. Use Garamond for the font, 24 for the font size, and black for the text color. Apply the Bold attribute and use Align Left. Type **Development Opportunities** in the text block.
23. Create a new document based on the RDATemplate and save the document as **Jobs.fla** in the Tutorial.07\Case4 folder. Add a text block on the Content layer, placing the text block on the Stage below the horizontal guide and between the vertical guides. Use the same font text attributes as in Step 22, and then type **Job Opportunities** in the text block.
24. Create two new documents based on the RDATemplate. Save one as **Health.fla** and the other as **Community.fla** in the Tutorial.07\Case4 folder. For each document, add a text block on the Stage, keeping it below the horizontal guide and between the vertical guides. Use the same text attributes as in Step 22. For the Health.fla document, type **Health Programs** in the text block and for the Community.fla document, type **Community Involvement** in the text block.
25. Save and publish each of the documents to create the **Development.swf**, **Jobs.swf**, **Health.swf**, and **Community.swf** files. Return to the RDAmain.fla document and test the Web site using the Test Movie command. Test each of the buttons and verify that the individual pages are loaded. Make any necessary corrections.
26. Submit the finished files to your instructor, either in printed or electronic form, as requested.

Review | Quick Check Answers

Session 7.1

1. XHTML or HTML
2. levels
3. False. When an SWF file is loaded at the same level that already has an SWF file playing, the new SWF file replaces the file that is currently playing.
4. Identify the goals and objectives for the Web site based on the needs of the client. Based on the goals and objectives, develop the content of the site. The content leads to the design of the Web pages, including the navigation system. Finally, build the site and test it to make sure all parts of the site work as designed.
5. by meeting with the clients and discussing what they want the site to accomplish
6. a diagram showing a sketch of how all of the site's pages are organized with lines indicating how each page links to the other pages

Session 7.2

1. a prebuilt document that installs with Flash and provides a way to quickly develop a new Flash document
2. to add instances from the external library to the library of the current document
3. rollover
4. True
5. hyperlinks
6. Create a separate movie clip with an animation, and then place an instance of the movie clip in the Over frame of the button's Timeline.

Session 7.3

1. a programming language within Flash that allows you to add actions to objects or frames in your document
2. `loadMovieNum("Staff.swf", 1);`
3. determines what action to take when a specific button event occurs
4. the Check Syntax button
5. the `loadMovie` action
6. name

Ending Data Files

Tutorial.07 →

Tutorial

- AC_RunActiveContent.js
- Home.fla
- Home.swf
- Main.fla
- Main.html
- Main.swf
- photo1.jpg
- photo2.jpg
- Photos.fla
- Photos.swf
- Services.fla
- Services.swf
- Teams.fla
- Teams.swf

Review

- AC_RunActiveContent.js
- JSPhotos.fla
- JSPhotos.swf
- MainPage.fla
- MainPage.html
- MainPage.swf
- picture1.jpg
- picture2.jpg
- Specials.fla
- Specials.swf

Case1

- AC_RunActiveContent.js
- Classes.fla
- Classes.swf
- Retreats.fla
- Retreats.swf
- SSSmain.fla
- SSSmain.html
- SSSmain.swf
- Supplies.fla
- Supplies.swf
- Welcome.fla
- Welcome.swf

Case2

- Home.fla
- Home.swf
- Instruments.fla
- Instruments.swf
- RCMmain.fla
- RCMain.swf
- RCMTemplate.fla
- Recital.fla
- Recital.swf
- Sheet.fla
- Sheet.swf

Case3

- flower1.jpg
- flower2.jpg
- ivy1.jpg
- Nursery.fla
- Nursery.swf
- Photos.fla
- Photos.swf
- WCmain.fla
- WCmain.swf

Case4

- background.jpg
- Community.fla
- Community.swf
- Development.fla
- Development.swf
- Health.fla
- Health.swf
- Jobs.fla
- Jobs.swf
- RDAmain.fla
- RDAmain.swf
- RDATemplate.fla

Objectives

Session 8.1
- Review the basics of ActionScript programming
- Compare ActionScript 2.0 and ActionScript 3.0
- Learn ActionScript 3.0 syntax
- Write ActionScript 3.0 code to create functions and handle events

Session 8.2
- Create links to external Web sites
- Create and test a Flash preloader

Session 8.3
- Create input and dynamic text fields
- Create an input form

Programming with ActionScript 3.0

Adding Interactive Elements to a Flash Web Site

Case | Admiral Web Design

Dan Jackson, owner of Jackson's Sports, meets with Aly and Chris and requests additional pages for the Jackson's Sports Web site. He wants a Resources page, which will contain hyperlinks to other sports-related Web sites. He also wants a page that team coaches can use to calculate the cost of team jerseys by entering the number of jerseys needed and choosing from various options to calculate and display the total cost.

Aly and Chris revise the design of the Jackson's Sports Web site. You will add the requested pages as well as a simple animation that will provide visual feedback while the site contents load into the Flash Player.

In this tutorial, you will learn how to use ActionScript 3.0 to add interactive elements to Flash documents. You will learn about the structure and syntax of the ActionScript programming language. You will write ActionScript code to control the navigation for the Web site, to create links to other Web sites, to input values, and to perform calculations.

Starting Data Files

Tutorial.08 →

Tutorial	Review	Case1	Case2	Case3	Case4
SportsWeb.fla	SoftballSite.fla	ScrapbookSite.fla	guitars.jpg piano.jpg SpecialsPage.fla trumpets.jpg	RevPhotos.fla flower1.jpg flower2.jpg flower3.jpg	Calories.fla

Session 8.1

Programming with ActionScript 3.0

ActionScript is a robust programming language that gives Flash developers an almost unlimited number of ways to make a Flash document interactive. ActionScript can be used to create actions to control multimedia elements such as buttons, and to control the way the different parts of a movie are played. Programming in ActionScript requires writing scripts that consist of actions, event handlers, and other programming statements to control how the actions are executed. In previous tutorials, you added actions to buttons that controlled animations in movies and controlled when and how an SWF file was loaded into the Flash Player.

In addition to controlling the order in which frames play in a document's Timeline or making buttons operational, ActionScript can be used to enable the viewer to input data, and then have the Flash Player process the data to return a result. ActionScript can also be used to change the properties of movie clips while they play in the Flash Player. For example, you can have a movie clip such as a graphic of a car that changes color when a button is clicked. With ActionScript, you can also test a condition and then execute different actions based on the result of the test. For example, you can create a script that compares an input value with a set value to determine what actions to execute.

In this tutorial, you will write ActionScript code to control multimedia elements, access external Web pages, and provide the user a means of entering and processing information in the Jackson's Sports Web site.

Comparing ActionScript 3.0 and ActionScript 2.0

ActionScript 3.0 is the latest version of the ActionScript programming language and is conceptually different from the previous version, ActionScript 2.0, that you used in earlier tutorials. ActionScript 3.0 has many more capabilities than ActionScript 2.0 and is designed to enable Flash developers to create highly complex applications. The Flash Player 9 plug-in uses the **ActionScript Virtual Machine 2 (AVM2)**, which is the Flash Player built-in code that plays Flash movies. Previous versions of the Flash Player use the original ActionScript Virtual Machine (AVM1). Improvements in the new AVM2 enable Flash Player 9 to run faster and more efficiently than previous versions. ActionScript 3.0 code will not run on the AVM1, so Flash movies using ActionScript 3.0 will run only on Flash Player 9 or later.

Tip

You can still run SWF files that contain ActionScript 2.0 or earlier in Flash Player 9.

In a previous tutorial, you used ActionScript 2.0 to create an event handler assigned to a button instance. The event handler carried out an action such as stopping or playing a movie when the button was clicked and then released. In ActionScript 3.0, you cannot add actions to a button instance. You also cannot add actions to movie clip instances. Instead, you add the actions to frames in the Timeline.

Working with Objects and Properties

ActionScript is used to control and modify objects. An **object** is an element in Flash that has **properties**, which are characteristics, that can be examined or changed with ActionScript. The multimedia elements you work with in Flash, such as buttons, movie clips, and text blocks, are considered objects. For example, a button has properties such as its width, height, and location on the Stage. An instance of a movie clip symbol has similar properties. ActionScript code can be written to read or change these properties in response to certain events, such as a mouse click, a key press, or when a certain frame in the Timeline is played. One example of a property for an object is alpha, which represents the transparency of a movie clip. Other properties include rotation, which controls the orientation of a movie clip, and visible, which controls the visibility of a movie clip. These properties can be examined and modified using ActionScript.

Referring to objects in ActionScript requires that you assign names to them. Recall that you can have multiple instances of one movie clip symbol, which means that multiple objects are based on one symbol. When using ActionScript to refer to a specific instance, you must refer to its instance name.

After you assign a name to an instance, you can refer to it in the action using dot notation. **Dot notation** links an object to its properties and methods. (Methods are discussed later in this session.) For example, if a movie clip instance has the name circle_mc, the code to change the alpha property of the instance to 30% is circle_mc.alpha = .30. The values for an object's alpha property range from 0 to 1, where 1 represents 100%. The dot (.) links the property to the particular instance or object.

Naming Objects Effectively | InSight

When naming an instance of an object, you should include a suffix that identifies the object's type. Flash recognizes the _mc suffix for movie clip instances, the _btn suffix for button instances, and the _txt suffix for text field instances. Although you are not required to use these suffixes, doing so takes advantage of code hints in the Actions panel. When entering ActionScript code, Flash displays code hints based on what is typed. For example, if you assign the name circle_mc to a movie clip instance on the Stage, and then use the name in the Actions panel, Flash displays code hints specific to movie clips. As you type the first few letters after the dot, the matching code is highlighted in the code hints list. The highlighted code is added to the script when you press the Enter key. This makes it easier to enter the correct code and avoid typing mistakes.

Aly and Chris have sketched a storyboard showing the design of the Jackson's Sports Web site, as shown in Figure 8-1. The sketch shows the new pages to be completed as well as the navigation of the site.

Jackson's Sports Web site storyboard | **Figure 8-1**

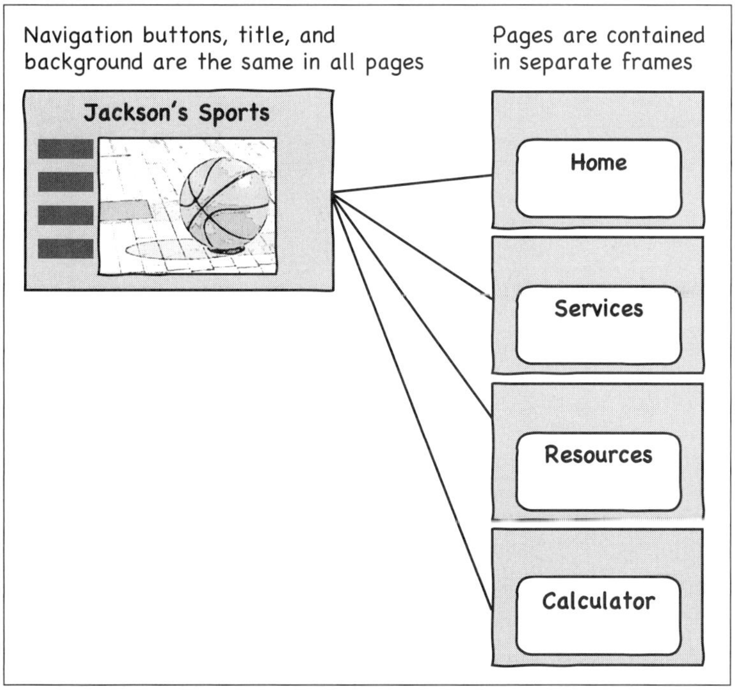

Aly asks you to review the new Jackson's Sports Web site that she and Chris created and assign names to the objects representing the buttons for the site's navigation. You will also extend the Timeline of the document to add the Resources and Calculator pages.

To preview the Jackson's Sports Web site, name the button objects, and extend the Timeline:

1. Open the **SportsWeb.fla** file located in the **Tutorial.08\Tutorial** folder included with your Data Files, save the file as **JacksonsWebSite.fla** in the same folder, and then change the workspace to its default layout. The first frame displays the content for the Web site that will be used later in this tutorial.
2. In the Timeline, move the playhead to **Frame 10**, if necessary, to display the Home page for the Web site on the Stage, and then, in the Timeline, move the playhead to **Frame 20** to display the Services page for the Web site. Each Web page in the site will be in a separate frame.
3. In the Tools panel, click the **Selection** tool, and then, on the Stage, click the **Home** button to select it. The name of the Home button instance, home_btn, appears in the Instance Name box in the Property inspector. You will assign similar names to the other button instances. See Figure 8-2.

Figure 8-2 Home button instance name

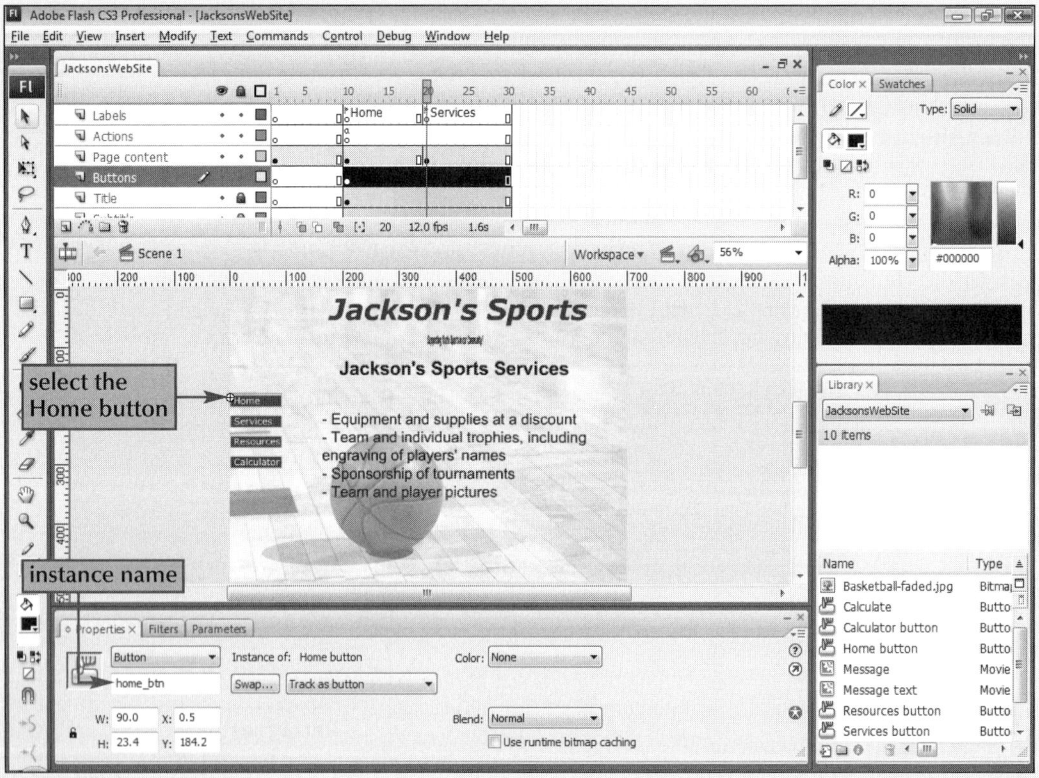

4. On the Stage, click the **Services** button to select it, and then, in the Instance Name box of the Property inspector, type **services_btn** and press the **Enter** key. The name services_btn is assigned to the Services button instance.
5. Repeat Step 4 to assign the instance name **resources_btn** to the Resources button instance and to assign the instance name **calculator_btn** to the Calculator button instance.

6. In the Timeline, insert regular frames at **Frame 50** of all the layers, and then, in the Labels layer, insert keyframes at **Frame 30** and **Frame 40**.

7. In the Labels layer, select **Frame 30**, and then, in the Frame Label box of the Property inspector, type **Resources** and press the **Enter** key. The Resources frame label appears in the Timeline next to Frame 30 of the Labels layer.

8. In the Labels layer, select **Frame 40**, and then, in the Frame Label box of the Property inspector, type **Calculator** and press the **Enter** key. The Calculator frame label appears in the Timeline next to Frame 40 of the Labels layer. Each frame that will contain content for the site's pages is labeled. See Figure 8-3.

Figure 8-3 Timeline with labels for the pages

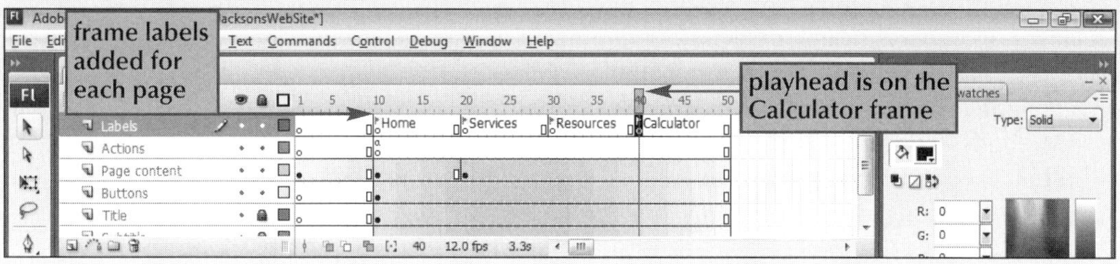

9. In the Page content layer, insert a keyframe at **Frame 30**, and then, on the Stage, replace the Jackson's Sports Services text with **Sports Web Site Resources** and delete the large text block in the center of the Stage. You will add the page content later in this tutorial.

10. In the Page content layer, insert a keyframe at **Frame 40**, and then, in this frame, replace the Sports Web Site Resources text with **Team Jersey Calculator**. See Figure 8-4.

Figure 8-4 Content for the Calculator page

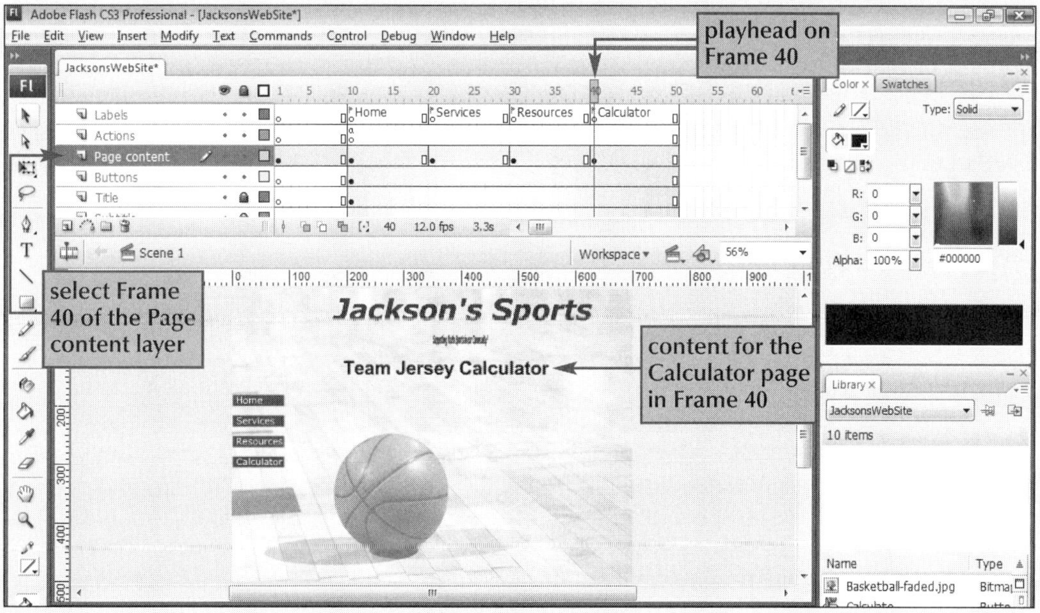

Using Actions, Methods, and Functions

An action is a statement, such as `gotoAndStop()`, that instructs an SWF file to do something. The terms *action* and *statement* are often interchangeable.

Functions are blocks of statements that process information and return a value or perform some action. Flash includes a number of prebuilt functions, such as the `trace()` function, which displays values in the Output panel and the `math.Random()` function, which returns a random number. You can also create your own functions. For example, you can create a function that accepts the temperature value in Fahrenheit degrees and returns the value in Celsius degrees. Then you can **call**, or execute, the function from different parts of the script in which it is defined. To use a function, you need to know what value or values to send to it and what value or values to expect in return. The values you send to a function are called **parameters**, or arguments, and are enclosed in parentheses. For example, the text "You are here" in the action `trace ("You are here")` is a parameter of the function. Not all functions require parameters. For example, the `math.Random()` function requires no parameters, so nothing is enclosed in the parentheses.

Methods are functions specific to a particular object. They are built-in capabilities of the object that perform certain actions or respond to certain events. Methods are similar to other functions and actions, but they are part of an object and can be used to control the object. For example, if you have a movie clip instance named circle_mc in the document's main Timeline that has 20 frames in its own Timeline, you can control which of the 20 frames will play. You do this with the `gotoAndPlay()` method for the movie clip. Using dot notation, you code the object name followed by a dot followed by the method's name. The following code tells the movie clip instance to start playing at Frame 10 of its Timeline:

```
circle_mc.gotoAndPlay(10)
```

The parameter value of 10 in the parentheses specifies to which frame the playhead will go. Because `gotoAndPlay()` is a method of the movie clip object, the movie clip knows how to respond when the method is executed. The `gotoAndPlay()` method is also considered an action in the main Timeline because the main document is considered an object. When using the `gotoAndPlay()` method for the document's main Timeline, it is not necessary to specify an object name.

The Jackson's Sports Web site will use functions to move the playhead to a specific frame in the Timeline by referring to frame labels. For example, the `gotoAndStop("Home")` action will move the playhead to the frame labeled Home. The label is displayed in the Timeline in the Labels layer. In the case of the Jackson's Sports Web site, Frame 10 contains the home page for the site. The content of each page of the Web site will be in a separate frame and will be referred to by its label.

Writing ActionScript Code

When writing ActionScript code, you need to follow certain rules, which are also known as the **syntax** of the language. As shown in previous examples, actions and functions are often written in mixed uppercase and lowercase. For example, the `gotoAndPlay()` function uses the uppercase letters A and P, whereas the remainder of the letters are lowercase. Because ActionScript is case sensitive, writing this function as `gotoandplay()`, with all lowercase letters, will generate an error message. Also, even though most statements work without an ending semicolon, it's good programming practice to include it. Ending the statements with a semicolon follows the format of other programming languages. Other required syntactical elements are parentheses, which are used to group arguments in methods and functions, and curly braces, which group a block of related statements together. Figure 8-5 shows a sample ActionScript syntax.

Sample ActionScript syntax **Figure 8-5**

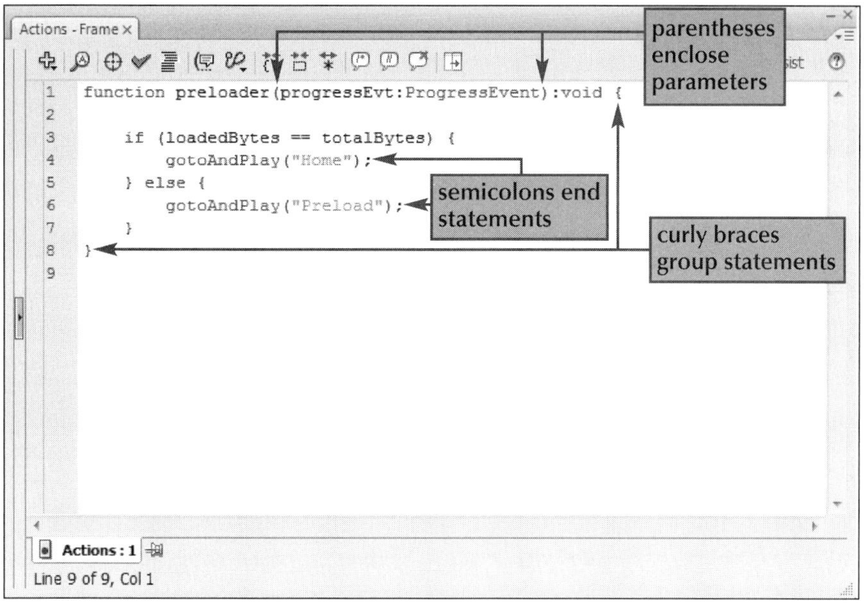

You'll review the actions in Frame 10 of the Actions layer of the Jackson's Sports Web site.

To review the actions in Frame 10 of the Actions layer of the Jackson's Sports Web site:

1. In the Timeline, click **Frame 10** of the Actions layer. The *a* at the top of the frame indicates that the frame contains an action.
2. Click **Window** on the menu bar, and then click **Actions**. The Actions panel opens and displays a script.
3. If necessary, click the **collapse** button in the vertical bar between the Actions toolbox and the Script pane. The Actions toolbox collapses and the Script pane expands. See Figure 8-6.

Figure 8-6 Script for Frame 10 of the Actions layer

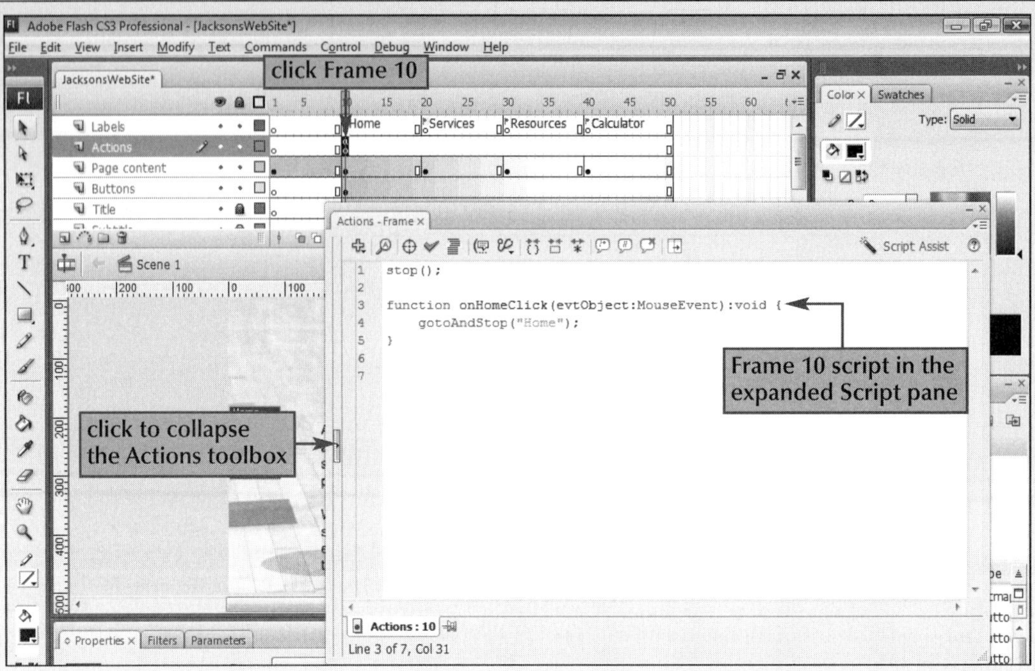

Tip

You can also double-click the vertical bar between the Actions toolbox and the Script pane to collapse or expand the Actions toolbox.

The first line of the Actions panel contains `stop();` which will stop the playhead on Frame 10 to prevent the movie from playing continuously. The third line contains `function onHomeClick(evtObject:MouseEvent):void {` which defines the onHomeClick function.

To define a function, you use the function keyword followed by the function name. A **keyword**, also called a reserved word, is a word that has a specified use or meaning in ActionScript and cannot be used in another context in a statement. The function name is a user-defined name and should be unique. The name should not start with a number, but it can include letters, numbers, the underscore character, and the dollar sign character. Within the parentheses following the function name, you specify the parameter of the function, which in this case is an event object with the user-defined name of evtObject. An **event object** represents an actual event such as the clicking of the mouse button and contains information about the event such as its properties. The event object must be assigned an event type—in this case, MouseEvent. Object types are coded using a colon character and followed by the type identifier. The event type, MouseEvent, distinguishes evtObject from other types of events.

InSight | Using a Standard Naming Convention

When assigning names to objects such as functions, variables, movie clips, and buttons, you should use a mixed case format where the first letter of the name is lowercase and the first letter each word that is part of the name is capitalized. This naming convention makes it easier to read names within the ActionScript code and is consistent with other programming languages.

A function can return a value, such as the result of a calculation, based on the actions in the function. The results of the function, such as a return value, must also be assigned a data type. If the function does not return a value, then you code the void keyword after the colon character to indicate no value is returned. The statements in a function must be enclosed in curly braces. In this case, the curly braces enclose the statement `gotoAndStop("Home");` which is the action to be performed when the function is called. Functions can include multiple statements, but this function requires only one statement. When the onHomeClick functions is called, the playhead will move to the frame labeled *Home* and the movie will stop playing. The function structure is shown in Figure 8-7.

Figure 8-7 **Structure of the onHomeClick function**

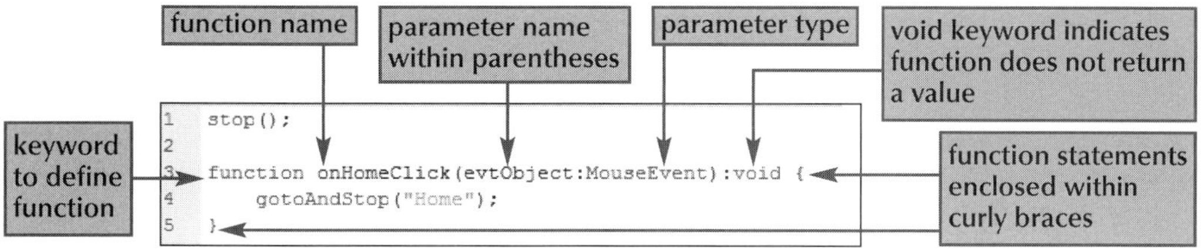

You will write similar functions to move the playhead to each of the frames representing the Web pages of the document.

To add new functions for the Jackson's Sports Web site:

1. In the Actions panel, click on line 6 below the closing curly brace, and then type the following lines of code exactly as shown to create a function that moves the playhead to the Services page:

```
function onServicesClick(evtObject:MouseEvent):void {
      gotoAndStop("Services");
}
```

2. Press the **Enter** key after the closing curly brace to move the insertion point to a blank line, and then type the following lines of code exactly as shown to create functions that move the playhead to the Resources page and the Calculator page:

```
function onResourcesClick(evtObject:MouseEvent):void {
      gotoAndStop("Resources");
}
function onCalculatorClick(evtObject:MouseEvent):void {
      gotoAndStop("Calculator");
}
```

   The functions have been added to the Script pane. You will check the code for syntax errors.

> **Tip**
>
> You can also copy and paste the code and then edit the pasted code to add the additional functions.

3. In the Actions panel, click the **Check syntax** button to check for syntax errors in the code you entered. A dialog box opens, indicating whether the script contains errors.

4. Click the **OK** button. The dialog box closes. The error-free functions appear in the Script pane. See Figure 8-8.

Figure 8-8 Functions added to Script pane

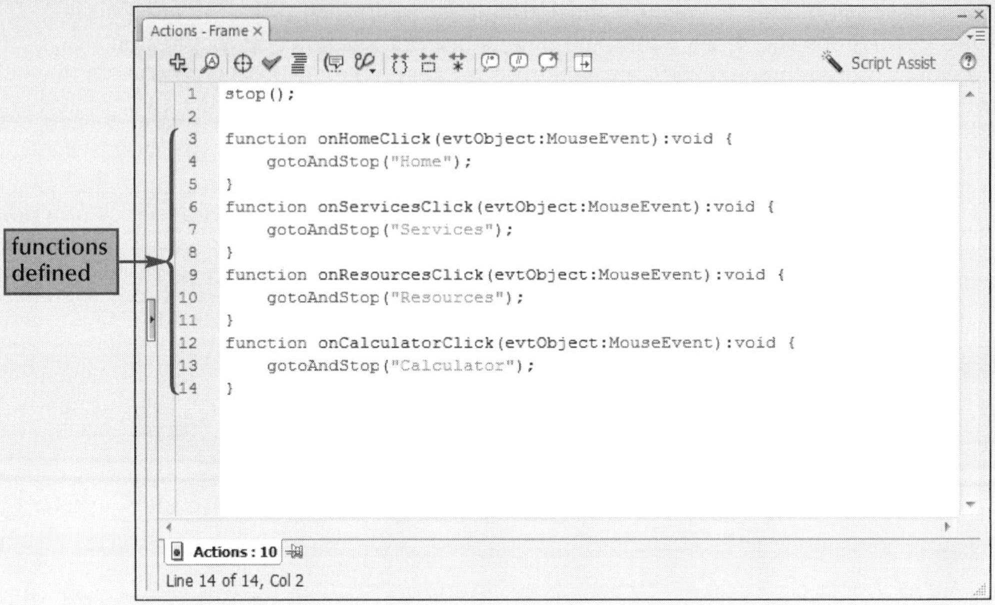

Trouble? If the script contains errors, there are probably typing errors in the functions. If the Compiler Errors panel is hidden behind the Actions panel, click the Actions panel title bar to collapse the panel. In the Compiler Errors panel, review the error message(s), and then close the panel. Click the Actions panel title bar to expand the Actions panel, compare the code in the Actions panel with the code shown in Figure 8-8, and then make the necessary corrections so that your code matches the code in the figure. Repeat Steps 3 and 4 until your code is error-free.

Adding Events and Event Handling

Events are things that happen when a movie is playing, such as when the user clicks a button or presses a key. ActionScript can respond to or handle an event by carrying out instructions based on the event. The code to respond to or handle events consists of three elements: the event source, the event, and the response. The **event source**, also known as the event target, is the object to which the event will happen, such as a button instance. The event is the thing that will happen to the object, such as a button click or a key press. The **response** is the steps that are performed when the event occurs. The Action-Script code you write to handle events must include these three elements.

Creating an Event Listener

In the Jackson's Sports Web site, clicking a button with the mouse is the event that will control which function is called. If the Home button is clicked, for example, then the onHomeClick function should be called to move the playhead to the Home frame. To call a function when a button is clicked, you need to create an event listener. An **event listener** is a method that the Flash Player executes in response to specific events. All objects that have events have an event listener.

To create an event listener, you first create a function to be called in response to an event, as you did in the previous steps. Then you use the object's `addEventListener()` method to establish a connection between the function, such as onHomeClick, and the event source, such as the home_btn instance. The `addEventListener()` method registers the function to be called with the event source to listen for a specified event. When the event occurs, the Flash Player can respond by calling the associated function. The `addEventListener()` method has two parameters: the event to listen for and the function to call when the event happens. The code for the event listener for the home_btn is:

```
home_btn.addEventListener(MouseEvent.CLICK, onHomeClick);
```

This code contains the three elements required to respond to an event. The event source is the home_btn, which is the instance name of the Home button, the event is CLICK, which is a property of the MouseEvent object and represents the clicking of the mouse, and the response is the call to the onHomeClick function. The `addEventListener()` method is called to register the onHomeClick function with the button instance. The code structure is shown in Figure 8-9.

Figure 8-9 Format of an event listener

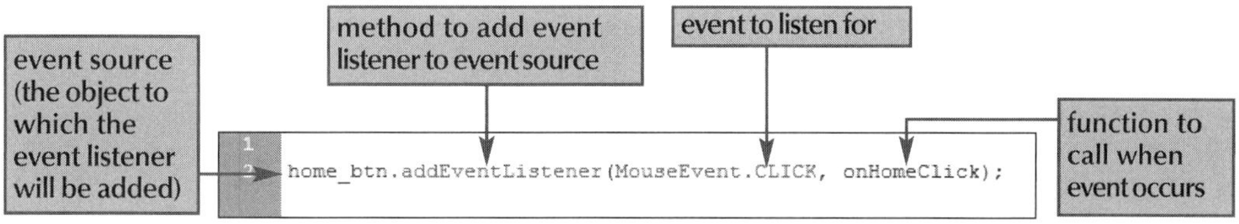

You will add the event listener code to register the functions with the mouse click event for the button instances.

To add the event listener code to the script:

1. In the Actions panel, place the insertion point after the closing curly brace at the bottom of the script, and then press the **Enter** key to move the insertion point to beginning of line 15. You'll enter the event listener code, starting on line 15.
2. Type the following line of code exactly as shown for the first part of the event listener for the Home button, as shown in Figure 8-10:

   `home_btn.addE`

   After you typed the dot, the list of code hints opened, and scrolled to first method that begins with the next letters you typed. In this case, the `addEventListener` method is selected in the code hints list.

Figure 8-10 `addEventListener` **method selected in the code hints list**

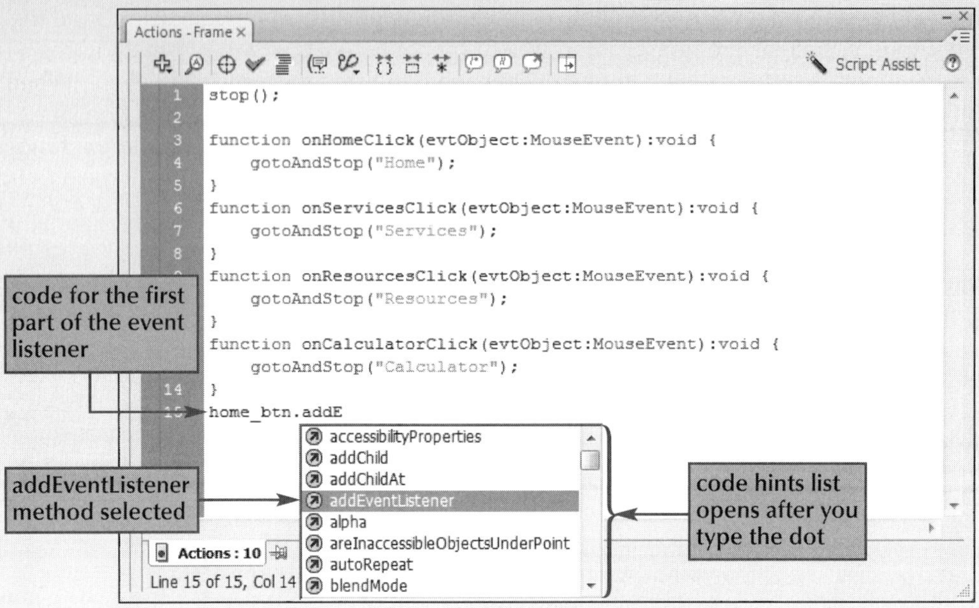

3. Press the **Enter** key. The rest of the `addEventListener` method name is added to the script.

> **Tip**
> You can also double-click the desired code in the code hints list to add the code to the script.

4. Type the following code for the event listener exactly as shown below, and then press the **Enter** key to insert a new line:

```
MouseEvent.CLICK, onHomeClick);
```

The complete code for the Home button event listener is `home_btn.addEvent (MouseEvent.CLICK. onHomeClick);`. Parentheses are not included for the onHomeClick function when it is used as a parameter in the `addEventListener` method.

5. Type the following lines of code exactly as shown to create the event listeners for the other buttons, pressing the **Enter** key after each line.

```
services_btn.addEventListener(MouseEvent.CLICK, onServicesClick);
resources_btn.addEventListener(MouseEvent.CLICK, onResourcesClick);
calculator_btn.addEventListener(MouseEvent.CLICK,
onCalculatorClick);
```

6. In the Actions panel, click the **Check syntax** button ✔ to check for syntax errors in the code you entered. A dialog box opens, indicating whether the script contains errors.

7. Click the **OK** button to close the dialog box. The error-free functions appear in the Script pane.

   Trouble? If the script contains errors, there are probably typing errors in the code. If the Compiler Errors panel is hidden behind the Actions panel, click the Actions panel title bar to collapse the panel. In the Compiler Errors panel, review the error message(s), and then close the panel. Click the Actions panel title bar to expand the Actions panel, compare the code in the Actions panel with the code shown in Steps 4 and 5, and then make the necessary corrections so that your code matches the code. Repeat Steps 6 and 7 until your code is error-free.

8. Save the document. You will test the Jackson's Sports Web site.

9. Click **Control** on the menu bar, and then click **Test Movie**. The movie opens in a Flash Player window. The Loading text appears briefly, and then the Home page opens.
10. Click the **Services** button to display the Services page, click the **Resources** button to display the Resources page, click the **Calculator** button to display the Calculator page, and then click the **Home** button to display the Home page.
11. Close the Flash Player window and return to the document.

Adding Comments

As scripts get longer and more complex, comments become increasingly helpful. **Comments** are notes within the ActionScript code that explain what is happening. Comments do not cause any actions to be performed and are not necessary for the actions to work. However, they are very useful to the programmer writing the code and to other programmers who might later modify the code. Single line comments are indicated by two forward slashes (//). Any text after the slashes in the same line is not interpreted by the Flash Player. Comments that span multiple lines are enclosed with the /* and */ characters.

You will add comments to the script in the Jackson's Sports Web site document.

To add comments to the Jackson's Sports Web site script:

1. In the Actions panel, place the insertion point to the left of `stop();` on the first line, and then type the following code, pressing the **Enter** key after each line to create a multiple-line comment.

```
/* ActionScript code to make the buttons in the
Jackson's Sports Web site functional.
The first action will stop the playhead to
keep it from advancing automatically */
```

2. Press the **Enter** key to add a blank line between the comment and the first line of code.
3. In the Actions panel, place the insertion point to the left of the word function on line 8 (which contains the onHomeClick function), type the following code, and then press the **Enter** key to create a single-line comment:

```
// These functions control the site's navigation
```

4. In the Actions panel, place the insertion point to the left of the home_btn on line 21 (which defines the first event listener), type the following code, and then press the **Enter** key to create a single-line comment.

```
// This code creates the event listeners
```

5. Save the document. See Figure 8-11.

Figure 8-11 Comments added to the script

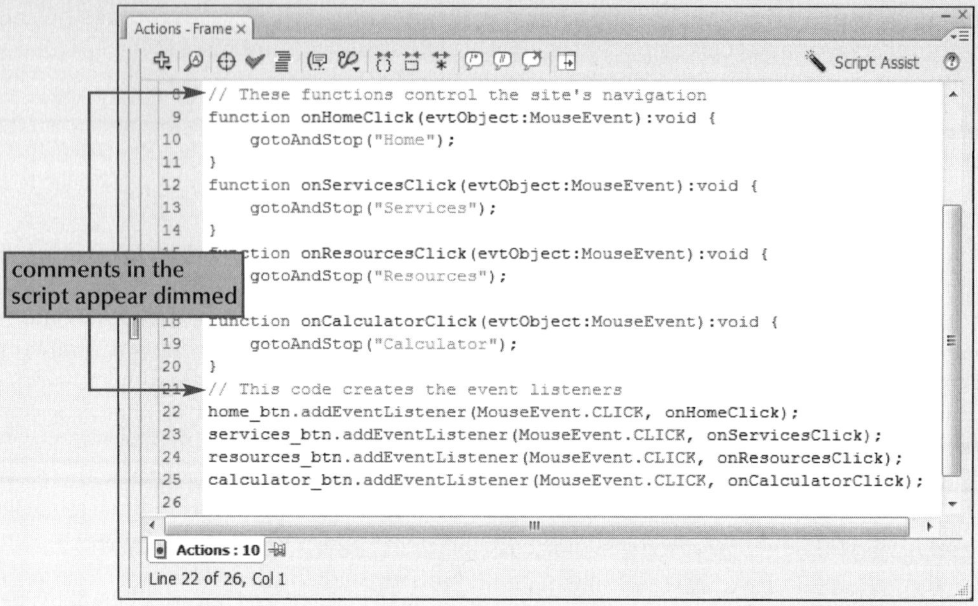

6. Close the Actions panel.

In this session, you learned the basic components and rules for the ActionScript programming language. You learned about actions, functions, methods, and event listeners. You entered code to make the Jackson's Sports Web site's navigation operational. In the next session, you will write ActionScript code for the two new pages that will be added to the Jackson's Sports Web site.

Review | Session 8.1 Quick Check

1. What is ActionScript?
2. True or False? In ActionScript 3.0, you can add code to a button instance to handle mouse events.
3. A(n) ________________ is an element in Flash that has properties or characteristics that can be examined or changed with ActionScript.
4. What is the advantage of adding suffixes to movie clip and button instance names?
5. Write the expression to change the alpha property of the Car_mc instance to 50.
6. What three programming elements are needed to respond to or handle events?
7. Why should you add comments to ActionScript code?

Session 8.2

Creating Links to Web Sites

Dan Jackson wants the Resources page of the Jackson's Sports Web site to include three links to Web sites on the Internet that might be of interest to his clients. A Flash document can include links in the form of buttons or movie clips that use ActionScript to direct the Flash Player to open the specified Web site. You will complete the Resources page by creating buttons that represent links to the external Web sites and adding the corresponding ActionScript code. When the viewer clicks a button, a browser window will open, displaying an external Web site.

You will start by creating three buttons and assigning names to the button instances on the Stage.

To add button instances to the Resources page:

1. If you took a break after the previous session, make sure the JacksonsWebSite.fla document is open, the workspace is set to its default layout, and the Actions panel is closed.
2. In the Timeline, click **Frame 30** of the Page content layer, and then deselect the title text. The Page content layer is where you will create the buttons for the Resources page.
3. In the Tools panel, click the **Text** tool, set the font to **Arial**, set the font size to **20**, set the text color to **black**, select the **Align Left** alignment, deselect the **Bold** attribute, create a text block below the title about **200** pixels from the top edge of the Stage and about **250** pixels from the left edge of the Stage, and then type **US Youth Soccer Online** in the text block.
4. In the Tools panel, click the **Selection** tool. The text block remains selected.
5. Click **Modify** on the menu bar, click **Convert to Symbol** to open the Convert to Symbol dialog box, type **USSoccer** in the Name box, click the **Button** option button, and then click the **OK** button. The text block is converted to a button symbol.
6. On the Edit bar, click the **Edit Symbols** button, and then click **USSoccer**. The symbol opens in symbol-editing mode.
7. In the Timeline, insert a keyframe in the Over frame, select the **US Youth Soccer Online** text, and then, in the Property inspector, click the **Bold** button **B**. The text is bolded, providing visual feedback when the user moves the pointer over the button.

   Next, you will draw a rectangle over the text block in the Hit frame to make it easier for the viewer to click the button. Otherwise, the viewer would have to move the pointer directly over a letter to activate the button.
8. Insert a keyframe in the Hit frame, click the **Rectangle** tool in the Tools panel, and then draw a rectangle with a black fill that is 90 pixels wide by 20 pixels high to cover the text block. See Figure 8-12.

Figure 8-12 **Rectangle in the button's Hit frame**

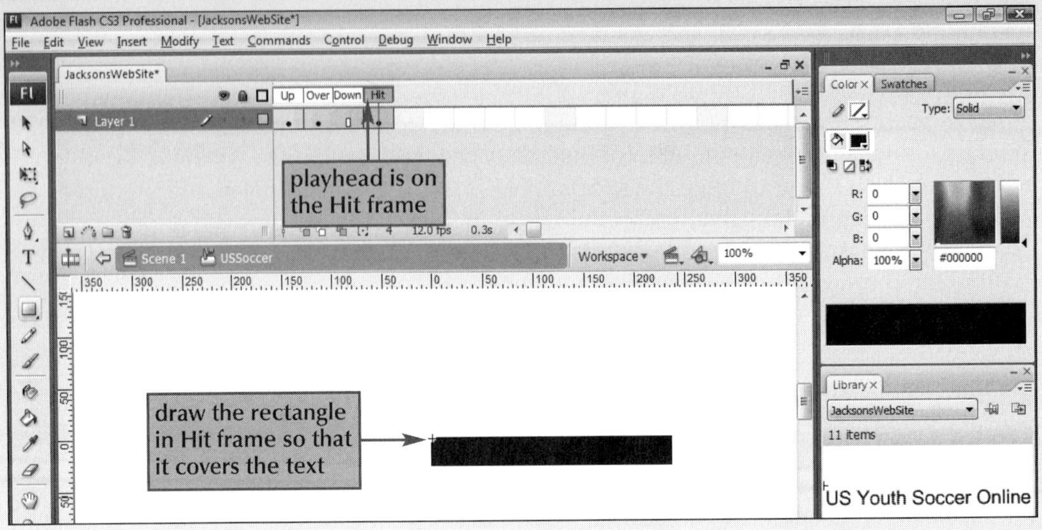

9. On the Edit bar, click the **Scene 1** link to return to the document's main Timeline. You'll create duplicates of the USSoccer button next.
10. In the Library panel, right-click the **USSoccer** button and click **Duplicate** on the context menu to open the Duplicate Symbol dialog box, type **ASA** in the Name box, and then click the **OK** button. A copy of the USSoccer button named ASA appears in the library.
11. Repeat Step 10 to create a duplicate of the USSoccer button named **NAYS**. The NAYS button appears in the library.

    You will modify the text in the Up and Over frames of each of the duplicate button symbols.
12. On the Edit bar, click the **Edit Symbols** button, click **ASA** to open the button in symbol-editing mode, click the **Text** tool in the Tools panel to select it, change the button text to **American Softball Association** in both the Up frame and the Over frame, and then click the **Scene 1** link on the Edit bar to exit symbol-editing mode. The button text is updated.
13. Repeat Step 12 to open the **NAYS** button in symbol-editing mode, change the button text to **National Alliance of Youth Sports** in both the Up and Over frames, and then exit symbol-editing mode.
14. Drag an instance of the **ASA** button from the Library panel to below the USSoccer button instance on the Stage, and then drag an instance of the **NAYS** button from the Library panel to below the ASA button instance on the Stage.
15. In the Tools panel, click the **Selection** tool to select it, press and hold the **Shift** key, click each of the three buttons on the Stage, and then release the Shift key. All three button instances on the Stage are selected.
16. Click **Modify** on the menu bar, point to **Align**, and then click **To Stage** if necessary to deselect it. The buttons on the Stage will align relative to each other.
17. Click **Modify** on the menu bar, point to **Align**, and then click **Left** to align the buttons along their left edges.

Tip

You can also use the Selection tool to draw a marquee around the three buttons on the Stage to select them simultaneously.

18. Click **Modify** on the menu bar, point to **Align**, click **Distribute Heights** to space the buttons evenly, and then deselect the button instances. See Figure 8-13.

Figure 8-13 Text buttons on the Resources page

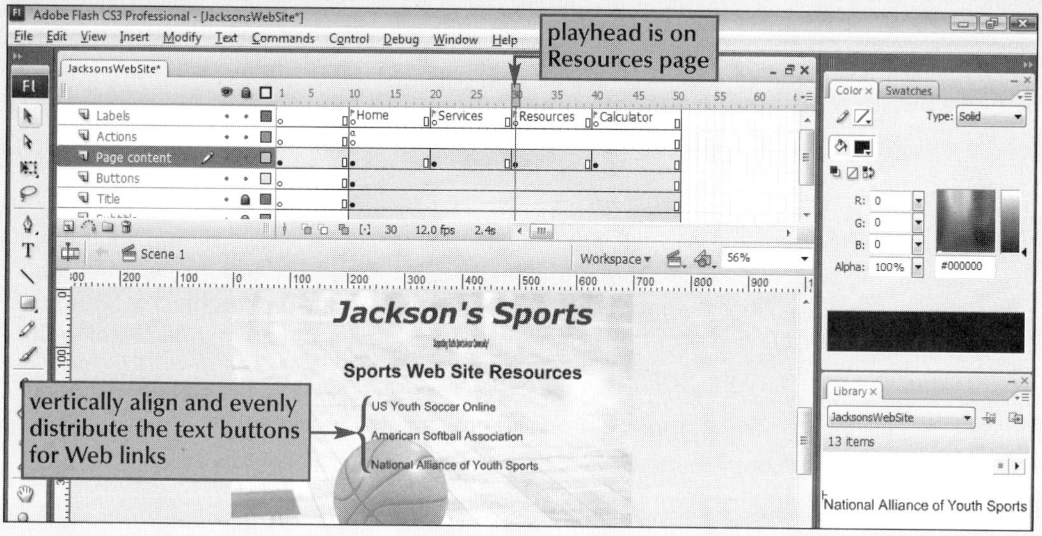

Each of the three button instance must be assigned a name before you can add ActionScript code that references the button instances. Also, Aly wants you to add a message for site visitors explaining that a browser window will open when a button is clicked to visit a Web site.

To add instructions and name the button instances to the Resources page:

1. On the Edit bar, click the **Zoom control arrow**, and then click **100%**. The Stage is magnified.
2. In the Tools panel, click the **Text** tool T to select it, set the font to **Arial**, set the font size to **10**, set the text color to **black**, deselect the **Bold** attribute, select the **Italic** attribute, select the **Align Left** attribute, add a text block above the USSoccer button instance on the Stage, type **Clicking a button below will open the Web site in a new window** in the text block, and then deselect the text. See Figure 8-14.

Figure 8-14 Instructions added to Resources page

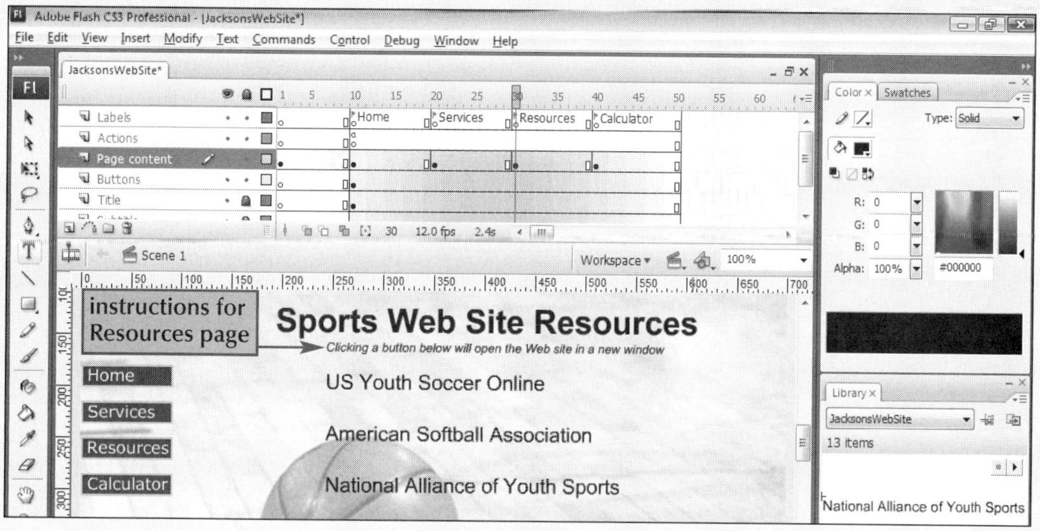

3. In the Tools panel, click the **Selection** tool , select the **USSoccer** button instance on the Stage, and then, in the Property inspector, type **soccer_btn** in the Instance Name box and press the **Enter** key.
4. Repeat Step 3 to name the **ASA** button instance as **softball_btn**, and then name the NAYS button instance as **alliance_btn**.

Using the URLRequest Class

To create a link to an external Web site, you need to create a function as you did in the previous session. The function will use the `URLRequest()` class to define an object with the value of the Web address of the site to which you want to link. A **class** is a blueprint for an object that describes the properties, methods, and events for the object. All objects in ActionScript are defined by classes. The ActionScript code for the function to link to a Web site is as follows:

```
function gotoSoccerSite(eventobj:MouseEvent):void
{
    var soccerURL:URLRequest = new
URLRequest("http://www.usyouthsoccer.org/");
    navigateToURL(soccerURL);
}
```

The first line in the code defines the function by listing the function's name and parameter. This is the same way you defined the functions in the previous session. The third line of the code creates a variable named soccerURL as an object that represents a Web address. A **variable** is a user-defined object that holds data and whose value can change while the SWF movie plays. You define a variable using the var keyword followed by the variable's name, which must be one word comprised only of alphanumeric characters, the underscore, or dollar sign characters. A variable must be **typed**, which means you need to specify what type of data it can contain. The data type of the variable is listed after a colon character. In this case, the data type is URLRequest, which means that the variable can only hold data representing a Web address.

The equal sign in the statement is an assignment operator and is used to assign a value to the soccerURL variable. **Operators** are used in ActionScript statements to tell the Flash Player how to manipulate values. On the right side of the assignment operator, the new operator is used to create an instance of an object based on the URLRequest class. Creating an instance using the new operator is known as calling the constructor method for the class. The **constructor** is a special method used to create instances of objects based on a class. The Web address to be assigned to the soccerURL variable is specified in the parameter of the URLRequest class.

The next line of the code is the `navigateToURL()` function, which will open a Web site in the computer's default browser using the value in its parameter for the Web address. In this case, the function's parameter is soccerURL, which contains the Web address specified in the previous line of the script.

You will add the code to create the functions for the Web site links in the Resources page.

To create a script with functions to control the Resources page buttons:

1. In the Timeline, click **Frame 30** of the Actions layer and insert a keyframe, click Window on the menu bar, and then click Actions to open the Actions panel. The Script pane is empty. You will add the code for the first function.

2. In the Actions panel, type the following lines of code exactly as shown to create a function to open the US Youth Soccer Web site.

```
function gotoSoccerSite(eventobj:MouseEvent):void
{
    var soccerURL:URLRequest = new
  URLRequest("http://www.usyouthsoccer.org/");
    navigateToURL(soccerURL);
}
```

3. Press the **Enter** key twice after the closing curly brace to insert a blank line, and then type the following lines exactly as shown to create two more functions that open the American Softball Association site and the National Alliance of Youth Sports site, pressing the **Enter** key twice between the functions and once after the third function:

```
function gotoSoftballSite(eventobj:MouseEvent):void
{
    var softballURL:URLRequest = new
  URLRequest("http://www.softball.org/");
    navigateToURL(softballURL);
}

function gotoAllianceSite(eventobj:MouseEvent):void
{
    var allianceURL:URLRequest = new URLRequest
    ("http://www.nays.org/"); navigateToURL(allianceURL);
}
```

4. In the Actions panel, click the **Check syntax** button to check the ActionScript code for syntax errors. A dialog box opens, indicating whether the script contains errors.

5. Click the **OK** button. The dialog box closes. The error-free functions appear in the Script pane. See Figure 8-15.

Functions added to the Resources script **Figure 8-15**

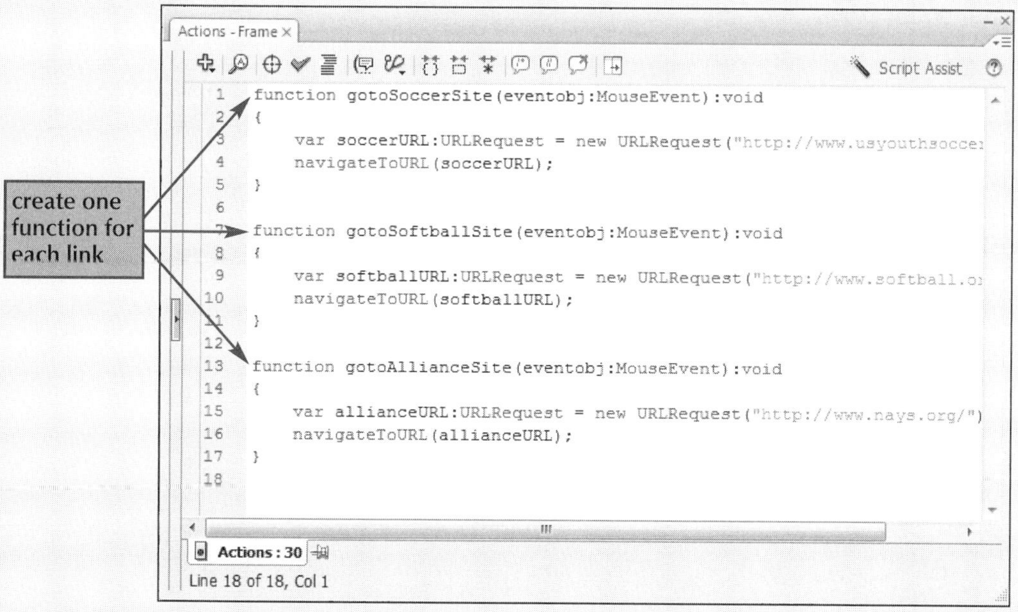

Trouble? If the script contains errors, there are probably typing errors in the functions. If the Compiler Errors panel is hidden behind the Actions panel, click the Actions panel title bar to collapse the panel. In the Compiler Errors panel, review the error message(s), and then close the panel. Click the Actions panel title bar to expand the Actions panel, compare the code in the Actions panel with the code shown in Figure 8-15, and then make the necessary corrections so that your code matches the code in the figure. Repeat Steps 4 and 5 until your code is error-free.

Just as you had to add event listeners to the code in Frame 10 of the Actions layer to make the navigation buttons operational, you need to add similar event listeners to make the buttons on the Resources page operational. The event listeners for the Resources page have the same format as the ones for the navigational buttons. You use the `addEventListener()` method for each button instance to register a button's CLICK event with the associated function. You will type the event listener code next.

To add the event listener code for the Resources page:

1. In the Actions panel, place the insertion point after the closing curly brace ending the last function, press the **Enter** key to add a blank line, and then type the following line of code exactly as shown to create the event listener for the US Youth Soccer button:

```
soccer_btn.addEventListener(MouseEvent.CLICK, gotoSoccerSite);
```

2. Press the **Enter** key after the closing semicolon to insert a new line, and then type the following lines of code to create the event listeners for the other buttons, pressing the **Enter** key after each line:

```
softball_btn.addEventListener(MouseEvent.CLICK, gotoSoftballSite);
alliance_btn.addEventListener(MouseEvent.CLICK, gotoAllianceSite);
```

3. In the Actions panel, click the **Check syntax** button to check the ActionScript code for syntax errors. A dialog box opens, indicating whether the script contains errors.
4. Click the **OK** button. The dialog box closes. The error-free functions appear in the Script pane.

   Trouble? If the script contains errors, there are probably typing errors in the functions. If the Compiler Errors panel is hidden behind the Actions panel, click the Actions panel title bar to collapse the panel. In the Compiler Errors panel, review the error message(s), and then close the panel. Click the Actions panel title bar to expand the Actions panel, compare the code in the Actions panel with the code in Steps 1 and 2, and then make the necessary corrections so that your code matches the code in the steps. Repeat Steps 3 and 4 until your code is error-free.
5. Save the JacksonsWebSite.fla document.

The code for the functions and event listeners to make the buttons operational is complete. You will test the links in the Resources page.

To test the buttons in the Resources page:

1. Click **File** on the menu bar, point to **Publish Preview** and then click **Default - HTML**. The Jackson's Sports Web site opens in the default browser.
2. In the browser window, click the **Resources** button to display the Resources page, and then click the **US Youth Soccer Online** button to open the Web site in a separate window. If necessary, switch to the window displaying the US Youth Soccer Web site.

Trouble? If an error message appears stating the page cannot be displayed, your computer might not be connected to the Internet. If necessary, connect to the Internet and repeat Step 2. If your computer is connected to the Internet, check the URL in the `URLRequest()` parameter to make certain it is correct. If you cannot connect the Internet, then read the remainder of the steps in this section.

Trouble? If an Adobe Flash Player Security dialog box appears stating that the Flash Player stopped a potentially unsafe operation, click the Settings button. A Web page displays the Adobe Flash Player Settings Manager. In the Settings Manager, click the Always allow radio button to select it, and then click the Edit locations button. In the box below the Tip, select the path of the JacksonsWebSite.swf file, copy the text, and then paste the text in the Trust this location box. Click the Confirm button. Close the Web browser, and then repeat Steps 1 and 2.

3. Switch to the browser window displaying the Jackson's Sports Web site, and then click the **American Softball Association** button to test that it opens the appropriate Web site.
4. Repeat Step 3 to test the **National Alliance of Youth Sports** button.
5. Close the browser windows to return to the JacksonsWebSite.fla document. The Resources page is complete. You have added the buttons and ActionScript code to open external Web sites in a browser.

Using a Flash Preloader

An SWF file, like an HTML file, is downloaded over the Internet from a Web server to the user's computer, known as the **client computer**, where the files will reside. A major factor that affects the amount of time a file takes to download is the size of the file, measured in kilobytes. A **kilobyte** is approximately 1000 bytes, and a **byte** is equivalent to one character of information. Flash Web sites typically contain various multimedia elements, such as graphics, animations, pictures, audio, and video. Each of these elements adds to the overall size of the published file. Even though the SWF files are compressed and contain vector graphics that tend to be small, they might still take some time to download.

Another factor that affects download time is the type of Internet connection used by the client computer. The type of Internet connection can be a broadband connection using a cable or DSL modem, which provides high-speed download capability, or it could be a much slower dial-up connection using a telephone modem, as is the case with many personal computers. When an SWF file starts to download from a Web server to a client computer, it is loaded into the Flash Player one frame at a time. The first frames start playing in the Flash Player as soon as they load, even though other frames of the file are still downloading. This is because of the streaming capability of Flash files. **Streaming** means that as the file is downloading, the initial content can start playing while the rest of the content continues to be downloaded, which reduces the wait time for the user. A problem occurs, however, when the client computer plays all of the loaded frames and then has to wait for additional frames to load. This can happen if a particular frame has a large amount of content such as bitmap images. The wait causes the Flash Player to pause the playing of the SWF file while additional frames load. This delay affects the way the SWF file plays and might confuse or frustrate the user. Also, if the wait is more than a few seconds and no visual indication appears that something is still loading, the user may think the Web site is not working and decide to go to another site. To avoid losing site visitors, Flash developers usually add a **preloader**, which is a short animation or message located in the first few frames of the Flash file. The preloader typically contains a short animation and the word "Loading" to indicate to the site visitor that the Web site is still loading. This visual feedback helps assure the site visitor that the Web site is loading while the frames of the SWF file continue to download. After all of the content has downloaded, the preloader stops and the rest of the SWF file plays. Several examples of preloaders are shown in Figure 8-16.

Figure 8-16 **Examples of preloaders**

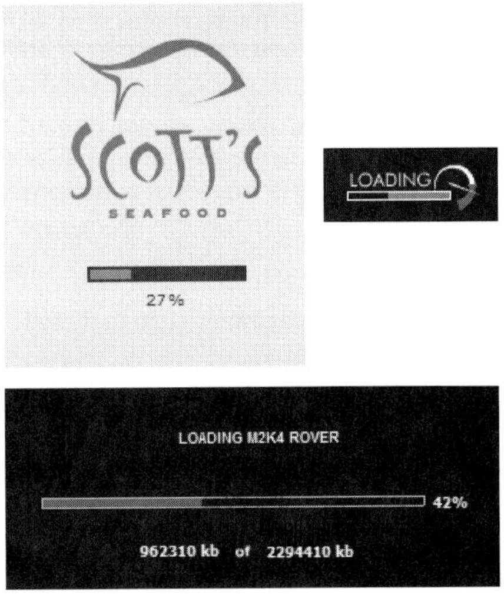

Creating the Preloader

Adding a preloader to a Flash file requires ActionScript code along with a loading message and/or an animation placed in the first frame of the Timeline. The preloader message and animation display only while the file is being loaded. A script can be added to a later frame in the Timeline to control the preloader and to check if all of the content has downloaded. The basic logic involves knowing how much of the SWF file has loaded and comparing that with the total size of the file. The amount of content that has loaded and the total size of the file can be measured in either number of frames or number of bytes, both of which can be examined using ActionScript. By checking how much content has been loaded and comparing it to the total size of the file, different actions can be performed. For example, if the number of bytes that have loaded into the Flash Player is equal to the total number of bytes for the file, the entire SWF file has loaded. At that point, the SWF file can play as designed. Otherwise, the preloader animation continues to play.

If the SWF file contains a large number of frames, you can create a preloader that checks the number of frames loaded. In the case of the Jackson's Sports Web site, the number of frames is small, so it is best to check the number of bytes loaded. To create the preloader code, the script will need to get the total number of bytes to be loaded and the number of bytes loaded. The number of bytes loaded will increase as more of the file is loaded into the Flash Player. As long as these two values are not the same, the preloader animation will continue to play. When the two values are the same, the SWF has finished loading. At that point, the preloader animation will stop and the rest of the frames in the movie will be played. The steps for the preloader code are as follows:

```
Get the total number of bytes
Get the number of bytes loaded
Update the preloader animation
If the number of bytes loaded equals the total number of bytes
   play the rest of the SWF file
Otherwise
   continue playing the preloader animation
```

These steps will be followed to create the code for the preloader for the Jackson's Sports Web site.

To get the total number of bytes, you will create a function with an instance of the ProgressEvent class as its parameter. The ProgressEvent class has the event type PROGRESS, which includes the properties bytesTotal and bytesLoaded. The bytesTotal property contains the total number of bytes in the SWF file. The bytesLoaded property contains the number of bytes loaded. These numbers will be compared to each other to determine if the SWF file has completed loading into the Flash Player. The numbers can also be used to calculate what percentage of the file has loaded.

You will start creating the script for the preloader in the first frame of the Actions layer by creating a function and defining two variables.

To create the first part of the preloader script:

1. In the Timeline, click **Frame 1** of the Labels layer, and then in the Property inspector, type **Preload** in the Frame Label box and press the **Enter** key. This label will be referred to in the script for the preloader.
2. In the Timeline, click **Frame 1** of the Actions layer, and then, in the Script pane of the Actions panel, type the following line of code exactly as shown and press the **Enter** key:

```
function preloader(progressEvt:ProgressEvent):void {
```

This code creates a function named preloader with the object progressEvt as its parameter. The progressEvt object is set as a ProgressEvent data type.

3. In the Script pane of the Actions panel, type the following lines of code exactly as shown, pressing the **Enter** key after each line:

```
var totalBytes:Number = progressEvt.bytesTotal;
var loadedBytes:Number = progressEvt.bytesLoaded;
```

The first var line creates a new variable named totalBytes whose data type is Number. The value of the bytesTotal property of the progressEvt object is assigned to the variable. The second var line creates a variable named loadedBytes with a data type of Number. The value of the bytesLoaded property of the progressEvt object is assigned to the variable.

Creating the Preloader Animation

The totalBytes and loadedBytes variables can also be used to control the animation used in the preloader. Recall from Session 8.1 that the properties of a movie clip instance can be modified using ActionScript. You can create a movie clip in the shape of a rectangle and then gradually increase the horizontal size of the rectangle to match how much of the file has been loaded. Because the rectangle instance is an object, you can modify the object's scaleX and scaleY properties, which represent the relative size of the object compared to its original size. The scaleX property can be used to scale the object horizontally. The property uses a fractional value such as 0.5 to represent a percentage of the object's original size. For example, a scaleX value of 0.5 changes the object to display 50% of its original size. So by changing the scaleX property of the rectangle from 0 to 1, the rectangle appears to grow horizontally from 0% to 100% of its original size.

You will create an instance of a movie clip in the shape of a rectangle with a registration point on its upper-left corner. The rectangle will grow horizontally, starting from the left side and growing to the right side. When the rectangle is back to its original size, the SWF file has finished loading.

InSight | **Calculating the scaleX Property**

To determine the value to assign to the scaleX property of the rectangle, you divide the loadedBytes value by the totalBytes value, resulting in fractional values ranging from 0 to 1. The result, which represents the percentage of how much of the file has loaded, can be assigned to the scaleX property of the rectangle. It increases gradually until the two values are equal, resulting in a value of 1, which means all of the file's content has loaded and the scaleX property of the rectangle is 100%.

You'll add a preloader animation to the Page content layer.

To add the graphic and code for the preloader animation:

1. Collapse the Actions panel to see the Stage, and then, in the Timeline, click **Frame 1** of the Page content layer.
2. Below the Loading text block on the Stage, draw a rectangle that is **300** pixels wide and **20** pixels high with a **dark green** (#009900) fill and no stroke. See Figure 8-17.

Figure 8-17 Rectangle for the preloader animation

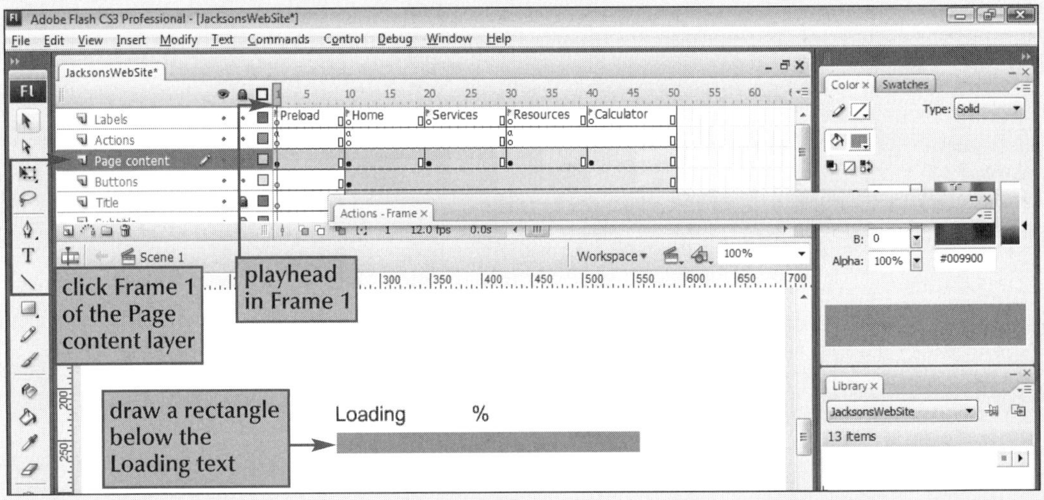

3. Convert the rectangle to a **Movie clip** symbol named **Rectangle** with the upper-left registration point selected.
4. In the Property inspector, type **loadBar_mc** in the Instance name box, and then press the **Enter** key to name the movie clip instance. The preloader movie clip instance is complete.

   You will add the code to change the loadBar_mc's scaleX property.
5. In the Timeline, click **Frame 1** of the Actions layer, expand the Actions panel, and then, in the Script pane at the end of the script type the following code exactly as shown, pressing the **Enter** key after each line:

```
var amtLoaded:Number = loadedBytes/totalBytes;
loadBar_mc.scaleX = amtLoaded;
```

The amtLoaded variable will hold the result of dividing loadedBytes by totalBytes. This resulting number is a fractional value that represents the percentage of how much of the SWF file has been loaded. This value is assigned to the scaleX property of the Rectangle movie clip, loadBar_mc, causing it to increase horizontally each time the loadedBytes value changes.

In addition to the loadBar_mc animation, you will add a special type of text box that will display a changing value, from 0% to 100%, indicating how much of the SWF file has loaded. You will add this text box and its associated ActionScript code in Session 8.3.

Completing the Preloader Code

The next part of the function is a comparison using a conditional statement. A **conditional statement** compares one value to another. Based on the result of the comparison, certain actions are performed. Conditional statements use **comparison operators**, such as ==, which is used to test for equality. This is different from the assignment operator =, which is used to assign a value to a variable. Other examples of comparison operators include >, <, and !=, which are used to test for greater than, less than, and not equal to, respectively. You create a conditional statement using the if keyword, which tests a condition. If the condition is true, the Flash Player performs actions within the curly braces that follow it. You can also include the else keyword, which contains the actions to perform when the condition is false.

The if statement compares the values of loadedBytes and totalBytes. If the values are not equal, the loading has not finished so the playhead is moved to the Preload frame, which is Frame 1. If the values are not equal to each other, the playhead moves to Frame 1. If the values are equal, then the loading has finished and the playhead is moved to the first part of the Web site, which is the frame with the Home label. You use the `gotoAndPlay()` function to direct the playhead to a specific frame, referring to a frame by its label. You will add the if conditional statement to the script next.

To add code to compare the loadedBytes and totalBytes values:

1. In the Script pane of the Actions panel, click at the end of the script, and then press the **Enter** key to add a blank line.
2. Type the following code exactly as shown, pressing the **Enter** key after each line:

```
if (loadedBytes == totalBytes) {
      gotoAndPlay("Home");
  } else {
      gotoAndPlay("Preload");
  }
}
```

The condition, enclosed in parentheses, compares the values in the loadedBytes and totalBytes variables. If the values are equal, the `gotoAndPlay("Home");` statement is executed, causing the playhead to move to the first page of the Web site. If the values are not equal, the `gotoAndPlay("Preload");` statement is executed, causing the playhead to move to the frame labeled Preload. This causes the script to run again. The closing curly brace on the last line closes the preloader function.

The function for the preloader script is complete. However, it will not work until an event listener is added to the script. Recall that event listeners were added to previous scripts to register button instances with functions to be performed when a button was clicked. The CLICK property of the MouseEvent event object was used as a parameter in the `addEventListener()` method. In the preloader script, you need to add an event listener to call the preloader function when a specific event occurs. In this case, the event is not when a button is clicked. Instead, the event is when a part of the SWF file has loaded into the Flash Player. The progressEvent.PROGRESS event will indicate when a new part of the SWF file has loaded. Because the event is dispatched or generated by a LoaderInfo object of the main Timeline, you need to register the event listener with the object. You can do this using the `addEventListener()` method of the loaderInfo object.

You will add the event listener to the script.

To add the event listener code to the preloader script, check for errors, and test the script:

1. In the Script pane of the Actions panel, at the end of the script, press the **Enter** key to add a blank line, and then type the following code exactly as shown.

```
loaderInfo.addEventListener(ProgressEvent.PROGRESS, preloader);
```

When content is loaded into the Flash Player, the PROGRESS event occurs and the addEventListener() method calls the preloader function. You will check for syntax errors before testing the script.

2. In the Actions panel, click the **Check syntax** button to check for syntax errors. A dialog box opens, indicating whether the script contains errors.

3. Click the **OK** button. The dialog box closes. The error-free code appears in the Script pane. See Figure 8-18.

Figure 8-18 Preloader script

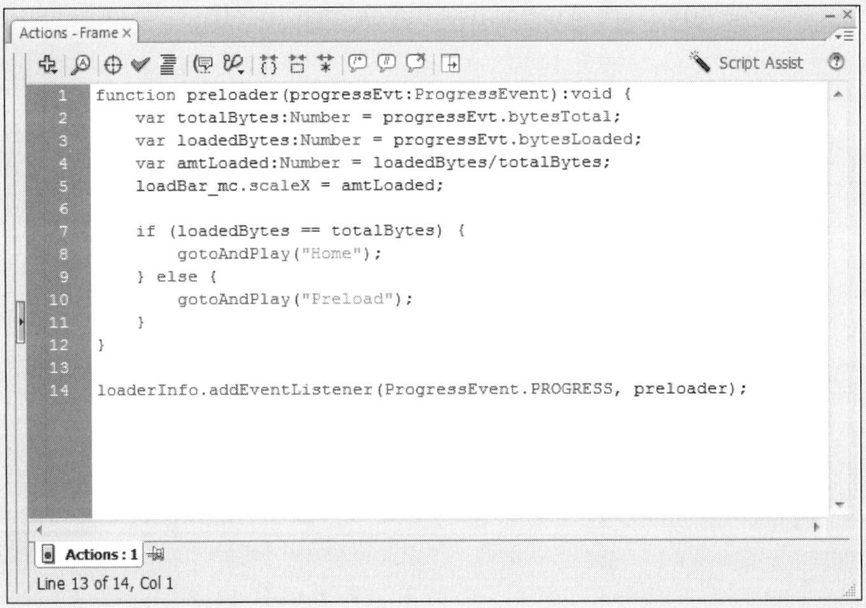

Trouble? If the script contains errors, there are probably typing errors in the functions. If the Compiler Errors panel is hidden behind the Actions panel, click the Actions panel title bar to collapse the panel. In the Compiler Errors panel, review the error message(s), and then close the panel. Click the Actions panel title bar to expand the Actions panel, compare the code in the Actions panel with the code in Figure 8-18, and then make the necessary corrections so that your code matches the code in the figure. Repeat Steps 2 and 3 until your code is error-free.

4. Save the JacksonsWebSite.fla document, and then close the Actions panel.
5. Click **Control** on the menu bar, and then click **Test Movie**. The SWF file plays in the Flash Player; however, the preloader appears for only a fraction of a second.

   Because the SWF file is loading from your computer's drive, the file's content loads instantly. As a result, the preloader animation is only visible for a very short time. This will not be the case when the SWF file is downloaded from the Internet. To test the preloader, you can use the Simulate Download command. This command simulates the time it takes to download an SWF file based on the type of Internet connection you select.
6. In the Flash Player window, click **View** on the menu bar, point to **Download Settings**, and then click **56K (4.7 KB/s)** if necessary.
7. Click **View** on the Flash Player menu bar, and then click **Simulate Download**. After a few seconds, the preloader animation plays. See Figure 8-19.

Figure 8-19 Simulated download process

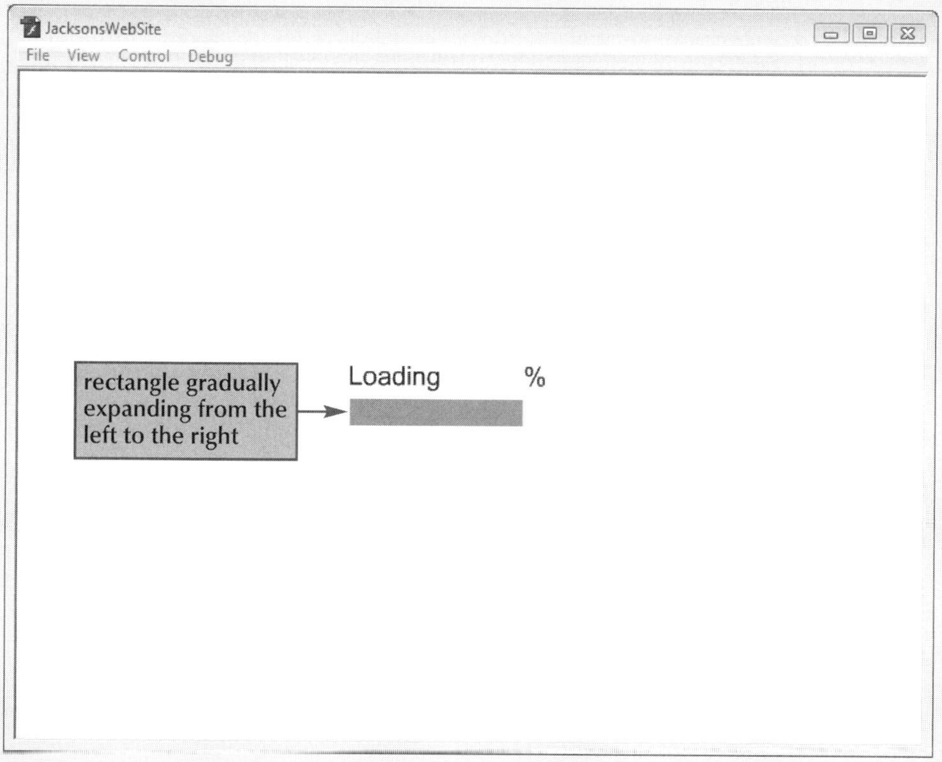

After the green rectangle is scaled to its original size, the home page of the Jackson's Sports Web site appears.

8. Close the Flash Player window to return to the JacksonsWebSite document.

The preloader for the Jackson's Sports Web site is complete. In this session, you used the `URLRequest()` function to create buttons with URL links to Web sites on the Internet. You also created a preloader using ActionScript and tested the preloader by simulating the download speed of a 56K modem Internet connection.

Review | **Session 8.2 Quick Check**

1. Write the ActionScript code to create a function named `gotoCourseSite()` that will use the `URLRequest()` class to open the Web site *http://www.course.com.*
2. What does it mean that a variable has to be typed?
3. What is a constructor method?
4. What is the purpose of a preloader?
5. An object's scaleX and scaleY properties represent the relative size of the object compared to its ________________ size?
6. Explain how you can simulate the downloading of an SWF file within Flash.

Session 8.3

Creating an Input Form

An input form is a common element found on many Web sites. An **input form** allows the user to enter data into text boxes. The data can then be submitted for storage and processing on a Web server. The server software sends results of the processing back to the user's computer to be displayed on the same form or on another Web page. A page developed with Flash can also allow the user to enter data, have the data processed, and return a result directly from the Flash Player on the user's computer. The page developer uses ActionScript to write the underlying functions required to create a form with several input fields coded to accept data from the site visitor, such as the number and type of items to be purchased. Other fields on the form display results based on the site visitor's input, such as a total price. Creating an input form requires the use of dynamic and input text.

Using Dynamic and Input Text

Text is an important element of a Flash document. All of the text you have created so far has been static text. Static text cannot be changed after the document plays in the Flash Player. Recall, however, that there are two other types of text in Flash: dynamic text and input text. Although static text cannot change, dynamic text can. Dynamic text can receive text in the form of characters or numbers from a Web server or from an expression in ActionScript and display the text on a Web page in the Flash Player. Dynamic text is defined to display the contents of a variable. The variable can be used in ActionScript to change the value displayed. For example, if a dynamic text block is assigned the variable Amount, you can code an expression in ActionScript that assigns the result of a calculation to the variable. The value stored in the variable Amount will then appear in the text block on the Web page. Input text is used to allow the user to enter text into the text block. This text can then be stored in a variable and used in an ActionScript script.

Based on Dan's request, you will create a form for the Team Jersey Calculator page for the Jackson's Sports Web site. This page will allow a user such as a team manager to enter several values for the type and number of team jerseys the team needs to buy. The page will contain a button that when clicked will use the entered values to calculate a total cost and display the result. One of the values that the user will enter is which type of jersey is desired. One option is a team jersey for $10.00 with the team name only. The other option is a team jersey for $12.00 with both the team name and a player number. Then, the user will enter whether the jersey will contain the name of the player for an additional $1.50 per jersey. Finally, the user will enter the number of players and number of coaches to determine the number of jerseys needed.

You will complete the Calculator page by creating the input and dynamic text blocks. You will also add a Calculate button and write the ActionScript code to make the button operational so that it calculates the total cost. You will start by adding the static text blocks for the page.

To create the static text boxes for the Team Jersey Calculator page:

1. If you took a break after the previous session, make sure the JacksonsWebSite.fla document is open, the workspace is set to its default layout, and the zoom is to 100%.
2. In the Timeline, click **Frame 40** of the Page content layer. The Team Jersey Calculator page appears on the Stage.
3. Deselect the title text block, and then click the **Text** tool [T] in the Tools panel, set the font to **Arial**, set the font size to **22**, set the text color to **black**, deselect the **Bold** and **Italic** attributes, and select the **Align Right** attribute.
4. Create a text block below the page title about **200** pixels from the top edge of the Stage and **500** pixels from the left edge of the Stage, type **Type of Jersey**, press the **Enter** key to create a new line, type **Enter 1 for team name only - $10.00 each**, press the **Enter** key to create a new line, and then type **Enter 2 for team name & player number - $12.00 each**.
5. Select the last two lines of the text block, and then, in the Property inspector, change the font size to **14**.
6. Create a text block about **280** pixels from the top edge of the Stage and **500** pixels from the left edge of the Stage, use the same text attributes as the first text block but change the font size to **22**, type **Include player names (Enter Y or N)**, press the **Enter** key, and then type **$1.50 per player**.
7. Select the second line in the text block, and then, in the Property inspector, change the font size to **18**.
8. Create a text block about **340** pixels from the top edge of the Stage and **500** pixels from the left edge of the Stage, use the same text attributes as the previous text block but change the font size to **22**, and then type **Number of players**.
9. Create a text block about **390** pixels from the top edge of the Stage and **500** pixels from the left edge of the Stage, use the same text attributes as the previous text block, and then type **Number of coaches**.
10. Create a text block about **440** pixels from the top edge of the Stage and **500** pixels from the left edge of the Stage, use the same text attributes as the previous text block, and then type **Total cost (w/o tax) =**.
11. In the Tools panel, click the **Selection** tool [arrow], and then, if necessary, reposition the text blocks on the Stage so that their right edges are aligned. See Figure 8-20.

Figure 8-20 Static text blocks

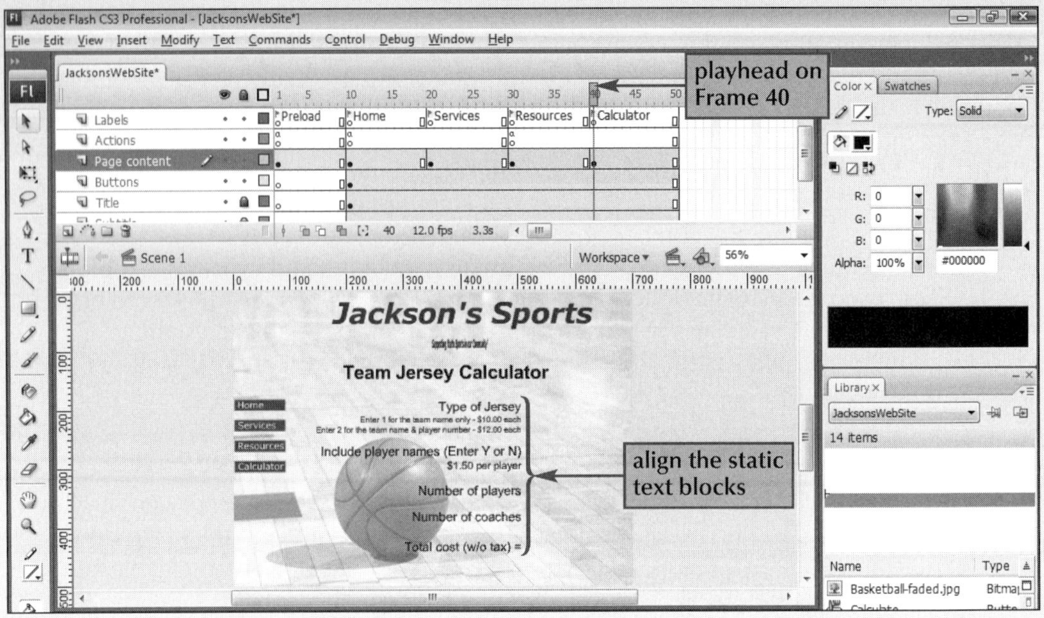

The static text blocks are complete. Each text block provides instructions to the user about the values that can be entered into the input text boxes. You will create the input text boxes next. You will also assign instance names to each input text box so that it can be referenced in the ActionScript code.

To create the input text boxes for the Team Jersey Calculator page:

1. In the Tools panel, click the **Text** tool, and then in the Property inspector, click the **Text type** button and click **Input Text**. The next text block you create will be for input text.
2. In the Property inspector, set the font to **Arial**, set the font size to **20**, set the text color to **black**, deselect the Bold and Italic attributes, and then select the **Align Right** attribute.
3. To the right of the Type of jersey text block, create a text block, and then, in the Property inspector, set the W and H dimensions to **70** pixels wide and **30** pixels high, select **Single Line** from the Line type button, click the **Show border around text** button to select it, type **1** in the Maximum characters box to set the input box to allow only one character, type **jerseyType** in the Instance name box, and then press the **Enter** key to assign a name to the text box. See Figure 8-21.

Figure 8-21 Input text block properties

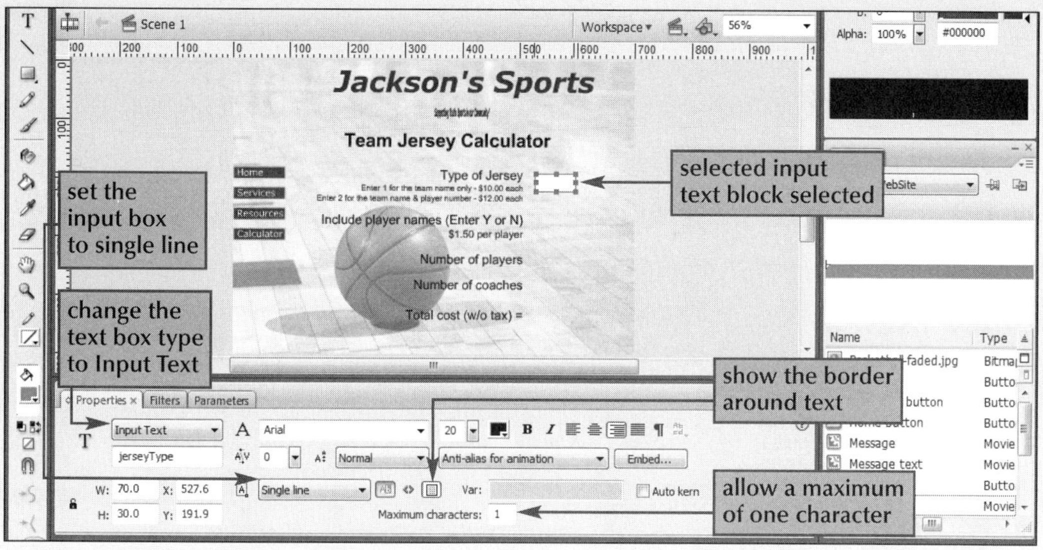

Trouble? If you have trouble changing the width and height values of the text block, click the Selection tool in the Tools panel, select the text block if necessary, and then change the values in the Property inspector.

You'll create additional input text blocks.

4. Repeat Steps 1 through 3 to create an input text block to the right of the Include player names (Enter Y or N) line, entering **playerNames** as the instance name.

5. Repeat Steps 1 through 3 to create an input text block to the right of the Number of players line, entering **numberOfPlayers** as the instance name and setting the maximum characters to **0**.

6. Repeat Steps 1 through 3 to create an input text block to the right of the Number of coaches line, entering **numberOfCoaches** as the instance name and setting the maximum characters to **0**.

7. In the Tools panel, click the **Selection** tool, and then, if necessary, reposition the input text boxes so that they are vertically aligned. See Figure 8-22.

Tip

Setting the maximum characters to 0 allows the input box to accept an unlimited number of characters, and not zero characters.

Figure 8-22 Input text boxes

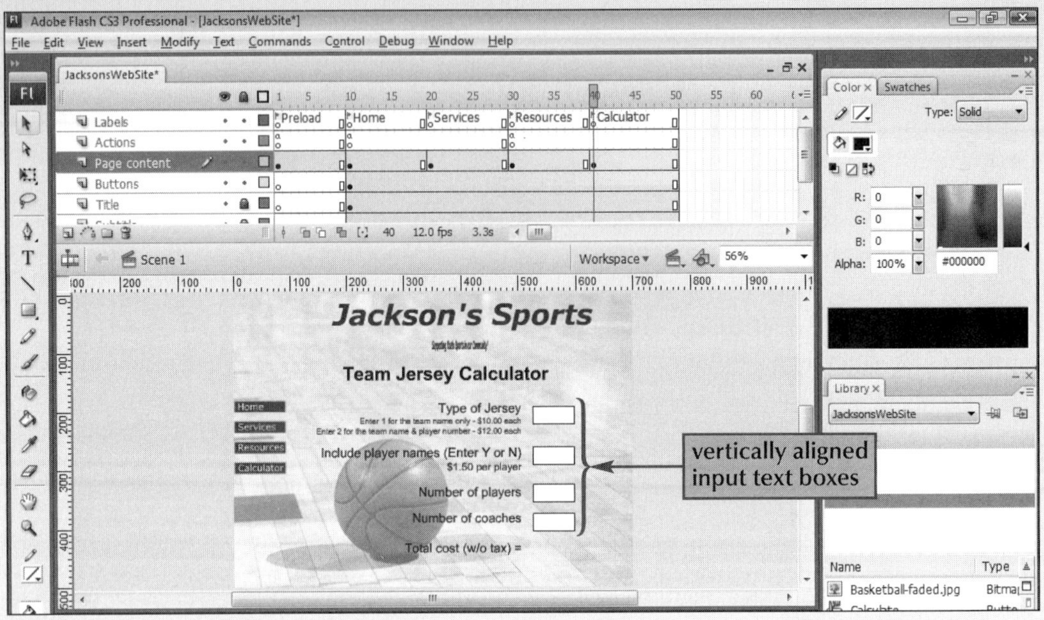

The input text boxes the visitor will use to enter data are complete. You will add a dynamic text block next. This text block instance must also be assigned a name. You will also create an instance of a Calculate button that Aly created.

To create the dynamic text box and add a button to the Team Jersey Calculator page:

1. In the Tools panel, click the **Text** tool T, and then create a text block to the right of the Total cost (w/o tax) = line.
2. In the Property inspector, click the **Text type** button and select **Dynamic Text**, set the font to **Arial**, set the font size to **20**, set the text color to **black**, deselect the **Bold** and **Italic** attributes, and select the **Align Right** attribute.
3. In the Property inspector, set the width to **70**, set the height to **30**, type **total** in the Instance Name box, and then, click the **Selectable** button to deselect it, if necessary.
4. Drag an instance of the **Calculate** button from the Library panel to the left side of the Total cost (w/o tax) = text block, and then, in the Property inspector, type **calc_btn** in the Instance name box and press the **Enter** key to assign a name to the button instance.

Writing ActionScript Code to Do a Calculation

The Calculate button requires ActionScript code to make it operational. The user will enter values in the input text boxes you created, and then click the Calculate button to compute the total cost for the jerseys. As you have done with previous scripts, you need to define a function. The function will process the values entered in the input text boxes and calculate a total cost that will be displayed in the dynamic text box. The first line of the script will create a function called Calculate. After defining the function, you will add several statements to define variables that will be used within the script. These variables do not represent objects on the Stage, but are used to hold intermediate values used as part of the calculations. Each variable is defined with the var keyword, a name, and the Number data type. The Number data type specifies that the variables will contain numbers.

To define the function and the initial variables for the script in the Team Jersey Calculator page:

1. In the Timeline, click **Frame 40** of the Actions layer to select it, click **Insert** on the menu bar, point to **Timeline**, and click **Blank Keyframe** to insert an empty keyframe.
2. Open the Actions panel, and then, in the Script pane, type the following line of code exactly as shown to define the function:

```
function Calculate(evt:MouseEvent):void {
```

3. Press the **Enter** key twice to insert a blank line, and then type the following lines of code exactly as shown to define the variables, pressing the **Enter** key after each line:

```
var price:Number;
var totalCost:Number;
var numberOfJerseys:Number;
```

Tip

You can also right-click the frame, and then click Insert Blank Keyframe to add an empty keyframe.

The first input text block will contain either a 1 or a 2 for the type of jersey. To determine which price to use for the jersey, you must use an if conditional statement. The condition that needs to be checked is whether the jerseyType value the user entered is 1 or 2. You will create two conditional statements; one to check for the value of 1 and one to check for the value of 2. Based on the results of the conditions, the price variable will be assigned a value of 10 or 12, corresponding to the cost of selected jersey.

Using Expressions and Operators

An **expression** is a statement that is used to assign a value to a variable. For example, the expression UserName = "Tom" assigns the text "Tom" to the variable UserName. When referring to text in an expression, it is enclosed in quotes. The characters within the quotation marks are considered string data, which is handled differently than numeric data. **String data** is a series of characters—such as letters, numbers, and punctuation—and is always enclosed in quotation marks. **Numeric data** is a number or numbers that are not enclosed in quotation marks. So, to assign a numeric value to a variable, you do not enclose the value in quotes. For example, the expression Amount = 20 assigns the numeric value 20 to the variable named Amount.

The equal sign in the expression is an example of an operator. Operators are used in expressions to tell Flash how to manipulate the values in the expression. There are several types of operators. For example, the equal sign is an example of an **assignment operator** because it assigns a value to a variable. ActionScript also has **arithmetic operators** such as +, –, *, and / that are used to indicate addition, subtraction, multiplication, and division, respectively. Another type of operator is a comparison operator, which is an operator used in conditional statements, as you learned earlier.

The script to calculate the results will use expressions and operators.

To code the statements to determine the price of the jerseys:

1. In the Script pane of the Actions panel, type the following lines of code exactly as shown at the end of the script, pressing the **Enter** key after each line:

```
if (jerseyType.text == "1") {
        price = 10;
        }
```

In this code, jerseyType is the name assigned to the first input text block and it contains the value entered by the user. The text property of the jerseyType object represents the value contained in the input box. The conditional operator == compares the input box value to the text value of "1". If the values are equal, the next line assigns a value of 10 to the price variable. You'll code a second conditional statement to check for a jerseyType value of "2".

2. Press the **Enter** key twice to insert a blank line, and then type the following lines of code exactly as shown, pressing the **Enter** key after each line:

```
if (jerseyType.text == "2") {
        price = 12;
        }
```

If the text value of the jerseyType object is "2", a value of 12 is assigned to the Price variable.

After the second if statement is performed, the price variable will contain either a value of 10 or 12 depending on the jerseyType value entered by the user.

The next action to perform is another if statement to determine whether the user entered Y or N. This determines if the player names will be included on the jerseys. If the user entered Y, you will add 1.50 to the price of the jerseys. Because ActionScript is case sensitive, you need to check for both a lowercase y and an uppercase Y. This will ensure that the correct value is calculated, regardless of how the user entered the letter.

There is no need to check for the letter N because if the user entered N, the price will not change. To check for two conditions within the same if statement, you use the logical operator ||, which represents the Or comparison. You will add the ActionScript code for the if statement next.

> **Tip**
>
> You can use shortcuts to combine assignment and arithmetic operators, such as Amount += 5 instead of Amount = Amount + 5 to increment the value in the variable Amount by 5.

To code the statement to check if player names will be included:

1. In the Script pane of the Actions panel, type the following lines of code exactly as shown at the end of the script, pressing the **Enter** key after each line:

```
if (playerNames.text =="Y" || playerNames.text == "y") {
        price += 1.50;
}
```

In this code, playerNames is the name of the input text box that contains the value the user enters to specify whether the names of the players will be included on the jerseys. The text property represents the value entered by the user. The || operator causes the condition to be true if either one of the comparisons is true. If the condition is true, the variable price is increased by 1.50.

The next two input text blocks contain values that represent how many players and coaches are on the team. These two values will be added together to get the total number of jerseys to be purchased. Before the values can be added, they need to be converted to numbers. Because the number of players and number of coaches are whole numbers, you will use the int() function.

Converting Values to Numeric Data | InSight

Values entered into an input text block are considered string data and not numeric data. That is, the values are not treated as numbers, but instead are treated as text characters. Using the + operator to add the two values will not yield the correct result if the values are not first converted to numeric data. The `int()` function can be applied to the values to convert them to integer numbers, which are whole numbers that do not include decimals.

After you have calculated the number of jerseys, you can multiply the number by the price of each jersey to get a total cost. You will add the statements to determine the total cost next.

To code the statements to determine the total cost of the jerseys:

1. In the Script pane of the Actions panel, type the following line of code exactly as shown at the end of the script:

```
numberOfJerseys = int(numberOfPlayers.text) +
int(numberOfCoaches.text);
```

   The numberOfPlayers and numberOfCoaches variables were defined in the input text blocks. The text property is used to get the value entered by the user for each text box. These values are converted to integers and then added together. The result is then assigned to the variable numberOfJerseys.

2. Press the **Enter** key twice to insert a blank line, and then type the following line of code exactly as shown:

```
totalCost = numberOfJerseys*price;
```

   The value in the numberOfJerseys is multiplied by the value in price and the result is assigned to the totalCost variable.

The final step is to assign the value in totalCost to the dynamic text block so that it will be displayed for the user. The dynamic text block can contain only string data. Because the totalCost value is a number, it must first be converted to string data before it can be assigned to the dynamic text box named total. To convert the number to a string, you apply the `String()` function to the totalCost value. The results of the `String()` function can then be assigned to the total dynamic text box. You will add this code next.

To code the statement to display the final result:

1. In the Script pane of the Actions panel, type the following line of code exactly as shown at the end of the script:

```
total.text = String(totalCost);
```

   The totalCost value is converted to a string and assigned to the text property of the total dynamic text box. The value will then be displayed to the user.

2. Press the **Enter** key, and then type **}** (an ending curly brace) to complete the script. See Figure 8-23.

Figure 8-23 Script for calculation

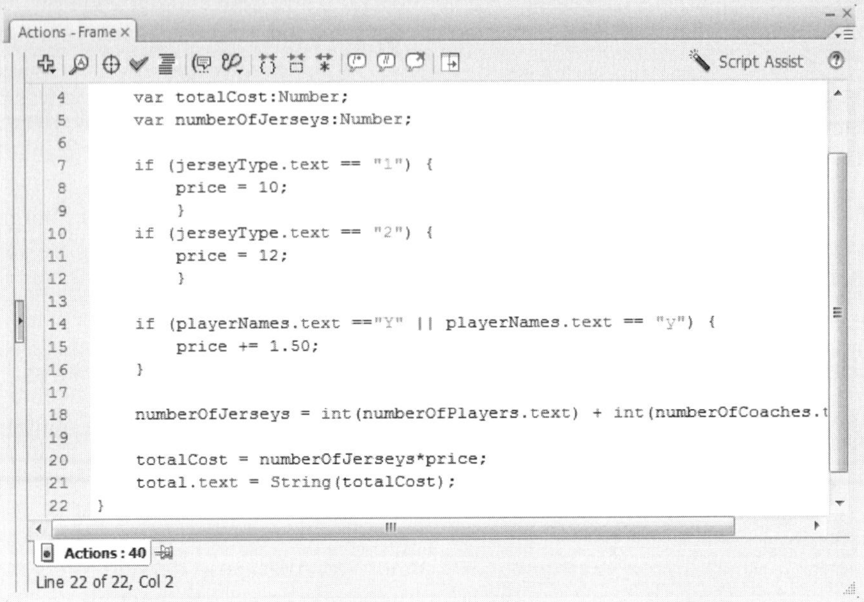

To make the Calculate button operational, you need to add an event listener. The event listener for the Calculate button has the same format as the ones used for the other site buttons. You will use the `addEventListener()` method for the calc_btn button instance to register the button's CLICK event with the Calculate function. You will type the event listener code next.

To add the event listener code, check for errors, and test the script:

1. In the Actions panel, place the insertion after the closing curly brace ending the Calculate function, and then press the **Enter** key to add a blank line.
2. Type the following line of code exactly as shown to create the event listener for the Calculate button:

   ```
   calc_btn.addEventListener(MouseEvent.CLICK, Calculate);
   ```

   Before testing the script, you should check for syntax errors and make corrections as needed.
3. In the Actions panel, click the **Check syntax** button to check for syntax errors. A dialog box opens, indicating whether the script contains errors.
4. Click the **OK** button. The dialog box closes. The error-free code appears in the Script pane.

   Trouble? If the script contains errors, there are probably typing errors in the code. If the Compiler Errors panel is hidden behind the Actions panel, click the Actions panel title bar to collapse the panel. In the Compiler Errors panel, review the error message(s), and then close the panel. Click the Actions panel title bar to expand the Actions panel, compare the code in the Actions panel with the code in previous sets of steps, and then make the necessary corrections so that your code matches the code in the steps. Make certain that the variable names and ActionScript keywords have the correct case and that the parentheses and curly braces are organized and paired correctly. Repeat Steps 3 and 4 until your code is error-free.
5. Save the JacksonsWebSite.fla document.

6. Click **Control** on the menu bar, and then click **Test Movie**, and then click the **Calculator** button to advance to the Team Jersey Calculator page.
7. Enter **1** for the Type of jersey, **Y** for Include player names, **10** for the Number of players, **2** for the Number of coaches, and then click the **Calculate** button. The Total cost field displays 138. See Figure 8-24.

Figure 8-24 Results of the calculation

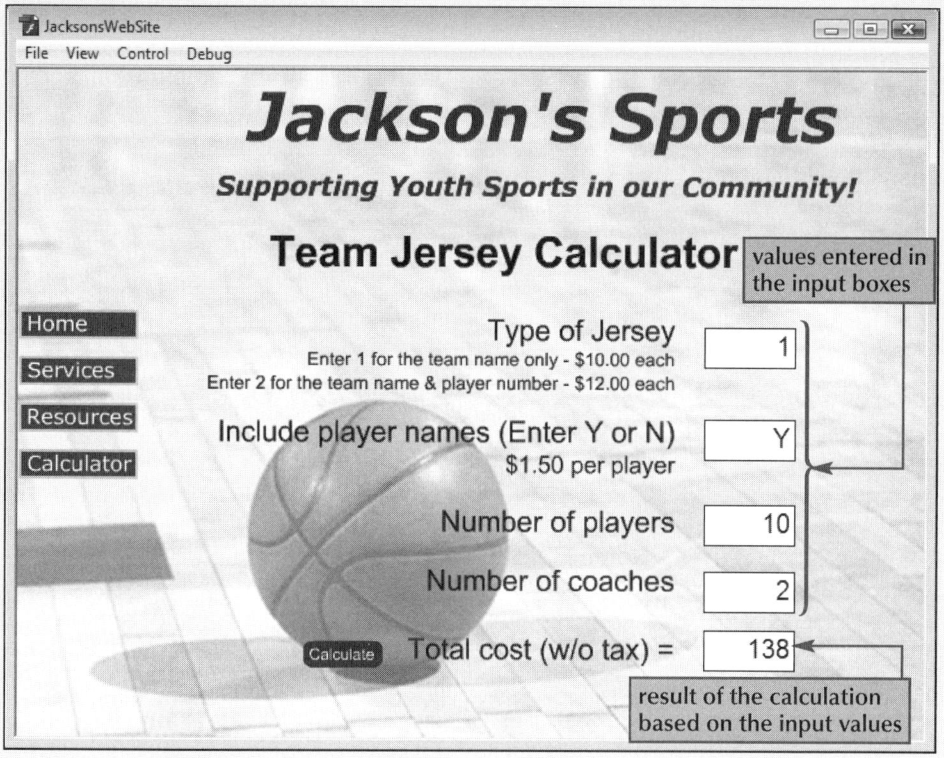

Trouble? If you don't get the correct results, make sure you enter the correct input values and also check the variable names of your input and dynamic text boxes. Remember that ActionScript is case sensitive. If the case of the variable names assigned to the text boxes is different from that used in the code, the result will not be correct.

8. Enter a set of input values of your choice, click the **Calculate** button to see the total cost, and then repeat with another set of input values.
9. Close the Flash Player window to return to the JacksonsWebSite.fla document.

Adding Numeric Feedback to the Preloader

In Session 8.2, you created an animation for the preloader to provide visual feedback to the user. In the animation, the scaleX property of a rectangle was changed based on how much of the SWF file had loaded into the Flash Player. In addition to the visual feedback, Flash developers often include numeric feedback showing what percentage of the file has been loaded. The same value used to change the scaleX property of the rectangle can be displayed as a percentage. To display the number, you need to create a dynamic text block similar to the one you created to display the results of the calculation in the Calculator page. You will add a dynamic text block for the preloader and then you will add thecode to calculate and display the percentage of the file loaded.

To add a dynamic text block to the preloader:

1. Collapse the Actions panel to view the Stage.
2. On the Edit bar, click the **Zoom control arrow** and click **100%**, and then in the Timeline, click **Frame 1** of the Page content layer.
3. On the Stage, create a dynamic text block between the Loading text block and the % text block, set the font to **Arial**, set the font size to **20**, set the text color to **black**, deselect the **Bold** attribute, select the **Align Right** attribute, and then deselect the **Show border around text** button, if necessary.
4. In the Property inspector, type **percent_txt** in the Instance name box, and then press the **Enter** key to assign a name to the text block instance. See Figure 8-25.

Figure 8-25 Dynamic text block

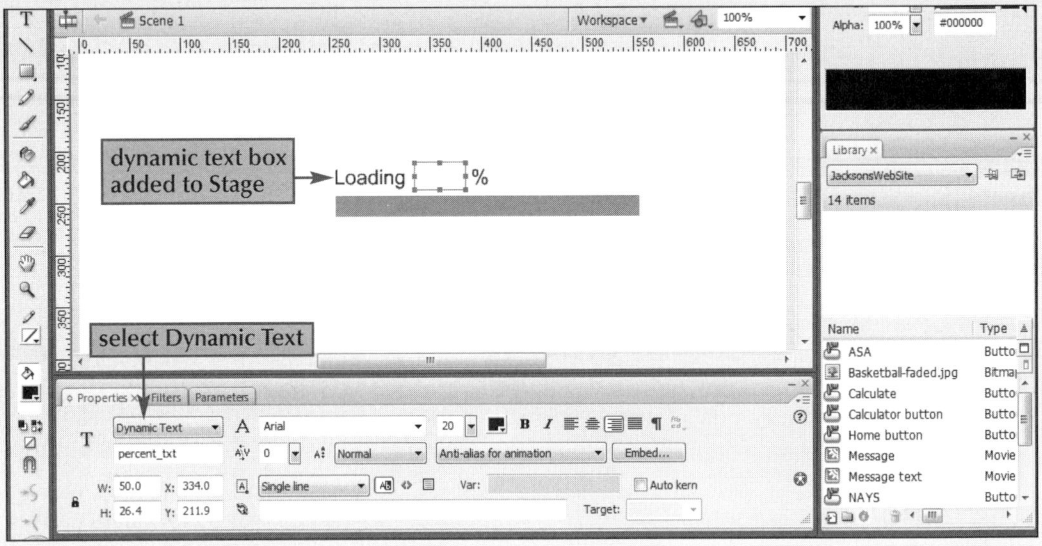

Next, you will add the code to the preloader function to calculate and display the percentage of the file loaded.

To add numeric feedback code, check for errors, and test the script:

1. In the Timeline, click **Frame 1** of the Actions layer, and then expand the Actions panel.
2. In the Script pane of the Actions panel, place the insertion point in front of the line with the if conditional statement, press the **Enter** key to add a blank line, and then type the following line of code exactly as shown:

   ```
   var percent:int = amtLoaded*100;
   ```

   This line creates a new variable named percent with integer as its data type. The value in amtLoaded is multiplied by 100 to change the amtLoaded value to a percentage. This percentage is assigned to the percent variable.
3. Press the **Enter** key to add a new line, and then type the following line of code exactly as shown:

   ```
   percent_txt.text = String(percent);
   ```

The value in the percent variable is converted to a string using the `String()` function and the result is then assigned to the text property of the percent_txt object, which is the dynamic text block instance on the Stage. The result is that the percent value is displayed in the dynamic text box instance.

4. In the Actions panel, click the **Check syntax** button to check for syntax errors. A dialog box opens, indicating whether the script contains errors.
5. Click the **OK** button. The dialog box closes. The error-free functions appear in the Script pane.

   Trouble? If the script contains errors, there are probably typing errors in the code. If the Compiler Errors panel is hidden behind the Actions panel, click the Actions panel title bar to collapse the panel. In the Compiler Errors panel, review the error message(s), and then close the panel. Click the Actions panel title bar to expand the Actions panel, compare the code in the Actions panel with the code in Steps 2 and 3, and then make the necessary corrections so that your code matches the code in the steps. Repeat Steps 4 and 5 until your code is error-free.
6. Save the JacksonsWebSite.fla document.
7. Click **Control** on the menu bar, and click **Test Movie**. The SWF file plays in the Flash Player.
8. In the Flash Player window, click **View** on the menu bar, and then click **Simulate Download**. After a few seconds, the preloader animation plays and the percent loaded value displays. See Figure 8-26.

Figure 8-26 Simulated download process

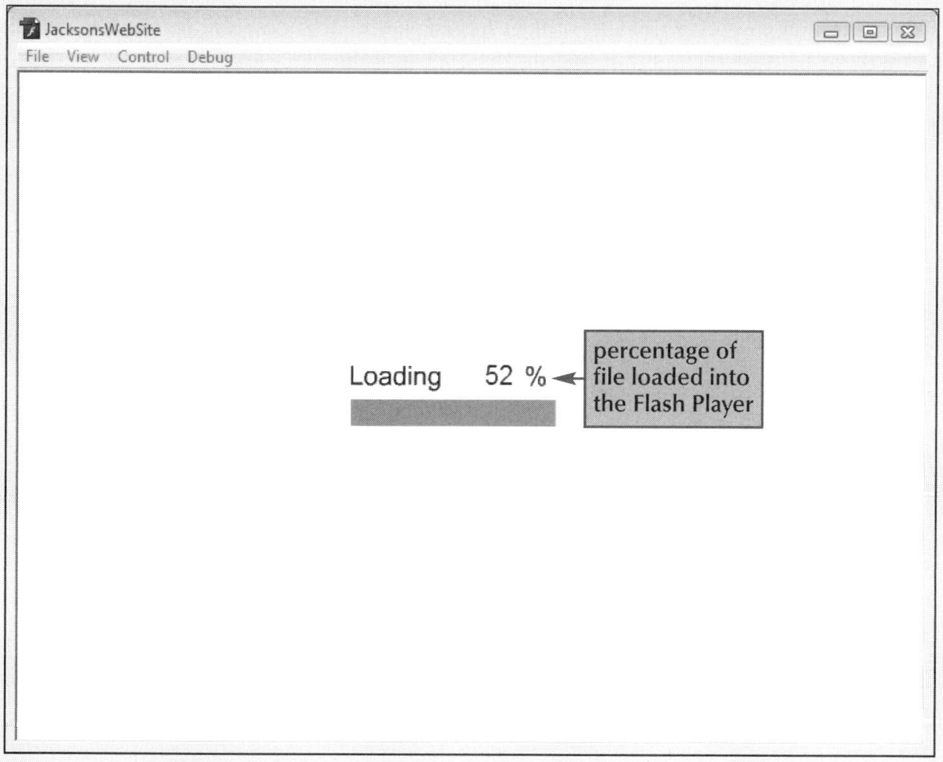

After the percent loaded value reaches 100%, the home page of the Jackson's Sports Web site appears.

9. Close the Flash Player window, and then close the JacksonsWebSite.fla document.

You have completed and tested the input form page that allows the user to enter values in input text blocks, calculates the total cost of the jerseys based on the values entered, and displays the result in a dynamic text block. You also added a dynamic text block to display the percent loaded value with the preloader animation.

Review | Session 8.3 Quick Check

1. What is the purpose of input text?
2. How can you limit the number of characters that can be entered in an input text block?
3. Write a statement to multiply the value in the numeric variable subTotal by 15 and assign the result to the dynamic text block with instance name of subtotal_txt.
4. Explain the purpose of the || operator in the following conditional statement: if (Code == "1" || Code == "2").
5. What is the purpose of the `int()` function?

Review | Tutorial Summary

In this tutorial, you learned the basic elements of ActionScript programming, how to create scripts to control objects in a Flash document, and the structure and syntax of a script written in ActionScript. You also learned about the differences between ActionScript 2.0 and ActionScript 3.0. You used ActionScript to make navigational buttons operational for a Flash Web site and to create links to other Web sites. You also created an input form using input and dynamic text blocks that enable the user to enter data and receive the result of a calculation. Finally, you created a preloader function to display an animation and numeric feedback while a SWF file loads in the Flash Player.

Key Terms

ActionScript Virtual Machine 2 (AVM2)
arithmetic operator
assignment operator
byte
call
class
client computer
comment
comparison operator
conditional statement
constructor
dot notation
event listener
event object
event source
expression
function
input form
keyword
kilobyte
method
numeric data
object
operators
parameter
preloader
property
response
streaming
string data
syntax
typed
variable

Practice | Review Assignments

Practice the skills you learned in the tutorial.

Data File needed for the Review Assignments: SoftballSite.fla

Aly has developed a different version of the Jackson's Youth Sports Web site with an emphasis on softball teams. Aly asks you to complete the Web site by adding links to the Web Links page, adding input and dynamic text boxes to the Player Trophy Cost page, and adding the ActionScript code to make the navigational buttons, the Web Links, and the Trophy cost calculate button operational. You also need to complete the preloader animation and code.

1. Open the **SoftballSite.fla** file located in the Tutorial.08\Review folder included with your Data Files, and then save the file as **JSoftball.fla** in the same folder.
2. In the Labels layer, insert keyframes at Frame 30 and Frame 40, and then add the label **Preload** at Frame 1, the label **Weblinks** at Frame 30, and the label **Trophies** at Frame 40.
3. On the Stage, select the Home button instance and in the Property inspector, name the instance as **home_btn**, select the Services button instance and name the instance as **services_btn**, select the Weblinks button instance and name the instance as **weblinks_btn**, and then select the Trophies button instance and name the instance as **trophies_btn**.
4. In the Actions layer, select Frame 10. In the Actions panel, insert the following comment before the first line:
```
//Keep the playhead from advancing automatically
```
5. In the Actions panel, insert the following comment on the line before the function statement:
```
//Button functions
```
6. In the Actions panel, on the line after the closing curly brace, type the following code:
```
function onServicesClick(evt:MouseEvent):void {
      gotoAndStop("Services");
}
function onWeblinksClick(evt:MouseEvent):void {
      gotoAndStop("Weblinks");
}
function onTrophiesClick(evt:MouseEvent):void {
      gotoAndStop("Trophies");
}
```
7. In the Actions panel, on the line after the last closing curly brace, type the following code:
```
// Event listeners
home_btn.addEventListener(MouseEvent.CLICK, onHomeClick);
services_btn.addEventListener(MouseEvent.CLICK, onServicesClick);
resources_btn.addEventListener(MouseEvent.CLICK, onWeblinksClick);
calculator_btn.addEventListener(MouseEvent.CLICK, onTrophiesClick);
```
8. Check the code for syntax errors, make any necessary corrections, and then collapse the Actions panel.
9. In the Library panel, make a duplicate of the asaYouth button symbol, name the duplicate **softballYouth**, and then edit the softballYouth button by changing the text in both its Up frame and Over frame to **Softball Youth**. In the button's Timeline, insert a keyframe in the Hit frame, and then draw a rectangle with a black fill and no stroke to cover the text block.

10. In the Library panel, make a duplicate of the asaYouth button symbol, name the duplicate **myTeamZone**, and then edit the myTeamZone button by changing the text in both its Up frame and Over frame to **My Team Zone**. In the button's Timeline, insert a keyframe in the Hit frame, and then draw a rectangle with a black fill and no stroke to cover the text block.
11. Edit the asaYouth button by inserting a keyframe in its Hit frame, and then draw a rectangle with a black fill and no stroke to cover the text block.
12. In the Page Content layer, select Frame 30, add an instance of the softballYouth button below the asaYouth button instance, and then add an instance of the myTeamZone button below the softballYouth button instance. Select all three button instances on the center of the Stage, and then, in the Align panel, deselect the To stage button, click the Align left edge button, and click the Space evenly vertically button to align the instances and distribute them evenly.
13. On the Stage, select the asaYouth button instance and name the instance as **asaYouth_btn**, select the softballYouth button instance and name the instance as **softballYouth_btn**, and then select the myTeamZone button instance and name the instance as **myTeamZone_btn**.
14. In the Actions layer, select Frame 30, and then, in the Actions panel, type the following code above the //Event listeners comment line:

```
function gotoSoftballYouthSite(eventobj:MouseEvent):void
{
    var softballYouthURL:URLRequest = new
      URLRequest("http://www.softballyouth.com/");
    navigateToURL(softballYouthURL);
}


function gotoMyTeamZoneSite(eventobj:MouseEvent):void
{
    var myTeamZoneURL:URLRequest = new
      URLRequest("http://www.myteamzone.com/teamwebsites/
      SoftBall.aspx");
    navigateToURL(myTeamZoneURL);
}
```

15. In the Actions panel, type the following code after the last line, and then check the code for syntax errors, making any necessary corrections:

```
softballYouth_btn.addEventListener(MouseEvent.CLICK,
      gotoSoftballYouthSite);
myTeamZone_btn.addEventListener(MouseEvent.CLICK,
      gotoMyTeamZoneSite);
alliance_btn.addEventListener(MouseEvent.CLICK, gotoAllianceSite);
```

16. In the Page content layer, select Frame 40, create an input text block to the right of the Add individual names (Enter Y or N) text block, make the text block 70 pixels wide and 30 pixels high, set the line type to Single Line, show the border around text, set the maximum characters to 1, and then name the input text box instance as **playerNames**.
17. Create an input text block to the right of the Number of players text block using the same dimensions and properties as the playerNames text box, except name the input text box instance as **numberOfPlayers**.

18. Create a dynamic text block to the right of the Total cost (w/o tax) = text block using the same dimensions and properties as the playerNames text box, except set the maximum characters to 0 and name the dynamic text block instance as **total**.
19. In the Actions layer, select Frame 40, type the following code above the //Event listener comment line in the Actions panel, and then check the code for syntax errors, making any necessary corrections:

```
if (trophyType.text == "1") {
      price = 5.95;
      }
if (trophyType.text == "2") {
      price = 8.95;
      }

if (playerNames.text =="Y" || playerNames.text == "y") {
      price += .50;
}

totalCost = int(numberOfPlayers.text)*price;
total.text = String(totalCost);
}
```

20. In the Page content layer, select Frame 1, deselect all the contents on the Stage, select the rectangle's green fill but not its stroke. Convert the rectangle's fill to a movie clip symbol named **Rectangle** with the upper-left registration point selected. In the Property inspector, name the Rectangle instance as **loadBar_mc**.
21. On the Stage, create a dynamic text block to the left of the % text block, set the font to Arial, set the font size to 20, set the text color to black, deselect the Bold attribute, select the Align Right attribute, deselect the Show border around text button, make the dimensions of the text block 70 pixels wide and 40 pixels high, and then name the text block instance as **percent_txt**.
22. In the Actions layer, select Frame 1, type the following code in the Actions panel before the //Event listener line, check the code for syntax errors, making any necessary corrections:

```
      loadBar_mc.scaleX = amtLoaded;

      var percent:int = amtLoaded*100;
      percent_txt.text = String(percent);

      if (loadedBytes == totalBytes) {
            gotoAndPlay("Home");
      } else {
            gotoAndPlay("Preload");
      }
}
```

23. Save the JSoftball.fla document and test it. In the Flash Player window, use the Simulate Download command to test the preloader. Click the Web Links button to go to the Web Links page. On the Web Links page, click each of the link buttons to open the linked Web sites in a browser window. (If an error message appears indicating an error opening the Web pages, the URLs for these Web sites might have changed since the printing of this text. See your instructor or technical support person for assistance.)

24. Click the Trophies button to go to the Player Trophy Cost page. In the Type of Trophy text box, type **1**. In the Add individual names (Enter Y or N) text box, type **Y**. In the Number of players text box, type **11**. Clicking the Calculate button displays 70.95 for the total cost.
25. Submit the finished files to your instructor, either in printed or electronic form, as requested.

Apply | Case 1

Add Web links, an input form, and ActionScript code to make buttons and Web links operational, and to perform a calculation based on input values in a Flash Web site for a scrapbooking store.

Data File needed for this Case Problem: ScrapbookSite.fla

Sandy's Scrapbook Store Web Site Sandy meets with John to discuss adding two new elements to the Web site, including a new page added with hyperlinks to Web sites with additional scrapbook information helpful to the store's customers. She also wants a page for customers to select from several options for the weekend retreats. These options include the type of retreat (one-day or two-day), the number of people who will attend, and whether the use of the store's tools will be needed for the retreat. The page will then display the cost of the retreat based on the selections.

1. Open the **ScrapbookSite.fla** document located in the Tutorial.08\Case1 folder included with your Data Files, and then save the file as **SandysSite.fla** in the same folder.
2. In the Timeline, insert a new layer above the Content layer and name it **Actions**. In the Actions layer, insert keyframes at Frame 10 and Frame 20. Insert a layer above Actions layer and name it **Labels**. In the Labels layer, insert keyframes at Frame 10 and Frame 20, and then add the label **Home** in Frame 1, the label **Resources** in Frame 10, and the label **Retreats** in Frame 20.
3. On the Stage, select the Home button instance, and then, in the Property inspector, name the instance as **home_btn**, select the Resources button instance and name it as **resources_btn**, and select the Retreats button instance and name it as **retreats_btn**.
4. In the Actions layer, select Frame 1, and then in the Actions panel, insert the following code and check the code for syntax errors, making any necessary corrections:

```
//Keep the playhead from advancing
stop();
//Button functions
function onHomeClick(evt:MouseEvent):void {
      gotoAndStop("Home");
}
function onResourcesClick(evt:MouseEvent):void {
      gotoAndStop("Resources");
}
function onRetreatsClick(evt:MouseEvent):void {
      gotoAndStop("Retreats");
}
// Event listeners
home_btn.addEventListener(MouseEvent.CLICK, onHomeClick);
resources_btn.addEventListener(MouseEvent.CLICK, onResourcesClick);
retreats_btn.addEventListener(MouseEvent.CLICK, onRetreatsClick);
```

5. In the Content layer, select Frame 10, and on the Stage, create a static text block within the blue rectangle at about 210 pixels from the left edge of the Stage and 270 pixels from the top edge of the Stage. Use Comic Sans MS for the font, 14 for the font size, black for the text color, and Align Left for the alignment. Type **Scrapbook Portal** in the text block.
6. Create another static text block below the first one with the same text properties. Place it about 210 pixels from the left edge of the Stage and 305 pixels from the top edge of the Stage. Type **Scrapbooks, etc.** in the text block.
7. Create another static text block below the second one with the same text properties. Place it about 210 pixels from the left edge of the Stage and 340 pixels from the top edge of the Stage. Type **International Scrapbooking Association** in the text block. Select the three text blocks, and then align them by their left edges and distribute them evenly vertically.
8. Convert each of the three text blocks into button symbols. Name the first text block symbol **ScrapPortal**, name the second text block symbol **ScrapbooksEtc**, and name the third text block symbol **International**.
9. Edit the ScrapPortal symbol, insert a keyframe in its Over frame, make the text bold in this frame, and draw a rectangle in the Hit frame to make it easier to click the button. Edit the ScrapbooksEtc symbol, insert a keyframe in its Over frame, make the text bold in this frame, and draw a rectangle in the Hit frame. Edit the International symbol, insert a keyframe in its Over frame, make the text bold in this frame, and draw a rectangle in the button's Hit frame.
10. On the Stage in the main Timeline, select the ScrapPortal button instance and, in the Property inspector, name the instance as **portal_btn**, select the ScrapbooksEtc button instance and name the instance as **etc_btn**, and then select the International button instance and name the instance as **assoc_btn**.
11. In the Actions layer, insert a keyframe at Frame 10, and then, in the Actions panel, type the following code to make the buttons operational and check the code for syntax errors, making any necessary corrections:

```
//Button functions
function gotoPortalSite(eventobj:MouseEvent):void
{
    var PortalURL:URLRequest = new
      URLRequest("http://www.scrapbookportal.com");
    navigateToURL(PortalURL);
}

function gotoEtcSite(eventobj:MouseEvent):void
{
    var etcURL:URLRequest = new
      URLRequest("http://www.bhgscrapbooksetc.com/");
    navigateToURL(etcURL);
}
```

```
function gotoAssocSite(eventobj:MouseEvent):void
{
    var AssocURL:URLRequest = new
      URLRequest("http://www.iscrap.net/");
    navigateToURL(AssocURL);
}
//Event listeners
portal_btn.addEventListener(MouseEvent.CLICK, gotoPortalSite);
etc_btn.addEventListener(MouseEvent.CLICK, gotoEtcSite);
assoc_btn.addEventListener(MouseEvent.CLICK, gotoAssocSite);
```

12. Create a new static text block below the third button. Use Comic Sans MS for the font, 10 for the font size, black for the text color, Align Left for the alignment, and apply the Italic attribute. Type **Clicking the buttons above will open a browser window.** in the text block.
13. In the Content layer, select Frame 20, create an input text block to the right of the Enter letter for the desired retreat option line. Place the text block about 430 pixels from the left edge of the Stage and about 260 pixels from the top edge of the Stage. Make the text block 40 pixels wide by 20 pixels high. Use Comic Sans MS for the font, 12 for the font size, black for the text color, and Align Right for the alignment. If necessary, select Single Line as the line type, select the Show Border Around Text button, and enter **1** as the maximum characters. In the Property inspector, name the text block instance as **retreatType_txt**.
14. Create a second input text block with the same dimensions and properties as the retreatType_txt text block. Place this text block to the right of the How many in your group? line and about 300 pixels from the top edge of the Stage. If necessary, set the maximum characters to 0 and name the text block instance as **attendees_txt**.
15. Create another input text block with the same dimensions and properties as the retreatType_txt text block, and place it to the right of the Include use of store tools for $8.95 (Y- yes or N- no) line and about 325 pixels from the top edge of the Stage. Change the maximum characters to 1 and name the text block instance as **tools_txt**.
16. Create a dynamic text block to the right of the Total cost (w/o taxes): line and about 355 pixels from the top edge of the Stage. Use the same dimensions and text properties as the input text blocks. Name the text block instance as **total_txt**.
17. Drag an instance of the Calc button from the document's Library panel to the lower-right corner of the light yellow rectangle, and then name the text block instance as **calc_btn**.
18. In the Actions layer, select Frame 20, and in the Actions panel, type the following code, and then check the code for syntax errors, making any necessary corrections:

```
//Calculate cost of retreat
function Calculate(evt:MouseEvent):void {

      var price:Number;
      var totalCost:Number;

      if (retreatType_txt.text == "F" ||
      retreatType_txt.text == "f") {
            price = 24.95;
            } else {
            price = 14.95;
            }

      totalCost = int(attendees_txt.text)*price;
```

```
        if (tools_txt.text =="Y" || tools_txt.text == "y") {
            totalCost += int(attendees_txt.text) * 8.95;
        }

        total_txt.text = String(totalCost);
}
//Event listener
calc_btn.addEventListener(MouseEvent.CLICK, Calculate);
```

19. Save the SandysSite.fla document, and then test it. Click the Resources button to display the Resources page. Click each of the links to open the Web sites in browser windows. (If an error message appears indicating an error opening the Web pages, the URLs for these Web sites might have changed since the printing of this text. See your instructor or technical support person for assistance.)
20. Click the Retreats button to display the Retreats page. Enter **F** for the type of retreat, **3** for the number of people in the group, and **N** for use of store's tools. Click the Calculate button to display 74.85 for the total cost.
21. Submit the finished file to your instructor, either in printed or electronic form, as requested.

Apply | Case 2

Create a Flash Web site with buttons that when clicked display the contents of previous and next frames for a music store.

Data Files needed for this Case Problem: SpecialsPage.fla, guitars.jpg, piano.jpg, trumpets.jpg

River City Music Web Site Janet meets with Alex to request a new Web site that will display musical instruments. Several pages will display special sales and the site user will be able to change the display from one special to another.

Alex asks you to help him modify an Instruments page by adding buttons to control the display of each special and by adding each special on a separate frame. Each special will display a picture of a musical instrument and a short message about the special. River City Music currently has three instrument specials.

1. Open the **SpecialsPage.fla** document located in the Tutorial.08\Case2 folder included with your Data Files, and then save the file as **Instruments.fla** in the same folder.
2. In the Timeline, insert three new layers above the Contents layer. Name the first layer **Buttons**, the second layer **Labels**, and the third layer **Actions**.
3. In the Timeline, select the Buttons layer and then open the Buttons Common Library. (*Hint:* Click Window on the menu bar, point to Common Libraries, and then click Buttons.) In the Buttons Library panel, open the playback flat folder, drag an instance of the flat blue back symbol to the Stage, place the instance below the text block at the center of the Stage, and then name the instance as **prev_btn**. Drag an instance of the flat blue forward symbol, place the instance just to the right of the flat blue back instance, and then name the instance as **next_btn**. Close the Buttons library panel.
4. Select both of the button instances, deselect the To stage button in the Align panel, if necessary, and click the Align top edge button. Lock the Buttons layer to prevent accidentally changing its contents.
5. In the Timeline, insert regular frames at Frame 10 of all the layers. Insert a keyframe in Frame 2 of the Contents layer, and then delete the bottom text block.

6. Import the **guitars.jpg**, **piano.jpg**, and **trumpets.jpg** files located in the Tutorial.08\Case2 folder included with your Data Files to the document's library. Drag an instance of the guitars.jpg bitmap from the document's Library panel to the center of the rectangle and place it above the buttons.
7. In Frame 2 of the Contents layer, add a fixed-width static text block to the left of the guitars picture. Make the text block's width about 100 pixels and place it about 190 pixels from the top of the Stage and about 80 pixels from the left of the Stage. Use Arial for the font, 14 for the font size, maroon (#660000) for the text color, and Align Left for the alignment. Type **Guitars are now on sale. Save up to 30% on name brands.** in the text block.

EXPLORE

8. In the Timeline, insert a keyframe at Frame 3 of the Contents layer. On the Stage, swap the instance of the guitars.jpg bitmap with an instance of the piano.jpg bitmap. Change the text in the text block to the left of the picture to **Used pianos on sale. Save 20% off their regular price. Tuned and refurbished.**

EXPLORE

9. In the Timeline, insert a keyframe at Frame 4 of the Contents layer. On the Stage, swap the instance of the piano.jpg bitmap with an instance of the trumpets.jpg bitmap. Change the text in the text block to the left of the picture to **Take an extra 15% off all trumpets. Also, get a free lesson with the purchase of a trumpet.**
10. In the Timeline, select Frame 1 of the Labels layer. In the Property inspector, assign the label **Begin** to this frame. Insert a keyframe at Frame 4 of the Labels layer, and assign the label **End** to the frame.
11. In the Timeline, select Frame 1 of the Actions layer. In the Actions panel, type the following code (this code stops the playhead at Frame 1; the function move the playhead to the next frame unless the playhead is on Frame 4, in which case the playhead will move to the frame labeled Begin):

```
//Keep the playhead from advancing
stop();

//Advance the playhead to the next frame
function onNextClick(evt:MouseEvent):void {
      if (currentFrame!=4) {
         nextFrame();
   } else {
         gotoAndStop("Begin");
   }
}
```

12. In the Actions panel, type the following code after the last line (the function moves the playhead to the previous frame unless the playhead is on Frame 1, in which case the playhead will move to the frame labeled End):

```
//Advance the playhead to the previous frame
function onPrevClick(evt:MouseEvent):void {
      if (currentFrame!=1) {
         prevFrame();
   } else {
         gotoAndStop("End");
   }
}
```

13. In the Actions panel, type the following code after the last line (this code creates the event listeners for the buttons):

```
// Event listeners
```

```
prev_btn.addEventListener(MouseEvent.CLICK, onPrevClick);
next_btn.addEventListener(MouseEvent.CLICK, onNextClick);
```

14. Check the code for syntax errors, and make any necessary corrections.
15. Save the Instruments.fla file, and then test it. Click the buttons to display each of the specials in the frames.
16. Submit the finished file to your instructor, either in printed or electronic form, as requested.

Apply | Case 3

Add ActionScript code to advance the playhead from one frame to another and add a preloader to a Flash Web site for a nursery.

Data File needed for this Case Problem: RevPhotos.fla, flower1.jpg, flower2.jpg, flower3.jpg

Westcreek Nursery Web Site Alice requests a different version of the photos page to display pictures of flowers and plants for sale. Because the number of pictures varies each week, only one button will be used. Each time the button is clicked, a different picture will appear. This will allow more pictures to be added without adding more buttons. You will modify a revised photos page by adding one picture with text per frame and adding a button to advance from one frame to the next. You will also add a preloader, which will display a message and an animation indicating the progress of the loading.

1. Open the **RevPhotos.fla** file located in the Tutorial.08\Case3 folder included with your Data Files, and then save the file as **WCPhotos.fla** in the same folder.
2. In the Timeline, insert a new layer above the Background layer and name it **Pictures**. Insert two more layers above the Preloader content layer. Name the first layer **Labels** and the second layer **Actions**.
3. (EXPLORE) In the Pictures layer, insert a keyframe at Frame 10. Use the Import to Stage command to import the **flower1.jpg** file located in the Tutorial.08\Case3 folder included with your Data Files. Click the Yes button to import all of the images in the sequence, which places each of the three pictures in separate frames.
4. In the Timeline, insert regular frames at Frame 12 of all the layers except the Pictures layer. In the Pictures layer, select Frame 10 and create a static text block in the lower-center of the picture. Use Arial for the font, 24 for the font size, white for the text color, and select the Bold attribute. Type **$9.95–$29.95** in the text block.
5. In the Pictures layer, select Frame 11, create a static text block in the lower-center of the picture using the same attributes as in Step 4, and then type **$4.95–$16.95** in the text block. In the Pictures layer, select Frame 12, create a static text block in the lower-center of the picture using the same attributes as in Step 4, and then type to **$3.95–$8.95** in the text block.
6. In the Actions layer, insert a keyframe at Frame 10. In the Labels layer, insert a keyframe at Frame 10, and then add the label **preload** in Frame 1 and the label **begin** in Frame 10.
7. On the Stage, select the Next button instance, and then name the instance as **next_btn**.
8. Select Frame 1 of the Preloader content layer, and on the Stage, draw a rectangle above the Loading text block. Use red (#FF0000) for the fill and do not include a stroke. Use dimensions of 345 pixels for the width and 30 pixels for the height. Convert the rectangle to a movie clip symbol named **loadBar** and, if necessary, select the upper-left registration point. In the Property inspector, name the rectangle instance as **loadBar_mc**.

9. In the Actions layer, select Frame 1, type the following code in the Actions panel, and then check the code for syntax errors, making any necessary corrections. The code will check and compare the bytes loaded with the total bytes and increase the scale of the red rectangle as the document is loaded. After the document is loaded, the playhead is moved to the frame labeled begin.

```
//Keep the playhead from advancing
stop();

//Preloader function
function preloader(progressEvt:ProgressEvent):void {
      var totalBytes:Number = progressEvt.bytesTotal;
      var loadedBytes:Number = progressEvt.bytesLoaded;
      var amtLoaded:Number = loadedBytes/totalBytes;
      loadBar_mc.scaleX = amtLoaded;

      if (loadedBytes == totalBytes) {
            gotoAndPlay("begin");
      } else {
            gotoAndPlay("preload");
      }
}
//Event listener
loaderInfo.addEventListener(ProgressEvent.PROGRESS, preloader);
```

10. In the Actions layer, select Frame 10, type the following code in the Actions panel, and then check the code for syntax errors, making any necessary corrections. The code will advance the playhead to the next frame each time the button is clicked.

```
//Keep the playhead from advancing
stop();
//Advance the playhead
function onNextClick(evt:MouseEvent):void {

      if (currentFrame == 12) {
        gotoAndStop("begin");
    } else {
          nextFrame();
          }
}

//Event listener
next_btn.addEventListener(MouseEvent.CLICK, onNextClick);
```

11. Save the WCPhotos.fla file, and then test it. Use the Simulate Download command to test the preloader. After the document loads, the first picture is displayed. Click the Next button to display the next picture.
12. Submit the finished file to your instructor, either in printed or electronic form, as requested.

Challenge | Case 4

Complete a Flash Web site by adding ActionScript code to compare user input against possible values and calculate a result.

Data File needed for this Case Problem: Calories.fla

Regional Dietetic Association Web Site While reviewing the Web site with the association's president, Katie suggests adding a simple calorie-burning calculator as an interactive element to the site. The calculator will enable the user to enter an activity, his or her weight in pounds, and the number of minutes spent on the activity. The calculator will determine and display the number of calories burned based on the values entered. The formula to determine the number of calories burned is as follows:

calories burned = exercise_factor x weight x minutes

The exercise_factor is a number assigned to each exercise activity that represents the rate of calories burned for that activity.

You will develop the new page for the Web site based on a document that Katie has developed.

1. Open the **Calories.fla** document located in the Tutorial.08\Case4 folder included with your Data Files, and then save the file as **CaloriesCalc.fla** in the same folder.
2. In the Timeline, insert three new layers above the Content layer and name them **Text fields**, **Button**, and **Actions**, respectively.
3. In the Timeline, select the Text fields layer and create an input text block to the right of the Enter letter for activity: text. Use Arial for the font, 14 for the font size, black for the text color, and Align Right for the alignment. Also, if necessary, select Single Line as the line type, select the Show Border Around Text button, and set the maximum characters to 1. Place the text block so that its left side aligns with the vertical guide and its top edge is about 110 pixels from the top of the Stage. Set the text block's dimensions at 40 pixels wide by 20 pixels high, and then name the text block instance as **activity_txt**.
4. Create another input text block with the same properties as the activity_txt text block but with the maximum characters set to 0. Place this text block to the right of the Enter your weight: text at about 165 pixels from the top of the Stage and name the text block instance as **weight_txt**.
5. Create another input text block also using the same properties as the activity_txt text block with the maximum characters set to 0. Place this text block to the right of the Time spent doing activity: text at about 195 pixels from the top of the Stage and name the text block instance as **time_txt**.
6. Create a dynamic text block to the right of the Number of calories burned is: text at about 250 pixels from the top of the Stage. Use the same properties as you did for the input text blocks except use white for the text color, make the text bold, and deselect the Show Border Around Text button. Make the text block about 60 pixels wide by 20 pixels high and name the text block instance as **calories_txt**.
7. In the Timeline, select the Button layer and then drag an instance of the Calc button from the document's Library panel to the Stage below the dynamic text block so that its left side aligns with the vertical guide. Name the button instance as **calc_btn**.
8. In the Actions layer, select Frame 1, and then in the Actions panel, type the following code. After the comments, a Calculate function is defined and a numeric variable named exercise_factor is also defined.

```
// Function to determine the exercise factor based on
// the letter entered for Activity
function Calculate(evt:MouseEvent):void {

var exercise_factor:Number;
```

EXPLORE 9. In the Actions panel, type the following code after the last line. The exercise factor used to calculate the number of calories burned is different for each of the possible activities. The user will enter a letter into the activity_txt input text box that represents the activity. The switch statement checks the value in activity_txt and compares it to the values in the case statements. If the value in activity_txt matches a value in the case statement, the statement following the case statement is executed. For example, if the value entered into the activity_txt input text box is either B or b, the value .039 is assigned to the exercise_factor variable. The break statement is used to exit the switch statement.

```
switch (activity_txt.text) {
case "B" :
case "b" :
        exercise_factor = .039;
        break;
```

EXPLORE 10. Type the following lines to check for the rest of the possible activity_txt values within the switch statement. Each set of case statements is followed by an assignment statement that assigns the appropriate value to the exercise_factor variable.

```
case "S" :
case "s" :
        exercise_factor = .052;
        break;
case "J" :
case "j" :
        exercise_factor = .075;
        break;
case "Y" :
case "y" :
        exercise_factor = .04;
        break;
```

EXPLORE 11. Type the following lines to complete the switch statement. The default statement causes a value of zero to be assigned to the exercise_factor if none of the case values matched the value in the activity_txt input text box.

```
default :
        exercise_factor = 0;
};
```

12. Type the following lines to convert the value entered into the weight_txt and time_txt input boxes into Integer values and assign the values to the Weight and Time variables, respectively.

```
// Convert input values into Integer numbers
var Weight:Number = int(weight_txt.text);
var Time:Number = int(time_txt.text);
```

13. In the Actions panel, type the following lines of code. The exercise_factor and Weight value, which is the person's weight, are multiplied. The result is multiplied by the value in Time which is the number of minutes spent doing the activity. The resulting value is the number of calories burned. This value is assigned to the text property of the calories_txt so that it will appear in the dynamic text box.

```
// Determine the number of calories burned
var Calories:Number = exercise_factor * Weight * Time;
calories_txt.text = String(Calories);
}
```

14. In the Actions panel, type the following lines to create an event listener and complete the code.

```
//Event listener
calc_btn.addEventListener(MouseEvent.CLICK, Calculate);
```

15. Check for syntax errors and make any necessary corrections.
16. Save the CalorieCalc.fla file and test it. Enter **S** for the Activity, **175** for the weight, and **30** for the number of minutes. Click the Calculate button. The number of calories burned is 273.
17. Submit the finished file to your instructor, either in printed or electronic form, as requested.

Review | Quick Check Answers

Session 8.1

1. a programming language that allows you to make Flash documents interactive by manipulating objects
2. False.
3. object
4. Flash will display code hints in the Actions panel when the names with suffixes are used.
5. Car_mc.alpha = 50;
6. the event source, also known as the event target, the event, and the response
7. Comments enable the programmer writing the code to document the purpose of each section of the code and is beneficial to other programmers who might have to modify the code at a later date.

Session 8.2

1.
```
function gotoCourseSite(eventobj:MouseEvent):void

{
    var courseURL:URLRequest = new
      URLRequest("http://www.course.com");
    navigateToURL(courseURL);
}
```
2. Variables should be typed to specify what type of data they can contain.
3. a special method used to create instances of objects based on a class
4. to provide visual feedback to the site visitor such as a short animation or message while the rest of the file's contents load into the Flash Player.
5. original
6. Use the Simulate Download command in the Flash Player to simulate the time it takes to download an SWF file based on the type of Internet connection you select.

Session 8.3

1. to enable the user to enter data into a text block
2. In the Property inspector, enter a number in the Maximum characters box to specify the limit for the number of characters that may be entered in the input box.
3. `subtotal_txt.text = String(subTotal * 15);`
4. The || operator causes the condition to be true if the value in Code is either 1 or 2.
5. to convert values to integer numbers, which are whole numbers that do not include decimals

Ending Data Files

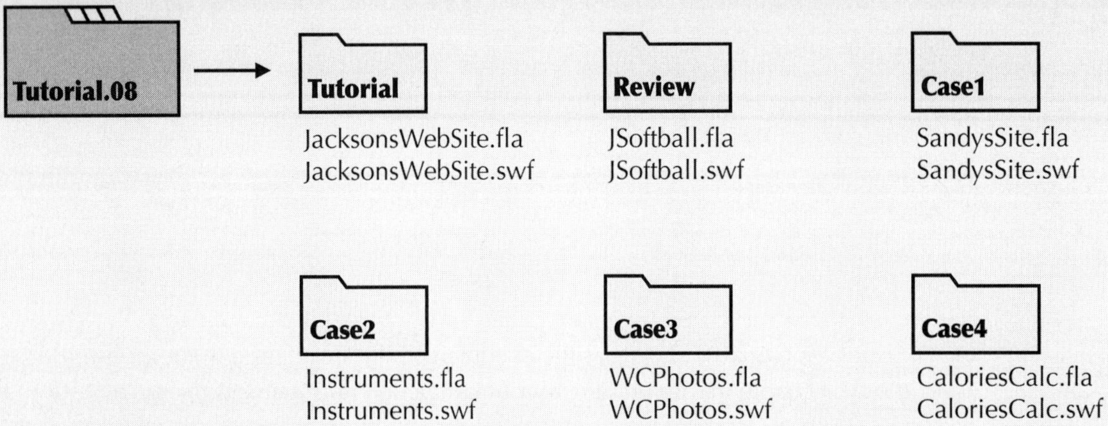

Objectives

Session 9.1
- Add Web links using the ComboBox component
- Add photos using the UILoader and Button components
- Add a ProgressBar component
- Add ActionScript code to control the components

Session 9.2
- Learn the basics of using digital video as it relates to Flash
- Import video into a Flash document
- Modify the FLVPlayback component and its parameters
- Add button components to control video clip selection

Session 9.3
- Prepare Flash content for printing
- Control printing with ActionScript

Using Flash Components and Video, and Printing Flash Content

Adding Web Links, Photos, Video, and Printable Content to a Flash Web Site

Case | Admiral Web Design

Dan Jackson wants to change to the Jackson's Youth Sports Web site. Aly and Chris ask you to revise the Jackson's Youth Sports Web site to incorporate the changes that Dan requested. You will add Web links to the home page, complete the Photos page, and complete the Videos page that will be used to display short video segments of youth sports games. The page will contain buttons to select from two video clips and will include controls to play and pause the videos and to mute the audio. Finally, you will create a page that displays coupons the user can print and then redeem at the store. Aly instructs you to use components to create these interactive elements in Flash.

In this tutorial, you will learn how to use components to create interactive elements, how to import video into a Flash document, and how to control the printing of individual frames in a Flash document.

Starting Data Files

Tutorial.09 →

Tutorial
bball1.mpg
bball2.flv
JSWebSite.fla
photo1.jpg
photo2.jpg

Review
NewSoftballSite.fla
softball_clip.avi
softballPhoto1.jpg
softballPhoto2.jpg

Case1
SandySiteDraft.fla
supplies.jpg

Case2
piano.jpg
piano_clip.mpg
RCMDraft.fla

Case3
flower1.jpg
flower1_sm.jpg
flower2.jpg
flower2_sm.jpg
flower3.jpg
flower3_sm.jpg
landscape.avi
WCDraft.fla

Case4
meal1.jpg
meal2.jpg
RDAJobs.png
RDAWebSiteDraft.fla

Session 9.1

Using Flash Components

Components are prebuilt movie clips installed with Flash that include a set of user interface and video components. These components are actually movie clips that have been exported with the .swc extension. Some of the components installed with Flash can be used to create user interface elements in documents. For example, the CheckBox component allows you to create check boxes that can be used as options a user can select on a form. When the user clicks a check box, a check mark appears in the check box. This information can then be processed using ActionScript. Using a component such as the CheckBox means you don't have to create the graphics and functionality that is already built into the component. Other components include the ComboBox, which displays a drop-down list from which the user can make a selection, and the ProgressBar, which displays the loading progress of content loading into the Flash Player.

InSight | Downloading Additional Components

You can add more components by downloading them from Web resources such as the Flash Exchange, which is an Adobe Web site with resources for Flash developers. You can also purchase components from other sources such as *www.flashloaded.com*. Downloaded components are installed using the Adobe Extension Manager. You can even create your own components by exporting a movie clip from the document's Library panel. The Flash Exchange and the Adobe Extension Manager are both accessible from the Help menu.

The Flash components are located in the Components panel. The first time you add a component to a document, simply drag an instance of the component from the Components panel to the Stage. The component's movie clip and other elements are added to the document's library. Then, you can add more instances of the same component by dragging them from the Library panel to the Stage. You can assign each instance a name and view or change its parameters using either the Parameters panel or the Component Inspector panel. Parameters are settings that can be changed for each instance of a component. The Parameters panel contains the most commonly used parameters based on the selected component. The Component Inspector panel can contain additional parameters not shown in the Parameters panel.

Reference Window | Adding a Flash Component

- Click Window on the menu bar, and then click Components.
- In the Components panel, double-click the components list you want to expand, if necessary.
- Drag an instance of the component from the Components panel to the Stage.
- Reposition and align the component instance on the Stage as needed.
- In the Property inspector, name the instance and enter width and height values.
- In the Parameters panel, enter the appropriate values.

Using the ComboBox Component

Based on Aly's instructions, in place of the Resources page you created previously for the Jackson's Youth Sports Web site, you will add a drop-down list of Web links to the home page, as shown in Figure 9-1. The user can then click an item on the list to navigate to another Web site.

Home page with Web links **Figure 9-1**

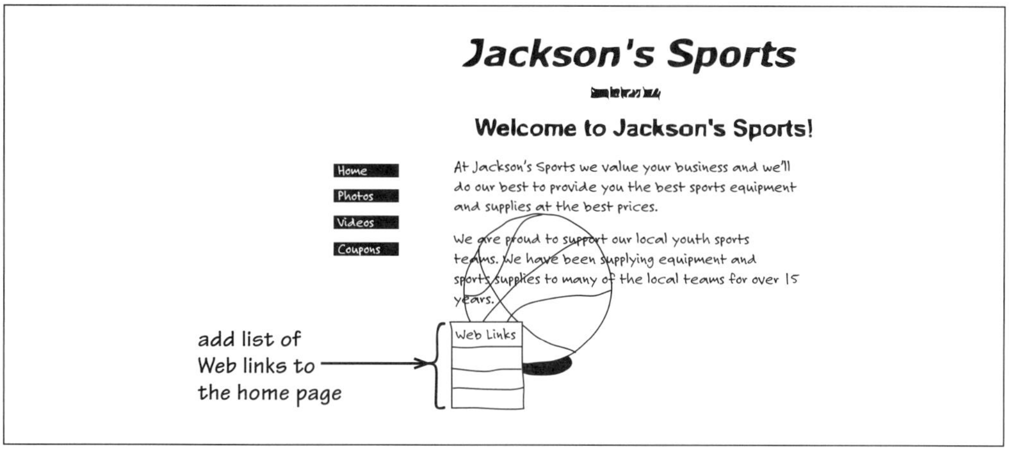

You will create the Web links by adding a ComboBox component to the home page, setting its parameters, and adding ActionScript code to make the items in the ComboBox functional.

To add a ComboBox instance to the Jackson's Youth Sports Web site home page:

1. Open the **JSWebSite.fla** file located in the **Tutorial.09\Tutorial** folder included with your Data Files, save the file as **RevisedSite.fla** in the same folder, set the workspace to its default layout, and then change the zoom to Fit in Window.
2. In the Page content layer of the Timeline, select **Frame 10**. The Home page content appears on the Stage.
3. Click **Window** on the menu bar, and then click **Components**. The Components panel opens.
4. In the Components panel, if necessary, double-click **User Interface** to expand its list of components. See Figure 9-2.

Tip

You can also press the Ctrl+F7 keys to open the Components panel.

Figure 9-2 Components panel

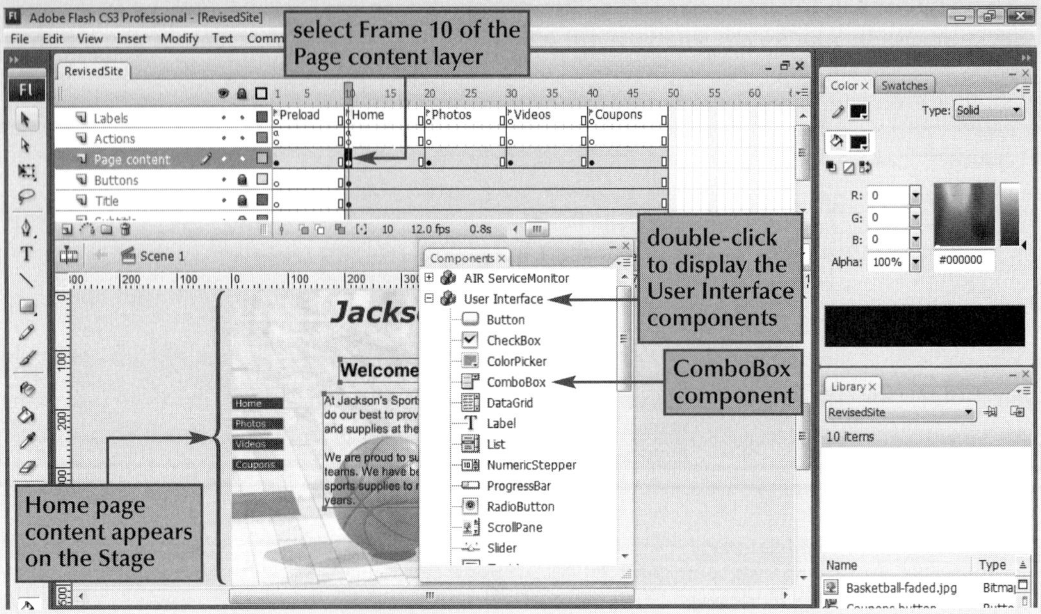

5. Drag an instance of the **ComboBox** component from the Components panel to the Stage, and then close the Components panel.
6. On the Stage, if necessary, reposition the ComboBox instance below the text block containing the welcoming paragraphs, aligning the left edge of the button with the left margin of the text block.
7. In the Property inspector, name the instance **webLinks_mc**, change the width of the instance to **120** pixels, and make sure the height is **22** pixels. The ComboBox instance is positioned and sized for the Home page.

The Parameters panel displays the parameters for the ComboBox instance. The dataProvider parameter defines the labels that will appear on the drop-down list and the values that will be associated with each item. The editable parameter, when set to true, enables the user to edit the items in the list. The contents of the prompt parameter will appear on the ComboBox instance on the Stage. The rowCount parameter determines how many rows to allocate to the drop-down list. You will enter values for the prompt and dataProvider parameters.

To set parameter values for the ComboBox instance:

1. In the Property inspector, click the **Parameters** tab. The Parameters panel appears, showing the parameters for the selected ComboBox instance.
2. In the Parameters panel, click the box in the column to the right of the prompt, type **Web Links**, and then press the **Enter** key. The Web Links text appears in the ComboBox instance on the Stage.
3. In the Parameters panel, double-click the box in the column to the right of dataProvider. The Values dialog box opens.

Tip

You can also click the magnifying glass button in the right column of the dataProvider parameter to open the Values dialog box.

4. Click the **Add value** button [+] to add an entry for label0, click **label0** in the Value column, type **Soccer**, press the **Tab** key to move the insertion point to the data value box, and then type **1**. The first value is added to the dataProvider parameter.
5. Repeat Step 4 to add two more values to the dataProvider parameter, using **Softball** for the second label and **2** for its value and then using **Youth Sports** for the third label and **3** for its value. See Figure 9-3.

Figure 9-3 Values dialog box

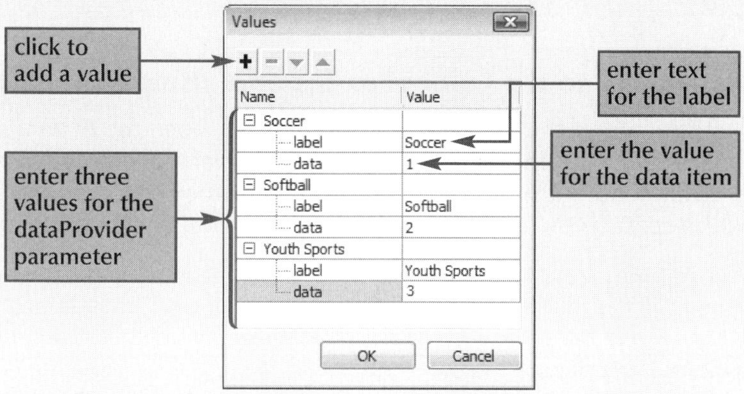

6. Click the **OK** button to close the Values dialog box. The three dataProvider values appear in the Parameters panel.

With the ComboBox component instance added to the Stage and its parameters set, you need to add ActionScript code to make the ComboBox instance operational. When the user clicks an item in the drop-down list, the value associated with the item can be checked using ActionScript code. For example, if a user clicks the Soccer item, the value of the ComboBox instance is 1 because that value is associated with Soccer. ActionScript uses the ComboBox value to determine which URL to use to navigate to a Web site.

To check which of the three URLs will be used, you can use a switch statement, which is helpful when you need to execute one of several statements or blocks of statements based on the value of the same expression. Each block of statements that may be executed is enclosed between a case statement and a break statement. Each case statement has a value associated with it, as shown in Figure 9-4.

Figure 9-4 Sample switch statement

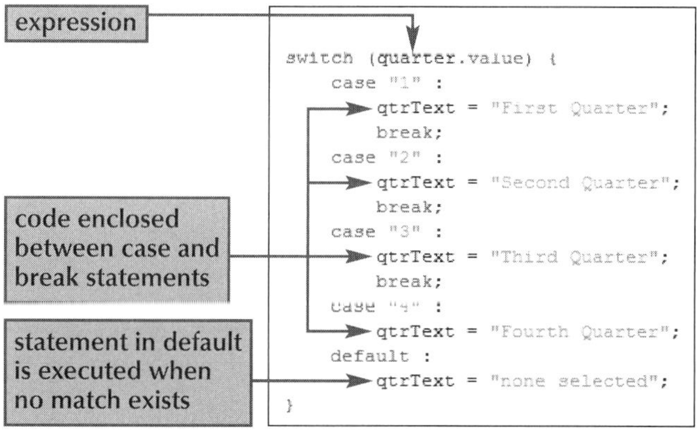

The expression is evaluated and its value is compared with the values in each case statement. If a match exists, the statements following the case statement are executed. The break statement is used to exit the switch statement. The default statement executes when there is no match. You will add a switch statement to check the value of the selected ComboBox item, which can be 1, 2, or 3. When a match is found, the associated code within the case statement assigns a Web site URL to a string variable. No default value is needed because a user can select only three possible values. After the switch statement, the value in the string variable is used to navigate to the corresponding Web site.

You will add the ActionScript code for the ComboBox instance.

To add functionality to the ComboBox instance using ActionScript:

1. In the Actions layer of the Timeline, select **Frame 10,** open the Actions panel, and then, if necessary, click the **collapse** button in the vertical bar between the Actions toolbox and the Script pane. The Actions toolbox collapses and the Script pane, which contains the code for the Web site's navigational buttons, expands.

Tip

You can click the Auto format button in the Actions panel to align and apply indentation to the code to improve readability.

2. In the Script pane, place the insertion point in the blank line after the last line of the existing code, and then type the following lines of code exactly as shown, pressing the **Enter** key after each line, to create the function that determines which URL will be used.

```
// Function to check which site was selected
function gotoSite(eventObj:Event):void {
      // Variable that will hold the URL
      var linkText:String;
      // Switch statement determines which URL to assign
      switch (webLinks_mc.value) {
      case "1" :
            linkText = "http://www.usyouthsoccer.org/";
            break;
      case "2" :
            linkText = "http://www.softball.org/";
            break;
      case "3" :
            linkText = "http://www.nays.org/";
            break;
      }
```

3. In the Script pane, type the following lines of code to create a URLRequest object that is used in the navigateToURL function. The URLRequest uses the URL assigned to the linkText variable in the switch statement.

```
//Open Web site using the selected URL
var siteURL:URLRequest = new URLRequest(linkText);
navigateToURL(siteURL);
```

4. In the Script pane, type the following lines of code to change the value displayed in the ComboBox instance after the Web site is opened. Without this statement, the ComboBox instance will display the label of the item selected by the user.

```
//Set ComboBox to display the prompt, Web Links
webLinks_mc.selectedIndex = -1;
}
```

5. In the Script pane, type the following lines of code to create an event listener. When a change occurs in the ComboBox instance, webLinks_mc, the gotoSite function is called.

```
// Event listener
webLinks_mc.addEventListener(Event.CHANGE, gotoSite);
```

6. In the Actions panel, click the **Check syntax** button to check for syntax errors in the ActionScript code. A dialog box opens, indicating whether the script contains errors.
7. Click the **OK** button. The dialog box closes. The error-free functions appear in the Script pane.

   Trouble? If the script contains errors, there are probably typing errors in the functions. If the Compiler Errors panel is hidden behind the Actions panel, click the Actions panel title bar to collapse the panel. In the Compiler Errors panel, review the error message(s), and then close the panel. Click the Actions panel title bar to expand the Actions panel, compare the code in the Actions panel with the code shown in Steps 2 through 5, and then make the necessary corrections so that your code matches the code in the steps. Repeat Steps 6 and 7 until your code is error-free.
8. Collapse the Actions panel, and then save the RevisedSite.fla document.
9. Click **Control** on the menu bar, and then click **Test Movie**. The Home page appears in the Flash Player window.
10. On the Home page, click each of the Web Links selections, as shown in Figure 9-5, to test them. The Web site that corresponds to the selected item opens.

Figure 9-5 Web links on the Home page

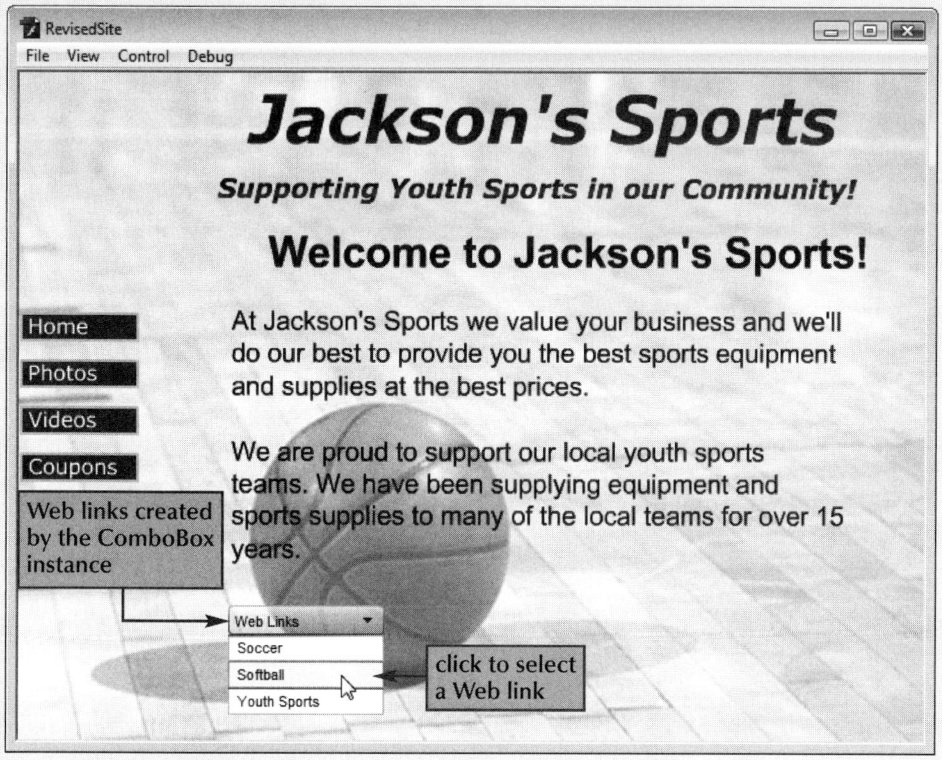

11. Close the Flash Player window and the browser windows.

Using the UILoader Component to Display Photos

The revised Web site created by Aly and Chris contains a Photos page to display youth sports team photos, as shown in Figure 9-6. You will add an instance of the UILoader component, which can be used to load content such as images and SWF files, to the page. The youth sports photos can be loaded into an instance of the UILoader component. You will then use the Button component to add buttons that control which pictures are loaded into the UILoader instance.

Figure 9-6 **Photos page**

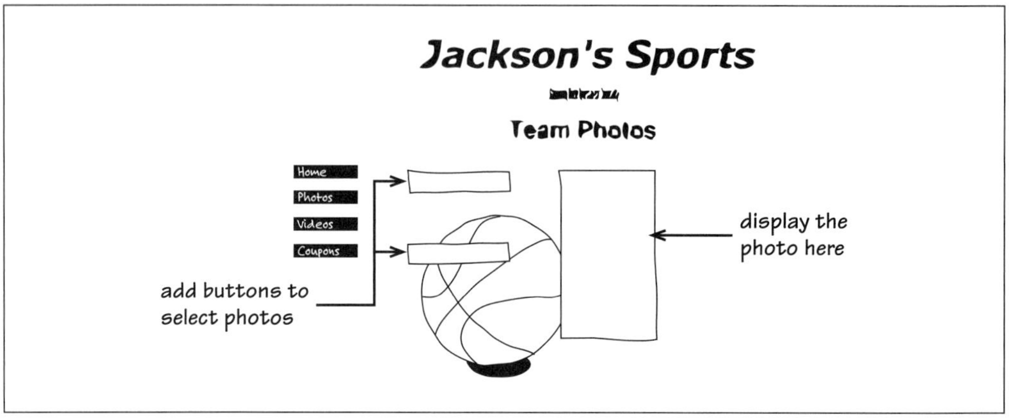

You will add the UILoader and Button components to complete the Team Photos page.

To add instances of the UILoader and Button components to the Team Photos page:

1. In the Page content layer of the Timeline, select **Frame 20**, The Team Photos page appears on the Stage.
2. Click **Window** on the menu bar, click **Components** to open the Components panel, and then, if necessary, move the panel to the right side of the Stage.
3. Drag an instance of the **UILoader** component from the Components panel to the Stage, positioning it about **180** pixels from the top of the Stage and **300** pixels from the left of the Stage.
4. In the Parameters panel, name the instance **loader_mc**, change the width of the instance to **165** pixels, and then change the height to **250** pixels.
5. Drag an instance of the **Button** component from the Components panel to the Stage, positioning it about **180** pixels from the top of the Stage and **150** pixels from the left of the Stage.
6. Drag another instance of the **Button** component to the Stage, positioning it about **220** pixels from the top of the Stage and **150** pixels from the left of the Stage, and then close the Components panel.
7. Select the first Button instance on the Stage, name the selected Button instance **photo1_btn** in the Parameters panel, and then repeat to name the second Button instance **photo2_btn**.
8. On the Edit bar, change the zoom control to **100%** to magnify the view of the buttons.

9. On the Stage, select the **photo1_btn** instance, and then, in the Parameters panel, click the column to the right of the label parameter to select the text Label, type **Photo 1**, and press the **Enter** key. The Button instance on the Stage changes to reflect the new label.

10. Repeat Step 9 to select the **photo2_btn** instance and change its label to **Photo 2**. The second Button instance on the Stage changes to reflect its new label. See Figure 9-7.

Figure 9-7 UILoader and Button instances

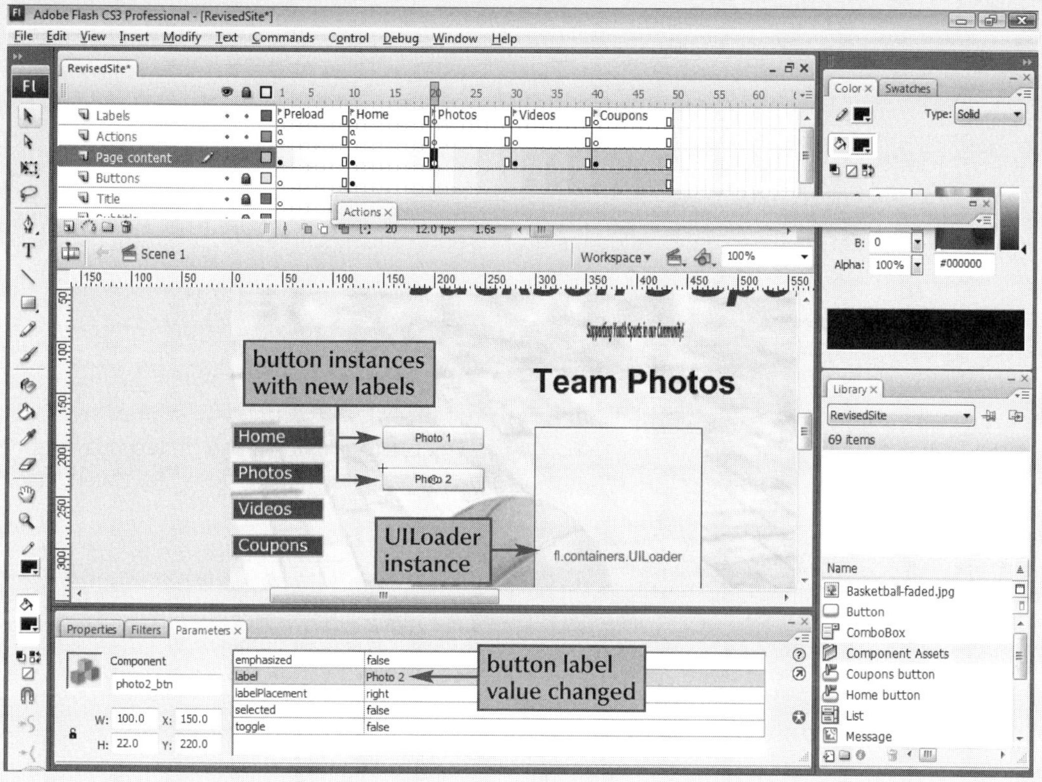

The UILoader and Button components are added to the document. To make the component instances operational, you need to add ActionScript code similar to the code you used for the Web links on the Home page. You create a function with a URLRequest object that contains the name of the photo file to be loaded. Then, instead of using the navigateToURL function, you use the load function of the UILoader instance. You then add an event listener to the button instance to listen for the CLICK event and to run the function that will load the photo.

To add ActionScript code to make the UILoader and Button instances operational:

1. In the Actions layer of the Timeline, select **Frame 20**, and then expand the Actions panel.

2. In the Script pane, type the following lines of code to create the functions that will create a URLRequest object with the photo's filename. The load method of the loader_mc movie clip instance will be used to load the photo into the UILoader instance.

```
// Function to load the first photo
function loadPhoto1(eventObj:MouseEvent):void
{
      var photoURLReq:URLRequest = new URLRequest("photo1.jpg");
      loader_mc.load(photoURLReq);
}
// Function to load the second photo
function loadPhoto2(eventObj:MouseEvent):void
{
      var photoURLReq:URLRequest = new URLRequest("photo2.jpg");
      loader_mc.load(photoURLReq);
}
```

3. In the Script pane, type the following lines of code to create the event listeners that will detect when each button is clicked and run the corresponding function to load a photo.

```
// Event listeners
photo1_btn.addEventListener(MouseEvent.CLICK, loadPhoto1);
photo2_btn.addEventListener(MouseEvent.CLICK, loadPhoto2);
```

4. In the Actions panel, click the **Check syntax** button to check for syntax errors in the ActionScript code, and then click the **OK** button to close the dialog box that indicates whether the script contains errors. The error-free functions appear in the Script pane.

   Trouble? If the script contains errors, there are probably typing errors in the functions. If the Compiler Errors panel is hidden behind the Actions panel, click the Actions panel title bar to collapse the panel. In the Compiler Errors panel, review the error message(s), and then close the panel. Click the Actions panel title bar to expand the Actions panel, compare the code in the Actions panel with the code shown in Steps 2 and 3, and then make the necessary corrections so that your code matches the code in the steps. Repeat Step 4 until your code is error-free.

5. Collapse the Actions panel, save the RevisedSite.fla document, click **Control** on the menu bar, and then click **Test Movie**. The Home page appears in the Flash Player window.

6. On the Home page, click the **Photos** navigation button to display the Photos page.

7. On the Photos page, click the **Photo 1** button to load the first photo, and then click the **Photo 2** button to load the second photo. Each photo, in turn, is loaded into the UILoader instance and appears on the Stage. See Figure 9-8.

Figure 9-8 UILoader instance operational

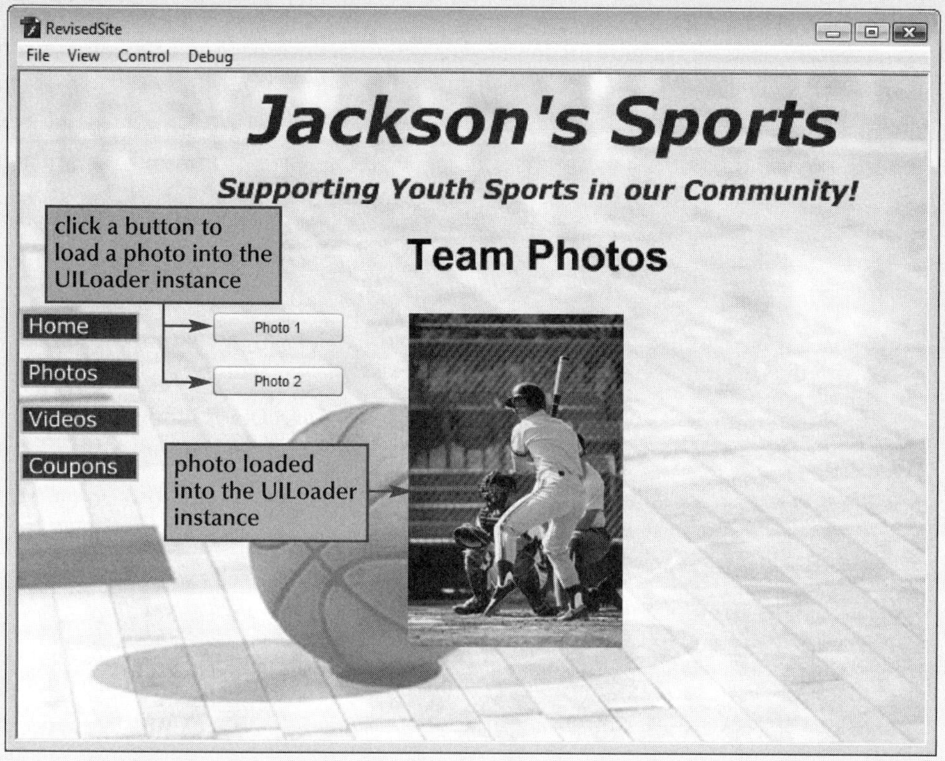

8. Close the Flash Player window.

Using the ProgressBar Component

The Photos page now displays photos in the UILoader instance each time a photo button is clicked. To improve the user experience with the Photos page, you can add a preloader that provides visual feedback when the photos are loading. This is helpful to someone using a slow Internet connection. To create a preloader that requires only a minimal amount of ActionScript and that shows the progress of the photos loading into the Flash Player, you can use the ProgressBar component.

The ProgressBar component can work together with the UILoader component to display the progress of loading content, such as a photo file, into the UILoader instance. As the photo file loads into the UILoader instance, the ProgressBar instance displays an animation depicting the progress of the loading. For the ProgressBar to detect the loading of the content, you enter the name of the UILoader instance into the source parameter of the ProgressBar instance. This establishes a connection between the two component instances.

You will add a ProgressBar component to display a preloader animation for the Photos page.

To add an instance of the ProgressBar component to the Stage:

1. In the Page content layer of the Timeline, select **Frame 20**, click **Window** on the menu bar, and then click **Components** to open the Components panel.

2. Drag an instance of the **ProgressBar** component from the Components panel to the Stage, close the Components panel, and then position the ProgressBar instance at the center of the UILoader instance on the Stage.
3. If necessary, in the Property inspector, click the **Parameters** tab to display the Parameters panel.
4. In the Parameters panel, name the instance **pbar_mc**, change the height to **10** pixels, click in the column to the right of the source parameter, type **loader_mc**, and then press the **Enter** key. The ProgressBar instance will use the contents of the UILoader instance as the source of the content whose progress will be tracked. As the content loads into the loader_mc movie clip, the pbar_mc instance will display a preloader animation.
5. Save the RevisedSite.fla document, click **Control** on the menu bar, and then click **Test Movie**. The Home page appears in the Flash Player window.
6. In the Flash Player, click **View** on the menu bar, point to **Download Settings**, and then click **DSL (32.6 KB/s)** to select the download speed for the simulation.
7. Click **View** on the menu bar, and then click **Simulate Download**. The Home page appears after a few moments.
8. On the Home page, click the **Photos** navigational button to display the Photos page. The ProgressBar instance appears on the Photos page.
9. On the Photos page, click the **Photo 1** button to load the first photo. The Progress-Bar instance displays an animation indicating the content is being loaded. When the photo appears, the ProgressBar animation stops, but remains visible. See Figure 9-9.

Tip

In the Flash Player window, you can also click the Ctrl+Enter keys to run the Simulate Download command.

Figure 9-9 ProgressBar instance on the photo

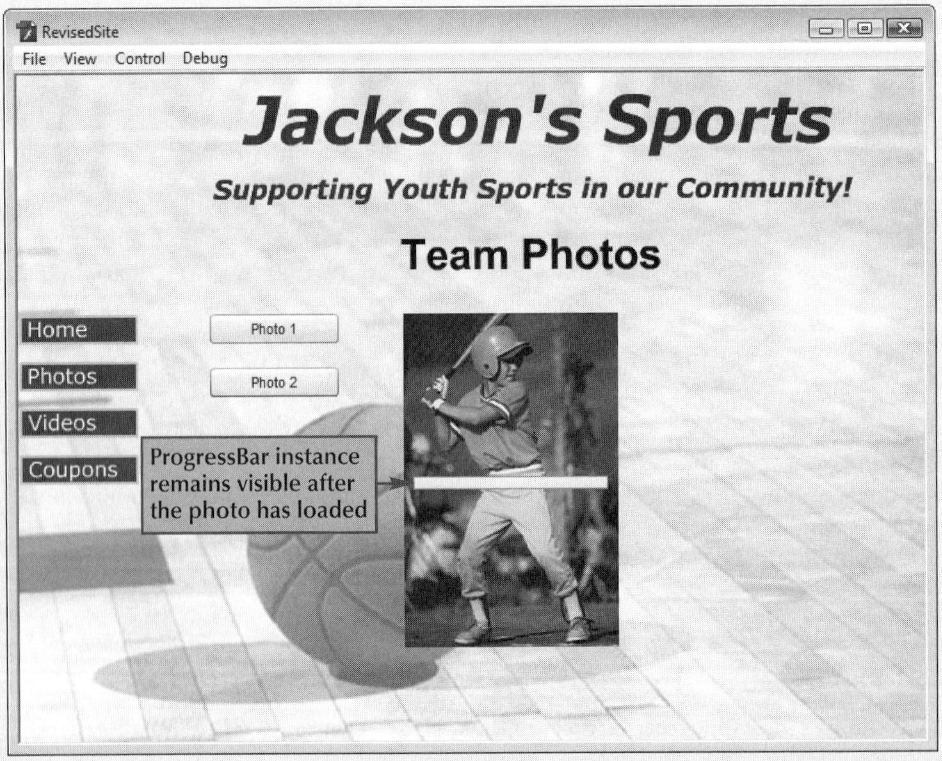

10. Close the Flash Player window.

The ProgressBar instance works as expected; however, it appears before and after a photo is loaded. To hide the ProgressBar instance before a photo is being loaded, you need to change its visible property to false. When a photo is about to be loaded into the UILoader instance, you change the visible property of the ProgressBar instance to true so that it appears. After the photo loading is complete, you change the visible property back to false. You also need to add an event listener that will check for the COMPLETE event of the UILoader instance, which indicates that the loading of the content into the UILoader is complete. When the COMPLETE event is detected, the event listener will run a function to set the visible property of the ProgressBar instance to false so the instance disappears from the Stage. You will add the ActionScript next.

To add ActionScript code to control the ProgressBar instance:

1. In the Actions layer of the Timeline, select **Frame 20**, and then expand the Actions panel.
2. In the Script pane, place the insertion point at the beginning of the first line, press the **Enter** key to add a blank line, and then, starting in the blank line, type the following lines of code to hide the pbar_mc instance when the Photos page is displayed.

```
// Hide the ProgressBar instance
pbar_mc.visible = false;
```

3. In the Script pane, place the insertion point after the opening curly brace within the loadPhoto1 function, press the **Enter** key to add a blank line, and then, in this blank line, type the following line of code to display the pbar_mc instance before the first photo is loaded.

```
pbar_mc.visible = true;
```

4. In the Script pane, place the insertion point after the opening curly brace within the loadPhoto2 function, press the **Enter** key to add a blank line, and then, in this blank line, type the following line of code to display the pbar_mc instance before the second photo is loaded. See Figure 9-10.

```
pbar_mc.visible = true;
```

Visibility set for the ProgressBar instance **Figure 9-10**

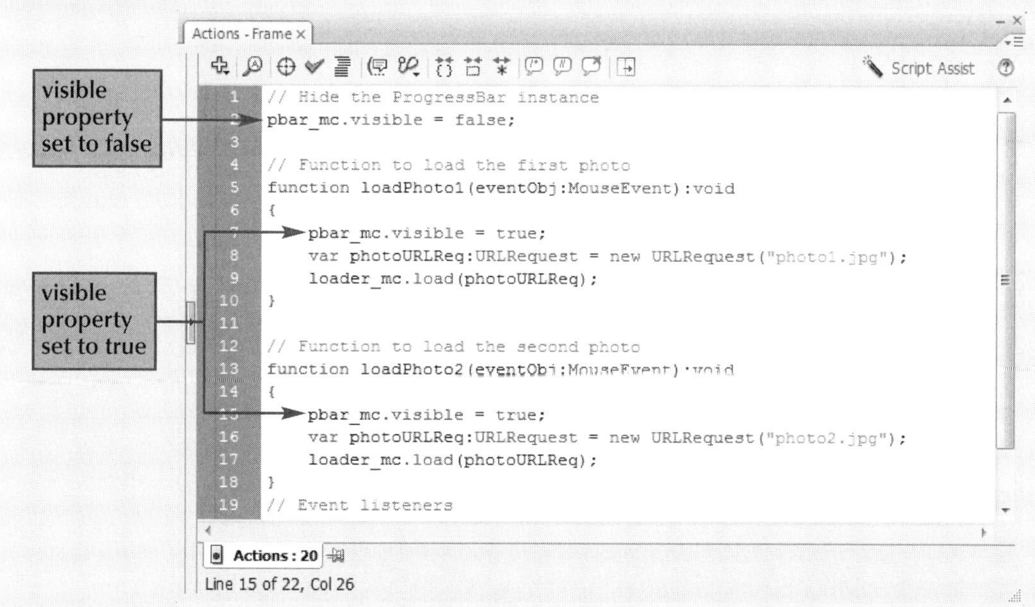

5. In the Script pane, place the insertion point after the closing curly brace of the loadPhoto2 function, press the **Enter** key to add a blank line, and then, starting in this blank line, type the following lines of code to create a function that will hide the pbar_mc instance when the loading of a photo is completed.

```
// When the loading is complete, hide the ProgressBar instance
function hideBar(eventObj:Event) {
        pbar_mc.visible = false;
}
```

6. In the Script pane, type the following line of code after the last line to create an event listener that runs the hideBar function when the COMPLETE event occurs for the loader_mc instance.

```
loader_mc.addEventListener(Event.COMPLETE, hideBar);
```

7. In the Actions panel, click the **Check syntax** button to check for syntax errors in the ActionScript code, and then click the **OK** button in the dialog box that indicates whether the script contains errors. The error-free functions appear in the Script pane.

   Trouble? If the script contains errors, there are probably typing errors in the functions. If the Compiler Errors panel is hidden behind the Actions panel, click the Actions panel title bar to collapse the panel. In the Compiler Errors panel, review the error message(s), and then close the panel. Click the Actions panel title bar to expand the Actions panel, compare the code in the Actions panel with the code shown in Steps 2 through 6, and then make the necessary corrections so that your code matches the code in the steps. Repeat Step 7 until your code is error-free.

8. Collapse the Actions panel, save the RevisedSite.fla document, click **Control** on the menu bar, and then click **Test Movie**.
9. In the Flash Player, click **View** on the menu bar, and then click **Simulate Download**. The Home page appears after a few moments.
10. On the Home page, click the **Photos** navigational button to display the Photos page, and then click the **Photo 1** button to load the first photo. The ProgressBar animation appears followed by the photo. The ProgressBar instance disappears after the photo is loaded.
11. Click the **Photo 2** button to load the second photo. The ProgressBar animation appears followed by the photo. The ProgressBar instance disappears after the photo is loaded.
12. Close the Flash Player window. The Photos page is complete.

In this session, you learned about components and how to use them in your Flash documents. You used the ComboBox, Button, UILoader, and ProgressBar components along with ActionScript to add Web links to the Home page and buttons to load player photos on the Photos page.

Review | Session 9.1 Quick Check

1. What is a Flash component?
2. What is the purpose of the dataProvider parameter of the ComboBox component?
3. In the ComboBox component, the contents of the ________________ parameter appear on the ComboBox instance on the Stage.
4. Which statement is used to exit a block of code in a switch statement?
5. Write the ActionScript code to hide a ProgressBar component instance named progress_mc.

6. For a ProgressBar instance to detect the loading of content into a UILoader instance, you enter the name of the UILoader instance into the ________________ parameter of the ProgressBar instance.

Session 9.2

Adding Video to a Flash Document

So far, the Flash documents you have created include a variety of multimedia elements, such as graphics, bitmaps, and sounds. You can also add video to Flash documents. Video can make a Web site more visually appealing and exciting. Before you work with video in Flash, you should understand some basic terminology and concepts about how video is prepared and in what format video can be imported into Flash. You need to consider the frame size, frame rate, and file size of video files. You also need to understand that using video on your Flash Web site can significantly increase a site's overall download time.

Using a High Quality Video Source File | InSight

The quality of the source, or original, file is critical to consider when using video in Flash. The better the quality of the source file, the better the result when the video is imported into Flash. You should start with a high-quality video file before importing the video into Flash.

You can use a digital camcorder to record video and then transfer the video from the camcorder's media to the computer. You can also connect the camcorder to a computer and record video directly to the computer. Another method is to convert video from an analog format such as a VCR tape into a digital format that you can store on a computer. However, whenever possible, it is best to use a digital source file. Converting from analog to digital can produce lower-quality video compared to video that is captured in digital format.

Regardless of the video source, you should edit the video using a video-editing program such as Adobe Premiere after it is transferred to the computer but before it is imported into Flash. Although Flash provides some editing options when video is imported, the options are limited. A video-editing program allows you to trim unwanted parts of the video or select part of the video depending on how you plan to use it. You can also change other attributes of the video, such as its frame rate and frame size.

Selecting the Frame Rate and Frame Size

A video's **frame rate**, which is similar to the frame rate of a document in Flash, represents how many frames play each second. Video frame rates vary, depending on where the video is played. For example, video played on television plays at 30 frames per second. However, video played on the Web plays at slower rates, typically varying between 10 and 15 frames per second. Frame rate also affects the size of the file. The higher the frame rate, the larger the size of the video file. For example, a 10-second video clip formatted at 30 frames per second contains 300 frames. The same 10-second video clip formatted at 12 frames per second contains 120 frames. Of course, the higher the frame rate, the better the quality of the video. Deciding on the frame rate to use is a balance between the quality of the video and the size of the file. Lowering the frame rate lowers the quality of the video but decreases the video's file size.

InSight | Selecting an Appropriate Frame Rate

Consider several factors when deciding the frame rate to select for a video. One factor is the video's content. Video with a minimal amount of movement can be played on the Web at rates of 10 or less frames per second. A video with very little motion might be someone talking in front of the camera. However, video with more movement, such as children playing a sport, is best played at frame rates between 12 and 15 frames per second. A second factor to consider is the target user's connection to the Internet. High frame rates do not play well with a dial-up connection because the connection speed cannot download the frames fast enough to play smoothly on the client computer. A faster, broadband connection can better handle higher frame rates. A final factor to consider is the capability of the client computer. A slow computer with minimal capabilities might not be able to support videos with high frame rates.

When editing video clips and preparing them for use in Flash, you should also determine what frame size to use. The **frame size** refers to a video's width and height dimensions. You can decide the frame size by considering the type of Internet access that target users will have and the length of the video. If you are targeting users with dial-up connections, limit the frame size of videos to something like 160 pixels wide by 120 pixels high. If the majority of the target users have faster connections, set the video's frame size to higher dimensions, such as 320 pixels wide by 240 pixels high.

Using Compression and Decompression

Another factor affecting the use of video over the Web is the size of the video file. The amount of data required to represent a few seconds of video can make downloading the video over the Internet a slow process. As a result, compression is used to reduce the size of the video file. Recall that compression refers to reducing the size of the file by removing redundant data. You can specify how much to compress a video when you edit it using a video-editing program. To compress video requires an encoder program, also known as a **compressor**. Before the video can be played, it needs to be decompressed with a decoder program, also known as a **decompressor**. A video compressor/decompressor program is called a **codec**. Various codecs are available to work with video. By default, Flash uses the On2 VP6 codec when you publish video content to Flash Player 8 or higher. If you publish video content to Flash Player 7, then Flash uses the Sorenson Spark codec. Videos published for Flash Player 7 will also run on more recent versions of the plug-in, but those published for Flash Player 8 or higher will not work on earlier plug-ins. The codecs used by Flash compress the video when it is published from Flash. The Flash Player contains the corresponding decompressor to decompress the video for playback.

Both the On2 VP6 and the Sorenson Spark codecs in Flash reduce the size of a video file while retaining the best quality possible. Because Flash uses codecs to compress video, it is best to avoid compressing the video before bringing it into Flash. When editing the video with a video-editing program, you should export it using as little compression as possible, because after you bring the video into Flash it is compressed again, further reducing its quality.

After you edit a video clip, you export it in one of several formats. Flash accepts several video file formats, including .mpg, .avi, and .dv. Other formats can also be used. For example, if your computer has the QuickTime plug-in installed, you can import video in the .mov format into Flash. Each video file format has different characteristics and might or might not include compression.

Delivering Video

For video to be available as part of a Web site, it must be uploaded to a Web server, just like the site's Web pages and SWF files. When you import video into Flash, you need to know the type of Web server the video will be uploaded to and how the video will be delivered to a client computer. This determines the method you use within Flash to prepare or encode the video. **Encoding** is the process of compressing the video. Flash provides three methods by which video may be encoded for delivery: embedded video, progressive downloading, and video streaming. **Embedded video** places the video in the Flash document, similar to the way that bitmaps are imported and become part of the document. When you publish the Flash file, the video is published as part of the SWF file and can significantly increase the size of the published file. Embedding video is recommended only when you are targeting site visitors with older versions of the Flash Player (version 5 or lower) and when the video clip is less than 5 seconds in length. When a video is encoded for **progressive downloading**, the video file is saved separately from the Flash SWF file you create to play the video. This method also makes it easier to change video content without having to change or republish the SWF file. The **video streaming** method requires that the video be uploaded to a Web server running Flash Media Server, which provides Web developers features to add interactive audio and video to Web sites.

Using the Import Video Wizard

After video is captured and prepared using a video-editing program, it is ready to be imported into Flash. The Import Video wizard presents a series of dialog boxes in which you select the video file, select the encoding format to use, crop and resize the video, and select prebuilt playback controls. The Video Import wizard encodes or converts a video file into the FLV or Flash video format and also creates an instance of the FLVPlayback component on the Stage.

Aly has prepared two short video clips of local youth sports to add to the Video page of the Flash document, as requested by Dan. You will use the Import Video wizard to create an instance of the FLVPlayback component, which will serve as the video player. The first video clip is in the MPEG format and will be converted to an FLV file by the wizard. You will then modify the FLVPlayback parameters and add two Button components to enable playing the two video clips in the same player, as shown in Figure 9-11. Finally, you will add the necessary ActionScript code to make the buttons operational.

Figure 9-11 **Videos page**

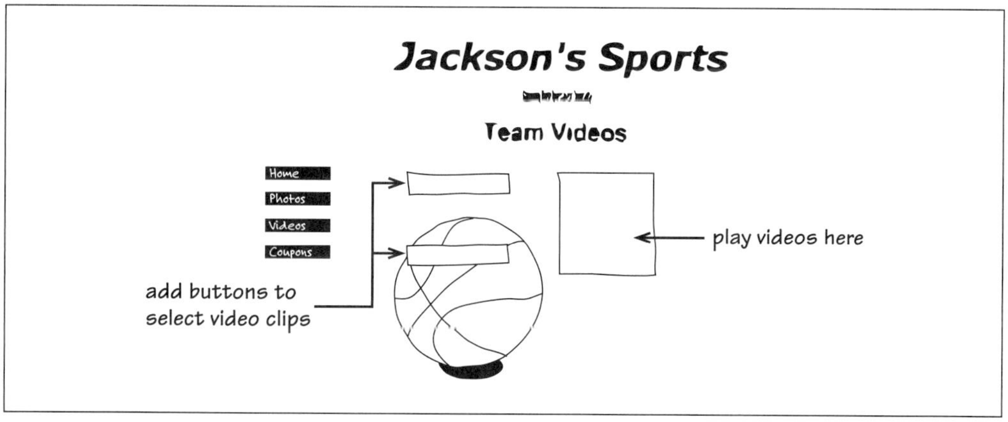

You'll start by adding the bball1.mpg video to the Videos page.

To select the bball1.mpg video clip using the Import Video wizard:

1. If you took a break after the previous session, make sure the RevisedSite.fla document is open and the workspace is set to its default layout.
2. On the Page content layer of the Timeline, select **Frame 30**. The Videos page content starts in this frame.
3. Click **File** on the menu bar, point to **Import**, and then click **Import Video** to start the Import Video wizard. The Select Video dialog box opens, prompting you to specify the location of the video file to be imported, which is either on your computer or on a Web server. In this case, the video file is located on your computer.
4. Click **Browse** button, navigate to the **Tutorial.09\Tutorial** folder included with your Data Files, and then double-click **bball1.mpg**. The video file is selected.
5. Click the **Next** button. The Deployment dialog box opens.

In the Deployment dialog box, you select how the video will be delivered to the Internet. The first three options—Progressive download from a web server, Stream from Flash Video Streaming Service, and Stream from Flash Media Server—require the use of version 7 or later of the Flash Player. When you select one of these options, the wizard converts the imported video file into a Flash Video file with the .flv extension. The second and third options require that the published files be uploaded to a Web server running Flash Media Server. The fourth option, As mobile device video bundled in SWF, requires the use of Flash Lite 2.0 or later and is meant for deploying content to mobile devices. The Embed video in SWF and play in timeline option embeds the video in the Flash document. The last option, Linked QuickTime video for publishing to QuickTime, is used to publish the Flash content and video as a QuickTime movie. The video files imported using this option must be QuickTime files with the .mov extension. The Flash document must then be published as a QuickTime file and not as an SWF file. The resulting file plays using the QuickTime plug-in and not the Flash Player. You will select the Progressive download option to deploy video for use on a Web server.

Selecting one of the first three options opens an Encoding dialog box in which you select a Flash video-encoding profile as well as options to add cue points and to crop and resize the video clip. **Cue points** are markers you set in the video to synchronize the video with animation, graphics, or text in the document. You select a profile based on whether the video will be played back using Flash Player version 7 or 8, and on the video and audio rates you want to use.

To select a deployment option for the bball1.mpg video:

1. In the Deployment dialog box, if necessary, select the **Progressive download from a web server** option, and then click the **Next** button. The Encoding dialog box opens, displaying a preview window and a list of video-encoding options.
2. Click the **Encoding Profiles** tab, if necessary, and then select **Flash 8 – Medium Quality (400kbps)** from the encoding profile list. In the preview area, extra areas appear above and below the video. You will remove the unwanted areas.
3. Click the **Crop and Resize** tab to display cropping options, and then, in the Crop section, click and hold the top crop arrow to display the slider, and drag the slider to change the value to **16**. The dashed outline in the preview area indicates how the video will be cropped. See Figure 9-12.

Figure 9-12 Crop and Resize tab of the Import Video wizard

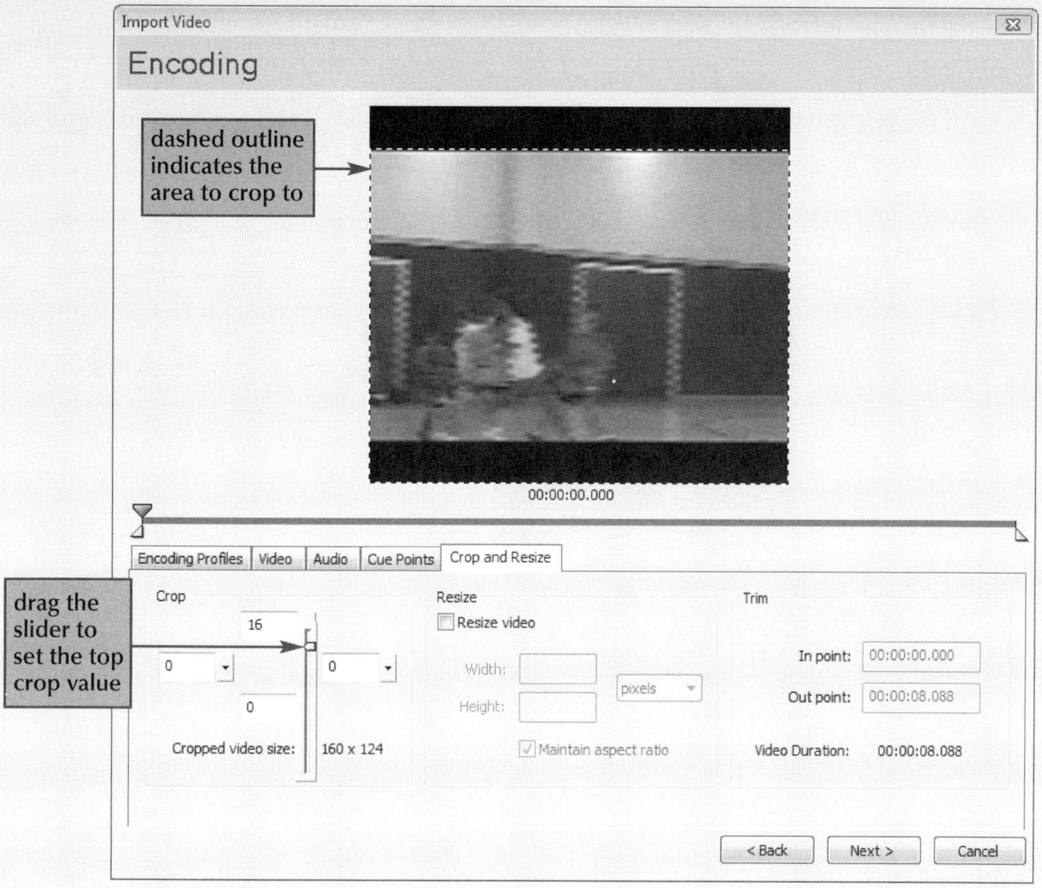

4. Click and drag the bottom crop arrow, and then drag the slider to change the value to **16**. The other crop values remain at 0. The encoding profile is complete.
5. Click the **Next** button. The Skinning dialog box opens.

In the Skinning dialog box, you select the type of playback controls to add to the Flash file. These playback controls are referred to as a **skin** and consist of an SWF file. The wizard makes it easy to add playback controls by providing many preconfigured skins from which you can select in the Skin list. You can also create a custom skin.

After you select a skin, the final dialog box in the wizard presents a summary of your selections and indicates what will be done when you click the Finish button. For the first three deployment options—Progressive download from a web server, Stream from Flash Video Streaming Service, and Stream from Flash Media Server—an FLV file is created and an instance of the FLVPlayback component with the selected playback controls is added to the Stage. The FLVPlayback component provides the display area in which the video is viewed.

Tip

You can change the FLVPlayback component's skin at any time by changing its skin parameter in the Parameters panel.

To select a skin and complete the Import Video wizard:

1. In the Skinning dialog box, select **SkinUnderPlaySeekMute.swf** from the Skin list. The skin is applied to the video component in the preview area. See Figure 9-13.

Figure 9-13 Skinning dialog box in the Import Video wizard

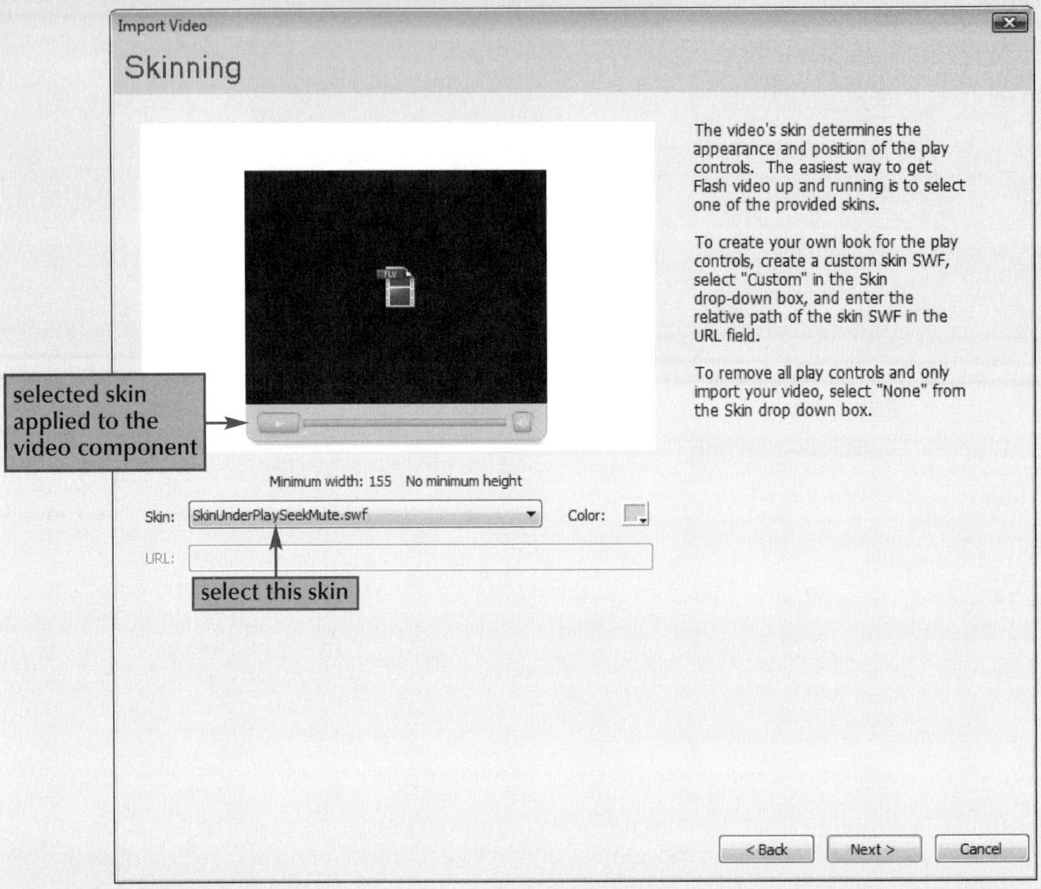

2. Click the **Next** button. The Finish Video Import dialog box displays a summary of the import process. In particular, note that a Flash Video file, named bball1.flv, will be created and a video component for the selected skin will be saved as a separate file.
3. Click the **Finish** button. A dialog box opens, showing the encoding progress of the video. When the process is complete, an instance of the FLVPlayback component is placed on the Stage.
4. Reposition the FLVPlayback instance to about **300** pixels from the left of the Stage and **200** pixels from the top of the Stage, and then, in the Property inspector, change the width of the FLVPlayback instance to **200** pixels and its height to **150** pixels. See Figure 9-14.

Figure 9-14 FLVPlayback instance added to the Stage

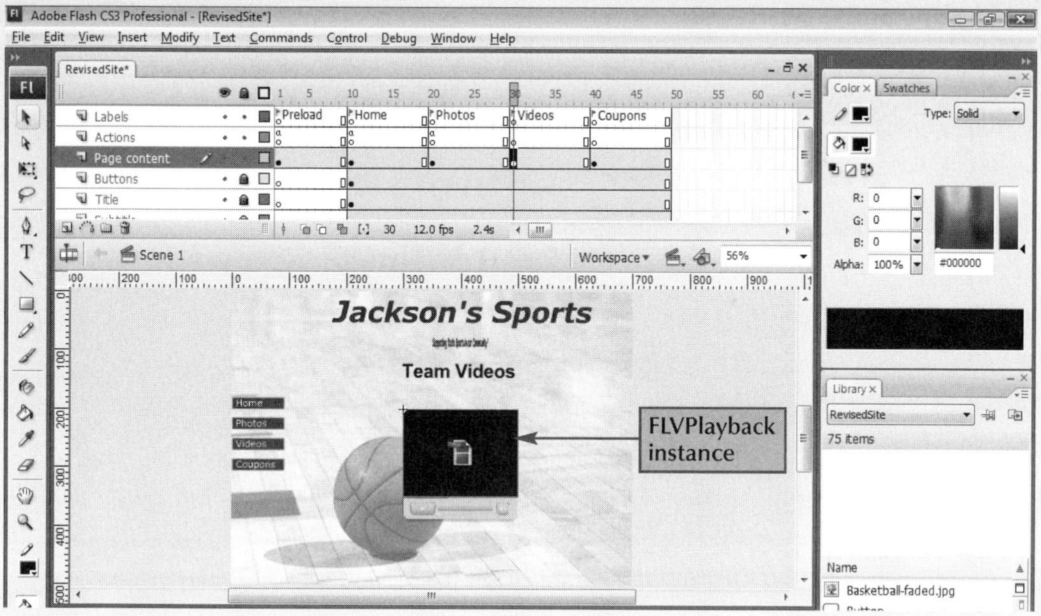

You will save and test the FLVPlayback component instance you added to the Videos page.

5. Save the RevisedSite.fla document, click **Control** on the menu bar, and then click **Test Movie**. The Home page opens in the Flash Player window.

6. In the Flash Player window, click the **Videos** button to advance to the Videos page. The Videos page appears and the video clip starts to play.

7. After the video stops playing, on the video controls, click the **Play/Pause** button to play the video again, and then click the **Play/Pause** button to pause the video. As the video plays, the small triangle under the seek bar moves to indicate the progress of the video. See Figure 9-15.

Figure 9-15 Video playing on the Videos page

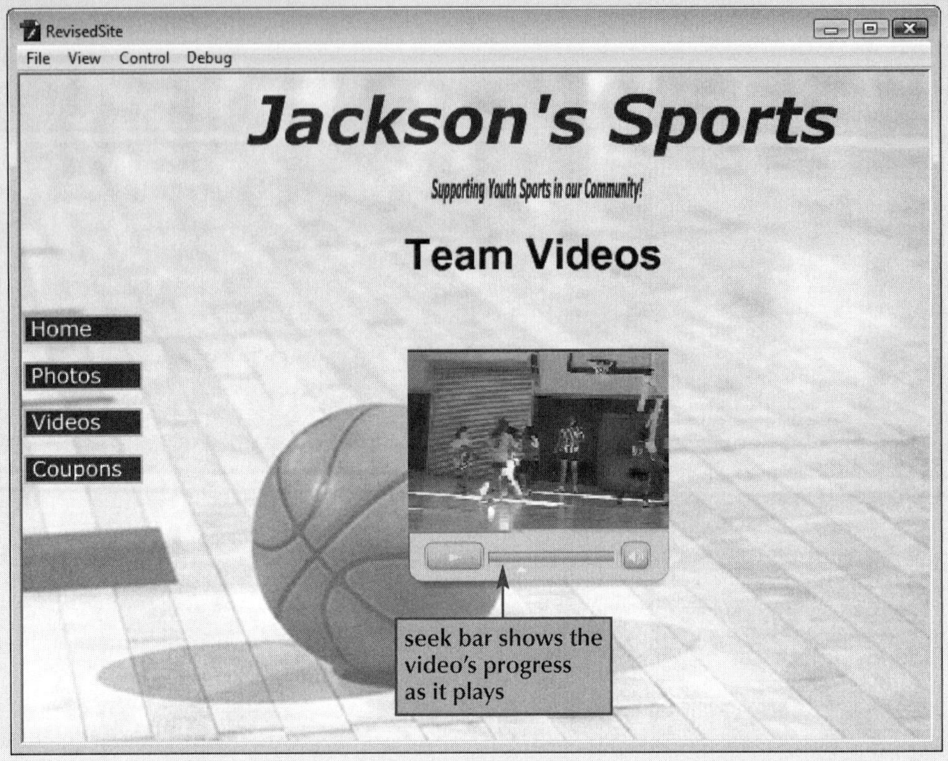

8. Close the Flash Player window to return to the Flash document.

The Videos page displays a video clip and includes controls to play, pause, and mute the video. Aly has a second video for the page. You will add two buttons and ActionScript code so that when each button is clicked, a different video plays, enabling users to choose between the two videos. Because the video you added to the page uses the FLVPlayback component, you can modify the component's parameters so that the video played is determined by ActionScript.

To modify the FLVPlayback's parameters and add Button instances to the Videos page:

1. On the Stage, select the **FLVPlayback** instance, if necessary, and then, in the Property inspector, click the **Parameters** tab. The component's parameters appear.
2. In the Parameters panel, double-click the box to the right of the skin parameter. The Select Skin dialog box opens.
3. In the Skin list, click **None**, and then click the **OK** button. The skin with the player controls is removed from the Stage.
4. In the Parameters panel, scroll down the parameters list, and then double-click the box to the right of the source parameter. The Content Path dialog box opens and the bball1.flv filename is selected. See Figure 9-16.

Content Path dialog box — **Figure 9-16**

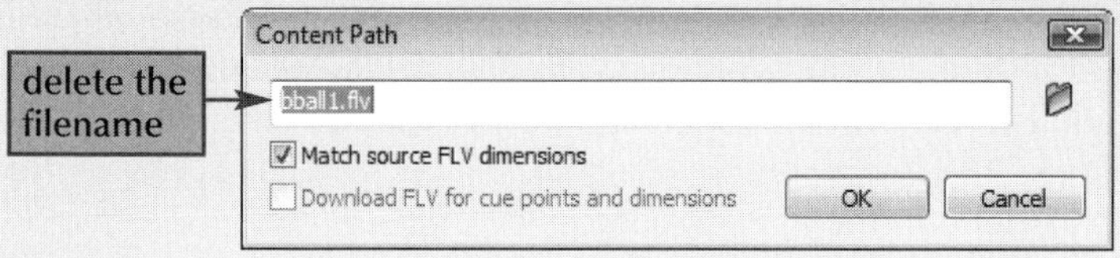

5. Press the **Delete** key, and then click the **OK** button. The source file is removed.
6. In the Parameters panel, type **videoPlayer** in the Instance Name box, and then press the **Enter** key. The name is assigned to the FLVPlayback instance, which can be referenced with ActionScript.

   Because you previously added an instance of the Button component to the document, the Button component is already in the document's library. You can add instances of the same Button component by dragging them from the Library panel.
7. Drag an instance of the Button component from the Library panel to the Stage, and then place the instance about **200** pixels from the top of the Stage and about **150** pixels from the left of the Stage.
8. On the Stage, select the Button instance if necessary, and then, in the Parameters panel, name the instance **videoButton1_btn**, click the box to the right of the label parameter, type **Video Clip 1**, and press the **Enter** key. The videoButton1_btn instance on the Stage is relabeled as Video Clip 1.
9. Repeat Steps 7 and 8 to create a second Button instance about **250** pixels from the top of the Stage and about **150** pixels from the left of the Stage, name the instance **videoButton2_btn**, and then change its label parameter to **Video Clip 2**. The videoButton2_btn instance on the Stage is relabeled as Video Clip 2. See Figure 9-17.

Buttons added to the Videos page — **Figure 9-17**

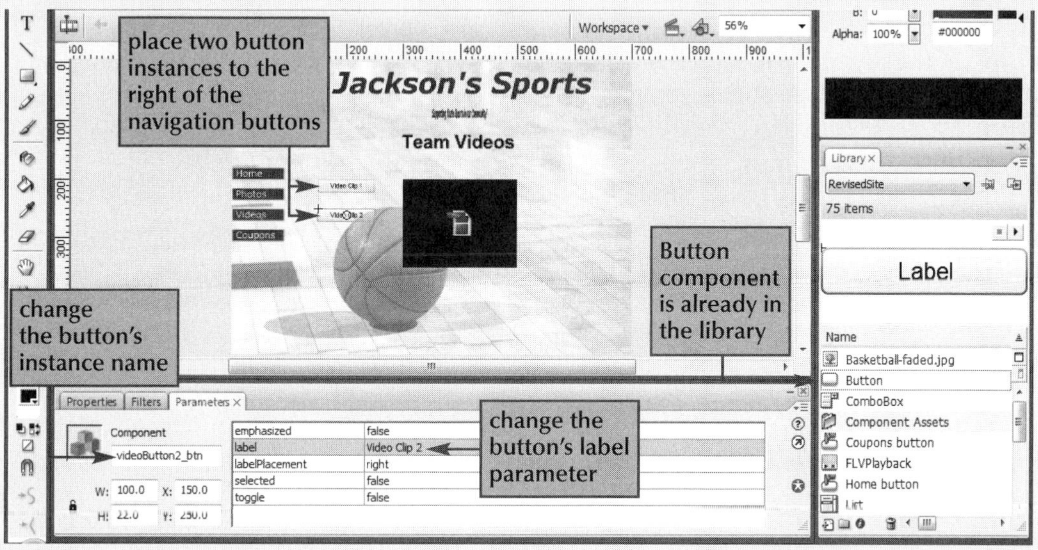

Next, you will add the ActionScript code that controls the loading of the video clips into the FLVPlayback component. The code will include two functions, one for each video. Each function will assign the name of the video clip to the source parameter of the FLVPlayback instance and it will assign SkinUnderPlaySeekMute.swf to the skin parameter. Event listeners will be added so that when a button is clicked, the associated function will run.

A video clip must be in the FLV format to play in the FLVPlayback component instance. When you used the Import Video wizard to import the bball1.mpg video clip and create an instance of the FLVPlayback component on the Stage, the bball1.mpg video clip was converted to an FLV file named bball1.flv. You can also use the Flash Video Encoder, a separate standalone program that installs with Flash, to convert videos into the FLV format without using the Import Video wizard within Flash. The Flash Video Encoder is especially useful when you have multiple video files to encode in the FLV format.

Aly has already converted the second video file that you will use in the Videos page, bball2.flv, into the FLV format. You will add ActionScript code to make the video clip buttons operational on the Videos page.

To add ActionScript code to play the two videos on the Videos page:

1. In the Actions layer of the Timeline, select **Frame 30**, and then open the Actions panel.
2. In the Script pane, type the following lines of code to define the functions that will load a video clip file and a skin into the FLVPlayback instance.

```
// Functions to add video clips and skin to FLVPlayback component
function playVideo1(eventObj:MouseEvent):void {
      videoPlayer.source = "bball1.flv" ;
      videoPlayer.skin = "SkinUnderPlaySeekMute.swf";
}
function playVideo2(eventObj:MouseEvent):void {
      videoPlayer.source = "bball2.flv" ;
      videoPlayer.skin = "SkinUnderPlaySeekMute.swf";
}
```

3. In the Script pane, type the following code to add the event listeners so that when a button is clicked, its associated function is run.

```
// Event listeners
videoButton1_btn.addEventListener(MouseEvent.CLICK, playVideo1);
videoButton2_btn.addEventListener(MouseEvent.CLICK, playVideo2);
```

4. In the Actions panel, click the **Check syntax** button to check for syntax errors in the ActionScript code, and then click the **OK** button in the dialog box that indicates whether the script contains errors. The error-free functions appear in the Script pane.

   Trouble? If the script contains errors, there are probably typing errors in the functions. If the Compiler Errors panel is hidden behind the Actions panel, click the Actions panel title bar to collapse the panel. In the Compiler Errors panel, review the error message(s), and then close the panel. Click the Actions panel title bar to expand the Actions panel, compare the code in the Actions panel with the code shown in Steps 2 and 3, and then make the necessary corrections so that your code matches the code in the steps. Repeat Step 4 until your code is error-free.

5. Collapse the Actions panel, save the RevisedSite.fla document, click **Control** on the menu bar, and then click **Test Movie**. The Home page opens in the Flash Player.

6. On the Home page, click the **Videos** button to advance to the Videos page, and then, on the Videos page, click the **Video Clip 1** button to play the first video clip. The video plays in the FLVPlayback instance and the video controls appear under the video. See Figure 9-18.

Figure 9-18 **Buttons and video player on the Stage**

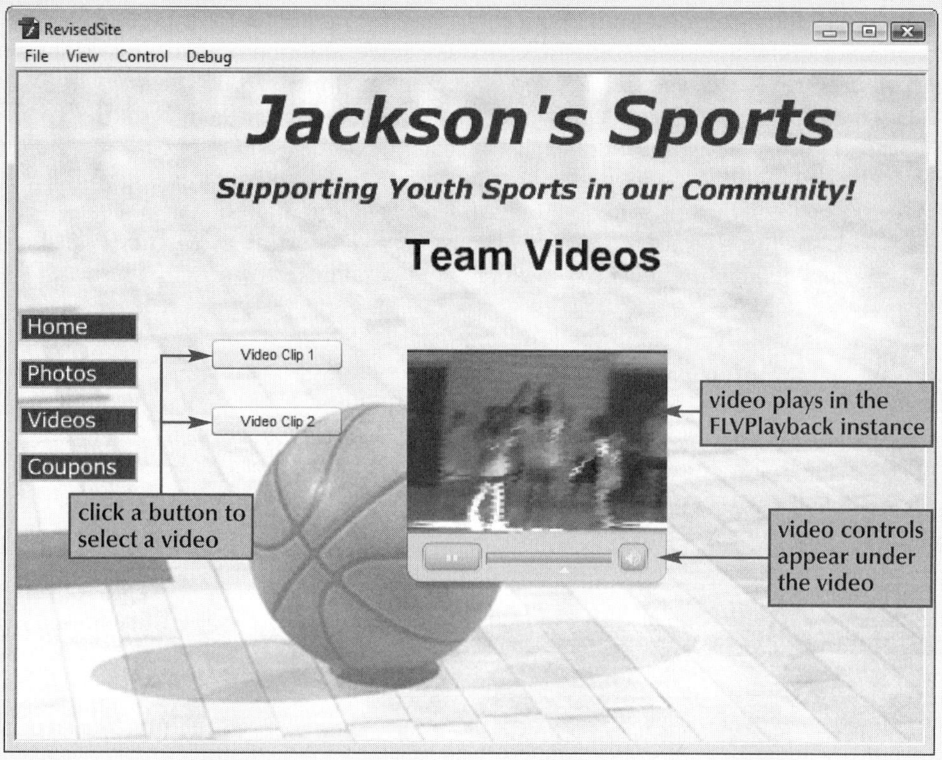

7. Click the **Video Clip 2** button to play the second video.
8. Close the Flash Player window to return to the Flash document. The Videos page is complete, and the Web site can showcase video clips of youth sports teams.

In this session, you learned basic concepts involved in using video and importing it into Flash. You reviewed the video formats you can use with Flash and different types of compression techniques. You imported a video file using the Video Import wizard in Flash, and then you modified the parameters of the FLVPlayback component to play two videos.

Session 9.2 Quick Check | Review

1. List three video formats that can be imported into a Flash document.
2. Why is it important to compress video files?
3. ________________ video places the video in the Flash document, similar to the way that bitmaps are imported and become part of the document.
4. What is a codec?
5. Which codecs are used by Flash?
6. ________________ are markers you can set in the video to synchronize the video with animation, graphics, or text in the document.
7. Which three deployment options in the Import Video wizard convert the imported video into a Flash Video file in the FLV format?

Session 9.3

Creating Printable Content

The graphics and animations created with Flash are meant to be displayed on computer screens and are usually not designed to be printed on paper. However, users often want to print part of the Flash Web site. Users can print the content of a Web site using the Web browser's Print command or using the Flash Player Print command. The Print command in the Flash Player can be disabled when the document is published.

When the Web browser's Print command is used, the content currently displayed in the Web page prints. However, if the content of the SWF file is designed to occupy most of the width of the computer screen, part of the content might be truncated, or cut off. This is because the layout of the computer screen is in **landscape orientation**, which means it is wider than it is tall. The printed page, however, is usually in **portrait orientation**, which means it is taller than it is wide and is meant to fit on a standard 8½ by 11 inch sheet of paper.

Instead of using the Web browser's Print command, the user can use the Flash Player's Print command, which is available from the context menu that opens when the user right-clicks SWF file content in the Flash Player. From the context menu, the user can choose to print the current selection so that only the currently displayed frame of the SWF file is printed. If the user chooses to print all contents, then all the frames of the SWF file are printed. This might not produce the desired result because the SWF file can contain a long animation with many frames.

InSight | Designing Printing Capabilities for Flash Documents

A Flash document should include options to print specific frames rather than relying on the Web browser or the Flash Player to control the printing of the SWF file. Provide buttons that the user can click to print specific elements of the Web site, which help prevent the user from becoming frustrated with undesirable print results. Depending on the site requirements, design certain parts of the Web site specifically for printing. For example, a store might want to place a map of the store's location on the Web site. The map can be designed to print on a standard sheet of paper. Or, a store might want to include a coupon on its Web site that the user can print and redeem at the store. Also, you can link to documents that are saved as Adobe Acrobat PDF files, which are already formatted for printing. In any case, if a Flash document contains elements that a user may want to print, be sure to design the printing capabilities into the document.

Creating Content for Printing

Dan requested that two coupons be added to the Jackson's Sports Web site that a user can print and redeem at the store, as shown in Figure 9-19. One coupon will be for 20% off summer sportswear. The second coupon will be for 10% off any item in the store. You will create the printable coupons and then create buttons to control the printing of the coupons.

Coupons page | Figure 9-19

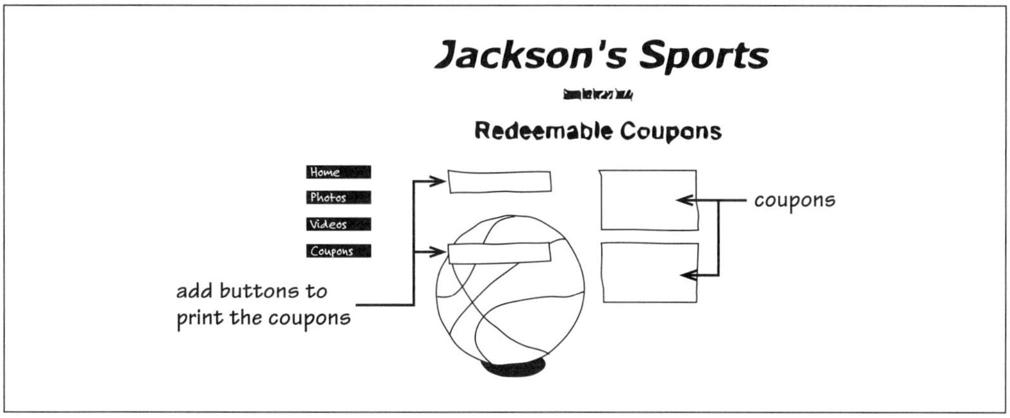

You'll start by creating the content of the first coupon in the Page content layer for the Coupons page.

To create the first coupon:

1. If you took a break after the previous session, make sure the RevisedSite.fla document is open and the workspace is set to its default layout.
2. Create a new movie clip symbol named **coupon1**. The symbol opens in symbol-editing mode.
3. In the Tools panel, click the **Rectangle** tool, change the fill color to **light yellow** (#FFFF99) and the stroke color **no stroke**, and then, on the Stage, draw a rectangle that is **300** pixels wide and **150** pixels high.
4. In the Property inspector, set the rectangle's X and Y values to **0**.
5. In the Timeline, rename Layer 1 to **background** and lock the layer, and then insert a new layer and name it **content**.
6. In the Tools panel, click the **Text** tool, and then, in the Property inspector, set the font to **Arial**, set the text color to **black** (#000000), set the font size to **30**, select the **Bold** and **Italic** styles, and select **Align Center** for the alignment.
7. On the Stage, type **Jackson's Sports**, and then, in the Tools panel, click the **Selection** tool and center the text block at the top of the rectangle. See Figure 9-20.

Figure 9-20 Text heading for the coupon symbol

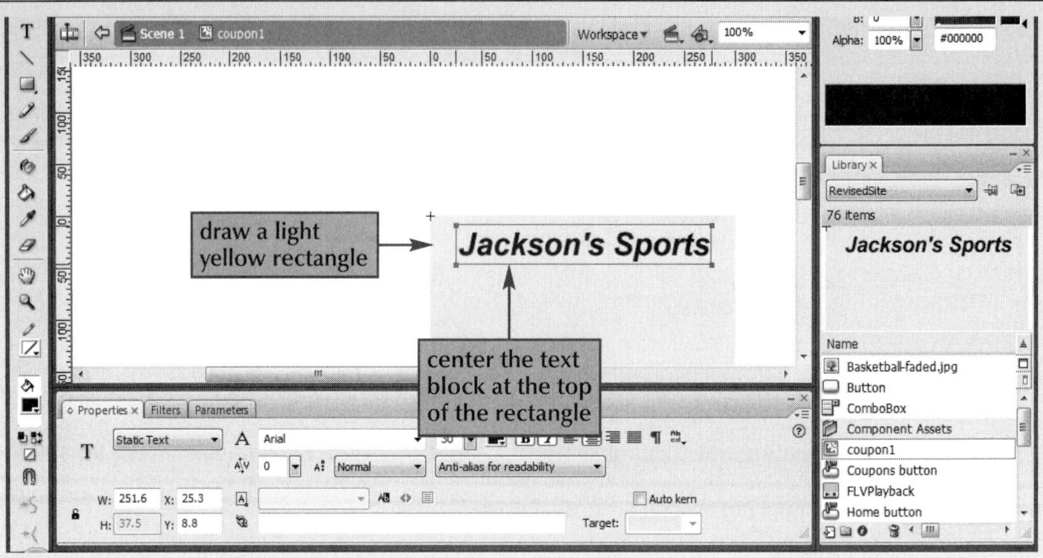

8. Deselect the text block, select the **Text** tool [T] in the Tools panel, and then, in the Property inspector, change the font size to **20** and deselect the **Italic** style.
9. On the Stage, create a text block at the center of the rectangle, type **20% off all**, press the **Enter** key to create a new line, type **Summer Sportswear!**, and then deselect the text block.
10. In the Property inspector, change the font size to **14**, deselect the **Bold** style, and then, on the Stage, create a text block centered at the bottom of the rectangle and type **Valid during September only!**.

    You will draw a border for the coupon next.

11. In the Tools panel, click the **Rectangle** tool, and then, in the Property inspector, change the fill to **none**, set the stroke to **black** (#000000), set the stroke height to **2**, and select a dashed line for the stroke style.
12. On the Stage, draw a rectangle just inside the sides of the yellow rectangle so that it forms a frame around the contents of the coupon.

    Next, you'll add the baseball and basketball symbols to the coupon.

13. Drag an instance of the **Baseball** symbol from the Library panel to the left side of the rectangle, and then drag an instance of the **Basketball** symbol to the right side of the rectangle. See Figure 9-21.

Coupon text and graphics

Figure 9-21

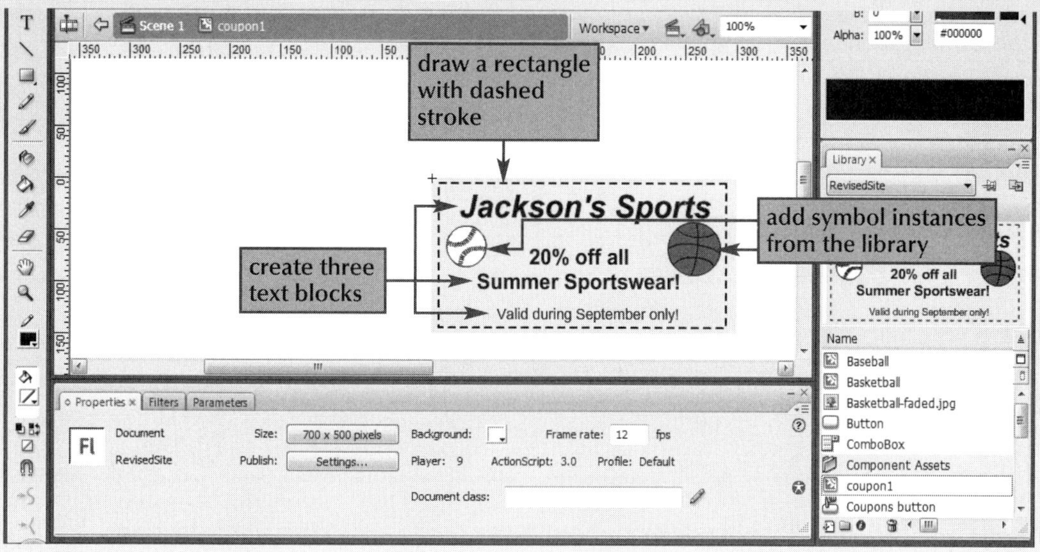

The coupon movie clip's background and content are complete. However, when the user prints the coupon, you don't want the background to print. You will add a second frame to the coupon movie clip that will contain the contents of the coupon but not the background rectangle. The second frame will contain the content to print.

14. In the content layer, select **Frame 2**, and then insert a regular frame. The text and graphics appear in Frame 2, but the background rectangle does not.

    Because you added a second frame to the coupon's Timeline, you need to add a `stop()` action to the first frame that will keep the playhead from advancing to the second frame.

15. In the Timeline, insert a new layer, name it **action**, and then, in the action layer, select **Frame 1**.

16. Open the Actions panel, type the following line in the Script pane, and then collapse the Actions panel.

```
stop();
```

The first coupon is finished. The second coupon will be the same as the first coupon except that it will be for 10% off any item in the store. You will copy the first coupon movie clip to create the second coupon. Then, all you need to do is modify the duplicate coupon movie clip's content.

To create a copy of the coupon1 movie clip for the second coupon:

1. In the Library panel, right-click the **coupon1** symbol, and then click **Duplicate**. The Duplicate Symbol dialog box opens.
2. Type **coupon2** in the Name box, and click the **OK** button. The duplicate symbol appears in the library.
3. Open the **coupon2** movie clip in symbol-editing mode, and then, on the Stage, edit the center text block so that the top line reads **10% off any** and the second line reads **item in the store!**.

4. Replace the text in the bottom text block with **Limit one coupon per customer per visit**. See Figure 9-22.

Figure 9-22 Second coupon

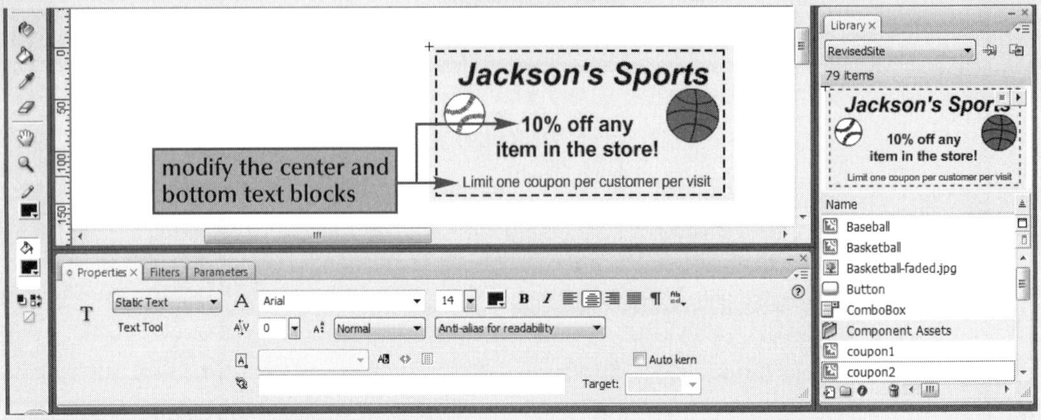

5. Exit symbol-editing mode, and then, in the Tools panel, click the **Selection** tool.

With the coupons complete, you are ready to add an instance of each coupon to the Coupons page. You will also add two instances of the Button component that will be used to control the printing of the coupons.

To create instances of the coupons and buttons:

1. In the Page content layer, select **Frame 40**, and then drag an instance of the **coupon1** symbol from the Library panel to the Stage.
2. Click **Window** on the menu bar, click **Transform** to open the Transform panel, and then, in the Transform panel, click the **Constrain** check box to check it, double-click the **width** box to select its value, type **50**, and press the **Enter** key. The movie clip is reduced to 50% of its original size.
3. Reposition the instance about **300** pixels from the left of the Stage and about **175** pixels from the top of the Stage. The coupon1 instance is in the correct position on the Coupons page.
4. Drag an instance of the **coupon2** symbol from the Library panel to the Stage, and then, in the Transform panel, double-click the **width** box to select its value, type **50**, and press the **Enter** key. The coupon2 movie clip is reduced to half its original size.
5. Reposition the instance about **300** pixels from the left of the Stage and about **260** pixels from the top of the Stage. The coupon1 instance is in the correct position on the Coupons page.
6. Select the **coupon1** instance on the Stage and name the instance **coupon1_mc** in the Property inspector, and then select the **coupon2** instance on the Stage and name the instance **coupon2_mc** in the Property inspector. The two coupon instances are named.
7. Drag two instances of the **Button** component symbol from the Library panel to the Stage, placing the first instance about **195** pixels from the left of the Stage and about **175** pixels from the top of the Stage and placing the second instance about **195** pixels from the left of the Stage and about **260** pixels from the top of the Stage. See Figure 9-23.

Figure 9-23 Coupons and buttons added to Coupons page

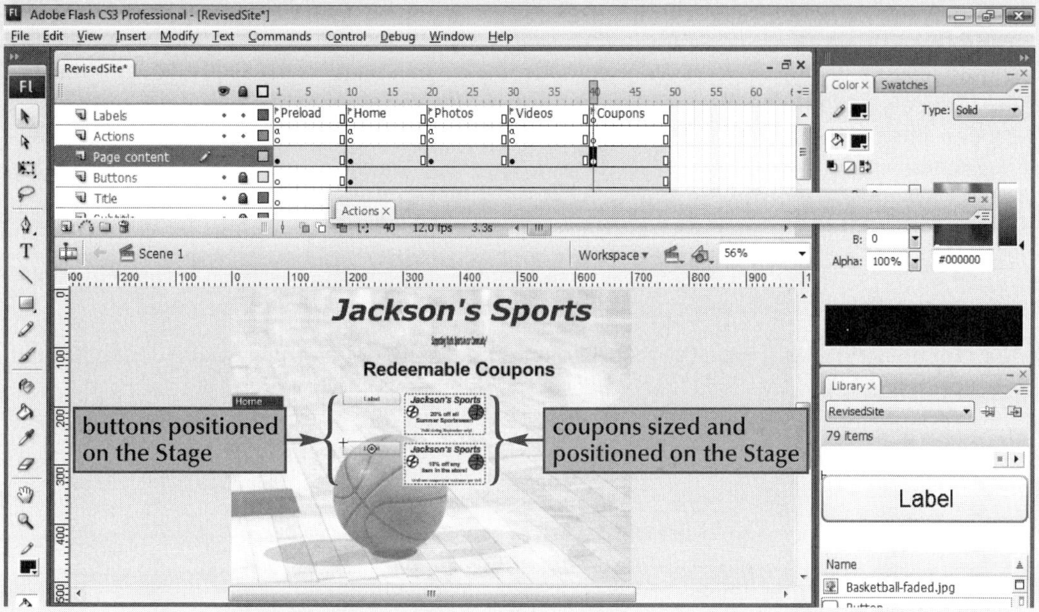

8. In the Property inspector, click the **Parameters** tab to display the Parameters panel.
9. Select the first **Button** instance on the Stage, and then, in the Parameters panel, name the instance **printCoupon1_btn**, click the box to the right of the label parameter, type **Print Coupon 1**, and press the **Enter** key. The first button instance is named and labeled.
10. Select the second **Button** instance on the Stage, and then, in the Parameters panel, name the instance **printCoupon2_btn**, click the box to the right of the label parameter, type **Print Coupon 2**, and press the **Enter** key. The second button instance is named and labeled.

Using the PrintJob Class to Control Printing

The Coupons page contains the two coupons and buttons. Next, you need to add the ActionScript so that when a button is clicked, the corresponding coupon prints. The Flash Player can communicate with a computer's operating system's printing interface so that pages can be passed to the print spooler. The **print spooler** manages the print jobs that are sent to the printer by the various programs running on the computer. To control printing within the Flash Player, you use the ActionScript printJob class and follow these steps in sequence:

1. Create an instance of the PrintJob class.
2. Initiate the printing process.
3. Add pages to the print job.
4. Send the pages to the operating system's printer.

You will create two functions, one for each coupon. Each function will create an instance of the PrintJob class using the new operator, start the print process using the `start()` method, add a page to the print job using the `addPage()` method, and then send the print job to the computer's operating system using the `send()` method. You should also include code to prevent an error being generated by the Flash Player if the user cancels the printing process. You can use an if statement that checks if the printing process has been initiated. If it has been initiated, the steps to print the coupon run. Otherwise, the steps do not run.

To add ActionScript code to print the coupons:

1. In the Actions layer, select **Frame 40**, and then expand the Actions panel.

Tip

You can click the Apply line comment button in the Actions panel to add the // comment characters to the Script pane.

2. In the Script pane, type the following lines of code to define the first function that will print a coupon. The third line defines a variable named myPrintJob1 of type PrintJob and assigns the variable an instance of the PrintJob class using the new operator. The `start()` method is then called for the myPrintJob1 instance. If the `start()` method is successful, the `addPage()` method adds the movie clip contents to the print job and the `send()` method sends the print job to the operating system.

```
// Function to print the first coupon
function printCoupon1(eventObj:MouseEvent):void {
     var myPrintJob1:PrintJob = new PrintJob();
     if (myPrintJob1.start()) {
        myPrintJob1.addPage(coupon1_mc);
        myPrintJob1.send();
     }
}
```

3. In the Script pane, type the following lines of code to define the second function that will print a coupon.

```
// Function to print the second coupon
function printCoupon2(eventObj:MouseEvent):void {
     var myPrintJob2:PrintJob = new PrintJob();
     if (myPrintJob2.start()) {
        myPrintJob2.addPage(coupon2_mc);
        myPrintJob2.send();
     }
}
```

4. In the Script pane, type the following lines of code to add the event listeners so that when a button is clicked, its corresponding function is run.

```
// Event listeners
printCoupon1_btn.addEventListener(MouseEvent.CLICK, printCoupon1);
printCoupon2_btn.addEventListener(MouseEvent.CLICK, printCoupon2);
```

5. In the Actions panel, click the **Check syntax** button to check for syntax errors in the ActionScript code, and then click the **OK** button in the dialog box that indicates whether the script contains errors. The error-free functions appear in the Script pane.

   Trouble? If the script contains errors, there are probably typing errors in the functions. If the Compiler Errors panel is hidden behind the Actions panel, click the Actions panel title bar to collapse the panel. In the Compiler Errors panel, review the error message(s), and then close the panel. Click the Actions panel title bar to expand the Actions panel, compare the code in the Actions panel with the code shown in Steps 2 through 4, and then make the necessary corrections so that your code matches the code in the steps. Repeat Step 5 until your code is error-free.

6. Collapse the Actions panel, save the RevisedSite.fla document, click **Control** on the menu bar, and then click **Test Movie**. The Home page appears in the Flash Player.

7. On the Home page, click the **Coupons** button to advance to the Coupons page, and then on the Coupons page, click the **Print Coupon 1** button to print the first coupon. The operating system's print dialog box opens.
8. Select the appropriate printer, and then click the **OK** button. The first coupon prints.
9. Click the **Print Coupon 2** button to print the second coupon, select the appropriate printer in the operating system's print dialog box, and then click the **OK** button. The second coupon prints.
10. Close the Flash Player window to return to the Flash document.

The first and second frames of the coupon movie clips printed. You want only the second frames to print because they contain the coupon without the filled rectangle as a background. To print the second frame of the movie clip, you need to specify the frame number as a parameter in the `addPage()` method. You can include three optional parameters in the `addPage()` method in addition to the name of the movie clip to print. The first optional parameter specifies the area to print, which can be defined by specifying rectangular coordinates. The second optional parameter specifies if the content is to print as a vector or as a bitmap. By default, the content is printed as a vector. If the content to be printed includes a bitmap, you can set this parameter to `{printAsBitmap:true}`. The third optional parameter is a number that specifies which frame to print. If you want to use this optional parameter without specifying the two other optional parameters, you need to use null as the middle parameters. The method to print the second frame of the coupon1_mc movie clip is:

```
myPrintJob1.addPage(coupon1_mc, null, null, 2);
```

You will add the parameters to the `addPage()` method for each coupon.

To add the parameters to the addPage() methods :

1. Expand the Actions panel, and then, in the Script pane, revise the `addPage()` method for the first function to include the following additional parameters.

   ```
   myPrintJob1.addPage(coupon1_mc, null, null, 2);
   ```

2. In the Script pane, revise the `addPage()` method for the second function to include the following additional parameters.

   ```
   myPrintJob2.addPage(coupon2_mc, null, null, 2);
   ```

3. In the Actions panel, click the **Check syntax** button ✔ to check for syntax errors in the ActionScript code, and then click the **OK** button to close the dialog box that indicates whether the script contains errors. The error-free functions appear in the Script pane.

   Trouble? If the script contains errors, there are probably typing errors in the functions. If the Compiler Errors panel is hidden behind the Actions panel, click the Actions panel title bar to collapse the panel. In the Compiler Errors panel, review the error message(s), and then close the panel. Click the Actions panel title bar to expand the Actions panel, compare the code in the Actions panel with the code shown in Steps 1 and 2, and then make the necessary corrections so that your code matches the code in the steps. Repeat Step 3 until your code is error-free.

4. Collapse the Actions panel, save the RevisedSite.fla document, click **Control** on the menu bar, and then click **Test Movie**. The Home page opens in the Flash Player window.

5. On the Home page, click the **Coupons** button, and then, on the Coupons page, click the **Print Coupon 1** button to print the first coupon, select a printer in operating system's print dialog box, and then click the **OK** button. The first coupon prints.
6. Click the **Print Coupon 2** button to print the second coupon, select a printer in operating system's print dialog box, and then click the **OK** button. The second coupon prints.
7. Close the Flash Player window to return to the Flash document.

The second frame of each coupon movie clip printed. Aly wants you to modify the ActionScript code so that the size of the printed coupons is larger than the coupons' original size. To print a coupon in a larger format, you need to temporarily scale the movie clip to a larger size, print the coupon, and then scale it back to the size originally set on the Stage.

You use the scaleX and scaleY properties to scale a movie clip. The scaleX property is the scale factor of the width of the movie clip and the scaleY property is the scale factor of the height of the movie clip. A scale factor of 1 represents 100%. To enlarge the size of the coupon movie clips to twice their original size requires a scale factor of 2 for both the scaleX and scaleY properties, which represents 200%. After the coupons are printed, you need to return the coupons to the sizes that they were originally set on the Stage. The coupon movie clips were reduced to 50% of their original size when they were placed on the Stage, so after they are printed, you need to set the scale factor back to 0.5, which represents 50%. The statement to change a movie clip's scaleX property to 200% is:

```
coupon1_mc.scaleX = 2;
```

You will add the ActionScript code to the print functions so that the coupons print at twice their original size.

To scale the coupon movie clips for printing:

1. Expand the Actions panel, in the Script pane, place the insertion point after the opening curly brace for the if statement in the printCoupon1 function, press the **Enter** key to add a blank line, and then, starting in the blank line, type the following lines of code to increase the size of the coupon.

```
 // Increase the size of the coupon to 200%
coupon1_mc.scaleX = 2;
coupon1_mc.scaleY = 2;
```

2. In the Script pane, place the insertion point at the end of the `addPage()` statement in the printCoupon1 function, press the **Enter** key to add a blank line, and then, starting in the blank line, type the following lines of code to reduce the size of the coupon. See Figure 9-24.

```
// Reduce the size of the coupon to 50%
coupon1_mc.scaleX = .5;
coupon1_mc.scaleY = .5;
```

Figure 9-24

ActionScript code to scale the coupon1 movie clip

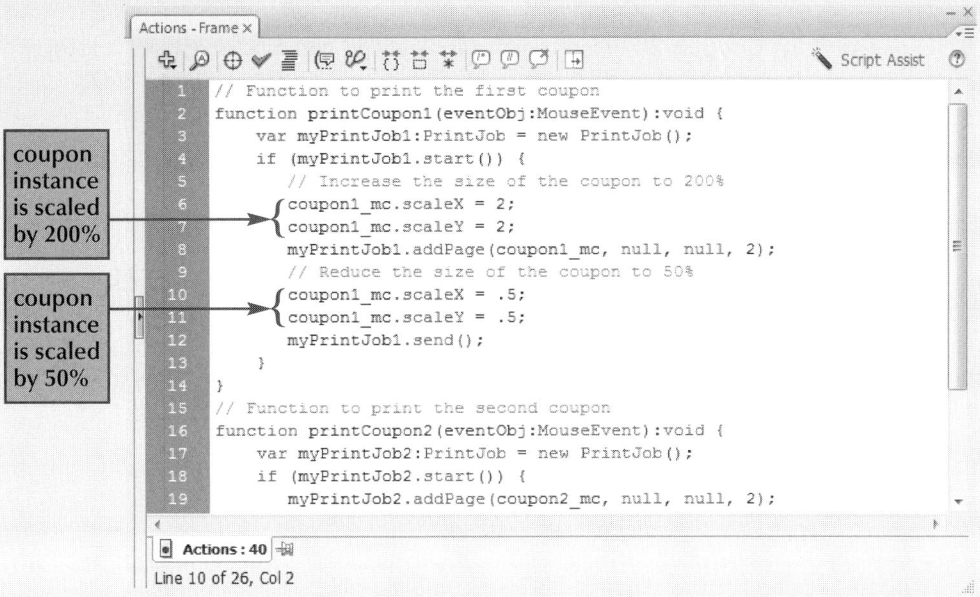

3. In the Script pane, place the insertion point after the opening curly brace for the if statement in the printCoupon2 function, press the **Enter** key to add a blank line, and then, starting in the blank line, type the following lines of code to increase the size of the coupon.

```
// Increase the size of the coupon to 200%
coupon2_mc.scaleX = 2;
coupon2_mc.scaleY = 2;
```

4. In the Script pane, place the insertion point at the end of the `addPage()` statement in the printCoupon2 function, press the **Enter** key to add a blank line, and then, starting in the blank line, type the following lines of code to reduce the size of the coupon.

```
// Reduce the size of the coupon to 50%
coupon2_mc.scaleX = .5;
coupon2_mc.scaleY = .5;
```

5. In the Actions panel, click the **Check syntax** button ✔ to check for syntax errors in the ActionScript code, and then click the **OK** button in the dialog box that indicates whether the script contains errors. The error-free functions appear in the Script pane.

   Trouble? If the script contains errors, there are probably typing errors in the functions. If the Compiler Errors panel is hidden behind the Actions panel, click the Actions panel title bar to collapse the panel. In the Compiler Errors panel, review the error message(s), and then close the panel. Click the Actions panel title bar to expand the Actions panel, compare the code in the Actions panel with the code shown in Steps 1 through 4, and then make the necessary corrections so that your code matches the code in the steps. Repeat Step 5 until your code is error-free.

6. Collapse the Actions panel, save the RevisedSite.fla document, click **Control** on the menu bar, and then click **Test Movie**. The Home page opens in the Flash Player window.

7. On the Home page, click the **Coupons** button, click the **Print Coupon 1** button on the Coupons page to print the first coupon, select the appropriate printer in the operating system's print dialog box, and then click the **OK** button. The first coupon prints.
8. Click the **Print Coupon 2** button to print the second coupon, select the appropriate printer in the operating system's print dialog box, and then click the **OK** button. The second coupon prints.
9. Close the Flash Player window to return to the Flash document.

The Coupons page for the Jackson's Youth Sports Web site is complete and site visitors can print the two coupons. Aly will show the completed Web site to Dan Jackson at their next meeting. She is confident he will be pleased with the finished site.

In this session, you created Flash content for printing. You used the PrintJob class to enable printing from within the Flash Player. You also specified which frames in the document to print and how to scale the content to print.

Review | Session 9.3 Quick Check

1. What two methods can be used to print Flash content?
2. Write an `addPage()` statement that adds the third frame of the map_mc movie clip to the print job.
3. Write the ActionScript statements to scale both the width and the height of the map_mc movie clip so that it is 150% of its original size.
4. True or False? If the Flash Player's Print command is used, only the current frame of the SWF file can be printed.
5. The print ______________ manages the print jobs that are sent to the printer by the various programs running on the computer.

Review | Tutorial Summary

In this tutorial, you used Flash components to add interactive elements to a document, including Web links, photos, a preloader, and buttons. You learned the basics of digital video as it relates to Flash and how to add video to a Flash document using the Flash video component. You made content in Flash printable. Finally, you entered ActionScript code to control the Flash components and the printing process.

Key Terms

codec
component
compressor
cue point
decompressor
embedded video
encoding
frame rate
frame size
landscape orientation
portrait orientation
print spooler
progressive downloading
skin
video streaming

Practice | Review Assignments

Practice the skills you learned in the tutorial.

Data Files needed for the Review Assignments: NewSoftballSite.fla, softball_clip.avi, softballPhoto1.jpg, softballPhoto2.jpg

Aly wants you to complete a new version of the Softball site she started for Jackson's Sports. You need to add Web links to the site's Home page in the form of a drop-down list. You will also add a photos page with softball team photos, a videos page to showcase team videos, and a coupons page with printable coupons for softball equipment.

1. Open the **NewSoftballSite.fla** file located in the Tutorial.09\Review folder included with your Data Files, and then save the file as **JacksonSoftball.fla** in the same folder.
2. In the Timeline, select Frame 10 of the Page content layer, drag an instance of the ComboBox component from the Components panel to the Stage, position the ComboBox instance about 320 pixels from the left of the Stage and 350 pixels from the top of the Stage, name the instance **softballLinks_mc**, and then change the width of the instance to 150 pixels. Do not change its height.
3. With the ComboBox instance selected, in the Parameters panel, enter **Softball Links** for the prompt parameter, and then enter the following label/data value pairs in the dataProvider parameter: **ASA Youth Softball**, **1**, **Softball Youth Magazine**, **2**, and **Sports Teams Web Sites**, **3**.
4. In the Actions layer, select Frame 10, place the insertion point after the last line of the existing code in the Actions panel, and then type the following lines of code to make the Web links operational.

```
// Function to check which site was selected
function gotoWebsite(eventObj:Event):void {
      // Variable that will hold the URL
      var weblinkText:String;
      // Switch statement determines which URL to assign
      switch (softballLinks_mc.value) {
      case "1" :
            weblinkText = "http://www.softball.org/youth/";
            break;
      case "2" :
            weblinkText = "http://www.softballyouth.com/";
            break;
      case "3" :
            weblinkText = "http://www.myteamzone.com/teamwebsites/
SoftBall.aspx";
            break;
      }
//Open Web site using the selected URL
var siteURL:URLRequest = new URLRequest(weblinkText);
navigateToURL(siteURL);
//Set ComboBox to display the prompt, Web Links
softballLinks_mc.selectedIndex = -1;
}
// Event listener
softballLinks_mc.addEventListener(Event.CHANGE, gotoWebsite);
```

5. In the Timeline, select Frame 20 of the Page content layer, and then drag one instance of the UILoader component and two instances of the Button component from the Components panel to the Stage. Position the UILoader instance about 300 pixels from the left of the Stage and 180 pixels from the top of the Stage. Position the first Button instance about 160 pixels from the left of the Stage and 180 pixels from the top of the Stage and the second Button instance about 160 pixels from the left of the Stage and 220 pixels from the top of the Stage.
6. Name the first Button instance **softballPhoto1_btn**, name the second Button instance **softballPhoto2_btn**, name the UILoader instance **photoLoader_mc**, and then change the dimensions of the UILoader instance to 165 pixels wide by 250 pixels high.
7. In the Parameters panel, change the label parameter of the first Button instance to **Photo 1** and change the label parameter of the second Button instance to **Photo 2**. In the Actions layer, select Frame 20, and in the Actions panel, type the following lines of code so that when a button is clicked, the corresponding softball photo will load into the UILoader instance.

```
// Functions to load photos
function loadPhoto1(eventObj:MouseEvent):void
{
      var photoURLReq:URLRequest = new URLRequest
            ("softballPhoto1.jpg");
      photoLoader_mc.load(photoURLReq);
}
function loadPhoto2(eventObj:MouseEvent):void
{
      var photoURLReq:URLRequest = new URLRequest
            ("softballPhoto2.jpg");
      photoLoader_mc.load(photoURLReq);
}
// Event listeners
softballPhoto1_btn.addEventListener(MouseEvent.CLICK, loadPhoto1);
softballPhoto2_btn.addEventListener(MouseEvent.CLICK, loadPhoto2);
```

8. In the Timeline, select Frame 30 of the Page content layer, and then start the Import Video wizard. Select the **softball_clip.avi** file located in the Tutorial.09\Review folder included with your Data Files. In the Deployment dialog box, select Progressive download from a web server. In the Encoding dialog box, select Flash 8 – Medium Quality (400kbps) for the encoding profile, enter 32 for the top and bottom crop values, and resize the video to 280 pixels by 163 pixels. In the Skinning dialog box, select the SkinUnderPlaySeekMute.swf file for the skin and gray (#CCCCCC) for the skin color. Import the video.
9. On the Stage, reposition the FLVPlayback instance about 250 pixels from the left of the Stage and 170 pixels from the top of the Stage.
10. In the Timeline, insert a keyframe at Frame 40 of the Labels layer. In the Property inspector, assign the label name **Coupons**. In the Page content layer, select Frame 40, and drag an instance of the coupon1 movie clip from the Library panel to the Stage. Reduce the size of the instance by 50% and name the instance **coupon1_mc**. Drag an instance of the coupon2 movie clip from the Library panel to the Stage, reduce the size of the instance by 50%, and name the instance **coupon2_mc**.

11. Position the coupon1_mc instance about 220 pixels from the left of the Stage and 180 pixels from the top of the Stage. Position the coupon2_mc instance about 420 pixels from the left of the Stage and 180 pixels from the top of the Stage.
12. Drag two instances of the Button component movie clip from the Library panel to the Stage. Place one button below the coupon1_mc instance and place the second button below the coupon2_mc instance. Name the first Button instance **printCoupon1_btn** and change its label parameter to **Print Coupon**. Name the second Button instance **printCoupon2_btn** and change its label parameter to **Print Coupon**.
13. In the Timeline, insert a keyframe at Frame 40 of the Actions layer. In the Script pane of the Actions panel, type the following lines of code so that clicking the buttons prints the corresponding coupon. Frame 2 of each coupon is printed at 200% of its original size.

```
// Function to print the first coupon
function printCoupon1(eventObj:MouseEvent):void {
    var myPrintJob1:PrintJob = new PrintJob();
    if (myPrintJob1.start()) {
         // Increase the size of the coupon to 200%
         coupon1_mc.scaleX = 2;
         coupon1_mc.scaleY = 2;
       myPrintJob1.addPage(coupon1_mc, null, null, 2);
         // Reduce the size of the coupon to 50%
         coupon1_mc.scaleX = .5;
         coupon1_mc.scaleY = .5;
       myPrintJob1.send();
    }
}
// Function to print the second coupon
function printCoupon2(eventObj:MouseEvent):void {
    var myPrintJob2:PrintJob = new PrintJob();
    if (myPrintJob2.start()) {
         // Increase the size of the coupon to 200%
         coupon2_mc.scaleX = 2;
         coupon2_mc.scaleY = 2;
       myPrintJob2.addPage(coupon2_mc, null, null, 2);
         // Reduce the size of the coupon to 50%
         coupon2_mc.scaleX = .5;
         coupon2_mc.scaleY = .5;
       myPrintJob2.send();
    }
}
// Event listeners
printCoupon1_btn.addEventListener(MouseEvent.CLICK, printCoupon1);
printCoupon2_btn.addEventListener(MouseEvent.CLICK, printCoupon2);
```

14. Save the JacksonSoftball.fla file and test the Web site to make sure the Web links work, the photos load, the video plays, and the coupons print. (*Hint:* If the Web site links do not work, the URLs for the sites might have changed since the printing of this book.)
15. Submit the finished files to your instructor, either in printed or electronic form, as requested.

Apply | Case Problem 1

Add Web links with a ComboBox component, a printable coupon with a Button component, ActionScript code to control the buttons and components, and a bitmap graphic with a mask to a Flash Web site.

Data Files needed for this Case Problem: SandySiteDraft.fla, supplies.jpg

Sandy's Scrapbook Store Web Site Sandy wants a coupon added to the Classes page of the store's Web site for 20% off the cost of one of the scrapbook classes. She also wants to add links to the Resources page without cluttering the page with individual buttons. John also suggests adding a picture showing scrapbook supplies as an example of what customers can expect to use when taking a class. You will add these new elements to the Classes and Resources pages for the Web site.

1. Open the **SandySiteDraft.fla** file located in the Tutorial.09\Case1 folder included with your Data Files, and then save the file as **ScrapbookWebSite.fla** in the same folder.
2. In the Timeline, insert two layers above the Content layer. Name the first layer **Actions** and name the second layer **Labels**. In the Labels layer, insert keyframes at Frame 10 and Frame 20, and then add the label **Home** to Frame 1, the label **Resources** to Frame 10, and the label **Classes** to Frame 20. In the Actions layer, insert keyframes at Frame 10 and Frame 20.
3. On the Stage, select the SSS Home button and name the instance **home_btn**, select the Resources button and name the instance **resources_btn**, and then select the Classes button and name the instance **classes_btn**.
4. In the Actions layer, select Frame 1, and then, in the Script pane of the Actions panel, type the following lines of code so that clicking the navigational buttons advances the playhead to the corresponding label.

```
//Keep the playhead from advancing
stop();
//Button functions
function onHomeClick(evt:MouseEvent):void {
      gotoAndStop("Home");
}
function onResourcesClick(evt:MouseEvent):void {
      gotoAndStop("Resources");
}
function onClassesClick(evt:MouseEvent):void {
      gotoAndStop("Classes");
}
// Event listeners
home_btn.addEventListener(MouseEvent.CLICK, onHomeClick);
resources_btn.addEventListener(MouseEvent.CLICK, onResourcesClick);
classes_btn.addEventListener(MouseEvent.CLICK, onClassesClick);
```

5. In the Content Layer, select Frame 10, drag an instance of the ComboBox component from the Components panel to the Stage, place the instance about 240 pixels from the left of the Stage and 250 pixels from the top of the Stage, name the instance **resourceLinks**, and then change the width of the instance to 170 pixels. Do not change its height.
6. With the ComboBox instance selected, display the Parameters panel, enter **Scrapbook Resource Links** for the prompt parameter and enter the following label/data value pairs in the dataProvider parameter: **Scrapbook Portal**, **1**, **Scrapbooks, etc.**, **2**, and **International Scrapbook Assoc.**, **3**.
7. In the Actions layer, select Frame 10, and then, in the Script pane of the Actions panel, type the following lines of code to make the ComboBox operational.

```
// Function to check which site was selected
function gotoWebsite(eventObj:Event):void {
      // Variable that will hold the URL
      var reslinkText:String;
      // Switch statement determines which URL to assign
      switch (resourceLinks.value) {
      case "1" :
            reslinkText = "http://www.scrapbookportal.com";
            break;
      case "2" :
            reslinkText = "http://www.scrapbooksetc.com/";
            break;
      case "3" :
            reslinkText = "http://www.iscrap.net/";
            break;
      }
//Open Web site using the selected URL
var siteURL:URLRequest = new URLRequest(reslinkText);
navigateToURL(siteURL);
//Set ComboBox to display the intial prompt
resourceLinks.selectedIndex = -1;
}
// Event listener
resourceLinks.addEventListener(Event.CHANGE, gotoWebsite);
```

8. Import the **supplies.jpg** bitmap located in the Tutorial.09\Case1 folder included with your Data Files into the document's library. Create a new movie clip symbol named **bitmap**. Drag an instance of the supplies.jpg file to the center of the Stage. Use the Transform panel to proportionally reduce the size of the supplies.jpg instance to about 60% of its original size.
9. Insert a new layer and name it **Mask**. Draw an oval on this layer that is about 145 pixels by 110 pixels. Use black for the fill color, and do not include a stroke color. Place the oval directly on top of the supplies.jpg bitmap. Convert the Mask layer into a mask layer. The Layer 1 layer should be converted into a masked layer, both layers should be locked, and the supplies picture shows through the oval mask. Exit symbol-editing mode.

10. In the Content layer, select Frame 20, and then drag an instance of the bitmap movie clip from the Library panel to the lower-right corner of the Stage.
11. Create a new movie clip symbol named **Coupon**. In symbol-editing mode, draw a rectangle at the center of the Stage using light pink (#FFCCFF) for the fill color and black for the stroke color. Select a dotted line for the stroke style, and use a stroke height of 2. Select the rectangle and change its width to 300 pixels and its height to 150 pixels. If necessary, change its X and Y coordinates to 0. Rename Layer 1 to **Background** and lock the layer.
12. Insert a new layer and name it **Graphics**. Add four instances of the triangle symbol. Place each instance in a separate corner of the rectangle. Use the Free Transform tool to rotate the instances so that the long side of each triangle faces the center of the rectangle.
13. Insert a new layer and name it **Text**. Create a static text block at the top part of the rectangle. Use Comic Sans MS for the font, 22 for the font size, and maroon (#660000) for the text color. Use Italic for the style and Align Center for the alignment. Type **Sandy's Scrapbook Store** in the text block. If necessary, center the text block in the top part of the rectangle.
14. Create a new text block in the center of the rectangle. Change the font size to 16, the text color to black, and the font style to Bold. Use Align Center for the alignment. In the first line, type **Take 20% off any**, and then press the Enter key. Type **Scrapbooking Class!** in the second line. If necessary, center the text block within the rectangle.
15. Create another text block at the bottom of the rectangle. Change the font size to 8, and do not apply the Bold or Italic styles. In the first line, type **Must be redeemed by March 31**, press the Enter key, and then type **Call for class availability**. If necessary, center the text block in the bottom part of the rectangle.
16. In the Timeline, insert keyframes at Frame 5 of all layers. In Frame 5 of the Text layer, add a text block below the rectangle. Change the font size to 16, do not apply the Bold or Italic styles, and use Align Center for the alignment. Type **Clip this coupon for great savings!** in this text block. In Frame 5 of the Graphics layer, add an instance of the scissors2 symbol, and place it on the lower-left side of the rectangle so that its midpoint is over the rectangle's stroke.
17. In the Timeline, insert a new layer above the Text layer and name it **Action**. With Frame 1 of the Action layer selected, open the Actions panel, add the following line so the playhead will stop at Frame 1, and then exit symbol-editing mode.
```
stop();
```
18. In the main document Timeline, select Frame 20 of the Content layer, and add an instance of the coupon symbol to the center of the Stage. Use the Transform panel to reduce the size of the instance by 50%, and then assign the instance the name **coupon_mc**.
19. In Frame 20 of the Content layer, drag an instance of the Button component from the Components panel to below the coupon instance on the Stage. Name the Button instance **print_btn**, and then, in the Parameters panel, change its label parameter to **Print Coupon**.

20. In the Actions layer, select Frame 20, and then, in the Script pane of the Actions panel, type the following lines of code so that when the button is clicked, the fifth frame of the coupon instance is printed.

```
// Function to print the coupon
function printCoupon(eventObj:MouseEvent):void {
    var myPrintJob:PrintJob = new PrintJob();
    if (myPrintJob.start()) {
        // Increase the size of the coupon to 200%
        coupon_mc.scaleX = 2;
        coupon_mc.scaleY = 2;
      myPrintJob.addPage(coupon_mc, null, null, 5);
        // Reduce the size of the coupon to 50%
        coupon_mc.scaleX = .5;
        coupon_mc.scaleY = .5;
      myPrintJob.send();
    }
}
// Event listeners
print_btn.addEventListener(MouseEvent.CLICK, printCoupon);
```

21. Save the ScrapbookWebSite.fla file, and test it to make sure the navigational buttons work, the resource links work, and the coupon prints. (*Note:* If the Web site links do not work, the URLs for the sites might have changed since the printing of this book.)
22. Submit the finished files to your instructor, either in printed or electronic form, as requested.

Apply | Case Problem 2

Add a video clip using the FLVPlayback component, a printable form using a Button component, and ActionScript code to control the components in a Flash Web Site.

Data Files needed for this Case Problem: RCMDraft.fla, piano_clip.mpg, piano.jpg

River City Music Web Site Janet requests a video clip be incorporated into the Recital page of the store's Web site to show an example of a piano recital. She also wants a recital hall reservation request form added to the site that can be printed so her customers can submit their recital reservation requests.

Alex instructs you to revise the Recital page of the Web site by adding the video clip and the printable form. You are to import the video clip into the document and display it on the Recital page, create the printable form and add a button to control the printing of the form.

1. Open the **RCMDraft.fla** file located in the Tutorial.09\Case2 folder included with your Data Files, and then save the file as **RCMWebSite.fla** in the same folder.
2. In the Timeline, select Frame 20 of the Content layer. Use the Import Video wizard to import the **piano_clip.mpg** video file located in the Tutorial.09\Case2 folder included with your Data Files. Use Progressive download from a web server for the deployment option.
3. If necessary, select Flash 8 - Medium Quality (400kbps) for the encoding profile. In the Encoding dialog box, click the Crop and Resize tab and then enter **34** for the top and bottom crop values.

EXPLORE

4. On the Crop and Resize tab, click the Resize video check box to check it, make sure the Maintain aspect ratio check box is checked, and enter 150 pixels for the width of the video.

EXPLORE

5. In the Skinning dialog box, select SkinUnderPlayMute.swf for the skin, and then change the skin color to gray (#999999).
6. After you import the video, reposition the FLVPlayback component instance on the Stage by setting its X coordinate to 320 and its Y coordinate to 200. In the Parameters panel, set the autoPlay value to false.
7. Modify the text block on the left side of the rectangle. Add a blank line below the existing paragraph, and then type **To reserve the hall for your group, click the button below to print the reservation form.** in the text block.
8. Open the Components panel and add an instance of the Button component to the Stage. Place the button below the text block on the left side of the Stage. Align the button's left side with the left side of the text blocks and name the instance **print_btn**. In the Parameters panel, change the button's label to **Print Form**.
9. Create a new movie clip symbol named **Recital Hall Form**. In the symbol's Timeline, rename Layer 1 **Form**, and then add a new layer and name it **Action**. In the Actions panel, add the following line to stop the playhead at Frame 1.
```
stop();
```
10. In the Form layer, draw a rectangle at the center of the Stage with a blue (#0066FF) fill and black stroke. Make the rectangle 90 pixels wide and 40 pixels high and set its X and Y coordinates to 0. Add a text block at the center of the rectangle. Use Arial for the font, 12 for the font size, bold for the font style, white for the text color, and Align Center for the alignment. Type **Reservation**, press the Enter key, and then type **Form**. If necessary, realign the text block over the rectangle.
11. In the Form layer, insert a blank keyframe at Frame 2, and then change the zoom level of the Stage to 50%. In Frame 2, draw a rectangle with no fill, a black stroke, a stroke height of 2, and a solid stroke style. Make the rectangle 600 pixels wide and 600 pixels high. Set the rectangle's X and Y coordinates to 0.
12. In Frame 2, add a text block inside the top of the rectangle. Use Monotype Corsiva for the font, 54 for the font size, black for the text color, Align Center for the alignment, and then type **River City Music**. Add another text block below the first text block. Use Arial for the font, 14 for the font size, black for the text color, Align Center for the alignment, and then type **Recital Hall Reservation Request**. Center both text blocks within the top part of the rectangle.
13. Create a new text block using Arial for the font, 14 for the font size, black for the text color, and Align Left for the alignment. Place the text block inside the left side of the rectangle below the first two text blocks, and then type the following:

    Name ________________
    Address ________________
    Phone ________________
14. Draw a rectangle over the text block with the Name, Address, and Phone lines. Use light orange (#FFCC66) for the fill color and no stroke. Make the rectangle 230 pixels wide by 90 pixels high, and position it so that it acts as a background for the text block.
15. Create another text block below the previous text block using the same properties. Type the following for the text block:

    Date of Recital ________________
    Time of Recital ________________
    Number of people attending ________________

16. Draw a rectangle over the text block with the Date of Recital line. Use the same fill color as the first rectangle and no stroke. Make the rectangle 240 pixels wide by 70 pixels high, and position it as a background for the text block.
17. Create another text block with the same properties as the previous one, and type the following in the text block:
    For office use only ________________
    Reservation Confirmed ________________
    Date Confirmed ________________
    Reservation Fee Paid ________________
18. Draw a rectangle over the text block with the For office use only line. Use a light yellow (#FFFFCC) for the fill color and no stroke. Make the rectangle 240 pixels wide by 80 pixels high, and position it as a background for the text block.
19. Import the **piano.jpg** bitmap located in the Tutorial.09\Case2 folder included with your Data Files into the library. Drag an instance of the bitmap from the library to the Stage. Place the instance to the right of the Name text block and within the rectangle on the Stage. Exit symbol-editing mode.
20. In Frame 20 of the Content layer, add an instance of the Recital Hall Form to the Stage. Place it to the right of the Print Form button instance and below the text. Name the instance **form_mc**.
21. In the Actions layer, insert a keyframe at Frame 20, and then, in the Script pane of the Actions panel, type the following lines of code so that when the button is clicked, the second frame of the Recital Hall Form movie clip prints.

```
// Function to print the form
function printForm(eventObj:MouseEvent):void {
    var myPrintJob:PrintJob = new PrintJob();
    if (myPrintJob.start()) {
        myPrintJob.addPage(form_mc, null, null, 2);
        myPrintJob.send();
    }
}
// Event listeners
print_btn.addEventListener(MouseEvent.CLICK, printForm);
```

22. Save the RCMWebSite.fla file, and then test it to make sure the video clip plays and the recital reservation form prints.
23. Submit the finished files to your instructor, either in printed or electronic form, as requested.

Challenge | Case Problem 3

Add photos and buttons using a ProgressBar component and UILoader component, customize the ProgressBar component, and then import a video to complete a nursery Web site.

Data Files needed for this Case Problem: WCDraft.fla, flower1_sm.jpg, flower2_sm.jpg, flower3_sm.jpg, flower1.jpg, flower2.jpg, flower3.jpg, landscape.avi

Westcreek Nursery Alice tells Amanda that she wants to have a short video clip of a sample landscape added to the Weekly Specials Web site to give potential customers an idea of the store's landscaping work. She also wants to have the Photos page revised to display thumbnails of the flower pictures to make it easier for potential customers to know what is on sale. Amanda asks you to import the short video and to complete a new Photos page that displays thumbnails of the pictures. She has prepared the small versions of the pictures to be used as thumbnails.

1. Open the **WCDraft.fla** file located in the Tutorial.09\Case3 folder included with your Data Files, and then save the file as **WCWebSite.fla** in the same folder.
2. Select the Home button on the Stage and name the instance **home_btn**. Select the Photos button and name the instance **photos_btn**, and then select the Landscaping button and name the instance **landscaping_btn**.
3. In the Timeline, insert a new layer above the Labels layer and name it **Actions**. Select Frame 1 of the Actions layer, open the Actions panel, and then type the following lines of code in the Script pane to keep the playhead from advancing and to make the navigational buttons operational.

```
//Keep the playhead from advancing automatically
stop();
//Button functions
function onHomeClick(evt:MouseEvent):void {
      gotoAndStop("Home");
}
function onPhotosClick(evt:MouseEvent):void {
      gotoAndStop("Photos");
}
function onLandscapingClick(evt:MouseEvent):void {
      gotoAndStop("Landscaping");
}
// Event listeners
home_btn.addEventListener(MouseEvent.CLICK, onHomeClick);
photos_btn.addEventListener(MouseEvent.CLICK, onPhotosClick);
landscaping_btn.addEventListener(MouseEvent.CLICK,
onLandscapingClick);
```

4. In the Content layer, select Frame 10, and then import the **flower1_sm.jpg** picture onto the Stage and place it about 85 pixels from the left of the Stage and about 155 pixels from the top of the Stage. Import the **flower2_sm.jpg** picture onto the Stage and place it below the first picture. Import the **flower3_sm.jpg** picture onto the Stage and place it below the second picture. Align the pictures by their left sides and make sure they are spaced evenly.
5. Select each picture in turn and convert it into a button symbol, using the names **flower1 button**, **flower2 button**, and **flower3 button**, respectively. Name the flower1 button instance **flower1_btn**, name the flower2 button instance **flower2_btn**, and the name flower3 button instance **flower3_btn**.
6. For each button symbol, edit the symbol, insert a keyframe in its Over frame, and add a text block on the center of the picture. Use Verdana for the font, 12 for the font size, white for the font color, Bold for the font style, and Align Center for the alignment. Type **Click Me!** in the text block.

7. In the document's main Timeline, make sure Frame 10 is selected in the Content layer, and then drag an instance of the UILoader component from the Components panel to the center of the Stage. Resize the UILoader instance to 250 pixels wide by 187 pixels high. Name the instance **picLoader_mc**.
8. Drag an instance of the ProgressBar component from the Components panel to the Stage and place it in the center of the UILoader instance. In the Parameters panel, name the ProgressBar instance **progressBar_mc**, change its height to 10, and change its source parameter to picLoader_mc. Do not change its width.

EXPLORE

9. In the Library panel, open the ProgessBar component in symbol-editing mode, double-click the small rectangle to the left of the Bar Skin label, increase the zoom level to 800%, double-click the stroke of the rectangle, and then change its color to green (#006600). On the Edit bar, click ProgressBar barSkin, double-click the fill of the rectangle, and then change its color to bright green (#00FF00). Exit symbol-editing mode.
10. In the Actions layer, select Frame 10, and insert a keyframe. In the Script pane of the Actions panel, type the following lines of code to make the picture buttons operational. Clicking a picture button will load the corresponding picture into the picLoader instance. The ProgressBar instance will appear temporarily indicating the picture is loading.

```
// Hide the ProgressBar instance
progressBar_mc.visible = false;
// Functions to load photos
function loadPic1(eventObj:MouseEvent):void
{
      progressBar_mc.visible = true;
      var picURLReq:URLRequest = new URLRequest("flower1.jpg");
      picLoader_mc.load(picURLReq);
}
function loadPic2(eventObj:MouseEvent):void
{
      progressBar_mc.visible = true;
      var picURLReq:URLRequest = new URLRequest("flower2.jpg");
      picLoader_mc.load(picURLReq);
}
function loadPic3(eventObj:MouseEvent):void
{
      progressBar_mc.visible = true;
      var picURLReq:URLRequest = new URLRequest("flower3.jpg");
      picLoader_mc.load(picURLReq);
}
// When the loading is complete, hide the ProgressBar instance
function hideBar(eventObj:Event) {
      progressBar_mc.visible = false;
}
// Event listeners
flower1_btn.addEventListener(MouseEvent.CLICK, loadPic1);
flower2_btn.addEventListener(MouseEvent.CLICK, loadPic2);
flower3_btn.addEventListener(MouseEvent.CLICK, loadPic3);
picLoader_mc.addEventListener(Event.COMPLETE, hideBar);
```

11. In the Content layer, select Frame 20, and then import the **landscape.avi** video file located in the Tutorial.09/Case3 folder included with your Data Files. Use the Import Video wizard, select Use progressive download from a web server for the deployment option.

EXPLORE

12. If necessary, select Flash 8 - Medium Quality (400kbps) for the encoding profile. In the Encoding dialog box, click the Crop and Resize tab, and in the Resize section, click the Resize video check box to check it. Make sure the Maintain aspect ratio check box is checked, and enter 180 for the width of the video.

EXPLORE

13. In the Skinning dialog box, select SkinUnderPlayMute.swf for the skin and select a gray (#CCCCCC) color for the skin. After you import the video, reposition the video component instance on the Stage by setting its X coordinate to 300 and its Y coordinate to 165.
14. Add a text block on the top part of the video clip. Use Arial for the font, 12 for the font size, white for the text color, and Align Center for the alignment. Type **Westcreek Nursery Landscaping** for the text. If necessary, reposition the text block so that it is centered on the top part of the video clip.
15. Save and test the WCWebSite.fla file. Use the Simulate Download command with a download setting of DSL (32.6 KB/s) to test the photos' ProgressBar. Click each photo thumbnail to see the ProgessBar display. After a photo loads, the ProgressBar instance is hidden. Also, make sure the video clip plays in the Landscaping page.
16. Submit the finished files to your instructor, either in printed or electronic form, as requested.

Challenge | Case Problem 4

Add photos, Web links, printable content, and the results of a calculation to an association's Web site, using components and ActionScript code.

Data Files needed for this Case Problem: RDAWebSiteDraft.fla, RDAJobs.png, meal1.jpg, meal2.jpg

Regional Dietetic Association Web Site Richard wants to limit the values that can be entered into the text fields used for a calorie calculation form. He wants users to select from a list values instead of typing in a value. Richard also wants to include a table of job listings that customers can print from the Jobs page. Katie develops a revised version of the association's Web site. You will complete the site by adding Web links, a page with photos, a printable job list, and a Calories Burned Calculator page.

1. Open the **RDAWebSiteDraft.fla** file located in the Tutorial.09\Case4 folder included with your Data Files, and then save the file as **RDAWebSite.fla** in the same folder.
2. On the Stage, select the Home navigational button and assign a name to the instance. Repeat this step for the rest of the navigational button instances: Photos, Jobs, and Calories.
3. In the Timeline, add descriptive labels in the Labels layer for Frames 20, 30, and 40.

EXPLORE

4. In the Timeline, select Frame 10 of the Actions layer, and then add code in the Script pane of the Actions panel to keep the playhead from advancing and to make the navigational buttons operational.
5. In the Timeline, select Frame 10 of the Page content layer, and then drag an instance of the ComboBox component from the Components panel to the Stage, placing it below the paragraph at the center of the Stage. Name the instance and type **RDA Web Links** in the prompt parameter.

EXPLORE 6. In Frame 10 of the Actions layer, add code in the Script pane to make the ComboBox instance operational so that selecting an item in the ComboBox list opens the corresponding Web site. Use the following URLs for the Web links. The value of the prompt parameter should appear in the ComboBox instance after an item is selected and the width of the ComboBox instance should be increased so that longest Web site name displays completely.
American Dietetic Association, http://www.eatright.org/
National Restaurant Association, http://www.restaurant.org/
Dietitian Central, http://www.dietitiancentral.com/
American Heart Association, http://www.amhrt.org/

7. In the Timeline, select Frame 20 of the Page content layer, and then drag two instances of the Button component to the Stage, and place them centered horizontally on the bottom part of the Stage. Name each of the Button instances and change the label parameters to **Photo 1** and **Photo 2**, respectively.

EXPLORE 8. Double-click the first Button instance to display its skins, and then double-click the Over skin. Increase the zoom level, and then change the color of the entire stroke of the Button's Over skin to orange (#FF6600). Return to Scene 1.

9. Drag an instance of the UILoader component from the Components panel to the center of the Stage, and then resize the instance to 200 pixels wide and 185 pixels high. Drag an instance of the ProgressBar component to the center of the UILoader component instance. Assign names to the UILoader instance and the ProgressBar instance. Assign the name of the UILoader instance to the source parameter of the ProgressBar.

EXPLORE 10. In Frame 20 of the Actions layer, add code in the Script pane to make the Button instances operational so that clicking a button displays the corresponding photo in the UILoader instance. The ProgressBar component instance should not display until a photo is loading and it should not display after a photo has completely loaded.

11. Import the **RDAJobs.png** file located in the Tutorial.09\Case4 folder included with your Data Files into the document's library.

12. Create a new movie clip symbol named **Jobs list**. In symbol-editing mode, drag an instance of the RDAJobs.png bitmap to the center of the Stage, reduce the size of the instance to 25% of its original size, and set its X and Y coordinates to 0. In the Timeline, add a blank keyframe in Frame 2 and drag an instance of the RDAJobs.png bitmap to the Stage and set the bitmaps' X and Y coordinates to 0.

13. In the Timeline, insert a new layer and name it **Action**. In Frame 1 of the Action layer, add a line of code so that the playhead will not advance to Frame 2. Exit symbol-editing mode.

14. In the Timeline, select Frame 30 of the Page content layer, drag an instance of the Jobs list symbol to the center of the Stage, and assign a name to it. Drag an instance of the Button component from the library to the Stage and place it below the Jobs list instance. Assign a name to the Button instance and change its label parameter to **Print Jobs List**.

EXPLORE 15. In Frame 30 of the Actions layer, add code in the Script pane to make the Button instance operational so that clicking the button prints Frame 2 of the Jobs List instance.

EXPLORE 16. In the Timeline, select Frame 40 of the Page content layer, then drag an instance of the Label component from the Components panel to the Stage, and place it about 230 pixels from the left of the Stage and 180 pixels from the top of the Stage. Change the text parameter of the instance to **Select activity**.

EXPLORE 17. Add three more instances of the Label parameter below the first Label instance on the Stage and align all four instances vertically along their left edges. Place the second instance about 220 pixels from the top of the Stage, the third instance about 260 pixels from the top of the Stage, and the last instance about 300 pixels from the top of the Stage. Change the text parameters of the three instances to **Select weight**, **Select # of minutes**, and **Calories burned**, respectively.

18. Drag an instance of the ComboBox component from the Components panel to the Stage and place it about 420 pixels from the left of the Stage and 180 pixels from the top of the Stage. Name the instance and change its prompt parameter to **Activities**. In the dataProvider parameter, enter the following label/data value pairs: **Baseball**, **1**, **Soccer**, **2**, **Jogging**, **3**, and **Yoga, 4**.

EXPLORE 19. Drag an instance of the NumericStepper component from the Components panel to the Stage, and place it about 420 pixels from the left of the Stage and 220 pixels from the top of the Stage. Name the instance and change its maximum parameter to 300, its minimum parameter to 50, and its stepSize parameter to 10.

EXPLORE 20. Drag another instance of the NumericStepper component to the Stage and place it about 420 pixels from the left of the Stage and 260 pixels from the top of the Stage. Name the instance and change its maximum parameter to 120, its minimum parameter to 0, its stepSize parameter to 5, and its value parameter to 0.

21. Create a dynamic text block on the Stage and place it at about 420 pixels from the left of the Stage and 300 pixels from the top of the Stage. Use Arial for the font, 14 for the font size, black for the font color, Show border around text, and Right Align for the alignment. Make the text block 72 pixels wide and 22 pixels high. Name the text block instance.

22. Drag an instance of the Button component from the Library panel to the Stage, and place it at about 320 pixels from the left of the Stage and 350 pixels from the top of the Stage. Change the label parameter of the instance to **Calculate**, and name the instance.

EXPLORE 23. In Frame 40 of the Actions layer, add code in the Script pane so that when the user selects an activity, selects a weight, selects the number of minutes, and then clicks the Calculate button, the number of calories burned is calculated based on an exercise factor associated with each exercise. The result of the calculation is then displayed in the dynamic text block. The exercise factors associated with each activity are **Baseball, .039, Soccer, .052, Jogging, .075, Yoga, .04**. The number of calories burned is calculated by multiplying the exercise factor by the weight and the number of minutes.

24. Save and test the RDAWebSite.fla file. Make sure the navigational buttons are operational. Also, use the Simulate Download command to test the photos' and the ProgressBar. Make sure the jobs list in the Jobs page, prints, and in the Calories page, select **Soccer** for the activity, **180** for the weight, and **30** for the number of minutes. Click the Calculate button to display a value of 280.79999 for the calories burned.

25. Submit the finished files to your instructor, either in printed or electronic form, as requested.

Review | **Quick Check Answers**

Session 9.1

1. a prebuilt movie clip installed with Flash
2. to define the labels that appear on the drop-down list and the values associated with each item
3. prompt
4. break
5. `progress_mc.visible = false;`
6. source

Session 9.2

1. .mpg, .avi, and .dv
2. The amount of data required to represent a few seconds of video can make downloading the video over the Internet a slow process, and compression is used to reduce the size of the video file.
3. Embedded
4. a compressor/decompressor program used to compress video and then decompress it for playback
5. Sorenson Spark and On2 VP6 codecs
6. Cue points
7. Progressive Download from a Web Server, Stream from Flash Video Streaming Service, and Stream from Flash Media Server

Session 9.3

1. the Flash Player's context menu or the Web browser's Print command
2. `addPage(map_mc, null, null, 3);`
3. map_mc.scaleX = 1.5;
   map_mc.scaleY = 1.5;
4. False
5. spooler

Ending Data Files

Tutorial.09 →

Tutorial

bball1.flv
bball2.flv
photo1.jpg
photo2.jpg
RevisedSite.fla
RevisedSite.swf
SkinUnderPlaySeekMute.swf

Review

JacksonSoftball.fla
JacksonSoftball.swf
SkinUnderPlaySeekMute.swf
softball_clip.flv
softballPhoto1.jpg
softballPhoto2.jpg

Case1

ScrapbookWebSite.fla
ScrapbookWebSite.swf

Case2

piano_clip.flv
RCMWebSite.fla
RCMWebSIte.swf
SkinUnderPlayMute.swf

Case3

flower1.jpg
flower2.jpg
flower3.jpg
landscape.flv
SkinUnderPlayMute.swf
WCWebSite.fla
WcWebSite.swf

Case4

meal1.jpg
meal2.jpg
RDAWebSite.fla
RDAWebSite.swf

Reality Check

Adobe Flash is a professional authoring environment for creating rich, interactive content for the Web including interactive graphics and advertisements with animation, sound, and video. You can even create entire Web sites using Flash, create online forms to gather data, or display photos in online galleries.

In this exercise, you will use Flash to create a Flash Web site with interactive graphics containing information of your choice, using the Flash skills and tools presented in Tutorials 1 through 9. Use the following steps as a guide to completing your Flash Web site and graphics.

Note: Do *not* include any personal information of a sensitive nature in any graphics or content that you create to be submitted to your instructor for this exercise. Later, you can update the graphics with such information.

1. Create a list of at least three goals for the Flash Web site.
2. Based on the goals of the Flash Web site, develop a list of objectives. Include the use of audio, video, and bitmaps as part of the objectives for your site.
3. List three characteristics of the site's target audience.
4. Develop an outline with categories and subcategories to correspond to the site's objectives.
5. Develop a storyboard that shows how the site's content and navigation will be organized.
6. Gather relevant graphics for the site's background and banner. Write the headings and content for each of the pages. If adding a photos page, gather and prepare relevant photos. Obtain sound effect clips and if using video in the site, obtain and prepare the video clip.
7. Sketch the site's design to show how the banner, navigational buttons, page headings, and site graphics will be organized.
8. Create a new document that is at least 600 pixels wide and 400 pixels high. Extend the layer in the document's Timeline to include 10 frames for the site's preloader animation plus an additional 10 frames for each of the site's pages.
9. Make Layer 1 the Background layer and insert additional layers, as needed, for content that will be the same on each page of the site such as the site's the navigational buttons.
10. Insert a layer for the content that will be different on each page, insert a layer for the actions, and insert a layer for the labels that will identify each page in the site. Rename each layer with an appropriate name.
11. In the labels layer, add appropriate labels to identify the preloader section, the home page, and each of the other pages of the site.
12. Based on the site's design, in Frame 10 of the Background layer, add a background graphic or image as well as other graphics to the document that will be the same in each page of the site.
13. Create a banner as a movie clip and include the site's title, a bitmap graphic, and a gradient. In Frame 10 of the Background layer in the document's main Timeline, add an instance of the banner to the Stage and align it with the top of the Stage.
14. Create a movie clip with a motion tween animation of an appropriate graphic and add an instance to the Background layer. This animation may be of a rectangle, circle, or other shape that displays on all pages of the Web site.

Reality Check

15. Create a Home button as a symbol. Include a simple animation in the button's Timeline that displays when the mouse pointer is moved over the button. Add a sound effect that plays when the button is clicked.
16. Duplicate and modify the Home button to create buttons for each of the other pages of the site. Add an instance of each button to Frame 10 of the document's main Timeline. Align and space the button instances on the Stage.
17. Assign names to the button instances and then add the ActionScript code to Frame 10 of the actions layer to make the navigational buttons operational.
18. Create a preloader animation in the first frame of the site that includes a graphic and a dynamic text field to display the percent of the movie's content that has been loaded. Add the necessary ActionScript code to Frame 1 of the actions layer to make the preloader animation work.
19. For each page in your site, create an appropriate page heading and add content and graphics pertinent to that page. Consider adding animated text to one of the pages and a graphic or animation to another page.
20. If appropriate for your site, in one of the site's pages, add a component to display multiple photos saved as JPEG or GIF files. Add buttons to enable the user to choose which photo to display. Include a component to display a progress bar animation as each photo is loaded. Add the appropriate ActionScript code to make the buttons and components functional.
21. If appropriate for your site, in one of the site's pages, create a form using input text and dynamic text to enable the user to enter data, click a button, and receive a result based on the data. Add the appropriate ActionScript code to process the input values and display the appropriate result.
22. If appropriate for your site, in one of the site's pages, create at least three URL links using a Flash component. The links should be to Web sites related to the site's content based on the objectives of the site. Add the appropriate ActionScript code to make the component functional.
23. In an appropriate page, import a video and add an instance of the video using the FLVPlayback component and an appropriate skin with playback controls.
24. Save the pages, and test them in the Flash Player. Adjust the pages, as needed.
25. Save and close the document, and then submit the completed Web site to your instructor, in printed or electronic form, as requested.

Creating a Banner, a Payment Calculator, and a Photo Page

Case | Discount Autos

Discount Autos of San Antonio has been in business for over 15 years providing quality, used vehicles. Located on the corner of Highway 151 and Alamo Parkway, Discount Autos' sales have been steadily increasing. To continue this trend in sales, a new marketing campaign has been developed by owner, Allen Bidwell. As part of this new campaign, Allen wants to improve the business's Web site. In particular, Allen wants a new banner developed for the site as well as a tool that potential customers can use to calculate their monthly loan payments based on a loan amount, the number of months for the loan, and the interest rate. He also wants the site to include an area to showcase auto specials, using pictures of vehicles and video.

Starting Data Files

AddCases → **AddCase.01**

Auto1.jpg
Auto2.jpg
Auto3.jpg
autos.mpg
SpecialsPage.fla

To create the new banner:

1. Create a new document with dimensions of 600 by 100 pixels.
2. Use the Color panel to create a linear gradient. Set the left gradient pointer to a light red color (#EB8458) and set the right gradient pointer to white. Create a rectangle using the new gradient as its fill and no stroke. The rectangle should match the size of the Stage and serve as a background for the banner. If necessary, reposition the rectangle so it is aligned with the Stage. In the Timeline, add a regular frame at Frame 60 to extend the layer.
3. Create a new layer for the title text block. Name the layer **Title**. Use a font such as Impact, use a text color such as maroon (#660000), and select italic style. Use a large font size and type **DI$COUNT AUTO$** in the text block. Center the text on the banner. Increase the line spacing slightly for the text making sure the text remains centered within the rectangle on the Stage.
4. Create a text animation with the dollar sign so that it alternately increases and then decreases in size for a pulsating effect. Start by breaking the title text block into its individual letters and then converting the left $ character into a graphic symbol.
5. Edit the dollar sign graphic symbol in symbol-editing mode and convert the $ character in the symbol to a movie clip. Insert keyframes at Frames 5, 10, 15, and 20. In Frames 5 and 15, increase the size of the dollar sign instance to 110% of its original size, being sure to constrain its width and height. Create motion tweens between each keyframe so that the dollar sign instance exhibits a pulsating effect throughout the 20 frames.
6. In the Title layer of the document's main Timeline, delete both $ text blocks, and then create a new layer named **Dollar signs**. In the new layer, insert an instance of the dollar sign graphic symbol between the letters I and C on the Stage, being sure to align the $ with the rest of the letters.
7. In the Dollar signs layer, insert another instance of the dollar sign graphic after the letter O in AUTO, being sure to align the $ with the rest of the letters in AUTO. In the First Frame box in the Property inspector, change the starting frame of the instance to 10.
8. Add a mask effect to the banner using a gradient that moves horizontally across the text. First select all of the letters in the Title layer (the $ symbols should not be selected) at the same time, and then convert the letters to fills. Copy all of the letters at the same time and paste the copies in a new layer above the Title layer. Name the new layer **Title2**. The copies should be in the same relative position as the original letters.
9. Insert a new layer between the Title and the Title2 layers. In this layer, draw a rectangle that is about the same size as the Stage. Create a linear gradient that is black on the ends and has a narrow white strip in the middle. Use this gradient for the rectangle's fill and do not include a stroke.
10. Convert the rectangle into a movie clip symbol. Create two motion tweens to have the rectangle move from the left side of the Stage horizontally across to the right side of the Stage for 30 frames and then back to the left side of the Stage for the next 30 frames.
11. Convert the Title2 layer into a mask layer. The layer with the rectangle should be masked. This creates a highlight affect on the title text in which the highlight moves across the text and back.
12. Save the banner as **DiscountAutosBanner.fla** in the AddCases\AddCase.01 folder included with your Data Files, and then test it.

To create a payment calculator:

13. Create a new document with dimensions of 250 by 300 pixels and a light yellow (#FFFFCC) background. Create a title text block using a dark red color (#990000), 0 for the letter spacing, and a font of your choice. Type **Discount Autos** for the text block and center it across the top part of the Stage.
14. Create a text block using Arial for the font, a smaller font size, and black for the text color. Type **Monthly Payment Calculator** in this text block and center it right below the title text.
15. Draw a rectangle with no fill, a dashed stroke style, and rounded corners. The rectangle should be slightly smaller than the Stage and should form a frame for the contents of the Stage.
16. Create four text blocks using a smaller text size. Align the text blocks vertically by their right edges. Type **Loan Amount** for the first text block, **Length of Loan** for the second text block, **Interest Rate** for the third text block, and **Monthly Payment** for the fourth text block.
17. Create an input text block to the right of the Loan Amount text. This will be used to enter the amount of the loan. Create another input text block and place this one to the right of the Interest Rate text block. This will be used to enter a rate. Make each input text block about 60 pixels wide and 20 pixels high. In the Property inspector, select the Show border around text option, and select Align right for each input text block. Name the first text block instance **loanAmount** and name the second input text block instance **interestRate**.
18. Create a dynamic text block to the right of the Monthly Payment text block. Make the text block about 60 pixels wide and 20 pixels high. In the Property inspector, deselect the Show border around text option, and select Align right. Name the text block instance **monthlyPayment**.
19. Add an instance of the ComboBox component to the right of the Length of Loan text block. This will be used to select the number of months for the loan. Name the ComboBox instance **lengthOfLoan** and make the instance about 65 pixels wide. In the Parameters panel, enter **Months** for the prompt parameter. Add the following labels and data value pairs for the dataProvider parameter: label:**36 mo.**, data:**1**, label:**48 mo.**, data:**2**, label:**60 mo.**, data:**3**.
20. Add an instance of a Button component to the bottom of the Stage and assign the name **calc_btn** to the instance. In the Parameters panel, type **Estimate** for the label parameter.
21. Add a new layer and name it **Actions**. Select Frame 1 of the Actions layer. In the Script pane of the Actions panel, type the following ActionScript code to calculate the monthly payment and place the result in the Monthly Payment dynamic text block.

```
 // Function to determine the monthly payment
function Calculate(evt:MouseEvent):void {
   var numberOfMonths:Number;
   switch (lengthOfLoan.value) {
   case "1" :
      numberOfMonths = 36;
      break;
   case "2" :
      numberOfMonths = 48;
      break;
   case "3" :
      numberOfMonths = 60;
      break;
```

```
};

// Convert input values into Integer numbers
var Loan:Number = int(loanAmount.text);
var Rate:Number = int(interestRate.text);
// Determine the monthly interest rate
var monthlyRate:Number = (Rate/12)/100;
// Calculate part of the formula using the Math power function
var factor:Number = 1- Math.pow(1+monthlyRate,-numberOfMonths);
// Calculate the payment; round to the nearest dollar
var payment:Number = Math.round((monthlyRate/factor)*Loan);
// Display the resulting monthyly payment
monthlyPayment.text = String(payment);

}
//Event listener
calc_btn.addEventListener(MouseEvent.CLICK, Calculate);
```

22. Save the document as **MonthlyCalculator.fla** in the AddCases\AddCase.01 folder included with your Data Files, and then test the monthly payment calculator.

To create a Specials Page:

23. Open the **SpecialsPage.fla** document located in the AddCases\AddCase.01 folder included with your Data Files, and then save the document as **Specials.fla** in the same folder.
24. In the Timeline, select Frame 1 of the Content layer and add an instance of the UILoader component to the center of the Stage. Name the instance **photos_mc.** This is where the auto photos will be loaded.
25. Add a ProgressBar component instance below the UILoader instance. Name the instance **pBar_mc** and type **photos_mc** in its source parameter.
26. Add a Button component instance below the ProgressBar instance. Name the button instance **next_btn** and change its label parameter to **Next**.
27. Select Frame 1 of the Actions layer, and in the Script pane of the Actions panel, add the following ActionScript code after the existing code. When the Next button is clicked, a photo will be loaded into the UILoader instance. The photo file names used are auto1.jpg, auto2.jpg, auto3.jpg. The ActionScript code uses the variable num for the value (1, 2, 3) in the filename. The ProgressBar instance displays only while a photo is being loaded.

```
// Code to load photos; set initial value of num to 1
var num:Number = 1;
// Hide the ProgressBar instance
pBar_mc.visible = false;
// Load photos function
function loadPics(eventObj:MouseEvent):void
{

   pBar_mc.visible = true;
   // Create the photo file name using the value in num
   var pic:String = "auto"+num+".jpg";
   // Load the photo into the Loader instance
   var picURLReq:URLRequest = new URLRequest(pic);
   photos_mc.load(picURLReq);
   // Increment the value in num
   num += 1;
```

```
   // If num is greater than 3, set it back to 1
   if (num > 3){
      num = 1;

   }

}
// When the loading is complete, hide the ProgressBar instance
function hideBar(eventObj:Event) {
   pBar_mc.visible = false;

}
next_btn.addEventListener(MouseEvent.CLICK, loadPics);
photos_mc.addEventListener(Event.COMPLETE, hideBar);
```

28. In the Content layer of the Timeline, select Frame 10. Import the **autos.mpg** video located in the AddCases\AddCase.01 folder included with your Data Files using the Import Video wizard. Use Progressive download from a web server for the deployment. Crop the video to remove unused areas and select an appropriate skin to include playback controls. Place the video at the center of the Stage below the Video text block.
29. Save and test the Specials page.
30. Submit the finished files to your instructor, either in printed or electronic form, as requested.

Ending Data Files

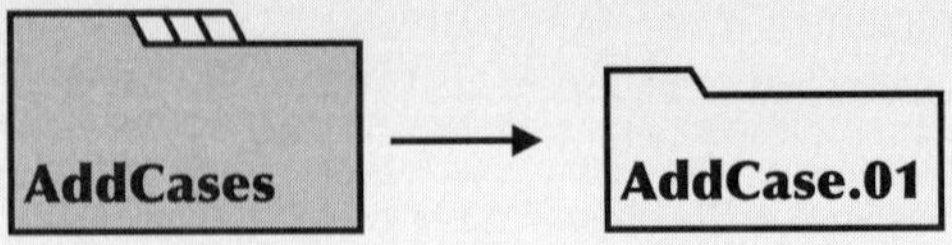

Auto1.jpg
Auto2.jpg
Auto3.jpg
autos.flv
DiscountAutosBanner.fla
DiscountAutosBanner.swf
MonthlyCalculator.fla
MonthlyCalculator.swf
SkinUnderPlaySeekMute.swf
Specials.fla
Specials.swf

Creating Flash Graphics for a Web Site

Case | Bexar County Zoo

The Bexar County Zoo of South Texas is a non-profit organization dedicated to providing quality care for their animal collection and offering an educational and recreational experience for its visitors. The zoo has been in operation for over 15 years and is accredited by the American Zoo and Aquarium Association. The zoo is open year-round and has recently redesigned its Web site. Cecilia Fuentes, zoo director, has requested several new elements be added to the Web site. One of these is a photo gallery showcasing several pictures of animals. She has also requested a banner advertising some of the new exhibits at the zoo.

Starting Data Files

AddCases → **AddCase.02**

bear.jpg
bearBig.jpg
butterfly.jpg
elephant.jpg
elephantBig.jpg
giraffe.jpg
parrots.jpg
rhino.jpg
rhinoBig.jpg

To create a photo gallery:

1. Create a new document based on the Modern Photo Slideshow template in the Photo Slideshows template category. Save the document as **zooPhotos.fla** in the AddCases\AddCase.02 folder included with your Data Files in the Flash CS3 file format.
2. In the Photos folder of the document's library, delete the existing photos. Import the following bitmap files located in the AddCases\AddCase.02 folder included with your Data Files into the document's library and place them in the Photos folder: **giraffe.jpg**, **elephantBig.jpg**, **rhinoBig.jpg**, **bearBig.jpg**.
3. On the Title, Date layer, select and replace the My Photo Album text with the text **Bexar County Zoo Photo Gallery**.
4. Select Frame 1 of the picture layer and add an instance of the giraffe.jpg bitmap. In the Property inspector, set its X and Y coordinates to 0. Select Frame 1 of the Captions layer and replace "The elegant seashore" text with **Joey the Giraffe**.
5. Repeat Step 4 to add instances of each of the imported zoo animal pictures into Frames 2, 3, and 4. Also, add an appropriate caption for each picture in place of the existing captions.
6. Save and test the photo gallery document.

To create an interactive banner:

7. Create a new document with dimensions of 350 by 265 pixels and a background color of yellow (#FFFFCC). Insert a new layer and name it **Border**. On this layer, create a green rectangular border around the inside edges of the Stage. Use a stroke style other than Solid and do not include a fill.
8. Import the following bitmap files located in the AddCases\AddCase.02 folder included with your Data Files into the document's library: **bear.jpg**, **butterfly.jpg**, **elephant.jpg**, **parrots.jpg**, **rhino.jpg**.
9. Create a new movie clip symbol named **bearAlpha**. In this symbol, insert an instance of the bear.jpg bitmap and use the Info panel to center it on the Stage. Select the bear.jpg bitmap instance on the Stage and convert it into a movie clip symbol named **bear_mc**.
10. In the bearAlpha movie clip Timeline, create a motion tween to fade-in the bear_mc instance from Frame 1 to Frame 5. Use a starting alpha amount of 50%. Insert a new layer and add a `stop ()` action to Frame 5 of this layer. Insert a new layer and add a text block centered across the top of the Stage. Type **Visit the Bear Exhibit!** in the text block.
11. Repeat Steps 9 and 10 to create movie clip symbols with a fade-in effect for each bitmap image. Name each movie clip based on the bitmap it contains: **elephantAlpha**, **parrotsAlpha**, **butterflyAlpha**, **rhinoAlpha**. Add appropriate headings for each movie clip.
12. In the document's main Timeline, insert a regular frame at Frame 20 of each layer and then insert a new layer below the Border layer and name it **Pictures**. Insert an instance of the bearAlpha movie clip. Align the instance with the edges of the Stage.
13. Insert a keyframe at Frame 5 of the Pictures layer and swap the movie clip instance on the Stage with an instance of the butterflyAlpha movie clip. Insert a keyframe at Frame 10 and swap the instance on the Stage with a elephantAlpha instance. Insert a

keyframe at Frame 15 and swap the instance on the Stage with a parrotsAlpha instance. Insert a keyframe at Frame 20 and swap the instance on the Stage with a rhinoAlpha instance.

14. Insert a new layer above the Border layer and name it **Labels**. In Frame 1 of the Labels layer, add the frame label **bear**. Insert a keyframe at Frame 5 and add the frame label **butterfly**. Create similar frame labels at Frames 10, 15, and 20, using **elephants**, **parrots**, and **rhino** for the labels.
15. Insert a new layer and name it **Actions**. Add a stop action in Frame 1 to prevent the frames from playing automatically.
16. Create a new button symbol named **picture1 button**. Draw a small triangle (about 20 pixels in width and height) for the button shape using a white fill and black stroke. In the button's Over frame, change the color of the triangle's fill and flip the triangle shape vertically to create a rollover effect. Insert a new layer and add a text block with the number 1. The text block should be inside the triangle.
17. Create a duplicate of the picture1 button and name it **picture2 button**. Change the text in the symbol to **2**. Create three more duplicates of the button. Name the duplicates **picture3 button**, **picture4 button**, and **picture5 button**, respectively. Change the text in the duplicate buttons to **3**, **4**, and **5**, respectively.
18. In the document's main Timeline, insert a new layer and name it **Buttons**. Insert instances of each button along the bottom of the Stage, inside the border. Align the button instances horizontally and name the instances as follows: **pic1_btn**, **pic2_btn**, **pic3_btn**, **pic4_btn**, **pic5_btn**.
19. In the Actions layer, select Frame 1 and type the following ActionScript code after the `stop ()` action. When the pointer moves over the pic1_btn instance, the onButton1Over function is called, which moves the playhead to the frame with the bear label.

```
function onButton1Over(evt:MouseEvent):void {
   gotoAndStop("bear");
}

pic1_btn.addEventListener(MouseEvent.MOUSE_OVER, onButton1Over);
```

20. Add the appropriate functions and event listeners to the code to make the rest of the button instances functional. When the pointer moves over a button instance, the playhead should move to the frame with the corresponding label and stop.
21. Save the banner as **zooBanner.fla** in the AddCases\AddCase.02 folder included with your Data Files, and then test it.
22. Submit the finished files to your instructor, either in printed or electronic form, as requested.

Ending Data Files

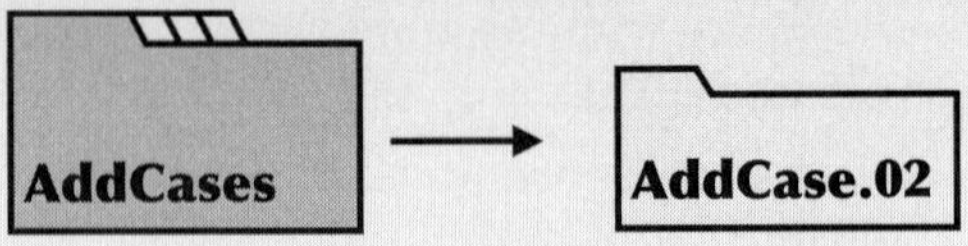

zooBanner.fla
zooBanner.swf
zooPhotos.fla
zooPhotos.swf

Glossary/Index

Note: Boldface entries include definitions.

T

U

V

W

X

Z

Task Reference

TASK	PAGE #	RECOMMENDED METHOD
Action, add to button using Behaviors panel	FL 338	Select button instance on Stage, open Behaviors panel, click [icon], in Behaviors panel, point to behavior type, click behavior, modify values in dialog box, click OK
Action, add using Actions panel in Script Assist mode	FL 225	Select frame or button instance, expand Actions panel, click Script Assist button to toggle on, click category in Actions toolbox, double-click desired action, set parameters
Actions, check for syntax errors	FL 331	In Actions panel, click [icon], click OK, check errors in Compiler panel
Actions toolbox, collapse or expand	FL 363	In Actions panel, click [icon]
Bitmap, change properties	FL 255	In Library panel, select bitmap, click [icon]
Bitmap, convert to symbol	FL 257	Select bitmap instance, click Modify, click Convert to Symbol, set options, click OK
Bitmap, convert to vector	FL 266	Select bitmap instance, click Modify, point to Bitmap, click Trace Bitmap, set options, click OK
Bitmap, import	FL 252	See Reference Window: Importing a Bitmap
Button, add ActionScript code	FL 329	See Reference Window: Adding ActionScript Code to a Button
Button, add from Buttons library	FL 212	Click Window, point to Common Libraries, click Buttons, drag button from Buttons library panel to Stage
Button, create	FL 217	See Reference Window: Creating a Custom Button
Button, test within program window	FL 213	Click Control, click Enable Simple Buttons, click button on Stage
Colors, select	FL 33	Click [icon] or [icon] to open color palette, click desired color swatch
Component, create instance	FL 412	See Reference Window: Adding a Flash Component
Component, set parameters	FL 414	In the Property inspector, click Parameters tab, set parameter values
Dynamic text, create	FL 388	Click [T], in the Property inspector, click Text type control, click Dynamic Text, create text block on stage
External Library, copy symbol	FL 315	See Reference Window: Copying Symbols from an External Library
Fill, apply	FL 67	Click [icon], select fill color, select Gap Size modifier, click object on Stage
Flash, start program	FL 6	Click Start button on taskbar, click All Programs, click Adobe Flash CS3 Professional
Flash, exit program	FL 43	Click File, click Exit
Flash document, close	FL 43	Click File, click Close
Flash document, create from template	FL 317	Click File, click New, click Templates tab, select category, select template, click OK
Flash document, export as image	FL 285	Click File, point to Export, click Export Image, select destination, type filename, select file type, click Save, set options, click OK
Flash document, modify	FL 29	Click Modify, click Document
Flash document, open	FL 9	Click File, click Open, select file, click Open
Flash document, preview by scrubbing	FL 14	Drag playhead in Timeline header

TASK	PAGE #	RECOMMENDED METHOD
Flash document, preview in Flash Player window	FL 10	Click Control, click Test Movie
Flash document, preview in Flash program window	FL 10	Click Control, click Play; or press Enter
Flash document, preview in Web page	FL 11	Click File, point to Publish Preview, click HTML
Flash document, publish	FL 280	Click File, click Publish
Flash document, test animation	FL 133	See Reference Window: Testing a Document's Animation
Flash document, test download in different settings	FL 383	Click Control, click Test Movie, click View, point to Download Settings, click desired setting, click View, click Simulate Download
Flash SWF file, display context menu	FL 5	Right-click Flash SWF file
Frame, copy	FL 115	Select frame or frames, right-click selected frames, click Copy Frames
Frame label, add	FL 232	Select frame, in Property inspector, type label in Frame box, press Enter
Gradient, create, edit, save	FL 271	See Reference Window: Creating, Editing, and Saving a Gradient
Gradient fill, apply	FL 273	Click , select gradient for fill color, click object on Stage
Gradient fill, transform	FL 277	Click , click gradient on Stage, adjust gradient
Grid, display	FL 26	Click View, point to Grid, click Show Grid
Grid, edit	FL 26	Click View, point to Grid, click Edit Grid
Grouped object, create	FL 33	Click , draw marquee around objects, click Modify, click Group
Grouped object, edit	FL 35	Select object, click Edit, click Edit Selected; or double-click selected object
Grouped object, exit edit mode	FL 35	Click Edit, click Edit All; or on Edit bar, click Scene 1
Guides, clear	FL 62	Click View, point to Guides, click Clear Guides
Guide, create	FL 27	Display rulers, drag guide from a ruler to Stage
Guides, edit	FL 28	Click View, point to Guides, click Edit Guides
Help, display contents	FL 42	See Reference Window: Using the Flash Help System
Image, export	FL 84	Click File, point to Export, click Export Image, select location, enter filename, click Save as type arrow to select file format, click Save
Input Text, create	FL 386	Click , in Property inspector, click Text type control, click Input Text, create a text block on Stage
Instance, create	FL 97	Drag copy of symbol from Library panel to Stage
Instance name, add	FL 360	Select instance on Stage, in Property inspector, enter name in Instance Name box
Keyframe, insert	FL 130	Select frame in Timeline, click Insert, point to Timeline, click Keyframe
Layer, insert	FL 115	In Timeline, click
Layer, rename	FL 115	In Timeline, double-click layer's name, type new name, press Enter
Layer, select	FL 115	Click layer in Timeline
Layer folder, insert	FL 114	In Timeline, click
Library panel, change to narrow view	FL 93	In Library panel, click
Library panel, change to wide view	FL 94	In the Library panel, click

TASK	PAGE #	RECOMMENDED METHOD
Library panel, open	FL 93	Click Window, click Library
Lines, draw with Line tool	FL 72	In Tools panel, click , select stroke color, draw on Stage
Lines, draw with Pencil tool	FL 64	In Tools panel, click , select Pencil Mode modifier, set stroke properties, draw on Stage
Mask layer, create	FL 162	See Reference Window: Creating a Mask Layer Animation
Motion Guide layer, create	FL 159	See Reference Window: Creating a Motion Guide Layer
Movie Explorer, use	FL 195	Click Window, click Movie Explorer, click Show buttons to select and deselect as needed
Object, copy	FL 76	Select object, click Edit, click Copy, click Edit, click a paste command
Object, flip horizontally	FL 132	Select object, click Modify, point to Transform, click Flip Horizontal
Object, modify anchor points	FL 39	See Reference Window: Using the Subselection Tool
Object, modify with Selection tool	FL 37	In Tools panel, click , drag a line or a corner of the object to change its shape
Object, move	FL 37	In Tools panel, click , select object, drag object
Object, reposition on Stage	FL 17	Drag object with , or change object's X and Y values in Property inspector
Object, scale on Stage	FL 22	Select object with , in Property inspector, change object's W and H values or in Transform panel, change object's width and height values
Object, select with Selection tool	FL 36	In Tools panel, click , click object; or draw marquee around object
Object, transform	FL 74	See Reference Window: Transforming an Object Using the Free Transform Tool
Objects, align on Stage	FL 225	Select several objects, open Align panel, click desired align button
Objects, distribute to layers	FL 180	Select objects, click Modify, point to Timeline, click Distribute to Layers
Objects, group	FL 66	Select several objects, click Modify, click Group
Objects, select with Lasso tool	FL 40	In Tools panel, click , click and drag to select objects; or click , click , click points around objects, double-click to complete selection
Onion skinning, turn on	FL 188	In Timeline, click
Oval, draw	FL 60	In Tools panel, click , select stroke and fill colors, click and drag pointer on Stage
Panels and panel groups, organize	FL 19	See Reference Window: Organizing Panels and Panel Groups
Panels, collapse to icons	FL 20	Click Collapse to Icons button
Panel, display	FL 19	Click Window, point to Other Panels, if necessary, click desired panel
Panels, set to default layout	FL 7	Click Window, point to Workspace, click Default
Primitive oval, draw	FL 71	In Tools panel, click , select stroke and fill colors, click and drag pointer on Stage
Publish settings, change	FL 280	Click File, click Publish Settings, select types and enter filenames on Format tab, select options on file type tabs, click Publish or OK
Publishing profile, save	FL 282	In Publish Settings dialog box, click +, enter publish profile name, click OK
Rectangle, draw	FL 55	In Tools panel, click , select stroke and fill colors, click and drag pointer on Stage

TASK	PAGE #	RECOMMENDED METHOD
Rectangle, specify rounded corners	FL 57	In Tools panel, click [button], in Property inspector, change Rectangle corner radius value, press Enter
Rulers, display or hide	FL 27	Click View, click Rulers
Scene, duplicate	FL 120	Open Scene panel, select scene, click [button]
Scene, rename	FL 118	Open Scene panel, double-click scene, type new name, press Enter
Scene, select	FL 119	On Edit bar, click [button], select scene
Snap to Objects, select	FL 62	In Tools panel, click [button] to toggle it on and off
Sound, add to button	FL 237	See Reference Window: Adding a Sound to a Button
Stage, change view	FL 23	See Reference Window: Changing the View of the Stage
Stage, move its view	FL 24	Click [button], drag Stage to new position
Stage, show all	FL 9	Click View, point to Magnification, click Show All
Steps, replay	FL 87	Open History panel, select steps in History panel, select object on Stage, click Replay button in History panel
Steps, undo	FL 89	Click Edit, click Undo or open History panel, move slider to previous steps in History panel
Stroke or Fill properties, copying	FL 68	See Reference Window: Using the Eyedropper Tool
Symbol, create	FL 91	See Reference Window: Creating a Symbol
Symbol, create duplicate	FL 95	In Library panel, select symbol, click [button], click Duplicate, type duplicate symbol's name, click OK
Symbol, edit	FL 95	See Reference Window: Editing a Symbol
Symbol, swap	FL 143	Select instance of symbol on Stage, in Property inspector, click Swap button, select symbol, click OK
Text, animate	FL 169	See Reference Window: Creating Text Animations
Text, create	FL 80	In Tools panel, click [T], in Property inspector, set text properties, click or click and drag on Stage to create text block, type text
Text, spell check	FL 83	Click Text, click Check Spelling
Text, split letters into individual text blocks	FL 180	Select text block, click Modify, click Break Apart
Template, create	FL 313	See Reference Window: Creating a Flash Template
Timeline, change its view	FL 112	On Timeline, click [button], click desired view
Timeline, hide	FL 53	On Edit bar, click [button]
Timeline Effect, add	FL 126	Select object or objects, click Insert, point to Timeline Effects, point to Assistants, Effects, or Transform/Transition, click effect
Timeline Effect, delete or edit	FL 126	Select layer with effect, click Modify, point to Timeline Effects, click Edit Effect or Remove Effect
Tool, select	FL 15	Click tool's button in the Tools panel or press tool's shortcut key
Video, import	FL 428	Click File, point to Import, click Import Video, follow steps in Import Video Wizard
Workspace, set to icons	FL 20	On Edit bar, click Workspace, click Icons Only Default
Web page, preview	FL 5	Start Internet Explorer or another Web browser, click File, click Open, click Browse, select HTML file, click Open, click OK
Zoom level, change	FL 24	Click [button], click [button] or [button], click specific area of Stage